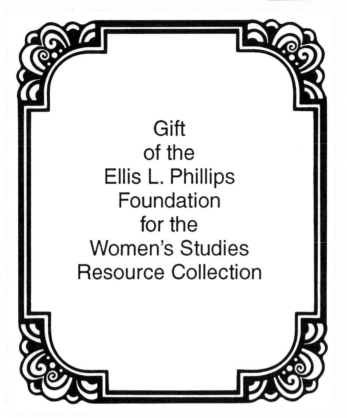

ALSO BY HELEN LEFKOWITZ HOROWITZ

Campus Life
(1987)

Alma Mater
(1984)

Culture and the City
(1976)

The Power and Passion of
M. Carey Thomas

The Power and Passion of
M. Carey Thomas

❖ ❖ ❖ ❖ ❖

HELEN LEFKOWITZ
HOROWITZ

Alfred A. Knopf
NEW YORK
1994

#2936l342

THIS IS A BORZOI BOOK
PUBLISHED BY ALFRED A. KNOPF, INC.

Library of Congress Cataloging-in-Publication Data

Horowitz, Helen Lefkowitz.
The power and passion of M. Carey Thomas / Helen Lefkowitz Horowitz.
p.   cm.
Includes bibliographical references and index.
ISBN 0-394-57227-0
1. Thomas, M. Carey (Martha Carey), 1857–1935. 2. Bryn Mawr College—
Presidents—Biography. 3. Women educators—United States—Biography.
I. Title.
LD7062.7   1894.H67   1994
378.748'12—dc20   93-39509
                                              CIP

Manufactured in the United States of America
FIRST EDITION

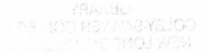

To

Jane Nuckols Garrett,

John Brinckerhoff Jackson,

and

the memory of Helen Solomon Atlas

I SHOULD hope that because our memories of Miss Thomas are so vigorous and so strongly etched she may escape the fate of the many heroes and heroines of the past whose immortality is little more than a name and a list of achievements, due to the misguided piety of their biographers. Those biographers have tried to erase from the record such qualities as seem to them uncomfortable or undignified or not in accordance with the conventional ethics of the day, and have succeeded in making of their heroes plaster saints. If those of us who have known Miss Thomas well do not succeed in passing on as a matter of biographical record some of the qualities which have made her unique and unforgettable in her own lifetime, then we shall have failed through wilful blindness to truth and shall be guilty of a criminal waste of rich and abundant material.

—HELEN TAFT MANNING
Address at Memorial Service for M. Carey Thomas

Contents

Preface

M. CAREY THOMAS in memory is as complex as she was in life. To Bryn Mawr students and alumnae she is the legendary founder, the ghost who inhabits the library cloisters, the presence still larger than life who directs the institution as by an unseen hand. To readers of Gertrude Stein she is the model for Helen Thornton, the dean of Fernhurst College. To modern students of women's studies she is the spunky girl of her journals and early letters who set out to defy the patriarchal world by skinning a mouse and becoming a new woman. Family members recall her with a mixture of affection, pride, fear, and anger. The 1947 biography that they authorized sought to obscure her image, perhaps to protect a reputation felt to be at risk in the first years after her death. To readers of Laurence Veysey's biographical entry in *Notable American Women*, Thomas is the heavy-handed college president who, whatever else she did, traveled with thirty-five trunks and used her position to foster nativism.[1] In her lifetime Carey Thomas inspired enthusiasm, awe, love, rage, and hatred. Almost sixty years after her death, she still does.

In presenting her life story, I have tried to be fair. To the degree that I can, I use her own words and attempt to inhabit her consciousness. I cannot absent myself: I am Jewish, middle class, a social democrat and a feminist, a wife and mother, and I live in the late twentieth century. I have sought to understand the daughter of Quakers, a passionate lover of women, a restless seeker of knowledge, power, and wealth, and one who proudly assumed some of the prejudices of the conservative elite. As a historian I try to empathize with someone from another world; as a human being I cannot help but judge as well as depict.

Do I like Carey Thomas? From the outset I have been asked this question, and I still search for the answer. I suppose that knowing her as well as I do, I share the range of feeling about her. I like her, even love her, at times. I have cried at her losses, and I have cheered her victories. I have thrilled to her words on women and creativity. But I have also quivered with rage at her lies and deceits. Some of her views and actions are repugnant to me. Yet I admire the institutions that she built—Bryn Mawr College, the Bryn Mawr School, the Johns Hopkins University School of Medicine—and I know that they have redeemed themselves from the restrictions she once imposed.

I chose to write about M. Carey Thomas not because of her formal accomplishments but because she was an intriguing, complicated person with an extraordinarily well-documented life. I relished the opportunity to focus on a single life, to see historical forces refracted through the actions and consciousness of an individual. I wanted both the immediacy of biography and the chance to see if, in writing a life story, new questions might emerge, new knowledge might be gained.

Researching and writing this book has been immensely satisfying. I have liked knowing Carey Thomas well, holding the many details about her in my head. I have enjoyed her familiarity and her otherness. I have felt that I have come close to understanding what it meant to live in another era. In addition, I believe that I have made an important contribution to the study of history in several salient areas.

The second wave of feminism has come at the same time as a major shift in sexual consciousness and the rise of the lesbian and gay movements. Understanding of the present has reshaped the questions asked of the past. Accompanying a heightened interest in the women of the turn of the century has been a desire to understand the thoughts, feelings, and actions of those who chose to love women. Because of the richness of the papers, I have been able to track Carey Thomas' awareness and some of her behavior in the critical period that spans the 1870s to the 1910s. At the same time that I have immersed myself in contemporary scholarship and theory, I have exercised great care to portray Carey Thomas' behavior, emotions, and self-conceptions in her language and thought as she moved through her life course.[2] In such contested terrain, my judgments are bound to be controversial. Knowing this from the outset, I have quoted Carey Thomas copiously so that those with differing approaches can draw on the material of this biography to document grounds for contradiction and thereby advance the debate.

I have explored the way that thought, belief, intimacy, and reading were intertwined. What has interested me is the powerful impact of reading on living a life. Reading helped to shape Carey Thomas' moral choices, reorient her religious convictions, and inform her understanding of her self and her emotions. Her reading of philosophy and science led her to question the religion of her childhood. Her parents were orthodox Quakers who accepted the literal truth of Scripture. As she read works and heard lectures that challenged her parents' faith, where would her questions take her? If she went outside revealed religion, how could she ground a moral basis for living? What were alternative sources of meaning? Science could question and explain, but could it guide action?

Carey Thomas and her friends read aloud Percy Bysshe Shelley, Algernon Charles Swinburne, and Théophile Gautier. Through their words, especially the poetry of Swinburne, Carey reached into her ardent nature and learned to distinguish herself from the women of her mother's generation. In an era before lesbianism was named and defined in medical literature, she understood her love for Mamie Gwinn and later for Mary Garrett as passionate, full of "rapture and fire." This study of Carey Thomas probes her reading and its relation to the development of her consciousness as a woman-loving woman. It does so with a sense that she was not alone in finding understanding of her passionate self in fiction and poetry.

Although I do not want to be an advocate for M. Carey Thomas, I hope that this biography will help restore her to her rightful place in the historical record. She was a heroine in her prime, widely celebrated in the press. On the age's many lists of the important women of the time, she held a prominent and secure place.[3] Today, as the recent biographical entry by Veysey suggests, she has fallen into eclipse. While her historical decline springs partly from an understandable reaction to her elitism, it also represents a serious historical injustice that needs to be righted. Thomas' educational achievements are misunderstood and wrongly devalued. Bryn Mawr College at its creation was a great advance for women. Most historians of higher education have seen women's colleges as retrograde institutions, modeling themselves after the most conservative male colleges. Not only is the notion of a unilinear path of educational progress from traditional college to progressive university a questionable assumption, the judgment about Bryn Mawr is dead wrong.

Carey Thomas envisioned Bryn Mawr as a women's University of Leipzig devoted to original inquiry, not as a Yale or a Haverford, neither of which she respected. Bryn Mawr College attracted great scholars to teach for a few years or a lifetime and freed them from administrative work so that they could continue research. It shaped students' study into a group system, a forerunner of the major, and prepared them for graduate training and important careers. From the outset it offered women graduate education in the liberal arts. Irrespective of the gender of its students, the Bryn Mawr graduate school was one of the leading institutions training scholars in the United States. Although this is the story of Carey Thomas, not of the college, for many years Bryn Mawr was the lengthened shadow of one woman. Whatever else Thomas deserves, she belongs in the pantheon of turn-of-the-century educational leaders such as William Rainey Harper, Charles William Eliot, and G. Stanley Hall.[4]

Women's historians have failed to rescue M. Carey Thomas' reputation from its historical demise. Undervaluing the changes that undergird middle-class and professional women's lives, many practitioners have focused on the factory and labor union and ignored the high school and college. Both are important: an understanding of changes in women's experience involves both industrialization and education. In this light, the creation of Bryn Mawr—offering to women scholarship of the highest standards and the graduate fellowships and training they could get nowhere else—was a major breakthrough in American women's history. Its founding is comparable in significance to the opening of the Lowell mills.

Carey Thomas achieved in many other areas: suffrage and feminism, women's associations, medical education. To discuss why she is not remembered in each requires a lengthier disquisition than a preface allows. Suffice it to say that she could be a difficult advocate and adversary. To some degree I want this biography to restore her to appropriate memory; it should, as well, help explain why others tried to forget her. But it insists that in one way she must be recalled. Thomas was a vivid, powerful voice in her day. In her speeches to audiences of women she focused on women, higher education, and creativity. Her biography will, I hope, make accessible to the late twentieth century an important lost strand of feminist thinking.

Although familiar with her life and its portrayals from earlier research, I held off from rereading depictions of her so that I could let her letters and journals shape the tale. After six years of research and writing, I returned to Gertrude Stein's early story *Fernhurst*, published only after her death, and it took my breath away. Stein told the story of Carey Thomas' tangled relationship with Mamie Gwinn, her intimate friend of twenty-five years, and Alfred Hodder. Stein presents an uncanny likeness of Carey Thomas in the fictional guise of Helen Thornton, as a woman who is "hard headed, practical, unmoral in the sense that all values give place to expediency and she has a pure enthusiasm for the emancipation of women and a sensitive and mystic feeling for beauty and letters."[5] Stein never to my knowledge met Carey Thomas or visited Bryn Mawr during the latter's lifetime. But she got so much right.

I teach college, and therefore I understand. If anyone outside my immediate family knows me, my students do, for they see sides of me in class I cannot but reveal. Stein learned about Carey Thomas from the young Bryn Mawr alumnae studying with her at Johns Hopkins medical school.[6] But although Helen Thornton speaks Thomas' words and looks and acts so much like her, she is, in the end, not Carey Thomas. Imagined without Carey Thomas' past, she lacks her depth and resonance, the vitality and rich complexity of the person who emerged from historical time.

Carey Thomas admired Gertrude Stein's writings, but never knew that she was the subject of one of her tales. Thomas herself attempted late in life to write her autobiography. Bits of it had been coming out for years in her speeches and writings. Some of Thomas' words found their way into her sister Helen Thomas Flexner's memoir, *A Quaker Childhood*.[7] In reading this material and the existing draft of four chapters of the autobiography and the notes that she made, I am convinced that Carey Thomas in her later years obscured as well as revealed. She had a selective memory, enjoyed mythmaking, and was capable of outright lies. She sought to frame herself as she would have wanted others to remember her. I have used this material warily and selectively. Thus there are legends about M. Carey Thomas that will not be repeated in this book.

When she died, Carey Thomas left instructions that her executors choose a biographer if her autobiography was incomplete. They kept the biography among friends, selecting Edith Finch, the companion of Lucy Donnelly in her later years. As this biography will reveal, Lucy as a young woman had lived and worked in an intimate friendship with Helen Thomas, Carey's youngest sister, and they remained close after Helen married Simon Flexner and Lucy became Bryn Mawr's distinguished professor of English.[8]

The authorized biography that emerged, *Carey Thomas of Bryn Mawr*, is an unsatisfying life story that never gives a clear picture of its subject. A letter of reply to art connoisseur Bernard Berenson, the husband of Carey Thomas' cousin, clarifies why. After reading the biography, Berenson wrote Finch guarded praise and suggested that she needed to write a second book about Carey as "a human being *an & für sich* [in and for herself]." Finch answered that she had done this in preparation: "I fancy Carey Thomas was one of those people, whom I deplore, who are born to succeed. But it was the sexual problems of which you speak, added to the circumstances of her life (the ones that can be publicly examined even now) that turned her to her particular sort of success. Though, whatever, doubtless it would have been, as you say, the counterpart to success in mines, railways or factories." Berenson had been fascinated by Mamie Gwinn, and so, too, was Finch. To Edith Finch, however, the attraction was negative. She saw Mamie as "evil—like the evil of Byzantium encrusted with gold and jewels and mosaic colour, glinting sombrely." Mary Garrett, by contrast, seemed to her only "an uncommonly respectable figure and correspondingly dreary."[9]

With so many negatives ringing in my ears, I returned to the letters of agreement in the Bryn Mawr College Archives between Edith Finch and Helen Thomas Flexner, representing the executors of Thomas' estate. In them I found Finch's acceptance of censorship. I began to understand the biography's artistry. Whenever the author confronted an important, controversial, or passionate moment, she threw up a cloud of verbal smoke to satisfy her censors and obscure a subject she did not like.

Fortunately the Finch biography did not end family responsibility for M. Carey Thomas' memory. Millicent Carey McIntosh, her niece, the president of Barnard College, and her last living literary executor, saw to it that the papers were saved after a fire damaged them. Under her encouragement, Marjorie Housepian Dobkin edited Thomas' early letters and journals in what remains a valuable edition, widely used as a text in women's history classes.[10]

McIntosh gave Thomas' personal papers to the Bryn Mawr College Archives. Under Lucy Fisher West's direction the papers were expertly processed and published in a microfilmed edition.[11]

Carolyn Heilbrun has reclaimed biography for the feminist project. She is right; the world looks different with a woman at the center.[12] Yet M. Carey Thomas as a subject cannot fulfill all feminist hopes, and I fear that my biography will disappoint some readers. Hers is not a heroic story, although it has many heroic elements. At times I imagined writing only the first half of the life. Had I ended the telling in 1899, the reader could leave Carey Thomas triumphant. Yet she lived on, and to be honest to the life I had to go on. The twentieth-century part of the story is far less appealing, but it exists, and I and my readers must face it. It is part of a past that we must understand. But just as Carey Thomas was not blameless in her younger life, in her maturity she was not unmixed evil.

As important as was Thomas' public life, at moments it pales beside the drama of her personal life. My second temptation was to tell only the personal story of her relations with Mamie Gwinn, Mary Garrett, and Alfred Hodder. While a few traditionally trained historians have questioned the appropriateness or the significance of research into private life, some of my coworkers in women's studies have admitted that they care little for reading the professional trials of a college president. I confess that I am gripped by the emotional tale of Carey, Mamie, Mary, and Alfred. And yet, I know that to separate passion from power in Carey Thomas' life story is to distort and trivialize. I have argued that she lived life at the pitch of Italian opera: to take away her professional struggles, deeds, and commitments turns *Tosca* into the afternoon soaps. Moreover, because of Carey Thomas' ambition, Mary Garrett's money, and Mamie Gwinn's intelligence, any severance of private from public makes the larger story unintelligible.

To what degree was M. Carey Thomas a representative woman of her age? To what degree was she sui generis? This is a harder question now than it was before I began to immerse myself in her words, before she as an individual became etched in my consciousness. There was always about Carey Thomas something of the weird duck: she never fit into the straitjacket of Victorian convention or of her own effort to be a lady. She was frankly ambitious in an era that glorified women's sense of duty. She was energetic, even brusque. She read more than seems humanly possible and continued throughout her life to read newly written books. She was free from many of the pressures other women felt to be good, obedient, and subservient to men. She was vivid. Students always noted that with her fine clothes and noble mien, she was spontaneous and perhaps a bit off. She broke the molds.

But there is much that she shared with many leading women in her day. She was a reader who ranged widely and dreamed big dreams. She went to college filled with hope, but after graduation endured a crisis of confidence as it became clear that the world had no use for her gifts. She shared her life with other women in an era that neither defined nor put limits on their love. She blended her personal life and work in ways that make them inseparable. She linked her own professional advancement to the cause of women. She confronted a public world that, while it often opposed her in specifics, celebrated her accomplishments and accorded her immense respect. She drew her strengths not only from her unusual family and unique personal resources but also from the powerful women's institutions that she herself helped build. She lived in the heyday of women's separate associations. Women's clubs, women's professional organizations, reform groups, settlement houses, and women's colleges were generating a power base for social, economic, and political action. This female world sustained a dynamic agenda that linked women's enfranchisement to social justice and peace.[13]

But, of course, she had to come first. She had to exist before there was a Bryn Mawr College. What is ultimately most remarkable about M. Carey Thomas is not what she did or said, but her construction of her self. Whatever reservations I have about her, I always come back to the hard fact that she was a pioneer. She operated in a world without models of who she could be and become. There is a sense, hard to recreate in today's densely textured world of contradictory female images, that Carey Thomas was utterly alone. She had to imagine herself, create herself. It is easy to forget what an immense task that was. In my terms she did not do it perfectly or at times even well. But she was heroic in the task she set.

Ultimately she built better than she lived. The institutions that she created and the doors she opened for women remain as a lasting legacy. We who follow her, and who—partly because of her—have well-traveled paths in front of us, have the responsibility to extend her life's work. As we continue her quest to uphold the highest standards of higher education for women, we must insure that "women" includes all women.

Acknowledgments

ALTHOUGH this is a biography by a single author, it is, more than any other project that I have been engaged in, a social product. It could not have been researched and written without the sustained contributions of individuals and institutions. From the first moment a biography of M. Carey Thomas was an idea, Knopf editor Jane Nuckols Garrett has given it thoughtful attention. Her questions and comments have helped shape my thinking throughout all the stages of research and writing. Our many talks included informal moments when I benefited from her broad understanding of life. Nikki Smith has been an exemplary literary agent, combining sage advice, solid help, and great conversation. Jisho Carey Warner and Melvin Rosenthal spared me errors small and large.

The M. Carey Thomas Papers in the Bryn Mawr College Archives made this book possible. I am grateful to Millicent Carey McIntosh for giving Thomas' personal papers to the college. The personal and professional papers were published in a microfilm edition under the direction of Lucy Fisher West. Not only did I have the 217 reels available for research, some whose length exceeded a thousand double-sided pages, I benefited throughout from West's meticulous preparation of the material and her thoughtful introductions to both the papers as a whole and each individual reel. While it was the quality of the papers that drew me to undertake the biography, West's thorough and well-considered treatment of them has sustained me. In the years since Lucy West's retirement, I have been ably assisted at the Bryn Mawr College Archives by Caroline Rittenhouse, the college archivist, and by Leo Dolenski, the manuscripts librarian. Caroline has fostered the project in numerous ways, tangible and intangible. I am grateful to her and to Jim Rittenhouse for their many kindnesses. President Mary Patterson MacPherson has extended to me the larger hospitality of Bryn Mawr College. This is in no way an official or authorized biography, however. Neither the archives, the college, nor any of its staff is responsible for my statements or judgments.

Although the bulk of my research was at Bryn Mawr College, I have benefited from many archives. In several places, the archivists gave me valued help beyond official duty. I gratefully acknowledge the Princeton University Libraries, and especially the contribution of Ben Primer and Judith Golden.

Nancy Weiss Malkiel extended gracious hospitality. The American Philosophical Society Library's treasures were unearthed with the help of Beth Carroll-Horrocks. Nancy McCall aided me ably at the Alan Mason Chesney Medical Archives of the Johns Hopkins medical school. Fiorella Superbi was of great assistance at the Berenson Archives, I Tatti, outside Florence. Again I am grateful to Judith Ann Schiff of Manuscripts and Archives, Yale University Library. I found valuable material at the Milton S. Eisenhower Library, Special Collections, Johns Hopkins University, and The Rockefeller Archive Center, North Tarrytown, New York. Barbara Chase opened up the Bryn Mawr School papers to me and shared her work with me. Ron Walters assisted me with arrangements. Lisa Timothy helped me locate material in the Lilly Library of Indiana University. On a trip she took to Vassar College, Joyce Berkman extended collegial friendship into research assistance. Interlibrary Loan at the Honnold Library of the Claremont Colleges and the Neilson Library of Smith College brought the microfilm reels to me.

The kind invitation of Peter Hughes gave me the pleasure of speaking to the English Seminar at the University of Zürich. I am grateful to Peter and to Anwen Hughes for their help in locating important Zürich sources. With the kind help of Werner Bramke, I was able to travel to the University of Leipzig. I want to thank Pit Lehmann for his invaluable research assistance.

Many scholars answered queries of a specific nature. I am especially grateful to Leon Katz, Brenda Wineapple, and Judy Walkowitz for their help. John Thelin and Armstead Robinson gave me timely advice. I benefited greatly from talking with Millicent McIntosh at an early stage of my research. Marjorie Housepian Dobkin offered her encouragement and sent me photocopies that she had used in her own work. Two Smith College colleagues have helped to enrich my education: Eleanor Terry Lincoln and Elizabeth G. von Klemperer. I am grateful to Gertrude Gutzmann of Smith and to Smith students Gretel Helena Schueller and Elizabeth Ann Nichols for their aid in translations from the German. A lunch with women's studies colleagues at Smith College proved enormously informative and I wish to thank Martha Ackelsberg and Ruth Solie, as well as visiting scholar Karen Blair, for their insights.

Over the course of many years of research and writing I have been assisted by Smith students. Each has made a special contribution. I wish to thank Adrienne Press, Wendy Kline, Jennifer Mezey, Ann Robbart, and Pamela Wyn for careful work. Both Wendy and Jennifer made summer research much more interesting by their critical readings. In the academic year 1992–93 I had the good fortune of having Susan Webster as a research assistant. Her thorough and cheerful work brightened the year and gave me a firm sense that I was on solid ground.

The two institutions of my employ during research and writing gave material help. I am grateful to the University of Southern California for providing research funds. In the five years that I have been at Smith College, I have benefited from a research leave, funds for travel and photocopies, provision for summer research assistance, and a leave of absence. It is a source of both pleasure and pride to teach at a college that values scholarship so highly.

Fellowships enabled the final writing of this book, and I am deeply thankful to two institutions. In fall 1992, I took a leave from teaching through a grant from the National Endowment for the Humanities. In spring 1993, The Spencer Foundation continued that leave. In addition, I am grateful to The Spencer Foundation for research assistance and travel funds. The year of full-time research and writing was greatly enhanced by the Spencer grant and by its intangible but very real moral support.

I have presented elements of my work to many audiences, and in each case I have gotten valuable comments and criticism. I wish to thank especially the Friends of the Neilson Library and the Project on Women and Social Change at Smith College, Bryn Mawr College, the nine Phi Beta Kappa chapters that hosted me, and the American Studies Association.

Readers have been extraordinarily kind, especially given the length of the draft manuscript. Jane Garrett read what must have seemed like an infinity of drafts. Both Lisa Alther and Lois Banner read it at two stages, and I profited by the issues that they raised. In addition, I was fortunate to have the good judgment of Mary Maples Dunn, Carolyn Heilbrun, Daniel Horowitz, and Nikki Smith. Each reader pushed me to clarify my thinking and my prose. I remain responsible, however, for errors and judgments that they could not correct. Many of my ideas in chapters 7 and 9 were worked out as I pondered "Nous Autres: Reading, Passion, and the Creation of M. Carey Thomas," published in June 1992 in the *Journal of American History*. I wish to thank again the readers of that piece for their careful help. I am grateful to the journal and its editor for permission to reprint portions of the article.

I have often thought that my life is an academic version of the Mom and Pop grocery store at the corner of childhood memories. For over thirty years I have been in a professional and private partnership with Daniel Horowitz. As I worked on this biography, he was researching and writing about the career of Vance Packard. We heard each other's stories and puzzled over each other's questions. His skepticism and good humor frame the context in which I considered M. Carey Thomas. Our children probably had more of the "store" than they might have wanted, but they rolled up their sleeves in due fashion and minded the counter. I am grateful to Dan for the life we have created. And to Ben and Sarah for sharing it with us.

My triple dedication is a tribute to three persons that I hold in high esteem. It honors Jane Garrett's more than twenty-five years as an editor at Knopf. It recognizes the great importance of J. B. Jackson's imagination and writing in my life and work. And it remembers my beloved grandmother, whose long and varied life remains for me an abiding source of strength.

The Power and Passion of
M. Carey Thomas

I Could Not Catch Thee

M. CAREY THOMAS was conceived "in full daylight." James Carey Thomas, eager to have a child after his wife had suffered a miscarriage, persuaded Mary Whitall Thomas to have intercourse at midday so that both might be at the "height of their physical powers." The mother ever afterwards wondered if this was the source of her firstborn's "irrepressible vitality and intense joy in living." So wrote M. Carey Thomas about her own genesis. Mary Thomas recorded the birth in these words: "Our precious little daughter was born the 2nd of First Month, 1857, and on the 3rd we named her Martha Carey Thomas, hoping that she may not unworthily bear the name which is held in such dear remembrance by us both." Named for her father's late mother, she was never called Martha. Carey was her adult name; Minnie, that of her childhood.[1]

The two accounts capture the spirit of M. Carey Thomas' beginnings. From the very first, she was a lively, willful being enfolded by enthusiastic love tempered with the deep piety of the Society of Friends. The atmosphere, as she later put it, was filled with "an entrancing mixture of sheerest unreason and beguiling goodness."[2] Mary was a young matron of twenty-one; James, a physician two years older. The two had married fifteen months before and settled in Baltimore. Both were Friends, commonly called Quakers. Mary Whitall had grown up in Philadelphia, the daughter of wealthy glass manufacturer John Mickle Whitall and his wife, Mary Tatum Whitall, both pious Friends. Mary's older brother James Whitall had brought home from Haverford College his roommate James Carey Thomas, the son of a well-regarded Baltimore physician and Friend. A few years later, after he had trained to become a doctor at the University of Maryland, sturdy, redheaded James Carey Thomas courted and won the hand of winsomely beautiful Mary. After a long engagement, the newly married couple moved into the Baltimore house that John Whitall built for his daughter. It was here that M. Carey Thomas was born.

Baltimore in 1857 was a thriving city of approximately two hundred thousand, the third largest in the young nation and one of the most important in the slaveholding South. James and Mary brought their baby daughter into a special corner of that city, the close-knit Quaker world of what is now known as Old West Baltimore. Its families dwelt in the comfortable brick houses on both sides of treelined streets placed on a diagonal to the city's grid. The angle was appropriate, for most Friends had long before freed their slaves, and some held Northern sympathies.[3]

When James Thomas' father died, the young physician, his wife, and his daughter moved to James' larger childhood home on Madison Avenue. Surrounded by Thomas kin, they lived close to the Baltimore Friends Meeting House on Eutaw Street, where both Mary and James were devout members. Their world soon expanded to include the Baltimore beyond their doors. Mary Whitall Thomas became active in the women's meeting and began to move outward to moral reform and temperance. James Carey Thomas was respected as a Quaker lay minister. Increasingly he played a part in the civic life of Baltimore as a Sunday school teacher at the Young Men's Christian Association and through his association with Johns Hopkins. Yet even as Mary and James moved into the larger city, they remained within the mentality of Friends. As M. Carey Thomas later noted in the course of reading family letters and journals, this was a world focused on "getting the baptism of the holy spirit. . . . The Civil War is scarcely mentioned."[4]

The first daguerreotype of Minnie, in a lace-covered white dress, sitting in a child's chair, captures a ghostly glimpse of Mary retreating from the image after placing her child. Mary's eyes are eager and loving, her hand ready to support Minnie if needed. In the diminutive form at center camera there is little of the older girl and woman, beyond the wide-spaced brown eyes and distinctive middle part of her shining light brown hair. The print captures the likeness of an appealing child, made momentarily serious by the demands of mid-nineteenth-century photography to remain still and unblinking.

As James and Mary Thomas looked upon Minnie, what were their hopes? As deeply religious members of the Society of Friends, above all else, they saw her as a child of God. Their strongest wish for their Minnie was the experience of conversion, what they called the new birth or new heart, so that she might know the Divine Spirit. Mary Thomas recorded Minnie's early utterances that gave grounds for hope. In August 1859 she wrote, "Minnie made her first little prayer tonight. She asked Heavenly Father to give her a new little heart."[5]

To watch for harbingers of spiritual rebirth, Mary scrutinized her daughter for signs of developing conscience and moral feeling. As a young child Minnie showed great promise. When she was almost three, she could express her struggle to do good as the conflict inside her of good and bad angels. Mary noted that when Minnie did something wrong she came up to her, put her hand on her cheek, and said, "Is you grieved, mamma? Why didn't I not do that? I want to listen to the good angels." Mary reported soon after that Minnie told her, "Mamma, I do want to be good *so* bad, but then the naughty angels will come in. I don't let them come in, but they just come in themselves."[6]

Minnie was a cheerful, playful, affectionate child, and her mother delighted in the reactions of her own parents and sisters. Mary recorded Minnie's first visit to her parents: "The little baby won her way into all hearts by her quiet little ways, and her good-humored little face." John and Mary Whitall enjoyed the advantages that their wealth allowed and drew their children and grandchildren to them each summer in Atlantic City. Mary Thomas began to spend six midsummer weeks under their roof, a practice she followed until her parents' death. In Minnie's first summer Mary experienced the delight of sharing her own child with her family. This was an important beginning: in the next two decades Mary gave birth to nine more children. Eight of James and Mary Thomas' ten offspring lived beyond their first year and into adulthood.[7]

Mary Thomas' parents were generous to their youngest daughter, Mary, and indulged their grandchildren. They visited frequently and welcomed their children with their growing families into their three homes. Much of the year they lived in Philadelphia, close to the Meeting. On the beach at Atlantic City, they had a cottage surrounded by several acres. It was their country place, the Cedars, on a large working farm in New Jersey that became the family center. Although the creed required members of the Society of Friends to abstain from secular music, art, drama, jewelry, and other adornments— restrictions that some families might take to the extreme of asceticism—the Whitalls did not deny themselves physical affection, play, or the pleasures allowed by a kind Father. At appropriate points, the Whitalls gave to each of their grandchildren treasured toys, such as an elegant hobby horse to Minnie when she was two. In their own houses, they allowed their grandchildren to play freely, turning up chairs in the parlor to defend imaginary farmyards from foxes and other predators.[8]

John Whitall delighted in his youngest daughter's first child. The Atlantic City summers that he provided gave them time together. When Minnie was three, her mother commented on her health and exuberance. Her greatest pleasure was bathing in the ocean, "a brave little girl she was, going in just as far as her mama could take her." Her grandfather called her "little sturdy," as he relished her "whole souled enjoyment of everything." John Whitall wrote affectionately to Minnie, but he also stated clearly the kinds of expectations that went along with love. As he sent his love to the family with the admonition "and keep a very large pile for thyself my darling, sturdy, dear grandchild," he besought Minnie to pray. She should ask help to be good and to love her Savior and to do nothing to "grieve his Holy Spirit." Love, abundant love linked with the demand to be good and to submit to Heavenly Father's will: this was the Whitall formula to reproduce in the next generation loving and pious daughters. Would it work?[9]

Minnie Thomas' great-grandmother Anne Tatum thought not. In the baby's second year, the mother of Mary Tatum Whitall wrote to Minnie a letter designed for her parents' eyes. The elderly woman was troubled. "Thou has been introduced into this state of being, under what would generally be considered, auspicious circumstances." She feared Minnie would not understand that "every temporal enjoyment brings with it a *balance*. I have desired thy beloved and loving parents in training their Immortal offspring may take a comprehensive view of their *high* responsibilities!" Anne Tatum, "now near the close of a long life," felt the need to persuade Minnie's "indulgent father and mother" to remember duty, discipline, and sacrifice. "The human mind is of such a texture as to require the discipline of the Cross in order to develop all its strength and power. Remember therefore our ancient motto—No Cross, no Crown!"[10]

Although Mary Thomas looked for signs of piety and self-sacrifice in her child in ways that her grandmother would have approved, the generations between Anne Tatum and Mary Thomas made a difference. The granddaughter's generation believed that children grew in Christ less through the discipline of the Cross and more through Jesus' saving love.

And as a woman of the mid-nineteenth century, Mary Thomas delighted in her daughter's abounding energy and growing intellect. Fascinated by Minnie's developing language, Mary jotted down her uses and misuses of words. When Minnie was three, she told her mother that her dinner was "lovlicious." Before Minnie was three, Mary Thomas taught her daughter her letters, creating a game in which Mary put a piece of paper with large letters on a pincushion for Minnie to stab with a long needle. At age six Minnie said her lessons to her mother nearly every day; she spelled, printed dictation on her slate, and did simple arithmetic.[11]

In Minnie's first years, mental and spiritual development were fused. Culture and religion in the Quaker household of her parents were one. The Society of Friends had split in two in 1827, into the liberal Hicksites and the Orthodox. The Thomases belonged to the Orthodox body of Friends, which believed itself the saving "remnant." In the 1840s both the Thomas and Whitall branches of the family had been powerfully influenced by the evangelical preaching of Joseph John Gurney. James and Mary Thomas and many of their family and friends were leaders in the Gurneyite renewal movement that brought Orthodox Quakers into the larger evangelical Christian world of thought and practice. Renewal theology placed an emphasis, new to Quakers, on the experience of conversion, what they called the new birth. Renewal Quakers established Sunday or First Day schools and became active in temperance and prison reform. They urged family worship, Bible reading, and informal prayer circles. Locked out of the established Orthodox Quaker institutions which were controlled by the rival Wilburite faction, they established their own beachheads—Haverford College outside Philadelphia, the New Garden School in Greensboro, North Carolina, and the *Friends' Review*. In these exciting times of intense discussion, organizing, and prayer, Mary and James lived a life of religious enthusiasm.[12]

Minnie liked her mother to say hymns to her before going to bed, as well as a poem of Elizabeth Barrett Browning. At age three she went to her first Meeting, where she sat very still and demonstrated great interest. Mary noted in her journal that at her second Meeting, Minnie laughed, "but redeemed her character again the last time by being a very good little girl." Just before she was five, Minnie began formal religious training at the Friends' First Day school conducted by a cousin. Mary reported that Minnie told her, "Mamma, we all have to confess in school, yes, we have to confess. If we know anything about Cain and Abel, or Adam and Eve, we have to confess it." When Minnie was five and a half, her mother reported that she regularly attended the class and enjoyed it. Her mother was proud that she read well and that she amused herself by long stretches of reading to herself.[13]

As new parents in mid-nineteenth-century America, the progeny of two established Baltimore and Philadelphia families, James and Mary Thomas saw Minnie as growing into a fitting daughter who would marry and have children of her own. They expected their firstborn to love her brothers and sisters. Mary approved of all signs of her daughter's caring, domestic side. After Minnie expressed her longing to stay always within the parental nest, her mother revealed her conventional expectations: "I am afraid she will change her mind some day, especially as she was inquiring very earnestly a short time afterwards what little boy she was going to marry."[14]

Although Mary derived much pleasure from her daughter's spirited nature, from Minnie's first months Mary's journal records a counterpoint—unease at Minnie's willfulness. The other side of her exuberance was a self-assertion that did not easily bend to parental authority. The meaning of Minnie's obstinacy went far beyond issues of family government. A pious Friend saw the relation between acceptance of earthly authority and of Divine. Confronting her willfulness, those who loved Minnie faced the question: was she to be saved?

Minnie's assertiveness began in infancy. When she was six months old, Mary Thomas tried to get her to sleep in a crib, but could not bear her cries. After Minnie turned one, Hannah Whitall Smith, Mary Thomas' older, more experienced sister, stepped in. She saw that Minnie got a bottle of milk at ten every night, was tucked up tight, and left undisturbed until morning. Although she cried a little for a few nights, she soon began to sleep soundly until six in the morning. A year later, Hannah was again visiting when Minnie refused

to go to bed. Mary Thomas attributed the problem to her child's being unaccustomed to a new nurse. As Mary reported, Hannah "took her in hand, and
triumphed at last." After resisting furiously for a few nights, Minnie gave up.
She was put in her crib with a mint drop in each hand and after her mother
kissed her on her lips would sing herself to sleep with the words "Dear mamma,
dear mamma."[15]

As an old woman, M. Carey Thomas remembered the incident differently.
It was her first childhood memory. She had been allowed to stroke her mother's
eyebrows as she went to sleep and during the night if she awakened. She
recalled that she was "shrieking at the top of my lungs as I always did when
my mother refused to have her eyebrows stroked" when the door opened and
"a menacing figure" stood beside her crib. In a stern voice such as she had
never yet heard, Hannah said, "Minnie, stop crying. Your mother will not
come if you cry all tonight and all tomorrow. Here is a mint drop." Hannah
so frightened her that she stopped shrieking and never again asked her mother
to let her stroke her eyebrows.[16]

The menacing figure above her crib, Hannah Whitall Smith, came to
have a unique place in Minnie's affections. A special tie bound them. In the
month before Minnie's second birthday, Mary noted that her daughter called
all her dolls Hannah and took them to bed with her. The following summer,
Minnie had her aunt's company and attention, devoting herself, in Mary's
words, "almost too much." Minnie got Hannah to go to the beach with her,
"and the zest with which she would caper off on a sturdy little trot was very
funny."[17]

In Minnie's first year, Hannah lost her elder child, five-year-old Nelly,
leaving her with only a four-year-old son, Frank, who would be ten at the birth
of his sister Mary. Hannah's husband, Robert Pearsall Smith, was emotionally
unstable. Into the empty space, Minnie came. Hannah delighted in her niece's
visits and wrote her loving letters. Hannah was devoted to Frank, but the loss
of what was then her only daughter continued to haunt her. Minnie also came
to have need of Hannah. At the end of Minnie's second year, Mary and James
Thomas had their second child, John M. Whitall Thomas. Minnie found
herself no longer the sole object of her parents' attention. Although Mary and
James held special love for their firstborn, they had less and less time. James
Thomas was a traditional father and provider, but his medical practice and
religious and civic concerns occupied him fully. Mary, attached as she was to
Minnie, was impelled by the demands of her faith and of her growing brood.

Hannah was no ordinary aunt. A deeply spiritual woman who had left the
Society of Friends to join the Plymouth Brethren, she was in 1861 on the
verge of the work that brought her renown as an evangelist and writer. She
identified with her niece's whole-souled enjoyment. When six-year-old Minnie was visiting Hannah, she and her brother and cousin walked to the woods,

paddled about, climbed rocks, "and got *perfectly filthy* for an hour or two."
As Hannah wrote to her sister Mary, "Min just reminds me of my young self
the whole time. She paddled almost up to her hips and could hardly drag
herself away." Perhaps Hannah also sensed in the exuberant girl something of
her own questing spirit. A revealing letter to Minnie at age four began with
her telling of her recent dream: "I thought thee *would* walk all by thyself along
a long board that reached out into the water ever so far, and I ran after thee
as far as I could go, but I could not catch thee until thee was way at the end,
and then thee was all sopping wet, and I dreamed I hugged thee up *so* tight."
The child venturing off on her own in a treacherous place, the aunt running
after, the child immersed, the aunt loving: Hannah never claimed to have
psychic powers, but her dream accurately presaged the future of M. Carey
Thomas.[18]

Hannah was an enthusiast. Hannah described to Minnie how she had
begun to pare peaches, and how her father and mother had joined her. Then
came Frank and cousin Johnny Whitall ready to help. What they really wanted
was to eat. "So I told them to have their mouths all ready, and whenever I
came across a nice ripe piece I called them over and popped it right in."
Hannah had broken with the Quaker prohibition of music and in her household sang psalms. In a later letter from Hannah to Minnie, thanking her for
her gift of a pincushion and her message that "thee thinks I am the beautifullest
woman in the world," she wrote, "I often want to see thee, my dear little light
of my eyes, and in the evenings I think it would be *so* sweet to have thee sitting
in my lap singing hymns to thee. Does thee remember how we used to sing
hymns at Atlantic City?"[19]

Mary Thomas thoroughly approved of the growing love between her beloved sister and her eldest child. She hoped that her older sister might help
bring her daughter to Jesus' ways and to self-control. Some of Hannah's letters
were designed to do just that, counseling Minnie to be good and to love Jesus,
but others may have encouraged Minnie's more ebullient side. The messages
that Minnie received from her Aunt Hannah were, in fact, deeply contradictory, as contradictory as Hannah's own extraordinary nature. Hannah pled
with the child to open her heart to Jesus. She encouraged Minnie to be caring
toward her brothers and to be domestic. Yet what is one to make of this
narrative that Hannah wrote to her sister when she had Mary's children
visiting? After letting the children get dirty, she had allowed Minnie to dress
as a boy. She wrote in robust humor to her sister that soon after Mary had
departed, "We proceeded to business and soon had thy little girl transformed
into a very handsome little boy." The children went out to dig in the sand,
but because there were only two wooden spoons for four, they began to quarrel.
To restore peace, Hannah agreed to take the children to the store to get four
wooden shovels. "The children had a grand time in the carpenter's yard,

playing on a high pile of lumber, rampaging and caracoling about in fine style, the Gorilla [John Whitall Thomas] among the rest." After the noon dinner Minnie stayed dressed as a boy. As she ran up and down the pavement in front of the house, the neighbors came out. They "wanted to know *his* name and all exclaimed 'what a handsome little boy.' I was looking out my window. Min would not tell her name as she evidently did not like to dispel the illusion, but Frank told them and they seemed perfectly astonished, and heartily amused. Min says she wants to turn into a boy and wants to know why she can't."[20]

Mary Thomas was deeply fond of her sister, but her dressing Minnie as a boy was more than she could take. She wrote Minnie a letter whose apparent humor only partly masked its uneasiness. Hannah's letter, Mary wrote, told her about "how funny you looked dressed up in Franky's trousers. It made me laugh very much to think of my little daughter looking so much like a little boy that the people did not know who she was." More disturbing to Mary than her daughter dressed as a boy had been Minnie's wish that she were one. Mary did not scold. In her characteristic manner, she told her daughter of a mother's positive pleasure in her as a girl: "I think I should have known her but I am sure I should love better to see her looking like a dear little girl. Thee don't think I'd like to have three boys and no little daughter, does thee? And what would Johnny and Harry do without any sister?" Her postscript added the further weight of James Thomas' potential concern. Mary told Minnie that she was sending Hannah's letter to him: "I don't know what he'll think of his little daughter being dressed up like a boy."

Although Quaker thought and practice had greatly extended the range of behavior appropriate to girls and women, it insisted on the absolute essence of male and female. To want to be of the other sex threatened the spiritual order. In language that Mary would later use, it was one of the delusions of Satan. As disturbed as she was, Mary did not let her feelings separate her from Minnie. Mary closed, "I hope those lips of thine don't get pouted out much. I shall want to give them ever so many kisses when I get hold of thee."[21]

In an image of Minnie from this period, a brown-eyed girl with a well-proportioned face, full lips, and clear jaw has her parted hair freshly brushed back over her ears and out of sight. She is posed in a white lace dress behind a delicate Victorian chair back. The representation captures a vigorous child in the frame of parental hopes. Daguerreotypes were taken not only to record a moment in an emerging child's development but also as a lasting token of a child who might be taken to the Lord at any minute. Death was a constant presence in the Thomas and Whitall families. Although Mary Thomas did not lose a child until her fifth died in his first year, she feared the Grim Reaper with every illness.

Before Minnie turned six, pride in her growing ability, pleasure in her zest, and anxiety about the state of her soul had become the settled themes of her mother's journal. The Christmas season of 1862 prompted Mary Thomas to reflect. Minnie had gone to two children's parties that she had enjoyed perhaps too much. "She seemed to enter so entirely into the spirit of party going, that I felt quite convinced it would be better for her to enjoy herself in a more rational way." Mary continued, balancing her daughter's difficulty in resisting temptation with her pleasure in reading the Bible, "I trust that our little daughter is growing daily in her desire to please her Savior."[22]

Although Mary and James Thomas were anxious about the state of Minnie's soul, they delighted in her. As Minnie approached her seventh birthday, Mary stepped back to summarize her satisfaction: "Minnie is growing [into] a very companionable girl. She reads a great deal and plays very nicely with her brothers and sits up in the evening to tea with her Father and Mother and beguiles them into allowing her to sit up much too late. She is a great pleasure and joy to us all."[23]

II

IN THE Thomas household, 1864 began well. Although the nation was torn by civil war, the Thomas family was moved only by its internal dramas. Mary Thomas recorded in her journal: "The year opened upon us very pleasantly enjoying our home and our children, delighting in our darling daughter, who seemed to grow dearer every day. I fear we thought too little of the rich blessings that were bestowed upon us, and settled down in the enjoyment of the gifts somewhat forgetting the giver." Grandmother Tatum had insisted that "every temporal enjoyment brings with it a balance . . . the discipline of the Cross." The payment that Anne Tatum had thought necessary for the Crown was about to be demanded. Into the indulgent and happy household came catastrophe.[24]

Mary Thomas recalled the scene: "Minnie came into the nursery . . . and said, 'Mamma, I'm going to be assistant cook.' " Minnie washed and put on an apron. She came in to kiss her mother. As Minnie left to go downstairs, Mary thought to herself, "What a darling, satisfactory, precious daughter." Then she wrote, "The vision of her dear little figure had scarcely left my mind before I heard a scream which filled me with horror. I rushed to the door and met my darling child in flames."[25]

Late in life M. Carey Thomas wrote her own account of the burn. She had gone into the kitchen to visit the cook. When the cook went to answer the doorbell, she asked Minnie to lift the lid off the kettle if the water boiled. As seven-year-old Minnie tried to do this, her apron caught fire from the coals. Afire, she rushed first to her father's office "and tried to put out the flames by wrapping myself in his big traveling shawl. But the folds were held together by [an] old-fashioned man's . . . safety pin which I could not unfasten. After sixty-eight years I remember, as if it were yesterday, the moment of utter terror when, enveloped in flames, I could not unfold the shawl. I rushed upstairs shrieking for my mother. She saw me at (as she told me afterwards) the head of the stairs burning like a torch with flames reaching high above my head." Mary smothered the flames with blankets. She herself caught fire but the nurse damped them with blankets. "Twice when my mother opened the blankets the flames burst out again." She sent one servant for cotton and linseed oil and others to try and find James, who was attending patients away from home. [26]

Mary cut off Minnie's clothes, wrapped her in cotton soaked in soothing oil and lime water, and laid her down. Mary wrote in her journal that as she comforted her daughter and gave her "assurances that she would soon be well," Minnie was "altogether calm and natural." Mary noted, without comment, Minnie's first thoughts: she said "she did not see why Heavenly Father was not with her then. He was with Shadrach, Meshach, and Abednego in the fiery furnace, and she thought He might have been with her." [27]

Minnie remained conscious until her father and another physician unwrapped the cotton. She was badly burned on her right leg and arm. M. Carey Thomas recalled, "I remember what seemed the burned flesh on my leg coming off when they opened the cotton wrapper, and after this I remember nothing more." In her telling she lay unconscious for many weeks. Mary noted in her journal that Minnie became feverish in the evening, and her mind began to wander. "Then began the struggle for life. For days and weeks she lay, and tossed on her bed of suffering, and we watched in agony beside her, not knowing whether she would be left to us." [28]

In the months that followed, as Mary cared for her precious Minnie, their early bond was restored. The three boys that had come between Mother and eldest daughter were entrusted to others, and Mary gave Minnie all she had. "The one [and] only desire of her heart seemed to be to have her Mamma near her, night and day I remained beside her, took every meal at her bedside for four or five months and never left her." Again and again in those months she sang to her:

> Oh her mother's ever near, never fear, ever, ever near
> And her Savior's ever near, never fear, ever ever near,
> Ever near ever dear, never never fear.

Each day Mary had to dress the burn. This was the most disturbing time of all, because "it hurt her intensely, she was so terribly excited and nervous." James Thomas was a physician, but dressing the burn was solely Mary's task. "I always did it, no one else could touch her, she always wanted her father in the room, but no one must touch her but Mamma." [29]

Minnie's pain was intense. At moments she sought release in death. Mary recalled, "Sometimes she would wake up and say, 'Oh, Mamma, I want to go so bad up to Heaven.' And I could not wonder, darling child, and yet I could not give her up if it was the Lord's will to let her remain." As M. Carey Thomas remembered these days in her autobiography, she recalled the anguish. Daily her mother had to pull the cotton off the burn. The dressing caused the wound to bleed profusely, and "every day my shrieks resounded." Because she would allow no one but her mother to touch her, Mary, "too, had to go through the daily agony of hurting me so terribly." Mary had asked her daughter to believe in prayer. Minnie now insisted that, two hours before the burn had to be dressed, her mother kneel down and pray to God "to make the next dressing less terrible." M. Carey Thomas explained, "I felt sure that if my mother who seemed to me so good and beautiful (that not even God could resist her) only prayed hard enough, God would not let my dressings hurt me so awfully." It did not work. "The pain never lessened, and, although I did not dare to let her omit prayers, lest by any happy chance God might hear her at last, my faith in prayer never recovered the shock I received from my mother's unanswered prayers." If it had been her own prayers, she would have thought it was her failure, "but when my mother prayed, I knew that there must be something wrong with God."[30]

Members of the family came to visit and help. Dr. J. R. Winslow stayed several nights. Hannah came and brought her baby, Mary, born just after Minnie's burn. Mary recorded that Hannah's "visit was a great comfort to us all, she amused Minnie with her stories and cheered us all up very much." Gifts came in abundance, but failed to amuse her because she could not play with them. Mary and James gave her a canary. As Mary wrote her mother, "It is impossible to refuse her anything that she seems to desire." Gradually the superficial burns healed, "but the large burn remained as it was." In the spring, to get Minnie out of doors and distract her, James Thomas had a basket made that fit into the carriage. A crib mattress was placed in the basket for Minnie's comfort. The basket made it possible for Minnie to travel, and she went twice to Philadelphia. In the summer she went with her mother to Atlantic City and to the Cedars. There Minnie took a daily ride. Her father, who had remained in Baltimore, wrote to her how glad he was that she could sit up and walk with her mother's help. "I am thankful that our kind Father in Heaven has healed thee thus much. Let us ask him to make thee quite well, if it is His will."[31]

Although Mary's attentive family did what they could, Mary knew that no one could take her place. "Day and night I was still with her. She could not be happy if I was out of her sight. Sometimes she would consent to let Aunt Hannah sing her to sleep, rubbing her foot the while, but 'I want Mamma' was generally the cry in such a plaintive little voice that it could not be withstood." During their days together Mary read aloud to her works such as *Grimm's Fairy Tales* and *Gulliver's Travels*. Minnie especially liked *The Arabian Nights* and asked her mother to read it again and again. As M. Carey Thomas recalled in her autobiography, her mother told her "that sometimes she felt as if she could not bear to read over and over stories [that] seemed to her so silly but that seemed to me full of enchantment." At nights when the pain was more intense Mary read and recited poetry.[32]

After the summer stay, Mary returned with Minnie and the boys to Baltimore, not to their house in the city but to a cottage outside. Minnie's condition worsened, and fear of a Confederate raid brought them back into the city. As they returned they passed several Union fortifications. In Baltimore the following day Minnie grew even worse, "great bumps rising up on her sore when the dressing was removed, which bled profusely." Their doctor was bewildered and advised the seashore. Leaving their sons with James' Aunt Julia, Mary and James took Minnie to Atlantic City, and in the next three weeks she improved. The family returned to the cottage outside Baltimore, where Mary slept with Minnie downstairs. Finally in September Minnie was able to get up and walk. When her Whitall grandparents visited the following month, they "were delighted to see darling Minnie walking about a little, though her sore was still very large, and very painful when being dressed."[33]

Without warning, in April 1865, Minnie took desperately sick with typhoid and lay in a torpor. Mary wrote that within hours she became so ill "that we gave her up almost." The danger passed; Minnie recovered. With deep gratitude, Mary Thomas recorded, "Our merciful Heavenly Father again gave us back our darling from the very verge of the grave, and we were able to bring our children all safe to our home in Baltimore again." In the months that followed, Mary reported to her family that Minnie looked thin and frail and seemed depressed. The wound in her right leg did not heal. It was not until December 1866, almost three years after the burn, that Mary could state that Minnie had returned to wholehearted enjoyment.[34]

To Mary Thomas, Minnie's burn was an act of God. "The Lord giveth, the Lord taketh away." As she relived it in the writing, she first thought of it as God's reminder of His gifts. She never blamed her Heavenly Father. Ultimately she was grateful that He chose to let Minnie remain with her awhile.

Late in her life as she composed her autobiography, M. Carey Thomas saw her burn as the divide between a carefree, happy childhood and a sentimental girlhood. "After eighteen months of enforced quiet, listening to reading and to the talk of my mother and her sisters and friends that went on around me, I got up a very different child a Romantic Victorian." With the cynicism of age, she asserted that she was her "mother's little acolyte," believing anything that her mother believed. Yet other memories of hers and the record of the time tell a different story.[35]

Her first cry had been that God had forsaken her. God let her be burned. He had been with Shadrach, Meshach, and Abednego in the fiery furnace. "He might have been with her." God would not end her suffering, but kept her on earth. Only her mother could help. A seven-year-old child in terrible pain, she held on to the one who meant comfort and hope. Minnie reenacted the earliest drama of life; and her mother did not fail her. Mary Thomas was at her side as she had been when Minnie was an infant. And this time, Aunt Hannah would not intervene to insist that Minnie fall asleep alone: "night and day I remained beside her, took every meal at her bedside for four or five months, and never left her." The child, deserted by God, clung to her earthly mother whose prayers God failed to answer. Just at the point when friendships and school might normally have pushed a daughter into an autonomous realm away from her mother, Minnie found herself utterly dependent on Mary Thomas, reliving their earliest days together before the birth of three brothers. And since God had not spared her as he had Shadrach, Meshach, and Abednego, and He had not answered her mother's prayers, at an existential level Minnie now had grounds for religious doubt.

The horror, the fear, and the renewed intimacy changed the way that mother saw daughter. In the years of Minnie's early childhood, her mother had balanced pleasure in her firstborn's enthusiasm and intellect with anxiety about her willfulness. With the burn, the struggle to subdue Minnie's will ended. As Minnie returned to health, Mary noted in her journal only signs of her well-being. From age seven until she went away to school at fifteen, Minnie Thomas' soul was left alone.

CHAPTER 2

Ain't Going to Be Sentimental

S PUNKY, religious, imaginative, affectionate, demanding: these words characterize Minnie Thomas at eight as she emerges from the journal that she dictated to her mother and aunt. Living within the close relationships of her family, Minnie seems a typical girl of her time. The antics of her youngest brother, Bond, amused her. Each new step of recovery gave her pleasure: going to Bible class, staying up late, putting herself to bed, doing the dishes. With her newfound freedom she had no wish to lose her mother's exclusive attention. As Mary Thomas reentered her own world of Meeting and reform, Minnie noted, "I did not much like Mother's going out." She delighted in the imagination. Her parents encouraged her love of poetry and mythology. Her father told her about the Greek gods; in January 1865, he read to her the story of Perseus and the Gorgons, but she did not like it "half as much" as the Wonder Book.[1]

Her autobiography tells a different story, one of the pain and heroism that Minnie Thomas was determined to hide. Beginning in the summer of 1865 she learned to walk again. Her right arm and the calf of her right leg completely healed, but a large open sore on her right thigh remained, eight inches long and three to six inches wide. "The summer of 1865 I persuaded my father to let me take off the terrible dressing and bandages and try to walk about my room for a little while every day." She wore a short jacket that left her legs unclothed. "I remember holding on to the chairs and furniture and hopping on my well leg across the open spaces of the room." Each day she walked farther and longer. Exposed for periods each day to the open air, her sore "got less angry and hurt less." She convinced her father to give up dressing the wound. "I was now determined, however much it hurt, to go about as usual, and I was rewarded for my courage. Soon I was able to walk without limping." She learned to skate and swim and play baseball with her brothers and their friends. If she ever fell or was hit by a ball, "the agony was almost unbearable." Hiding her pain, she did not let it make a difference in what she did. "Had it not been for my indomitable determination to act as if I was well I should have been a cripple all my life." The wound did not heal completely until she was fifteen. During those years she never mentioned her struggle or her suffering, even to her mother.[2]

The reward was play, delightful play. By the fall of 1865 she returned to First Day school and to regular school. Although her diary records frequent feelings of "mortification" at forgetting her text or at being stupid, the primary activity of her days was play. In the indulgent, child-centered Thomas household, the adults left Minnie and her brothers alone to devise endless games. They were the modern Greeks repelling the Turks in Sebastopol. They were the Hebrews against the Philistines. The illustrations in Flaxman's *Homer* gave them "an inexhaustible supply of heroic battles." In one exploit, frequently retold by Baltimore kin, the children commandeered the family's winter supply of potatoes to use "as ammunition for a great Homeric battle in our front hall." Expecting Mary to be out for the morning, the Thomas children took the part of the Trojans; their friends, the Greeks. Mary returned early and met at her front door an older woman whom the children of the family called Aunt Harvey Ellicott. Mary "prayed on the doorstep that we might be up behaving well and opened the door with her latch key to find herself and Aunt Harvey in the midst of a terrific battle with potatoes flying in every direction. They were bombarded with potatoes from . . . above in the second-story landing before we even knew anyone had come. Aunt Harvey's bonnet was knocked off and her spectacles broken and our Mother got a black eye." Such incidents occasioned "sympathy for our father and mother for having brought into the world such imps of darkness."[3]

During these years Mary was busy not only with constant pregnancy and repeated childbirth but also with her own emerging career as a religious leader and reformer, which often took her out of the house. As she came home she feared opening her front door, and well she might: at different times she found Minnie with her two front teeth knocked out, Harry impaled on the railing, Bond with the prongs of a garden rake sticking through his foot, and John with a broken shoulder. Moreover, there was a good deal that Minnie and her brothers kept from their mother. They were not supposed to watch the servants conduct a rat hunt with terriers and sticks, but they did. They played in the stable yard, forbidden ground presided over by the two African-American coachmen of her father and uncle. Their worst adventure did land them the punishment of being put to bed for the day. Unwilling to tolerate one of John's fierce outbursts of temper, his siblings tied him up, buried him in the sand, and forgot him; as the tide came in, he almost drowned before his loud cries alerted rescuers.[4]

Despite the disapproval of her older, more conservative Baltimore relatives, Mary was determined to give her children wide freedom. In September 1865 she lost a son, James Whitall Thomas, born the previous March. She had almost lost her daughter, her beloved eldest child, but God in his mercy had restored her. M. Carey Thomas recorded in her autobiography that some believed that the burn was "God's punishment" on her parents for the way they had brought her up.[5] Mary knew better, and once Minnie began to recover, Mary no longer had the desire or will to restrain her daughter's exuberant nature.

A good part of the year Minnie was with her mother's family, away from Baltimore eyes. At Atlantic City they could enjoy what M. Carey Thomas later recalled as "a desert of sea and sand." There were the ocean to bathe in and ships to sail. They had the run of the Whitalls' New Jersey farm, the Cedars, with its fields, woods, and pond. There were trees to climb and horses to ride. For Mary Thomas and her sister Hannah Whitall Smith, the Whitalls converted a double house they called the Barracks. To it Mary and Hannah brought their growing broods to spend much of the summer. At New Year's the entire family gathered in Philadelphia for a Whitall feast.

II

For five years of play and school, Minnie ignored her journal, but at age thirteen, when she returned to diary-keeping, her liveliness had a clear direction. She announced her intentions at the outset:

> Journal kept by Jo March
> Commenced June 20th 1870
> *Ain't going to be sentimental*
> *"No no not for Jo" (not Joe)*
> *Not for Jo March if she knows it*
> No No No[6]

In her diary, Minnie assumed the persona of Jo March, Louisa May Alcott's alter ego in *Little Women*. By so doing she declared her independence from conventional notions of womanhood. Jo is the tomboy daughter, the reader and writer, who cuts and sells her hair, and writes and sells her words to provide for her impoverished family. Unlike domestic Meg, pious Beth, and vain Amy, Jo is not "sentimental." She relishes action, not emotion. She is plucky, impulsive, and literary. All very much like Minnie Thomas in her early teen years. For two years Minnie kept a diary as Jo March, where she tried to say exactly what she thought, without preaching. She hoped it would be for her eyes only. In her large and entangled family, this was difficult. She began its second volume with the hopeful intention, "I am going to do my best to seclude it from the public gaze."[7]

Camera images of Minnie from this period err, for by their nature they negate her most essential quality, her vitality. Yet they do show that she was coming to look like the Thomas side of her family. Many years later in her memoir, Minnie's much younger sister described them: "The Thomas family all had hair that gleamed in the light. We were inclined to be short and sturdy and were energetic and quick in our movements. . . . We laughed aloud gaily." Except for her height—Minnie was to grow to five feet, four and a half inches, taller than the average female of her time—the family word portrait fit her. Moreover, she had her father's clear, well-defined features: widely spaced brown eyes under dark arched brows; a large, straight nose; and full, sharply defined lips. At least for the camera, she carried herself well. In her day she would not have been regarded as pretty, for she was neither fragile nor exquisite. She was unquestionably fair and comely.[8]

As did her model Jo at the outset of Alcott's rendering, Minnie scorned conventional femininity. Her cousin Bessie King was ready for play, but both girls frequently had to contend with Bessie's widowed father. Bessie was the daughter of her parents' closest friend, Francis T. King, a prominent Quaker known for his work to advance higher education. M. Carey Thomas later recalled Bessie's beauty, the "glow in her cheeks," and her blue eyes and soft brown hair. Minnie told her diary, "After breakfast King came up. I was delighted to see her. We climbed about a little and then went on top of the house and sat under the shade of a chimney" and learned a poem. The two went to Bessie's father's office to see if they could go rowing. Mr. King asked about their companions. When the girls answered "the boys," Mr. King told them they were "entirely too big and all that sort of stuff. . . . People seem to think that girls don't want any fun and even if they do want to row and climb they are shocked and say it isn't *LADYLIKE*." Against this pressure Bessie and Minnie vowed to "resist to the last."[9]

Their main recreations were climbing on the roof, rowing, skating, walking on stilts, riding, and shocking the neighbors. Although Minnie's family allowed her to take the carriage, Bessie's father did not. One November day, angry at all the things forbidden to them by Mr. King, Minnie recounted that she and Bessie "went to a store and bought lots of *bad* candy, came back, lay on my bed, and ate it from a *sense of duty*, of course. Then we went into the yard, swung on the trapeze, and walked on stilts. We stood at the back gate on them and astonished passersby." They also acted out dramas taken from the books they were reading. They built forts of books and used chess pieces as soldiers. They went through all of Sir Walter Scott's novels, acting out the scenes they liked best.[10]

By age thirteen, Minnie's intellectual abilities were becoming apparent. On June 20, 1870, she reported that she had gotten four prizes when school closed for the summer. She delighted in Romantic poetry and memorized her favorites, such as "The Cloud" by Shelley. She was a great reader and read for pleasure. Home voices, however, urged reading for self-improvement. One autumn day she went with her friends to the Mercantile Library and withdrew *Green Mountain Girls*, but when she returned the book with her mother, she called it "the most trashy immoral miserable *Yankee* bad book I ever read" and reminded herself, "I really *must* not waste my time on such *trash*." Mary Thomas believed that Minnie should read for profit, not for pleasure. While Minnie was chatting with Bessie, she "didn't watch Mother who got out Josephus' four great big volumes for me to read—the idea; but we compromised and got out A *Prince of the House of David*."[11]

Late in her life M. Carey Thomas noted that her childhood and youth were lived exclusively within the Society of Friends. "Until I went to boarding school and college I knew no one who was not a Quaker." She further judged Baltimore to be a peculiarly insular, Southern world. Yet, with the exception of a sole reaction to a popular novel, her journal records little that is distinctively Southern. Moreover, it suggests diverse intellectual influences impinging upon her. George Peabody had given to the city the Peabody Institute, which, when it opened in the late 1860s, combined a library, a music school, and a lecture program. In her early teen years she went there with her parents to lectures, even when this meant late nights and no time to prepare her lessons for the next day. Loving poetry as she did, she was excited that James Russell Lowell was coming to lecture. Yet during his address she found talking to Bessie more compelling: "we had so much to tell each other it was a great trial to listen to Lowell." The scientific series during the 1870–71 season won her genuine admiration and fired her ambition to become a scientist and physician.[12]

Searching for experiments, Minnie found a book written for boys that gave her ideas, and in late November 1870, she tried to produce a mouse skeleton. Her journal contains a full narrative of what became in Baltimore a legendary event. First Minnie put out a trap and caught a live mouse. Her friends would not kill him, "so I heroically dropped the trap into a pail of water and rushed out of the room." As she waited for the mouse to die, Bessie and she roasted chestnuts, and then, going outside, "bared our glittering knives and commenced operations." They had not counted on the mouse's fur being soft, and found they could not make a hole in it. "It made us sick and our hands trembled so we couldn't do a thing." Realizing that their squeamishness "was *feminine* nonsense," they forced themselves to continue, and, although it disgusted them, they got the skin off "elegantly, just like a glove." Forgetting their high scientific calling, they ran about holding the skinned mouse by the tail, chasing a friend. After boiling the carcass, they picked off the meat, saved the tongue and eyes to examine under a microscope, and put the skeleton on the window to bleach. Pleased with their accomplishments, the two girls resolved "to spend our money in instruments instead of candy, and . . . invite our friends to our experiments." Minnie decided to become a chemist.

But triumph quickly turned into disaster. A maid threw away the tongue and eyes and "worst of all, woe, woe is me," the skeleton smashed after it fell out of the window. When Bessie told her father about the mouse, he gave her a grave look and said, "Bessie, Bessie, thee is losing all thy *feminine* traits." Minnie, who by then had returned to domestic pursuits, commented, "I'm afraid I haven't got any to lose for I greatly prefer cutting up mice to sewing worsted."[13]

Minnie's religious heritage did not dampen her curiosity and high spirits or impede her access to the larger culture. It meant, however, that outside influences were subjected afterward to Quaker interpretation. At the dinner table or on the walk home from a lecture, elders commented on what they heard, and they bent or rejected it according to the faith. By her teen years, however, Minnie Thomas kept her own counsel. She listened to elders, but sifted and challenged that which went against her own inner light.

One of Minnie Thomas' most revealing journal entries came in January 1871. She went to hear the orator Anna Dickinson lecture on Joan of Arc. Although Minnie perceived that Dickinson "got carried away by her own eloquence," she liked the talk. The militaristic content went unmentioned in this Quaker daughter's journal. Instead Minnie focused on Dickinson's call for women's rights. In her address she had stated, "that if a boy had genius and talent and splendid abilities" and went to his parents to tell them he must go forth to improve the world, "they would dry their tears and send him forth with their blessing." However, "if a girl grown up in the same way with the same talent, same genius, same splendid abilities, should in the same way express her desire, they would put her in her chamber, lock the door and put the key in their pocket and think they had done their duty!" Dickinson's message struck Minnie strongly, reaffirming her sense of wrong. She wrote in her journal, "Oh my, how terrible, how *fearfully* unjust that seems. A girl [should] certainly do what she chooses as well as a boy." And then, in what would become a characteristic response, Minnie thought of herself as a counter-example: "When I grow up, we'll see what will happen."[14]

On the walk home Minnie's ire was provoked by Dr. Morris, a family friend who joined them. All the way home he talked about the "sacred shrine of womanhood and that no matter what splendid talents a woman might have she couldn't use them better than by being a wife and mother and then went off in some highfalutin stuff about the strength of women's devotion, completely forgetting that all women ain't wives and mothers, and they, I suppose, are to fold their hands and be idle waiting for an *eligible* offer." This got Minnie Thomas' dander up. Her comment: "Bah! stuff! and nonsenses!"[15]

In 1870, Minnie had five brothers and sisters to share not only parental attention but also family resources. Even within the relatively homogeneous, prosperous community of the Society of Friends, some had more than others.

Minnie began to take pleasure in those wealthier than she and to develop strategies for receiving their gifts. Her interest in science required, as she put it, "money, money, money, even for the privilege of blowing one's self up." When a school friend gave her some minerals for her collection, Minnie's first thought was of their expense. She commented to her journal, "I was ever so much obliged, wasn't it splendid? I took them home and father said they were very valuable."[16]

Although Minnie showed little distress at her failures either to be a good student or to be morally righteous, she did try to keep within bounds, at least at Meeting. At this point, she accepted fully her family's religious heritage. Trips to Philadelphia, especially the one centered on her grandparents' family celebration of the New Year, coinciding with her birthday, caused her to reflect and to make resolutions. On January 1, 1871, for example, she resolved to study harder, to read fewer novels, and to be a better Christian. "I do want to be a *real* Christian not a half a one and to really let my light '*shine*' and not keep it under a snuffer of naughtiness all the time."[17]

Minnie constantly stated her intention to become "better," but also resisted efforts to make her so. The following day, despite the Philadelphia influence, she stayed up late with Bessie, and in their towel fight she broke one of her grandmother's fine vases. She and a cousin got on top of the house and shot walnuts at the door of a neighbor, angering the neighbor's cook, who scolded an innocent African-American child. "Oh, it was so exciting for if we got caught My! the consequences! but it was such fun."[18]

Although her high spirits held the potential for trouble, her parents seem to have put little pressure on her during these years, and she remained in an indulgent environment. A letter from her cousin Frank clarified the contrast between her home life and the stricter atmosphere of Haverford College where he was a student. The college's managers had come up with a new list of rules, forbidding the students to whistle and sing. "Bessie and I were congratulating ourselves we weren't there for we would have been suspended."[19]

As her behavior grew more rowdy, her piety found a new expression. When she turned fourteen she began to write poetry. Her high ambition and her love of Romantic poetry did not a poet make. Interest in her poetry is psychological, not literary. For the adolescent Minnie, poetry became a medium to express her high thoughts. Her first poem set the model for those to come. In "Snow-flakes," she perceives the snow as God's messengers from heaven to earth. The message that they bring is obedience to God's will:

> *Little snow-flakes you can teach us*
> *In your simple childlike way*
> *That what ere our Father tells us*
> *Only straight way to obey*

Ultimately the snowflakes teach the lesson of death and trust in the afterlife. The snowflakes trust their Sender to go down to the unknown. Humankind must trust God that when called, they will ascend to heaven, "that glorious upper country," hidden from the sight of the living.[20] Her poetry fit the Quaker mold exactly. She did not show the poem to her mother or Bessie. She gave it to her aunt Mary Thomas, who then sent it anonymously to the religious periodical *Leisure Moments*. A month later Minnie had the pleasure of seeing her words in print.

Her poetic profession of conventional piety may have loosened its hold over her behavior. At the point that "Snowflakes" was published, tensions within Minnie between mischief-making and goodness—what she had once believed were the pulls of the bad angels and the good—became more intense. Though sometimes phrased in the religious terms of being a good Christian, goodness took a new, secular direction. At odds were Minnie Thomas' high spirits that rebelled against authority and her mounting ambition to become a cultured woman.

Dinner table conversation at the Thomas house fed her aspirations. An English guest provoked intense discussion about the value of women's education. "Mother, of course, was for." Francis King and the Englishman agreed "that they didn't see any good of a woman's learning Latin or Greek, it didn't make them any more entertaining to their *husbands*." To these men, women's domestic duties were enough to fully occupy their lives. "They talked as if the whole *end* and aim of a woman's life was to get *married*, and when she attained that *greatest state of earthly bliss*, it was her duty to amuse her husband and to learn nothing, never to exercise the powers of her mind, so that he might have the *exquisite* pleasure of knowing more than his wife." The men had couched their argument in different terms. To the skeptical Minnie this smacked of hypocrisy: "of course, they talked the usual cant of woman being too *high*, too *exalted* to do anything and sit up in perfect ignorance with folded hands and let men worship at her shrine." Minnie translated their "highfalutin" language into a more candid appraisal: "women ought to be *mere dolls* for men to be amused with, to kiss, fondle, pet, and love, just maybe, but as for association with them on terms of equality, they wouldn't think of such a thing." She felt forced to admit that she had stretched the two men's words a bit: "Now I don't mean to say that these two men believed this but these were the principles they upheld."

The guests' words ran against Minnie's awakened sense of women's rights, fueled by Anna Dickinson and supported by her mother and her aunt. Her reaction is important not just because it is the visceral response of a lively fourteen-year-old girl in 1871, but because it set the course of M. Carey Thomas' life's work. "I got perfectly enraged: how *unjust*—how *narrow minded*, how *utterly incomprehensible* to deny that women ought to be educated and worse than all to deny that they have equal powers of mind. If I ever live and grow up, my *one* aim and concentrated purpose *shall* be and is to show that a woman *can learn, can reason, can compete* with men in the grand fields of literature and science and conjecture that opens before the nineteenth century." She could do all this and remain "a *true*" woman.

In a grand flourish, Minnie contrasted her ideal woman with "the trifling ballroom butterfly . . . the ignorant rag doll baby" that the two men admired. In Minnie's conception, the ideal woman had plumbed the depths of human experience through learning. She was "the woman who has fought all the battles of olden time over again whilst reading the spirited pages of Homer, Virgil, Herodotus." She had "sympathized in the longings after something beyond mere daily existence found in the works of Socrates, Plato, and Aeschylus." She had "reasoned out all the great laws which govern the universe with Newton, Arago, Galileo." She had "mourned with Dante, reasoned and speculated with Schiller, Goethe, and Jean Paul." She had been "carried away by Carlyle and 'mildly enchanted by Emerson.' " She had "idealized with Milton and emerged with strengthened intellect from the intricate labyrinth of geometry, trigonometry and calculus." Inspired by her dream of educated womanhood, Minnie Thomas set out her own course of study as her "firm, fixed purpose."[21]

What is fascinating is that fourteen-year-old Minnie Thomas' list is male and secular. She had been excited by Thomas Carlyle's *On Heroes, Hero-Worship, and the Heroic in History*, and took his examples of the "Man-of-Letters Hero" as models of aspiration. As did many other girls in her time, she sought and found imaginative ideals in the high deeds of men portrayed in literature.[22] None of the great thinkers she names are religious heroes. Redeeming power inheres in the great works of the Western tradition, not in the Holy Scriptures. For this daughter of two pious Friends, the Quaker frame of reference had moved to the background.

Questions about the Bible did come up at the table. Two weeks later, at dinner, the family discussed evolution. Mary Thomas had organized a school for Quaker children, including four of her own, and had brought Rebecca Marble to teach it. She was a guest at dinner, along with James Thomas' younger brother Allen. By her account, Minnie still held the literal interpretation of the story of Adam and Eve. To her surprise, not only did her Uncle Allen and Miss Marble express their belief in evolutionary theory, her father did not defend the biblical story of creation. Minnie found this exciting and decided to become a geologist. Clearly she had been talking to her teacher about her ambitions. Embedded in the entry is a new element—college. "Oh my, I *must* go to Vassar. Miss Marble [says] that she thinks I might possibly be prepared to enter the freshman class by next summer if I study real hard till then." In far-away Baltimore, the first great college for women, in Pough-keepsie, New York, exerted its pull.[23]

Yet during this time of high aspiration, with its first talk of college, a conflicting drama was unfolding. Minnie was getting into scrapes in school. By early May 1871, the class, with Minnie Thomas as leader, had gotten out of hand. The girls and boys, on opposite sides, sent notes, shot popguns, turned books into weapons, swiped handkerchiefs, and sprinkled water on each other. One morning, when Minnie arrived at school, the boys had written "beware" on the wall in chalk. The girls and boys hid each other's hats. Minnie found her new hat covered with coal in the cellar and ruined. She took it philosophically: "I have learned to take joyfully the spoiling of my goods."[24]

Between this and the next scrape a new element was added to the plot. Rebecca Marble, whom Minnie always called "splendid" in her journal, was falling in love with Allen Thomas. With his father dead, James Thomas had assumed the role of family elder, and much of the courting between his younger brother, a professor at Haverford, and Minnie's teacher took place in the Thomas house, right under curious Minnie's nose. One Saturday in May, Miss Marble and Minnie made and iced a coconut cake. The young teacher stayed for dinner, and the relatives on James' side came. Minnie's curiosity and excitement mounted. Minnie declared her pleasure: "What fun it is to watch 'em. If they ain't in *love, they like* each other anyway."[25]

A few weeks later, Minnie learned that Rebecca and Allen were engaged. After the two came for dinner, Minnie pondered the new development and puzzled over love. It seemed strange that "two people, only having seen each other such a short time, should profess to love one another better than anybody else in the world." She wondered whether it was happier to fall in love or stay single. The one thing that she did know was that she enjoyed watching and that "romance enlivens up this prosaic world of ours a heap."[26]

The engagement was set, but the drama was not played out. Minnie's mischief at school had continued. A squirt-gun fight angered Miss Marble, and she kept them in during recess. School was supposed to end June 16, but the parents thought the children should remain longer, and the year was extended to June 20. When Minnie's class was informed of this, they "raged, fussed, and exploded with anger." She and four other ringleaders got colored chalk and wrote "20th" everywhere, including the ceiling and the school furniture. They wrote on the blackboard "the hateful 20th pshaw pooh disgust" and put the number 20 on their right shoulders. Minnie confided to her journal that she never gave a thought to whether Miss Marble would like it or not.[27]

Miss Marble did not. The class's misbehavior went beyond what she would tolerate. She gathered the class with a bell and said, "I consider the words that have been written on the blackboard an insult to the school, to myself, and to the scholars. Will the authors please to *erase* them." The five, including Minnie, did so, and for the first time Minnie felt momentary remorse. Later in the day when she caught the children fighting, Miss Marble threatened that if there was any more bad behavior, she would send notes to their mothers. Now it was Minnie who hit her flash point and told her teacher that "I didn't care a cent. Mother knew all about it, and if she didn't, I'd tell her." Minnie left school in a rage that she vented at home. Mary Thomas took it all in good humor, but without defending her daughter. Mary Thomas clearly understood Minnie as having given in to the devil's temptation, for she said that despite the children's fun, "the trail of the serpent is over it all."[28]

Fired by high ambition to go to college, inspired by a teacher who was about to become her aunt, but running around at school with squirt guns and writing words on the blackboard: nothing too unusual. What is unusual is the way her elders handled it, how they reined in Minnie so that she did not buck.

Rebecca Marble took Minnie to see a friend's insect collection. On the walk she gave her a note. The teacher wrote rather than spoke because a letter would allow Minnie to think over its contents and would enable the writer to tell Minnie how much she loved her. Miss Marble perceived that Minnie's reaction to the note to her mother demonstrated that the girl was not aware of the "serious light in which such things look to me, and which I really believe to be their *true* light." Miss Marble preferred not to write to Minnie of her recent actions but only of the "noble girl thee really is in mind and heart." She would bend Minnie back to her true nature: "The school-girl's character has much to do with the making of the woman, I would have all little annoying things driven away from thine." She felt that she might not be the best guide, for she loved Minnie too much to discipline her appropriately. She wanted to shift the burden of authority from external to internal. She wrote, "Let the knowledge of what is right be thy law both in school and out, and thy inward monitor, that which gives the most severe reprimand: be 'a *noble Christian student*'!" Minnie confided to her journal that the note "completely changed my views and made me love Miss Marble more than ever."[29]

This incident tells much about Minnie Thomas and more about the Quaker world that nurtured her. As a girl Minnie was given both much guidance and wide latitude. The hand of discipline was light. When she trespassed a boundary, her elders dealt with her carefully, tactfully, and lovingly.

III

THE SUMMER of 1871 was a happy time. The pressures impinging upon her in Baltimore were released. She visited Anna Shipley, the daughter of one of her Aunt Hannah's close friends in Philadelphia, and enjoyed getting to know her.

Bessie went with Minnie in July to Atlantic City, and she had the good company of Frank. The young people swam in the ocean, read in trees, and hunted bugs. Hannah nurtured Minnie's ambition to become a doctor. Ever ready to encourage free play, Hannah gave the girls an old camp meeting tent that they used as a bath house, while the boys used the woods. Bessie kept to the feminine sport of croquet, but Minnie played cricket with the boys. In the rough game she wore out her clothes. When Mary threatened to make her a cricket suit of red flannel, rather than being upset by the thought of wearing jacket and pants Minnie reacted that she wished she would. One day, after she had been declaiming women's rights' principles, the horse she was riding reared, tossed her off, and fell on her. Determined to prove to her companions that women did not scream, Minnie crawled out from under the horse "much to their astonishment."[30]

As Minnie returned to school in the fall of 1871, she did not return to the reckless behavior that had led her into conflict with Miss Marble. Her turmoil moved inward and centered on her gender and her ambitions. While Frank now entered Princeton, her cousin Whit went to a school in Providence, and a male friend to Haverford, she was stuck in Baltimore and back in Miss Marble's classroom. In a school oration Minnie spoke her mind. As she spoke for all girls, enumerating their grievances and their lack of rights, she suggested that she was facing conventional expectations about feminine behavior. "In the first place if a girl gets tired of doing nothing and joins in some of her brothers' games, jumps a few fences, climbs a few trees, she is called, oh horrible name, a 'tomboy.' " She is not allowed to hunt. She is told that such expressions as "jolly" are "shocking" and "unladylike." If she whistles, she is reminded, "Whistling girls and crowing hens never came to a good ends." Worst of all, while her brothers get an education, home life makes it hard for her to study, and she is told that college is a waste of time. Minnie exhorted the girls in her class to study hard and for the boys to acknowledge female intellectual equality. In her ringing ending she cited an authority who argued that men of the future will have to carry arms to keep women from their rights: "So boys get ready your pistols and sharpen your swords while we girls will sharpen our wits."[31]

Her journal gave less adorned vent to her feelings. Life seemed unbearable. She was tired of study, disliked all her acquaintances, and found growing up into conventional womanhood distasteful: "Girls never can have any fun. They can't play or else everybody thinks they're tomboys, and I haven't had one nice game since I came home, and I am nearly fifteen, and each year I have less fun and am more grown up." The pressures on her to conform or to be deviant were both distasteful: "I ain't good and I ain't bad, I ain't a *tomboy* nor I ain't *ladylike*, and I'm everything that's disagreeable, and I do want a little excitement."[32]

Minnie projected onto college the excitement she sought and began to ache to go to Vassar. How different it was for her male cousins. The world forced boys to go to school, but did not allow girls. She wondered where college would lead her. She had no real alternative to becoming a doctor. She was determined not to be dependent upon her parents or marry, and she did not want to teach school. She could think of nothing worse than "living a regular young lady's life." Education and a profession would cut her off from conventional society, but at age fourteen she did not care: "I *despise* society, and I *detest* girls."[33]

Life in the late nineteenth century was just too humdrum. Perhaps inspired by the vision of Joan of Arc, Minnie wished she had lived during the medieval period and died in the Crusades, a strange ambition for a Quaker daughter. Men in the nineteenth century cared only about moneymaking, she thought, and had as little to offer her as conventional girls. "You'd about as soon catch one of them risking his life and charging at the head of his troops as you'd catch a young lady saying anything sensible." As Minnie tried to balance her conflicting inner drives, she wished that she were "either awful bad or awful good." If bad, she would "have lots of fun"; if good, she could go to twelve Meetings a day and enjoy them, "which I don't do now." In the midst of this agonizing there were conventional pleasures, especially the birth of her sister Helen Whitall Thomas. In October of 1871, she wrote in her journal, "Ellie is six weeks old and just as sweet as possible. She laughs and coos, and altogether is cunning."[34]

Minnie decided to be a flirt. The Yearly Meeting at the end of October brought to Baltimore two young men. She attracted the attentions of Franklin McCoy, and he walked her home and asked for the porcelain miniature picture of her that he found in the house. She refused and found him foolish—a "goose"—for becoming enamored of her. A friend of Rebecca Marble, who had gone to Vassar, was visiting. Minnie became excited about college, and Mary supported her. Minnie wrote to Frank, "Mother has positively promised me that I shall go when I'm seventeen. Ain't that *elegant*?" She agonized about Vassar. If she did not get to go, she would "commit suicide or do something dreadful." Now her flirtation appeared in a new light. By it she had betrayed her dream of Vassar: "I don't believe I'm any better nor less foolish than the rest of girls, for look how I ~~carried on with, flirt~~ behaved with Franklin. . . . I despise it, and after all my air castles, too." Distaste for the present and longings for a different life overcame her. She fancied a world where the air was pure oxygen, where "our life would sweep through its fevered burning course in a few hours, we would live in a perfect delirium of excitement and would die vibrating with passion."[35]

At this point Minnie drew close to Frank. Encouraged by Hannah, in 1866 the Whitall cousins had formed a society, the S.S.S. (for Snip, Snap, Snorum), pledged to fun. Minnie had become a full-fledged member by 1870, when the group drew up its rules, selected the arbutus as its flower, and wrote its history. In her letters to Frank, Minnie constantly reminded him of his membership in the S.S.S. and its motto "primus ludus, supremus ludus, semper ludus," or first, last, and always play. Minnie made her usual trip to Philadelphia to celebrate the New Year with the Whitalls. As she turned fifteen, Philadelphia ceased to be for her a place of piety, and became one of good times among peers. She and Frank sat in the dark to await 1872, while "Frank told me his love secrets. He is very much in love with Anna Shipley." Minnie judged Anna as she had Rebecca Marble: "perfectly splendid." And as she had with her uncle and teacher, Minnie enjoyed observing the budding romance.[36]

Hannah shifted her energies from encouraging godliness in the young to fostering their social life. She gave them what she called a "row." She invited a crowd for tea and then, after the refreshments, left the house. The spirited youth turned out the lights and played hide and go seek. Minnie hid in Frank's closet with Anna. They were not found for a long time, so they had a good talk. Minnie's aunt Sarah Whitall Nicholson, known as Aunty Hal, reported to the family that when she passed by Hannah's house at nine in the evening, there were no lights on, but "every now and then she heard a thundering noise against the front door and a perfect chorus of shrieks and yells until she was afraid the policeman would come."[37]

Anna's ladylike ways required Minnie to put her to a test. Minnie bragged about the fun she had climbing on Baltimore roofs, egging Anna on. The two girls climbed out on the roof and ran over those of the attached houses. When they came to a high wall with a big drop to the roof below, even Minnie was afraid. But she "hung and dropped so as to see if Anna would." Anna got high marks: "though I know she hasn't been used to climbing, [she] did it without the slightest hesitation. Hurrah for her!" Once back in Baltimore, Minnie confided to her diary that Anna was "just too nice for anything, and I'm perfectly in love with her, the way she speaks and all. Oh, she is too splendid. I like her better than any girl, of course, excepting Bessie."[38]

She wanted Anna to come for a visit. With elaborate detail, Minnie schemed to convince her parents to allow her to invite Anna and Frank to the house when the adults took the younger children with them to Yearly Meeting in Philadelphia. Minnie wrote to Frank excitedly that her mother—who was "really just as fond of fun as Aunt Hannah" though lacking her "gift of regardlessness"—was almost convinced. Frank could tell his mother, but must keep it from their grandmother, "for if I have father and mother alone I think I can persuade 'em to but if Grandma or Aunty Hal puts in their veto I'm a dead dog." Minnie outlined for Frank the many attractions of the plan: they would have the house and the horses and carriages to themselves, they could go fishing, and they could go to the market to choose their food. Minnie was worried that Frank's attraction to Anna might spoil the visit and cautioned him to act "perfectly free and easy" with her. It all worked, and they had fun. Minnie was delighted with Frank. "He is so much more wide awake, full of theories and everything and altogether is by far the nicest fellow I've seen."[39]

At one level Minnie was abetting Frank in his budding love affair with Anna. Throughout these months she alternately teased him about his affections and goaded him into confiding his feelings. For example, she pled with him in November, "I don't know what I *shall* do if thee don't tell me about that romantic adventure, thy letter fairly made me unhappy, I wanted to know so much. Oh, Frank, *please, please, please, please* do then. It will be perfectly *barbarous* if thee won't, after raising my curiosity up to such a pitch." She cajoled in all the ways she knew: "Ain't there *any* inducement I can offer thee? I'll *never* tell, *never* show thy letter to any one and, oh, if thee don't, I'll think thee's perfectly horrid, and I won't invite thee on at Christmas, *so there*."[40]

During the April visit he told her more than he had done before. What he said was so compromising that at some point M. Carey Thomas crossed it out (just as she cut out a passage about Anna from a letter to Frank written at the same time). The few legible words suggest that he might have told her about the physical side of their courtship. This was most titillating to Minnie, and her excitement had as its object Anna as well as Frank. She followed Frank's revelation by this declaration, the final words of which she later crossed out so that they are illegible: "I do believe I'm a perfect goose! I think I must feel towards Anna, for instance, like a boy would, for I admire her so, not any particular thing but just an undefined sense of admiration, and then I like to touch her, and the other morning I woke up and she was asleep, and I admired her hair so much that I kissed it. I never felt it so much with anybody else." A few months later, as Minnie wrote to Anna reminding her to send the lock of her hair that she had promised, she admitted, "thee don't know but I'll kiss it."[41]

Although a "goose," the word she had first used for the smitten Franklin McCoy, at fifteen Minnie did not comprehend being "in love" with Anna as ruling out a future relationship with a male. Between New Year's Eve and the Philadelphia Yearly Meeting, she thought about writing to Frank. She decided, "Frank is ever so nice. Whenever he and I are *alone*, we have such nice times." She contrasted her cousin to "the general run of boys" that she found "horrid." She had been thinking about whether she would want to fall in love. She quickly qualified, "though, of course, such a thing never *would* and never *shall* enter into my doctoral brain." But if she did, "who on earth would there be to fall in love with?" She had only one comment for the Baltimore Quaker boys she knew: "Ugh."[42]

It is very difficult to determine what Minnie Thomas knew about sex as a girl. Her journal is silent on the subject until the entries she wrote as a young woman. By the time that she wrote her autobiography, M. Carey Thomas' reading of Freud had informed her of the importance of sex in childhood development, and consequently she made an effort to set down her early sexual knowledge. In composing her autobiography, Thomas jotted down images immediately upon waking in the morning. In one set of images, she listed the Bible, the adultery trial of Henry Ward Beecher, and her childhood request of Bessie King, who had lived on a farm, to tell her the difference between bulls and cows. Two other items on the list—"Mother and sleeping spoon-fashion" and "Lying———fashion: Did it bring babies?"—may have been her questions from childhood as she was trying to figure out what made her mother pregnant. They suggest that in the informal Thomas household she had seen her parents lying together in bed.

The autobiography also tells the story of accidentally overhearing at age twelve a conversation between her mother and Aunt Harvey Ellicott. She heard Mary say, "I will not have more children than we can take care of and bring up properly. I cannot bear it any longer. I will tell the Doctor (as she always called my father) it must stop." To this, Minnie heard Aunt Harvey reply, "My dear, you will say no such thing. Unless you are willing to have him go to other women, you must go on bearing it and have just as many children as the Lord sends." Childbirth was painful for Mary and it took her many weeks to recover. Thomas wrote that she did not understand what her father could do to prevent more children, but she resented him for refusing to do something her mother wanted. Mary was not seeking birth control but a cessation of sexual intercourse. Birth control, although available and understood in a physician's household, was morally unacceptable to her as a refined Christian woman. In the same passage, Thomas also recalled overhearing her Aunt Hannah say that "she could not bear the kisses—they were the worst."[43]

All of this was written from distant hindsight, when Thomas was in her seventies. Intriguing, vivid, suggestive of her mother's and aunt's distaste for conjugal relations, it tells of Thomas' consciousness as an older woman. Her memory (or, possibly, imagination) stands, however, in contrast to the romantic consciousness that Minnie Thomas portrays in her own adolescent journal. In its pages she chronicles her girlhood reading of contemporary fiction that moved her in conventional ways. Dinah Maria Craik's *Hannah*, for example, an intensely romantic book, provoked her thinking about love. The novel was set in England and involved the love between Bernard and Hannah, the sister of his late wife. English law forbade their marriage, but Minnie reports, "they loved each other so wildly and passionately." What appealed to Minnie was the intensity of their inexpressible love: "they couldn't hardly see each other, and, oh, they suffered so. It seems to me that if I ever fell in love it must be like that and with such a splendid passionate man as Bernard." Their intense love, under the ban of incest in England, ultimately triumphed in the freer air of France.[44]

In her own life, had Frank ceased to be Laurie to her Jo and become Bernard to her Hannah? A tantalizing possibility. Minnie was drawing close to Frank. Unlike all the horrid boys that she knew at meeting, Frank cared about all the things she did. They were very much alike. To the fifteen-year-old Minnie, love involved the association of sameness, not the coming together of opposites.

As Minnie mused on the love of Hannah and Bernard, her thoughts turned, however, not to Frank, but to Bessie. The two girls had talked about romance. They walked the streets at dusk, feeling as if they had "discovered the secret of perpetual motion and could walk on forever." When they had parted, Bessie had said, "I go my way and thou thine." Minnie wondered if, at a later time in their lives, they would part in a different way. As Minnie defined their closeness, she saw it as identity: "Now, almost all our interests are the same; we care for the same pursuits; we like the same books; we have the same ideals, almost." As Minnie moved out from the orbit of her immediate family, she sought above all to recreate the bond that she had once had with her mother. As firstborn, she had known Mary Thomas' exclusive love. The burn had restored her mother to her for an interlude. But as Minnie recovered, Mary Thomas returned to her manifold duties as wife, mother of a large brood, and devout Friend. With Bessie, Minnie could vie more successfully. They were, as Minnie put it, "so jolly and nice together." When she wrote this in her journal, she added, "and love (at least I love Bessie) each other so." The parenthetical catch in Minnie's voice suggests a fear that her strong feeling for Bessie was not fully returned.[45]

Four days later she felt more secure. Bessie and she had tried to skate, but had found the skating to be poor. They came inside Bessie's house and sat together by the fireplace. It "was dark . . . it was so quiet, and we had hold of each other's hands and talked about anything, and it seemed as if we could sit there forever, and whenever Bess and I get together all alone we have such nice times, and I do love her so much." After she returned home, Minnie tried to capture the moment in a poem that fused her hopes for the future with her love of her cousin. The flames in the fire became a portent of their futures. Each was a strand, weaving together possibility and reality. The flames of each intertwined.

> *And again the skeins got tangled*
> *For behold when the weaving was done*
> *Our work was so mixed with each other's*
> *That instead of two it was one.*

So may it be in our futures—
May our lives so intertwine,
That ne'er may the words be spoken
"I go my way, thou goest thine"![46]

Her love of Bessie was not exclusive. In these same weeks Minnie was corresponding with Anna and thinking of her, so much so that Bessie was becoming jealous. In Minnie's mind, love for a male should not enter "her doctoral brain," for it threatened her future. Love for females, in contrast, became intertwined with her aspirations. As she wrote about Bessie in her journal, she typically shifted to the plane of her high hopes for the future. With Bessie, she could imagine a future in which the two of them joined together in a great work. In a photograph from this period, Minnie sits next to a standing Bessie. They look severe as they face the camera. Their hair pulled tight, both wear white collars and dark jackets, perhaps hoping that if they looked in front of a camera like men, they could dream men's dreams.

In March the two girls went to the last sewing meeting, a female Quaker gathering for a secular task. With no "horrid boys" to interfere, they began to fantasize about their lives. They had assumed new names, Rush for Minnie, Rex for Bessie. After supper the two went alone into the meeting house. To susceptible Minnie, the empty room was filled with romantic possibilities: "a solemn gloom hanging over," the windows letting in just enough light "to cast a dim uncertain shadow on the long rows of empty benches. . . . Under every bench in the recess of every shadow there seemed to lurk strange fantastic figures and forms that had taken refuge from the glare and bustle in this perfect stillness." Minnie and Bessie began to "build air castles." They walked up and down the aisles and talked.

They dreamed of "what we wanted to be and do and formed plans how, after we had come home from Vassar, having taken bright honors, we would do everything." They would live together, devoting themselves to study. They would "have a library with all the splendid books with a bright wood fire always burning, dark crimson curtains and furniture, great big easy chairs where we could sit lost in books for days together." They would be authors and have "a great large table covered with papers." They would be scientists and have "a laboratory where far into the night we would pour over crucibles mixing our mystic ingredients and perhaps making discoveries which should effect the whole world." In this setting they would "live, loving each other so and urging each other on to every high and noble deed or action and till all who passed should say, 'Their example arouses me,' their books ennoble me, their deeds inspire me and behold they are women!' "[47]

That these were only dreams for the future made Minnie's heart ache. As she longed for her realized future she asked, "Why can't two girls love each other and live together and help each other in life's struggle just as well as a man and a woman!" She feared that one of them, most likely Bessie, would fall in love with a man. Vassar loomed as Minnie's goal. She wanted it so much that "it even mingles with my very dreams."[48]

As her ambitions reached a fevered pitch, Minnie began to meet some resistance from her parents. Her mother, who had always supported her and upheld the cause of women, pulled back. When she and Bessie asked for a scientific laboratory, her mother answered, "Oh, you can't, you're *girls.*" Minnie was furious: "when I heard that, I ground my teeth and swore (affirmed) that no one should say that of us. As if we hadn't as much sense, invention, and perseverance as boys." The two girls got immediately to work and fixed up one of James Thomas' electrical machines and made a Leyden jar.[49]

Minnie's father began to challenge her ambitions by reminding her of religious opposition to women's self-assertion. After a meeting in late March 1872, Minnie had stated that she thought Saint Paul was "very unjust to women and that I disbelieved him as far as I possibly could anything in the Bible." James Thomas answered her that Paul was right, "that the man *was* the head of the woman, as Christ is the head of the church, that God made it so, that a woman was weaker than a man, the woman was made for the man not man for the woman." As he continued, he specified that men had "power, strength, force, intellect," and women "sweetness, gentleness, gracefulness, beauty, love." James insisted that "a wife must reverence her husband, that the man always took the lead and was made by God to do so." Coming from any male, such a statement would have angered Minnie. Coming from her father, "it made me so mad, almost beside myself."

Minnie compared herself to all the boys whom she knew, and fumed at the presumption of their superiority. Her father's argument rested on male "*brute* strength," but this had no validity, for it would favor a prize-fighter over a gentleman. It was "*too* unjust, *too* horrible." Minnie did not believe it. She knew that she had "as much sense as any boy I know . . . and more too." If she lived, she would show "who'll be worth the most. It seems to me I'd die if I could do *anything* to show that a woman is equal to a man."

Again, in what had become a pattern in her thinking, Minnie made the logical leap from an assertion of female equality to a fear of female dependence. After she stated her determination to prove women's worth, she shifted: "If I have to give up my freedom in the slightest degree *I'll never marry*, and I don't expect to anyhow, for if Heavenly Father spares me my senses I'll never be dependent on anyone, man or woman, if possible." In 1872, at age fifteen, she based her dream of the future and her opposition to her father's support of Paul on a set of articulated principles: "I am thoroughly and heartily woman's rights and never expect to change my opinion."[50]

Frank accepted Minnie and her aspirations. The son of the beloved aunt who had encouraged her to venture far in the water, Frank joined Minnie as she read and dreamed of the future. Minnie could talk to Frank, knowing that he did not laugh at her ideas or ambitions. After the unchaperoned visit in April, she wrote to him recalling their interesting talk. "All those sorts of things and theories are perfect fascinations, and, oh, there is so much to learn and find out, and what a field for discoveries!" She asked Frank to make a bargain. They would read up on what interested them and compare notes in the summer and that way push each other. Frank had the advantage of Princeton and intellectual companionship, unlike Baltimore where Bessie and she were derided for reading.[51]

As Minnie envisioned the future, Frank would become a great lawyer; she, an esteemed doctor: the S.S.S. would become known "throughout the world, as having produced the greatest lawyer and doctor ever seen" since the Greeks. In letters to Frank, Minnie revealed her primary motive for studying so hard. At fifteen Minnie Thomas was curious and had a lively intelligence, but did not see learning as an end in itself. "The books we read," she wrote to her cousin, "the knowledge we get, are the weapons for the Ego to fight with when the time comes . . . now is the time when we are forging our swords."[52]

One important development in Frank's life Minnie could not share— though her family hoped it would not be long before she would. Frank had experienced the new heart of religious certainty. Minnie wrote to him that she remained unconverted. He had gotten ahead of her "because I can't quite do it, though I really think I want to, and it would be real nice if we could start together, but I can't."[53]

In the summer of 1872 Minnie and Frank were especially close. Early in the summer Anna's father took his daughter and the S.S.S. on an excursion through the Pennsylvania Dutch country. There, as M. Carey Thomas remembered in her autobiography, she and Frank had tussled and fallen together to the ground. "We both realized that something had happened to us. After that a strange enchantment possessed us," and they wanted only to be alone in each other's company. Writing in September 1872 Minnie recalled in her journal that when they returned to the Cedars, she and Frank spent days and evenings together: "The whole long day we'd lay in the hammock and on the grass and read and talk and dream. . . . All through the long twilights we sat under the trees and read and read and read like we ourselves seemed lost in the story, and when it was too dark to see we talked of ourselves, our past, our futures, and how we were going to help each other on and stick by each other." In her autobiography, M. Carey Thomas remembered that they often talked until ten P.M., bid their grandparents good night, and then retired to her bedroom to continue their talk. Mary and Hannah began to get "anxious" about their "close companionship."[54]

They were on the sixth book of *Paradise Lost* when Frank caught typhoid. On August 8 he had been ill for ten days. Minnie wrote in her journal that in the early afternoon, as she was napping on the sofa, her family woke her and told her, "Get up, Frank is dying." She went into his room and from one-thirty to four watched him as he lay still. Hannah stroked his hair and put her hand on his forehead. "He breathed fainter and fainter and at last stopped. We all sat still for a few minutes. Then Aunt Hannah and Uncle Robert closed his eyes, and we all went out."[55]

Minnie was unprepared for Frank's death. In her journal Mary Thomas recalled that while others in the family came gradually to anticipate his end, Minnie fought against the knowledge: "She *could* not believe that Frank was going to die, she *would* not think of it." The call that awakened her from the nap thus "came with all the terrible pain of a sudden shock." To Mary, the death of Hannah's child made her afraid for her own. But she knew that for Minnie the loss was different, she would have no one to take his place.[56]

A month later as she wrote in her own journal, Minnie was still feeling the shock. "Oh, it seems too dreadful. I can hardly believe it. Frank's and my lives have so intermingled ever since we were children, and we planned all our future together and everything and to think that I'll have to go on all alone. . . . I loved him so so much and now I'll never see him anymore." She regretted the words unsaid. "It wouldn't have been so bad if I could only once have told him how nice I thought he was and how much I loved him, for I don't believe he half knew."[57]

Frank's funeral on his eighteenth birthday was dreadful. "I can never forget the dull heavy thud of the earth as it fell upon the coffin." Others close to Frank found comfort in the belief that Heavenly Father had taken him for his own. But Minnie wrote in her journal simply, "All is over now, and life goes whirling on again but it will never be the same to me as it was before."[58]

The death of Frank closed a door in Minnie Thomas' life. Within her expressive family she had begun to fall in love with a young man. This was balanced by her love for her cousin Bessie and for Anna—a mix typical for a girl of fifteen in her day. Minnie also dreamed of college and a career. In 1872 many lively girls shared this dream. What if Frank had lived? In the inbred Quaker worlds of Baltimore and Philadelphia, marriage of cousins was common. Might Minnie and Frank's love have developed and led to their early marriage? It is certainly possible. Had it happened, is it likely that M. Carey Thomas' life would now find its way into biography?

CHAPTER 3

We Want Scholars

QUITE precipitously after Frank Smith's death, Mary and James Thomas decided to send their precious daughter to the Howland School, a Quaker academy for girls in Union Springs, New York, run by Robert B. Howland. Hannah Whitall Smith had planted the idea long before, seeing a notice of the school in the *Friends' Review* and sending for the catalogue. Minnie and Frank had talked it over and, as she wrote to her Aunt Hannah, "one of the last things he said to me was that he thought I'd better go." But James and Mary only made their final decision a week before Minnie was to enter.[1]

It was not easy for Minnie to leave home. As she wrote to Hannah, "I had no idea how hard it was to go away and leave 'em all. It's terrible." Bessie, who had finished Miss Marble's school the year before Minnie, had spent an unprofitable year, and her father had already decided to send Bessie to Howland. Francis T. King knew of the school through his support of the New Garden School (later to be Guilford College) in Greensboro, North Carolina. Mary Mendenhall, the daughter of Nereus Mendenhall, New Garden's guiding light, was a student at Howland. At school's opening, Francis King and Mary and James Thomas escorted their daughters, who were to room together. Mary wrote in her journal that the three "were delighted with the school and left the girls there with good hope that it was for the best."[2]

Minnie quickly became absorbed in her new world. She took the classical course. She studied Cicero in Latin, but—despite years of private tutoring—had to begin Greek again. In her literary course, she reported to her teacher what she read. She worked hard, yet, as she noted in her journal, "Sometimes the grindstone stops . . . and we have jolly fun Friday, and Saturday, and Sunday, for we have just the gayest set of girls here; oh, I do love fun so much, and I do really like study, too, and they don't gel I'm afraid."[3]

In her first term Minnie reported the happy news that—after eight years—the wound from the burn had healed completely. Her parents rejoiced. James wrote, "How good it is to hear that thou art quite well of the burn—which has been such an episode in thy life—and yet which has not I trust impeded thy progress in any direction." In his eyes, Minnie had gained from her experience, for it had called forth "thy mother's constant companionship," the source, James felt, of "the greatest stimulus to thy mental appetite." James assessed the balance: "If few girls have had so great a trial, few have had such a Mother!"[4]

During the Howland years, money was scarce in the Thomas household. Mary had gone into debt with the school run by Rebecca Marble and had to be bailed out by her father. With the birth of Frank during Minnie's first year away, eight children shared the resources of a Baltimore physician. James worked very hard. Mary often described her husband's deep fatigue as he lay on the couch in the evening while she wrote. But much of what he did as a doctor and as a Quaker minister was pro bono, not for income. As Mary wrote to Minnie to explain why money was so short, "Patients won't pay, and so we are poor in this world's goods, but rich in being heirs of a glorious heavenly inheritance." There never seemed to be a lack of essentials. Good food abounded. The house was always filled with the company of an extended family and visitors. Servants eased Mary's strenuous days. But she found that there was no cash surplus that allowed her to be as generous to her eldest child as a mother might have wished.[5]

When James sent Minnie money for books or to pay the Howland bill, Mary always cautioned her daughter to be careful with any change. She should write letters on thin paper that required fewer stamps. Minnie had written that she needed new shoes. Mary could not deny this necessity to her daughter and instructed her to go ahead and have the shoes made. But she could not enclose the funds to cover the bill. Mary wrote, "We will send thee the money sometime, though it is a *very scarce* article at present here. . . . Thee must remember that thee is a *costly* girl, and a very *dear* one. . . . I have not one dollar in my purse and am not likely to have for some time to come."[6]

At one point James Thomas almost became the editor of a religious journal, which would have supplemented his income. But Mary cautioned her daughter not to be too hopeful, for this prospect might prove a "chateau in Espagne." Although the extra money would provide Minnie a chance for college, most likely Vassar, Mary feared that writing weekly for the journal "would be too much for Father's discursive and fitful genius." John Whitall had helped out his daughter's household many times, and at another point when Minnie asked for money, Mary counseled Minnie to imitate what must have been Mary's usual approach to her father: "If thy finances are low, I think now would be a good time to write to Grandpa. He will understand the hint and the X [ten dollars] will be forthcoming."[7]

Minnie clearly had little hesitation about asking her family for the things of the world. She wrote to a friend that she was taking to Howland "two real pretty pieces of crimson Brussels" for her room. Her gain was Mary's loss, but this did not trouble her. "Mother is not quite resigned to my taking them yet and looks longingly at the two parlor doors, in which they fit so prettily; but I hope soon to reduce her to a becoming resignation. What a great thing submission is!"[8]

For a pious Friend, issues of money and consumption were bound up inextricably with religious injunctions of simplicity. When Minnie wrote for books or shoes, her mother accepted these as needs, but when she asked for money for a purpose that Mary regarded as frivolous or against the creed, her response was different. After Minnie requested funds for a ring, Mary replied, "I am disappointed that thee has not the moral courage to face the music and the independence to say that thee does not care enough for the ring to go directly counter to thy Mother's wishes. Perhaps thee could not say that in *truth*, and that is what disappoints me." Mary was not forbidding Minnie; she was trying to influence her. Minnie might be able to get her father, without Mary's consent, to pay for the ring. But she should take into account both her mother's feelings against jewelry and her father's lack of money. Mary was careful not to make Minnie's decision a test of their relationship: "I shall not love thee less, darling, if thee still hankers after the ring."[9]

The manner in which Mary Thomas dealt with the ring was characteristic of her guidance of her fifteen-year-old daughter. Mary normally attempted to shape Minnie's choices, but not to make them. As Minnie arranged her travel plans from Howland, either to come home or to make visits, Mary and James wrote to her the variables and their opinions, but normally let Minnie's judgment prevail. To the daughter, however, the line between home counsel and control was not clearly drawn. As she explained to Hannah, the reason she could not visit her on the trip from Howland to Baltimore was that her parents did not want her to travel alone: "though they say we can do as we choose, yet it is evident which they think best."[10]

As Minnie entered Howland, Mary tried to help her establish open, easy relationships with her schoolmates. Mary was delighted that many of the girls were Quakers: "I have a very decided preference for Friends for friends." In her very first letter, Mary counseled Minnie to be less formal in her approach to others and to "drop the *Miss*" in favor of first names, as it was more homelike. She worried about Minnie's snobbery and judgmental spirit. She wrote, "Thee has got a little up into the airy mind in thy opinion of the teachers and girls there. I expect some of these girls thee looks down upon are thy superiors in some things." Bessie was different. She was a friend, a Friend, and a member of the family. When Minnie complained about Howland food, Mary suggested that she be philosophical about it. Although Minnie should not show any outward disgust about meals among the girls, with Bessie she might show her true feelings: "Thee and Bessie can blow out about it when you get into your own room."[11]

Minnie entered Howland with her old heart. She had not experienced the baptism of the Holy Spirit that her family had hoped for her. As she wrote to Hannah, "I do want to be a *realer* Christian but I ain't consecrated yet a bit. I think it's harder for me than anybody else."[12] Mary Thomas was entrusting her daughter to Friends in the hope that Minnie might improve her mind and manners and possibly enter into the Kingdom. During Minnie's Howland years, Mary herself continually experienced religious renewal. She reported to her daughter the many meetings in which she delighted in the Lord. She thrilled at the new meanings she found in biblical texts. She reported proudly her growing ability to speak in Meeting. She hoped that at Howland Minnie might imitate her and exert her influence for good.

Frank Smith's death continued to hover over the Thomas household. In February 1873, James and Mary named their newborn son Frank Smith Thomas at Minnie's request. The loss of her beloved nephew had reawakened in Mary anxiety about her daughter's spiritual state. Hannah was writing a religious biography of Frank, *The Record of a Happy Life*, the book that launched her public career. During its composition Mary feared that the account of Frank's life might make it appear that Minnie shared his high estate. When she read the book she was relieved that it virtually ignored Minnie: "I am glad there is nothing in the book that makes thee out better than thee is." Frank's life turned him from "the best, the noblest, of all the grandchildren" into a saint. Hannah's portrayal became a text for Mary, giving her the inspiration and the means to guide Minnie. When her daughter complained that the prayer meetings at Howland were "cold and dead," Mary suggested that she look on pages 78 and 86 of Hannah's book to see how Frank had turned them around at Haverford.[13]

Mary interpreted Minnie's discontent and restless searching for knowledge and meaning as a sign of distance from the Savior. She longed for Minnie to "get into 'the liberty,' " the term Frank had used for faith. Minnie was a divided spirit, wanting salvation and resisting it. Only one path lay to inner reconciliation, the total acceptance of God's dominion. Mary perceived that Minnie feared consecration because it threatened her intellectual independence, and she countered that faith would, to the contrary, release Minnie's mind from its shackles. Because Frank's conversion had taken place at Haverford, Mary hoped that Minnie would experience rebirth at Howland.[14]

If Howland was opportunity, it was also fraught with dangers. Minnie might be careless with her lamp and cause a fire. She might study too hard and injure her health. Mary particularly urged that Minnie not take German, and she regularly offered warnings about overwork, illustrated by examples of girls who had failed to heed. Minnie must not sit outside on the damp grass or talk at night after going to bed. She should lock her door and bolt her windows at night. It was difficult for her to give up daily oversight of her daughter. "I don't want thee, my darling, to take the lead in any wild goings on, I am so afraid of something happening, your getting on fire, or getting colds, or making yourselves notorious by your pranks. I know how full of fun thee is." At home, Mary had been able to protect Minnie by her counsel. Now that she was away, Minnie had only her own judgment to guide her. Mary hoped that she would incorporate all the guidance she had received: "Remember thee has to think *my* way and thine, too, now."[15]

Most frightening of all, away from the Quaker nest, Minnie might hear, see, do, and believe what was wrong. Mary and James Thomas' religious views were being influenced by evangelical currents. Heaven and hell were literal places. Satan was loose in the world. Their unconsecrated Minnie was at risk. Mary repeatedly implored Minnie to write to her fully, every detail. Bereft of her darling daughter, knowing all about Minnie's life was a great comfort to her, and it allowed her to try to influence Minnie and protect her from evil.

As Minnie described the spiritual state of those about her, Mary gave her guidance. Mary's greatest concern was the Greek and Latin teacher, Zaccheus Test, who was preaching unorthodox doctrines to the students. He was no stranger to Mary. In the small, tight-knit world of Friends, doctrines of others were well known. In one way, Mary Thomas' letters to her daughter during the Howland years can be seen as a running dialogue with Dr. Test. As he began to give Bible instruction, Mary became anxious, and in mid-February 1873, she cautioned her daughter not to accept his views. He was teaching that there was no Satan. Mary countered that Satan was real, and though "a creature, and God the Creator," he was "a creature with great powers." The Bible also made plain eternal punishment and the coming of salvation through Christ Jesus.[16]

By Minnie's second and final year, Mary worried increasingly about Test's influence and that of Jane M. Slocum, the teacher of metaphysics and political science. Mary was very close to her brother James Whitall, Minnie's Uncle Jim, and he reinforced her fears. He had been talking with other Friends. Dr. James E. Rhoads, a physician and Indian rights reformer later to be an important presence in Minnie's life, told him "he would not have a daughter at Howland under Dr. Test's influence, and Miss Slocum's. He would prefer the conservatism of Haverford." Mary was now very troubled about Minnie's soul. James Thomas joined in Mary's battle with Dr. Test and responded to his daughter's questioning of original sin by arguing that Adam had given his descendants a propensity to sin. In the conversion experience, Christ bestows "the blessing of the new birth," and "we are made partakers of his sinless nature." James especially mistrusted spiritualism, for Satan was loose, as well as "evil spirits capable of transformation into what may seem angels of light."[17]

Mary and James were right to fear, for Minnie was without anchor in a sea of threatening forces. In the summer after her first year, Minnie wrote

Anna Shipley an honest letter about the state of her faith. Minnie wrote that although her faith was weaker than it had been a year earlier, it was more worth having because it had been tested. She had lived among girls at Howland who had raised questions that had caused her faith to waver. But because her earlier training and experience were imbued with Christianity, her belief had been somewhat restored. However, it had not returned in the old way. She believed "in God and Christ and the general inspiration of the Bible and that is most *truly* the word of God." But the specifics, what she called "the minor points," she no longer accepted: "I don't and can't believe in eternal punishment nor in an eternal principle of evil personified by Satan."

Minnie knew in her heart that these were not really minor points. Not to believe in Satan or hell was to question the fundamental structure of her parents' belief. As she wrote to Anna, "Though it seems to *me* I am nearer the truth than I was before, yet my Christianity is not *definite*. After death is a perfect blank, almost." She could not understand how preachers could believe in "such a material Heaven and Hell." Though she occasionally longed for the time when Adam and Satan and the angels were real, that time had passed. "I doubt if many people would call me a *Christian*, but I should be very sorry to think that the 'old old story' was nothing to me." In fact, she confessed, her faith was more in doubt than she had first intimated. At times "I do feel that Christ is my Saviour, but at others I doubt everything, then again I forget all: I am so passionately fond of fun."[18]

Mary became fully aware of the dangers besetting Minnie at Howland when Bessie King returned to Baltimore in the spring term of Minnie's senior year and declared that she believed, as did Zaccheus Test, that revelation worked within the individual soul. To Mary this was unsound and she repeated her belief in the Bible as truth based on God's word. Dr. Test should return to teaching only Latin and Greek. She called on her daughter to gather a Bible class of the evangelical girls to "band together to defend the *Truth*." Minnie, of course, was in no position to defend her mother's truth. Despite Mary's warnings, she had found Test's preaching an inspiration. In her journal she penned a tribute as she left Howland: Dr. Test, she wrote, "has given us a glimpse of a grand and noble theology which will remain with us."[19]

Evil took many forms beyond Zaccheus Test. Lecturers tempted the students with reports of earlier eras that had not been blessed by the light of the Gospel. There were books it was better not to read. Mary suggested "The Ode to Duty" as an alternative to Elizabeth Barrett Browning's *Aurora Leigh*. At times it seemed to Mary that Minnie was taking "too much liberty" in her reading, that her choices were deliberately perverse. "I think thee really prefers an unsound book, to a sound one."[20]

In fact, Minnie did. She was, as she wrote to Anna, determined to range freely: "Yes, it *is* very hard to keep from being narrow; but it is one thing that

I am determined to try and do." In the summer after her first Howland year, she proudly listed the course of reading designed to broaden herself: it included Matthew Arnold's *Culture and Anarchy*, George Eliot's *Romola*, a novel in French by George Sand, and the poetry of William Wordsworth.[21]

Mary's attempt to control Minnie's reading was somewhat out of character, given the family's broad tastes in literature and their regular attendance at public lectures. More in keeping was her objection to the distractions of entertainments such as opera, that to Mary joined "affinity to Ahab to an alarming degree" and threatened to dissipate "the life of Christ in your souls." About cider, she warned, "Thee knows the dangers of getting a fondness for such things are *fearful*." Most alarming of all, in Mary's eyes, were the costumed frolics in which her darling daughter dressed as a man.[22]

Minnie wrote home about an entertainment that she and Bessie organized, a costume party in which they asked the guests to come as ladies and gentlemen. With Bessie's help, Minnie made herself a suit of men's clothes: black pants and dress coat, white vest, lavender silk cravat, gentlemen's cuffs, yellow kid gloves, and a black felt crush hat. She parted her hair on the side and applied a black mustache. "Altogether I made an elegant gentleman," she boasted. The girl whom she squired wore a dress of light silk, and "as she is very pretty and blushed whenever I spoke to her, it was splendid." At the party the guests ate and danced. Minnie proposed a toast. "Thee don't know what fun it was to stand up there in my lavender cravat and dress coat and make a speech." Such an evening was not to Mary's liking. Against this temptation of Satan, she wrote, "Thee knows how I feel about thy dressing up as a man. It is very repugnant to my taste. I do suppose it is great fun but I think it is not nice. It would be simply disgusting if any men were present, and I don't like it anyhow." As she closed, however, she reassured Minnie, "Thee is a dear precious daughter if thee does dress up as a man."[23]

Mary's influence was not enough in this instance. Minnie continued to take the male role. After learning that Minnie had been dressed as a man in a mock wedding, the mother departed from her usual practice of allowing Minnie to exercise her own judgment. Mary wrote, "I am both surprised and *mortified*." Because she had written to Minnie her full disapproval, she had been certain that Minnie would never dress as a man again. "I shall now be forced to make it a *positive command*. It *must not* be done again." Mary made it clear that she would accept no arguments or exceptions. "It is *perfectly disgusting* and revolting to me. . . . Some of the delicacy is brushed off thy character, darling daughter, and I can't help grieving over it. . . . I love thee too devotedly to be able to bear thy not being altogether womanly and lovely."[24]

What was the issue here? Years before Mary had reacted sharply when Hannah allowed Minnie to dress in Frank's trousers. Now her daughter was again away from home, but this time the danger was even greater. Quaker practice frowned on all forms of artifice. Because it emphasized the soul's harmony with the Divine, the creed blurred any distinction between thought and action. The Thomas family bent proscriptions on secular literature read at home and went frequently to lectures, even of unbelievers, but never indulged in theater or opera. Staged performances, in their depiction of fantasy, posed a particularly strong threat to the soul. Mary had sent Minnie to Howland with every expectation that she would be under Friends' control. Minnie was not only going to costumed performances, she was taking part in them. And most offensive of all was her assuming the part of a man. Confounding male and female essences was a terrible temptation, making Minnie peculiarly vulnerable to Satan's power.

In addition, there was propriety. Mary had given Minnie an unusual range of freedom to indulge her love of skating, walking on roofs, and shocking the neighbors. At critical moments, however, she had begged her daughter to conform to custom and to present herself in proper form. Mary was especially sensitive to criticism by Bessie's family, for, as she wrote to Minnie about another issue, "they are so particular, thee knows." Bessie's presence at How-land gave Mary immediate grounds for anxiety. In addition, she worried about news of her daughter being broadcast to other families. "I am positively ashamed to think of all the letters that have gone to all the homes describing my *own* dear daughter dressed up as a man!"[25]

A fascination with the sexual might lead a twentieth-century reader to rivet on Minnie's pleasure when her partner blushed; an interest in feminism might highlight the way that Minnie relished offering a toast in her black dress coat and lavender cravat. These are undeniably important foreshadowings of the adult woman. But Mary did not see them. Her concerns were twofold, faith and propriety. Confusion of male and female violated a spiritual canon; and, now that Minnie was growing into a young woman, Mary feared scandal if men were present. At issue for Mary in cross-dressing was the heightened eroticism of exposing oneself in pants. Prostitutes revealed their bodies in this manner. When Mary wrote, "It would be simply disgusting if any men were present," it was of the dress of fallen women that she was thinking.

In her thoughts of her absent daughter Mary Thomas was absorbed in protecting her body and soul, but fifteen-year-old Minnie was engaged in more worldly dramas. Her school photographs speak of her social aspirations at Howland, presenting a fashionable Minnie. She went to a studio several times while she was at Howland to have photographs taken as mementos for school friends. In the images, her clear, regular features offer no trace of the animated, eager schoolgirl. For the first time one can see the emergence of deep lids over the eyes, which would give her face one of its most salient features in maturity. In the photographs Minnie wears elaborate clothing, with bows at neck and waist. In one pose, her long brown hair is braided in the crown that she wore for many years. In another, a half-profile from the rear, her hair is dressed uncharacteristically grandly, upswept in full curls.

Minnie went to Howland with her beloved Bessie. The two roomed together and assumed that they would remain each other's best friend. But strains between them surfaced early, worrying Minnie's parents, whose closest friendship was with Francis King. Both Minnie and Bessie formed passionate friendships with others. Years later Carey Thomas wrote in a letter, "When Bessie and I reached Howland, devotions were rife. Bessie was made love to by Harrie Tilden and responded sufficiently to make me fly from our room whenever she appeared; and, of course, I was treated in just the same way by Libbie, who was seven years or more older and a woman, while I was a child of fourteen." It took only a few visits from Libbie and a little teasing, "and I knew from a slight touch of personal experience what was going on about me." In retelling her Howland experiences, Thomas turned herself into the naïf, even to the point of making herself a year younger than she was. She suggested that she innocently entered an environment where "devotions were rife." In contrast to her adult self-portrayal, however, the fifteen-year-old Minnie of her letters and diaries—who had already been "in love" with Anna and Bessie—was prepared on entering Howland for such a world and eager to partake in its pleasures.[26]

Minnie's special friend at Howland was Libbie Conkey, a young woman from Rochester, New York. They studied together. After supper they often went to a room in the gallery of the gymnasium and talked. A poem of parting that Minnie wrote to Libbie at the end of the first winter term suggests that she became attracted to her in the early autumn. The brevity of their encounter intensified the romance:

> All we did was touch and meet,
> And now we must part—my sweet,
> From each-other.

At the close of her first year at Howland, Minnie devoted her journal entry almost exclusively to Libbie. Her words suggest that she was aware of the intense quality of her feeling and that she took a male role in the relationship. "The girls said we 'smashed' on each other or 'made love,' I don't know. I only know it was elegant. She called me 'her boy,' her 'lieber Knabe,' and she was my 'Elsie.'" With Libbie back home in Rochester, Minnie was left with only letters. In her longing, Minnie wrote Libbie a poem at the end of the 1873 spring term, recalling

> Memories of our friendship, dear,
> How at first we were drawn near,

How our lives touched one another,
How we learned to love each other,

*   *   *

Kiss me "good-night" as of old!
Let me feel thine arms enfold![27]

In March Minnie had written to her mother about her feelings for Libbie. Mary had encouraged her: "I guess thy feeling for Libbie is quite natural. I used to have the same romantic love for my friends. It is a *real* pleasure." Later in the spring, Mary wrote sympathetically about Minnie's loneliness in Libbie's absence: "I know thee misses her, but guess it is just as well for thy studies. Lovers cannot be very good students."[28]

Although Minnie continued to have intense feelings of longing for Libbie, she gradually became close to Carrie Ladd. Unlike her other close friends, who had been mirrors of herself, Minnie found Carrie to be different, and the friendship was never as intense as that with Libbie. In the second year Carrie had to share Minnie with a host of others. Bessie and Minnie were the pioneers of their set. After their first year, cousins Mary Carey and Bessie Nicholson joined them, as well as Anna Shipley. Initially Minnie had been uneasy about Anna coming to Howland and had tried to discourage her, but by the fall of her senior year, Minnie was sending jaunty letters to Anna, whom she called her "golden-haired Romola," trying to entice her. Anna came, but the two decided to keep some emotional distance. In April Anna took ill and had to return to Philadelphia without graduating. Minnie wrote to her that she thought "it was very well we decided to have a real warm friendship instead of a 'smash' for I never could have stood philosophically thy worshiping like the old Romans at many shrines." By not becoming "smashes," they had kept what they had: "As it is now, I do not think our other friendships make any difference in ours for each other."[29]

Although Mary fully accepted Minnie's love of her female friends, she feared any connection that, out from under her parental roof, her daughter might make with a male. She urged Minnie to treat "all the men and boys with supreme indifference." Knowing Minnie's high spirits, she added this caution: "no fondness for fun ought to lead a girl into the slightest compromise of her dignity." In the spring of her senior year, when Minnie was helping to plan a frolic, Mary wrote "I hope the ball will be a ladies party only. *Do try*." Mary's proscriptions presumed that Minnie would marry. What she wanted was a proper match. After her daughter's visit to Hannah in the fall of 1872, Mary asked teasingly if a youth Minnie had met was all that her "fancy painted him? I don't think thee will meet thy fate there." When Minnie met her "fate," the term Mary used for a husband, she should be properly introduced.[30]

Minnie was not thinking about marriage, however. As much as she loved her mother, she did not want to reproduce her mother's life. Minnie loved reading and ideas. Although Mary normally expressed happiness with her life, her busy days and nights left her no time for contemplation. She wrote, "I am kept so busy all the time I do not even get time to *think*. It seems to me it would be a perfect luxury to sit down and just think up a great many things, but the leisure never comes." The Thomas household was peopled and indulgent. Mary reported a constant round of family visits, as many as three or four a day. Guests from out-of-town were welcomed, finding beds where they happened to be. During the Howland years Mary reported the regular use of Minnie's room. Mary's way was informal and child-centered. One day when all five boys were at home, joined by a visiting cousin, she wrote to Minnie, "They are all having a good time and I enjoy having them ever so much. But, oh, the pillow fights! The tumult is something astounding." Once, as Mary was writing to Minnie, the boys broke a window. Mary's jaunty reply captured the spirit of the Thomas household: "but that is better than one of the commandments, as Father says."[31]

Daughter and mother began to travel along increasingly separate paths. Mary Thomas was moving beyond her Quaker world into temperance reform. These were years in which the Baltimore Meeting of which she was a leader resisted the revival movement within Quakerism. Personally stirred by the revivalist message of holiness, Mary Thomas went out into the broader society. In the spring of 1874 she called a women's meeting at the Aisquith Street Presbyterian Church. Daily meetings followed that led to the formation of the Maryland Women's Christian Temperance Union. She and her coworkers held a daily midday prayer service for working and business men downtown and prayed with soldiers and with prisoners in the house of correction. They demanded a separate building for women prisoners and they closed a notorious concert hall. Minnie loved her mother, but she wanted a more rarefied future for herself.[32]

Higher education was what would make such a future possible. Minnie continued to dream of college. But looming as a cloud over her desire for Vassar was the low state of family finances. Believing that the family was rushing Minnie through Howland to save money, James Whitall sought to intervene to give Minnie a third year. Mary knew that this might arouse false hopes in her daughter that Uncle Jim might pay for Vassar. Minnie must not misinterpret. His concern was not for her higher education but was fear of her "breaking down. He trembles for an over-wrought brain."[33]

While Minnie was at Howland, the male members of the Thomas family were helping form Johns Hopkins University. The large bequest of Johns Hopkins, a Baltimore Friend, had been entrusted to the community's leaders, headed by Francis King, Bessie's father. James Carey Thomas became a member of the board of trustees. In March 1874, James wrote to Harvard, Yale, and Cornell for information. In June 1874, President Charles W. Eliot of Harvard University visited Baltimore to advise on university policy. Mary told Minnie that Eliot had delighted his hosts. But he had done more. One of Minnie's several hopes was to attend the new university. Eliot dashed that. Mary wrote, "You will have to give up the idea of having women in the college. Eliot says, and I think it is true, that coeducation does very well in communities where persons are more on an equality, but in a large city where persons of all classes are thrown together it works badly, unpleasant associations are formed, and disastrous marriages are often the result." Mary went on to encourage Minnie to think of Vassar: "I think female colleges are infinitely preferable. We are not beholden to the men for stimulus or association but can paddle our own canoe."[34]

As Minnie began to face the return home, she asked her parents if she might invite Carrie Ladd to live with her. They refused. Mary wrote to her James' reaction to his daughter's entreaties: " 'Min is a sweet child, but she does try a vast number of expedients; she might be said to have a prolific mind.' " For the rest of his life James confronted that "prolific mind." Aware that Minnie had not consecrated her soul to Christ at Howland, by the close of Minnie's senior year Mary longed to have Minnie back in the safety of home.[35]

At the end of the term, Minnie's future was given a new, clear direction. From the outset, Jane Slocum had been important to her. "From the very beginning she seemed to like me and helped me in every way. . . . Some times I have thought she let me come closer to her than the other girls for when I would go to bid her goodnight she would draw me to her and kiss me and tell me my love helped her more than I knew." As Minnie was taking her final examination in political economy, Miss Slocum watched her and asked her when she finished to come to her parlor. What she said gave Minnie her future. She had watched Minnie carefully from the outset and had been pleased with her recitations and examinations. "Both have showed that you go to the root of things and understand them. . . . You have good habits of study, and now I think I have found out what you can do. . . . What we want in the cause of women are not doctors and lawyers (there are plenty of those), we want scholars." Minnie had a good start, comparable to that of a boy. "Now I want you to be a great scholar. I don't think you will be content to merely receive and not originate. You have a great deal of time, and none of it is lost if you work steadily for your end. I want great things of you."

Minnie was moved, for she valued Miss Slocum's judgment, and "the thing she wanted was the one thing I had dreamed of." Their parting gave Minnie promise of her teacher's continued attention. When she kissed her after commencement, Miss Slocum put her arms around her and said, "Goodbye precious, remember I shan't ever give you up." Several months later, Minnie renewed the promise that she had made: "I will devote my life to study and try to work some good from it."[36]

II

COMMENCEMENT at Howland sent Minnie back home with her future undecided but her goal precise. Convinced that the cause of women needed more scholars, Minnie needed to take the first step and go to college. She had dreamed of Vassar since she was a fourteen-year-old in Rebecca Marble's school. While at Howland she had frequently reminded her mother of this, and Mary had herself encouraged the idea of a women's college rather than a coeducational one. But Miss Slocum advised Cornell, which had just opened its doors to women, rather than Vassar or the two new women's colleges— Smith and Wellesley—scheduled to take their first students in the fall of 1875. (Haverford and Princeton, where her brothers and cousins were students, were all-male; Swarthmore was the coeducational college of the Hicksite Friends.) Perhaps it was the Quaker connections of the founder, Ezra Cornell, that gave the university in upstate New York a special hold, or the boldness of the experimental university and the prestige of its newly assembled faculty. It may have been Miss Slocum's sense that Minnie might be more fully tested in the difficult environment of coeducation. Because Minnie's one moment of wavering caused her to consider the University of Michigan, it seems likely that Miss Slocum saw the coeducational university as setting the highest standard available to women.

Influenced by her teacher, Minnie now set her sights on Cornell. In August, as she wrote to Hannah on the anniversary of Frank's death, she set the tasks ahead. In three weeks she would return home "and then I will begin study again. I look forward to Cornell now, as that is the highest place open to ladies. The more I study the more I care about it. I should love to spend my life in it. That was what Miss Slocum wanted me to do." Minnie began a yearlong campaign to convince her parents to let her go to Cornell. Miss Slocum was her strongest ally. At the Howland commencement she spoke to James Thomas. By September he had promised Minnie that on his visit to Cornell to study its methods for the new Johns Hopkins University he would find out about entrance requirements. Minnie was hopeful. "I think," she wrote to Anna, "it will rest entirely on my own choice whether I go or not. Mother is willing, except for . . . missing me, and father is trying, persuading, but some times I see signs of his (not my) relenting."[37]

Miss Slocum spent the winter holidays with the Thomases. Minnie found her pleasant and liked the fact that Mary and James admired her. Jane Slocum had a law degree, which gave her prestige. The Thomases invited over the

Johns Hopkins board and President Daniel Coit Gilman. Minnie was delighted that Miss Slocum "gave it to them royally on coeducation." Her visit, however, did not settle the issue of college. In late January, Minnie wrote to Anna that the controversy was coming to a head. Discussion was painful, for Minnie was learning what it meant to go against "custom and precedence." Her parents feared it might "be wrong, to say nothing of the *wrench.*"[38]

In April Miss Slocum wrote about Cornell, and Minnie relayed to Anna, "I think it has helped to resign Father and Mother a great deal to the necessity." President Gilman added his encouragement. At tea at the Thomases in May he not only talked about his ideas about the university, "he talked so nicely about Cornell and promised me a letter of introduction to his friend Mrs. White," the wife of President Andrew D. White. He whetted Minnie's appetite by telling her that Cornell's professor of classics, James Peck, was "one of the most learned men we have."[39]

The year at home was one of hoping, studying, and waiting. Minnie had to prepare for entrance examinations, made the harder by her attempt to register as a junior. She stayed close to the home nest. She especially appreciated the help of her uncle Allen Thomas, who worked with her on Greek and taught her double entry bookkeeping. The year was not totally bereft of social pleasures. She had a visit from Libbie Conkey. In anticipation, she teased Anna, "Don't thee envy me, Anna?" adding with an asterisk, "Of course the person changed to suit." In the code-language about passionate friendships that she and Anna understood, Minnie wrote to Anna that although she and Libbie had seen each other both in Rochester and at the Howland commencement, they had not been able to really "see" each other: "The other girls were always around. Perhaps *thee knows* what that is!"[40]

In some ways the year threw Minnie back to the issues and concerns of her life before Howland. As she returned to her parents' household, she reentered the religious atmosphere of her childhood and its insistence upon her new heart. She wrote to Hannah in the summer of 1874 of the dilemma that plagued her relationships with those she loved: "I expect there is one thing more thee would like to hear, Aunt Hannah, that is, that I am consecrated to the Lord. But I can't tell thee that, one time last term I did think I was, but then it passed away." Even when she tried to put the strongest light on her weakened faith, her corrosive doubts intruded. She continued, "However, I do think I believe in Christ, and it is as much as I can do to hold on to that some times." But she knew that did not satisfy. Minnie feared that her aunt might interpret her failure to be consecrated as a lack of familial love. To counter that possibility Minnie wrote, "Dear, dear Aunt Hannah, I do love and admire thee so. And I thank thee for thy kindness to me more than thee can ever know. From the time thee used to call me the 'light of thy eyes' till now I have loved thee next to Father and Mother." This was the essence of

Minnie's problem. In wanting so deeply for their precious Minnie to find happiness in the Lord, her parents and aunt appeared to make belief in evangelical Christianity the test of Minnie's love for them. In her clearest moments Minnie tried to separate the questions that she had about belief from the certainty she felt about love.[41]

The connection was not easily severed. Nor could Minnie always be so clear, even to herself. A part of her wanted to believe. But try as she might, she was far from the faith of her childhood. As she brooded about the state of her faith, no longer as confident as before her Howland years, she wrote this telling comment, "How well I remember my half distressed delight when I read the first infidel verses I ever met with in the raving of Shelley. Yet such thoughts are very familiar now."[42]

The prose and poetry of Percy Bysshe Shelley had begun their corrosive work. As a young child she had memorized his shorter poems. Now she read his longer works. In her retirement, as she listed "the great liberal influences of my emancipation," M. Carey Thomas wrote, "first of all came Notes to Queen Mab." An early Shelley poem, *Queen Mab* was suppressed at its publication in 1813 as a revolutionary work. It offers an indictment of past and present and a vision of a just and democratic social order. It is searingly anti-Christian. It goes beyond anticlericalism to hold up for ridicule and ignominy the sacred myths of the Judeo-Christian tradition. Shelley's extensive notes to the poem address a range of issues: political justice, opposition to marriage, a universe governed by necessity—all of which informed Minnie Thomas. Most dramatically, the notes declared, "There is no God!"—at least not in the Christian sense—and submitted proofs that belief in God was a passion contrary to reason. Shelley proved to be a powerful dose to Minnie Thomas. A few years later she would write to a friend, "You know I have Shelley to thank, and through him Godwin, for almost all the light I walk by."[43]

In this year of religious doubt after Howland, Minnie continued to observe the outer forms of worship, but she could no longer call forth the inner spirit. "In sort of a dream I go to Meetings and hear talkings of Christ and his love and nearness. They believe it." "They," not "I": she had moved far away. And yet she would not avow her disbelief. Although Bessie was willing to call the Quaker creed "illogical," Minnie could not, for she knew it as "the belief of those I love dearest and best." As she tried to sort out her position, she set forth for the first time what became her mature position. Christianity was, at one level, an enthusiasm, as was Hinduism. Only Christianity was better "than any of the rest." Its glory was its believers' "personal delight, their lives, the nobility of the Bible, the gloriousness of His life and creed." What made Christianity wrong was that it was exclusive, relegating all non-Christians to damnation. And it was too specific. Its concrete detail jarred her sensibility:

"Many of the hymns are like profanation to me—God is high as heaven and deep as Hell. . . . How dare they speak of him with a familiarity which his own most beloved disciples dared not use."[44]

Separated from traditional faith, she turned to literature. She confided in her journal her pleasure in reading and her passionate responses. As she finished *Sintram*, she "lay back and sobbed and cried. I could not help it."[45] The tale of a man's defeated aspiration to triumph over sin struck close to home. She read the Romantic poets, the *Iliad*, and John Ruskin's *Modern Painters*. She attempted at moments to set down in her journal thoughts about art and life, but they read as odd and distant words for a passionate girl of seventeen.

Even more painful were the times in which Minnie doubted the course that she had set for herself. One March day, after she and Bessie had disagreed about a philosophical question, she realized that she differed from the girls of her acquaintance. "Sometimes I think I have begun upon those problems of the 'equations and inequalities of life' too soon. I do not think it is the happiest thing for a *girl*, especially, to get interested in study." She seemed engaged in an unending process in which she always felt she knew too little. Unsupported and isolated, she felt for that moment, "I would rather die than anything else, I think, for there is so much opposition to the only thing I care for . . . it is so impossible to get the highest culture by one's self, and I have to see thousands of boys enjoying and often throwing away the chances I would give *anything* for."[46]

In mid-June, however, all the uncertainty about her future and self-doubt vanished. She bragged to her journal as if to a sympathetic friend, "Well it is *done!* on the 13, 14, 15 of last June I passed the entrance examinations at Cornell University for the admission into the Classical Course." In retrospect the year of preparation looked altogether different. The summer before "it seemed impossible, but the whole of this year, with a steady unalterable determination that surprised myself even, I have been working for it." She now reviewed the year and the full extent of the struggle that she had undergone. "Father was terribly opposed and last Christmas when Miss Slocum was at our house said he never, while he lived, would give his consent. Many and dreadful are the talks we have had upon this subject, but Mother, my own splendid mother, helped me in this as she always has in everything and sympathized with me." Minnie's family framed the issue in terms of duty. "Again and again last winter did the old difficulty of deciding between our 'duty to ourselves and others' come up, for it was not a religious duty, of course, to go to Cornell, and some times it seems as [if] it ought to be given up." Although many relatives thought so, Minnie ultimately knew, "I *could* not."

Because the issue remained unresolved for so long, the practical problems of preparation for the examinations got jumbled together with the emotional issues. It pained Minnie that her father had opposed her going, "for I love him dearly and cannot bear to disappoint him." Many years later, she created the legend that her mother had promised to cry until he relented, but her journal gives only a vague depiction. "How it was done I do not know . . . if it had not been for Mother I am sure he would not have consented, but about three weeks before he gave up, and I began to prepare for the examinations." The delay put her in a frenzy, and she studied every moment before the tests, even on the train trip to Cornell. She emerged victorious and felt understandably proud of herself. She reported that Professor Peck had told her that she passed "a splendid examination" in Latin. She did well also in algebra, geometry, geography, arithmetic, grammar, and spelling, passing at almost the highest mark. The professors complimented her parents, and she enjoyed Robert Howland's pride in her as a graduate. It was ordeal and triumph: "The strain was terrible. . . . And it was an inexpressible satisfaction to pass well."

While Minnie took the examinations, her parents explored the university. The campus was at the time a grouping of about five sturdy gray stone buildings, set on rolling countryside complete with cliffs and streams. Sage College, the handsome new residence for women, was nearing completion, its more romantic form in harmony with the new Gothic buildings of Andrew White's presidency. "Mother was delighted with it and I think Father was pleased." James Thomas remained uneasy, however, and on the last night before he left, said, "Well, Minnie, I'm proud of thee but this University is an awful place to swallow thee up."[47]

The Thomases had arranged their visit to Cornell to coincide with the opening of Sage College. In writing to Anna after her return home, Minnie told her how pleased she was at the university, the festivities, and the new hall. "It really does seem a splendid university, and the professors and their wives are men of culture besides learning." George W. Curtis had spoken, giving a "most thrilling and logical appeal and argument for coeducation at the Inauguration." Minnie liked Sage College, pronouncing it "splendid" and admiring its "elegant parlors," dining room, gymnasiums, reception rooms, and "loveliest" student rooms. She approved of the promise that she would be treated as an adult, making the rules and regulations with the other students.[48]

Her immediate future set, she returned to study so that she might do well in the placement examinations in the fall. As eager as she was for college, she occasionally regretted having to work so hard in the summer. In a July letter to Anna, she wrote, "I am in a very bad humor. I want to be in swimming with the boys, instead of sitting up here untwisting Plato's *vague* Socratian ethics." But a month later, her zest for study (and her iconoclasm) had returned. She wrote to Anna, "My own virtuous Zac, how thee needs a contaminating influence like me to drag thee from embroidery, to be a 'restraint' upon thy 'pious meditations,' " and to join in reading novels and eating candy. "Lately it has been a joy to *live*—in fact I have had a *baptism* of life. I feel so gloriously well and even sitting up here and studying is fun."[49]

The approach of college did not signal the end of her parents' efforts to bring Minnie into the fold. She continued to keep herself at a distance, holding herself aloof from their religious enthusiasms. One evening in August 1875, she came close to entering their universe. Then she drew back angrily. The letter she wrote to Anna the same night revealed both her own conflicted consciousness and the religious environment of her world of origin.

First she set the scene: "Charles Coffin, Dr. Rhoads, Edward Earle sitting in three arm chairs on one side of a narrow aisle down the center of parlor, Mother, Aunt Hannah, and Rhoda Coffin in three arm chairs opposite." Charles and Rhoda Coffin were Indiana Friends, leaders in the Gurneyite renewal movement; Edward Earle, from Massachusetts, was a Quaker active in Indian rights. James E. Rhoads, from Pennsylvania, was an important Gurneyite. From this solemn gathering, Minnie initially stood aloof, but then became drawn in. "I, outside, knew that affairs of nations, society, and soul were being settled, and I penetrated and took seat at opening of aisle." In an elliptical manner, she reviewed the talk: "Sanctification, manifestation of Holy Ghost, baptism of fire, how *far* does 'save to uttermost' mean. Is 'old man' ever stone dead. Dr. Rhoads thinks Paul not to be understood literally, Aunt Hannah, freedom of *conscious* sin. Is the highest outpouring of Spirit accompanied with physical feeling? General opinion, not *necessarily*. All: if it is, we want it." The conversation would have had heightened meaning had Minnie known the part that Dr. Rhoads was later to play in her life.

Minnie had a moment of intense religious illumination. "Then came upon me like a flash of lightning what for months I have been trying to make Aunt Hannah remember, or to grasp myself. Her explanation of being 'crucified with Christ.' To me, it was a revelation of . . . a *Paulish*, figurative text before." The assembled, seizing what might be the beginning of her spiritual rebirth, began to pray. Minnie described it to Anna: "Then followed the natural effect from the six efficient causes there present—prayer meeting. Rhoda Coffin prayed for me, showing *astonishing* knowledge of my spiritual condition." Suddenly Minnie felt betrayed. Rhoda could have known what she did only because she had learned it from one of Minnie's Howland classmates who had used her as a text. What followed was for Minnie an extraordinary statement: "Very likely, wouldn't trust my own Mother if she wanted an illustration. Doctors of souls are like doctors of men: professional zeal makes them forget the individual in dissecting and analyzing the disease."

Minnie's final comment to Anna about this lost moment: "Exeunt. What a queer thing it all is, religion and irreligion." Four days later she was back to her core insight. In her journal she stated that religious enthusiasm was "simply another form of the trances of the Neo-Platonists and of the absorptions of the Buddhists into Brahma." Then she added something new, suggesting the possibility that her tolerance was turning into active disbelief. She wrote that the emotional and intellectual sides of human nature were so "delicately balanced" that the slightest pressure sent one into a "morbid sentimentalism" or into a "cold denial of anything beyond the poor horizon of . . . observation." Never sentimental about religion, was she now beginning to feel "cold denial"?[50]

Mary, who had longed for Minnie's consecration, must have been sorely disappointed by her daughter's temptation and resistance. What was wrong? Why did Minnie—surrounded by every influence for good—resist? The human heart remains a mystery, and at its core lie belief and unbelief. It is easier to trace consequences than causes. Yet for M. Carey Thomas there are some clues. Embedded in her mother's diary is Minnie's anguish at age seven, when her pain told her that God had forsaken her. He had allowed her, unlike Shadrach, Meshach, and Abednego, to burn. He had not answered Mary's prayers that the dressing not hurt. At no point after that did she feel the certainty of God's abiding love. As Minnie recovered, her parents loosened their brake on her willfulness. As much as she loved her mother, she remained devoted to fun and to intellectual exploration that began to take her far from home. She was forming intense bonds with girls of her own age. As Mary's pressure on Minnie's soul mounted at Howland and during the year at home, daughter began, at some level, to fight mother. Faith became part of the struggle; lack of faith, a critical way that Minnie saw herself as different from Mary.

Mounting tension at home added to Minnie's eagerness for college. She was, as she wrote to Anna, "in a fever of impatience for Cornell to commence."[51]

CHAPTER 4

A Complete Convert to "Coed"

MINNIE THOMAS entered Cornell with a new name. Before leaving home she talked it over with her father. She was ready to leave "Minnie" behind, and her father agreed. He did insist, however, that she not adopt a new one but rather drop the Martha that she never used and the Minnie by which she had been called and take her middle name as her given one. He suggested that she call herself Carey Thomas and sign her name M. Carey Thomas. Her father's choice was an intriguing one, for, by it, he was encouraging his daughter to rename herself after him. She was the only one of the children to carry his family middle name. The younger Thomas children accepted the new name quickly, sending, as Mary wrote, their "love to *Carey*, correcting me for my misnomer." To her parents and to her Baltimore friends she remained Minnie for many years.[1]

When she arrived in Ithaca to take placement examinations, she stayed with Professor William Channing Russel, the professor of literature and vice president of Cornell, and made arrangements to dwell at Sage College. The opening of the women's residence was delayed because bedding and crockery for the hall had not yet come. In going to Howland, she had convinced her mother to loan her two pieces of crimson carpet. At Cornell she made a larger grab at family resources. Despite the scarcity of cash in her indebted parents' household, Carey set her sights on a three-room suite costing four hundred twenty dollars for the year, a price comparable to 60 percent of a worker's annual income. She wrote to her father for permission but, before she received his answer, she secured the three rooms, following, she insisted, the advice of Professor Russel. Carey's arguments for the expensive suite were that it would give her a friend nearby, Margaret Hicks, an architecture student she had met at entrance examinations in June, a beautiful parlor, and "the prestige of having a nice room at first."[2]

Although Howland had taken her away from home, it had brought her into association with others of her tradition and social class. As a university, Cornell, by contrast, attracted a varied student body. To her parents, Carey expressed pleasure at new associations, bragging that she was in the same institution as Ulysses S. Grant's son and a Chinese prince. But who was she at Cornell? To be the daughter of a leading Quaker physician and lay minister from Baltimore carried little weight.

Her insecurity about how others perceived her can be seen in her first communication home about her new world. Ruth Putnam was also staying with Professor Russel. She was a "rara avis . . . daughter of the great publisher and sister of Dr. Putnam Jacobi, the great New York lady doctor." Before they had known each other two hours, Ruth had questioned her on her family. Ruth professed "great amazement" that Carey was Quaker because she spoke "like a lady who had been out a great deal in society." Carey added that Ruth "evidently thinks Friends are cooks or something." Though she never put it quite this way, having a three-room suite filled with fine things would convince those around her that she was high born.[3]

In her first letter to Anna Shipley, Carey insisted on her great satisfaction, "it is worth everything to be here." In the preceding week she had withstood the difficult test of reading an essay aloud to her male classmates. She encountered great courtesy: men in her classes treated the women with deference and even waited to open doors for them. A few mornings before, she had arrived early at analytical geometry. Fifteen men were "talking and laughing rather loudly." As she entered, "every hat was taken off and their whole manner changed." Carey pronounced herself "a complete convert to 'Coed.' "[4]

When President Charles W. Eliot of Harvard had warned Mary Thomas of the "disastrous marriages" that often resulted from coeducation, he was playing upon parental fears that away from familial supervision, young collegians might choose partners from backgrounds different from their own. Carey Thomas attended Cornell in its early years of coeducation, when the institution treated the women students much as they did the men. She was one of twenty women in a class of 240. In its first year Sage College, the new residential hall for female students, opened board to all takers to add to revenues. This meant that male students dined with the coeds. When Carey wrote home with the news, she assumed that her father would be shocked. He took the news calmly, but Mary did not. She wrote, "I think it is dreadful and wish they could keep them out." She cautioned, "Do be very reticent, and not take any more notice of them than is absolutely necessary." Carey acted to make her mother proud: she took her seat at the end of a table and "barricaded" herself between Ruth Putnam and Margaret Hicks.[5]

Before Carey had left home, James and Mary Thomas had extracted from her a promise that at Cornell she would avoid all social contact with male students. They called this her "rule." James and Mary feared that their spirited daughter might destroy her reputation as a lady by unchaperoned contacts with men or that she might fall in love with someone they regarded as unsuitable.

So frightening was the prospect that they abjured their usual practice of giving Carey leeway to make decisions. Her "rule" was the price Carey had to pay for Cornell.

Since age fourteen Carey Thomas had looked to college as the place where she might become the important person she dreamed of being. She envisioned that college would set her off from the masses of ordinary humanity. If she had not gone to college, she would have been condemned to being a "blighted being."[6] Miss Slocum had fired her with the specific ambition to become a scholar and directed her to Cornell. The new university offered to young women an education unusual in the 1870s. In contrast to the traditional liberal arts curriculum of colleges, Cornell was committed to establishing the parity of all study, including practical subjects. Carey Thomas, however, pursued a classical course at Cornell as rigorous as the one required at Vassar or Yale. In her two years of study, she concentrated on Greek, Latin, mathematics, literature, and philosophy, and was one of five in her class to receive the bachelor of arts degree.

Cornell in the 1870s was an exciting intellectual world that from the outset challenged Carey Thomas. In late September she wrote home about her work. She noted a lecture on old Gothic by Hjalmar Hjorth Boyesen, a young professor of literature, emerging on the national scene as a writer of fiction and a literary critic. Mathematics with Professor William E. Byerly was a particular delight. She was studying analytic geometry and found it to be "the explanation of so much that I have wondered about before . . . it is a revelation!" She wrote to Anna that she was spending her spare time in the library reading books explaining mathematics, seeking to gain an "intellectual understanding" of the field. Another letter reported that she, along with Ida Bruce, constituted the highest class in Greek. She was doing outside reading in Latin and Greek. Her only complaint was the "ordeal" every three weeks of composing an original essay.[7]

Carey Thomas studied hard and enjoyed her work. She wrote home in January 1876, "Last week went like a flash. My lessons are really such a pleasure that the time goes faster when I study them than otherwise."[8] Her studies were both broad and deep. She wrote her notes in bound notebooks. They reveal advanced work in mathematics and science, as well as in literary studies. The notebook for Byerly's course in calculus contains theoretical discussion of the nature of a variable and pages of detailed equations. In physics she studied electricity, and her notebooks contain sketches of elements of experiments. Mathematics and science did not daunt her; one could well imagine her following these courses with graduate training or medical school.

However, as Carey Thomas set her sights upon becoming a scholar, she thought of the study of language and literature. Notebooks for these courses reveal, on the one hand, close attention to classical texts and, on the other, broad speculation and aesthetic theory. In Latin and in the Greek course taught by Professor James Peck, the notebooks contain line-by-line examinations of major works, such as *Oedipus* and *Agamemnon*, as well as discussions of form and meaning. Courses in literature, taught by Professors C. C. Shackford and Hiram Corson, treated some of the same texts, but in a different manner. Notes for Shackford's course in literature are particularly full. He was not one of Cornell's new lights, but rather a hold-over from an earlier era. He opened up to Carey Thomas the world of Shakespeare, leading to a lifelong interest. His authoritative voice speaks through Thomas' notes in ways that were to echo in her own subsequent lectures in literature. "All true artists," he intoned, "embody with special tendencies the everlasting truths." The true test of a work of art is "its universality."[9]

Carey Thomas particularly enjoyed Professor Corson's course in later English literature, taken the second semester of her first year. Corson treated technical elements of poetry: meter, rhyme schemes, use of words; but in addition offered bold statement and broad-ranging speculation. Although never acknowledged as a mentor, Corson influenced her later scholarship and teaching. He introduced her to Alfred Tennyson's "Morte d'Arthur," declaring it "the most exquisite example of blank verse since Milton." He discussed poetry in language that was to resonate in her teaching: "Tennyson pays more attention to tone than any other poet. Hence he is rather harmonious than melodious. Keats abounds in melody we love to linger over . . . but he is not harmonious."[10]

Corson's course in literature spilled out in many directions. He gave lectures three hours each week that delighted Thomas. Topics he assigned led to discussion. For example, in January 1876, she wrote home that conversation about the leading characters in Elizabeth Barrett Browning's *Aurora Leigh* had led to a debate in which she had taken the position that poetry was more important than philanthropy because the poet inspired the work of doing good. Corson's wife taught French informally, had the students play French games, and organized a student play in French. In her second year, Professor Corson read nineteenth-century British poetry in the evenings. Thomas wrote home after hearing him read, "I think I enjoy poetry more than anything else." To undergraduates of Thomas' generation, Corson was a liberating force. When Anna railed against Walt Whitman, Thomas retorted that she must not judge a poet by excerpts. She had decided to read Whitman carefully, for Corson "says that a union of Bret Harte and Walt Whitman would make *the* American poet."[11]

Carey Thomas' notebooks reveal that she was hardly the devoted acolyte. She doodled, drawing repeatedly a rather dashing man's head. She tried out various monograms with her initials. She exchanged notes with friends, particularly with Ida Bruce. She wrote her own and Bruce's names repeatedly, once within a drawing so that they looked like the names of authors on book jackets. Once she wrote to a classmate, "I don't like to answer if no one else does." She was clearly bored at times and restive in the classroom. One philosophy lecture provoked Thomas to write, "This is stupid." The person beside her answered, "True." Thomas continued, "I gave up skating for it, and we have known everything he has said."[12]

Carey Thomas' college thesis, written in the spring of 1877, was an essay on Greek and Roman civilization. It contrasts the glory of Greek civilization and the emptiness of Roman power. Its themes, dealt with in broad sweeping terms, were ones already well worked in existing literature. It treats sympathetically the Romans' effort to learn from the Greeks. It praises Roman achievements and asserts their enduring influence on Western civilization. Its language is an accurate mirror of college lectures.[13]

Perhaps because her "rule" cut her off from some of the social events of the university, in a most unusual way Carey Thomas' extracurricular and curricular life merged. She could not dance with men, but while others did, she could talk with her young professors. H. H. Boyesen became an important intellectual companion. But more generally, for women in the 1870s, Cornell was a hospitable world in which work and play were blended. Thomas went to see Professor Peck to talk with him about the difficulty that she, unaccustomed to his drill, was having in his advanced Latin course. Mrs. Peck invited her to stay for tea. Professors' wives and daughters often called. President Andrew White gave entertainments in which talk ran to literature.

Lectures, readings, heady talk were supplemented by wide reading for pleasure. Later in her life, when M. Carey Thomas described her college life, she recalled "those stretches of unoccupied leisure, those long unfilled afternoons and evenings and nights" devoted to "voracious and limitless reading of poetry and unending discussions of abstract questions." She listed her college idols: "Wordsworth and Shelley and Keats and Browning and Swinburne and Victor Hugo were the poets of our college days; George Eliot and Balzac our novelists, and Matthew Arnold, Emerson, Carlyle, Ruskin, and Herbert Spencer our seers and prophets." In remembering her college days, she was recalling both the books that formed the content of courses and those she read for sheer pleasure.[14]

II

CAREY's "rule" meant that she was a bystander to some of the social life of Cornell. She kept a calling card from Edmund Le Breton Gardiner with an undated invitation to ice-skate, and toward the end of her life she recalled skating so skillfully with a young instructor in physics that "people used to stop skating to watch us." She did not dance with men or go on excursions with them, however. At times it was hard to abide by her self-denying ordinance. In November she wrote to her parents that she had "a real temptation" when Gardiner and two other men invited Ruth Putnam, Margaret Hicks, and her for a country drive: "I hesitated a little for I wanted to see it dreadfully, and the girls insisted upon my going. But at last I decided that I also did not care to be under that obligation to the gentlemen, and, besides, it would be breaking my rule of not going out with students, so I refused." She was glad she had refused when she saw them drive off, after a third coed was found, "a couple on each seat in true tête-à-tête fashion."[15]

In abiding by her "rule" Carey stood outside the mores of coeducation and had to watch her classmates from a distance. In January of her first year, she stepped beyond reticence to try and get others in Sage College to follow her lead. As she saw a Miss Mitchell, one of the young women on her corridor, going out to skate with a man, she stopped her to argue that this would have an improper influence on others. When Miss Mitchell replied that Carey had convinced her, but that she did not want to tell her escort she had changed her mind, Carey answered, "It will be a good lesson to him, and it's *splendid* in you, Miss Mitchell." In adopting the language of social propriety, Carey established herself as a lady in the eyes of her peers.[16]

In February of her first year, Carey complained to her mother about the cost of keeping her "rule." Mary reassured her that, though it involved sacrifice, she was certain that Carey would be better off if she were consistent. "If it is thy invariable habit to refuse such invitations, no one can complain, and thee will be saved *lots* of trouble. Father and I would be greatly troubled by the knowledge that thee might be going with Tom, Dick, and Harry. And thee would not find, darling, that it *paid*." Both elements of the calculus were important and reemerged repeatedly: parental fear and Carey's profit.[17]

For Carey the cost of having nothing to do with men at Cornell was both that she missed masculine company and that she had constantly to watch her female friends leaving with male partners. When Miss Hicks went off with a male companion on a drive, Carey was left alone without her. Carey had come to Cornell with her own rule: she was not to waste time with another smash. This rule proved impossible to keep. In October Carey wrote home about her full social life. Cornell professors and their wives paid calls that had to be repaid. The evening before, President White's daughter had come to Sage College for a tea, attended by about thirty male and female students. Dancing in the parlor followed. "I waltzed a little with some of the girls, *of course*, and it was fun. Almost every evening about half past ten or eleven Miss Hicks and I have a waltz up and down the dark hall." As she was writing the letter, Margaret Hicks, who roomed next door, came in her room and joined her in letter-writing. "She is very nice, and I believe I am getting rather devoted to her, but I am as yet struggling against it." The two had spent afternoons studying together in Cascadilla glen, a scenic spot near the campus. A few weeks later Carey wrote that they had gone out tramping in the fields and in the evening read Swinburne's *Chastelard*. She had moved a lamp onto a bookcase near her bed so that the two could "lie there and read as nicely as can be."[18]

What she did not write to her parents was that she had once again fallen in love. This she confided to Anna: "Well, I have been and gone and done it, I may as well confess. Ever since the first I have struggled against it. I made up my mind that up here, at least, I would not have a friendship that was in the least absorbing. It takes time and I don't approve of them." When she met Margaret Hicks, she knew she would like her, "but not one advance did I make." In the first week at Cornell, in the course of conversation, "I said that I had made up my mind not to have any more intimate friendships, and she took that as a hint and carefully avoided showing that she liked me." Margaret Hicks fell in love with her. "It was dancing and Swinburne that did it." She taught Carey how to waltz "and we waltzed and waltzed together." They would study and then "about half past nine we would finish studying and she would undress and put on her trailing wrapper and come in to my bedroom and we would lie there and read." One evening as they were lying together reading Swinburne, "I made an unguarded remark and was perfectly astonished at the way she responded, and then I gave up. . . . She cares for me in a different way I think from any of my other friends, more like I cared for Libbie."

Carey went on to write to Anna of her friend's beauty, describing her eyes and complexion. Because she and Anna were always interested in "each other's love affairs," Carey wanted to tell her about her new beloved. Margaret Hicks was "altogether an ideal smash, and I love her, and we have quite nice times." They had decided not to let others know: "they are in perfect ignorance, especially when every night she comes along the dark corridors to bid me good night."[19]

During her Cornell years Carey did not keep a journal, something that, as she neared graduation in June 1877, she regretted. At that point she set down the record of her involvement with Margaret Hicks, suggesting its central importance in her life at Cornell. She recalled her commitment not to fall in love again, her introduction to Miss Hicks in June before entering college, and their early encounters in the fall. She then retold the story she had written to Anna, but with one important difference. One night, as they were reading aloud in bed Swinburne's *Atalanta in Calydon* and learning several of the choruses, "we had stopped reading later than usual and obeying a sudden impulse I turned to her and asked, 'do you love me?' She threw her arms around me and whispered, 'I love you passionately.' She did not go home that night, and we talked and talked. She told me she had been praying that I might care for her."[20]

Care for Miss Hicks she did. Carey nicknamed her Clytie, because once, when she looked at her standing by a bust of Clytemnestra, she saw a resemblance. Their relationship proved intense and stormy. Carey often criticized Margaret's easy acceptance of others, and this led to tearful recriminations. What Carey never alluded to directly was that Margaret was being courted by a man. Carey had a rival for Margaret's affection, Karl Volkmann.

Margaret also had her rivals. Carey enjoyed having two admirers vie for her attention. During her first year at Cornell she sustained her Howland friendships and returned there for visits. On one occasion she described to Anna her anticipation of Washington's Birthday festivities at the Howland School. The event was an all-female fancy-dress tea-party for which she was having a new dress made. She was to be waited on with flowers by her escort. Margaret Hicks was asked by a former female acquaintance "who is quite a lady killer." Her own invitation came from a Howland student with a smash on her so intense that "she does not eat one thing when I am down there and raves about me . . . and says she is miserable when I am with her and perfectly wretched when I am away." Carey then told Anna of a triangular weekend when Carrie Ladd came to visit and she and Margaret Hicks hid their affection for each other. With this, she enlarged on her feelings for Margaret Hicks. "Thy 'rival' Miss Hicks is still a fascination and we are constantly together, reading and studying Greek and learning poems. . . . She is so pretty . . . that no matter on what sublimated subject I am raving, I am always conscious of her prettiness, and thee knows . . . one likes to forget the objects of sense." This long letter of multiple entanglements—and the very act of writing about them to Anna—was designed, in part, to revive Anna's love. Carey closed with the reassurance, "Yes, I love thee very dearly. . . . Goodbye, I give thee a spiritual kiss, my Romola, right on thy golden hair."[21]

As she wrote to her parents, Carey was more guarded in her disclosures. Yet what she wrote disturbed them, for it indicated their daughter's engagement in a secular world that exposed her to the dangers of the senses. Mary accepted Carey's absence from home to attend college with equanimity greater than she had during the Howland years. Mother still feared for her darling daughter's soul and wrote long, loving sermons, but the desperate tone of earlier letters eased. Mary continued to counsel Bible group, friendship only with Christians, caution with dangerous texts, and avoidance of unprofitable subjects; but she lightened her oversight and softened her language.

Mary raised an alarm, however, when she learned that Carey had waltzed. After this, she counseled Carey not to write about waltzing in the body of a letter, but on a separate sheet; that way Mary could keep such matters from her own mother. Mary herself wanted to know all that Carey did, and she professed not to be shocked, but dancing clearly went beyond her limit. She did not see how "the love thee is forming for waltzing will be of any use to thee in any way." She would much prefer that Carey walked outdoors. In contrast to a brisk walk, waltzing "only *feels nice*, purely sensual." It was "beneath the pursuit of a child of God."[22]

As disturbed as she was by waltzing, Mary was relieved that Carey had refused to dance with a man. Though clear that Carey was not to socialize with college men, Mary sent mixed signals to Carey about her female friendships at Cornell. Soon after Carey's first year began, Mary wrote, "I hope thee will have a real good time this term, and cultivate some nice girls as *friends* not as sweethearts. Tell me all about them, which thee likes the best." Yet this was in the abstract, not the particular. After Libbie Conkey came to visit Carey at Cornell in the spring, Mary commented, "I am glad thee had such a lovely visit from Libbie, and that she was so pretty and satisfactory. It is a benediction to have people pretty, even if they are not much else. Was Madgie [Hicks] jealous?"[23]

Mary never suggested that she regarded Carey's romantic friendships as wrong. Eager as she was for Carey to profit by her unique chance at Cornell, she feared her intense attachments as distractions from study. A conversation that Carey had with Hannah Whitall Smith during the summer before entering Cornell suggests another family fear. She and her aunt drove along the beach in the moonlight, talking "among other things about *smashes*." Hannah fully accepted them, she told Carey, for she had "always had those sorts of friendships, feels capacity yet, thinks they are all right." There was one danger, however. Hannah warned her that the kind of "nature" that yields to a "smash" was "apt to fall in love." What Hannah meant was that Carey's passionate nature might find the wrong channel: a man. It was this that she warned against. Carey promised her aunt, "Yes, ma'am, *I shall be careful*." In the women's world that Carey shared with her mother and aunt, passionate love for another woman was allowed, even valued; love for a man posed risks and danger.[24]

Sex, scandalous sex, was very much on Mary's and Hannah's minds, for allegations of impropriety had come home full force. Robert Pearsall Smith, Hannah's husband, had become a lay evangelist and enjoyed immense popularity in Europe. Hannah, who had joined her husband on the Continent and in England in his revival meetings, had now returned with him to the United States. They returned not in triumph, but in disgrace. Public accusations flew in England that in his religious ecstasies Robert had laid his hands on prayerful female bodies. The European tour of victory for the Lord had turned into personal tragedy. Robert had been read out of the English holiness meetings and the aristocratic homes that had once thrilled to his words. Mary carefully understated the scandal to Carey: "Aunt Hannah has had some trouble about some very disagreeable things which have been in some of the papers about Uncle Robert. A young lady who came to him for spiritual help complained of impropriety in his conduct and conversation, though at the time she did not manifest the slightest displeasure, which was very remarkable if there was any real ground of complaint." Newspapers in England, in opposition to the holiness doctrine of freedom from sin, had given the incident wide publicity. Although it was "all very disagreeable . . . I think it will blow over soon." It did not. Robert retreated into private life, never to emerge from the shadows. Hannah gradually returned to prominence and to England, but in a very different spirit.[25]

Hannah and her immediate family interpreted Robert's fall from public esteem and her own compromised position in varied ways. Mary's letter to Carey spoke only of the love that most of the family extended to Hannah and Robert and her own efforts to placate her brother James, who presumed to judge. The letter from Hannah that Mary enclosed to Carey suggests that Hannah was confused and felt somehow responsible for Robert's shame. Carey herself worried only about Hannah and wished she could save her from trouble.[26]

Hannah's troubles may have begun to affect her sister's consciousness in subtle ways. In addition, Mary's reform work in brothels and saloons, coupled with her inability to control her fertility, may have altered her feelings. During her eldest daughter's first year at Cornell, she was pregnant for the tenth (and last) time, a pregnancy that made Carey fear for her health. M. Carey Thomas' autobiography contains this recollection: On returning from Howland or Cornell, "I would give my mother a frightened glance. If she were wearing a short velvet jacket she wore before her babies were born, I would rush away to my room and sob until my Mother would come to find me and join her tears to mine." Mary's letters to Carey at Cornell contain far less about her husband than they had three years before.[27]

Moreover, Mary more frankly states her affiliation with the women in her family and community. In the summer after Carey's first year at Cornell, Mary wrote to her that John, home from Haverford, was not having much fun. She had not had the long talks with him that she and Carey shared in her upstairs parlor. Her sons were simply not as satisfactory to her as her daughters and she confessed that she could not talk to them, for they were not "as nice as girls 'say what you will.' " After Carey had returned to Cornell, Mary, in an aside, declared her own attraction to women. Using language that linked her with her daughter, she wrote Carey about James' friendship with the president of Johns Hopkins: "Father and Gilman are as thick as ever. I call it a smash. *I* have no one to smash with, now that Esther has fallen. I do not find that she fascinates me as she used to at all. I can get along without seeing her with perfect equanimity."[28]

Although Carey's "rule" prohibiting social events with male students al-layed much family anxiety, Mary worried about her daughter's contact with her male professors. In the course Carey Thomas had with Professor William E. Byerly, a recent Harvard Ph.D., she was the only student. Mary wrote her disapproval: "I do not at all like thy having the lecture *alone*. Tell me exactly how it is managed. . . . Is no one in the room but thee and Byerly? If that is the case, I think it is *objectionable*." She did not interfere and force her daughter to withdraw, but she did give her a lesson about how she might protect herself. "It will require the utmost care on thy part to prevent his becoming too intimate. Let no considerations of gratitude for the interest he takes in thy studies induce thee to permit the slightest approach to familiarity. Check it at once by a marked displeasure: coldness of manner will at once convey thy displeasure, and he will respect thee all the more for keeping him at a distance." Mary's fear was not unfounded. The young, single male faculty at Cornell entered the coeds' social world fully: they called, they came to tea, they skated, and they served as escorts to the dances.[29]

Carey's letters carry no suggestion of interest in Professor Byerly, but do report that he called on Ida Bruce and later escorted Cornell women students to the dances. Attentions to Carey came from Professor Boyesen. Boyesen later told Carey that her father, whom he had met when James brought Carey to Cornell, was very interesting to him because he was "so utterly different from anything he had seen before." Boyesen joined the male students eating at Sage College, and stayed with them for conversation, singing around the piano, and dancing. One evening as after-dinner dancing in Sage began, Boyesen asked Carey to waltz. Carey reported to her parents that she told him "that I was obliged to him, but I did not dance the round dances. He flushed crimson but I do not think he was angry for he sat down and talked very interestingly about Swinburne, Rossetti, etc." They began a literary flirtation that lasted Carey's two years at Cornell.[30]

Word of this got to Anna in Philadelphia. Carey quickly countered Anna's teasing about men: "As for my falling in love, Anna: please don't laugh about it for it is too serious a matter. . . . Why, when I have disliked gentlemen all my life, I should make an exception here is beyond me. I have even stopped having literary rhapsodies with Professor Boyesen, not because I consider it perilous but because I am afraid people may not know their purely aesthetic character." In fact this was premature. In the fall of her second year, Carey wrote again about Boyesen, whose newly published story she recommended to Anna to read. Boyesen and she had had a long talk: "I am always carried away, while I talk to him, in perfect sympathy with him. We fairly raved together over *Daniel Deronda* and George Eliot; but when I go up stairs and think over him, I do not trust what he says, somehow. I should like so much to believe in him and in his genius but there is something so—I can't tell what about him."[31]

Rumors about them did flourish. In April of her second year, a Cornell student looked at the books of the hotel in Trumansburg to see "Professor B—— and Miss Thomas." He came back to Cornell to spread the word. Boyesen set things aright by saying that he was "very much mortified, that it was too bad for me, but that he himself had an elegant time." Later when visiting Anna, a young Haverford acquaintance who attended Harvard told Carey that he had heard that she and Boyesen were engaged. Years later, Carey wrote to an intimate friend that she had stood beside the copy of the statue of Moses in Sage College and made a decision "*not* to learn to care for Boyesen, whom I was perilously near falling in love with." At the end of her life she listed Boyesen as one of her "lovers" on the list she compiled for her autobiography. Despite these statements at many years' remove from Cornell, there is little evidence from the record at the time that Carey was interested in Boyesen as a possible suitor. His real importance derived from the stimulus and direction he gave to her intellectual life.[32]

Carey and Margaret Hicks had declared their love for each other over a volume of Swinburne's poetry that Boyesen had lent. This was a time in which Carey read widely, both aloud to Margaret, lying with her on the lounge, and to herself. Carey frequently listed her reading: on one occasion, Herbert Spencer's *First Principles*, August Wilhelm von Schlegel's *A Course of Lectures on Dramatic Art and Literature*, Richard Watson Gilder's *The New Day*; on another Victor Hugo's *Les Misérables*, Edgar Allan Poe stories, Johann Wolfgang von Goethe's *Sorrows of Young Werther*, an unspecified work of William Makepeace Thackeray, and the poetry of Elizabeth Barrett Browning. For some of these books, Boyesen guided the choice. When she wrote to Anna, she sought to pass on his inside information. The work of Gilder, one of the few contemporaries on her list, she recommended to Anna as "one of Boyesen's coterie. Do read it!"[33]

Carey provided almost no commentary on her prose reading at this point. Only statements written afterward clarify that the texts of Positivism were reshaping her consciousness. Poetry, by contrast, evoked intense personal response noted at the time. Swinburne's *Atalanta in Calydon*, Elizabeth Barrett Browning's *Sonnets from the Portuguese*, Robert Browning's *Pippa Passes*, and Gilder's love sonnets were the language of her intimate friendship with Margaret Hicks and correspondence with Anna Shipley. Educated young people of sensibility in the 1870s translated elements of this broader literary culture into a specific discourse of feeling and heightened emotion. They slid without break from reading poetry and discussing it to talking about themselves and their passions.

III

CORNELL provided a two-year respite from the religious pressure of home. As a result, the university allowed her a temporary tolerance of Christianity. In her household Carey had been the religious outsider, resisting her family's pressures for specific belief. At Cornell, she kept her outsider stance, but, to her surprise, found herself in opposition to the secular, agnostic atmosphere of the university. As she wrote to Hannah, "Everything is so different here from at Howland or anywhere else. The sense of free moral agency is crushing some times."[34]

The course in moral philosophy that was taught to all juniors and seniors by William D. Wilson, a minister who served as college registrar, angered her. She wrote to Anna, "The slurs he casts at Christianity and God . . . make my blood *boil*." He made aspersions against Christians. His discussion of perfectionism insulted Thomas, as did the laughter it evoked. "If he fairly combatted Christianity I wouldn't care, but to have him, whenever he mentions God, say 'if there is any such' . . . infuriates me."[35]

Carey Thomas' ire at such comments may have encouraged her to reconsider religion. With Margaret Hicks and the women on her hall she formed a Bible study group that read and talked together on Sundays. Though she insisted that she did not do so "from the least *atom* of Thomas evangelizing spirit," the aim of the gathering was religious inquiry. To her surprise, she learned that of the other five women, only Margaret Hicks was a true Christian: two were avowed atheists; one, a Unitarian; and one, "nothing in particular." She also listened, she felt with profit, to Henry Ward Beecher when he came to preach and, toward the end of her final year, heard one of Felix Adler's controversial lectures on history through the Old Testament.[36]

For these two years, Carey was free of the religious scrutiny of her Baltimore household. Though more open to religion, she remained, as she explained to Anna, "neither cold nor hot, not thoroughly convinced of the 'Evidence of Christianity.' "[37] In time, the poetry and the prose read in her Cornell years formed the basis of the secular culture that took the place of religion, but while she was at Cornell, religion, art, and philosophy coexisted side by side.

Later in her life, M. Carey Thomas wrote of the pall cast by Dr. Edward Hammond Clarke's writings, just in these years, about the ruinous effects of college on female organs. Although there is no evidence that Clarke caused Carey to rein herself in, it is clear that Mary and James took his injunctions to heart. They worried that hard study would destroy Carey's health. The one time that they interfered with her plans was when they forbade her to stay at Cornell for the summer after her second year to study and compete for a Latin prize. They feared that her "health might be utterly broken by it . . . that her brain would be overwrought." They did not object, however, to her larger goals for herself. As Mary closed the letter that gave the decision about the Latin competition, she wrote lovingly, "It is, as thee says, a great bother having children with independent bents of their own. If you will only all turn out good noble Christians, I shan't mind the little accessories in the way of A.M.'s and M.D.'s, etc."[38]

As Carey Thomas prepared to graduate, she paused to reflect. On June 12, 1877, she tried to summarize in her journal what the two years had meant to her. Going to college had been her goal since age fourteen. Now, at twenty, she had attained her prize. It was an important moment, one that she had long anticipated. It was, as she put it, "the one purpose that runs through my journals." She graduated from a university with a degree that she believed was of greater value than one from Vassar. Yet in contrast to her sense of success at her graduation from Howland three years before, she judged her Cornell years more temperately. They had not been easy, for she had entered behind, especially in Latin. Cornell had, however, been worthwhile. "Altogether I have learned a great deal and it has been thoroughly profitable to be here. It has given me a new outlook. Though I feel very far from a good Latin and Greek scholar, yet I do see light somewhat."

Yet whatever intention she had of summing up her intellectual achievements was lost as she turned to her personal life. She judged that "Cornell missed all that glorious culture that one reads of in college books." The university had not offered her the college life of fiction. Outside of a handful of women students, she had met few people that she did not regard as beneath her socially. Except for H. H. Boyesen, the men were "second rate, 'half cut,' Bessie would say."[39]

These musings at the end of her college years suggest the increasing importance that class distinctions were coming to play in Carey's consciousness. By establishing herself in a three-room suite and by refusing to socialize with male collegians, Carey positioned herself outside the ambit of Cornell undergraduates. She somehow ignored the overcrowded, indebted, democratic household from which she had come to translate her parents' fear of her leaving the Quaker fold into aristocratic protectiveness. While Mary was seeking to turn sinners from drink in prisons and on street corners, her daughter was creating an aloof air of command.

In the group photograph with six friends, Carey's elegantly pleated light-colored skirt is spread in front of the darker-hued dresses that form the background. While the others generally tilt their heads to look slightly downward, Carey's face is perpendicular to the floor, emphasizing her strong jaw. Her gaze under her deeply lidded eyes is straightforward. Seated with her arm resting on another's lap, she makes room for her broad shoulders.

By the end of her college career Carey's sharp tongue and efforts to establish herself as a lady had led Cornell women outside her circle of friends to fear her, and this caused her momentary concern. She learned that they thought her "cold and proud," and she felt that something was amiss because those who did not know her became frightened when she came in the room. From her own reports, it seems they had learned the lessons she had to teach.[40]

In her final journal entry for Cornell, Carey turned to her intimate friendship with Margaret Hicks. It was here that she set down the lengthy narrative of their first declaration of love. Now, at the time of parting, Carey was mystified by her feelings. At one level, she questioned whether or not it were "best for people to care about each other so much." As she listed the negatives, it is clear she was thinking at the level of practicality. The relationship lasting the two years of college had wasted her time, which she could have better spent in reading. Moreover, their quarrels, especially about the propriety of accepting male attentions in college, had given her pain. Perhaps with her mother's calculus in mind—does it pay?—Carey reflected that it had been a shame in college "to be distracted by such things."

Carey could not understand why she could not control her own passion. She was "mastered by it." Her other romantic friendships had contained an element of idealism, expressed in her poetic effusions. But Margaret Hicks' ordinariness prevented this. Though she was lovely and pretty, Margaret was not serious. Having no deep intellectual interests, she probably would not be successful as an architect. Essentially she lacked strength of character and self-assurance. "I think she will probably get married." With such an escalating catalogue of unfavorable traits, why had Carey been so enamored of her? Essentially, she did not know. "I just fell in love with her." Gradually, after the night Margaret Hicks had declared her love, she got "fonder and fonder of her," going against her own "better judgment." Ultimately, she wrote, "I cannot tell why it was."[41]

Carey's need to set down her confusions about Margaret Hicks distracted her from close examination of what college had meant to her. It would be a mistake to take her own words at face value, however, and assume that affairs of the heart overrode her ambitions and commitments at Cornell. Beneath the surface of her journal lay two critical issues.

Carey Thomas felt let down. Although Cornell had given her ideas, appreciations, and an intense friendship, it had not transformed her. As she left, she thought that this might have been her fault and scolded herself for not using her time fully. She could not see that she wanted what Cornell could not offer. She was beginning a spiritual quest to replace the religious certainty that eluded her. Cornell had given her an opportunity for intellectual growth, but what she desired was the hard rock of certainty, the feeling of true knowing that could conquer all doubt. In addition, she had a psychological need that college could not meet. In a most curious fashion, Carey Thomas felt empty. Her mind was a void to be filled, and Cornell had not filled it.

Perhaps this is why she did not consider following the path of her Cornell mentors. Despite the influence of Boyesen, Corson, and Shackford, it never occurred to her to teach belles lettres and write. As she thought about the next step, graduate study, she set her sights on classical philology. Preparing to obey Miss Slocum's injunction to be a scholar, she turned to the prestigious study of classical languages, a highly technical form of scholarship that aspired to become a science.

Carey Thomas had a deep anxiety centering on the question of the next step. Upon graduation, she had no clear sense of direction. College had not given her a firm sense of how she might move toward a life work. The fault was less that of Cornell than of the larger society in which it was embedded: the university offered its students high intellectual ideals; the society outside resisted the ambitions and seriousness of women college graduates.

IV

As CAREY THOMAS faced an unknown future, she had an extraordinary mother who moved beyond her own life history to sympathize with her daughter's ambitions and fight for their realization. Mary Thomas' own life was full. She was a "Public Friend," expressing her Quaker faith through preaching and reform outside of home and Meeting. She was fired by religious enthusiasm, taxed by work for reform, and burdened by service as daughter, wife, and mother. Yet she focused on Carey and counterpoised her struggles with loving guidance and information. Mary and James were also unusually well placed within a Quaker milieu that was developing new institutions for higher education.[42]

A letter to Carey in November 1875, from both Mary and James, conveys the blending of their public and private worlds and their guidance of their daughter. Mary wrote that she was sitting in her messy parlor as her daughters did their lessons, when she heard noise in the hall. "I had just time to hustle everything under the table and rise serene to meet Reverdy Johnson and Gilman." Reverdy Johnson, Jr., was a leading trustee of Johns Hopkins University and chairman of the executive committee; Daniel Coit Gilman, the initiating president. As Mary entertained them, conversation turned to Carey. Gilman told her that he had taken "great pleasure" in informing a professor of Greek at Oxford about Carey and the other women studying Greek in Baltimore. They then talked about the new university, Johns Hopkins, that Mary was assured was to be "pushed forward with energy." James continued the letter, wishing Carey to learn in detail about the plans that, as a trustee, he was helping to shape.[43]

Johns Hopkins University mattered not only because James was on its founding board and a confidant of President Gilman, but also because of the possibility that it might educate the family's daughters. Mary reported that she had anticipated that Gilman would not mention women in his inaugural address, but that he had stated, "without making any definite declaration for the University," that he looked on Girton College of Cambridge University "with the greatest interest, and confidently expected to see a Girton in Baltimore." In the spring of 1876, Mary suggested to Carey that she and Ida Bruce might apply for a fellowship at Johns Hopkins: "They have 10 fellowships and 35 applications but no women!"[44]

In Carey Thomas' second year at Cornell, the Johns Hopkins board and the president debated the university's policy regarding the entrance of women. Bessie was living at home, hoping to be able to attend. Mary reported to Carey in October 1876 that Bessie King visited President Gilman to apply, "but that one of the trustees objects so decidedly to coeducation that they will have to discuss the whole matter." Mary disclosed that relatives on the board—James, Francis T. King, and Galloway Cheston, James' uncle,—supported "giving women the benefit of the *University* advantages" but not admitting them to the college. Although Mary was uncertain of the outcome of the board discussion, she feared that Gilman would not support women as strongly as she desired.[45]

By late November, Mary had much more to report. Her letter is significant not only because it conveyed her and her immediate family's involvement, but also because of the inside story that it told. "They had the woman question up at the Johns Hopkins University board the other day and had a most interesting discussion." The board was divided, although the weight of opinion was "on the woman side." Reverdy Johnson, Jr., and Charles J. M. Gwinn were "totally unwilling to let women in, in any way or shape." Again, James Thomas, Francis King, and Galloway Cheston supported the admission of women. Gilman asked the board to "leave the matter to his discretion . . . to make such arrangements for special cases as would seem best." Johnson, speaking privately to James after the meeting, said that "he expected Bessie King would be up there the next morning asking admittance, but Father said Bessie had made other arrangements for the present and the question might not be put to the practical test for some time." Mary cautioned that Carey must keep all of what she had written confidential, and James penned a postscript to reinforce the warning. What neither Mary nor James stated, but both knew, was that Carey Thomas' future was at stake. A decision about the admission of women to graduate work would set the terms under which she might pursue her second degree.[46]

Another new educational venture that involved James Thomas and his kin held even greater potential import for Carey Thomas. In April of her second year at Cornell, Carey learned from her mother that along with a visit to John at Haverford College, outside Philadelphia, "Father and cousin Francis and

Uncle Jim met Dr. Taylor there to prospect for the girls' college." Joseph Wright Taylor, a wealthy bachelor from Burlington, New Jersey, and a member of the Haverford College board of trustees, was thinking of establishing a Quaker college for women. He found little interest among the Wilburite Friends in Philadelphia, but he successfully drew in Gurneyite Haverford Trustees James Carey Thomas, Francis T. King, and James Whitall.[47]

Mary's attention to Taylor's college was particularly keen because she knew that Carey was in some uncertainty about her life's work. During the Cornell years, neither mother nor daughter mentioned marriage or potential prospects. Clear to both of them was Carey Thomas' dream of a future career that in both their eyes required the single state. The specific form her work would take, however, remained problematic. In November of Carey Thomas' senior year, Mary lovingly wrote that she trusted "our Father will find a place of happiness and usefulness in the world and fit thee to fill it." Carey Thomas was being encouraged by Miss Slocum to prepare herself for a professorship, but Mary thought it a dead end. Mary wrote in March 1877, "Miss Slocum's idea of a woman's holding a chair in a regular university is chimerical, unless the race of wise men dies out."[48]

Thus a women's college held a special promise. Mary continued, "There is to be someday a grand Quaker Female College, founded by Dr. Taylor near Haverford, I guess. A chair in that would be fine thing. It is a secret as yet, I believe, so do not speak of it." Taylor's endeavor, opening as Bryn Mawr College in 1885, began and remained very much a family matter.[49]

CHAPTER 5

If Everything Were Given Up and for Nothing

IN BALTIMORE Carey Thomas sought to continue formal education and enter the graduate program of Johns Hopkins University. On September 22, 1877, she applied. President Daniel Coit Gilman was courteous and promised that he would bring her application before the trustees within the month. She wrote in her journal the following day that she was in a state of "great anxiety to know whether all these advantages are to be shut forever, or even for a time" to women. In her favor, her father was an influential trustee and a confidant of President Gilman. Yet key trustees opposed coeducation. The board devised a compromise: Carey Thomas was admitted as a candidate for the second degree, "to have the direction of studies by the University Professors, and the final examination for degrees without class attendance in the University." In other words, she might consult with professors but she was barred from graduate seminars. Professor Basil I. Gildersleeve, Johns Hopkins' distinguished classicist, agreed to accept her as a student.[1]

As she anticipated the work ahead, she was enthusiastic. She wrote to Anna Shipley in late October 1877 that she was about to embark upon the study of philology. Quickly she accepted Gildersleeve's judgments about former scholarship. "Philology," she explained, "means something very different from inspiration, not that I undervalue it. Indeed I am trembling on the brink of plunging into it." The work ahead would be difficult. Gildersleeve had made it clear that he intended a degree from Johns Hopkins to be as valuable as that from a German university. He had assigned several books, one of them in German, a language she did not know, and gave her until Christmas to learn enough German to read it. Then he would begin working with her. She exclaimed, "The die is cast. If I enter upon this, I give up medicine forever and become—a scholar." She began reading the *Odyssey* in Greek with Bessie King, renewing their friendship. In early October she wrote in her journal that reading the Greek classic was like being "in the Holy of Holies."[2]

By November, however, her enthusiasm was gone. She set and kept a serious work schedule. She studied six days a week from nine A.M. to three P.M. On three mornings she worked with Bessie, reading Greek classics; on alternate mornings she studied German and Greek. Two afternoons a week she heard Gildersleeve lecture at the university. Her labors gave her no pleasure or satisfaction. She wrote in her journal that she was deeply discouraged, especially by her imperfect knowledge of Greek. The detail seemed mindless. "I cannot bend my mind to it and yet, I *must*."[3] This mood did not leave her. As the academic year progressed, she became more and more disheartened.

Carey found it difficult to live at home after two years at Cornell. The casual informality of the Thomas household grated, a daily reminder of the difference between her aspirations and reality. In December she wrote in her journal, "Our household is not constructed right. I do not think there is ceremony enough observed." She found many details neglected, the food not cooked properly, and the younger children misbehaving at meals. Her seven brothers and sisters made the gracious living she desired an impossibility: "if people realized that to have more children than they can afford to train and support properly was a greater crime than anything else I am sure it would be better."[4]

The months that followed were extraordinarily difficult ones. Barred from seminars, Carey Thomas studied on her own, attended formal lectures, and had occasional conferences with Gildersleeve. She became increasingly depressed and bewildered. She struggled to take up the faith of her parents and to find some reconciliation between Christianity and reason. Instead, her religious uncertainty deepened, throwing her into a state of crisis. Because she lived in her mother's household, religious difference became religious conflict, setting daughter and mother at odds.

Carey Thomas endured. But she almost did not. She almost sank. What made her different? Why did she, unlike the bulk of talented, ambitious women of her generation, emerge intact at the end of these years of trial? In the answer must be her capacity for friendship. In Baltimore she turned to others and created the female friendships that sustained her for the rest of her life.

During Carey's Cornell years, Bessie King had expanded her world to include three women outside the circle of Friends: Mary Garrett and Mamie Gwinn, both daughters of Johns Hopkins trustees, and Julia Rogers, Mary's closest friend. Once Carey was in their midst they constituted themselves the "Friday Evening." Every second Friday, the five women, joined at times by Carrie Ladd, now teaching in Baltimore, met in one of their homes to talk about their jointly conceived novel to which each contributed chapters.

For the group photograph of the five, the photographer placed Mamie, dressed all in white, in the chair at the center and arranged Carey, Julia,

Bessie, and Mary around her, leaning toward her to make a composition. Carey sits somewhat as she had at Cornell, with her shoulder out and her arm on a lap. Dressed as she is in dark clothes, the head appears large, the body sturdy but neither slim nor fat. Again her face is straight front, her eyes direct. It is an uncompromising look at the camera by a person determined to be taken seriously. Another image from the same period, with her face in partial profile, shows Carey to be quite handsome. With her dark eyes opened wide, the line of her jaw at an angle, and her hair upswept in a crown of shining braids, one can appreciate the perfect proportions of her features, almost see the intensity of the eyes. As Mary's daughter, Carey Thomas associated beauty with the delicate countenance of her mother. She carried the sturdy, handsome face of the Thomas side, and with it the Thomas magnetism.

Bessie and Carrie had been among her most intimate friends, two of the five romantic friendships of her young life. In the Friday Evening circle Carey found the two sustaining friends of her adulthood, Mamie Gwinn and Mary Garrett. But Carey was no longer fourteen nor away from home. As an adult, she learned that intimacy took longer, built more gradually, and required the sustenance of trust.

The Friday Evening gave Carey a context in which to think out some of the dilemmas of choice. The joint novel was largely an occasion for these talented women, in their early twenties and living with their families, to meet and talk seriously about life, religion, vocation, and, not incidentally, marriage. Carey's contribution to the collective work provides an entry point into their thinking, or at least into Carey's thinking, for her collaborators' chapters are largely scenes and interludes, while hers tell the primary story.

At the time she began her venture into fiction, Carey had found new intellectual passions. She wrote in her journal, "My interest is now in the first part of the present century, Godwin and Shelley, etc." Mamie Gwinn had introduced her to William Godwin, and Carey was moved by his *Enquiry Concerning Political Justice*. After reading it, Carey wondered how she could have failed to see the inequality and suffering all around her. The primary impact of Godwin, a British political philosopher of the late eighteenth century, however, was religious rather than political. What Carey found in his work was that his effort to establish a secular basis of ethics in the greatest good to the greatest number offered her an alternative to Christianity's grounding of moral life in the Gospels. Carey read his *Memoir of Mary Wollstonecraft* and *Caleb Williams*. She was also reading *Frankenstein* and *The Last Man*, by Mary Shelley, the daughter of Godwin and Mary Wollstonecraft and the wife of Percy Bysshe Shelley. These works raised questions about sexuality, morality, and women's rights. Both Godwin and Wollstonecraft challenged the institution of marriage. Mary Shelley was conceived out of wedlock, although her parents did marry. Wollstonecraft was the writer of *A Vindication of the Rights of Woman*, a searing critique of the life and miseducation of conventional women that Carey read a few months later.[5]

Carey wrote two chapters, one immediately following Mamie's stage-setting opening and the other at the close, which give two separate stories of male love. Both play on the theme of idealism versus carnality. The first is a fictionalized rendering of the words and life of William Godwin and Mary Wollstonecraft, renamed Gratian Warren and Mary Allston. Mary's great love for Gratian, a philosopher espousing revolutionary ideas, leads her to follow him and live with him and his son without the sanctification of marriage. On his deathbed Gratian confesses that he has wronged her. Mary narrates that he believed that "when love and sympathy is as perfect as ours the outer tie of marriage is only a symbol. . . . Such love as ours can never change." Although he has shared his life and home with her in complete chastity, his death would leave her alone. People would not understand their purity. Moreover, he has violated the terms of their cohabitation, not in deed but in thought. Immediately before he dies, Gratian declares that their friendship has been more than friendship: " 'I love you,' he added, holding me close to him and pressing his lips to mine in long, lingering kisses, as he had never done before."[6]

Carey's second story centers around Gratian Warren's son Percy, suggested by the poet Percy Bysshe Shelley. The story is told by a messenger who heard Mary Allston's tale and who has long loved her. He goes in search of Percy, who is pursuing pleasures of the flesh under the tutelage of Marron de Motrée, a woman of the world. Carey reveals her vision of female danger as, in the narrator's voice, she describes the courtesan: "Marron bent toward me with that exquisite studied grace, which from the days of Aspasia to the present has made men as wax in the hands of such as she. Pure and noble girls and wives and mothers scorn to bend themselves to all the tastes and senses of a man." Marron took the narrator to see Percy at a revealing moment: "Percy drew the girl to him and we both caught the glance with which he looked at her. There was deep love and reality of passion in his eyes." Marron suggests, however, that Percy is not really in love and describes him as a "genius" with "a clear directness of vision." Such a man, "withheld by no tradition," was "sensitive to the least influence, passionate, sensuous. Pleasure is now his only rule."

The death of his stepmother brings Percy to Mary's grave. After reading his father's papers, he is transformed. Revealed to him was "a vision of the possibilities of man, the harmonious march of reason. Superstition, luxury, love of women were veriest chaff beside it." Percy now dedicates himself to his father's work and goes alone. The narrator learns at the end that he has become a poet: "The Delphic fire has touched his lips."[7]

Both stories suggest that Carey was deep into fantasies of heterosexual love and struggling to reconcile its possibility with idealistic aspiration. Through the conventions of the romance she indulges in passionate embrace and then draws back. Both the Godwin figure, the reformer, and the Shelley figure, the poet, sublimate their passion. Capable of love, they choose to rise above carnality to dedicate themselves to the world. What is odd in her stories is that, in imagining her characters as male, their dilemmas do not fit their situation: men can both love and work.

Conversations of the Friday Evening closely paralleled the text. In early February, the group met to discuss Mamie's chapter, which raised for them the question of marriage. Carey reported in her journal that Mamie "believes in free love, according to Godwin's view," but she rejected children. Mamie argued that "if a man cared enough for her to wish to be her intimate friend, she would consider him a beast if he did not agree." Mamie's provocative comment set them off and they discussed the matter until eleven in the evening. "We all concluded there is something wrong about the present relations of marriage and yet none of us accepted Miss Gwinn's views." Carey made it clear that she did not think that it was the wedding proper that was at issue, but rather the moral results that might follow. "It *does* seem to me that free love will (and platonic friendship I think we may leave out of the question because I am afraid it is not possible with men) degrade matters and above all women."[8]

About ten days later Carey continued the discussion with Mary Garrett. They had been to the theater, the first time for Carey, signaling a decisive break with Quaker tradition. Carey was in raptures and talked with Mary until three in the morning about life and love: "There seems no solution of the question of marriage, for it is difficult to conceive [of] a woman who really feels her separate life work to give it all up when she marries a man, and yet I think—a fact which I used to ignore—that it is and must be a giving up." The question was a particularly live one for Bessie because she was being courted. Carey felt herself deeply torn. "Oh, it is a real question, I think. Julia and Mary and Bessie and I all feel it. Will the solution be that we will be four old maids? If a woman has children, I do not see but what she will have to, at least for some time, give up her work." The problem for Carey was deepened by the weakening of her sense of future mission. As she thought about "doing" and "life work" she pondered, "Yet, after all, what is it to be?" She felt that she could do something, but so did every young person. "Think, if everything were given up and for *nothing*."[9]

II

CAREY did not admit it in her journal in February, but "everything" had come into her life. She was in love with a man, a brilliant, attractive, sympathetic man of her background and social standing: Francis Gummere.

On March 24, 1878, late at night, Carey Thomas wrote in her journal.

The entry began with comments, becoming repetitive, on the conflicts between the study required for a graduate degree and the pleasures of literature. She noted delight with a poem by Dante Gabriel Rossetti. Her writing suddenly became irregular, the characters of different shape. "Now I want to write down something that has been quivering on my pen every time I take it to write in my journal." To anyone who might read her journal, she pleaded, "I hope if anybody takes up this book they will have the honor not to read it." What she had to say went against the construction of her life: "Last summer after coming from Anna's, that something came, at.least the suspicion of it against which I have always prayed."

She had almost divulged the secret in November. As she set down her deep discouragement in her new work at Johns Hopkins, she had written this at the end of the entry: "Then, too, unexpectedly I have had a great trial this Fall, and all my most dear and firmly held beliefs seem to prove null and void."[10]

A few weeks before, she had written about Frank Gummere in her journal for the first time. The October 1877 entry was a guarded one, designed to shield a private matter from prying eyes; but even as she tried to mask her feelings, she expressed a great deal. The entry is an intriguing combination of admiration for Frank Gummere and jealousy of his opportunities as a man. She had seen him at Anna's, and his talk of Harvard had filled her "with envy." She wondered if he would be successful. "He is full of enthusiasm for all my favorite things, poetry, literature. My pet books are his favorites, and altogether we are very congenial on literary and theological subjects." He was thinking of studying in Germany. She wished she "were a man for that; because *Germany* is shut to ladies along with the Johns Hopkins University and a few other of the very most glorious things in the world." She concluded in words she voiced throughout her life, "yet I would not be a man."[11]

Now in March 1878 she set down the history of her friendship with Francis Gummere. They had first met in Atlantic City. Carey could not remember the date, but an August 3, 1873, letter to Anna Shipley fixes it exactly in the summer between Carey's two years at the Howland School. At age seventeen, Frank had graduated from Haverford College, where his father was president. He had worked in an iron foundry and was then reading law in Philadelphia. On the day they met they sailed together and then talked about their hopes: he, for Harvard; she, for college. They talked about study and work and men and women. Frank told her that Tennyson had expressed it best. Carey got her book of Tennyson and he read the part, "not like in like but like in difference." She saw him again at a party at Anna's. They talked of books, and he walked her back to her aunt's house in Philadelphia. He and his friend Richard Cadbury sent a poem to Carey and others at Howland. On a late-afternoon visit with a friend, she had declined a dinner that included Frank, because she had not wanted to be the guest too many. This had been mistakenly relayed to Frank as her desire to avoid him. He became upset because, as Carey was later told, "he had talked about his devotion to me, that, of course, he had had no right and I was angry with reason. He would never see me again." He did not call on her.[12]

She saw him next in the summer of 1875, when she went to Haverford College to attend a lecture by her uncle Allen Thomas. Frank had just finished a year of study at Harvard, where he had taken a second B.A. Their first encounter was on the train. "We were sitting talking when Mr. Gummere came though the car and passed us with a fierce bow. I thought of all his anger and the wretched misunderstanding and my heart stood still with excitement." As the party disembarked, Frank asked Anna to walk with him under his umbrella, but she refused and walked with Carey. During and after the talk, "Mr. Gummere sat over to the right by himself, 'glaring' at us as Anna kept whispering to me." Later, he came nearer "and for a little while we talked each to someone else, with our backs to one another. Then he turned and held out his hand. 'Miss Thomas, I want to congratulate you on your examination and admission at Cornell.' " He asked to walk to the station with her. "I was about to refuse but Anna whispered 'go Min' so I went. It was pouring rain, and Mr. Gummere in talking would forget the umbrella every now, and I remember the lightning flashed very much as we were going down the steps under the bridge and Mr. Gummere was telling me what to study at Cornell, and we both walked off the boardwalk."

Later that summer during a visit with Anna at Windon, the Shipley country house, Frank and Dick Cadbury arrived for a visit. The young people were very much on their own, because Anna's parents were away. They had a ride and a talk, "the nicest we have ever had." They talked about religion: "He was in great doubt and perplexity. I, of course, was, too, and, oh, we talked perfectly freely about it!" They spoke of poetry. Frank said something about Shelley's *The Cenci* that shocked her. They got home before Anna and Dick and went to get some water. "Mr. Gummere said he could not tell me what a nice ride he had had." In the evening, the four played a game and sat on the porch talking and reciting poetry in the moonlight. After Anna and Carey tried in vain to recall a Wordsworth poem, Frank recited "The Garden of Proserpine" and "Hymn to Proserpine," two Swinburne poems "which haunted me for two years until I found them last year in *Laus Veneris*." Carey recited a Browning poem "and got intolerably frightened in the midst." At such moments, as earlier when she and Margaret Hicks fell in love, the language of poetry was the language of courtship.

Much later Carey learned that her difficulty in reciting the poem had been interpreted by the young men as springing from her particular interest in Frank. When Anna and Dick wandered off, she talked again with Frank. She noted in her journal surprise that she could remember everything: "I can see the trees shaking. . . ." Frank and Carey parted, shaking hands and wishing each other well as Carey prepared to go to Cornell and Frank to teach.

During his years of teaching at the Friends' School in Providence, Frank traveled for the summer in Europe. In June 1876 Frank wrote Carey "a very splendid letter," regretting not being able to join a camping trip. Carey decided not to answer it. In July 1877, after Carey had graduated from Cornell, she was again at Windon visiting Anna when Frank and Dick came to visit. This time, however, she found herself distressed in ways she scarcely understood. Anna's parents were not at Windon, nor was the older woman who had chaperoned the last visit, and "it was horribly embarrassing." So the two young women let the men stay only one night. Anna and Dick formed a couple and left Carey alone with Frank. "Then, for the first time, I felt embarrassed. It was such a ridiculously novel-like position and for the first time, I think, I felt conscious." Carey felt that she should not have allowed Anna to let the young men visit. "Father had objected to my coming, and that and the thought of the way Mr. Gummere had looked upon me before made me resolve to be as cold and careful as possible and show him that I did not care about him, which indeed was true."

Although she had been aware of male attention before, this was different. The two were alone, their interest in each other suggested by that of their absent friends who formed a "couple." With her knowledge of male-female love from fiction, Carey could only see it from the perspective of the romantic novel. Frank's look frightened her. Bewildered, she resorted to the behavior she had practiced with men at Cornell: coldness.

Carey's anxiety grew worse in the evening. The four talked amusingly about poetry, but when Anna and Dick left Carey and Frank alone, "I felt again the position I had placed myself in, for it was evident Dick and Anna cared most to be together and there were Mr. Gummere and I left." Carey assumed her cold manner, "but Mr. Gummere (he sat in a great big rocking chair and moved it nearer and nearer as he talked) was so splendid that every now and then I would forget; but I think probably he was disappointed a little." At ten the two went in the house and made lemonade, and Carey said she would retire. "It was dreadful to me to stay there. Mr. Gummere frightened me a little, though I don't know why, but I felt as if it would be a relief to get away."

The next day, the four had a picnic. When she was again alone with Frank, the two looked at a book of Tennyson poems. "It was embarrassing because Anna would leave us together, and I was not like myself, I felt, all the time." In the afternoon, when Dick urged Frank to swim, Frank tried to have time alone with Carey, by reminding her of a letter he wanted to show her, "but, of course, I could not help him out and would not." The two young men went off to swim. When Anna and Dick again left the two at tea, Carey's awkwardness returned. Afterwards they looked at Carey's Cornell photographs and spoke of H. H. Boyesen, the Cornell professor of English, to whom Frank had heard she was engaged. "I gave him a full description, and yet all the while I was conscious that I wanted to make up with Mr. Gummere, though there was nothing to make up." Mr. Gummere barely shook hands when they parted.

Faced with a young man whom she admired, who was clearly interested in her as a woman, Carey became frightened and confused. A week later Carey accidentally ran into both men at a Philadelphia library. Carey felt herself blush and "knew that I felt a little differently toward him." The blush embarrassed her enough to deny Dick Cadbury's report of it to Anna: "It is a base libel . . . I *never* blush."[13] In her journal Carey recalled that she had not dared to say that she regretted missing Frank at Atlantic City. "I tried to get courage to tell him I received his letter and thank him for it but I could not bring myself to mention it." Frank and Dick left, but not before she had completed her "indifferent role." Carey told Dick that she remembered the sail on which she met him but intentionally denied that Frank also had been there.

Some kind of moment had passed. Just as Carey recognized her attraction for Frank, her coldness had begun to erode his hope. He did not write. In the months that followed, Carey regretted her frosty manner and her flippant remark. She thought about Frank constantly—while she was studying, in the "limitless time to think between the turning over the leaves of a Greek dictionary," and especially when she went to bed at night. "My theories have given way, positively. I cannot help thinking about him." She deeply regretted her coldness and feared its consequences: "I think most probably things were so unfortunate last summer, and I certainly must have shown him my coldness and constraint, that he will think I have changed and get engaged to some other girl (the way with men!)."

And yet she was profoundly ambivalent. "I do not think I would marry him anyhow," which was the reason that she had been cool to him the previous summer. She would have "to give up . . . my dearest work that has lain next my heart from my childhood." And yet her work was so "indefinite." At least she could try, "I can at least give up everything for it." Having said this, she could express how utterly she admired Frank. "He is literary and enthusiastic, a passionate worshiper of poetry and a writer of it. He is interested [in] the same things as I am. He is struggling with the same old problems of life and religion, he is brilliant and so cultivated. . . . He has a little of the divine fire, I think, and hence is utterly removed from all other people I know."

At two in the morning Carey began to close the entry. Writing her thoughts had reawakened feelings in her that she had been struggling to suppress since she first faced them in the autumn. Recalling that difficult time, she wrote, "It was an awful trial. I cried and cried myself to sleep often because I could not stop thinking about him." It was the first time she had ever experienced anything so powerful. "You see," she explained to her journal, "I never came to anything before I could not, partially at least, manage." Moreover, her feeling for Frank flew in the face of her own avowed principles: "Then, it is so perfectly absurd to come to *me* who have always declared against it." She stated a philosophical hope that Frank would become engaged to another, only immediately to express her "intolerable desire" to know if she would see him in the summer. She concluded with this lament: "I am utterly at a loss. I have prayed about it with all the little faith I have and struggled against my foolishness (and yet it is not foolishness and I like it and that again is the worst of it) but it is no use and now I am going to wait and see."[14]

Carey's journal entry said much, but it did not say all. Several key elements are missing. It did not tell that Frank Gummere was receiving special benefactions from the important Friends who were planning a Quaker women's college. In the fall of 1877 Gummere was teaching in Providence, in the hope of preparing himself for a position at Haverford College. Feeling that he needed more training than a single postgraduate year at Harvard, he wrote to Joseph Wright Taylor, who in the small, closely knit world of Friends would have known Gummere as the son of the late president of Haverford. Taylor urged him to remain for the time being in Providence and suggested that he and others had something important in mind for Gummere in the future. A. K. Smiley, designated as a future trustee of Taylor's college, then paid for Gummere to go abroad for eight months' study in Germany. Carey had written enviously of Frank's trip in her October journal entry. In March, as she reconstructed the history of her friendship with Frank Gummere, jealousy of his opportunities, in contrast to the restrictions upon her, may have been too painful to express.

Nor did the journal do more than hint at the relation of Frank Gummere to one of the most important influences in her life, Swinburne's poems. When she met Frank and Richard Cadbury in the summer of 1873, both fancied themselves aesthetes, and they read, memorized, and imitated the poetry of Shelley and Swinburne. In 1875 Frank recited poems that "haunted" her for two years. Both were Swinburne's presentation of the Proserpine myth. In "Hymn to Proserpine," a Roman worshipper of the goddess of the Underworld bewails her displacement by the mother of Christ. The cult of the Galilean has conquered Rome, bringing its gray shadows, its pale Virgin, and its martyred saints to replace the intense colors and sensuous delights surrounding the old Roman gods. As he awaits death, the Roman refuses to accept the new faith: "I kneel not, neither adore you, but standing, look to the end." "The Garden of Proserpine" celebrates death, a death that is an end, a "sleep eternal / In an eternal night." It contains some of Swinburne's most quoted lines, asserting a pre-Christian Roman vision:

From too much love of living,
From hope and fear set free,
We thank with brief thanksgiving
Whatever gods may be
That no life lives for ever;
That dead men rise up never;
That even the weariest river
Winds somewhere safe to sea.[15]

These two poems were published in 1866 in England in Swinburne's *Poems and Ballads*. Carey found them in *Laus Veneris*, an American edition of *Poems and Ballads* that highlighted the poem of that title. She purchased it and a book of his later poems on December 23, 1879.[16] Both in England and in the United States, *Poems and Ballads* created a scandal. Unlike Shelley, Swinburne did not write treatises in verse. He presented his poems not as testaments to his own beliefs, but as experiments with the verse forms and mentalities of other ages. However, the poems' celebration of paganism—an outrage to Christianity—and their intense, unconventional eroticism shocked many readers.

In poetry and in life, Swinburne crossed boundaries and deliberately sought the perverse. Many of the best-known poems in the volume—"Anactoria," "Faustine," "Laus Veneris," "Dolores"—link love and pain; and the pleasure of pain and the pain of pleasure were to be Swinburne's most enduring theme. In "Anactoria" Swinburne recasts a poem of Sappho, the Greek poet of the seventh century B.C. In the poem Sappho rages against her beloved female disciple who has turned to another. In Swinburne's hands, anguish is mixed with lust, and in over three hundred lines the Greek poet reaps her imagined vengeance:

That I could drink thy veins as wine, and eat
Thy breasts like honey!

    *   *   *

         . . . oh that I
Durst crush thee out of life with love, and die,—
Die of thy pain and my delight, and be
Mixed with thy blood and molten into thee![17]

In "Anactoria" and other poems Swinburne portrays a world of sexual ambiguity and same-sex love. The poem "Hermaphroditus" was suggested by the statue in the Louvre of the Greek mythological figure, the son of Hermes and Aphrodite, who became united in one body with a nymph, one of the mythological female nature spirits. Swinburne plays with the way that male and female are blended in the god, evoking longings that cannot be satisfied:

> *Love stands upon thy left hand and thy right,*
> *Yet by no sunset and by no moonrise*
> *Shall make thee man and ease a woman's sighs,*
> *Or make thee woman for a man's delight.*
> *To what strange end hath some strange god made fair*
> *The double blossom of two fruitless flowers?*[18]

"Sapphics" is based on the legend of Sappho and her school of women disciples devoted to the worship of Aphrodite. Swinburne tells of Aphrodite's reluctant flight from the island of Lesbos, her "hair unbound" and her "feet unsandalled." Sappho, the tenth Muse, sang a song for her. Sappho did not see Aphrodite, shaken and weeping, as she left, but

> *Saw the Lesbians kissing across their smitten*
> *Lutes with lips more sweet than the sound of lute-strings,*
> *Mouth to mouth and hand upon hand, her chosen,*
> *Fairer than all men*

Above them soared her song:

> *Newly fledged, her visible song, a marvel,*
> *Made of perfect sound and exceeding passion,*
> *Sweetly shapen, terrible, full of thunders,*
> *Clothed with the wind's wings.*

"Such a song was that song" that the other Muses and gods, "All reluctant, all with a fresh repulsion," fled from her and Lesbos, leaving the land "barren / Full of fruitless women and music only," singing "Songs that break the heart of the earth with pity."[19]

Poems and Ballads opened to Carey Thomas a poetic world of vivid images, an often pagan world in which Swinburne explored and exploded conventional boundaries between desire and pain, men and women. To one familiar with Greek mythology and medieval lore, nothing in the poems is arcane or obscure. To Carey Thomas, searching for moorings and for a way of understanding her emotions, Swinburne's poetry could offer confirmation both of her religious doubt and of her passionate feelings toward women and men.

Finally, Carey's avowal of Frank Gummere's presence in her life and imagination was written prior to an evening that she spent with Mary Garrett and Julia Rogers, reading about sexual relations between men and women.

On April 1, Mary and Julia came to tea. The three young women retired to Carey's room with *What Women Should Know*, by Eliza B. Duffey, and about fifteen of her father's medical books.[20] They read from eight until eleven-thirty in the evening. She explained in her journal that they had done this because they were "old enough to know all about the different forces of life." To work for good, Carey felt she "must not be blindfolded," and "if passion and sensuality are real factors," she needed to understand them. She believed that "to the pure all things are pure, and, after all, in purely natural phenomena, what can be degrading."

She was unprepared for the shock of what she learned: "the revelations of vice and hateful, disgusting things that we had not the faintest conception ever existed were too much." She went to bed ill. "I had eaten of the fruit of the tree of the knowledge of good and evil, and it seemed as if there was no such thing as ever believing in purity and holiness again, or ever getting my own mind pure again." In the next few days she was unable to get what she had read out of her mind. Everything seemed governed by "this own hateful, beastly impulse of men." For a few days she felt in despair. "Thoughts of the things I had read kept coming up in spite of the perfect abhorrence with which I regarded them."[21]

Duffey's book is one of many advice books of the period that supported conjugal relations in marriage within the context of the love between husband and wife.[22] Doctor Thomas' medical books may have clarified that sexual intercourse was not governed by the desire for children and was more frequent in marriage than Carey had imagined. Because of their focus on pathology, the books may have contained extended discussions of venereal disease. In addition, they may have considered methods of birth control and a range of sexual practices. To read books normally reserved for doctors or for women on the verge of marriage was an unusual step. Particularly if she read of venereal disease and its causes and symptoms, it is not surprising that Carey Thomas initially found herself revulsed.

More important than her first reaction is how Carey began to incorporate her new knowledge and relate it to herself. Essentially she cast it out. Sex belonged to men. Their nature was carnal. In contrast, women had the capacity to love. Although married women might begin to experience sexual feeling of a subdued nature through sexual relations, women who kept themselves from men were protected from sexuality. Carey had enjoyed several smashes and after "dancing and Swinburne" she had declared herself passionately in love with Margaret Hicks, but she did not see this as having any relation to sexuality.

This is clarified by a journal entry written a month before she confessed to her journal her feeling about Frank Gummere and prior to her reading of her father's medical books. Here Carey departed from her usual form and wrote an essay in her journal on friendship. Her formulation gives important clues about her psyche. It clarifies the difference between the mental universe of the nineteenth century and that of the late twentieth. Carey began by asserting transcendentalism's tradition of radical individualism: each person alone, mired in daily affairs, attempts to confront the universe, only to lapse back into essential loneliness. From this trap, "one loop hole" allows the self to escape into an upper region: "a true, intimate, devoted friendship between man and man, woman and woman. We are carried out of self and see through another's eyes."

Friendship between women is purer than that between a man and a woman. Heterosexual love contains "an element of selfishness, of self-gratification." But women know that they have each other only briefly and without possession. At this point Carey reviewed her great loves, for Libbie Conkey, Carrie Ladd, and Margaret Hicks. She had loved each one intensely, but now only a calm liking prevailed. For the first time since she went to Howland, she was without such a friend. She could not pour out her thoughts to another with "complete sympathy of love . . . and clasped hands and loving eyes and close kisses and admiration."

In the late twentieth century to speak in such a manner suggests erotic feelings, sex. Beginning with such behavior—"clasped hands and loving eyes and close kisses and admiration"—desired or real, current writers follow a sexual trajectory whose potential end is orgasm. But for a nineteenth-century woman, such behavior led up another spiral: it followed an intellectual tradition, traceable since Aristotle, of ideal friendship. Carey continued: women's caring for each other meant "bowing before another's spirit in many things . . . and self-sacrifice, tenderly drawing the thought up to yours where you feel yours to be highest." Such a friendship meant "making thought and your soul life a real thing," it made a person "feel noble and generous, living in another, not self-centered." Through ideal friendship one could approach truth.[23]

To suggest that Carey was denying sexual feelings would be a misreading, through eyes blinded by a later era's understanding of sex. Carey's culture did not label women's feelings for each other, however passionate, as sexual. Ignoring all that appears to the present as erotic, white middle- and upper-class women believed they could "smash" or be "in love" with each other on the high plane of ideal friendship. That they admired each other's bodies, waltzed, kissed and caressed each other, and suffered intense feelings of jealousy and anguish was disassociated in their minds from sexual desire.

But was her feeling for Frank not sexual? Here Carey was more clearly threatened. Yet the culture of her age did not describe women's feeling for men in its romantic, preconsummated stage as sexual. It was admiration and affection, not desire. This was clear in Carey's effort, as she closed her April meditation on sexual knowledge, to deal with her feeling about Frank. In coping with what she had learned from medical texts, Carey took the high road of female purity in opposition to male lust. "I am sure it is hard, inexpressibly hard, but, I am sure, it is every woman's duty to face things, and in women's knowing all about it and being pure and noble themselves and restraining, as they only can . . . lies the only safety of the future salvation." She wrested one compensation. Heretofore she had felt herself hampered by social forces in her intellectual competition with men. Now she felt she had an advantage: "A woman by the mere fact of her womanhood seems higher morally and physically than a man, and therefore the time he has to spend in struggling against his lower nature she has to advance in." But given male lust, what counterforce was there? The pleasure-pain principle derived from William Godwin on which she had relied no longer seemed enough "to keep people in a morally lofty life." It was inadequate because it made "physical injury . . . the only measure of purity and up to that point all will be right." With no religion to turn to, she longed for "one great unity . . . the only hope we have against utter sense worship."

Her final statement gives a last clue to the meaning of this episode. "It had always seemed to me possible, if a man and his wife chose, . . . to live as friends in a beautiful companionship and pure and lofty things and for *no other element* to enter; but I believe, I am afraid I am convinced, that this is not possible." Carey had been pondering a marriage without sexual intercourse for some time, as her imagined story of Mary Allston and Gratian Warren suggested. On another occasion she had written that "platonic friendship . . . is not possible with men." Her father's books may have confirmed that a chaste marriage was undesirable or impossible. Whatever fantasy she had had that she might live with Frank Gummere without physical union was now dispelled. Were they to marry, she and Frank could not live on the plane of ideal friendship. [24]

Frank Gummere threatened Carey's construction of her self, the meaning of her past, and the vision of her future. From her early teens she had foresworn marriage. She would do great deeds. A scientist, a doctor, an artist, a writer could not marry, for marriage brought dependency upon a husband. By the 1870s some methods to prevent conception were known, especially in the medical community. But women of her religious and moral training regarded birth control as unacceptable, the recourse of the prostitute. Marriage thus meant the suffering of pregnancy, the travail of childbirth, and the burden of children. She had adored her mother, but never her life of chaos and unfinished sentences. To be famous and an example to her sex she must remain a feme sole. But a feme sole was not really a woman alone. She had learned the joys of ideal friendship. From her new understanding of the male sex drive, she realized that such friendship was only possible between women.

Frank Gummere was brilliant—with the "divine fire"—and eminently eligible. He was, like Percy Warren, a poet. Did Carey imagine herself as the girl he embraced? Could she resist for her sake, more than for his? Her Aunt Hannah had warned her that passionate girls prone to smashes were the kind likely to fall in love with a man. Was that true of her? If she did allow herself to love him and to commit herself to him—"everything"—what was then the purpose and meaning of her life? But if she did not, and her ambitions proved as ashes—"*nothing*"—then where would she be: "if everything were given up and for *nothing*"? To put it simply, marriage would make it all—years of hope, study, sacrifice—for nought. Yet marriage promised personal happiness. And when scholarship seemed tedious and the outcome uncertain, marriage offered a palpable, known alternative.

III

CAREY THOMAS' dilemma cannot be separated from her two years of crisis after college. Like other ambitious women of her era, she had sustained her sense of mission through school and college. But, after college, what? Ambition, particularly ambition for a career as vague as scholarship, was difficult for a young woman to sustain in the unsupportive atmosphere of home.

Scholarship was certainly tedious. In her hope to become a "noble woman" by becoming a scholar, she had not confronted how long and narrow the road would be. In the first year home, she realized that she had chosen graduate work in Greek not by conscious choice, but by "a sort of blind instinct." Her background in Greek, however, was defective, even counting her studies at Cornell. She entered Johns Hopkins late, and, working under Gildersleeve, took on the major Greek authors. To be successful she had to study at least eight hours a day, not the literature she loved, but grammar and detail. After working so hard to get into Johns Hopkins she felt she must not fail. Yet, as the first year of study progressed, she lost the interest to succeed. Though there were "so many books . . . waiting to unfold their treasures," she "must learn to write correct, lifeless Greek."[25]

The split that was evident at Cornell between dry scholarship and vital literature took a new, bewildering form. She loved modern languages and literature. The new scholarship gaining prestige and leading to university positions was philology. She was forcing herself to master classical philology at Johns Hopkins, and it led her to experience intense alienation in her studies. As the life of scholarship began to pale, she began to dream of the possibility that she might become a creator of literature: "A mere scholar, a mere teacher—let men who take it up as a trade do that! But we do need light, we do need thought expressed in everlasting forms." Chained to her Greek texts, Carey Thomas was longing to break free to become a writer.[26]

The problem was, as she half knew, she had no talent. Recipients of her poems may have cherished them, but only because they were acts of friendship or love. The Friday Evening novel is significant for the insight it sheds on Carey Thomas' state of mind, but gives no indication of any literary talent except that of Mamie Gwinn.

Torn by tedium and frustration, Carey Thomas began to doubt her powers. She had no one to whom to turn for guidance or support. Professor Gildersleeve was a distant but cool force, critical of her work and lacking any comprehension of the difficulties under which she labored. Not unusual for graduate school. But barred from seminars, she had no other university resources: no recitations; no discussion or debate; no fellow students to validate her choices or to commiserate with her. Day after day she confided to her journal that she felt that she had not done enough or that she had wasted much of her day. She tried to summon her old gods: "Ambition! All my old dreams and plans come to my aid!" Incantations did not work. Carey Thomas continued to judge herself harshly for not studying hard enough.[27]

What she failed to understand was that her friends were drawing her into their world, a wider world of culture. She had always enjoyed literature: her parents' household had allowed that secular pleasure. Now, under the influence of Mary Garrett and Mamie Gwinn, she opened herself to the forbidden pleasures of theater and music. Her first theatrical performance stunned her by its beauty. In February 1878, despite her parents' disapproval, she went in a party of seven, including Mary, Julia, and three gentlemen, to see Helena Modjeska in Camille. "It came up and went beyond anything I had imagined. I utterly lost all idea of locality." Although she felt some qualms about the play's moral message, "the whole thing was raised by the purity of the passion, and I could see no imaginable harm in it, and, oh, it is such a mighty pleasure!" Because Quaker strictures against theater had barred her from one of life's joys, she felt she had been defrauded. A few weeks later she heard Beethoven's Seventh Symphony at a concert at the Peabody, again with Mary Garrett, and felt pleased that she could now appreciate music.[28]

As Mary Garrett introduced her to music and drama, Carey felt drawn to her. The daughter of Rachel and John Work Garrett, the head of the Baltimore and Ohio Railroad, Mary was several years older than Carey and infinitely wealthier. She divided her time between Montebello, the Garrett estate in Clifton, a suburban neighborhood in Baltimore; the city house on Monument Street at Mount Vernon Square in central Baltimore; and Deer Park, a summer retreat in Garrett County, Maryland. In the group portrait of the five friends of the Friday Evening, Mary, wearing glasses and clad in a print dress, appears larger than the others, older, almost matronly. Few images and virtually no descriptions of her survive. Late in life, Mamie recalled her as suffering from a sense of inferiority and not a social success.[29] Except for Carey, no one ever spoke of her as charming or appealing. But she was very rich.

Carey quickly came to like Mary "more and more." In March 1878, as she sat next to her at the Peabody concert, Carey felt drawn not only to the music but to Mary. "I do believe I am falling in love with her. She is so, well, just what attracts me." Riding horseback with her later in the month, she pronounced Mary "lovely. I do not know when I have admired a girl so much. Her fearlessness on horseback really gives me a sensation of real, warm admiration. I should so like to have an earnest friendship with her." In lieu of the reading she was supposed to do, Carey wrote Mary a sonnet in her honor about the birth of their friendship. It is a deeply respectful poem, almost as if it were written to a patron.[30]

In 1878 Mary was studying for the Harvard examination given in New York City. The exam did not lead to entrance to the university, but certified accomplishment. For some young women who studied privately, it emerged as an important marker of educational attainment. Mary was constrained by a powerful father who looked to her for companionship, but on his terms. She admired Carey's freedom to go to Cornell and to enter Johns Hopkins. Carey, on her part, was deeply envious of the advantages that Mary's wealth allowed. In June 1878 Mary went to Europe with her parents. Carey wrote to her, echoing Matthew Arnold, "I am sure it is the royal road to that culture of sweetness and light that we are all of us striving for." Since Mary had already experienced its advantages, she would now be ahead of her friends. In fact, as John Work Garrett's daughter, Mary had unusual opportunities. Later in the summer Carey received a letter detailing Mary's social life in England. Mary described being taken to tea by Robert Browning and Alma-Tadema, talking to Burne-Jones, picnicking with Herbert Spencer. To Carey, the letter was "like a breath of culture upon a waste of savagery."[31]

A later irregular sonnet written about Mary Garrett tells some of what she meant to Carey in 1878. The Mary Garrett of the sonnet is calm, serene, and slow of speech, but strong and imperial. Undemonstrative, her

> *Caresses come but seldom—her smile thrills*
> *All tenderest harmonies, all unexpressed.*
> *A visioned calm doth hold her will's*
> *Impervious might—her spirit is at rest.*

"Unexpressed," for a reason: while Carey gossiped with Anna that Mary was in love with Dr. Murray, a suitor, she insistently ignored that Mary was attached. She was linked in an intimate friendship with Julia Rogers, who resided and traveled with her during these years.[32]

Although she held Mary Garrett in esteem, in the summer of 1878 Carey fell in love with Mamie Gwinn. The daughter of Charles J. M. Gwinn, Maryland's attorney general, and the granddaughter of Reverdy Johnson, a United States senator and ambassador, Mamie was seventeen, four years younger than Carey. She was brilliant, elusive, and precocious; moody, restless, not easily satisfied. And she was beautiful, with a languid beauty, set off by pale skin and soft dark hair. Educated at home, she had been given the leisure to indulge her love of poetry.

Mamie lived on Mount Vernon Place, one of Baltimore's most elegant streets. Her parents' townhouse, very near that of the Garretts, was only blocks away from Carey's family house, but the two came from quite different social milieux. From serving on boards together, their fathers knew and respected each other, but to the Gwinns, the evangelical world of the Thomases was alien territory. Mamie's father was a Presbyterian, her mother an Episcopalian; the family attended worship in her mother's church. By age seventeen Mamie had become a convinced skeptic and follower of Godwin. Despite her youth and lack of formal education, Mamie was more than able to keep up with a college graduate. She took it upon herself to move Carey Thomas farther from the faith of her parents.

Carey invited Mamie to visit her in July 1878, at the summer home of her recently widowed grandmother. When Mamie wrote to confirm arrangements she asked Carey the name of her grandmother, a request that measured the social distance that separated them. Mamie's letter encouraged Carey's religious doubt, quoting Shelley by way of argument. As she anticipated their time together, Mamie wrote, "There is a great deal I want to tell you of Godwin or rather talk of when I see you." She continued, "Shelley is inspiration: Godwin strength. Every word of his is a tonic." Pleased that Carey liked Shelley's *Alastor*, she wrote, "I am glad of everything that widens the distance between you and the faith of the past."[33]

The visit was an important one. Carey noted in her diary, in lines that recalled her smash with Margaret Hicks, "It is the old story over again. We talked and read Swinburne." But Atlantic City was not Cornell, and the pressure of evangelical faith surrounded Carey. One day at sunset the two read Swinburne's "Hymn of Man," from *Songs Before Sunrise*. Written to promote Italian unification, the poems of this volume followed the Shelleyan tradition of atheism linked to political radicalism, a world made right by human action. Immediately after Mamie's visit, Carey wrote in her journal that Swinburne's poem was "a paean of triumph over the vanishing of the Christian religion. To Mamie it was elixir, to me poison: though I could not help the bewildering beauty of it carrying me away." The two talked late into each night. "I am devoted to her, as I feared I would be."[34]

Carey had been fascinated by Mamie ever since the February meeting of the Friday Evening when Mamie declared that she shared Godwin's belief in free love. Mamie initially seemed wrapped up in herself. Carey hoped Mamie might "break down the barriers and care for someone and be broad enough to comprehend another." Alternately Carey grew critical of her "impersonality, her want of reference to others, her old mocking standpoint," and feared falling in love with her. Mamie was "a terrible temptation," she wrote in her diary. "She represents all that side of my nature I am trying to suppress, the roving through literature and study, seeking out whatever the bent of my fancy leads to, and the dilettante spirit, the complete contradiction to the steady working spirit I am endeavoring to summon." At this point Carey was trying to rouse herself to work by calling to mind the energy of the Northern young women she had known at Cornell, who "never meditate or lounge but go straight ahead and work and *do* something." Mamie represented the opposite pull, the undisciplined seeker of pleasure through books, willing to pause, to meditate and lounge. But by July her love for Mamie had "made her lovely." Carey was tantalized by Mamie. "She is the cleverest—damnably clever, I used to think; now I think gloriously clever—girl I ever had anything to do with, beyond doubt. She has the keenest literary sense. She is fantastic in too many ways."[35]

Several years after Carey Thomas' death, Mamie Gwinn recalled their first meeting. Though both their fathers were among the twelve founding trustees of Johns Hopkins University, the two had not met, for Carey's "mother's policy had kept her isolated" in unfashionable Quaker schools. Mamie viewed Mary Thomas harshly, seeing her as "brusque and queer, and likely to make queer decisions," such as allowing Carey to go to Cornell. Mamie recalled that Carey "too, was brusque and queer, and in her worldly clothes ill dressed, when I first met her." Mamie had not liked her on first sight. Late in her life she could recall little about their meeting except for "the visitor's sledge-hammer voice, her comely profile as she drove away." Mamie remembered well, however, that "tradition says that I reported upon reaching home the sudden advent of a horror." Mamie remembered that Carey, in turn, told her friends about Mamie, and the four agreed to ask her to join their literary club. Mary Garrett's mother was dispatched to call upon Mrs. Gwinn to seek her permission.

When the Friday Night convened, Mamie and Carey met a second time. Mamie recalled, "I soon ceased to dislike her; she had all her life, at least in tête à tête, the art of turning crudity into a certain charm." They began to see each other almost every day. Mamie regarded herself as immensely more cultured than Carey, despite Carey's Cornell degree. What Carey offered to the others was the possibility of self-support, allowing them to "escape alike a husband's and our parents' rule." Carey also appealed to Mamie because she liked her "for just the traits my mother most disliked in me." Carey complimented her ability and assured her that she was "more beloved" than members of her family.[36]

There were moments in the early days of their relationship when Carey became deeply depressed. One day in early May 1878, she wrote "I never had such a fit of the blues in my life. Yesterday I walked with Mary Garrett, and it was insufferable, I could not say one word. Then to tea at Mamie Gwinn's, and it was worse." They went to a play that failed to rouse her. After she returned home, she "descended into the depths."[37]

Contributing to her confusion and sense of despair was her full acknowledgment of the loss of Christian faith. For years she had churned. She had awaited a rebirth that had not come. Prodded by her Howland teacher, she had come to question the reality of heaven and hell. She had read widely beyond Quaker bounds. But because she had questions and not answers, when Carey renounced the faith of her parents, she was left with an intellectual and emotional void.

Matthew Arnold was some help. Carey had read Arnold's books of criticism before and during her Cornell years, including *Culture and Anarchy*, perhaps his best-remembered work. In Arnold she found an appreciation of ancient Greek civilization that fortified her own. In May 1878 she read *Literature and Dogma* for the third time. In her state of religious uncertainty, Arnold's arguments now had new cogency. She wrote in her journal that his book expressed what she had been coming to understand in the last five years. The Hebrews emphasized the "power outside of man that makes for Righteousness." As she set out her reasoned understanding of Christianity, she paraphrased Arnold. She no longer accepted the divinity of Christ. Christianity was based on false premises. Jesus was a great man with "more thirst for righteousness, more attainment of it than any other man." But he was human. "He was misunderstood. His disciples made him, forced him to be a god." Knowledge of his deification by his followers caused him to want to die. It was the task of culture to separate his teachings from the words of his disciples. "Then for the first time the true Christ-man is ours. There it is, my creed."

It was, as Carey knew, a joyless creed. In contrast to the ecstatic faith of her mother, Arnold's words brought only "the calmness of despair." It was for her, however, the only honest emotion. She had tried hard to believe in traditional faith, but could not. She misquoted Arthur Hugh Clough's lines,

We are most hopeless who had once most hope
And most beliefless who had once believed.[38]

Arnold did not solve the problem of morality. What was its basis, without religion? "If all right and wrong is relative, and we must believe it is, then the great horror of sin, the great admiration of Righteousness is gone." To declare one's independence from a creed's interpretation of a sacred text unleased the self in a moral wilderness, a universe without meaning. "It does seem no use. There is the phantom!"[39]

Arnold and Clough could take Carey only so far. She hungered for more. As she reached out for answers, she searched in two realms. As a lover of literature she found in poetry sources of inspiration to refashion her emotional and aesthetic life. But despite her passions and enthusiasms, belles lettres was not enough to satisfy her. She needed the intellectual foundation that she found in the science and speculation of her day. Her Quaker background had not forbade discussion of the new science of evolution. James Carey Thomas was a physician and interested in the new thought. But while her parents sought ways to reconcile science with their Christian faith, Carey took it pure. Years before, Shelley and Thomas Paine had battered down the walls. Now, in July 1878, Herbert Spencer entered.

Carey Thomas' reading of Spencer, a contemporary British philosopher, had begun in her first year at Cornell, when she took up his *First Principles*. In the summer of 1878, as she thrashed over questions of religion, she returned to Spencer. This time she read his *Principles of Sociology*, published in 1876 to immense acclaim. Spencer's treatment of religion made her very angry. On July 6 she wrote that she "threw down Herbert Spencer" and went to the library to escape into a novel. She expressed her distress in her journal: "I feel as if I could shoot him with my little pistol. I *hate* him for the way he speaks of 'the manufacture theory of creation' and the glorious old Greek gods." Yet his logic, she had to admit, "does convince," especially his derivation of ideas of immortality and God from dreams. She allowed herself the exclamation "Heavens" and then caught herself: "when I say heavens it has no meaning, it is only a derived term from men whose ancestral homes were on high hills." In July 1878 this iconoclasm was more painful than liberating.[40]

The next day she wrote to Mary Garrett a full reaction to *Sociology*: "It is wonderful. Yet I read it almost choking him with anger. He tears down with the most contemptuous sarcasm the Jehovah of the Hebrews and the glorious old Greek gods who have been to me inspiration and joy. . . . I can find no flaw in his logic; therefore I think we are bound to accept it." Spencer not only overturned the Christian myth of creation but also spoke disparagingly of a classicist's passion, the Greek gods. "His Explanations do spoil for me the glory of the old pantheon—'god by god goes out discrowned and dis-anointed.' "[41]

Carey Thomas' renunciation of traditional faith left in its wake a longing for the world that was now lost to her. As she read Spencer in her grandmother's summer cottage, her sense of loss became intense. Despite her disbelief, she was deeply moved by her grandmother's mental universe. As Carey read the Bible to her, she choked over the line from a psalm, "He that keepeth Israel shall neither slumber nor sleep." She wrote in her journal, "The whole beauty and comfort came over me." And yet her doubt would not go away. Christianity had "no proof. All Christians I see are afraid to listen to doubts. It is a continual struggle to them to hold on. . . . I pray every night, 'Oh, God, if it is true make me realize it,' and all the time the realization, the possibility even seems further off." Living with her grandmother confronted her with the contrast between their worlds. Not only did the older woman have faith, she had a traditional woman's life. Carey listened to her stories and conversations with friends with loving attention. Yet she measured the distance between them: With "never a word of abstract thought," her grandmother was "utterly untouched by the throbbing needs of the day, the exquisite poetry, the angry 'what have we [to] do with this man.' " She wondered if, someday, she might become like her.[42]

Although she seemed not to recall, twice before—in the intervals before Howland and before Cornell—she had confronted such doubts and despair. In all three times the symptoms were the same: religious uncertainty, restlessness, self-doubt, and the sense of being utterly alone. Yet this time, there were two differences. Carey Thomas had no immediate realizable goal ahead of her, only an indeterminate one. And she was playing for keeps. She was readying herself for life; but it was a life that seemed to recede from her grasp. The only thing that had made her future real was her imagination, and it was failing her. She had taken her dreams from literature and now was confronting life as lived. Carey Thomas at twenty-one had no corporeal models, no living women to show her how to become what she wanted to be, no actual person to convince her when she doubted that she could develop her mind and emerge as a scholar. Miss Slocum could inspire her, but only to go beyond her own achievements. At the most fundamental level, Carey Thomas was utterly alone.

What about Hannah Whitall Smith, her beloved Aunt Hannah? Always an important force in Carey's life, Hannah herself was in an uncertain time of trial as she picked up life's pieces after Robert's disgrace. Hannah was, in fact, adding to the pressure by continuing to work for Carey's conversion. In mid-August 1878 on a camping trip to the Adirondacks with Hannah, Carey's crisis came to a head. One evening around eight she took a canoe out into the middle of the lake, over a mile from shore. As she wrote in her journal a week later, "The sunset glow had died away and it was a clear starlit night. The little waves broke against the keel. I was thinking of the fact that I had wasted this year in struggles to believe in Christianity, useless, hopelessly so. I was in horrible doubt about the university. It is quenching soul and spirit to go on, it is risking all upon my being able to write." Here her script became irregular; the formation of words, jerky. "A horrible blank, no god to pray to, no shrine of Apollo to go to. A life of rasping at home if I can't believe, and that is impossible at least now. Suddenly, as suddenly as a possession, came over me the temptation to upset the boat."

No one would deem it suicide, for accidents happened frequently. "I shall never forget how the waves sounded and the stars looked. I came so near doing it, I tremble to think of it." But at this moment, she found some kind of answer. "Sudden thy shadow fell on me." There came to her "as a stealing melody some use and beauty into life. All the old fighting to believe died away. It lay behind me, a cast off garment." The reconciliation that she had longed for came. She understood faith as "a belief in the needs of man, in his soul." At the base of all religions was the heart's longing. All were good; none—"if they do not shackle"—were wrong. None had all truth, they were "only notes in the chorus." "Godwinism, its core, the heavenly secret of Shelley 'to fear himself and love all human kind,' the secret of Christ, 'a dying daily, self renunciation' are all one. It is worth working for, worth living to work out that. . . . I rowed back."[43]

The moment of reconciliation was short. Carey rowed back into a conflicted, painful existence. Every issue was charged. What did it mean that she continued to think of Frank Gummere and longed to see him again? Could they be friends on the ideal plane? Why, if her life's work was to be scholarship, could she not concentrate on Greek? As a pioneer did she have a responsibility to continue in her anomalous status at Johns Hopkins? Could she hope for Mary Garrett? Was Mamie worthy of her love? Would that love take her away from study? Did she have any special gift to give to the world? Could she be a writer? Could her parents, especially her mother, accept her?

In this time of confusion, Hannah allowed Carey to read her diary of the 1850s, and Carey transcribed whole passages from it into her own journal. What she learned from her reading was that Hannah had been deeply unhappy after her marriage. At age twenty, she had written, "I am too young to be married. The cares of life have come upon me so soon that they have crushed all the joyousness of my spirits." Hannah despaired of her condition, confiding to her diary that she remained rebellious and impatient because she could no longer devote herself to study and become "a thoroughly educated woman." She had to lay aside Greek, mathematics, and reading to fulfill her duties as wife and mother. She struggled to subdue her spirit and to submit to her husband's will. The children were trials to be borne. Hannah cried out during her second pregnancy, the more regretted because Robert had agreed that she should bear no more children for several years: "This is the end of all my hopes, my pleasing anticipations, my returning youthful joyousness." By copying these passages into her own personal record, Carey testified to their significance. She did not comment except to write, "It is a revelation."[44]

IV

ON OCTOBER 7, 1878, Carey Thomas wrote a letter to the Johns Hopkins trustees withdrawing from the university. In it she wrote a full explanation of her leaving in the hope that her act would "not be prejudicial to any other applicant." Her admission to graduate study was coupled with a condition that excluded her from the Greek seminar and advanced instruction. She was dependent solely on the help that Professor Gildersleeve "at the expense of his own time, which, notwithstanding his great personal kindness, I hesitated to encroach upon." Now, after "a trial of one year," during which she received no other aid than his advice in reading, she was convinced that "under the present regulations the assistance referred to cannot be obtained."[45]

Carey wrote to Anna that she had had a long talk with Gildersleeve, and he had advised her to withdraw. He informed her that she could anticipate no additional privileges in the coming year. He understood her discouragement as she worked in isolation. In contrast to her limited opportunities, he described the advantages that he was able to give to his five graduate students. "It absolutely did seem too cruel to sit there and hear of all his classes and lectures, to feel the inspiration he was to his students and to know that, on account of the narrow prejudices of a few members of the board, I was shut out from this paradise."[46]

The action, so long debated in her mind, resolved nothing. Although, she wrote, it seemed a necessary step, as she talked to Gildersleeve, "it almost broke my heart to be so near and yet so far from all his inspiration." She set herself a schedule. Each day she gave two hours to writing, followed by Greek, then German; she studied French and English for four hours in the evening. Her new freedom was deeply tinged with sadness: "A great sense of sorrow is still over me from the university, but perhaps it is best. At all events, it was inevitable."[47]

A conventional Baltimore social life offered itself, and eligible men came to call. A gossipy letter to Anna mentioned the attentions of Messieurs Halsted, Roland, and Tomlinson, three men who ultimately appeared on the list of "Lovers" compiled in her last years as she worked on her autobiography. Given her state of mind, however, such calls were not even a distraction. She was recruited by the young men of Gummere's circle to write for *The Quaker Alumnus*, an ambitious effort to create a youthful version of the *Friends' Review*. Her lackluster contributions were a piece on home study and a half-hearted plea for continued commitment to Quaker colleges.[48]

In the months that followed, failure loomed. Carey Thomas tried to renew her flagging energies and commitments. She wrote and despaired that she had no real ability. She mooned over Mamie Gwinn and caught herself falling into lassitude. She congratulated herself that Frank Gummere was far away and then regretted that they had not spoken. In midwinter this cycle of misspent time and recrimination, of longing and self-criticism was broken by her mother, who confronted her again with the issue of her religious apostasy.

Late in the evening of January 11, 1879, Mary Thomas spoke harsh words. Carey reported in her journal, "She says I outrage her every feeling, that it is the greatest living grief to her to have me in the house, a denier and defamer of the Christ whom she loves thousands more than she loves me." Ill faith intermingled with ill works; mother also castigated daughter for her behavior and demeanor. She judged her as "merely selfish, . . . a finder of fault in the house." Carey enumerated the charges: "that I barely tolerate Father, that I am utterly and entirely selfish, that I use the house of which I take the best of everything and Father and herself for my purposes and then care no more for them." Mary also accused Carey of being dangerous to her brothers and sisters, making "the other children unbelieving."

These were years in which Mary Thomas' intense religious feeling had propelled her into religious revivals and temperance reform. She had experimented with inner devotions and began to attend Methodist services. She held parlor meetings in her house. In 1878 when the evangelist Dwight Moody came to preach in Baltimore, his primary supporters were James and Mary Thomas. According to her grandson, James Flexner, Mary Thomas became Moody's chief organizer and speaker for the women's meetings. She was to emerge from these apprentice years as the respected and powerful president of the Maryland Women's Christian Temperance Union.[49]

With something of her public fervor she declared to Carey that she no longer loved her "except as a child." To treat her as if she approved of her, Mary told her, would make her "untrue to her Savior." Carey was distraught. "Oh heavens, what a religion that makes a mother cast her daughter off!" In her anger, she thought again of suicide. "I do believe I shall shoot myself. I almost think I will; there is no use of living and then Mother would see in the morning that she had been cruel."

Even Carey could not deny that some of what Mary had said was true, that she might be selfish. But the accusation that she had defamed religion in the house was false. "I call the gods to witness I never said a word against religion in her presence." Carey went to meeting and tried to influence the children for good. She felt that she in fact was the injured one: "I am treated by father and mother as a dog, an interloper." If she did not believe in the good in herself, she would have been lost. She had not rejected faith so much as faith had eluded her. Carey was suddenly utterly alone. She could not leave the house, for she had no training and no money. Yet how could she remain at home? The day before, her father had told her "that he shuddered to think of me in the house speaking words against his Savior." Her parents' harsh rejection of her was "the fruits of that cruel system" that put belief above love.

"I would rather die before I treated anyone so. I am all alone. Oh, what shall I do?"[50]

Mary could not allow such conflict to rend her household through the night. Carey had begun writing in her journal at eleven-thirty in the evening. After she closed, "Mother came up . . . and we determined to try again. She was lovely and we will be different." Yet something had happened. The bond of trust between them, threatened for years, had now snapped. Even in the early glow of reconciliation Carey partially understood this. "I will be different but it is hard to bring back a feeling. I used to be so passionately devoted to her and I wish I could be again. I will try and be good."[51] A month later, though her parents now tried to be kind, the wounds remained. Carey was deeply unhappy.

Mary was troubled about whether or not she had done the right thing and turned to her sister. Hannah did not reassure her completely: "It is hard to know whether what thee did was best or not, but I guess a 'faithful testimony' is always good in the end, even though it may seem severe. And it is a great gain to have got the barrier out of the way between Minnie and thee." Hannah saw that the issue lay elsewhere. The problem was not so much a conflict over religion, as Carey's need to find an independent means of earning a living. Hannah wrote, "If I were Minnie I would get my own living, if it killed me. I have always said that real independence can only come in this way, and I see it more than ever." Hannah was not certain, however, as to how her niece might come to support herself. "How on earth is the thing to be fixed?" she asked. Although Hannah agreed with Mary that for the time that Carey remained at home she had to respect her parents' wishes, she hoped that Mary would not judge her daughter so harshly. Mary had a right to demand that Carey yield, but she should not condemn Carey: "When you think of her and her present views, do remember me. I was just as radical as Carey, and even when I was a good deal older too, and was just as *set* in my views. She will come out all right I am sure."[52]

What was becoming clear to Hannah was not, however, apparent to her niece. In Carey Thomas' head the whole round of issues continued to rattle— a squirrel cage of recrimination for not working, anger that she lived in a vacuum where study found no support, growing fascination for Mamie Gwinn, unrequited admiration for Mary Garrett, and silence about Frank Gummere. He was not far from her thoughts, however. A letter from a mutual friend asking her to come to Philadelphia to see Frank left her confused. "I was completely disconcerted by this letter and my slain enemy returned. I discovered I was as much in a turmoil about Mr. Gummere as ever."[53]

Carey asked the friend to bring Frank to visit her in Baltimore. As she anticipated the visit, all the issues about him returned. Two new elements had entered, however. She had heard a rumor that in Providence, where he had been teaching at the Friends' School, he had fallen in love; and he was about to go abroad again, this time with a special mandate from Joseph Wright Taylor.

On March 24, 1879, Gummere met Taylor. According to Gummere's account, "He then and there made me a proposition I had never dreamed of: he informed me, he designed me for the presidency of his college. As nearly as I can recollect, he laid his hand on my shoulder and said: 'Thou knowest I am building a college at Bryn Mawr (words at least, to that effect): we must have a head for it: I think thee is the man.' "

Carey may not have known the exact words, but she would have known their essence. She, in fact, may have been the necessary midwife. In August 1878, after confessing her love for Frank to Bessie King, she spoke to Bessie's father, Francis T. King, the president designate of the board of trustees of Taylor's future college: "I could not help telling Cousin Frank that I thought Mr. Gummere would make the best president for the new Taylor College. I can do that much for him at least."[54] By the time that Gummere had his interview with Taylor, Carey knew both that he was in line for something important at the future college and that he would be going abroad.

It was immediately following the meeting with Taylor that Frank Gummere's visit to Carey was to take place. What Carey thought she wanted was a return of their former friendship. She decided to take the encounter as a challenge. "The whole thing is a test of my firmness, to meet a man whom I am in love with, a little, after nearly two years when he has stopped caring for me, in the presence of two men who know all about Mr. Gummere's former preference for me and who will watch me attentively." It would be her last trial. She had thought and dreamed of Frank for four nights. Once she saw him, it would be "all over," and she could return to work.[55]

The possibility of seeing Frank again brought to the surface the first mention of what must have been brewing for some time. Carey Thomas was trying to get abroad. She brought it up in her journal obliquely. Again she churned the revolving issues of her despair: she lacked inspiration and companionship; she was cut off from study; and she feared she could not write. Then she made this curious statement, "The whole conjunction of Mr. Gummere's visit strikes me as fatalistic. I am hopeless in regard to going abroad unless I myself make the money."

And then an even more curious statement, "It would make a difference in Mr. Gummere's prospects in the Taylor College if he were engaged to me. If he should still care about me there could be no likelier time for me to accept him." An altogether novel idea: Frank Gummere and she would marry to improve his chances to become the president of the new women's college. It was an academic Quaker young woman's perfect fantasy of the vicarious life and—perhaps more to the point—a means, however encumbered, of getting abroad. Immediately she pushed it to the side. She would continue to try to be someone in her own right. Though she might fail, she would "rather do what I think is best, follow my daemon into ruin and unhappiness. . . . I want freedom to live as I please, where I please, to think as I please."[56]

With Carey at a fever pitch, Frank changed his mind. He had, by his own account, been stunned by Taylor's proposition and may have needed to consult with his Harvard counselors. He told Carey that a telegram called him to Cambridge, and he sent his "deep regret." Frank was, in fact, experiencing deep personal crisis. After consulting with advisers, he thought Taylor's words over and "felt a certain shrinking from the responsibilities entailed." His health began to fail. He wrote to Taylor to propose that, after a period of study abroad as preparation, he take "the chair of English Literature alone, without any such addition of executive functions." Taylor promised the chair to him and, with two others (probably David Scull, Jr., and James Whitall), paid for him to go abroad to study. On the basis of a "general, not legally binding promise of the position referred to," Gummere left for Germany.[57]

As Carey learned of this, it put new pieces of the puzzle that is M. Carey Thomas on the table. Frank Gummere was going abroad to study: she would, too. If you cannot join him, imitate him and beat him. Beginning in the spring of 1879, Frank ceased to be the fantasied object of love, challenging the construction of her life, and emerged as the competition. What he did, she would do, but better. As he prepared to embark, she determined to go abroad.

She now had a goal that, like her dream of Vassar and Cornell, located a new life. Freedom was again a place, this time, Europe. There she would prepare to become a professor. In the back of her mind, not to surface again for several years, Carey Thomas registered the fact that someone was going to be the president of Taylor's college.

German universities were attracting many eager American students—more than ten thousand over the course of the nineteenth century. By the late 1870s it was a primary route to American university positions. It was, therefore, natural for a college graduate hoping to become a professor to set sights on Germany. A male college graduate, that is. In 1879, although some German universities allowed women to attend as auditors, it was unlikely that they would allow women to take degrees. A small number of women were studying in places such as the University of Leipzig, including a few American women, but it was an unusual and uncertain step.[58]

Nonetheless Carey Thomas moved decisively. Clear about her course, she again had to convince her parents. This time, she found a most unlikely ally. In June 1879 her grandmother Whitall summoned her to Philadelphia to meet a Mr. Jones who could talk to her from personal experience about study in Germany. Mr. Jones was a most encouraging witness: his own young-looking wife lived abroad with "no difficulty," and in Germany a person could manage on $600 a year, or almost $9,000 in 1994 dollars. It is probable that Hannah, understanding that Carey needed to find a way to support herself, figured out that she should study abroad and return to teach and then convinced her mother to help. Before Carey said a word, her grandmother promised to contribute part of the necessary annual $600—roughly $200 to $300—for Carey to study abroad. The deed was done. "Now, unless Father and Mother lose their resolution, it is sure." Her parents gave their permission.[59]

Mary Thomas was clear, but James' resolution wavered. Unlike her campaign to go to Cornell, Carey's task this time involved assuaging his feelings, not gaining his permission. She had to confront his sense that in letting her go he was neglecting his duty. As Carey reported to Mary Garrett, the two had "a tremendous talk." James said "he could not stand it, that it was wrong to let me go alone, that it was horrible to think of the anxiety of knowing I was out of reach and help if anything happened." Once again her mother came to her aid. She took the whole responsibility of Carey's going on herself. Thus absolved, James relented. Carey understood well what was at stake. A man, even of her father's "liberality," felt that to allow his daughter to study abroad meant a "sacrifice of paternal authority, responsibility, [and] traditional feeling about women." At age twenty-two, this seemed to her another example of "the misery and oppression of a girl's life." She felt that to combat it there needed to be "invectives like those of the French Revolution."[60]

Carey faced one last hurdle. She had to convince someone from her circle to accompany her abroad. At some level Carey's decision to go abroad echoed in each of the other four friends. Bessie King and Mary Garrett dreamed of study in Europe but their fathers were unsympathetic. Julia Rogers considered it, but temporarily withdrew. For a brief time a New York friend of Mary and Julia, Gertrude Mead, emerged as a possible companion. In late July Carey received word that Gertrude would not join her; but more importantly, that her beloved Mamie would. Mamie Gwinn had decided to study in Leipzig, and had convinced her parents to let her go.

Throughout the painful year, Mamie had become increasingly important to her. In the fall of 1878 as Carey had tried to work, she had attempted to put away her infatuation. In mid-September, she had declared to her journal that Mamie was "as unsatisfactory as moonshine." Their meeting was embarrassing. "I caught myself kissing her as in a trance from a habit of affection." After staying for four hours Carey left disgusted, wishing, on the one hand, that she was free of Mamie, and on the other, that her feeling for her might return. But within a month she was in love with Mamie again, declaring to her journal, "There is a passionate devotion between girls I feel sure."[61]

Mamie charmed Carey, not only with her beauty but also with her poetic ability. Carey confided to her journal that Mamie ran "more of a chance of success than any one of us I think. There is something rare and exotic in her genius." Carey wrote to Anna, "Mamie is downright satisfactory and excites me all the time by being on the verge of genius." Her poems "come nearer to real poetry than any I have ever seen. They are far beyond Mr. Gummere's, Mr. Boyesen's and, of course, my own." In verses dedicated to Mamie, Carey told of Mamie's handing her a poem she had written. As she read it, she envisioned Mamie "violet crowned," standing upon a height:

> And those dark eyes so close to mine,
> Were kindled; her lips trembled with the birth
> Of mightiest thrilling song—the bread and wine,
> Which was herself, She break and gave. Ere long
> The people bent them toward her and upturned
> Dull, hungering eyes and faces. At her song
> I wept and stood with them who yearned. [62]

Mamie showered Carey with affection, but she could be harshly critical. She was graceful and feminine. Carey's frank and solid manner could offend her. After one such outburst, Carey was in despair. "She said I swung my arms very much, bowed too low, pushed away a person's hand, did not look at him, that is, half turned away; sat with my legs crossed and my arm over the back of a chair and threw back my head when I talked." [63] Brown-eyed, vital, enthusiastic Carey was not ladylike.

In January 1879, the two spent the night together and talked through the night. Mamie told her, "I love you dearly, more than any one else, but I do not love you all I can love." Mamie's words struck Carey hard and pained her. She made a vow she could not keep, "I shall never give up to my love for her as I have. It is because I have that she feels that way, and because she has that I do. Nor more shall it happen, though I doubt if anything can change it now." At this early point Mamie believed that she loved Carey devotedly, but that Carey was not her grand passion. [64]

Passion is what Carey felt. Her love for Mamie swept her away. As she thought about her feelings for Mamie, she used the words "give up to my love for her" and let "it happen"—language that suggests surrender. Her hope that she might resist this love was short-lived, and in February she wrote in her journal, "Mamie and I have been getting more and more devoted and absorbed in each other. I never shall care as much for anyone again, whatever is the upshot. Her perfect love and gentleness and real desire for what is best, her cleverness, and our sweetest love. It almost breaks my heart that we cannot be more together and that, as it is, our love is a distraction and a drawback to both of us. When I see her, I am wrapped in languid happiness, and when she goes I feel unnerved for all effort and work."

Minnie Thomas as a young child,
Mary Whitall Thomas retreating to
the right, c. 1858

*The likeness of an appealing child,
made momentarily serious by the
demands of mid-nineteenth-century
photography to remain still and
unblinking*

Minnie Thomas in girlhood

*A vigorous child in the frame of
parental hopes*

Opposite: The five friends of the Friday Evening, c. 1879; Mamie Gwinn is at center, and posed around her are, clockwise from lower left: Carey Thomas, Julia Rogers, Bessie King, Mary Garrett

Again, an uncompromising gaze into the camera by a person determined to be taken seriously

Above: Carey Thomas and Mamie Gwinn, May 23, 1879

A joint studio portrait recording their early intimate friendship

Mary Garrett (left) and Julia Rogers

Proserpine by Dante Gabriel Rossetti, 1874

In 1883 Carey Thomas described the recurring female figure in Rossetti's paintings, "with its sensuous mouth and intellectual forehead . . . the same wonderful eyes and more than wonderful neck, which curves and undulates and upbears the 'small head of flowerlike.' " These women were to Carey "all inhabitants of a land of dreams"

Algernon Charles Swinburne,
London Stereoscopic Company

Found in Mamie Gwinn Hodder's papers

Much of the time Carey felt her love for Mamie as an absorption, distracting her, keeping her from work. She continued, "It takes sometimes two or three hours' hard work to escape from her atmosphere: sometimes I determine not to see her again, but then she is so sweet and pure I cannot see how it can be a disturbance; but it is." In her later years, Mamie wrote that she had been drawn particularly by Carey's "passive side," by which she meant that part of Carey that loved poetry and art. Carey may have feared the effect of this on her resolutions to work. But by the summer, knowing she was to go abroad, Carey was more willing to take time away from study, and Mamie became a delight. In midsummer she wrote that she and Mamie had spent days in the park reading together. "Mamie is lovely. I am wrapped up in her again. I never expected to have as perfect a friend." Mamie had been constant and caring, when Carey found herself moody and dull. Mamie was becoming devoted. "Her excessive love makes me feel how little I deserve anything. Whatever afterwards happens Ich habe genossen das irdische Glück—Ich habe gelebt und geliebt," which can be translated as "I have partaken of earthly bliss—I have lived and loved."[65]

In July Mamie struggled with her mother to get her consent to a year abroad. Mathilda Gwinn was deeply hurt by her daughter's desire to leave her and threatened to cut her off if she did. Propelled by love of Carey and distaste for the society life she would lead at home, Mamie pleaded for permission to go. Mary Thomas and Hannah Smith wrote to Mrs. Gwinn to encourage her to allow Mamie to accompany Carey. By then, Carey was imagining a life abroad with Mamie. "Your letter," she wrote to Mamie in mid-July, "made my heart beat decidedly faster because I want to see you, not a little while but for good and always." The following week, she wrote encouragingly, "Yes, dear love, our love shall be a help to everything we really care for and, being what it is, is a greater power for good. No, I am nothing but glad and I believe there is happiness and good work and completeness ahead and it will be inexpressibly sweet to have us go toward it together." Mamie had sent her photograph. Carey wrote that she cared so much for Mamie that she could hardly bear to look at it. It would mean a great deal if anything happened to Mamie. "But nothing will happen. You shall live to be mine and the gods'. I cannot do without you."[66]

Carey and Mamie booked August 22 passage on the Red Star Line's *Vaderland*. Uncertainty clouded their departure, however. Mamie's mother retreated from her approval, murmuring in Baltimore that she planned to adopt another daughter; and Mamie became ill. The last weeks were terrible. Carey felt all the agony of her decision. She wrote to Mary Garrett, "I am ashamed of myself to mind going so much. I look at the house and children with a 'last time' feeling and talk to Mother with a 'one word more' kind of sense." She feared members of her family would die before she returned. And she understood that, after a three-year absence, she would reenter her house a stranger. Her one deep consolation was that in the final weeks at home her mother put aside philanthropic duties to devote herself wholly to being with her.[67]

Faced with the crisis of Carey's departure, James and Mary Thomas turned to their faith, their rock but also the wedge that divided them from their eldest daughter. Again they confronted Carey's irreligion. At Carey's last First Day Meeting they prayed for her. Carey regretted that she could not soothe her father by testifying to a faith she did not feel. In the last week, as Mamie got ill with violent cramps, vomiting, and diarrhea, James found his opening and begged Carey to wait at least another year. He had secretly nourished a hope that if Carey found a new heart, she would stay home. Again he appealed to his wife. As Carey wrote to Mary Garrett, "He asked Mother the other night if she thought I would stay if I were suddenly converted. Mother said 'No,' so there is no other hope [on his part] but Mamie left." As late as August 18, Carey wondered whether or not she would go ahead if Mamie were ill the day they were to leave.[68]

In the pain of these last days, Carey made an embarrassing grab for Mary Garrett. Ignoring Julia's claims, she wrote desperate letters trying to set a time for the two of them to be alone. Carey got a visit, but with Julia in tow. Breaking her resolution of two years and "every announced principle," she sought physical closeness and sat with her head on Mary's shoulder. Back in Baltimore, she feared the consequences and wrote to Mary, "I shudder to think what [is] Julia's opinion of me . . . I think you will perhaps temper justice with mercy."[69]

During the visit Julia had made clear her displeasure over Carey's intimate letters to Mary. As a testament to their relationship, Mary shared with Julia all her communications, including those from Carey. As Carey steeled herself for her journey and long exile abroad, what she most wanted was a completely private correspondence with Mary. In letters that Mary might give to Julia, Carey tried to convince her to carry on an intimate correspondence, one shielded from Julia's eyes. As a reward Carey promised that "you shall hear everything of interest, I mean scandalous or otherwise, love affairs, of which, of course, there will be none, quarrels with Mamie, which I hope are as improbable as love affairs, whether I am really disappointed in Germany, which no one else shall hear, if it be so, in fact, everything." Yet in the delicate situation she was in, Carey could hardly write all. "I am afraid I have stopped to think between the lines, the things one does not say need consideration as well as the things one does, and I think you can read between the lines."[70]

On August 22, Sarah Nicholson, Carey's "Aunty Hal," wrote to Hannah: "Poor Min goes today. I can't help pitying her, after all. It seems dreadful to me, and I expect she will rue it, too, some day, especially with that awful burden of Mamie Gwinn on her. I can't conceive how they *could* bring their minds to let her go, but I suppose seeing she is as she is, it is really more comfortable to them to have her go than to have her uneasy at home." Tugged by home ties, uncertain until the last minute about whether Mamie could travel, troubled in her relation to Mary Garrett, and ill with diarrhea, Carey Thomas boarded the steamer. Not a propitious beginning.[71]

The Desire of My Heart

O N AUGUST 22, 1879, Carey Thomas and Mamie Gwinn departed on the *Vaderland* bound for Antwerp. Mary Thomas went to see them off at the dock, parting with them as they entered the boat that took them to the steamer. She wrote to a sister, "Minnie's sad, sad face haunted me." Mr. Gwinn went out to the steamer, and he reported to Mary that Mamie and Carey were comfortable. The pilot sent Mary a note that the two had cheered up. After saying goodbye to Mamie's father and seeing the trunks safely in the stateroom, but before the steamer began the journey, Carey wrote to her mother her gratitude "for giving me the desire of my heart . . . the fulfillment of all my dreams."[1]

This time Carey would not be disappointed. The dreams she held for herself were to be realized.

I

CAREY THOMAS' sojourn in Europe proved to be the decisive event in her life. Much about her up to 1879 had been unusual. But the record of her peers— in Baltimore, Howland, and Cornell—clarifies that Carey Thomas was one among a number of gifted, spirited young women, few of whom would make their mark upon the public stage. Disciplined study in Germany and Switzerland set her apart. For over three years she attended lectures, read, wrote, and took examinations in a difficult field. She returned home with a clear and unambiguous license to obtain a high position: a Ph.D. summa cum laude from the University of Zürich.

She also came home profoundly changed. Not only did she find her calling in the public world, she consolidated her conflicted personal life. Away from parents and Baltimore, she tried out a complex self in Europe and it worked. In her study she pursued scholarship with diligence and enthusiasm. She schemed for a position and dreamed of a college in the image of a European university. And, joined to Mamie by a special bond, she imagined herself a poet and an aesthete, especially in their long months of travel.

Reconstruction of Carey Thomas' experience abroad comes largely from her letters to her mother. It was a guarded relationship. Carey provided her mother with a complete and rich travelogue. She conscientiously tried to set down all her impressions of foreign life and to describe fully the works of art that she so carefully studied. She was forthright about her university experiences and her ambition to become a scholar. None of this was dangerous. About aspects of her inner life, however, she was more circumspect. Having entered treacherous waters too many times, Carey kept from her mother the state of her irreligion. She seldom discussed her hopes to be a poet. And normally she veiled her feelings for her female friends.

Nonetheless, because she was so far away, and letters provided her the only way she could communicate with her mother, her lengthy weekly letter is a rich record of the critical period in which she emerged into adulthood. So much was up in the air when she embarked. Could she realize her promise? Could she manage on her own? Could she sustain a relationship with Mamie more stable than the complicated and frequently tempestuous one of the past? Could she become the person that she longed, ached to be?

Her initial letters give little indication of what was to come. In addition to scene paintings, they describe Carey's pursuit of culture and her typical anxious responses to a new situation—criticism of others and efforts to establish her class position. The voyage itself began with a strong dose of sickness that made her miserable and homesick. But once arrived in Antwerp, Carey was in ecstasy. Europe was exactly as she had imagined it. She wrote to her parents her first impressions. She was struck by the quaintness and oddity of the town streets where women in traditional garb knitted stockings as they walked and dogs roamed four abreast. Almost immediately Carey and Mamie sought culture. By seven-thirty each morning they were out looking at paintings in churches. They got currant buns along the way for their makeshift lunch, returning to their rooms only for the five o'clock evening table d'hôte meal. Carey and Mamie traveled under the wing of a Baltimore family going abroad, and many of Carey's first comments focused on the family's crudeness. Their chaperons hated pictures. "They throw away money in royal style and drink unlimited wine."[2]

Whatever scorn Carey intended, it was problematic whether such wine-drinking was more dangerous than Carey's picture-viewing. The Quaker tradition of her family had allowed good food; solid, even handsome possessions; and appropriate, though restrained dress. It rejected visual art, secular music, and theater as seductions of the devil or of popery. Carey immediately announced that she was an aesthete who accepted no limits. Carey and Mamie went to Antwerp Cathedral and heard "the most glorious high Mass." She knelt to the host. She declared that Rubens' *Descent from the Cross* "more than fulfills my expectations. It makes one's eyes fill with tears every time one looks at it." Although implements of torture on view at the castle reminded her of the Inquisition, the bad side of Catholicism, yet "Art can never pay its debt to it for its cathedrals and lovely Madonnas and Christs. If I wanted to convert a skeptic I should send him to Europe."[3]

From Antwerp, Carey and Mamie traveled, escorted, to Brussels and then alone to Cologne and from there to Stuttgart. They had arranged from home to improve their German in an educated household for a month before beginning formal study at Leipzig. Even during that period of waiting, Carey found her deepest hopes for Europe verified. She wrote to her mother that she wished she could convey to her "the difference in the atmosphere here, the literary atmosphere, I mean. One has a sense of history being unraveled and antiquities dug up and a continual stir of conflicting philological theories." It was not possible for an American to know much, for "we have merely the dry bones." Her compatriots were "like men shut up in a prison, and studying about the grass and sky." Unquestionably Carey was determined that the Europe of reality fit the Europe of her anticipation.[4]

In Stuttgart, Carey made arrangements to board in Leipzig. She received flowery letters of introduction written by Andrew D. White—Cornell's absentee president who was serving as the American minister to Berlin—to the Leipzig professors of his acquaintance. Much to her pleasure, the letters paid tribute to her father and to her own position as "a very noble specimen of an American lady."[5]

On October 15, Carey and Mamie arrived in Leipzig and immediately went to their boarding house. It proved unsatisfactory, and after several weeks Carey leased a three-room suite at 7 Wintergarten Strasse, a street leading away from the main railroad station, only a few minutes' walk from the university. They rented from Frau Pochhammer, the daughter of a prominent professor. They were waited on by the household servant, and they used the house's supplies for a simple breakfast and supper, paying only cost. From the restaurant across the way, they secured their midday dinner meal, selected from the bill of fare and served to them with clean linen and silver in their own rooms. Carey was justly proud of herself for her skill in getting such an excellent arrangement close to the university. Although she later turned against Frau Pochhammer, the lodgings served the two scholars well as a comfortable and convenient place to live and work during their Leipzig years.[6]

Leipzig was a bustling metropolis as well as the home of one of Europe's greatest universities. A city of slightly under 150,000, it was the most important commercial and industrial city in Saxony and the center of Germany's book publishing industry. Elegant neighborhoods gave Leipzig something of the look of Budapest or parts of Paris, but Carey saw its grittier side. Her first description made no effort to glamorize the city. She wrote to Mary Garrett that it was "a city of soft coal, as dirty as Cincinnati." If Mamie or she went outside for ten minutes they returned with soot on their faces. When it rained, the streets were covered with black mud. To reach the university they crossed a large ungrassed square, the Augustusplatz, in front of the academic buildings. "Across this, stream the students in every direction and we with them, splashing through the soft churned slime. Our dresses, short as they are, don't dry from one day to another."[7]

The university, founded in 1409, held new and difficult challenges for Carey Thomas. She and Mamie Gwinn were interjecting themselves into a foreign, male world with little help and support. Women had begun attending German universities as auditors in the late 1860s. The University of Leipzig, under the Ministry of Education for Saxony, received 38 women in the 1870s. In 1873 and 1874 a couple of women earned Ph.D.'s, although by Thomas' arrival this privilege had been withdrawn. The men of Leipzig were not imbued with Cornell's ethos of democracy. The rules were not set by a benevolent and sympathetic American university president. By their presence, Thomas and Gwinn were violating centuries of student culture. Initially the male students received them politely. But in the manly world of Leipzig, the two women were conspicuous. When they walked across the square five hundred male heads turned "like a field of wheat in the wind."[8]

In letters to her mother Carey emphasized how well she was managing. For example, early in the term a young man who she assumed was from Poland or Russia approached Mamie and her with a question about women in Leipzig. Carey answered and he walked on. She wrote home that, following this conversation, he politely refrained from speaking to them in the lecture hall. Students seemed to wish to treat them courteously, but feared ridicule. Although the men often opened doors for her, "oftener I see them hesitate and then walk through determinedly." Mamie told her that a man who made way for her shrugged his shoulders angrily.[9]

However, a letter to Mary Garrett written two weeks later tells a quite different story. At the outset Carey warned Mary that she, Julia Rogers, and Bessie King "must be secret as the grave" about what she was about to write. The male students were causing Mamie and her much distress. In one of the lectures a man on the bench in front of them turned around repeatedly and stared at them; in another the man next to them did not take notes, he was so busy staring; in a third, where Carey was the only female, a man with a black beard seemed to be trying to stare her out of the lecture. "It may be that the students take this way of getting rid of the girls." Carey could not be moved. Mamie, however, was more vulnerable. The behavior of a fat man who sat next to her in one of her lectures was so distressing—he sat with his legs apart as close to her as possible and touched her hand several times—that she felt she had to withdraw from the series.

Several incidents at night frightened Carey and Mamie. The worst happened as they returned from the opera. As they turned into their street, they found it deserted. "We came suddenly around the corner face to face with two men, rather gentlemanly looking, who started, spread out their arms and said 'Damen, erhabene Damen' [Ladies, most revered ladies] and looked as if they were going to prevent our going past." There was no one to whom to cry out for help. Carey and Mamie "dodged them and rushed along the street into our house and upstairs, and the men half came after us and then stood looking to see where we went. . . . If we had not been so quick I am sure they would have amused themselves by frightening us very badly." Gradually Carey learned what was safe and how to limit unpleasantness and danger. Although it was difficult, she took on the European's expressionless street face, learning "to look perpetually at nothing."[10]

Carey's primary means of protecting herself was to ignore all men who sought acquaintance without a proper introduction. By this she insured that she was neither insulted nor distracted. Over the course of the three years, a number of young men attempted to get to know her, asking to call, making demonstrative bows, seeking to attract attention. Carey wrote to her mother that these efforts followed a clear pattern. "The various stages are the following: a student takes pains to open doors and stand back; he neglects his lectures and looks at one attentively for a month or so. Then he waits till he meets us face to face some day and makes a magnificent bow. We look at him in blank unrecognition, and he is disconcerted and gives up." Although Carey never yielded, she once admitted that she had been sorely tempted. By midpoint in their second year, Carey and Mamie won a grudging acceptance from their male contemporaries. "I think the men in our class . . . are getting to have a sort of contemptuous affection for us." They now let Carey and Mamie pass freely. More than that, the men extended courtesies: they removed their caps, picked up fallen gloves, and attended to the young women's comfort by closing blinds and shutting windows. "They accept us as established nuisances, now."[11]

Refusing acquaintance with male students did involve some loss. As she began to become more serious in her work, Carey realized that she missed the mutual aid that students normally gave one another. She had no one but Mamie with whom to share books, to talk over the lectures, to learn the ropes.

From time to time Carey reported on a number of European women at the university and two Americans—Harriet Parker, the daughter of a professor of Greek in Iowa, and Eva Channing, a Bostonian, in residence with her mother but not pursuing a degree. Relations with the Channing women were polite but distant. Carey had little use for the daughter, but occasionally found the mother, a well-read Boston clubwoman, interesting. The Channings, in turn, were critical of the two scholars from Baltimore. They used one visit to upbraid Carey and Mamie for their self-imposed isolation: "They think it very wrong of us not to speak to the students, not to bow to them and allow them to call."[12]

Although Carey Thomas made her way among the students with little contact, she received a kind and generous reception from the professors. Her letters of introduction proved invaluable. During her first autumn, Professors Curtius and Ebers and their wives graciously invited her to their entertainments. Professor Georg Curtius and his wife had Carey to tea several times. Carey wrote to Anna Shipley that he was "the foremost champion of the women in the University," and he and his wife obviously gave a personal interpretation to their responsibility for women students' welfare. In contrast to these simple visits, Professor Georg Ebers' dinner was considerably grander. Professor Ebers was well known to Carey, not only as a scholar but also as a writer of popular romances. When she arrived at his house, she was escorted to the sofa, a place of honor where "Ebers devoted himself to me." The professor inquired about President White and spoke heatedly about the want of American copyright to protect the royalties of foreign authors. Carey's pleasure at his attentions was marred by the German custom requiring all to rise and be presented when a newcomer entered the room. In general the men stood and the women were seated. A singer in extreme décolleté provided some distraction to the rather formal gathering as she periodically entertained the guests. The men and women rejoined at dinner, and Carey was seated next to a professor at the university. During the sumptuous meal he gave her useful information about taking a degree, and his friendship with H. H. Boyesen gave them a common subject. Carey fully enjoyed the evening and was distraught when she was called for at eleven: "We were both very much provoked we had to go. I quite enjoyed talking to some men again, so being forced to go was a 'third misfortune.' " The evening proved to be a unique event in Carey's life abroad, giving her firsthand experience of the combined delights of scholarship, money, and class in a society that valued all three.[13]

Carey Thomas' normal routine involved few social occasions. She arose at six-thirty each morning, filled her bag with the special *hefts*—paper in ten sheets later sewed together and bound—and took a quick breakfast of egg and tea in her rooms. She strode quickly to the university, a walk of five minutes. Mamie Gwinn followed at a more leisurely pace, meeting her at a lecture later in the morning. Thomas usually spent four hours a day at lectures, writing furiously like the German students throughout each hour. The rest of the day she read. Through Professor Ebers she gained access to the large reading hall filled with periodicals, and there between lectures she read the latest scholarly journals. She and Gwinn could each borrow twelve books from the university library. She took her midday dinner with Gwinn in their rooms. About half the afternoons she returned for more lectures. On the other afternoons the two scholars donned their wrappers and slippers and studied in their rooms from one-thirty until ten. Their supper was simple fare of cold meat or bread and honey.

It was a quiet life filled with hard work and few distractions. But something important began to happen. In the past two terrible Baltimore years Carey Thomas had reached the bedrock of religious doubt and had begun to build a conception of order. Although Herbert Spencer had made her angry, she believed him. In her later years, she listed Spencer as one of "the great liberal influences of my emancipation," joining Shelley, Godwin, and Arnold in her pantheon.[14] They and Swinburne loosed her from her religious moorings. But in addition, she learned from Spencer three elements that became an essential, though largely unexpressed, part of her creed. It was natural law, not divine revelation, that ordered the universe. Humankind could uncover the workings of natural law through the scientific method. And that law pointed to progress, in both nature and civilization. Carey Thomas lost her Christian faith. She replaced it with positivistic, evolutionary science.

It was with new faith that she now approached scholarship. She was initially drawn to the classics, because the ancient languages were the most prestigious studies in the older liberal arts curriculum. Cornell had given her a stimulating education, opening her up to new currents in literature and philosophy. She had longed for an education that Cornell could not give, at least in the humanities, providing the hard rock of truth. She might have made a good nineteenth-century scientist, but science was never considered, perhaps because it was connected to becoming a doctor, a profession that she had rejected. As she brought her longings for scientific truth to the study of literature, the University of Leipzig was prepared to satisfy her.

In Leipzig she was introduced to the study of literature through the history of peoples, their myths, and their languages. The education had two elements, comparative literature and philology. Comparative literature, as Carey Thomas understood it, was the study of great themes, tracing them through their permutations in the literatures of Western Europe. It was "a revelation," she wrote to Anna Shipley, that Greek stories and legends were repeated during the Middle Ages in different languages, the Stoic notion of morality forming the prototype for all later treatments of morality. Friedrich Zarncke was a popular professor. Thomas wrote home that he was the "students' pet," and that those attending his lectures applauded him as he came into the room. In her mind Zarncke's reputation was well deserved, for he made each point interesting. From the outset Zarncke's lectures on the Middle Ages excited her. "Questions about which I never thought before are assuming undue importance: who were the people settled on the shores of the Black Sea during the early first centuries of the Christian era, Goths, or what other German tribe?" She was beginning to get a sense of the Middle Ages. "I never realized the enthusiasm with which the people rushed from heathendom and savagery to a religion that drew out the gentler elements, how the creative imagination grasped it and scattered it abroad in hundreds of beautiful legends and poems . . . celebrating the adoration men pay to maidenhood and the reverence they give to a mother's love in the Virgin Mary."[15]

By February, Zarncke was tracing Renard the fox and the animal epic in stories of India, Greece, France, and Germany. He had been lecturing on the minnesingers. As she read these love songs from the twelfth century, they appealed to her poetic imagination. Thomas summarized these lectures in two articles in *The Quaker Alumnus*. She lauded the thoroughness of German scholarship kept current by scholarly journals and conveyed through lectures, and she discussed the guiding motif of comparative literature, explaining to her American audience that "the mass of tradition underlying literature is common material which each nation fashions as it will."[16]

Although Zarncke remained Thomas' favorite, she was also learning from other professors. In the five terms in which she studied in Leipzig she listened to the full cycle of lectures given by Zarncke, Curtius, Ebers, Wilhelm Braune, Richard Wülcker, and others. She worked most closely with Wülcker, the professor of English. A student of Zarncke, Wülcker was a younger scholar in the first year of his position. Thomas found him unappealing and pronounced him "insufferable." Older, more established scholars, such as Zarncke and Ebers, were more to her taste. In February 1880 she reported home that Ebers was lecturing on the romances of King Arthur and Charlemagne and had drawn up "great family trees for the different geste cycles," the medieval epic poems centering on a hero. It was these works that led her to her thesis.[17]

The second element of her training was the study of the evolution of language, what is today historical linguistics, but in the nineteenth century was called philology. In the 1870s and 1880s the University of Leipzig was the center of comparative philology. Curtius, a distinguished Greek scholar, established a school of linguistic study based on the evolution of sounds. Zarncke championed the cause of the opposition, who took the nickname the "Young Grammarians."[18] Thomas' work centered on comparative literature and philology based on medieval German, French, and Anglo-Saxon. Gwinn later argued that Thomas had been forced to shift from classics because it required a far longer period of study. What Gwinn did not understand was philology's great appeal. Abroad Thomas learned of the scientific study of language: language followed rules. If she could master those rules, she could reach truth.

She wrote to Anna Shipley that "all Germany has gone philologically mad.

Being in Rome, I have gone to work with the rest." She was digging up Sanskrit roots, mastering the rules, and learning Anglo-Saxon, high German, and Gothic. She bragged about her advantages. While scholars in England and America were learning "as complete gospel truth" the law promulgated by the early Germanic philologist Jacob Grimm, she was tracing its "later developments and contradictions."[19]

By May of her first year, Thomas reported that she was "struggling manfully with this new philology." She explained: "There are two factions, enemies to the death, Curtius and the conservatives who believe that *a*, *i*, and *u* were the original vowels from which all others were derived, and the new school headed by Zarncke, which thinks . . . *e* and *o* are the aboriginal vowels. An *a* is now hunted down and explained into an *e* or *o*." In the university, it was a heated battle. "Party spirit runs high, worse than Republicans and Democrats." As a Zarncke loyalist, Thomas believed in his theory. The problem was that the Curtius faction had written the textbooks, and Zarncke students had to work things out themselves. Although a part of her wished to become a writer, Thomas found herself captivated by English and German philology: "I see no halfway course. I shall soon be in, head and ears."[20]

In Leipzig Thomas sensed a student culture utterly different from that of Cornell, one devoted, obsessively devoted, to study. Her position as a woman and her self-imposed isolation may have distorted her view. She was aware of less scholarly aspects of Continental student life, for she reported that the top floor of a university building served as a prison for duelers and for those joining political societies. And, although she never entered a student beer hall, she lived across the street from a restaurant and watched students on "beer travels," late night roams from one hall to another.[21]

But the only world she knew at first hand was that of the high seriousness of potential scholars. The students allowed themselves minor diversions in the lecture hall. When a professor said something they did not understand, they shuffled their feet to ask him to repeat and explain; they groaned disapproval; and they mocked each other by echoing coughs and sneezes. But they lived only for their academic work. "Such a studious set I never saw. They take notes without a breath in between. The only conversation before lectures seems to be about notes and books." She felt as if she were "in the center of the revolution of this great scholastic organism, that it is a world in itself." As excited as she was by study, she began to pull back: "I see the great danger of being drawn in, sucked down into merely receptive study."[22]

In this first year abroad there were moments in which Thomas felt completely fulfilled. In February 1880 she wrote home, "I feel head and shoulders above my former self. I feel as if I had on seven-leagued boots, as Goethe says of the gods." In the poem she quoted, Goethe's gods stride "from mountain, to mountain in thunder." This was for Thomas a metaphor for the literary life. To "stride from one height of thought to another" was "a continual pleasure. . . . I am so happy." Moreover, it was a shared pleasure, as Mamie Gwinn had declared herself as happy as she.[23]

Thomas' growing confidence came at the moment that her ambition began to crystallize. Joseph Wright Taylor died January 18, 1880. Mary Thomas' letter informing her daughter stated that he had left virtually all his property to the women's college in Bryn Mawr, Pennsylvania. It raised this tantalizing question: "I wonder if Frank Gummere's chances will be injured by his death."[24]

On February 7, 1880, Thomas wrote a letter to her parents laying out what was starting to work in her mind. She began with a rather simple question: What should be her secondary field of study? She was clear that her primary field was English literature. As she delineated the dimensions of choice, she revealed her developing plan.

As she saw it, study in Germany and her own strengths and inclinations prepared her to become a professor. But she could see herself in only two colleges, Smith and the future women's college at Bryn Mawr. Taylor College, as she called it, gave her the advantage of closeness to her parents and the creativity of a new enterprise. But Frank Gummere had already been promised a place as its professor of literature. "Now, of course, Frank Gummere having received the appointment in English literature, I must take some other subject unless I wish to cut myself off from Taylor forever." The plan she sketched was to develop "the department of general literature." Here she had the edge because of her knowledge of languages. "Frank Gummere, of course, treats English literature from its Germanic side. He knows no French, Italian, nor Spanish, and only a college graduate's Greek." Thomas, by contrast, knew not only Greek, Latin, German, and French, but planned to learn Italian, Spanish, and Provençal. She could begin such a study in Leipzig, but she would have to continue in Italy and take her degree at Göttingen.

To embark on such an ambitious scheme, she wanted the certainty of an outcome. "Thee sees it is really important for me to know now because I must begin to work toward a degree. I wish it were possible for father to lay the matter before the trustees of Taylor College." Although she would be willing to promise to resign if she proved an ineffective teacher, "I would not be willing to take any inferior position or at any less salary than, for example, Frank Gummere, because I shall have had all the advantages he has and my subject will be a most difficult one, for which I should try to prepare myself even if it required six years."

She warned her parents about the need for secrecy, especially around members of the family, but if they thought it appropriate, they might discuss her concerns with James Whitall, who was not only a powerful member of the Taylor board and one of Francis Gummere's benefactors but also a potential source of funds to allow Thomas to spend extra years in Europe. In dilating on what this might mean, Thomas allowed herself the most positive statement that she had expressed since encouraged by Miss Slocum at Howland: "I never felt as if I had the training for a position I should care for before. After these three years it will be different."[25]

This canny letter staked out Thomas' claim for a Taylor professorship and set her against Gummere, who was preparing for the chair in English literature promised him by the founder. Taylor's death meant that a board of trustees had the authority to make the decisions. Thomas was not just writing to her mother, but to the wife and sister of two powerful trustees, James Carey Thomas and James Whitall.

Carey had written to Mary Garrett about her ambitions in a different vein. A professorship was very appealing: "It is an incitement to thought, it secures independent money and three months of the year, at least, of inspiration." To Mary, she separated herself from philological study and linked teaching to her artistic passions. During this period Carey was encouraging Mary and Julia to come abroad and to join their studies with hers and Mamie's. The language that Carey used to describe her new calling clarifies the degree to which Swinburnian aestheticism had replaced the Quaker faith of her youth. As a professor, "one can teach one's religion, highest beauty in literature and Art, from the lecture platform."[26]

II

FRANCIS GUMMERE, so recently the object of romantic anguish, now set the standard by which she fixed her ambition. Carey Thomas was aiming for a professorship such as he had been promised. Frank was no distant memory. He was in Leipzig, auditing the same lectures, skating with her, visiting with her in her rooms. He was now engaged to Amelia Mott. To her mother she mentioned him only in passing. On one occasion Frank told her of the efforts of a male student to attract her attention, rumpling his hair and then walking back and forth in front of her as she sat in the front row. On another she noted Frank's courtesy in securing for her, while she was away, a front seat in the lecture hall.[27]

Writing to Mary Garrett, Carey put her relationship with Frank in a different light. In February 1880 she wrote that she and Frank had their "last skate of the season." They walked for a mile or so and followed a river in the woods. In the sunset they "had it all out—marriage, Godwinism, Christianity, etc. I concluded he might as well hear a woman's standpoint for once, so I told him." She found him "very good and really pure, I think, even in thought." Frank was protecting her reputation in his letters home, and she sought to be equally protective. In order not to hurt his appointment at Taylor

College, she warned Mary not to let anyone know that they discussed religion. It troubled Carey that in their Saturday evening visits in her room he talked so freely that Mamie could hear through the door; for their next talk she would get cotton for Mamie's ears. In answer to the implicit question, Carey insisted, "I am completely, radically over caring about him, only I am not as ashamed of it as I was when I wrote to Julia because he is yet, oh, Lucifer, how art thou fallen, far the nicest man I know. I think perhaps he is not as clever as Mr. Cadbury, but he is completely congenial."[28]

To Anna Shipley, who knew him well, Carey wrote of a changed man. In contrast to Richard Cadbury and her female friends, Frank had "gone halfway over to the Philistine camp," a phrase that Carey used in these years to suggest those who rejected the aestheticism of Algernon Charles Swinburne and Dante Gabriel Rossetti. He had a new sober manner: "I think he has lost a great deal of his enthusiasm, but no doubt Dr. Taylor and Amelia will find him all the more satisfactory." When Frank came to call, he abided by the proprieties, bringing with him his male chum "to chaperon him."[29]

Mary had some doubt about Carey's feelings, and in an April letter Carey was careful to clarify that Frank no longer cared for her and often talked of his fiancée. Several months later, in an offhand comment, Carey revealed to Mary that she had once been in love with Frank. She wrote, "You know, Mary, that I could not and would not ever fall in love again." Love was for her now, as it had been for Goethe, only a "dichter liebe," the love of a poet, an emotion useful for its literary value.[30]

To study with the distinguished scholar Ten Brink, Gummere left Leipzig for Strasbourg, a university closed to women. Thomas could not follow, but she did consider trying. In June 1880 she wrote home that she longed to hear Ten Brink. "I think I shall ask Mr. Gummere to ask him if ladies could not possibly attend the Strasbourg lectures."[31]

A letter from Frank, written from Strasbourg in August, shows him to be both friendly and deeply insensitive. He positively crowed over the "superior advantages" that Strasbourg, from which Thomas was barred, offered over Leipzig: "The atmosphere of study here is much sharper—more ozone about it—than in Leipzig." He reported that in the English course, "the best men are in it, and the seminar is a *real* seminar with disputation and critical work." He proposed that he and Thomas continue to write each other about what they were learning in their universities. "Our interests lie so near together, the army of Germanists in America is so small, the Philistines so many and mighty, that our combined sympathetic work will be brought into play." And then he added, in a sentence that must have been particularly galling to Thomas, "And, by the bye, I wish you could think of some work at Taylor College, Bryn Mawr, I should say." Although he was worried about his position at the future Bryn Mawr College, now in doubt after Taylor's death, he believed

"David Scull and James Whitall are very good friends to me and will not, I think, let me be thrown over." He then closed with a report that he would be traveling with "Richard F. Mott and family," a delicate way of including Amelia Mott. He did not mention that he had written to trustee David Scull for some kind of commitment, informing him that he had sold stock and a bookcase to finance the trip with his fiancée and stating his need of five hundred dollars to obtain his degree.[32]

Over a long period, Carey's friends, excepting Mamie, had counseled her to end her friendship with Frank. In the strongest terms her mother repeatedly questioned its propriety. In December 1880, with Frank in Strasbourg, Carey finally, albeit grudgingly, agreed. A long letter to Mary Thomas began with Carey's preference for women and her devotion to Mamie. As she allowed herself to address Mary's argument, she gave rein to what must have been her fantasy. Mary had stated that it was wrong for an unmarried woman to engage in a literary friendship with a man. Carey saw the danger: "there is always more intensity in a man's friendships for a woman than for another man, and I suppose it is just possible that it might result in his wife's . . . sinking into his mistress and his friend changing into his love (excellent, were it not for the wife)." Although Carey denied that this pertained to her relationship with Frank Gummere, it provides one clue to her behavior. It suggests that Carey— intent on retaining her autonomy, repulsed by thoughts of sexual intercourse with a man, and choosing the life of the mind over marriage—imagined herself as Frank's true love, satisfying his spiritual needs, while Amelia Mott served his lower nature as "mistress."[33]

The August 1880 letter was Carey Thomas' last personal communication from Francis Gummere. After her return from abroad, they were to live and work at close range. Gummere became a distinguished professor at Haverford and a leading folklorist. They were both to attend the same Quaker Meeting and the same public events, but Gummere was to avoid ever speaking to her. A clear report came in 1898, and it is telling. Carey wrote to Mary Garrett that she had heard at Haverford, "Mr. Gummere read a poor poem in exactly the same tones that so affected me at eighteen. That was the escape of my life." Whatever she felt in 1880, breaking free from confinement was the ultimate interpretation that Carey placed on the effect on her of Frank's engagement and marriage to Amelia Mott.[34]

III

ALTHOUGH Frank's letters sustained a collegial tone, Carey received provocative letters from his close friend Richard Cadbury. Carey had spent time with Richard when he was squiring Anna Shipley, and in June before she left for Europe they spent an afternoon together, rowing and getting soaked in a thunderstorm. Richard clearly was taken with Carey, but knowing Carey's "requirements as to certain correspondents" and admiring Carey's commitment to become a scholar, he agreed to keep his letters on a high plane. "I feel quite confident I can keep my friendship for you perfectly unmixed with any thoughts that would wrong you, and if they possibly should come I will respectfully retire."[35]

Carey's correspondence with him reads nothing like her letters home. In Leipzig, Carey allowed herself a flirtatious correspondence with Richard. It began when he was in Paris, writing poetic drama; it continued after he returned to Philadelphia and more mundane concerns. Carey's letters to Richard expressed a deep identification with him, centering on her reactions to the glories of European art and her desire to be a writer. They are passionate letters. More than any others they reveal the intensity of her aesthetic experiences.

To Richard she denied that scholarship mattered to her in any inner sense. She wrote about her aspirations to create. Despite the excitement she experienced as she listened to lectures at the University of Leipzig, she framed the conflict exactly as she had in Baltimore: study versus original work. She distanced herself from Germany, which she likened to "scholastic Europe in the Middle Ages," although she admitted, "It may be I shall be drawn in and race with the rest." Her real joy was poetry. The meaning of Europe was the inspiration that it allowed. She tried to convince Richard not to return home. "Don't go back to America! I, a woman, in Leipzig, and not alone, feel as if my goal were ten times as near here. The glimpse of pictures and cathedrals I have had flashed light into what was before unformed mass. Material that in America one must laboriously amass from poetry here lies at hand." In Carey's understanding, the subject of poetry was the European landscape and its history. Americans knew it only through literature, but the sojourner in Europe could experience it firsthand. She wrote to Richard that in the Gothic cathedral she "*felt* what sent men on the Crusades. . . . To *feel* a thing is far beyond knowledge." In her new enthusiasm she asserted that Swinburne, Alfred Tennyson, William Morris, Dante Gabriel Rossetti, Théophile Gautier, and Charles Baudelaire "have not felt strongly enough, have not put themselves, their impassioned ecstasy and agony into their work. [It is] perhaps because they could not, that their works are 'cheap show.' " She was setting her sights on Greece, Rome, and Venice, where she would store up her impressions for poetry. "Don't you think that thoughts come from every new sensation?" To Richard she revealed that late at night after Mamie fell asleep she tried to compose. Her poems were as yet unworthy, "mere spelling, putting word and word together."[36]

Richard's efforts to write a poem in the Swinburne manner made Carey envious. She criticized it carefully and promised to send him anything that she wrote in return. As early as her first November abroad, however, she knew the prospects were not good. "My experiments or rather the experiments I hoped to try here have come to an abrupt close." She needed all her time for study and to soak up impressions. She was clearly daunted by the examples before her. She wrote to Richard about Swinburne's poetic dramas: "*Atalanta* is modern in the best sense but *Erechtheus . . .* is truly *Greek*. If one has the lyrical power, that form is a wonderful one, but one which only Shelley and Swinburne have thus far been able to use." As a result, she had written nothing. In a more hopeful mood, Carey had earlier written to Mary Garrett. She felt that her reading of Swinburne was inspiring her efforts at poetry: "I feel as if my daemon had broken out of his bottle." She had sketched out her dramatic lyric, its scene set in Venice.[37]

How serious was Carey's hope to become a writer? Was it merely a part of her romantic correspondence with Richard and Mary, or did she feel it more deeply? Perhaps it was both. Carey's poetic aspirations related to the inner life that she shared with her intimate friends, male and female. In the past, with Francis Gummere and with Margaret Hicks, Carey used the poetry of Tennyson, the Brownings, and Swinburne as the language of feeling. As she reached out to Richard and Mary, she again picked up the skein. Because Carey and Mamie communed daily, no steady written record of their relationship exists. But when either took ill, the other stopped study to read poetry aloud.

Carey recorded her secret hope to be a creative artist most fully in her letters to Richard, but it existed apart from him. Although she gave an occasional hint in her letters home, Carey ultimately expressed her aspiration to her parents in the frame of a double plan. She would study, receive her degree, and attain the professorship that would allow her to live independently. That was required by the family's lack of money. She wished she were wealthy, or even could count on an annual income of six hundred dollars for life, so that she could give herself to art. But she was not and needed the income from a position. Despite her need to teach and write scholarly works, she hoped to be able to do something more. In the winter of her second year, she wrote that if she followed her plan of work, "I am almost sure of being able to be a successful professor and of writing on my subject in time." She continued, "Of course, this is not what I hope to do. I mean not *only* this, but even if I can only do this I shall be far more satisfied with it than with an ordinary life." Then she held out this possibility: "If, however, I develop a ray of genius for writing, perhaps thee will see me sitting up there in my study and scattering an occasional sonnet or novel upon the world too ecstatic to do anything else. I had rather live on a potato and sleep on a board and do ideal work than make millions other ways."[38]

What Carey Thomas did was to make an understanding with herself. During the term she would pursue scholarship, as diligently as any German

man in the university. But in the four months of university vacation each year she would travel, storing up impressions that she would later turn into poetry and fiction. In the early spring of her first year abroad she wrote to Richard, "I have decided now to make comparative literature my center, one might call it my circumference, and therein is its charm. Travel all vacations, four months of the year, take time for writing-practice, and take a degree at the end." Because she was a woman, her parents were "willing to extend the time to four years if needful."[39]

Carey never revealed this scheme to her parents. They had only agreed to give her six hundred dollars a year for three years, and this supplied no reserve beyond her living expenses in Leipzig. How could she justify the added outlay for travel? Carey began a complicated campaign to convince her parents that she was forced into travel by Mamie's pressure, that it cost little more than staying in Leipzig, and that she could borrow the extra amount from Mamie and pay her back in a future year. As early as November, Carey wrote that Mamie's mother was sending a much appreciated twenty dollars with her letters. She warned her parents not to talk to Mrs. Gwinn about expenses. They would not be able to convince Mamie's mother that they could not afford to let Carey travel. "She insists on thinking it is because thee thinks that I shall get all in Heaven anyway, and earth makes no difference." Carey agreed that she could refuse Mamie's demand, but added that "it seems hard when so little enables one to see so much." And she promised, "Next year I shall have no difficulty in living on much less."[40]

The first goal was an early spring trip to Italy during the long university recess. As March approached, Carey and Mamie made plans, booking pensions in Rome and Naples. One by one they faced the problems in their way. Carey's was money. Although she could not demand the extra, she could get it by pretending not to want it for herself. In late February, after reviewing her accounts, she wrote, "I came to the conclusion that I ought to give up Italy but really it does seem like depriving Mamie of perhaps her only chance." Carey did not insist on the trip, but nonetheless persisted. "I am very much troubled to know what to do. It would cost a hundred dollars extra. But then if I let this opportunity go I am afraid of never seeing Rome, Florence, and Naples." Finally she reported, "Mamie has been weeping over my doubts concerning Italy. She is very resigned and sweet if I think I ought not to go." Then Carey promised that if she went ahead to Italy, she would pay back her parents by economizing in future years.[41]

Carey and Mamie both faced parents who were opposed to their traveling unchaperoned. Carey offered statement after statement from her professors and their wives that it was perfectly respectable for two girls to go to Italy unaccompanied. Finally, she produced her trump card. Mrs. Gwinn had been so anxious about Mamie's trip to Italy that she had submitted to Reverdy

Johnson's judgment. In triumph Carey wrote that this conservative foe of women at Johns Hopkins University felt that Mamie and Carey should go, and Mrs. Gwinn had relented. Carey cautioned her father to say nothing about this. With plans made, Carey gave herself over to the study of art and Italian.[42]

Carey's canny manipulation of her parents for the money to travel repeated at long distance what she had learned in her household. As the eldest daughter in a large, prosperous, but debt-ridden family, she had discovered how to snatch. She knew better than to do so directly, as she had done at Howland with her mother's two pieces of crimson Brussels. She did so by showing what a good girl she was, how little it would cost, and by turning pleasure, Italy, into duty, her obligation to Mamie. Although this may leave some distaste about Carey's capacity for deception, her use of indirection, and her selfishness, it was absolutely essential to her success. Long before age twenty-three, Carey Thomas had learned how to get what she wanted. Had she been a more direct and more generous person, she would not have traveled to Italy, not gotten to study in Europe, not gone to Cornell. She would have remained in Baltimore as a traditional woman. Only by breaking through the texture of goodness and duty was it possible in the 1880s for an intelligent and strong-minded young woman to get what she needed to achieve in the public realm.

For the moment what she had gotten for herself was Italy. How she reveled in it! As the train neared Rome, she wept with joy. Rome was all that she had dreamed. She and Mamie dedicated themselves to art, visiting and revisiting the papal palace and the Sistine Chapel. Carey described herself and Mamie as the Siamese twins, never leaving each other's side, even at the cost of quarrels and disagreements about where to go and the route to take. Although Mamie saw the ruins as only "bricks and dirt," to Carey they were imbued with artistic and historic meaning. She enthused to Richard Cadbury about Italy: "Rome, Naples, Capri, Pompeii, Castellammare, Sorrento and Paestum—I have seen them all. At Paestum, I felt for the first time the Doric column. . . . Lizards, blue Mediterranean through the spaces, acanthus growing over the ruins. It was just as one would have had it." "Like a flash," the distinction between the classic gods and heroes revealed itself.[43]

This first trip was a lover of literature's visit. Carey and Mamie searched out the places described by Virgil and the tombs of poets. Carey read Nathaniel Hawthorne's *Marble Faun*, and it was often in her mind as she walked in the Borghese Gardens. Carey wrote to Richard that she had visited Shelley's grave and "had the degradation of *feeling* all the sentimental trash one reads about it. You know I have Shelley to thank, and through him Godwin, for almost all the light I walk by."[44]

The Italy of this visit stayed with Carey forever. What was it that so captivated her? The literary associations certainly, but also the vitality. Italy was fun. She described her happiest day: on the island of Capri, she and

Mamie secured donkeys to go up the steep hills to see the ruins of the villa of Tiberius. She enjoyed the uninhibited exchange between the old woman leading her donkey and the peasant women along the path. And the blue sky and the light.

Her greatest adventure was the exploration of the ruins of Cumae, so frightening that Baedeker warned against it. It was a chance to see the river entrance to the mythical Hades, and Carey determined not to miss it. The excursion was guided by several Italian men. Carey wrote home, "I made up my mind to go, so one of the men caught hold of my hands and held me on his back in that way. We went staggering down into the horrible black water up to his waist. After wading through, he put me on a stone in the midst of the flood and showed me the Sibyl's bath. Then for a moment I was left in darkness and far down the rocks I saw a light glimmer. He had taken the torch down to show me the path to Hades, a dreadful hole going into the bowels of the earth." Carey then polished off her day by eating thirty oysters, with appropriate feeling for their historic associations. In Italy the Minnie who had skated, walked on stilts, and scampered over Baltimore roofs was reborn as Carey the energetic, passionate, indefatigable traveler.[45]

Seen from the outside, she and Mamie were two proper American young women students using their vacations wisely as they stayed in women's pensions and examined works of art. This is how she tried to portray herself to her parents. But it is only a partial picture. Yes, Carey and Mamie looked at paintings and sculpture and compared their impressions with those of Ruskin and Hawthorne. But to Carey this had a meaning different from appreciation. She saw herself storing up impressions that she hoped would one day burst into poetry. To Richard Cadbury she confided that studying for a degree in Germany was the small price that she must pay for Italy. "Before the pictures, the constant springs of new intellectual and emotional life; and in the open air, a faun life, a background, a setting, a wherewithal to furbish forth one's imaginations. . . . I *know* that I shall have a better chance because of Italy. If I could I would never leave it."[46]

Yet it would be a mistake to see Italy as a means to any end. Carey tried to clarify this in a subsequent letter to Richard. She had been wrong to suggest that she was using her travels to store up material for poetry. "It is reaching the spot predestined by all one's longings. It is feeling tropical life in one's veins and mellowing, feeling that if a year of such life were granted one, some gorgeous flower must bloom a poem, or a statue."[47] Something deeply personal happened to Carey in her years abroad, something she particularly identified with Italy. She expressed it as "tropical life in one's veins," "mellowing," and "faun life." She dreamed that Italy would be the wellspring of poems that she would later write. Although the poems were never written, Italy remained associated with art, leisure, Mamie, and the pleasure of their life together.

Germany, by contrast, was the place of work. For eight months of the year, Carey Thomas threw herself into it. One must read Carey's statements in context to understand that her love of Italy made her commitments in Germany no less strong. In fact, she continued to work with enthusiasm. With Professor Curtius' aid she and Mamie Gwinn applied to study in Leipzig for a second year, and again Andrew White wrote in her behalf. Carey Thomas in her second year attended a full set of lectures and worked intensively with Wülcker and Zarncke. In contrast with her Johns Hopkins' experience, she was welcomed fully into all classes. Wülcker admitted her into his seminar and even gave her his notes for lectures she had missed. She also participated in Zarncke's seminar. She reported home that two times a week he held a quiz that was for her "splendid fun." Zarncke took a verse and called on a student to recite. For an hour, Zarncke questioned the student, leading him on "until in some wonderful way of Zarncke's own the whole thing is made as clear as daylight." Thomas was a full participant in the exercise. Zarncke had not yet called on her, "but I should not care if he did, as I am prepared." At a later time, however, when Zarncke asked her to be one of the evening readers, she decided against it. "I thought that perhaps the men might make it disagreeable for me." Because only six of the fifty-six students read, "it seemed putting myself forward." Zarncke was extremely cordial and offered to assist her. With this stimulation and encouragement, she felt, as she wrote to Mary Garrett, that she was now "on the inside track" of university work.[48]

Carey Thomas now had a divided consciousness. In her first two years abroad, Italy and Germany formed its poles. Germany represented science, the long hard hours of study to become a scholar. Italy was poetry, idealized passion, the core of her inner life.

CHAPTER 7

In My Way, Not Thine Exactly

O N JULY 12, 1880, Carey Thomas paid her mother an odd compliment. Carey reported that when Mamie had heard of Mary's broad appreciation of literature, she had exclaimed, "Why, I didn't know any one who did not belong to *us* . . . believed that." Carey explained that by *us*, she and Mamie meant "*nous autres*—the Gautier, Rossetti school." This is a telling sentence. Although it was a throwaway line in a letter devoted to other purposes, as with many such gestures, it had a major underlying import. As Carey seemingly was attempting to establish a bond of connection with her mother, she was declaring her independence from her. She was announcing that she and Mamie belonged to a coterie linked to the French novelist Théophile Gautier and the British Pre-Raphaelites.[1]

The context for Carey's self-revealing tribute begins in February 1880. In Rome, Carey Thomas got the news that an article she had written was to appear in *The Nation*. She had published some pieces in *The Quaker Alumnus* but this was the first time that she had reached out to a non-Quaker audience. The unsigned piece in *The Nation* was really only a paragraph describing a frieze excavated at Pergamus and held by the German government. But to Thomas it offered the promising prospect that she could earn money by writing about her experiences and reflections in Europe for American periodicals. The article reached her in April. Though she was very pleased, she did not like the additions that her mother had made and wrote to her that they were "rather too romantic for the severe style I want to cultivate." She immediately began to write another piece and in June sent it off to her parents to forward first to *The Atlantic*, then to *Scribner's Monthly* and *Harper's New Monthly Magazine*. Her parents were shocked at its content. Mary Whitall Thomas reacted swiftly and clearly: "Naked female backs and thighs and knees are not subjects that ought to be discussed promiscuously." It was not that Carey Thomas herself should not think such words—the letter reflected no condemnation of the daughter's state of mind—only that she must not express them publicly. To do so was to breach a code. Her frank language would offend and disgust her friends and relatives. Mary wrote, "Imagine Uncle Reverdy reading it!!," thinking of Reverdy Johnson, Jr., Mamie's highly regarded uncle. Isolated, Carey and Mamie had forgotten that they lived in a world filled with "wicked and impure people." By going abroad to study, Carey had placed herself in a position that "to say the least is a little questionable." As a result, she must take particular care to do nothing that might offer conservative critics any grounds of criticism. James Carey Thomas reacted even more strongly. Mary reported that "he was astonished that thee should think for one moment of publishing such a thing." It would be "fatal to the cause thee wishes advanced."[2]

Carey disagreed. She had left out the word "breast" for her mother's sake but felt that Mary was too strict about other points. To leave out mention of the body and discussion of popes' wives and daughters would take away the only entertaining aspects of the piece. "If thee met it and didn't know it was mine, I am sure thee would have been amused." Immediately after this statement, Carey declared her allegiance to the Gautier-Rossetti school.[3]

In the famous preface to his novel *Mademoiselle de Maupin*, published in 1835, Gautier set out the principles that were to govern all his writing. "Nothing is really beautiful unless it is useless," he declared. It was a declaration of aesthetic independence. Art is not a tool of politics, religion, or philosophy; the aim of art is the exploration of ideal beauty. Heady words when they were first published, they still had power in 1880. They proclaimed the supremacy of art and beauty against the claims of family and Quaker Meeting.[4]

And Rossetti? Carey Thomas' conjunction of Gautier with Dante Gabriel Rossetti, the British poet and painter, is curious, and it is one that would not ordinarily have been made in 1880. Although Carey enjoyed Rossetti's poems and responded to his paintings when she saw them two years later, in the 1880 letter to her mother Rossetti was a stand-in for the more controversial Algernon Charles Swinburne. Very soon after the letter to her mother, Carey wrote to Mary Garrett a long letter about her dreams of art. Mamie was then reading aloud to her a Swinburne chorus, and Carey wrote, "It is lovelier than even my remembrance of it. I do not think any one of the past generation can realize the rapture and fire which this new Pre-Raphaelite school strikes to our hearts."[5] In talking to her mother about art, even in an aside, Rossetti, the leading Pre-Raphaelite, was a safer choice than Carey's true artistic passion, Swinburne. More than any of his English contemporaries, Swinburne had insisted on the utter independence of art from standards outside itself, on the necessity that art be free of service to religion and morality. Swinburne's poetry had long shaped Carey Thomas' consciousness.

The sense of herself as one of "nous autres" was an important part of Carey Thomas' self-definition. Beyond a devotion to ideal beauty, what did the phrase mean to her? The answer involves both art and love. By "nous autres"

Carey Thomas meant a band of devoted female souls committed to the pursuit of art. To be one of nous autres meant both attachment to aesthetic principles and commitment to building a life with women.

It was abroad that Carey made a final resolve never to marry. Family letters were filled with the upcoming marriage of her cousin Bessie Nicholson. Her Cornell smash Margaret Hicks interspersed her letters with college gossip about engagements and marriage. In August 1880 in the Milan cathedral Carey opened one of Margaret's letters in the anticipation of pleasure. As Margaret confided her indecision about whether to pursue architecture or literary studies, Carey was beguiled, only to be jolted by the letter's end: Margaret was giving up her life's work because she was engaged to Karl Volkmann, their Cornell contemporary.

Carey immediately answered Margaret. "In one way your engagement was no shock," she wrote, for "since that first fall term at Cornell I have known that Mr. Volkmann was in love with you." The major source of the conflicts between Carey and Margaret at Cornell was out in the open. Though not surprised, Carey was "bitterly disappointed" for she had hoped that Margaret "would care more for other things." Carey then wrote in a way that revealed a great deal about how she in 1880 interpreted the ending of her relationship with Francis Gummere. "I think that every girl falls in love with one of the first two or three men who have ever fallen in love with her. This has been substantiated by the experience of every girl I have ever known. If she does not yield to it and devotes herself to other things, she is as sure to get over it as men are." But while men recover to turn their attentions to more accommodating women, the young woman who refuses marriage can devote herself to work. Though she did not idealize work, Carey believed that "each one has his or her independent thought life to live and, of course, must be able to express this freely in some work." To marry was to stifle this basic human need. Although the single state might not be necessary forever, it was for the present. "Now I do not think there is a man who realizes that liberty and money, independence and 'life work' are as much to a woman as to himself. Every time I have expressed this to a man he says 'is it *possible* women feel so. I always thought that a girl when she fell in love gave up all that and considered her husband's work hers.' " As Carey bid Margaret "good night," she closed, "You know I wish you every happiness even though it be of the last kind that I should ever have chosen for you. What right have I to choose? None. Only the fancied right that having cared for you very much during two very pleasant years gives, and after all that is four years ago."[6]

Carey rather flippantly wrote home that she always knew that Miss Hicks would marry Mr. Volkmann "as soon as she got out of my influence. . . . I shall give her up, of course." But she could not dismiss her that easily. With great passion Margaret Hicks wrote back, answering every one of Carey's

arguments. She had found in Karl Volkmann her "life's love," and he sympathized with her aspirations that were as dear to him as his own. No direct
response survives. Carey paid close attention to Margaret's letter, however, for
three months later she referred to it. What is significant is the context.[7]

In Baltimore, tantalized by thoughts of Francis Gummere, Carey had
seen the decision not to marry as renunciation. Her response to Margaret's
engagement recalled that spirit in its advocacy of a young woman's refusal to
yield to a man's love. But by the time Carey wrote, the summer of 1880, she
had actually moved on to new ground. Living an intense life with Mamie in
Europe, she was reinterpreting her choice as the positive selection of a woman,
not a man. Three months later, on a November day after Mamie had nursed
her through a severe headache by reading poetry to her, she wrote to her
mother that Bessie King had a theory that one should wait until age sixty to
marry in order to have a companion in one's old age. Though this had its
points, Carey believed "in sticking to one's principles at all costs." Then she
went on to suggest that "sticking to one's principles" did not involve any loss.
Recalling Margaret's words, Carey suggested that she had a "life's love." Carey
wrote, "If it were only possible for women to elect women as well as men for
a 'life's love,' as Miss Hicks writes, all reason for an intellectual woman's
marriage would be gone. It *is* possible, but if families would only regard it in
that light!" Carey thought that a woman made a better partner for another
woman: "A priori women understand women better, are more sympathetic,
more unselfish." Taking a step back, and indirectly telling her parents that she
herself was thinking of Mamie in this vein, she wrote, "I believe that it will
be, indeed is already becoming, one of the effects of advanced education for
women."[8]

Carey resumed her thoughts about marriage to a man in February 1881.
This time the provocation was Richard Cadbury. In letters from Philadelphia
he pressed the case for marriage. Though he spoke in the abstract—"the sweet
privileges of wife and mother are the duty of every woman"—he obviously left
some ambiguity in Carey's mind (and that of her mother) as to his intentions.
Carey answered him that he simply did not know the life of girls. They live
under the domination of their fathers, have a few short society years, feel no
sense of direction, and turn to marriage as a lesser bondage. "Public and family
opinion is such as to force them into marriage, as a profession." Such marriages
did not lead to happiness. Through the women of her family, she had heard
of "hundreds of unhappy married women—the majority are unhappy."
Women are like men, and "a life devoid of wider interest is a blank, be it
married or unmarried." Thinking of her mother, she wrote that religion had
partly filled the void, "but eight children do not, any more than they would
yours."

She corrected Richard, "It is no woman's *duty* to marry; whether she be in love or not, it is her duty to consider true marriage, if you choose, a completion to life, but a completion which may come or may not but will surely not come if she marry without love, or if the man whom she loves be in any way a hindrance to her attaining the highest that she desires. . . . Exactly so, I think it is with a man." Then she stated her full revision. "In a transition state I think it would be quite often a *duty* and a pleasure not to marry until the supply of part of either sex equaled the raised demand." With this she concluded that Richard's provocative tone required their correspondence to end.[9]

Carey had sent Richard's letters to her mother. Mary Thomas had long urged Carey to break off the correspondence. Carey had refused to do so. She saw no reason why it was necessary, and "besides, it would be basest treachery." She did agree to send her his last letter "just to show thee how nice he is—in my way, not thine exactly." As Richard pressed Carey about marriage, Mary suggested to Carey that she might think about the idea. Carey was taken aback: "How thee can say, mother, knowing my theories as thee does, that I would be happier married, I cannot understand. Could thee think I would give up all I care for and have lived in, or does thee think I have been pretending? I feel absolutely *no* need of marriage. I could not find a man as nice as my girl friends."[10]

For what other reason, Mary had implied, did she continue to correspond with Richard? Carey answered, "The reason I cling to my 'Bohemian friendships' is that I don't want to get one-sided." Friendship was one thing; marriage was another. "Marriage means loss of freedom, poverty, and a *personal* subjection for which I see absolutely no compensation. Thee need not try to persuade me that thee would be happy in it without thy religious interest. Suppose thee had to sacrifice this, would thee do it? So please do not think so. . . . Thee must make up thy mind, sweetest mother, to have one old maid daughter." Thinking perhaps of Richard, she added, "If I only don't fall in love, for I wish to be spared the struggle, though, of course, the result would be the same." Two days after writing to her mother, Carey had a change of heart about ending her correspondence with Richard. She wrote him a light-hearted note, apologizing for mounting the rostrum in women's cause, and agreeing to "shake hands across the ocean" if Richard in turn would cease his "impertinences."[11]

Although Carey could speak in the abstract about the choice of a woman for a "life's love," she seldom wrote directly about her feelings for Mamie. In the spring of her first year abroad, when she thought that Julia Rogers might join them in Leipzig, she admitted that, although she would accept Julia into their ménage, "Of course, selfishly I should rather live as Mamie and I have been, because I love Mamie far more dearly and we agree together perfectly." As Christmas of her second year approached, Carey felt depressed and worried.

She was thinking about many elements of her life, her isolation from other university students, her anxiety about where she would take her degree, the restrictions that studying for the degree would place on her travel, and the effect of that on Mamie. She was afraid for Mamie to travel alone. Her guard lowered, Carey wrote, "I should not care if I did not love her, but I must say, as far as I can be outside of thee and Father, I am wrapped up in her. She has faults, of course, but she just suits me."[12]

Through revealing details or asides, some glimpses of Carey and Mamie's domestic life together in Europe come through the veil of discretion. The veil is thick, however, for Carey Thomas shared her era's reticence about references to the body. During her pregnancies while Carey was away from home, her mother had given only the faintest hint of her condition. Carey herself, through euphemisms, referred to menstruation only when she experienced some complication she regarded as related. Thus statements relating to private aspects of her life abroad with Mamie only come by indirection. When Carey answered her mother's query about how she dressed, she reassured her that she looked quite proper in the brown outfit that she wore to lectures. On returning home, however, she and Mamie immediately retired to their wrappers. Carey's was her very worn red one. Since Mamie's two from home had fallen apart, she put on "her gorgeous black Antwerp silk one with lace and cherry ribbons." Carey commented, "We both enjoy this gorgeousness." For the Christmas break in her second year, Carey and Mamie planned to visit James Thomas' younger brother and wife, Richard and Anna Thomas, then living in Vienna. Carey was astounded that Anna planned to house the two of them in her pension in the room of an unknown Miss Darling. "Mamie says she knows she can't undress for embarrassment. . . . It will be a great trial to us that we can't leave our clothes in their two little round rings on the floor."[13]

Although she preferred nude statues, actual human nudity embarrassed her. Carey relayed home a story told by Gertrude Mead of her medicinal bath taken in Berlin among nude women. By contrast, baths in Vienna and New York were "managed with decency. Everybody has on a chemise." In 1881 in Rome, however, when she took a Roman bath with Mamie, she commented to her mother that she was not embarrassed; but she did not mention whether or not it was taken partially clothed. Private bathing in the parlor-study of their Leipzig suite was primitive to one who knew the pleasures of a bathroom and servants. Carey described that after heating the water in a saucepan on the stove, "each performs our ablutions in a basin on a chair, with our backs to each other." In a characteristic Careyism, she followed, "We revenge ourselves [against the landlady] by using as much water as possible." What this suggests is that throughout their four years in Europe, Carey and Mamie retained some level of personal modesty about their unclothed bodies.[14]

In Carey's case, more than modesty was at issue, since Carey had been badly burned over much of her body as a child. From her first year at Howland until middle age, there is no reference in any of her correspondence to the burn or to the scars that it left. Weakness and pain that the scar tissue caused much later in Carey's life and the medical records of its treatment shed some light. The scars from the burn covered her right thigh and hip and extended to her lower abdomen. It may have reached her mons veneris, preventing there the growth of pubic hair. Nineteenth-century clothing, even that worn in swimming, always covered the scar tissue, adding perhaps an additional reason for Carey to remain dressed. Although at a deeper level there is no way to know what the scars meant to Carey, there is no hint at any point in her life that they caused her to feel inadequate in any way or of lesser worth than others.

Carey did not, however, seem beautiful to herself, though she acknowledged and admired the beauty of her mother and of other women. Her face was, in Mamie's word, "comely"; her brown eyes, vivid. Through posed studio photographs one can perceive something of her good looks; but not the intensity, the animation, the hunger for life. Her movements were energetic; her gestures, emphatic; her carriage, informal and unstudied. It was her vivacity and the light in her brown eyes that drew others to Carey.[15]

Mamie was beautiful by nineteenth-century standards. Helen Thomas' childhood memory of Mamie in these years was as tall, slender, languid, with pale skin and dark curly hair. Mamie's personal wealth allowed her to indulge her sense of style, the "gorgeousness" that Carey admired in her black Antwerp silk wrapper.

It was in their travels that Carey and Mamie's deep emotional bond was forged. Energetic and restless as she was, Carey had few moments in her long life when she was completely, totally satisfied. She had such a moment in September 1880 when on a gondola in Venice with Mamie she reached the apotheosis of personal happiness. The two hired a "pet gondolier" by the day; each evening, after the day's sightseeing was done, he rowed them up the Grand Canal and into the lagoon. Carey wrote to her mother, "We feel as if we were sailing out into eternity." As she tried to convey such earthly pleasures to her mother, she put it in Mary Thomas' language: she must come to Italy and see it herself, for "there won't be any Venice in Heaven." To Carey, such exquisite delight was beyond anything the Christian afterlife could offer.[16]

Mamie was profoundly identified with both travel to Italy and with poetry. In Baltimore, Carey had fallen in love with her in the familiar way, "We talked and read Swinburne." Mamie was intensely literary. She knew English poetry well and wrote poems that Carey admired. In her work mode, Carey feared her as "a terrible temptation," an epitome of the "dilettante spirit." It was Mamie's influence above all that drew Carey to imagine a part of herself as an artist and to think of the travel in her years abroad as cultivating aesthetic sensibility.[17]

Mamie chafed under the restrictions of the academic year. By November of their second year it was clear that she would not try for a degree abroad. As Carey wrote to Mary Garrett, "She hates the work."[18] Without Carey's driving ambition or her love of scholarship, Mamie turned away from graduate work to read the literature that pleased her and to focus on travel during the long vacations. With her, especially on trips to the Italian sun, Carey imagined herself an artist and free spirit.

How cautiously Carey wrote of this to her parents. In July 1880 she carefully informed her mother that she had seen many theatrical performances and had read the most forbidden of contemporary literature. In order to do so, she framed her confession in moral terms. She first dealt with theater. She had seen a great deal of it in Germany for it was cheap and good. She heard many famous singers and actors. "The result is that I have *almost* lost my desire to go, and three times Mamie and I have left before the end from sheer boredom. . . . The theater now seems to me the stupidest and most innocent amusement, rarely to be preferred to a book. Before, it was fairyland. See how much better my present state is."

Next, she faced the issue of "improper books." She would raise a daughter to read the authors that she had read: Honoré de Balzac, Alfred de Musset, Gautier, Gustave Flaubert, and Émile Zola. She had read them because they were available and quoted and because she "considered a literary education incomplete without them." She had just finished Zola's *L'Assommoir* and *Nana*. "Instead of doing me any harm, I feel as if such books had done me good. They have deprived me of any desire to read a book because it is improper." More important, they had performed the function that in her 1878 private diary she had given to her father's medical books: "They have so opened my eyes that I . . . feel better able to take care of myself and to regulate my own life. . . . Instead of being a great unknown factor in literature, all books on such subjects assume their proper place." Though such books were useful, they ranked "below ideal books, as a book on disease, useful as it may be, from its nature stands below a poem." For a person with literary judgment they are not harmful. "Such a one will be sure to emerge thinking them distasteful and stupid. I never read a more stupid book than Zola's *Nana*. Yet, like the theater, so long as I had not read them (or samples of them), they possessed an attraction which has now *utterly* vanished."[19]

On analysis, this letter is most clever. It seeks common ground with Mary at the same time that it establishes that Carey has acted in direct violation of her wishes. Moreover, Carey really gives no quarter. What she suggests is that by delving into the forbidden contemporary literature and theater, she has lost her unnatural attraction to them. Though she does register disgust at Émile Zola's *Nana*, whose extreme realism did offend her, she does not comment on her reaction to Zola's other works, which she admired, or to other authors.

In letters to Mary Garrett, Carey wrote of the many books by Zola that she was reading during this period, along with Flaubert and Balzac. Although she found *Une Page d'amour* only "mildly interesting," *La Faute de l'abbé Mouret* was, she stated, "a novel that takes the breath of one's imagination." She saw much theater in her years abroad. Her reaction to Sarah Bernhardt as Camille hardly fit the high-minded tone she took with her mother. To Mary she wrote, "Do you remember the quick tigerlike way she has of drawing Armand's face down to hers; it makes one shiver from head to foot. No, I never was so moved."[20]

Why would Carey write to her mother about theatergoing and novel-reading at all? She may have feared that, through friendship and university associations, word of her aesthetic ventures would get home. By owning up, she forestalled her parents' anger and presented her actions in an acceptable light. In addition, the part of Carey who was an aesthete felt the need to make some contact with home, even if she distorted her own image.

II

HOME REMAINED very important to her, but in her first two years abroad Carey's relations with her parents were complicated by repeated reminders that she did not compose the center of their universe. It came to her most dramatically when she was awaiting word on her plan to bring her desire for a position at Taylor College in Bryn Mawr to the attention of the trustees. When Mary Whitall Thomas received her daughter's letter, she was confronting the awful fact of the death of her own mother. On February 17, 1880, Carey got the news. Mamie brought the letter when she met Carey at Zarncke's lecture. Carey opened it just as Zarncke entered the lecture room. She spent the hour "choking with tears." Mary Whitall's death came as a tremendous shock. Carey was relieved that her grandmother had not suffered, "but it does seem perfectly dreadful to me not to have been there and . . . never to see her again." Carey mourned, "Nothing ever can take her place." Coming three years after the death of her husband, Mary Whitall's passing meant the end of the family that had gathered each New Year's Day. "This seems to me the final breaking up of the family."[21]

A week later, Carey still felt desolate. Any hope of an afterlife did her no good. As she wrote to her mother, "It is not the *least* consolation to me to feel that there may be a possibility of seeing Grandma again as a disembodied spirit. Without her cap and rocking chair and loving bright words I can't imagine her." With little sense of the injury her words might cause, she wrote that her only comfort was that she could feel so bereft only twice more—when Mary and James Thomas died.[22]

Her grandmother's death caused Carey enormous anxiety. In the months that followed, she had terrible nightmares about the death of her father and siblings. In fact, she had cause. Margaret got scarlet fever; Grace, the mumps; Frank was also stricken, and his hearing was affected. Carey fretted about each child and about her mother's health. Her fears threatened to drag her down during a time of personal exploration, growth, and pleasure.

When she returned to Leipzig after her first vacation in Italy Carey immediately began a summer campaign to secure her next trip. This was a difficult task given that she had overspent on the first and was indebted to Mamie. After her grandmother's death, part of the Whitall estate came to Mary Thomas, but it was tied up in property; and Carey no longer had the two to three hundred dollars a year that her grandmother had promised her. Further complicating Carey's campaign was a growing sense of her mother's estrangement. Her first response was anger. On May 30, after looking over her mother's letters, she wrote, "I have come to the conclusion that thy letters get less and less nice. I suppose thee is displeased at something in my letters or perhaps thee is too busy even to take an hour a week to write at leisure." Carey was jealous of the other claims on Mary's time and demanded her share. She knew it was not only family ties that kept Mary from writing longer letters, it was her religious and reform work; "but even I cannot help wishing for more of thee although I am so far away."[23]

Much to her shock and chagrin, Carey learned that Mary Thomas had written skimpily because she had been ill. All of Carey's fears welled up. She wrote immediately, expressing her regret at having accused Mary of neglect. "The one thing I am perfectly sure of is that [I] love thee more dearly than anything else, and I just could not live if thee died while I was away." In this June 22 letter Carey revealed the depth of her feeling for her mother. "I don't believe any of thy other children can love thee as much because thee has not been with them as much as thee has with me, and anyhow it is different." Carey recognized that her irreligion had caused a wedge to come between them. As if returning to their painful late-night talk of eighteen months before, she again put the burden of alienation on Mary's shoulders. "And then to think that something so involuntary, just a little change, or not being able to believe as much as thee does in one direction, should make it impossible for me ever to be satisfactory to thee sometimes almost makes me despair."[24]

Carey acknowledged again her intolerance and selfishness in Baltimore in the face of parental forbearance and generosity. Then she shifted the plane to her ambition. "I see myself how dreadful it must be to have a daughter who wishes to do all sorts of out-of-the-way things and who really would (and I don't know that I can do anything with them eventually) be very miserable without books." In a most curious statement, Carey suggested that her combination of drive and affection made her—as a woman—hell to live with: "If I were a man and married such a woman as I am, I think I should cut my throat, and the worst of it is that I neither can help caring about study, nor can I help wishing to be satisfactory to thee."[25]

Carey unleased a flood of homesick commentary on her life abroad. Then, in a most curious reversal, Carey snapped out of her mood, "I am not unhappy. I am happy, in one way happier than I ever was, and Mamie is as satisfactory as any friend or husband could be. It is only that my heart aches to see thee, and father, too, but he's a man and so that's different. I wish to kiss thee and see thy pretty soft hair and everything." Such intimate memories evoked again her homesickness. Carey ended with a heartfelt plea, "Please don't give me up."[26]

Carey's anguished letter reveals elements of her emerging consciousness. Her love for her mother remained for her the central bond, different from the love for her father. It was a love more intense because Carey was the eldest and because she had repossessed her mother after her life-threatening burn. In her mind, nothing should erode or challenge that love. Yet Mary had the other children, a career as a minister and reformer, and enthusiasm for an evangelical faith that left Carey cold. Mary's continued insistence that her Carey give herself to Christ and accept the Quaker creed meant that daughter could never satisfy mother. It was a wound that could not heal. And now Carey sensed that her love of books and her ambition were being defined in the same terms. Mary had supported her daughter's struggle for higher education—at Howland, Cornell, and Johns Hopkins—and she had won Germany for her. But now, as Carey studied abroad and began to develop her plans to take a degree, she sensed that to follow her daemon set her at odds with her mother. Although she had dreamed since girlhood of a life as an independent woman, her long sojourn in Leipzig was her first clear violation of feminine codes. At some level Carey understood that her commitment to scholarship and art threatened a basic tenet of the female world, that relationships were more important than ambition or ideas. Thus she imagined herself as the murderous husband of a wife who loved both him and books.

As Mary and James Thomas began to realize, in living and traveling abroad with Mamie, Carey was clearly creating a way of life quite different from that of Baltimore Friends. In trying to characterize Richard, Carey had called him nice "in my way, not thine exactly." The phrase serves as a hallmark of the growing difference between herself and her parents.

Carey liked to dwell on some of the more amusing forms of generational difference. She constantly teased her mother about Mary's preference for clothing statues with discreet—and to Carey, disfiguring—fig leaves. At one point she noted, "Mamie and I have been holding an animated discussion today as to why our mothers, and indeed the past generation generally, never sit with their legs over the backs or arms of chairs, as we and all the girls we have ever known do. We have concluded that it must be mysteriously connected with wearing chemises and disliking to look at nude statues and all your other charming inconsistencies."[27]

If such teasing worried James and Mary about the direction that Carey's thoughts were taking, it was not because in 1880 they feared for her character. They worried about her reputation. While she was abroad they continued to instruct her in the ways of their conservative world. They repeatedly explained to her that a woman in her position must take special care so as not to be misunderstood. The reputation of a woman alone was at great risk. Nothing Carey Thomas should do, say, or wear should confirm suspicions that she deserved reproach. Word of any impropriety in dress or manner could get back to Baltimore.

It is for this reason that they sought to censor anything that she might write from abroad. After they muffled her prose in the summer of 1880, Thomas wrote no more articles. She took from this experience a lesson that proved central to her development. What she might write should never be either merely aesthetic expression or a way of making money. Printed words framed the public perception of her as a person. That perception was one that she must cultivate carefully if she was to advance her ambitions.

To this lesson in the ways of the world she was adding instruction from Mamie about class. Carey had once accused Margaret Hicks of having no discrimination. Now she stood similarly accused by Mamie. In Mamie's eyes Carey simply could not see that Eva Channing and her mother were beneath their notice, or, as she later put it, that they were "a glaring fact" that Carey perceived as "a delicate nuance."[28] Mamie set out to tame Carey's public persona. She would rein in Carey's intensity and spontaneity in her relationships with others. In part this sprang from jealousy: Mamie wanted to have Carey all to herself. But in part Mamie was offering guidance in Baltimore upper-class feminine behavior. Alone with Mamie, Carey might read Swinburne and Rossetti; but in public, she must learn to cloak herself in restraint.

Tutored by Mamie, Carey found she had lessons to teach her parents about form. By her second year abroad Carey began to imagine her future. Although she had never met a woman who embodied what she wanted to be, she was coming to have a clear notion of her. She was to be an aristocratic scholar living an independent life of culture and creativity. Unfortunately, as her parents talked of her in Baltimore, they interpreted to their world that she was in Europe preparing to teach.

Carey learned of this when Mary Garrett came abroad with her parents in the summer of 1880. Carey and Mamie met the Garrett entourage in Switzerland. As Mamie, instead of joining Carey on a strenuous climbing expedition, visited with the senior Garretts, "Mr. Garrett told Mamie that the only sensible explanation he had heard of my going abroad was father's. He said I wanted to '*teach*.' Mr. Garrett then went on to say that, of course, with a large family as father had, etc., and talked most disagreeably." Mamie clearly saw that James Thomas' portrayal of Carey was a violation of upper-class codes of gentility. Carey continued the report: "Mamie was furious and said, of course, that there was no need of my teaching and that I never expected to *teach*, but only if I found it a means of influence to become a professor, just as she herself would like to, etc." After Carey talked with Mary about her father's mistaken understanding, "Mr. Garrett's manner changed. Before, he treated me more as a dependent." Carey attempted to clarify this to her mother. "So far from '*wishing* to teach,' I consider it a great misfortune, only second to Mary's and Mamie's, who can't get even the liberty that gives. . . . If father is hard pressed, let him say that I desire to be a *scholar*."[29]

The distinction was a difficult one for Carey's parents, and it took another round of letters to set them straight. Carey tried to place her position on a ground higher than that of society's standards. "Thee ought to know how little I care of anyone's opinion in Baltimore. I am already consigned to perdition, anyhow," she wrote in October 1880. The issue involved, however, "the cause of women." Carey Thomas must never seem to be driven by the need to support herself. "To say that I am in Germany fitting myself to teach has but one interpretation: Mr. Garrett's. To say I wish to be a scholar has no disadvantage." She was in Europe to imbibe culture and to become a scholar fit for creative work. Yes, she might become a college professor, but this was not teaching. It existed on a higher plane of value and thereby carried "theoretical weight."[30]

Carey was—and remained—grateful for her mother's encouragement that gave her Europe. Grateful, yet continually, naggingly unsatisfied. Pushing, always pushing for more, Carey constantly returned to her limited funds, her desire for travel, her need for culture, her obligations to Mamie. The Thomas household was, as always, in debt. James Whitall gave to his sister Mary $1,000 to pay her overdue bills in 1880 (and repeated this in years to come), a sum equivalent in today's dollars to roughly $15,000. He also contributed the $200 to Carey that his late mother had given. Carey saw the money coming to Mary as opportunity. Mary could travel in Europe. A second thought, never expressed, was that Carey might broaden her own sights and use additional money for travel. Europe was culture, and she must store it up for the long life ahead. On her return to Leipzig at the end of their April 1880 trip, Carey wrote, "I could die much more contentedly now, and, as Mamie says, it is even happier to live knowing that such a place as Italy exists, though one *is* exiled." In the following year Carey dealt with her feeling of exile by returning to Italy at every opportunity. In the intervening months she anticipated the next trip, in which she would "let the palaces and statues and Italian sun and color soak in."[31]

And yet, there was the other side. Carey Thomas was finding herself, not only as the lover of art in Italy, but also as the scholar in Germany. At times she found it difficult to attain the proper balance of study and travel. Mamie planned their trips and was always seeking more time for them to be away. Mary Garrett, then in Europe, was more sympathetic to Carey Thomas' ambitions. On the last day of 1880, Carey wrote to her: "A change has come over the spirit of my dream this year. I have leapt into a passionateness which I only knew before by fits. I do not care for anything except to try for the realization of some dreams. I hardly care to tell Mamie how fully this is so lest she should think the traveling she enjoys so intensely is a bore to me. It is not so." Carey went on to use the biblical language that was still a part of her. "It is only that I feel as if all that might come afterwards . . . is a selling one's birthright." Carey did admit that if she could see Mary, however, away from the Garrett entourage, "then perhaps my hunger for the potage would be too great to control." In this complicated image, not only was she telling Mary what a temptation she was, she was saying something about the claims of scholarship and travel. Carey Thomas felt like Esau: scholarship was her "birthright"; travel loomed like the mess of "potage" that she might trade for it, the immediate gratification that sacrificed her larger goal.[32]

Less than two weeks later, she again wrote to Mary, this time seeking some reassurance as she presented her claims against Mamie's. "Today I went into Mamie's study and found her sitting with her hands full of candy, weeping and eating both at once." Anticipating the Easter break, Carey Thomas had told Mamie that she must stay in Leipzig to work. Each vacation she found herself losing ground, for it took weeks to catch up the "broken threads" of her work. "It sounds improbable, but philology is such horridly confused stuff that it is true." In her first year, long vacations did not matter. But in her second year, it had changed. "Now, if ever, work tells." By traveling so much, Carey Thomas was delaying her degree. "I believe if I had studied right through I could have tried for my doctorate this winter. Now it will be next winter, and if we travel this spring and summer, it will be the winter after that—four years." It could not be solved by their separating; Mamie could not travel alone. Even in this letter, however, devoted as it was to pleading her case for scholarship above travel, Carey expressed the other side: "Lectures seem dry bones after the realities of the Belvedere and of the Dresden gallery."[33]

In the summer of 1881, however, Carey and Mamie were to have little time alone and no Italy. Mary and James Thomas came abroad, brought by a desire to see their daughter, the English Yearly Meeting, and the doctor's need for a respite from overwork. Carey had longed for this chance to see her mother and for her mother to see Europe. She wrote lengthy letters of instruction, telling Mary Thomas just how she should travel and what she should see. A complicating factor was the younger children. Once Carey knew that her advice that they be left at home had not been taken, she lobbied for their remaining with a family in England. Mary's plan differed, and she brought Helen, called Nell, and Frank to Leipzig to stay with Carey and Mamie while she and James traveled in Italy. Carey had suggested this the year before, but once it impended she took a different view, opposing it on the grounds that it was unfair to Mamie. However, Mamie relented and, in return for a week in Paris with Carey, agreed to take the children to the park each day.

Carey's letters reveal little about this visit. But after her eldest sister's death, Helen Thomas Flexner remembered it clearly in her memoir *A Quaker Childhood*. She had been very close to Carey in Baltimore; but in Leipzig found her a distant, "unapproachable" figure. While Carey studied, Frank and Nell were watched by Mamie. Helen Thomas recalled her sense of Mamie: "Her very appearance fascinated me. Tall and exceedingly slender with crinkly black hair and pale skin, she was quite different from anyone I knew . . . languid." Mamie read Swinburne's poems to Helen; Helen memorized "The Garden of Proserpine."[34]

It was on Sundays, when Carey joined Mamie and the children, that conflict erupted. Carey secured Sunday breakfast by dashing across the street and purchasing it at a shop. Nine-year-old Nell objected to food purchased on the Lord's day. She was shocked at Carey's proposal that they attend a concert in the Rosenthal, the city's great park, and insisted that to do so was a sin that her mother would not want her to commit. By Helen's telling, Carey responded, "Did not Mother tell thee that thee was to obey me? . . . I wish thee to go to the concert. If it's a sin, it is my sin, not thine. Run get thy hat and come along!" Nell felt most violated by Carey's dressing Frank as a girl so that he might enter the public bath with them during the hours reserved for women. When Nell insisted that "Frank's masquerading as a girl would be acting a lie, Carey's face suddenly lost its look of gay energy and grew very stern and the voice in which she spoke to me was vehement." Calling Helen "a very self-willed, disobedient little girl," Carey insisted that her opposition was "outrageous," that she would not be "bothered" with her "foolishness any longer," and proceeded to take both children to bathe. To Mary Garrett, Carey was candid about the children: "Frank and Nell are the most absurd little prigs. Mamie and I consider it our mission to liberalize them."[35]

Nell accepted Carey's indignities in the expectation that Mary Thomas would defend her youngest daughter's Quaker righteousness. When her mother returned, Nell patiently bided her time while Carey and Mary talked. Nell realized that the two had much to say to each other after two years. Moreover, "the importance of my sister to my mother had always been a basic fact of my life." However, Nell was shocked when she finally presented her case to Mary, and Mary took Carey's part, not hers: "Thy duty was to obey her and not to make things more difficult for her by objecting. It was not thy business to judge." In the two years that Mary had lived apart from Carey, she had grown in acceptance of her eldest daughter.[36]

Once the late summer break allowed Carey to leave Leipzig, she traveled with her parents to Switzerland and England. From the outset she had known that Leipzig was only for preparation, that, though open to women as auditors, the university did not allow women to take degrees. The University of Zürich offered women the Ph.D. On this trip she met with professors at the university and made provisional plans to return.

To Carey the trip was primarily memorable because it brought her closer to her mother. From Zermatt she wrote to Mary Garrett, "I find Mother even more liberal than before. We had our theological talk which I knew must take place last night, and it was far better than ever before, and now I have a light heart." Time with her mother cleared the air, and Carey could become less guarded. After her family's departure for home, Carey was able to joke about her aestheticism in the resumed correspondence. As she and Mamie toured England, examining art and visiting literary sites, she wrote to her mother, "Now that thee has seen these broken blocks of blackened marble and these dark old pictures that I am so wrapped up in, I am afraid thee won't care as much to hear about all the ~~idolatrous~~ ardent emotions they excite in my mind." When the two took an unexpected side trip to Liverpool, Carey did not have to hide the reason, that they had gone to see Ellen Terry and Henry Irving perform Alfred Tennyson's *The Cup*. She openly referred to her adulation of Sarah Bernhardt and her good luck. In London, "Fortune favored us: 'that wicked woman' was playing there just as we arrived."[37]

Mary and James Thomas came abroad at the midpoint of Carey Thomas' sojourn. Their presence gave her a chance to catch up with herself and consolidate the gains of the first two years abroad. Carey Thomas was now the hardworking scholar with ambition for public position; and she was the lover of Art and the arts, the passionate traveler, the free spirit, and the intimate friend. Europe gave her complex nature room to develop unimpeded.

CHAPTER 8

Dr. M. C. Thomas!

CAREY THOMAS' visit to England in the late summer of 1881 was memorable not only for the pleasures of being with her parents and seeing the sites of British literature with Mamie Gwinn; it also included an audience with her uncle Jim. James Whitall had continued in his father's glassworks, Whitall, Tatum and Company. After the death of his parents, James assumed the position of head of the Whitall family and tried to provide for some of the most important unmet needs of his sister's large household. It is difficult to track fully the contributions that he made to Carey Thomas' education and travel and to the added luxuries that his sister Mary enjoyed. He had always been generous. When Carey was at Howland, he had helped with the bills. During the four years in Europe he underwrote some of Carey's extra expenses.

He was also a trustee of Bryn Mawr College, the new name for the women's college founded by Joseph Wright Taylor, as was Carey's father, James Thomas, his close friend and former Haverford roommate. James Whitall's power on the board arose from his wealth and his location in Philadelphia. He was one of Francis Gummere's benefactors. As Carey Thomas first began to have thoughts about specializing in comparative literature, she asked her mother to address her queries to Uncle Jim. James Whitall traveled abroad in the summer of 1881. In early September 1881, as she was visiting Ely, Lincoln, and York, Carey Thomas met up with him. They had a most satisfactory private talk. She summarized it in a letter to her mother, written just after Mary's departure: "He said just what he said to thee, I imagine. I think he agreed with me that there surely would be such a chair wanted, and he said that he could see that especially in a girls' college it would be of great importance."[1]

James Whitall's encouragement made an important difference to Carey Thomas. Although always interested in plans for the college, after her conversation with her influential uncle, she approached Bryn Mawr's development with a new seriousness and intensity. While she was still in England she had a look at the women's colleges of Oxford and Cambridge with an eye to Bryn Mawr's needs. In contrast with the inadequacies of Newnham, she was impressed by the arrangements at Girton, shown to her by the principal, where each student had two rooms. Thomas judged the Girton students to be "of a much better class" than those of Newnham. Julia Rogers was studying Greek and Latin at Newnham. Normally never one to respect Julia's opinions, Thomas quoted her as deeming the Newnham students "second class."

Carey Thomas found Oxford University to her liking. She admired the men in their caps and gowns. She looked into their rooms from outside the window, "such luxurious rooms with mantel pieces hung with china, and easy chairs and lounges and elegant desks." As she saw the men in their sporting costumes and watched them at leisure in their boats, she felt terribly jealous of their opportunities. She had been given Germany, but England—were she a man—would have offered her something more. "Germany is the place to train a scholar, but England is the place to educate a gentleman. I can imagine nothing nicer in this world than to be a rich healthy young Englishman at Oxford. Almost for the first time I felt as if nothing could make up for not having been born an English *man*. I do not wonder that England has the poets and authors she has, with her scenery and parks and cathedral towns and universities and beautiful mists."[2]

Much of what Carey was feeling was her missed opportunity to be Shelley or Swinburne. Bound up in her ambition to be a poet was her association of literature with scenery, education, and social class. Had she merely been a failed artist this would have been of little significance. M. Carey Thomas, however, was to write her aspirations into the design of Bryn Mawr College.

After her conversation with James Whitall, Carey Thomas felt a clear sense of purpose: to get the degree. When she returned to Leipzig, she put the poetic muse behind her, stopped traveling, and applied all her efforts to preparing for the Ph.D. examination. It was a long and difficult pull and had many steps. She had to write a thesis, a piece of original investigation. She had to find a European university willing to grant a Ph.D. to a woman. She had to remove herself to that university, learn the specifics of its requirements, and prepare herself for the sequence of doctoral examinations. Finally, she had to defend the thesis and to undergo the ordeal of written and oral examinations, the latter in German. A daunting prospect.

Carey Thomas had gone to Leipzig because the university allowed women to hear lectures. It did not, however, grant them degrees. The University of Göttingen, by contrast, appeared willing to grant degrees, but barred women from lectures. The very difficulties pushed Thomas to try for the Göttingen degree. As she wrote to Mary Garrett, "*because* no other woman has a German degree I care more for it." In the expectation that she could take her degree, Thomas made several day trips to Göttingen to seek advice on her thesis from the university's professors. She received cordial treatment, especially from the wives, but gained little useful information. Göttingen was experiencing a change in its professor of English, and Thomas was caught in the transition. Attempting to be helpful, Leipzig professor Richard Wülcker advised her on a thesis topic. He suggested one that she researched for three months, only to find that Jacob Grimm had written on it and, worse, that contemporary scholars regarded it as an insignificant question. Wülcker's misguidance caused Thomas not only time, but anxiety, and she doubted whether she could trust him. By December 1881 Göttingen still had no resident professor, and Thomas worried that she might have to look elsewhere. With so much uncertainty, she became discouraged and angry that her difficulties arose from her "being a woman."[3]

By early February, Carey Thomas was back on track. She had a thesis topic that both Wülcker and Ebers thought excellent, a comparison of *Sir Gawayne and the Green Knight*, an English romance poem written in the 1300s, with French poems of the mid-twelfth century. She began work immediately and ordered books from other German universities. Mamie Gwinn, who had originally come to Leipzig intending to get a degree, never put herself through any of the formal hurdles. As Carey Thomas began to write her thesis, Mamie Gwinn sought museums and concerts.

During the March 1882 vacation Gwinn went to Berlin, and Thomas remained in Leipzig to prepare her thesis. After ten days of steady and lonely work, she pronounced her thesis almost finished. She had enjoyed the work, especially reading the medieval poems of chivalry. "It is like a different world: the ladies 'white as whale bone,' the knights 'stately as bears.' When they fall in love the knight steals to the lady's room each night, sometimes for a year, and yet the finest courtesy is observed. They commit 'no sin' till after 'being wedded with a ring.' " By contrast, her thesis she pronounced dry, but adequate: "I have read over a number of other dissertations, and mine is undoubtedly as good as the rest of them."[4]

Sir Gawayne and the Green Knight is a substantial piece of work. Carey Thomas subjected the English poem to the philological scholarship she had learned at the University of Leipzig. Through textual analysis she determined that in the 1370s a single author composed four poems: *Sir Gawayne and the Green Knight, The Pearl, Cleanness,* and *Patience.* She demonstrated a full command of primary sources and of current scholarship and, in the process, made clear her linguistic ability in modern German and French and medieval French and English. Following the research paths of German scholarship, she counted common words, noted distinctive mannerisms, and demonstrated similarities of rhymes, thought, and expression. She clarified the influence of William Langland's *Piers Plowman* on the author of the poems and used its 1377 edition to date the four poems.[5]

The middle section of the thesis examined *Gawayne* in the light of the French romance *Perceval* by Chrétien de Troyes and pointed out the English author's debt to the French source. Thomas regarded this as her most important contribution. *Gawayne* had always been cited as a "striking instance of an English author's originality." She proved "almost every incident borrowed."[6] Finally, the thesis treated the English tradition of King Arthur and the Knights of the Round Table. Thomas explored the part that *Sir Gawayne and the Green Knight* played in early English poems, in poems based on Chrétien de Troyes' *Perceval* and other French sources, and in Alfred Tennyson's *The Idylls of the King*.

In such a technical study, designed to meet the requirements of the German Ph.D., very little of Carey Thomas' love of literature could come through. And yet at a few moments it did. For example, in discussing the earliest poem, *The Pearl*, she wrote that it "has its source in that sunny and transparent sphere which encircled the Virgin, and in which a more disinterested fancy painted to itself the lot of the divinity it worshiped, eternally happy." One can sense Thomas' real sense of discovery as she probed the meaning of the Green Knight's color, its associations with peace and with wonder. As she treated the Gawayne tradition in English literature, she showed a strong interest in comparative national traditions. In contrast to his French counterpart, the English Gawayne, "instead of desiring peace that the young knights may practise lovemaking and chivalry, looks upon it as a time for good works." In a passage that would have been of considerable interest to English readers, she pointed to Tennyson's direct borrowing from Chrétien de Troyes and the manner in which the nineteenth-century English poet departed from the noble and generous Gawayne to present an irresponsible knight whose courtesy had "a touch of traitor in it."[7]

With the thesis manuscript in hand, Carey Thomas traveled again to Göttingen, this time to meet the new appointment in English literature, Professor Vollmer. He was courteous—as well as being "young, good looking, a complete dandy"—and agreed to find out definitively whether or not a woman might take the degree. They discussed Thomas' preparation, and he pronounced her dissertation "a good subject." He suggested that they walk to the dean's office to learn if she could take her examination for the degree. She wrote home: "He put on an immaculate pair of light kids and a stove pipe and offered to carry my Cornell diploma and Leipzig lecture book." Thomas learned from the Göttingen dean that, despite the fact that there was no formal bar and that she had fulfilled all of the Göttingen requirements, because she was a woman, "the whole faculty, forty-three men, will have to express their opinion on examining a lady. Is it not dreadful when *formally* there is no objection?"

Carey Thomas had to write a petition for the dean to present to the faculty.

She and Professor Vollmer drafted it, and she then returned to Leipzig to await an answer, which she was told would come in three weeks. Although Thomas hoped for a yes, she was prepared: "If 'no' comes we will pack up and leave at once for Zürich."[8]

The no came, and Carey Thomas and Mamie Gwinn went to Zürich. Mamie had been waging her own battle. Her absence from Baltimore weighed heavily on Mrs. Gwinn. Could she remain in Europe a fourth year? Carey feared that Mamie would have to return to Baltimore while Carey completed her degree and then come back to Europe once Carey was free to travel. Ultimately Mrs. Gwinn agreed to let Mamie stay abroad.

By June the two were settled in a boarding house at 43 Plattenstrasse in Zürich. A small, vertical city of less than eighty thousand, rising above its lake, Zürich was Switzerland's intellectual center and the home of an important university that, uniquely in Europe, welcomed women as students. Plattenstrasse, at mid-elevation, held handsome tree-shaded villas providing comfortable residences for students. Immediately upon arriving, Carey Thomas began her siege of preparation for the exams. She was reassured that her thesis was appropriate, but learned that, because she had only five-and-a-half terms in Leipzig, she had to have at least a half-term's residency in Zürich, delaying her examination until the fall. It was for the best, because she had new preparations to make, to meet Zürich's requirements in Old English and Old German. As she confronted the new demand, she was stoic: "It is a nuisance, but still I do not regret the trouble."[9]

Zürich gave Carey Thomas a chance to get some perspective on Leipzig. She attended lectures at Zürich that she felt were advantageous to her, those of Heinrich Breitinger, Heinrich Schweizer-Sidler, and Adolf Tobler, among others. As she closed out the summer, she wrote home, "Thee must not think that Leipzig was poky for any reason except that we had heard all the cycle of important lectures." She profited by the Zürich lectures and even learned that certain of Professor Zarncke's philological theories were wrong; yet the advantages of Zürich were "no compensation for my glorious Zarncke." Her admiration knew no bounds. "He is the most brilliantly clever person I have ever seen and to this add a genial magnetic naïveté which is charming."[10]

Carey Thomas handed in her dissertation before the August break, so the professors would have time to read it at leisure. Carey and Mamie then went to Italy again. Her brother Harry had come abroad, and Carey took off a week to travel with him, showing him Verona and Venice. Carey enjoyed herself and was pleased with her younger brother's development, his love of pictures and poetry as well as medicine. Being with Harry made her homesick, and she wrote to her mother, "Seeing your representative Harry and finding him so nice makes me think that after all, in spite of all my books and pictures and my lovely Florentine hills, which are softer than ever before, it is a great deal to give up, being at home." The pull home reminded her of her inadequacies. She pledged that when she actually returned home, she would become a different, reformed Carey: "*After* my degree I shall set my spiritual house in order. I shall begin by taking a cold sponge bath every day, never talking slovenly English, and so on. From the outside in I shall order my mind and spirit. In loving you I do not need any reform."[11]

Except for the excursion with Harry, the summer of 1882 was one of work, not play. Carey Thomas and Mamie Gwinn located themselves in Florence. Thomas found it difficult to study there: "How far away and contemptible books seem among really lovely things!" Her capacity for self-discipline was tested to the full measure. She maintained a regimen of nine hours of study a day, allowing herself only the pleasure of a two-hour morning walk with Mamie. Preparation for the examination was distasteful work. It was not original scholarship, but "hateful memorizing and cramming—five languages—with all their declensions and literatures, historical and actual."[12]

In mid-October Carey Thomas returned to Zürich, leaving Mamie in Florence. She missed her, but, as she put it, "My selfishness was not gigantic enough to persuade her to come with me simply to have the pleasure of kissing her good night and good morning, for that was all I should have time for."[13] Life for women at the University of Zürich held rich possibilities for friendship, for although Thomas was one of only five female students in philosophy, there were women from many parts of the world studying medicine. Open to women since the 1860s, the university had become a female educational mecca. In her boarding house Carey Thomas made friends with Emma Culbertson, a young woman physician from Boston, a Vassar graduate, completing her medical studies. Carey also had the company of the mother and two sisters of Ruth Putnam, an acquaintance from Cornell's Sage College.

Almost immediately Carey Thomas received the good news that the Zürich faculty had accepted her thesis. Richard Avenarius, the dean, told her "that he had rarely, if ever, heard the chief professors speak in such high terms of any thesis, of the learning, or rather wide reading and clear critical arrangement shown in the treatment of the subject matter; in short, they were delighted with it." The ordeal now began. She had to prepare a second work in English literature. If this were accepted by the entire faculty, she would then proceed to a half-day written examination at the university. Finally, she would undergo a three-hour oral examination by the professors.[14]

Carey Thomas sometimes referred to the second study as a thesis. She took great pains with it, but, in fact, it was designed to be a paper "to be prepared in three days' time with the aid of books of reference" in her own rooms in Zürich. She chose to write on Algernon Charles Swinburne. Responding to possible parental censure of so controversial a topic, she assured her mother that her "essay will not be printed so thee need not fear for my reputation."

She wrote to Mary Garrett to send her Swinburne books, for most of her own were packed in a chest in Leipzig. She had brought with her to Zürich only *Poems and Ballads* and *Essays and Studies*.[15]

The work that resulted—"Swinburne's Place in the History of English Poetry"—is a fine study, demonstrating a full reading of Swinburne's poetry and prose and an understanding of what was written about him. It is written with clarity and grace. What makes it of larger interest is its breadth and distance. It sees Swinburne as writing within both the French and the English poetic tradition. It discusses his relation to the Pre-Raphaelites and to the movement of English Hellenism. It treats the change from the early, dramatic Swinburne poems, written before 1871, to the later, more abstract poems that were intended "to make converts" to the cause of political freedom.[16]

The paper is reticent about the controversial content of many of Swinburne's early poems. It discreetly mentions that "The Leper" was one poem "unhesitatingly condemned" and that "Dolores" "contains the exposition of that part of Swinburne's poetry which is most repellant to the mass of readers." It sees "Fragoletta," "Hermaphroditus," and "Faustine" as representing "an un-English group of strange feminine, or half-feminine ideals." Despite this hesitancy, the impact of Swinburne on the writer is clear. The paper describes his lyrics in *Poems and Ballads* as "overwhelming, glowing, deeply dyed." It contains this appreciation: "Swinburne's lyrical genius has always seemed to me like what Marlowe's might have been had he lived, and lived after Keats and Shelley. In the whole of Swinburne's works I doubt if we can find a faulty or unmelodious line."[17]

The great difficulty in the work, however, is its authorship. Letters from Mamie Gwinn to Carey Thomas make clear that Gwinn was, at the very least, a collaborator and, at the very most, the principal author of the Swinburne paper. An October letter from Gwinn informed Thomas that "this morning I wrote some three pages of your Swinburne." Gwinn sent off the manuscript of her draft to Thomas and continued in the following days to write additions and corrections and to make suggestions. In a long undated letter she wrote: "I send you the result of having thought of you all day yesterday." She included an abstract of a note on "Proserpine": "I still think it instructive, but as you can see from the argument, a longer business than I supposed—an appendix more than a note—and I don't know that it's worthwhile, at least I won't work it out until I hear from you." She offered to proofread, in words that can only make a reader of Thomas' unedited prose smile: "I am seized by anxiety as to your punctuation, and terror as to your spelling."[18]

Gwinn urged Thomas, in copying the material into her own hand, not to change her words or the order in which she placed them: "I'll go over it for you, but don't let me see too much havoc made of my ideas. *Please* keep my arrangement." She especially noted those parts she felt Thomas ought to include. "Don't omit therefore my Baudelaire episode or any of my French quotation from Gautier or anything else. Stuff into the text about the *Songs Before Sunrise*, which has to contain the substance of all the change that insures a notice of the increasing Northern and English character of his poems, and the positive definition of his relation to France, in short his positive recognition of the actual circumstance of his life." Gwinn noted those elements that Thomas had drafted that ought to be eliminated. "I don't think you can use your Michelangelo's frost and fire. It really isn't fair or true: and you certainly can't use any of the rest of your things." Gwinn ended with this encouragement, "I am sure you will do well if you stick *to me.*"[19]

The question is, of course, did Carey Thomas "stick" to Mamie Gwinn? No drafts in either Thomas' or Gwinn's hand exist. Thomas did retain mention of Baudelaire and Gautier. She did not, however, discuss the *Songs Before Sunrise* in the terms that Gwinn suggested. Gwinn herself realized that Thomas had not included everything when she learned of the length of the finished work. As she wrote in mid-November, "The Swinburne was certainly good unless you cut out most of mine, which, from the length (or shortness), I am afraid you did."[20]

Although she may not have copied all that Gwinn wrote, that Carey Thomas used Mamie Gwinn's words is certain. The October letter makes specific reference to a passage that Gwinn had written that she felt Thomas ought to change. Thomas did not make the change Gwinn sought, and the statement Gwinn had originally made stood. More telling, the paper has Mamie Gwinn's style all over it. In her letters and lectures Gwinn often used certain polite mannerisms, such as "as it were," seldom found in Thomas' prose. Gwinn used dramatic metaphors. This sentence is undeniably Gwinn's: "Swinburne's management of meter is always original but as elsewhere we sometimes feel a French motive, altered and, as it were, recast, so here in some of the beautiful short measures we recognize that sharp quaver, as of a stretched violin string, which occurs so often in modern Italian poetry." Where Thomas might hedge in her prose, Gwinn was capable of the bold, declarative statement: "Swinburne whose poems have hitherto wandered upon most secret and widely diverging paths appears before us suddenly in a too dense compactness of subject." Moreover, as *Sir Gawayne and the Green Knight* demonstrated, Carey Thomas could construct intelligent sentences, but she never soared. The essay on Swinburne soars. At moments its remarkable prose bears the unmistakable mark of Mamie Gwinn: "Despite the great beauties of *Songs Before Sunrise*, there is a defect felt, or at least a blank surprise. I have indicated that a broad torrent of strong white day-light has obliterated the many and deep dyed colours of old. In the *Songs Before Sunrise* the briefer poems, in the new short-lined vibrating measure, are really preferable; because the others with their large grasp and scope, and swinging much-undulating outline seem, so to speak, *bleached*."[21]

Thomas added to Gwinn's words those of her own. There are infelicities of phrase that Gwinn would never have constructed. Elements that Gwinn mentioned in her letter do not exist: in the paper, there is no German and little French; there are no appendices or long notes alongside poems. Moreover, there is mention of Thomas' teachers and of the tradition of Anglo-Saxon ballads that she had studied. The Swinburne paper is thus a blend of her work and Gwinn's.

It was Carey Thomas, not Mamie Gwinn, however, who got the full credit. In his evaluation Breitinger praised the paper for its evidence of "wide reading" and "superb memory." He wrote that Thomas "shows complete independence from the views and research of her predecessors, astuteness in a series of fine comments about Swinburne's diction and metrical composition, and a wealth of ideas" that contribute to an understanding of Swinburne. Although unpublished, "Swinburne's Place in the History of English Poetry" stands under M. Carey Thomas' name in the files of the University of Zürich. It contributed an important element to the Ph.D., the basis of her professional life, the sine qua non of her future career. Gwinn's unacknowledged collaboration brings to mind the silent assistance of wives to the work of many male scholars. In her case there is a special poignancy, for, in a curious way, the fact that Thomas got the sole credit for the paper haunted Gwinn for the rest of her life. Carey Thomas never returned to the study of Swinburne. Until her death, Mamie Gwinn tried to write about Swinburne, but never published a word.[22]

Writing the paper in a three-day period proved to be a very rough experience, and Carey Thomas was ill with a headache and fever for the subsequent three days. She received the ministrations of the most prominent woman doctor in Zürich. In addition, the Putnam women saw her through these days, giving her medicines and reading to her. Thomas bounced back, and a week later took her six-hour written examination in German philology "most satisfactorily."[23]

At this point Carey Thomas began to "get very much excited." She had sensed "from the manner of the professors" that she had a chance of a degree with honors. In the week between her written and oral examination she "became more and more nervous" and could not eat or sleep. Dr. Culbertson took her in hand. Thomas took everything she dosed out, including strychnine and valerian.

On the day of the examination Emma Culbertson saw to it that Carey Thomas drank two cups of strong tea without milk. She dressed carefully in the brown brocade and velvet she had worn at her Cornell commencement. Culbertson walked her to the door of the examination room. Thomas entered a large room and sat at the end of a long table. For the next three hours Zürich professors examined her, one by one. For fifteen- and thirty-minute intervals she was successively tested in Anglo-Saxon philology, English and Anglo-Saxon historical grammar, German philology, Gothic, High German, German literature, Middle German, and English literature. Carey Thomas felt confident from the outset. "As soon as I got into the room I felt perfectly calm and was able to answer with perfect distinctness. I made almost no mistake and knew everything they asked. All the laws of the development of Gothic out of Indo-Germanic were never clearer to me than at the moment of the examination." Although the examination was more theoretical than she had anticipated, it was, she felt, "severe but fair."[24]

As the clock struck six, Richard Avenarius called the examination to a close. Carey Thomas left the room, and the professors decided her fate. She felt confident that she had passed with honors, and she even dreamed she might possibly merit a degree magna cum laude. The short wait was excruciating. "I never, never felt such a sensation of choking anxiety." At the end of five minutes she was summoned. She entered the room and stood at the end of the table. The dean rose and stated that "he had the pleasure of welcoming me . . . as a doctor of philosophy of the University and of informing me that the faculty had bestowed upon me the highest honor in its power to give, 'summa cum laude.' He then handed me my documents and shook hands. I left at once."[25]

This was Carey Thomas' moment of triumph. Over and over again in the telling she returned to the rarity of a summa. It was given only once in twenty-five or forty years, certain of the professors had never witnessed it, no woman in any field had ever received it at Zürich. All of this, calculated to be sure to enhance her future opportunities, was an effort to get others to understand how it felt. It must have felt wonderful. A young American woman alone in a room of twenty male professors, answering their learned questions in German, answering perfectly, and meriting the very highest honors. Four years before she had experienced the nadir of utter despair, questioning her intellect and her will. Now she conquered the learned men of Zürich in a public demonstration of her intellectual powers. As she began her letter to her parents the evening after the examination, she wrote, "Hail the conquering hero comes." She signed it at the close, "Dr. M. C. Thomas!" And followed with a critical postscript, "Be sure and tell Uncle James."[26]

According to custom, Thomas paid for the printing of the thesis in a small edition in Zürich. The book form Sir Gawayne and the Green Knight took, however, is deceptive. The evaluation she received made it clear that she needed further research if she were to develop the thesis into a published work that could make her scholarly reputation.

Breitinger, her official Zürich reader, gave the thesis high praise for Thomas' "expenditure of diligence" and "astuteness," but did not necessarily accept its conclusion. In her arguments about the chronology of the poems, Thomas was going against Professor Ten Brink, a revered authority. Breitinger made clear his reservations: "it is difficult to reach a decision purely out of inner reasons . . . definitive decisions will be only possible through newly discovered evidence." In treating Thomas' discussion of the influence of *Perceval*, he offered both praise and suggestions for improvement. He found that Thomas "succeeded in a satisfactory way with this proof," but he warned that not all the parallels that she had drawn were of equal weight. Breitinger found that the final section treating Tennyson had "fewer difficulties but also fewer rewarding and meaningful questions." At a number of points, Thomas wrote in the text that she was unable to obtain an original source. Breitinger noted the missing material and lamented the deficiencies of his university's libraries.[27]

Her Zürich professors gave her much encouragement. Avenarius, the dean, had conveyed their commendations prior to the November examinations. When she visited her examining professors before leaving Zürich, they praised her extravagantly. Dr. Heinrich Schweizer-Sidler told her he was "amazed" at her philological knowledge. He "hated" to have her leave Zürich; "he had never supposed above all a woman would show such a philological talent." Thomas promised him that she would keep him informed of her work and let him know her professional progress. Her professors urged her to take a year of study in the British Museum to develop her thesis into a book.[28]

Within a month, Carey Thomas' pleasure in her work had largely evaporated. Rereading her thesis, she found it "too stupid, too unimaginably dull!" Her summa had a new meaning. She deserved "*more* than the highest degree to have an intelligent being for four months of her life eat dust and grovel in the mole holes of the earth to collect *such* data." She insisted that her parents read it. "Thee and Father *must* read it. . . . Harry shall administer it in doses of a page a day. It is the least you can do, when I had to write it." Perhaps she was steeling herself for her parents' denigration of her work, for she reminded them that "they thought it splendid at Zürich." She joked that after reading it, they would have "all the conditions for a Greek chorus on the vanity of the overvaulting ambition of man."[29]

After the examination, she met Mamie and left for the French Riviera. They were quickly bored, and by late December they decided to go to London. Thomas got a reader's ticket at the British Museum. She read the latest books and hoped to find material for turning her thesis into a book. The British Museum was, she wrote to Mary Garrett, "the thing I have always wished for, every possible English book and periodical." She hoped at a later time to spend a year in London. "I could work up my dissertation into a very tolerable 'contribution to knowledge' had I even four months there." However, revising the dissertation was not really on Carey's mind. She and Mamie only spent a short time in London, and they were on a pleasure trip. Their real goal was the retrospective exhibition of Dante Gabriel Rossetti's paintings at the Burlington Fine Arts Club.[30]

From London Carey and Mamie went to Stuttgart to the house where they had begun their European sojourn. They hoped to perfect their speaking German, but they were restless and unhappy in a household they felt they had outgrown. Carey wrote to Mary that she had doubts about her future. "I used to think I would care so much to be a scholar. Now that I am sure that I can work in that direction I cannot decide. By the Mediterranean, before Rossetti's pictures, amid the chatter of German nothings . . . I have been thinking about it."[31]

As planned, Carey and Mamie went to Paris. Because Carey had prepared for her Ph.D., Mamie had lost travel in the spring and summer vacations. The choice of Paris was hers by virtue of her earlier sacrifice. Carey, however, set great hopes by Paris. It was the place where she was to resolve the question of her future. Although she attended the Sorbonne lectures of Gaston Paris, the noted French philologist, her real goal was art, not scholarship. As she wrote to Anna Shipley, she was going to Paris for lectures and to improve her French, "but, of course, most of all for the Louvre." With Mamie she found an apartment close to "George Sand's attic and the room where Gautier, Gérard de Nerval, Arsène Houssaye, and the young Romanticists cooked their sausages and developed their theories." Gertrude Mead joined them for *la vie bohème*. Carey wrote to Mary that she and Mamie were following "after strange gods . . . not strange, but new because they are connected with Gautier and Baudelaire . . . new to us. I mean the Romantic school of painters . . . whom Gautier so 'fanatically,' say the reviews, admired."[32]

Carey hoped that in Paris she would live the life of the creative artist. Her immediate model was Richard Cadbury, who had written a long narrative poem in Paris. In April, after she had finished her thesis, she had written that she would give poetry a try. "I owe it to my—folly, we will say, to give it a fair trial and I want to begin in Paris." If she failed, then the appreciation of "poems and art and music" would remain, any one of which was enough "to make one's life happy." By contrast, scholarship was not sufficient. "Take Zarncke, the ablest scholar I ever expect to see, almost a genius, and yet I would not care for his success." Again German scholarship seemed worthless, made of "numberless nothings." After writing her thesis, she was confident that she could be "a successful scholar in the field of Old English or Old French," but she wondered if that was what she wanted: "I do not feel as if it were worth giving one's life to and taking it away from at least the meditation on higher things. To those of us who have but one life, and not the life to come, it makes a whole world's difference what we do with that one life."[33]

There is no evidence that in Paris Carey ever took pen to paper to write poetry. Her experiment in living the life of an artist failed. In the summer of

1883 Carey, Mamie, and Gertrude traveled in Brittany, but Carey was ill much of the time. They returned to live in a French household and practice the language. In the early autumn, Carey and Mamie went to England for the British Museum, shopping, and sightseeing, including a visit to the Jersey coast to stand at the site of some of Swinburne's most notable poems.

Although Carey Thomas was pleased that her French was good enough to understand Gaston Paris' lectures, in terms of her scholarship the experience was disheartening. During her summer illness, she wrote to her mother that "one illusion has been entirely shattered. I shall never take up the Romance philology; it is impossible for anyone but a born Frenchman, Italian, or Spaniard." Her training in Germany was "totally different" from the methods of the Sorbonne. Not only different, but by her lights in August 1883, in unspecified ways, inferior. During the months in Paris she did not do research. She worked at learning to speak French, something she regarded as a necessity for a "cultivated person," but she only accomplished it imperfectly.[34]

Looked at from the perspective of the larger life, Carey Thomas' decision to leave Zürich immediately and to pursue art, not philological study, had far-reaching consequences. Once she removed herself from the scholarly world in which her thesis was valued, she lost heart. She began to question her choice of a career. By attending lectures at the Sorbonne, she put herself in the camp of a rival school, causing her to doubt the methods she had so laboriously learned. Mamie was always a pull toward travel and away from scholarship. One can understand Carey's need of a vacation and rest. One can sympathize with the desire to try out poetry away from the pressure of preparation for the Ph.D. Nevertheless, the full year of dilettantism after the Zürich examinations proved fatal to her early scholarly ambitions.

As early as November 1880 Carey Thomas had written to Mary Garrett: "I suppose even a touch of the creative power is the deepest pleasure we can know and the recognition of it the next greatest joy—in pictures and poems. With one or the other life would be very sweet . . . and then comes the hope of helping others." As Carey Thomas thought about what her life work should be, she was working with three categories that she put in a hierarchy. At the top was art, the life of the creative genius, the poet that she dreamed of being. On the second tier was appreciation, what today is called criticism, but what in Thomas' day could be pursued only as technical scholarship. Finally, there was "helping others," a broad, indefinite realm inherited from Thomas' family, which she reinterpreted as working to improve the life of girls. For three years, interrupted by vacations, she prepared herself for scholarship. During the vacations and in the year following her Ph.D. she hungered for art. And always she kept in mind her chance to use her education and experience to do something for girls.[35]

II

CAREY THOMAS' final admonition to her mother after receiving her summa—
"Be sure and tell Uncle James"—clarifies that she did not take her Ph.D. at
Zürich in a vacuum. Rather she took her degree in the context of her family's
involvement in the establishment of Bryn Mawr. In 1881–82, as she wrote
her thesis, reviewed, and readied herself for the examinations, plans for the
Quaker women's college were crystallizing in the minds of the male members
of the Thomas-Whitall family. Paralleling Carey Thomas' successful ascension
to the Ph.D. was her assault on Bryn Mawr.

It is in this context that Carey Thomas' letters to her family were written.
Mother was James Whitall's sister; Father was a member of the Bryn Mawr
College board of trustees; even Bessie was the daughter of Francis T. King,
the president of Bryn Mawr's board. At some level, Carey Thomas was always
aware of this. Her most private letters became part of a larger strategy to gain
for herself a position. Thus they obscure as well as reveal. After the summer
of 1881, Carey's letters home become more tricky to read. Those parts of her
inner life that might jeopardize an appointment by a board of Orthodox Friends
went under cover. That they remained alive are betrayed only by hints or slips
or by curious, circuitous efforts to take the moral high road.

Two obstacles to Bryn Mawr stood in her way. The first was her known
lack of faith. Taylor and his trustees conceived of Bryn Mawr as a Quaker
college and presumed in planning that its faculty would be drawn from the
Society of Friends. As every member of her extended family well knew,
Thomas did not accept the principal tenets of the creed. It is at this point
that Carey Thomas began—in letters to her own mother—a campaign of
dissimulation about her religious beliefs. The first foray was modest, merely
an avowal of her personal history and a statement of the relative worth of
Quaker teachings. "As for my views, thee knows I have an affection for the
Society of Friends which an outsider could never feel, and I believe its views are
more in accordance with the Bible than those of any other denomination."[36]

The second obstacle would have appeared even more formidable to one
less ambitious and less ruthless. There was no place for her. Francis Gummere
had been sent to Europe by the trustees to prepare for the college's chair in
literature, and Carey Thomas knew it. How could she create a place for
herself? In her letters home during her first two years abroad she had argued
for a second position, one in comparative literature. As she prepared for her
examinations in her third year, these arguments ceased. She now assumed
there was only one position. Francis Gummere became the person to beat.

It is at this point that Thomas shifted in her correspondence from friendly
mention of Frank to hostility. In September 1880, he had written to the board,
making it clear that he was "the party proposed to, not the proposer." Twenty-

six and engaged, he bore some responsibility for his widowed mother and his aunt. He intended to complete his doctorate quickly and needed to know his future prospects. Was there a job for him at Bryn Mawr or not? In the interim before the college opened, would Bryn Mawr pay him a salary? At the October 1880 meeting the board appropriated five hundred dollars to "assist Frank B. Gummere in preparing himself to take a Professorship in the Bryn Mawr College." This was followed in the spring of 1881 by an agreement to pay him five hundred dollars for the following academic year, with permission to take other work. This Thomas would have known from her father and uncle.[37]

Carey Thomas now demeaned Gummere's hurried Ph.D. and harshly criticized anything that he wrote. Unquestionably she hoped that Mary Thomas would discuss this with her brother. Moreover Thomas fought to keep the board from making a lasting commitment to Gummere before she finished her degree. In an undated fragment from this period to her mother, she wished that her father "could find out, could ask Uncle Jim and Cousin Frank if there would be any chance of their leaving the position unfilled for a few years. . . . If it be given right away to Mr. Gummere, it will be settled without its being in the least proved that it is given to the best person, and I can never work there, unless he be turned out." What about the promises to Frank Gummere? Thomas suggested that the trustees offer him the German professorship and encourage him to begin teaching at Haverford. In searching for grounds to convince the trustees to keep a post open for her, she argued that her sex gave her a special qualification. "It seems to me that being a woman's college, the only woman who will probably want a position there should not be excluded by a hasty appointment." Was Thomas overstepping a line? At the close of her letter, she asked her mother if she approved. "Tell me what thee thinks. I do not think I am bound to sacrifice what I feel to be my calling to the dislike of possibly disappointing Mr. Gummere, does thee?" Francis Gummere received no definite appointment. In March 1882, still in Leipzig, Thomas learned that the college was not to begin until 1885. She hoped that by then she would "be able to make myself *very desirable*."[38]

From her mother's letters Carey Thomas also learned about those being looked over for president. She did not comment on James Whitall's visit to her father to sound out if he were interested. (He declined because of his medical and religious obligations in Baltimore.) But she fought suggestions of others she considered ill suited or weak. Far from the scene of important decisions that might shape her life, Thomas felt powerless. And she used the resort of the powerless: gossip and social proprieties. She opposed one woman because she was divorced; she suggested that the prospects of a man being considered might be dampened if Mary looked at his actions at Howland; and she tried to persuade her parents not to put forward Allen Thomas. These machinations from afar show Thomas at her worst: competitive, but covert;

manipulative; dissimulating, even in one of her most intimate relationships; narrow-minded when it served her; willing to sacrifice close relatives and former friends. Were this all, M. Carey Thomas might be dismissed as a venomous young woman out only for her own interests. [39]

But it was not all. Carey Thomas understood that Joseph Wright Taylor's will offered a special opportunity for women that could be lost under the wrong hands. Already in 1881 and 1882 she had a vision of what Bryn Mawr College could be. And she knew, perhaps better than anyone else, the forces arrayed against these possibilities.

Settled in Zürich in the summer of 1882 and beginning her final preparation for her examinations, she wrote at great length to her mother some of her fears and hopes for Bryn Mawr in a letter clearly intended to influence the board of trustees. Encouraged that the trustees were moving slowly, she began her argument that the new women's college treat its students in a manner different from that of Haverford, which she had regarded from her girlhood as a backward male college where ill-qualified professors presided over dissatisfied, restive students. She stated that there should be no mandatory attendance required at lectures, and grounded her liberality on her judgment that, unlike boys, "girls manage themselves; they are only too anxious to work."

Carey Thomas disclosed for the first time her scheme for Bryn Mawr. She would make it the outpost of Leipzig in America. She would bring wholesale to the college the "new grammarian" movement of philology. She conveyed the enthusiasm that she held for the science of words. She did not want a professor of Latin and Greek to "be brought up in old fogy English and American ideas." Rather, that person should be trained in and teach "the *new philological* methods which are simplifying everything." She explained, "If that were so, thee sees, and if I had the German and French, the two professorships would play into each other's hands—the same theories, the same rules and everything gloriously clear and simple and on the triumphant winning side, before which the old theories and rules with exceptions are going down like a row of nine pins."

It is in this letter of July 23, 1882, written four months before her final Ph.D. examination, that Carey Thomas gave her first hint that she was thinking of herself as more than Bryn Mawr's professor of literature. In the midst of her scheming about the appointments in philology, she broke through, "Oh dear, if I had the organization of the college, I am sure I could make it the greatest success." Because the college was new, she would have the ability to shape it without having to deal with an existing faculty. "Now here is a new rich endowment, which need not have one backward movement from turret to foundation stone and has the chance of offering girls something they can get nowhere else."

To the potential criticism that her curricular aspirations for Bryn Mawr went beyond the capacities of college students, Thomas had two answers. The first was that there was no real incompatibility between offering courses at the highest level and those at an elementary one, if the latter were properly taught. As she put it at a later point in the letter: "here is a chance of giving milk to the babes and strong meat to the strong if the trustees are only wise."

She then proposed her scheme of graduate fellowships to attract advanced women scholars to the college. She informed her mother with this injunction, "Do talk to Uncle James and Father about a system of fellowships." She then set out the plan, "Even ten, consisting of free board and two or three hundred dollars over would give a tone to the college and bring advanced students there. It would raise Bryn Mawr at once above all the other girls' colleges and draw the very pick of their graduates there to put all their strength into the college. . . . [It] would inspire the professors and the very beginners." She added, "It is my idea and I am proud of it and wish the credit of it when the fellows of Bryn Mawr have become a power."

As she wrote, her ambitions soared—not only for herself, but for the college. She dreamed of a unified advance "of having the whole college go forward keeping step." It would be a place that offered in America what Leipzig had given her abroad. "I do *so want* girls to have the opportunity for culture without having to exile themselves for years to obtain it."[40]

In August 1882 Carey Thomas wrote a long letter to Allen Thomas, now the librarian of Haverford College. She feared that the trustees of Bryn Mawr might choose him as president. Her letter was an affectionate one and contained important news of her struggle for the Ph.D. It was also indirectly an effort to establish the legitimacy of her claim against his. In her eyes Allen Thomas was untrained and weak, and without saying it, she wanted him to know. She wrote about the strenuousness of her preparation for the Ph.D. and the quality of her training. She outlined all the hurdles yet to be leaped. She also praised her Leipzig mentor Zarncke. She had been fortunate enough to study under him, for he had opened up to her the new field that united the disparate studies of English philology, German, and Old French, what she called "the new philology." The movement was "carrying all before it. It certainly simplifies everything; it is like evolution in science." What she was arguing was that as a Zarncke student, she had received the word, she was anointed.[41]

In establishing her claim, Carey Thomas told more about herself than just her ambition. She also confirmed the source of the appeal of scholarship. In breaking with the religion of her parents, Thomas had been drawn in two directions, aestheticism and science. In Europe aestheticism, linked to Mamie Gwinn and travel, held strong attraction. The counter-pull in these years was science. Thomas read Herbert Spencer as well as Algernon Charles Swinburne. In the place of the divine revelation of her parents, she tried to substitute the facts of animal and human nature. She turned to science and to its popularizers to explain the universe. Interpreters of Charles Darwin gave her an explanation of origins and a progressive pattern of history. What the "new philology" did was to apply this kind of thinking to literature. Just as a scientist studied the origin of species and their transmutations over time, so the philologist studied the origin and development of words. In the past Thomas had split her love of literature from study. In Europe, even as she pursued literary scholarship, this split continued. But now scholarship had a new meaning: it was a source of truth.

A few months earlier, immediately after finishing her thesis, Carey Thomas had written of her work to Mary Garrett. The letter is remarkable for, although neither Thomas nor Garrett was religious, Thomas wrote to her of scholarship as revelation. She stated that the study of philology had been difficult and occasionally seemed meaningless, but that it all added up. "I see the links; things which have baffled me before are now clear." Thomas wished she could tell Garrett, without boring her, what her scholarship had done for her. "It is like the 'open sesame.' " All the languages of Europe "are all so wonderfully connected that one system of verbs . . . runs through the whole." Although the system was not fully worked out for Latin, Greek, and the Romance languages, "for the others it is marvelous to see how the same principles reappear. These principles are difficult to master but when once understood, 'there is light.' "[42] She had never found the "new heart" that her Quaker family desired, but she had found "light."

In writing about philology to Allen Thomas, Carey Thomas reported, "Mamie begins to put her fingers in her ears when I start to ride this hobby of mine." Many years later Mamie wrote that during these years Carey was not "seeking scholarship or culture or even pleasure; she was seeking simply a degree, for feminist, careerist and financial reasons."[43] Although Mamie's words were of the twentieth century, some of the thought behind them derived from their conflicts in the early 1880s. Mamie did not share Carey's enthusiasms or her needs. Mamie had been raised not by devout Quakers but by an Anglo-Catholic mother and a Presbyterian father who accepted his wife's ritual. She had come to culture early. She pursued it as a source of beauty, not as an alternative to revealed religion. As she studied abroad, Mamie listened to lectures as they pleased her and read as she liked; she was not working for a degree. Nor was she seeking to fill a void left by the departure of a material heaven and hell. She did not need the scientific methods of the nineteenth century as sources of truth. She could have Swinburne without Spencer. Carey, however, could not.

In September, Carey Thomas received from her mother a letter of James Whitall that encouraged her hopes, and she began to address the religious concerns of the trustees. They felt an obligation to abide by the terms of Joseph

Taylor's will. Moreover as good Orthodox Quaker patresfamilias, they were preoccupied with the proper protection of daughters of the faith. Carey Thomas wrote home that there was no incompatibility between the highest standards of education and a college founded for Quaker daughters. "I do not see what there could be in Dr. Taylor's will that would oppose the plan of making Bryn Mawr admirable. It need not be any the less guarded, because it is good." An excellent women's college would "increase the power of Friends." That it was under Quaker auspices would assure parents. The college could, in fact, be more advanced because it was a Quaker college. "Not only Friends but other careful mothers would feel a confidence that it would not prove a second Harvard to their daughters. . . . High as it might be, and the higher the better, there would be no danger." It should not, however, limit its student body to Friends. It might, like Johns Hopkins University, select its students through entrance examinations.

Again Carey Thomas imagined herself as Bryn Mawr's head. "The president of a new college . . . should be like the architect of a building and make every part in keeping." Mary Thomas had suggested that it would be difficult to attract a qualified faculty. Her daughter knew differently. "Thee must not say that the professors cannot be found because they *can* be found. I myself, if I could go into the matter, could find them and be sure that they would be suitable and that the college would have one impetus and one thought." Thomas realized that the trustees might select an unsuitable man, but she knew she was right for the position. "I feel as if my training had fitted me for it."[44]

The Ph.D. summa cum laude stimulated Carey Thomas all the more. In Zürich she instantly became a public figure. She took pleasure in the publicity, the anticipated account in the newspapers of Zürich. She heard reports that women connected with the university regarded her summa as a triumph for their sex, and she was stared at on the street. Carey Thomas relished being an exemplary woman. "The fact that no woman had ever received a 'summa' before made it as nice a thing for women in general as it was for me in particular and I care as much for the 'cause' as for myself."

With no break in thought, Carey Thomas shifted from Zürich to Bryn Mawr. "Of course, I suppose it is impossible and that they would never give it to me, but I should love to have the presidentship of Bryn Mawr. I believe I could make it the very best woman's college there is." If the board were not composed of members of the family and friends, she would write and propose herself. The thought that she was only twenty-five and had never been employed played no part in her thinking. She was qualified by Cornell, Leipzig, and Zürich. In her eyes she had, in fact the three credentials necessary: she was young and therefore in touch with the issues of the present; she had studied abroad; and she was a woman. In a manner calculated to appeal she closed.

Her ambitions were not for herself but for the college. She held hope that "this new opportunity for women may not be wasted—and a little Orthodox Quaker pride that we shall be the people to provide the highest woman's college."[45]

As Carey Thomas knew, it was the "we" that was at issue. Was she a Quaker? As she attempted to make herself acceptable to the Bryn Mawr board, she had declared her affection for the tradition and her relative regard for its tenets. But ambitious as she was, she knew better than to pretend to her mother's version of the faith. In the months after her exam she tried to establish grounds for toleration and to declare an abstract loyalty to the Society of Friends. In defending her brother John, now launched in a job and setting up his own household prior to his marriage, against the accusation that he had failed to attend Meeting regularly, Carey argued for his right to make his own decisions. She made it clear that in taking a stand for the right of each person to follow an individual course of conscience, she was engaging in "an abstract discussion." She wrote, "Personally I like to go to Meeting once a week. I believe it helps one."[46] It was an outright lie. In her years abroad she did not attend Quaker worship.

Early in 1883 Thomas got a letter from James Whitall. The Bryn Mawr board of trustees had made Dr. James E. Rhoads—a prominent physician, Indian rights reformer, and leader in the Gurneyite renewal movement within Orthodox Quakerism—the paid executive responsible for ongoing oversight of the emerging college. As key board members, James Whitall and James Carey Thomas retained a deep sense of concern for the new enterprise, writing each other during this period their thoughts about when the college ought to open and what its budget might look like. Whitall advised his niece to write directly to Rhoads about Bryn Mawr. Although he did not state it, Francis Gummere had now removed himself completely from Bryn Mawr by a letter of resignation to the board. Whitall did not pledge to assist his niece; he only wrote in double negatives that he felt that a letter would not be unsuitable and that it was only fair that she be able to act as if she "had no relations among the trustees."

In the letter he sent a copy of Joseph Taylor's will. Taylor had specified that he wished the teachers of the women's college he was endowing to "inculcate the doctrines of the New Testament as taught by Friends," and the trustees had adopted a resolution that confirmed this sentiment. As Carey Thomas confronted this potential bar to her future, she again sought middle ground. In a letter to her mother she repeated her arguments for high educational standards, against repressive governance, and for opening the college to all qualified young women. She did, however, make this concession to sectarianism: "The religious influence which undoubtedly will exist will not deter students who find there what they cannot find elsewhere and may have great influence upon them."

She returned to her own religious position: "As thee knows my views have been much modified since coming abroad. I believe thoroughly that the doctrines of Friends more than any others are in accordance with those of the primitive Christian Church." She was thus a "Friend." However, she saw her mission as teaching, not preaching. She argued on general grounds that a person could not do both. After declaring her unwillingness to embody the religious mission of the new college, Thomas made a most curious statement. If her parents approved, she would write to Dr. Rhoads. "Thee knows that whatever I have anything to do with, I hope thee and Father will always have a great interest in and, if as Uncle James says, he should wish to see an enlightened Christian influence like thine there, I can see no surer way of obtaining it than by appointing your daughter president."[47] Was Carey Thomas seeking to gain the Bryn Mawr presidency by riding in on her mother's pious skirts?

Carey Thomas continued to mount her campaign in Paris. In May 1883 she seemed clear about her future. She wrote to her mother that she wanted to write only good works, as had her model Théophile Gautier: "he never wrote a line that he need be ashamed of." Her mentor Zarncke established a similar standard in scholarship. As she set her sights for Bryn Mawr, the issue was the same—quality. She was going to write to Dr. Rhoads to suggest herself as president of Bryn Mawr. Realizing that "the central task of the office was to organize the intellectual life of the college," she would set out her "desires for the college," and only if they were found compatible with those of the trustees would she be willing to take the presidency.[48] Underlying her campaign for Bryn Mawr was her commitment to the new scholarship. Whatever doubts she had about her Leipzig training when she thought about revising her thesis dissolved when she contemplated Bryn Mawr College. She would bring Leipzig's new philology to America.

Carey Thomas had begun to draft the letter to Dr. Rhoads in March 1883 while she was in Stuttgart. He was well known to her. She had encountered Rhoads and his Orthodox Quaker opinions during her Howland years, and he had been present when her family tried to lead her to rebirth through prayer immediately before Cornell. In June the letter was still unsent. She explained to her parents that she only wanted to mail it when she had expressed herself exactly right.[49] The interim provided time to rally her family. She wrote to Uncle James and to Bessie King so that Bessie would be prepared to influence her father.

On August 14 the long letter was ready. "My Dear Friend," she wrote, taking care to use proper Quaker "thee-thou" idiom, "My old desire to see an excellent woman's college in America has made the management of Bryn Mawr from the time of its first endowment a matter of great interest to me." It was for this reason she was writing to him in regard both to the college and to herself. In stating her purpose in writing the letter, she distorted her past to conform to the image of the lady she wished to convey. She had gone abroad, she wrote, "meaning only to pursue study for its own sake," but "gradual training under German scholars who in a certain sense aid in making the science which they teach" led her to "doubt whether it would not be a more justifiable way of life, to aid in procuring this liberal education for other women, than merely to pursue my studies quietly at home." Her success at her Ph. D. examinations and her summa made her feel that she might "without presumptuousness" offer herself as a candidate for the Bryn Mawr presidency.

She wrote with "less hesitation" because of her conviction that "it is best for the president of a woman's college to be a woman." A male president "feels all the circumstances by which it differs from a man's college as limitations only; a woman sees definitely the especial needs, aims, interests, opportunities and possibilities." She offered her education and her opportunity "not only for study but for observation and for comparison of methods" as a counterbalance to her "comparative youth which to thee perhaps may seem a disadvantage."

The rest of the letter, written "simply as a woman much interested in Bryn Mawr," stated her vision of the college and the plans that she had carefully worked out over the preceding two years. She argued that the college must begin with a full number of professors and high standards. There must be no preparatory department. All the entrance requirements must be well publicized one or two years in advance. In imitation of Johns Hopkins, at least ten fellowships for graduate students should be established, offering them two to three hundred dollars and board and residence. The graduate fellows' presence would help give the new college "the requisite scholarly atmosphere," raise standards, and push professors to continue original research.

Finally, Carey Thomas broached the most sensitive issue of all, Joseph Taylor's will that seemed to limit the faculty to Quakers. "We must not deceive ourselves; an excellent college within the limits of any one sect or society is an exceptional thing, and must be obtained by exceptional measures." What she proposed was that initially the college begin with "provisional professorships," open without regard to religion and held largely by men. As the Quaker women graduates of the college became scholars, they could gradually replace their male professors. As a new institution and one offering graduate studies, Bryn Mawr ought to be better than the Quaker male colleges and "proud if it gives to such of its women as are scholars not only a training but a career." Thomas made the case for a college to foster women scholars, at the same time that it offered a general education. Such a college would be in keeping with the sect: "The Society of Friends has no deeper claim upon the gratitude and loyalty of its members than its steady equity and liberality toward women."

By early October, Thomas received Rhoads' initial response, written after a meeting of the executive committee but before consideration by the trustees. It was a kind, respectful letter. "All recognize the propriety and advantage of having a woman at the head of Bryn Mawr College," Rhoads wrote. "They equally appreciate thy eminent ability as a student and thy extraordinary acquirements as shown by the degree accorded thee." Rhoads wanted Thomas to know at the outset the concerns of his colleagues. "The most serious difficulties which arise are as to thy youth as compared with the 'young' presidents of Harvard and Johns Hopkins, and thy lack of experience as a teacher and in the practical management of an Institution." Although the trustees would receive the proposal at their meeting two weeks hence, they would hold only a preliminary discussion, awaiting Thomas' return before making any decision.

Although the presidency was in some doubt, Rhoads reassured Thomas that she would play an important role in the life of Bryn Mawr. "I feel sure that all the trustees will earnestly desire thy connection with the college in such capacity as will secure to it thy most efficient aid; and that they will value at its full measure thy warm interest in the college, and in some degree discern thy ability to advance its welfare." Rhoads was careful to put some distance between himself and the trustees, reminding Thomas of their conservatism in regard to female education. Rhoads hoped that "their caution and slowness will not appear as any want of just appreciation." To assure Thomas that her counsel was taken seriously, Rhoads told her that the executive committee had already acted upon her specific suggestion about a circular.[50]

Carey Thomas took Rhoads' letter as a positive sign. Her hope was buttressed when James Whitall wrote to her with advice, in case the trustees decided in her favor. He was, in fact, working quietly behind the scenes in her behalf, as this letter to her father suggests: "I sincerely hope that Carey will wait until she hears from Dr. Rhoads in reply to her letter. I trust that *you* will *also* do this." James Whitall continued with advice to his brother-in-law: "I have awaked to the necessity of our calling her no longer 'Minnie.' This name gives too much the impression of her being extremely young, and only a child. I think *we must all try* to make the effort to call her 'Carey.' "[51]

In her final weeks in Paris, advised by Mary Garrett, she attended to her wardrobe with her new duties in mind. If the trustees sent her a positive signal, Thomas thought of spending a week in London to look over educational treatises. Within short order, she received another letter from Rhoads that outlined the financial situation of the college, and she decided to visit Cambridge. But by late October a letter from Rhoads informed her that "the general meeting seems to have been rather adverse." After this discouraging news, Thomas changed her plans and spent her last remaining week abroad in London, reading at the British Museum and going around with Mamie to the picture galleries.[52]

CHAPTER 9

Nous Autres

AS CAREY THOMAS studied for her Ph.D. and set her sights on Bryn Mawr, she began to develop a public persona; but what kind of person was she in her intimate relations?

The Ph.D. required long hours of disciplined reading, writing, and memorization. Much of the work excited her, but some was admittedly a "grind." Thomas settled down, determined to accomplish her goal. At critical moments—writing her Gawayne thesis and studying for her examinations—Thomas worked alone. But she never traveled alone. She journeyed as part of a twosome with Mamie Gwinn, a twosome devoted to art. In her travels and in her relationship to Mamie she allowed herself to remain the lover of art, as she put it in July 1880, one of "*nous autres* . . . the Gautier, Rossetti school."

While Carey Thomas had pursued a degree in philology, Mamie Gwinn attended university lectures and read widely. Hers was a literary, not a scientific, education. She translated poems, including those of Charles Baudelaire. She read every word written by or about Algernon Charles Swinburne. Although she respected scholarship, she buttressed that side of Carey that reveled in travel and dreamed of a life of art. Carey and Mamie shared the fantasy that they might live the bohemian life of artists. Carey dreamed of becoming a poet. The two wrote the paper on Swinburne for the Zürich degree. They traveled to the Jersey coast in search of sources of his poems. They chose Paris for their final year abroad, and they settled in rooms on the Left Bank near those that Théophile Gautier had inhabited, and viewed the paintings that he had praised.

As Carey created a new identity for herself in Europe under Mamie's influence, what was she learning from the writers they admired? What were the personal lessons of "the Gautier, Rossetti school"? Gautier's *Mademoiselle de Maupin* was a book of special import, not only in the realm of aesthetic theory. Carey had read it in December 1878, and owned a copy.[1]

In Gautier's *Mademoiselle de Maupin*, the heroine of the title dresses as a man to learn men's ways. As Théodore de Serenne, she rides, fights, drinks, and dines with men, and learns of their crudity and utter contempt for the women they profess to love. Rosette, the sister of one of Théodore's companions, falls in love with her, as does Rosette's lover, the poet d'Albert. The male poet suffers sharp feelings of self-loathing before he learns that the "man" with whom he has fallen in love is a woman. However, for the two women, there is no such pain. In one scene, narrated by Maupin/Théodore, Rosette lures her to a rural retreat where they partake of wine and sweets. Rosette sits in Maupin's lap, "her arms round my neck, her hands interlaced behind my head, and her lips pressed to mine in a maddened kiss. I felt her half-naked and insurgent breasts leap against my breast, and her fingers tighten about my hair. A thrill ran right through my body and the nipples of my breasts grew hard." The only regret that Maupin feels is that she is physically unable to consummate this love.[2]

In addition to Rosette, Maupin wins the love of Ninon, a girl just entering puberty, and she spirits her away from a vicious mother. Ninon, dressed as a boy, serves Théodore as her page. Ninon's innocence allows her to think she is Théodore's mistress: "Her illusion was made perfectly complete by the kisses I gave her." To the erotic play among adult women is thus added that of an older woman to a girl, one "so diaphanous, so slender, so light, of so delicate and exquisite a nature," that she makes even the beardless, effeminate Maupin/Théodore seem masculine by comparison. Théodore takes "a malicious pleasure" in keeping Ninon "from the rapacity of men. . . . Only a woman could love her delicately and tenderly enough."[3]

To d'Albert, Maupin/Théodore's passionate embrace of women makes her all the more desirable. Nothing in her past is understood by him as casting a shadow over her future as his perfect mistress. She comes to him pure, declaring herself "as virgin as the Himalayan snows." In his pursuit of her d'Albert applies well the vast sexual experience that much of the earlier sections of the novel graphically describes. Their single night of repeated love-making is the passionate climax of the novel. What writers write, however, is not what readers necessarily read. Although Gautier's masculine audience may have been satisfied by the book's outcome, certain of his female readers may have learned a good deal about their own passionate responses to women. At the end of December 1881, after a visit from Gertrude Mead that would prove to be provocative, Carey asked her mother to send *Mademoiselle de Maupin* to Gertrude along with *Madame Bovary* and a book on mythology. Carey was never a neat person, and she often did not know where her immediate possessions were. Yet, after more than two years away from home, she could tell her mother just where *Mademoiselle de Maupin* was located. In her autobiographical notes penned late in her life, M. Carey Thomas left a short list labeled "Youth" and "Sex": *Mademoiselle de Maupin* is one of its four entries.[4]

Swinburne's poetry, important to both Carey and Mamie, dealt with forbidden themes. Sappho's love for Anactoria was imagined with intense sadomasochistic passion; Hermaphoditus' state, with sad longing. Though she read these poems, Carey Thomas did not comment on them directly. The paper that she and Gwinn composed for her Ph.D. gives knowledge only that she read, understood, and admired them. That Swinburne's concern with male and female were of interest to her is apparent from a statement in a letter to her mother in late February 1881. Carey was reading Tennyson's new book of poems. She wrote, "Swinburne admires it greatly. He says 'Rizpah' is glorious, that it shows that all great poets are bisexual, that in it Tennyson has the tenderness of woman." To Carey, Swinburne could not have paid Tennyson a higher compliment.[5]

Although Carey admired Dante Gabriel Rossetti's poetry, his greater importance to her was as a painter. In 1883 Carey and Mamie traveled to London to see the exhibit of his paintings. After viewing the exhibition and seeing his sister, the poet Christina Rossetti, in the galleries, Carey wrote home, "Oh, Mother, Rossetti's pictures are so wonderful. . . . Having seen them will make a difference in my whole life." Her rapturous letter to Mary Garrett was filled with her response to Rossetti's paintings. For three weeks, she wrote, she sat "before them day after day and absorbed as one can imagine a sponge thrown into an ocean of depth and colour gradually expanding till every cell is full of light." She was fascinated with the woman's face, modeled after the wife of William Morris, reappearing in many of Rossetti's important paintings, "with its sensuous mouth and intellectual forehead . . . the same wonderful eyes and more than wonderful neck, which curves and undulates and upbears the 'small head of flowerlike.' " Rossetti's women were to Carey "all inhabitants of a land of dreams." The beauty of the paintings was revealed only to those who brought "the desire" of their "hearts. . . . It was our desire, and it is quite impossible for me to talk about the pictures calmly." Mamie was sending the catalogue to Mary. From it Mary would see "how many and how desirable they were for those of us who care for dreamers of dreams and seers of visions."[6]

Not only was Carey's response to "the Gautier, Rossetti school" a critical ingredient in her desire to become a poet, it informed her intimate relations. In the final two years abroad, Carey and Mamie consolidated their loving friendship. The time of discovery had passed, and the two settled into a secure and satisfying intimacy. Carey normally had little reason to comment on their closeness, but when she did she thought in terms of a marriage. In February 1882, as they schemed to get away from work for an excursion, Carey wrote to her mother that they hoped for "some cheap little journey of a week or two somewhere, 'a wedding trip upside down,' as Mamie says."[7]

However they regarded themselves, the world took another view. Unmarried Baltimore women from their circle—even those who had studied abroad—were expected to return home to serve and to keep their mothers company. Carey's parents were unusual in accepting their daughter's drive for independence. But Mamie had a conventional mother who assumed her return to the household. Carey wrote Mary Thomas, "If Mamie and I could only go through the marriage ceremony together, then Mrs. Gwinn would not feel any more abused than Aunty Hal [whose daughter Bessie had moved out of the house upon her marriage to a man] does, if Mamie lived away from her all her life." She put their personal struggle in broad perspective: "That is one thing the emancipation of women will bring with it, women can elect each other or a man just as they please." Then she added, "I must say though that our ménage would have to have a more solid money basis than at present."[8]

What were Carey's feelings for Mamie in these years? Carey did not write in her journal when she was abroad. In her letters home she seldom wrote directly about her life's loves, but she did give some hints. In March 1882, immediately before Mamie Gwinn's departure for Berlin to allow Carey Thomas to write her thesis unencumbered, the two took off a half day and went with cream chocolates and a book of poems borrowed from Eva Channing to the Rosenthal, Leipzig's beautiful wooded park. The poems, by Channing's friend Lulu Jennings, who wrote under the pseudonym Owen Innsby, were "love sonnets" to Mrs. Bell, a Boston woman. Carey wrote home unselfconsciously, "They are both swells, and this girl has had a passion for Mrs. Bell for years. The poems are charming. *The Nation* and the *Academy* have both praised them most highly, though wondering how it is possible that one woman can feel so toward another. The editor of *The Nation* at least has discovered her name. As love sonnets they are nice because they *are* by a woman and lack that horrid sensuousness of men's love sonnets." Carey concluded that as far as she was concerned, the Boston girl's passion for a woman was not misplaced: "There are so many nice girls in the world. I have yet to meet a man who compares to them and certainly I know both Mr. Cadbury and Mr. Gummere well enough to judge."[9]

Unquestionably Carey felt passion for Mamie. Early in their love she had written in her diary, "There is a passionate devotion between girls I feel sure."[10] By the time of their March 1882 afternoon in the Rosenthal, they had shared rooms for two-and-a-half years and, at least at some level, thought of themselves as married. Letters home tell of their domestic life. They ate three meals a day together; read in the same room in their wrappers, occasionally with Mamie's head in Carey's lap; nursed each other in sickness, reading poetry to each other; accompanied each other to medical examinations; crawled into the same bed during a storm; and kissed each other each morning and night. Only extraordinary circumstances put them in the same bedroom or bed: fear or uncooperative hosts or landladies. To share a bed was not something they expected or desired. They were nineteenth-century women who valued their privacy as well as their intimacy.

Their days and nights in each other's company offered them time and leisure to express their passion for each other in their own manner. A critical void limits understanding Carey's feelings and her physical expressions of love. No letters from Carey Thomas to Mamie Gwinn survive from these years. When Carey and Mamie returned their letters to each other, Carey destroyed her letters to Mamie. Mamie kept some of Carey's letters, but they date only from the years after 1883. Carey's letters to Mamie in Helen Thomas Flexner's papers predate the European sojourn.

Carey retained a small selection of Mamie's letters, and these tell a great deal. Mamie took a spring vacation alone in 1882 so that Carey Thomas could prepare for her Ph.D. Her letters give a telling sense of Mamie's state of mind during this period and of the affection that she bestowed upon Carey. When Mamie was in Berlin in March 1882, she missed Carey terribly and begged her to hurry up her work and join her. The letters are alternatively begging, pleading, enticing, reassuring, and playful. For example, in one letter she wrote, "My love, my little-big love! 'Tis 11:30 but I am awake, and longing for you." She wrote of the opera schedule that they could enjoy together were Carey there. "My darling, I am so forlorn in my rising up and my lying down, my going out and my coming in! I lie on the sofa and don't undress simply because I am a coward and am miserable undressing without you." If money was a problem, Mamie promised to help pay for Carey's travel. "I am starved, frozen up, numb for lack of Cecil Schimmerle. Ah, if she would come! No, I wouldn't be naughty: she should study as much as she likes, and I would nestle on the floor, with my head on her lap." "I am a ghost. Everyone else has his, her, their Cecily—vieni, i cara—carissima, felicissima notte." In these letters Mamie showered Carey with pet names: Cecil Schimmerle, sugar Cecily, pet, my pettest, pink, birdie. As Carey later explained it, Cecil Schimmerle, Mamie's special name for Carey, was derived from Cecil and the Leipzig diminutive Sümeli.[11]

During the years abroad Mamie sought to have Carey utterly to herself. She strongly opposed friendship with the Channing women. She grew at times deeply jealous of Mary Garrett's claims on Carey. A serious threat emerged when Gertrude Mead came to visit the two women in Leipzig and later in Paris. Carey was attracted to her, admiring Gertrude's bohemian intensity. Much later Carey wrote that Gertrude attempted to take her from Mamie. (In 1896 Carey made an analogy between Gertrude and another woman who sought to break up two women's friendship through "making the wildest sort of love" to one of them.) In addition, Julia Rogers was studying in England, and despite the jealousy Carey felt for Julia's bond to Mary Garrett, Carey felt some responsibility to be hospitable to her. In Berlin, despairing over Carey's ties to Julia, Mamie wrote, " 'Tis only by ignoring outside people and things that we can sustain our unanimity, but that makes me only the more regret that we are not together the whole of this very last time in which there *are* no outside people." She continued, "I'm devoted to you, and the more impossible it is for me to comprehend or follow your relations to people, the more I cling to the individual love that is left."[12]

In 1879, anticipating their life abroad, Carey had written to Mamie, "You shall live to be mine and the gods'. I cannot do without you." Initially she feared Mamie as a temptation, pulling her away from steady work. In January 1879 after a conflict, Carey confided to her journal her anguish: "I shall never give up to my love for her as I have. . . . No more shall it happen though I doubt if anything can change it now." In her Baltimore journal and abroad in a letter to her parents, she described herself as "wrapped up" in Mamie. Such words reveal Carey and Mamie's passionate love for each other.[13]

No record exists of Carey's and Mamie's physical intimacy beyond a kiss and a head nestled on a lap; yet no record determines it was absent. Carey and Mamie may have been physically intimate beyond the kisses and caresses about which Carey wrote. They were immersed in a culture that set no limits on female physical or psychic closeness. They admired poetry and fiction that graphically described women's passionate physical response to each other. Sharing quarters abroad for four years, Carey and Mamie may have enjoyed private pleasures of which there is no record.

At this point in their lives, Carey and Mamie could not have considered themselves lesbian in the twentieth-century sense of the word.* In their own nineteenth-century terms, they loved each other passionately, chose to live together, and at some level gradually came to regard themselves as married to each other. They had the same tastes, shared the same reactions to poetry and art, and found in poems and paintings confirmation of their union. In their minds they were committed to each other with the highest type of love.

It is important to comprehend the context in which Carey Thomas expressed her feelings at different points in her life, the set of categories and descriptions that guided and shaped her evolving self-conception. At age twenty-five Carey understood her love of Mamie as part of a larger sense of herself as a passionate woman who loved women. Blessed with unusual parents who supported her aspirations for education, she had escaped the temptations and bondage of marriage with a man. Her loving relationship with Mamie offered her the best of marriage. She saw herself as committed to a life lived among women. She had no language to categorize herself, but her reading of poetry and fiction gave her an imaginative context in which she might understand her present and envision her future with Mamie.

---

*I hope that it is obvious to the reader that no judgment is being offered here. I am arguing that the theoretical framework that allowed a twentieth-century understanding of lesbianism was not available to Carey Thomas or Mamie Gwinn in the late 1870s and early 1880s. In the 1890s, however, Carey Thomas' reading of the medical literature did change her self-conception (see chapter 15).

The notion that women loved women best of all was embedded in her family—her mother's closeness to her own sisters, her mother and aunt's special affection for their female children and their nieces. In her family, such love for women was sustained even as young women fulfilled the biblical injunction and society's expectation in marriage and motherhood. As a typical young woman reached early maturity, the women of her family prepared her for courtship and marriage. But as Carey went to Cornell and then abroad, her own ambition and desire to achieve as a woman coupled with her parents' fears for her reputation broke this pattern. In the years after Cornell, she herself, without confiding in her mother, silenced her attraction to Francis Gummere because marriage would end her dream of scholarship and power. As she fell in love with Mamie, she returned to her youthful focus on a special female friend. No one around her suggested that this was inappropriate or wrong. In fact, the opposite message was given. Only when Mamie was allowed to go with her to Germany could Carey's parents countenance her study abroad.

But Carey Thomas was a different woman from her mother. She was more passionate and more sensual. Mary Thomas imbibed the religious and sentimental culture of antebellum Quakerism. Carey had read widely in the newer texts of rebellion and aestheticism. Shelley, Swinburne, and Gautier had shaped her consciousness. Through Gautier, she knew of the possibility of a woman's erotic response to another woman. Through Swinburne she knew of the intensity of Sapphic love. Her self-designation as an aesthete, as a member of the "Gautier, Rossetti school" takes Carey Thomas beyond the "female world of love and ritual" of her mother's generation into the new passionate, sensual, erotic mentality of the late nineteenth century.[14]

The years in Europe gave Carey an interlude in which she consolidated a self in partnership with Mamie. But she was not cut off completely. Abroad she continued to face the universal expectation that a woman should marry. Letters from home about Bessie Nicholson's marriage, Margaret Hicks' confession that she was engaged, Richard Cadbury's provocative statement about "the sweet privileges of wife and mother" as women's duty, and Mary Thomas' gentle nudging reminded her of women's traditional estate. The Atlantic Ocean distanced her from these pressures, and she framed a response: the right of women not to marry in order to pursue an independent thought life.

In Europe Carey also saw an alternative to marriage with a man: the established pairing of two women that some, though never Carey, later in the century called the "Boston marriage." She frequently commented in her letters about the traveling women in the pensions of Italy. She liked what she saw, especially the qualities of the English. She wrote home from Florence, "Nothing is so attractive as these hale, cultivated English spinsters who are so ladylike and yet so independent, who range over the face of the earth and seem so well and full of enjoyment." At times she found herself admiring individuals, such as a woman photographer living in the Florence pension with a woman artist. Given the social distance that Carey normally put between herself and others, however, it is unlikely that she learned very much about the inner nature of the friendships of these women.[15]

However, in 1882 in Zürich, while Mamie remained in Italy, Carey became close to Emma Culbertson, the Boston doctor finishing her studies who not only guided Carey through the ordeal of the Ph.D. examination, but gave her some sense of herself. Carey wrote her mother that Dr. Culbertson had "a most devoted friendship with a Dr. Smith who studied here five years and then took the direction of the Boston hospital where Dr. Culbertson was under her." Both women were surgeons and were going "into partnership," professional and personal, when Dr. Culbertson returned to Boston. Dr. Culbertson was deeply homesick for Dr. Smith. Carey found it "charming" that "they are going to pass their lives together. It is the way it should be and will be when more women enter professions. They will choose to live with each other and go off and make homes. I think another woman supplies every need a refined woman feels without her having to undergo the ordeal of marriage, loss of freedom, money, and, what I think, the highest kind of life."[16]

The language that Carey used here is significant. Looking on the world from her European outpost, Carey perceived marriage to a man as only "ordeal." By November 1882, as she wrote of Emma Culbertson, she only slightly rephrased the thoughts on marriage that had crystallized at least twenty-one months before, when in a letter to her mother she had opposed marriage on almost the exact same grounds as meaning "loss of freedom, poverty, and a *personal* subjection for which I see absolutely no compensation."[17]

When Carey used the phrase "personal subjection" she had two elements in mind. One was an uneasiness about male sexual desire that had first surfaced when she read her father's medical texts in her Baltimore years. Carey did not write of this directly in her years abroad but it came out in her reaction to the friendship that her cousin Mary Smith cultivated with Walt Whitman. In January 1883 in London, Carey got word that Hannah Whitall Smith had received Walt Whitman in her parlor. Carey wrote to her mother, "I am struck dumb at the thought that Aunt Hannah is entertaining Walt Whitman." Unquestionably, Whitman was a great poet. "I, of course, should be charmed to entertain him but to think that one of you should receive in your house the man who has written more grossly indecent things than perhaps any other man whose books are printed in an open manner, this consoles one for many things."

Despite her commitment to aesthetic freedom from moral constraints, Carey had a great deal of trouble with Whitman's poems. A late-twentieth-century reader is attuned to evidences of Whitman's homoeroticism, but it was Whitman's open portrayal of male lust for women that Carey found deeply offensive. As she put it, "He takes the view that everything that is, is lovely and of good report, and upon principle he glorifies the sexual functions. He rejoices that he has vigour enough to be the husband of all women alive. He longs to call out to every unmarried girl, etc. I am using, of course, most euphemistic language. He calls things by their names without scruple. I remember yet how he phrases Rossetti's line which was so objected to that he omitted it in later editions, 'monstrous maidenhood intolerable.' "[18]

Yet in understanding Carey's link between marriage and "personal subjection," more was at issue than unease at male sexual desire. In the early 1880s marriage in Maryland remained a union of power and subordination. "Loss of freedom" was real. Not only did the full burden of house and child care fall on the woman, but residues remained of legal inequalities rooted in the common law's declaration of women's legal death in marriage. Men controlled household resources. Women continued to be trained to patterns of deference to male authority. Although Carey had experienced unusual privilege, she knew that her ability to sustain scholarship or to pursue the love of art was contingent upon remaining single. Thus to Carey the choice not to marry was the choice of "the highest kind of life" over "personal subjection."

II

CAREY could dismiss Margaret Hicks' engagement as the true indication of her weakness of character; but how did she explain to herself that her own most loved mother had married? She found it hard to reconcile. Once, after Mary Thomas had made disparaging remarks about the "loneliness" of Carey's new single friend Gertrude Mead, Carey retorted that the source of her unmarried state was not in any unattractiveness in Gertrude, for she had had many suitors, but in Gertrude's lack of interest: "Men are really not nice enough for intellectual girls. Thee and Aunt Hannah were captured young before you had time to develop." All around her Carey saw matrons who seemed to be "women in bondage." Mary Thomas had survived marriage with personal freedom intact only because she was exceptional. "Thee knows *thee* is an extraordinary woman and has wonderfully overcome the drawbacks of matrimony, but there are not many such." What had saved Mary Thomas in her daughter's eyes was her commitment to religion, a commitment compatible with her marriage.[19]

Although, on some level, Carey came to terms with her mother's married state, she judged the extent of Mary Thomas' childbearing more harshly. Obviously she approved of her mother's first parturition, but she believed that human stock weakened down the line. In the spring of 1883, as Mary Thomas wrote of the younger children's sicknesses, Carey responded, "It is a proof, is it not? that even strong healthy people ought not to have more than four children because our strength goes in a descending scale down." As Carey thought of seeing the younger children again, she continued—with a lack of self-insight that must have made even a loving mother wince and dread the future—"I feel as if I should be very nice too. Thee must remember these four years have taught me a great deal besides Old German."[20]

Indirectly and directly Carey told her mother that she was no longer the selfish young woman who had troubled the home nest four years before. She quoted Gertrude Mead's praise for her warmth and kindness. However, her letters home reveal that on key issues she had not grown more benevolent.

As the Thomas children grew older and larger, the Madison Avenue house in Baltimore felt cramped and crowded. Carey's room had been fully occupied in her absences at Howland and Cornell. While she was abroad, her brother Harry lived in it. In 1882, as Carey contemplated returning home, she wondered how the house might accommodate her need of privacy and a separate study. She also worried about the house's relative tastelessness. She counseled her mother to redecorate the dining room and drew on Mamie's words for support. Carey had asked Mamie if the room was "disgraceful." In stating her assent, Mamie said that it reminded her of another household's "habit of breakfasting in their pantry."[21]

By the time she reached Zürich, Carey received good news. In the settlement of his parents' estate, James Whitall established a trust for his sister Mary that was to pass to the children on her death. Carey rejoiced, for it meant that she had some security for the future. The money would, she wrote, "at least enable the unmarried and non-self-supporting ~~members~~ girls of thy family to live in the story below the attic in their old age. It is lovely of Uncle James."[22] Carey hoped that the interest would allow the family to live within their income and begin to pay off some of their debts. Mary Thomas had different intentions and used the money to expand the Madison Street house. She also saw that Carey got an extra $100 to $150 for travel, a sum equivalent to $1500 to $2200 in today's dollars. Carey counseled Mary on ways that the renovated house might illustrate the family's social status. She suggested an internal plan that would prevent the servants from having to enter rooms to get to other rooms. Delighted that her mother intended to get her a new bed and bureau, she hoped that the new pieces would be blue and suggested Paris as the place to buy her rug.[23]

As further details of the estate settlement came to Carey, she learned that James Whitall had actually signed a deed transferring the funds. Two dangers appeared. If Mary Thomas should die before her husband, the money was to go to James Thomas. Carey wrote quickly, "do not forget to remake thy will so that we may have some place of refuge from that phantom second wife who, I feel sure, would never exist; but still." Even if Mary outlived her husband, there might be nothing for her eldest daughter, for Mary had a penchant for unwise investments in silver mines. While Carey was at Howland her mother had invested and lost; now she was trying again. Carey wrote to try and dissuade her, suggesting that such risky investments were "like Monte Carlo gambling."[24]

Although Mary Thomas may have welcomed Carey's involvement in the plans to alter the house and accepted her concern with protecting future resources, she could not have helped being troubled by Carey's desire to protect herself from family obligations. As Carey began to think about her trip home, she made it clear that she wanted to arrive only after the Yearly Meeting and her brother John's wedding. When James Thomas' stepmother was in Paris in June 1883, Carey was faced with the possibility that she and Mamie might have to attend the elderly woman on the journey home. Carey sought her mother's intercession, putting her reason on the ground of loyalty to Mamie: "Nothing could make me let Mamie room with a stranger and take a state room with Grandma which I am afraid she might expect. My first duty is to Mamie." Since she could not subject Mamie to a three-person stateroom, Mrs. Thomas would have to stay in a room nearby. She asked her mother to make different arrangements and scolded her for letting Mrs. Thomas travel to Europe without a paid companion.[25]

Carey was slightly kinder when her Howland teacher Jane Slocum came to Paris. She had not seen her in six years, and she owed her a great deal. Out of a sense of duty, she took her around to areas of Paris she might not discover by herself, but Carey begrudged the time and effort that such obligations took. Toward the end of her life, M. Carey Thomas reflected on friendship as she drafted her autobiography. Provoked by her recollection of the great influence on her of her childhood teacher Rebecca Marble, she asked herself why she had not seen her in her adult years when she and Rebecca had lived only a mile apart. She answered, "When I have felt that I have got all I can from a person I lose interest in them and pass on." She tried to explain this in terms of a growing divergence in view, then added this revealing statement: "I feel that it is a waste of time to associate with them." Both Rebecca Marble and Jane Slocum had altered her life with their teaching and encouragement. That Carey Thomas could discard them conveys much about her.[26]

Carey's misplaced judgment that she was no longer selfish arose from her isolation abroad from the claims of ordinary family life. In Europe she had little cause to be reminded of her selfishness, at least by her mother. Yet Europe was the location of one of her most self-centered actions. Before departing for Europe, as she was falling in love with Mamie, Carey quietly began to nurture an admiration for Mary Garrett. Mary, slightly older and exceedingly wealthier than Carey, introduced her to theater and opera. Carey composed a respectful sonnet for Mary and treated her as a revered and respected friend. What she seemed to ignore was that Mary was attached. She was linked in an intimate friendship with Julia Rogers, who resided with her during this period. As Carey prepared for the journey and what she anticipated would be three years abroad, she incautiously stepped over the line and was corrected by Julia. Undeterred, Carey sought an intimate correspondence with Mary.

Abroad Carey wrote intentionally frank letters to Mary and sought her advice. To her "Mentor," Carey wrote candidly about her meetings with Francis Gummere and forwarded Richard Cadbury's letters. She never alluded to her feeling for Mamie. Mary was critical of many of Carey's relationships. She urged Carey to break with her Howland and Cornell friends. Carey tried to defend herself and her youthful smashes. Carey cast out suggestive references, attempting to catch Mary. Having always lived at home, Mary had not been tempted as she had: "Oh Mary, if you had been to boarding school or college, you would see how hard it is. No, if you had, perhaps I should have been saved all my troubles and—." Mary, though affectionate and kind, ignored Carey's gestures.[27]

Carey's letters are exercises that seek in the many ways she knew to draw Mary to her and away from Julia. Carey had to be extremely careful, to write in hints and asides, for Mary let Julia read all her letters. Nothing is said directly; all is suggested. The tone of Carey's letters is introspective, thoughtful, allusive, poetic. Places are codes (not always cracked) for stages in their relationship. As Carey writes, "it is hardly worthwhile to tell you that I care, more than I did last summer at Germantown, and that I thought was impossible, but then West Chester comes in between," she knows that Mary will recall what happened at Germantown and West Chester, but hopes that Julia will not.[28]

Carey was invariably solicitous about Mary's health, grown suddenly delicate. When they met in 1875, Mary had been robust. Carey had especially admired the jaunty way she rode horseback. But in studying for the Harvard examinations, Mary had a breakdown that made her unable to concentrate. In addition, she experienced severe menstrual pain. Carey hoped Mary might come to Europe for travel and study.

Mary came abroad with her parents in the summer of 1880. In August Carey and Mamie traveled to Switzerland to meet the Garrett party. Initially Carey found it very awkward. As she wrote to her mother, "Mary kissed me from among the crowd in the dark. We were all three so embarrassed that evening that we could hardly speak." The following day Carey grew more at ease with Mary. But, quite unexpectedly, an accident changed the course of Mary's life, rendering her an invalid at a critical period in her life. She was climbing with Carey and two men, Mr. Gurney and Mr. Carrington, the latter an English clergyman who was Mary's "established escort" during her travels. Carey was in the midst of a wonderful day. "We lay on the rocks and subjected to the elements and in the midst of snow and ice. It was really like being up in the clouds." They walked for two hours on a glacier. "Mr. Gurney and I ran races, and Mr. Carrington held me by the hand, and we rushed like wind over the glassy snow. Unfortunately he took Mary and somehow she fell and sprained her ankle, broke a number of tendons." Mary bravely continued on the excursion as they reached a second glacier and climbed up a second elevation. When she returned to the hotel, her injury was very painful, but she only called a doctor the next morning. Her parents were very upset. Mamie's criticism allowed Carey to voice her own feelings: "As Mamie says, it *is* dreadful to think that a woman is such a slave that she is not even allowed to hurt herself without her owners becoming enraged."[29]

Carey had hoped that Mary could break free from her parents and travel with Mamie and her to Italy. But the ankle did not heal. For the next eight months Mary remained abroad, largely in France. Her injury prevented her from engaging in exercise that might have relieved the mental and gynecological distress she continued to suffer. The doctors she consulted abroad blamed her for overtaxing her female brain. Carey sympathized with Mary, for she remembered her own severe time of trial in Baltimore a few years earlier, but she refused to see Mary's condition as a female problem. She warned Mary to be skeptical about conservative English doctors who predicted dire consequences for women who studied: "Every doctor in the world might tell me what you were told and I should not believe it. You *can* have done nothing to bring on such lifelong consequences." Because Frank Gummere suffered from the same problem, it could hardly be rooted in female anatomy. When Mary wrote about a doctor's recommendation for uterine surgery, Carey's response was clear. "It does not seem to me certain that the womb is displaced or anything of that kind; because you know Mr. Gummere when he returned from Germany was that way. He could not read the simplest book or remember anything," a condition that lasted over a year.[30]

The August 1880 visit with Mary did not include Julia Rogers, who had remained in the United States while the estate of her grandmother was being settled. In December 1880, Julia joined Mary, who by then was gaining strength. Carey Thomas had planned to study, not travel, during the spring vacation of her second year abroad. But when March 1881 arrived, she and Mamie went to Rome to meet Mary and Julia. It turned out to be a horrendous reunion.

In Rome Julia confronted Carey, accusing her of seeking a "special friendship" with Mary. At issue were the difference in Carey's letters to the two women, Carey's demand that her letters be withheld from Julia, and Carey's requests for time alone with Mary and without Julia. Mary defended Julia.

Caught off guard, Carey flew into a rage. Civility was restored. Julia attempted to go on as before, even traveling with Carey and Mamie in Italy. Her manner was cold, however. As Carey wrote to Mary, "Do you know Julia never once kissed us good night after you left. I followed her to the door once in Naples, but she asked me what I wanted and my heart failed." In her letters to her mother at the time, Carey regarded Julia as an evil presence during their travels, an incomprehensible source of minor misfortunes. She wrote, disguising the conflict, "Traveling with Julia rather introduces a serpent into our Eden." Months later, after her parents' visit abroad, Carey was able to vent her spleen: "Julia herself has no idea of her crimes. I do not think she can realize how they seem in the eyes of an honorable person. . . . We have not had a break and shall not have, only . . . Mamie and I shall never again talk to her intimately."[31]

In the months that followed, Carey attempted to explain herself to Mary, now back in Maryland. She defended her desire to write intimate letters to Mary and talk with her alone. She placed the burden on Mary. "I think I have something to forgive." If the persons had been different, if, for example, Bessie King and Carey had met, and Bessie had asked for time alone to talk with Carey, and Mamie had pressured Carey so that she had only had three talks with Bessie, "I should feel as if I had in some way failed in my friendship to her." Had Mary told her that because she and Julia were soon to part company, they needed time alone, Carey would have accepted it and would not have come to Rome. What she resented was the language that Mary used when she talked to her in Rome. Mary had suggested that there was something wrong in Carey's desire for a special relation with her. "I think you should . . . not have said what you did about 'a sensible friendship.' To my knowledge our friendship has always been 'sensible.' If it is unsensible to wish to talk to a friend sometimes alone (and above all when that friend is you because you certainly do talk more freely alone), then I do not think I know what friendship is." Denying that she had ever tried to take Mary from Julia, Carey wrote, "I have hitherto liked and admired your friendship for each other, and . . . the last thing I would dream of doing, even supposing the impossible, that I had the power, would be . . . in any way coming between you. I cannot believe that an intimate friendship like yours or like Mamie's and mine shuts out the possibility . . . of any other companionship during one's life, and I feel as if your and Julia's friendship and Mamie's and mine were for life." Ultimately she asked Mary to forget "what I did and said that I should not have" in Rome. Having been taken aback by Julia, Carey admitted, she "may have done a hundred things."[32]

There was a long silence from Mary. As months went by and she did not write, Carey continued to send her a regular letter, attempting to take a light tone. Finally in late August, Mary wrote that she did not wish their correspondence to stop. In response Carey wrote a letter in September that may have been too personal either for Mary to have saved or for an older M. Carey Thomas to have kept with her papers, for, uniquely, it is missing. Mary's response, received in October, was deeply painful to Carey: "You say, unless I can write to you as a friend you would prefer that I should not write at all. I could not write to you in any other way if [I] tried, and if I could, I should not care to write." Mary had in turn unleashed hostile feelings toward Mamie. It was now Carey's task to defend her intimate friend, but in doing so she pointed out carefully that she did not share with Mamie the contents of Mary's letter. She ended with emotional pleading. She was distraught over Bessie's illness and also over the change in her relationship with her mother, as "statues and pictures and mad ambition have raised a sort of mist between myself and Mother." Her love of works of art struck her as a weakness: "there could be no excuse for the passion I cannot help giving them, no excuse except its sanctification in reproduction (like sexual passion)." As she closed the letter, she admitted to having had a "sobbing fit" over it. She wished Mary were there for a good-night kiss. "There is 'nothing between us' now, is there?"[33]

Mary, obviously troubled that Carey's feelings for her were not "sensible" and that she was not writing simply "as a friend," did not answer Carey's October letter until mid-March. In the vacuum, Carey continued to write monthly newsy letters. On New Year's Eve, however, she allowed herself a personal appeal. She begged Mary to write now and then "to bridge over this chasm of two years. It is a long time, when two years lie behind it—and *Rome* between." She wondered if her recent letters had been unsatisfactory, written as they were jointly to Julia and Mary and not to Mary alone. She once again attempted a special friendship. Would Mary keep from mailing Carey's letters to Julia, studying in England? As she closed, she suggested that perhaps Mary misunderstood something. "You cannot have misunderstood the fact that I love you and am not willing to give up our friendship."[34]

In time Carey resumed distant, careful relations with Julia and cautioned her mother to do the same. When Mary and Julia traveled to Europe a second time in the summer of 1883, Carey and Mamie did not see them. Carey's summer illness worked better than adoration and pleading, and Mary returned to a regular correspondence, answering each of Carey's letters immediately.

It was in Rome that Carey had recognized for the first time the extent of Mary Garrett's wealth. A sculptor was doing a bust of Mrs. Garrett at a cost of twelve hundred dollars, a sum double Carey's annual allowance abroad. Mary's father traveled in what Carey described as "an elegant private carriage with coachman and footman at his disposal," and when he needed permission to see a work of art, used a courier to gain it. Mary herself was accompanied by a personal servant who brushed her clothing and dressed her.[35]

In Paris, as Carey prepared to return to Baltimore, she was reminded of the difference between Mary's riches and her own comfortable but limited means. As she planned her final assault on Bryn Mawr, Carey gathered a fashionable wardrobe, writing to her mother, "I only wish to look nice, even a little nicer than usual if I am to be president of Bryn Mawr." Mary Garrett sent her a list of what she should buy, where she should shop, and the prices she should pay. Carey queried her mother about what to do. She had only two suitable dresses, one for winter and one for summer. She was thinking of purchasing an ulster, a winter cloth coat, a dark brown winter suit, and an evening dress. She contemplated a black silk dress for evening, but felt that the price of $100 (or almost $1,500 in 1994 dollars) was too much. But the obverse struck her as well. As she was agonizing about her decision, she recognized some of what it meant to be very rich. Mary and her friend Lou Knox had each spent between $250 and $300 for a dress at Worth's. Mary's father had given her a set of Braun photographs of great works of art, valued at $1,000. Mary's wealth meant something even more personal: Mary sent as a gift to Carey in Paris a Rossetti watercolor. Mary herself bought an important small Rossetti watercolor, *Mary in the House of St. John.*[36]

On the eve of departure, the details of purchases and fittings—costing approximately $300—helped distract Carey from facing an unknown world. She longed to be home and see her mother, but she also knew that a unique period in her life was concluding. She wrote to her mother about her sadness at ending her life abroad with Mamie: "Our life of study and looking at pictures has been exceptionally ideal. We have only seen each other and thus have only met with agreement instead of disagreement." Though she looked forward to seeing her mother and the work ahead, she knew she would miss what she had known. "Parting from Mamie will be very hard . . . although we shall be so near each other. She has been and is and, I think, always will be the very friend I should have chosen out of all the world."[37]

Carey Thomas had found herself in Europe. She had alternatively lived the life of the scholar, the artist, and the schemer for Bryn Mawr. She had shared a rich intimacy with Mamie and imagined one with Mary. Could the existence she had known abroad be sustained in America? As she prepared to board ship, she wrote to her mother, "Thee need not fear that I shall not like *home.* It is America I shall find it hard to bear."[38]

CHAPTER 10

When We Were All Young Together

✦✦✦✦✦

W HEN CAREY THOMAS returned to Baltimore at age twenty-six, she had not evolved a single fixed identity. She imagined herself in three quite distinct ways. She was the scholarly Doctor Thomas of the Ph.D., living out the ideal she had set for herself at age seventeen under Miss Slocum's tutelage. She was the aesthetic Carey, envisioned in late adolescence but created abroad in union with Mamie Gwinn, who dreamed of a life of art. And she was a third self, soon to be called Dean Thomas, committed to the cause of women, perhaps the most deeply held of all because conceived as a child and nurtured in the reform household of Mary and James Thomas.

On her return from abroad, Carey Thomas did not make a fully conscious choice for one of these lives. Somehow she hoped that she could live them all. In Europe she had partially done so: she had prepared effectively for her Ph.D., she had traveled and soaked up impressions, and she had schemed for Bryn Mawr. Yet at some level she knew that in leaving for America the delicate balance achieved in Europe would be difficult to sustain on home ground.

She was right. In the first decade back in America the active, reforming self, committed to broadening education for women, scaled creative heights. This is the M. Carey Thomas of Bryn Mawr College who has merited biographical attention in the past. With Mamie Gwinn's assistance, her scholar persona rose to meet the challenge of organizing courses and writing lectures. In time, however, it began to atrophy in response to the unremitting demands of her office. Her artistic spirit and its sustaining personal relations went under deep cover to be indulged in secretly at home and more openly as she traveled abroad each summer with Mamie.

I

ON NOVEMBER 25, 1883, Carey and Mamie landed in Baltimore. Their journey home had been by a roundabout route, and fog detained the ship near

Newfoundland for seven days. Carey was ill during the week of waiting. On the day she landed in Baltimore, Harry went down to the wharf to wait for the ship. He telephoned when he sighted it, and James and Frank went immediately to the dock. Mary and the rest of the children waited for Carey at home. After four years away, Carey did not recognize Margaret, Bond, or Grace. Mary reported to her sister Hannah, "Carey is lovely. She is *delighted* with the house and the children and her room."[1]

In Carey Thomas' years abroad, her aunt Hannah Whitall Smith had remained in the background, a supportive but unobtrusive presence. By the 1880s Smith's energies flowed to "the cause" of women's rights, and she sent her niece *The Women's Journal* and copies of her own speeches on women. Hannah Smith wrote an article on Carey Thomas' achievements that she did not publish; its private circulation, however, spread the news effectively among the Quaker community. A few months before Carey's return, when she was in Paris without real prospects of a job, Hannah Smith and James Whitall offered her a position as teacher to their daughters the following year. It was with great care that Carey answered Hannah that she ought not accept because she needed to give her time to prepare for Bryn Mawr and scholarship and that such work might damage her reputation. She assumed that her aunt understood her ambition. In the midst of elaborating on why she should be president of Bryn Mawr College, Carey Thomas wrote baldly, "I believe that often the right man gets, by hook or by crook, into the right place." Carey knew that her aunt could see the importance of Bryn Mawr, even when her mother might not.[2]

In the weeks after Carey Thomas' return to Baltimore nothing happened to resolve the question of Bryn Mawr. In Europe, Thomas had received two letters from Dr. James E. Rhoads, the college's provisional executive, one encouraging, the other cautious, but it was clear that all decisions awaited her return to America. Throughout December, silence persisted. In January, Hannah Smith decided the time had come for her to act, as she put it, to stick her " 'oar' into the Bryn Mawr pie." It was an opportunity she seized. No one on the Bryn Mawr board of trustees, not even her brother James Whitall or her brother-in-law James Carey Thomas, asked her advice. As Hannah Smith put it, "They would not consult a *woman*, I suppose, to save their lives." She interviewed Dr. Rhoads and let him know that he was not qualified to be president of Bryn Mawr, but that Carey Thomas was. On January 9, 1884, she wrote to the men chosen by Joseph Wright Taylor: "I do not believe the board of trustees are aware of the intense interest with which their course is being watched by the women of this country." Putting them on warning, she turned to the presidency. Two elements were critical to the success of the new college: its president must be a person of broad literary culture and a woman. Only one choice was possible, M. Carey Thomas. She was a Friend, an enthusiast for women's education, a person devoted to literary pursuits, and an unusually independent woman. "In fact, she seems to me to have been born, and educated, and *made*, for just this post. And not to take her would seem to me almost like a flying in the face of Providence."[3]

Hannah Whitall Smith knew her friends and relations and was realistic enough to understand that although these Orthodox Quaker men could not ignore her counsel, they might not heed her. Some compromise would have to be struck. If the board thought Thomas too inexperienced in business they might appoint an officer, such as the president of the board, to "take the pecuniary part of the management under his carry, leaving the literary and educational part to Martha Carey Thomas."[4]

On January 15, 1884, she wrote to Carey Thomas to "stick an oar into *thy* pie too," to prepare her niece to accept a position less than that of president. It was her guess that the trustees would insist on Rhoads as president, but would ask Thomas to share his authority, giving her a "sort of tentative position at first." Hannah Smith counseled her niece, "I cannot help thinking it would be wise for thee to agree to it. Thee could then *prove* thy capabilities, and could make thyself so absolutely necessary to them that they would have no alternative finally but to make thee president."

The aunt's arguments were a wonderful combination of opportunism and idealism, exactly pitched to the niece's ear. Carey Thomas should follow her advice, because it was her path to the presidency. In practical terms, she was taking little risk, for she could leave the position. By accepting what was offered, Thomas could soon work her way "into the very highest, and could have things go pretty much as thee might please." Smith urged her to agree to the trustees' terms "for the sake of woman. There is no one else but *thee* to save this college to our sex, and I beg of thee to throw thyself into the breach." For a brief time, Thomas should be prepared to use "woman's usual weapons . . . management and influence."[5]

Rhoads moved quickly. Eight days later, Mary wrote Hannah: "Dr. Rhoads is upstairs now talking with Minnie!! but do not breathe it." The formal action of the board took almost three more months. On March 14, 1884, the trustees appointed M. Carey Thomas professor of English and dean of the faculty, to serve under James E. Rhoads. After consulting with Johns Hopkins' President Daniel Coit Gilman, they had created an office virtually unknown in America. In the formal minutes they spelled out the dean's duties: "Until the opening of the college, as well as after it shall be in active operation, she shall assist the president in arranging the details of the courses of study, and in the adoption of the best methods and means for imparting the instruction to be given in the college." She was offered the salary of $1,000 a year—over $15,000 in today's dollars—a respectable sum for a beginning academic salary in 1884, but far less than the $4,000 of President Rhoads.[6]

James Thomas came home at ten P.M. with the news. Before his daughter got formal word or had a chance to think out her response, the newspapers announced the trustees' decision. Mary wrote Hannah the following day: "Carey was elected Dean of the Faculty of Bryn Mawr College yesterday and the newspapers have announced the fact today, which is very remarkable and very disgusting to her, who had hoped to break it gently to her friends. . . . I suppose the fates are upon her, and she will do it, though I think she has a thousand misgivings lest she is greatly narrowing her career."[7]

Despite all her scheming and planning, Carey Thomas was taken aback. As she wrote to Mary Garrett, "Before I had at all decided what to do," Philadelphia and Baltimore papers reported on her appointment. To Thomas' surprise, family and friends offered congratulations. Hannah Smith wrote, "The Papers rejoiced my heart yesterday with the announcement of thy Deanship! I herewith make my manners, and congratulate, not thee, but the coming women of our nation on the stride that has been made in their advancement by this step. In plain words, I am unspeakably delighted and encouraged and hopeful." Carey Thomas answered that she was confident she would be able to work with Rhoads, and she expressed her appreciation for her aunt's aid.[8]

Carey Thomas' response was, however, more complicated. As she wrote to Mary Garrett, it was secretly conditional: "Although I do not say so, I shall not consider the thing irrevocable until I have tried my utmost to organize it well and partially at least succeeded." After taking counsel with President Gilman at Johns Hopkins, she planned to travel to Vassar, Smith, Wellesley, and the Harvard Annex. She was to write a report to the trustees "in which I hope to be able to persuade them of a few primary principles." Her subsequent task was to be the selection of the first faculty.

As she pondered the steps ahead, she wrote to Mary, "The things we care for lie neither in degrees nor scholarship, and our heart is therefore not in them." As she listened to Felix Mendelssohn's *Elijah*, all at once, her "hesitation in regard to Bryn Mawr seemed ~~selfish and~~ cowardly." The dream of the artistic life abroad would have to be given up for at least five or six years. The change in her life was overwhelming. "I have realized why and how Europe ruins an American. A constant longing is not a good condition for work, and to wish for things that one cannot have is a fruitless employment."[9]

At the point that the trustees acted, Carey Thomas believed she was still trying to answer the major question in her life: which of the contending identities would she become? Would she pursue the ideal through art in Europe, scholarship in research libraries, or the active life of service for women in America? In Europe with Mamie Gwinn, she had blended scholarly preparation in Leipzig and Zürich with vacation travels soaking up European literary scenes and pictures. Both blurred into an imagined future of the independent cultured woman. Carey and Mamie had come back to America with an understanding that they should sustain in Baltimore, as best they could, their aesthetic and scholarly lives and return abroad as quickly as possible.

Yet even in Europe, as Carey Thomas schemed for Bryn Mawr, a third nature was working, propelled by a restless, driving ambition that could not be contained in the quiet of a library. She had initially maneuvered to become the professor of literature, but, as her work in Leipzig and Zürich progressed, she sought more. She dreamed of the power to transform what had been intended as a conservative Quaker college for girls into a cosmopolitan center for the latest European scholarship dedicated to the cause of women. In appointing her dean, the Bryn Mawr trustees unleased her reforming passion.

II

IN EUROPE she imagined Bryn Mawr as Leipzig in miniature. Compelled by the "light" of philology, she now had truth, the "open sesame" that unlocked the secrets of language and culture. She planned to bring European-trained scholars to the college, to establish a graduate school, and to create graduate fellowships. As she had put it, this was "strong meat to the strong" that she would place alongside "milk to the babes," the normal courses of the liberal arts curriculum for undergraduates. Because women need not be monitored, she could recreate the freedom of the German university without the license of the male German student.

She and Mamie Gwinn must have talked of this endlessly, in Europe and in Baltimore. At some point in one of their conversations, probably between when she was chosen dean and before the board formally appointed her, Carey Thomas picked up Mamie Gwinn's literary notebook and wrote out her scheme. There was $28,000—roughly $425,000 in today's dollars—available for the first year, after setting aside $10,000 for capital expenses. She planned to spend $16,500 on professorships in the following five fields: ancient philosophy and literature, including Greek, Latin, and Sanskrit; German philosophy and literature, coupled with Anglo-Saxon and Early English; romantic philosophy and literature with later English literature and composition; history and political economy; and mathematics. Each professorship was to be supported by a graduate fellow and a tutor. In the sciences, she anticipated borrowing professors from Haverford and the University of Pennsylvania to teach courses. The order of the professorships made her plan clear. Bryn Mawr was to be a school of philology, covering the three important language groups: ancient, Germanic, and Romance. History and mathematics were to serve as necessary supplements.[10]

Carey Thomas began a notebook for her thoughts, observations, and interviews. Her conversations with Rhoads made it clear that certain principles ought to guide the foundation of the new college. She searched for words to give an acceptable justification for her scheme. With deliberation and precision, Thomas wrote the principles in a logical order, using a different shade of ink to set questions and establish categories. She began with the brute fact that the small return on the endowment made it "impossible to organize all departments equally well." The trustees were committed to protecting the principal of Joseph Taylor's gift, forcing the college to start small.

Carey Thomas approached the college from the model of Johns Hopkins, Leipzig, and Zürich: hire a few specialists in key fields as professors, pay them very well, and limit their duties to allow fresh scholarship. She determined to make the positions ones of prestige and high salary so that the best-trained scholars would seek them. She noted to herself, "Institutions and professors are valued and ranked by the salaries which they give." To the five professors she added associates and instructors. She planned to appoint faculty only on the basis of a firsthand knowledge of the quality of scholarship and teaching, paying no attention to "recommendations or personal considerations."[11]

Rhoads thought about a curriculum that mirrored that of the university in the small, representing all fields. Thomas planned to specialize in the study of language. She found new parlance to justify this focus. Putting aside her belief in philology's intellectual power, she argued that languages were those "studies which cultivate the taste, judgment" of the "girls and women of the upper classes" for whose benefit Taylor endowed the college. To language she added philosophy, mathematics, and history. She deemphasized the sciences, because women students did not desire them and because she knew that a "thoroughly equipped" scientific department was not possible in Bryn Mawr's early years. Having logically considered the issues, she wrote her conclusions in the notebook. Adding that "as no institution is theoretical, but wholly practical in its working," she determined to visit existing women's colleges to see not only "the work being done . . . but the workers themselves—the professors and teachers in their classes."[12]

The following week she met, at his invitation, with Daniel Coit Gilman, the president of Johns Hopkins University. He offered her abundant advice about the organization of the college and the nature and selection of faculty appointments. Carey Thomas listened carefully and took notes but was skeptical about the intentions of a man whose failure to support women in the university had forced her to withdraw. Gilman elaborated about Bryn Mawr's chance to evolve something new for the education of American women. Thomas privately disagreed. She noted that there was a "fallacy" in Gilman's thinking. Men's colleges, because they had worked on common educational problems for many generations, were the best guide for women's colleges. Gilman had much to teach her about appointments, and she noted his advice that she look to the long term: "*Appoint* no professors without reference to their usefulness ten to fifteen years hence. Impossible to get rid of them." Assistant professors should be hired for a definite period of time, three or five years. Countering Thomas' willingness to disregard the sciences, Gilman insisted that no college worthy of its name could fail to have strong appointments in language, science, mathematics, and metaphysical philosophy. He expressed some skepticism about Thomas' plan for graduate fellows, but she largely passed it off to his limited notion of women's colleges and his "dislike to see Johns Hopkins University copied." Gilman attempted to discourage her scheme of special disciplinary libraries connected to classrooms, arguing that it drew strength away from the central library.[13]

Dr. Rhoads came to Baltimore to spend the weekend. They settled on Thomas' trip to the eastern women's colleges. She began regular visits to Philadelphia to consult with Rhoads. Although the opening of Bryn Mawr was seventeen months away, the trustees were ready to begin making appointments. Carey Thomas leapt right in to defeat premature decisions.

She entered Baltimore's Peabody Library with a new task, preparing lectures. She wrote to Mary Garrett, "I am deep in English philology, i.e., getting up English presentations of what I know only through German scholarship." Her new position gave intellectual companionship. With James Rendel Harris, Johns Hopkins' professor of New Testament Greek and paleography, she had "a little gossip every now and then" at her desk. Henry Wood, a Leipzig Ph.D. who taught English at Johns Hopkins, worked next to her and he grew "alternately enthusiastic or indignant" over Anglo-Saxon scholarship. To Mary, Carey Thomas wrote about Wood, "He is not a rival, I mean in lines of work, so I spur him on." Living at home, the constant sociability of the Thomas household made progress difficult. "I am so dissatisfied with the amount of reading I accomplish and with our incessant company to dinner. I think I shall shave my head and shut myself up in my study."[14]

Although envisioning herself as a refined woman of culture, Carey Thomas immediately threw herself into the life of action. The "little sturdy" who had so delighted her grandfather, the tomboy who had walked on stilts and had run along the roofs of Baltimore, was once again afoot.

Carey Thomas set out for the women's colleges, determined to learn everything they had to teach Bryn Mawr. Her first stop was Vassar College in Poughkeepsie, New York, where, much to Mamie's displeasure, letters from Gertrude Mead had eased the way. Thomas tried to understand Vassar from top to bottom, looking at hardwood floors as well as curriculum and standards. She attended classes, talked over course assignments, and evaluated each professor, with half an eye to potential usefulness to Bryn Mawr. Her notes were unsparing. For example she judged one philosophy professor to be "a nice man but a wretched teacher. His logic recitation is a farce." She noted that the mathematics professor held recitations that were "brilliant," but was "for some reason not popular quite. . . . Too old for us." Thomas paid attention especially to questions that Rhoads had posed about requirements, hours of teaching, student preparation, and offerings in art. She queried faculty on salary and learned that her $1,000 hardly measured against the $2,500 and housing offered to Vassar professors. She sought reactions to her proposed innovations, especially her plan of graduate fellowships and her ideas about allowing students to choose their courses.[15]

Carey Thomas' response to the pioneer women's college was complex. Vassar offered the full college curriculum, taught by professors, to undergraduate women. To this it hinged a vast building and a system of governance inherited from the female seminary. To fill the building, Vassar was forced to accept preparatory students, intensifying efforts to control students. Thomas rankled at Miss Goodsell, the lady principal, whom she found "not agreeable, little souled, not literary or scholarly, too fond of rules and system," but she warmed to the professors, especially the famed astronomer Maria Mitchell. Thomas wrote Mary Garrett, "It was a sensation to sit opposite Maria Mitchell at table, or to be in her study and see her lying on the couch at full length speaking sarcastic, rather bitter, wholly loyal things. I felt, little as personal enthusiasm is in my line, that I would do anything to show my reverence for her and I think I shall be guilty of keeping the tiny bunch of flowers she gave with what she says is her customary remark, 'A bunch from my garden, Miss Thomas, my *whole* garden.' " Mitchell worked with defective equipment, limiting her scientific achievements, but she was an extraordinary influence on Vassar students. Admiration for her made the sophomore class choose calculus in order to be able to take her course on mathematical astronomy. More generally, Thomas found that the women professors outshone the men: "Perhaps men cannot teach women easily." On the whole, despite Vassar's "intolerable rules," she liked its collegiate tradition. "Vassar seemed to me monastic and charming. I can't express how it impressed me, but unlike anything else I had ever seen."[16]

From Vassar, Carey Thomas went to Smith College in Northampton, Massachusetts. When the trustees began planning for the physical Bryn Mawr, they had consciously drawn on Smith's plan of a large academic building, topped by a tower, surrounded by student dwellings. At Smith Thomas explored the institution for all the useful knowledge it contained, visiting classrooms, interviewing faculty, looking at benches. Unlike Vassar, Smith was headed by a dynamic president, L. Clark Seelye, who was convinced that he had the answers to the critical questions. In ten years he had increased Smith's enrollment from 14 to 250, and he was beginning to receive significant benefactions. The secret, he insisted, was that Smith cottages, small-scale domestic residences where students lived and ate, were completely self-supporting, paying interest on the funds invested in their construction and furnishing. By contrast, Merion, the future residence hall at Bryn Mawr, was so expensive that it could never pay for itself. To properly supervise the college, Thomas noted, "President Seelye has learned to be fireman, architect, building stone mason, gardener." It was, she put it, "the only way." Seelye gave Thomas details about chairs, asphalt on walks, and other exalting topics. Carey Thomas was convinced. She wrote in her notebook, "I intend to build other cottages where I shall allow the girls to pay more and have two rooms apiece. Boarding arrangements must be made to *pay*" in order to encourage gifts to the college. To her mother she wrote that she feared that Rhoads would never be like Seelye, who knew more about the college's buildings and furnishings than the custodians. If Rhoads could not learn, she would. "I am *determined* to run economically as Smith does."[17]

But all was not glorious at Smith. The faculty did not measure up to buildings and grounds. There were no women professors. Seelye argued that he had tried, but could not find "suitably educated women," and when he did, they married and left. Smith had women teachers, but though the male professors received $2,500, the women's salaries began at $500.[18]

Thomas questioned students and teachers. She had inside help, for she was introduced by a distant cousin to her circle of undergraduate friends. Thomas took tea at a Smith cottage, talking to twenty-five students, and attended a college theatrical. She got privileged information from the women teachers, and it made her boil with rage. The standards were low, and the teaching poor. She wrote to Mary Garrett, "It is a chance wasted. I dislike to think about it, these 250 girls getting husks. . . . I cannot express to you my despair over women so clever, so enthusiastic, and so little chance. None of these girls can be scholars because they are not started right, their education is in the hands of men who *do not care*. There is not one strong woman in the place, not even one really well-educated woman." Carried away, she concluded, "I am conscious of a strong impulse to—well, to put it barely—to wring the necks of most of the professors and teachers in Smith College."[19]

Carey Thomas' next stop was Wellesley, the only college headed by a woman. There she spent little time with buildings and housekeeping, as Wellesley in 1884 was architecturally quite similar to Vassar. She focused instead on faculty and administrative structure. Wellesley organized its all-female teaching staff into departments headed by a full professor who taught only her specialty and who was given full authority over the assistants and instructors. Unlike Smith, Wellesley had not found it difficult to get female professors. Low faculty salaries were offset by the beauty of the setting and the chance to specialize. Thomas was harshly critical of the professors with the exception of one, about whom she noted, "I *think* she is good. Keep eye on her." She had long envied Alice Freeman, Wellesley's second president. But meeting her, she hedged: "Talking to her, listening to her, driving with her in her phaeton I feel her ability and non-ability in a breath."[20]

As critical as she was of "the stopping halfway, of the so far and no further of these girls' colleges," Carey Thomas was inspired by Wellesley's community of women. She wrote to Mary Garrett, "To sit, as I sat today, in chapel, and look down upon a woman president, reading prayers to an audience of five hundred women and seventy professors and teachers—all women, not a man's influence seen or felt; or to watch the girls in trousers swinging on rings, twirling on bars, a newer race of athletes—ushers in a new day." Referring to Tennyson's poem depicting an all-female community, she was moved by "the devotion to study of these girls and women professors in this Princess-like community of Wellesley."[21]

As Carey Thomas realized, this was no mere fact-finding trip. The missionary zeal she criticized as déclassé in her mother breathed in her. She found herself caught up in the cause of women. From Northampton she wrote to her mother, "I am only afraid of getting too much interested in it. I suppose I can't help being a woman and so caring for them to have the best, and Smith is not the best." Stirring in her was the ambition, denied by the trustees, to be Bryn Mawr's president. She wrote to Mary Garrett that if she had Bryn Mawr in her own hands, she could fill it with students and "not a girl would go to Smith." But she knew that even if she were president and gave her life to the college, "afterwards a President Seelye might step in and undo all." Her enthusiasm and passion for the cause of women were, she felt, "the curse of belonging to an unfree race." From Wellesley she wrote of feeling "the rush of passionate (because no less foolish word expresses it) interest in what is being done for girls." In high excitement she wrote home, "I find it difficult to think of any thing else but Bryn Mawr. I never felt so strong a capacity for managing anything. Oh, if I but had it all to do!"[22]

The competitive streak that had earlier pushed Carey Thomas to best Francis Gummere welled up. Bryn Mawr was not to stop halfway. It was to be better than Smith. If James Rhoads could not do something, she could. She would learn it all. From faculty and curriculum to entrance standards and furnaces, Bryn Mawr would set the standard.

Carey Thomas' final college visit was to the Harvard Annex in Cambridge, to be renamed Radcliffe College in 1893, where she listened to lectures. Stella Gilman who had aided her husband, Arthur Gilman, in the founding of the Annex, gave Carey Thomas a reception. As she met the Harvard faculty associated with the women's school, she wrote home that she had found them "charming in regard to women's education." Several of the young men had attended the University of Leipzig in her years and had known of her from the lecture hall. As she scouted for Bryn Mawr appointments, she was delighted to see William E. Byerly, who had taught her mathematics at Cornell and was now a warm friend of the Annex, and she asked others if he was willing to move. She talked to Dr. Dudley Allen Sargent about Bryn Mawr's gymnasium. She met with members of the Harvard faculty to discuss educational strategy and appointments. Professor Francis J. Child insisted that a college was its faculty and its books, not its campus. Clement Smith argued for a three-thousand-dollar salary for professors, sabbaticals, and an aggressive search for faculty. Carey Thomas was smitten. She wrote to Mary Garrett that she found the men "more pleasant to me than the women. In colleges they are more cultivated." She was a little more sensible after a morning with Ellen Swallow Richards, a scientist on the faculty of the Massachusetts Institute of Technology, who gave her introductions to other women educators. "It is a delight to see how women help each other. We shall soon be a power."[23]

In Boston, Mamie joined her for sightseeing and picture viewing, with Mary Smith, the daughter of Hannah Whitall Smith, in tow. They went to an afternoon at the Boston Women's Club, where, in addition to notable women such as Abby May, Thomas found her Leipzig acquaintance Eva Channing and Carrie Ladd from Howland. She wrote to Mary Garrett that she regarded Marion Talbot as "the most attractive" of the "many clever women" that she met in Boston, and yet she was "not drawn to any one of them." She began writing a report to the trustees while still in Boston. Mamie and she went to Newport for five days at a Friends' boarding house. There amid the cliffs and the ocean, Thomas continued writing.[24]

III

On June 7, Carey Thomas presented her report to the president and trustees. Although Thomas made every effort to cast her findings in a calm and ordered fashion, through the typescript gleams her passion to get Bryn Mawr right. She had imagined the academic soul of the college for a long time. Her college visits gave her authority to contend for it. In addition, the tour gave her new insights into the material body of buildings and budgets.

Carey Thomas had listened hard, absorbed well, and now argued strenuously. Seelye had convinced her of the necessity of a college "run on paying principles." Though, to Thomas' regret, the expensiveness of Merion Hall prevented a fair return on its investment, she hoped that future halls would follow the Smith policy. Each hall, with its own separate kitchen and dining room, should be run by a lady-in-charge as if it were her own house. Bryn Mawr should also charge varying room rates depending upon the quality of the accommodations. Students should be able to select rooms according to their "needs and means," just as they make other choices. Thomas drew on (and falsified) her own experience in Sage College at Cornell to argue that "it made no social difference whether a girl had one, two, or three rooms. I had three: many of my friends had but one." With tuition at $100 a year, the annual fee including room and board came to $350 or $400, considerably higher than the $275 it cost to go to Wellesley.[25]

Although Smith's domestic department gave to Bryn Mawr "our most natural and our best model," neither Smith, Wellesley, nor Vassar had much to offer in scholastic organization. "Everyone has said to me that Bryn Mawr would succeed if it supplied what these colleges lack." The Harvard Annex, though presenting "none of the attractions of college life," was the academic exemplar. Despite its high fees, it already had forty-one students. Given Joseph Taylor's purpose to educate future teachers and to give women "all the advantages of a college education which are so freely offered to our young men," Harvard and the other important colleges for men were the real guides. Thomas argued strenuously that teaching be limited to ten hours a week so that the faculty could remain scholars. "Unless the professor steadily continue his studies . . . he ceases to be a college professor, and becomes a schoolmaster." Thomas recommended that at Bryn Mawr all the important fields constitute departments to be placed in the hands of "scholars able to guide their students in higher study," aided by instructors and assistants.[26]

Carey Thomas insisted that the program of graduate fellowships she had recommended from the outset would greatly enhance Bryn Mawr's reputation. She proposed that the fellowships be given only to those of "marked ability," college graduates or possessors of a certificate, who have begun postgraduate study. Graduate fellows would bring "proved scholars into relation with the students." Graduate fellows would help attract and retain a well-qualified faculty and would keep professors alert and abreast of their fields. Thomas urged the trustees to create a graduate fellowship in each department. Scholarship by faculty and by graduate students required a library that was not to be merely one of general literature, but "a collection of tools." Its quality served as the true "measure of the scope of a college." Thomas suggested a compromise between the John Hopkins system of special libraries located in classrooms and the more typical general college library.[27]

In 1884 the course of study of women's colleges remained largely a sequence of required courses, known as the classical curriculum. Thomas advocated the group system followed by Johns Hopkins. Although not defined in the report itself, the trustees knew that the Baltimore university had introduced a compromise between the elective system being pursued at Harvard and the traditional classical curriculum. In addition to meeting general requirements in languages, mathematics, natural sciences, and English, a Johns Hopkins student selected a track—classical, scientific, legal, mathematical, or literary—that laid out a clear sequence of courses. Thomas proposed to the trustees that Bryn Mawr "adopt unconditionally the theory of Johns Hopkins."[28]

Carey Thomas urged the trustees not to establish many undergraduate scholarships for needy students, reminding them of Taylor's will establishing the college for the "young women of the upper classes." Scholarships, a likely area for future benefactions, were a drain on present endowment. Rather than support students who could not afford college, Thomas recommended a prize for the gifted, a European scholarship of six hundred dollars to be given each year to a Bryn Mawr graduate. As Bryn Mawr was to start with first-year students, the college did not have to select a European fellow for four years, but publishing an announcement of the fellowship in the circular would attract students and serve as "a mighty factor in the higher scholarship of women."[29]

Bryn Mawr differed from a university not in the quality of courses taught, but in their number. Starting with few students, Bryn Mawr must begin with very few departments, but "each of these should be in itself a model one," built on the quality of the faculty, the graduate fellows, the library, and scientific laboratories and collections. Thomas' original opposition to the sciences had evaporated under the weight of Gilman's arguments and her visit to colleges. She recommended that Bryn Mawr begin with a school of languages, including Greek, Latin, English, German, French, and the remaining Romance languages; a school of sciences, including chemistry, biology, zoology, hygiene, and botany; and departments of mathematics and history.[30]

Finally, Carey Thomas tackled the difficult subject of entrance examinations. Confronting an earlier trustee decision that set examination standards lower than those of Wellesley, Smith, and Vassar, she had to demonstrate to the board its mistake and get agreement on a higher standard. "A college is ranked among other colleges by the difficulty of its entrance examination." Thomas pushed the trustees to authorize ones similar to those of Harvard, the Annex, and Johns Hopkins.[31]

As she composed the report, Carey Thomas wrote to Mary Garrett that if the trustees did not support her resolutions, "How glad I shall be to return to my books again, and how much more satisfactory they are."[32] Such words are not to be taken seriously. Carey Thomas was now fully committed to Bryn Mawr. She was in it for good. At the trustees' meeting Carey Thomas met with complete success, winning every round. To Mary Garrett she outlined the full victory. The trustees, "after a fierce struggle," passed her financial plan. They established the professorships, created five graduate fellowships, set up only three scholarships of two hundred dollars each, founded the European scholarship, and made the entrance examinations more rigorous. "All of which I consider wonderful. The crisis is now over. Dr. Rhoads is completely in sympathy with me."[33]

More than she realized, Carey Thomas was fortunate in having James E. Rhoads as her chief collaborator. Bryn Mawr's founding president was an exemplary man. He began his career as a physician, but his highly successful practice caused him to question a life whose prosperity was based on others' ills. One morning during the Civil War, he awoke to find himself paralyzed. Total rest and travel abroad began his recovery; dedication to reform completed it. He turned to the causes of the Society of Friends: the education of freedmen, Indian rights, and education. At the time he became a trustee of Bryn Mawr he was editor of the *Friends' Review*. During the long period of Bryn Mawr's incubation, he served on the executive committee, as vice president, and ultimately as the paid executive to oversee the initial phases of the college. Whatever Carey Thomas thought of her qualifications, James E. Rhoads was the natural choice of the board for the college's first president.

In partnership with Carey Thomas, he was a superb choice. They were a grand team. Thirty years Thomas' senior, he brought to his work sympathy for her educational goals, judiciousness, innate kindness, and tact. With him Thomas could put her imagination into high gear, knowing that he would carefully examine her work, think through the proper course of action, and prepare the ground with his fellow trustees. Though he generally accepted Thomas' vision of Bryn Mawr, he was never a rubber stamp: he arrived at his agreement independently, after careful consideration. And he was never reluctant to amend when he felt it necessary. His knowledge of his colleagues and the trust that they held in him made Rhoads the perfect translator of Thomas' plans and the ideal mediator between the headstrong female dean and the conservative male board.

Carey Thomas immediately plunged into her next task, faculty appointments. The trustees were willing to make appointments for the academic year 1885–86 as early as spring 1884, but, to Thomas' mind, they were the wrong appointments, and she fought successfully to prevent them. Now that the report was accepted, the battle for appointments began in earnest. She had already secured Emily Gregory of Smith College for botany. She sought advice of Johns Hopkins professors, spending evenings with Marshall Elliott, Ira Remsen, and Maurice Bloomfield, among others. In early July she received word that Edmund B. Wilson, a biologist at the Massachusetts Institute of Technology, was coming to Bryn Mawr as associate professor. Charlotte Angas Scott from Girton received the appointment as associate professor of mathematics. Thomas' next task was to select the full professor of history and political science. She had taken counsel with Herbert Baxter Adams of Johns Hopkins, developed a list of six candidates, read their publications, and had interviews with three. She refused to consider a woman Ph.D. because she was a woman. ("How can a political zero teach politics, an ineligible statesman, statecraft?") Woodrow Wilson, recommended by Adams as "by all odds the best one we have had," about to receive his Ph.D. in history from Johns Hopkins University, received the appointment.[34]

The trustees met in late August, and again Carey Thomas got them to agree to her plans. Each time she battled the trustees she came away with growing appreciation of Rhoads. As she wrote to Mary, "Dr. Rhoads grows ~~nicer and~~ more and more satisfactory every time I see him. I think he will make an excellent president." In the division of labor that she worked out with him, she carried the academic plan and the appointments. She felt both the burden and the opportunity. She wrote to Mary, "I have to do everything in regard to scholastic affairs. To decide between two men and three women, all with Harvard or Cornell degrees, high recommendations and at least one year's study abroad is distracting me this evening. Which of them will teach Latin the best? How can I tell without seeing the third and fourth candidates?"[35]

Her next task was to write the Bryn Mawr circular to incorporate the changes that she and Rhoads had pushed through the board of trustees. She completed this in late August and took it to Philadelphia for Rhoads' approval. He was pleased with it, and Thomas left for a well-deserved vacation. While she was away, some of the trustees reopened issues that Thomas thought were resolved, especially the limitation on special students. Thomas was forced to try and reconvince the trustees of the rightness of the plan. In September she wrote to Mary Garrett that the trustees were uneasy about the requirements. "Each time they hear the arguments they are warmed into enthusiasm, which cools in the interval." Ultimately she reached a compromise with the board that allowed initial students, who had prepared under the old rules, to enter and make up deficiencies under the new rules for graduation. Thomas pronounced herself pleased with the result, though "one or two 'trustee' constructions have crept in."[36]

With the basic structure of the college set, Carey Thomas spent the autumn of 1884 interviewing Johns Hopkins faculty members about suitable candidates for professorships, and preparing lectures on English literature. After problems with her eyes cost her six weeks of work, she got glasses.[37] She was besieged by inquiries from prospective students, those applying for graduate fellowships, and applicants for jobs. She negotiated salaries and contracts and cultivated her former German professors to encourage them to recommend candidates for positions. In the spring, she worked closely with the faculty to establish the curriculum, develop their courses, and select their graduate fellows. With Rhoads' guidance, she drafted the first official program.

In the midst of these larger questions, she had time for small, but, for her, telling details. She had no say in the siting of the college and the planning and placement of its initial buildings. The founder and his advisers had situated the college on a secluded but accessible site in the Philadelphia suburb of Bryn Mawr, on land initially settled by Welsh Quakers and platted by the Pennsylvania Railroad after the Civil War. The trustees had hired Addison Hutton, architect of important Haverford College buildings, to design structures modeled after Smith College "in 'Quaker lady' dress." Inheriting buildings that she could not alter, Thomas was determined that within them college women should lead a fitting college life. She insisted that Bryn Mawr students *not* make their own beds. It was a symbol to set Bryn Mawr off, to announce that women scholars were no longer expected to save money by doing their own housework. Although Rhoads was sympathetic on every other point, Thomas found it difficult to convince him that students should not perform such a simple chore. He argued strenuously that the ten dollars per student it cost to support a servant whose sole task it was to make their beds would require a higher room charge or put the college in debt. But in the end, though there was no public announcement, Thomas won.[38]

Carey Thomas' achievement in 1884–85 gave meaning to the victories of the preceding spring and summer. She gathered a young faculty remarkable in its training and promise. Thomas had an unerring eye for quality, and she made few mistakes. To earlier appointments, she added Edward W. Hopkins and Paul Shorey in classics, Edward H. Keiser in chemistry, and J. James Stürzinger in Romance languages. She herself held the position in English literature. She saw to it that graduate students of excellent promise received fellowships.

On September 23, 1885, all was ready. On thirty-two acres near the Bryn Mawr railroad station stood three-story Taylor Hall, its gray stone enlivened by gables, chimneys, and a tall square clock tower. Nearby was Merion, a large vernacular dwelling with corresponding gables and chimneys but also welcoming porches trimmed in wood. Thirty-six young women, including Grace and Margaret Thomas, had successfully taken their entrance examinations and prepared to enter the new college as undergraduates, joined by eight graduate students. In ceremonies befitting the occasion, James Carey Thomas offered prayer, James Rhoads welcomed the students and faculty, and Daniel Coit Gilman and James Russell Lowell lent their dignity in opening addresses.

In her blue-fronted academic robe and Zürich hood, M. Carey Thomas sat proudly on the platform. The Bryn Mawr before her was the personal triumph of her imagination. The early foundation of Bryn Mawr was her purest act: cognition turned into will. She had thought it out in quiet moments abroad. In the eighteen months between her appointment as dean and the opening of the college, she turned conception into policy and personnel. Joseph Wright Taylor had provided the endowment, and the board of trustees oversaw the early buildings. Carey Thomas, aided by James Rhoads, took that material base in hand and turned what was intended to be a polite sectarian women's college into a dazzling center of new scholarship.

Fifty years later, she remembered the early Bryn Mawr "when we were all young together." She put her achievements this way: the male trustees whom Taylor had selected "had set out to produce a well-behaved fowl resembling those already living in neighboring barnyards, but found that they had hatched a soaring eagle instead."[39]

CHAPTER 11

Content, Not Lonely,
in the Passionate Land

BEGINNING in March 1884, as M. Carey Thomas began to build Bryn Mawr College, she saw her work as committed to the cause of women. What became of the aesthetic Carey who dreamed of a life lived for art? She was there, but under deep cover.

There was no way that Dean Thomas could exist otherwise. She had to succeed in the particular world of Orthodox Quaker men who composed the Bryn Mawr board of trustees. No distant body, they included her father, uncle, and several cousins. As she "thee-thou'd" them and President James Rhoads, she had to present herself as a serious and scholarly Quaker daughter, outwardly conforming to the manners and traditions of the creed. The artistic life that the aesthetic Carey valued was anathema to them. She reveled in Wagnerian opera, performances of Sarah Bernhardt, contemporary French novels, and the poems of Algernon Charles Swinburne. They found the mere existence of a piano a threat to basic order. Because of this, she had to keep her deanly and her aesthetic natures separate and her devotion to art hidden from view.

Inner forces, as well as outside pressure, forced the spirit that aspired to art into retreat. Bryn Mawr was an enthusiasm. Carey Thomas plunged into its planning with a reckless abandon ill-fitted to the artistic life. The work of organizing and administering a college came to fill Thomas' days and a good part of her nights. Beginning in September 1885, she embarked on an exhausting round each academic year. Moreover, she always added, never limited. She used all her personal relations to gain her ends, and thus what might have been renewing friendship and home ties in Baltimore turned into work. During the nine months of the academic year there was no surcease.

Yet throughout it all, Carey sustained—hidden from view—a slim strand of her aesthetic self within the intricate world of intimate friendships. In her own mind the passionate and the aesthetic were intertwined, sometimes fused. As she reached maturity, Carey Thomas was a complicated, even divided, person. Her close personal relations partook of her complexity. As a passionate dean, committed to the cause of women, Thomas exhibited energy, imagination, breadth, a capacity for logical thought, clarity, and calculation. As a friend and lover, the passion, imagination, and calculation certainly were there. Logic and clarity at first seem harder to find, but that is because Carey lived by different rules and at fever pitch.

She remained in the Thomas house on Madison Avenue in Baltimore until Bryn Mawr opened in September 1885. Although she managed to see Mamie almost every day, visits in parental homes were quite different from their intertwined life abroad. Vacations and travel with Mamie were more satisfactory. In the first months after she was appointed dean, Carey Thomas struggled to maintain a life devoted to scholarship, but constant interruptions and distractions made her feel she was accomplishing little. She tried to hold on to the certainties of Europe, but they proved elusive in the harsher light and bustle of America. Europe had given her Mamie Gwinn and, especially in the two years preceding her examinations, clear, unambiguous work. America brought her the confusion of the Thomas household and the return of old emotions and commitments.

By spring 1884 the rhythm of her life began to alter. She had a new and complicated job to learn that began to take her away from home. Initially it was the excursion to the New England women's colleges and an occasional trip to Philadelphia to consult with Rhoads. Gradually during the 1884–85 academic year, she spent more time in Philadelphia and Bryn Mawr and less in Baltimore.

From the outset Mamie feared Bryn Mawr. On January 16, 1884, the day after Hannah Smith's letter urging Thomas to accept a position under Rhoads, Mamie wrote a note from Mount Vernon Place with a different message: "Oh, Cecily, for my own sake, I do so wish they had let it alone." As Carey began to be caught up in the creation of Bryn Mawr, Mamie felt the difference in her friend immediately. Mamie had worked hard to cultivate Carey's aesthetic self, only to see it now overcome by the organizing and scheming of the reformer.[1] In the spring of 1884 as Thomas began to visit schools, she started with the Trenton Normal School, at James Whitall's request. Mamie was vexed at being left alone and at Carey stooping so low as to examine a normal school. She reminded Carey of their life together, "I took up Gautier yesterday afternoon and read especially . . . 'Thébaïde' and 'Ténèbres,' which names pray remember." She missed Carey exceedingly: "My study misses your footstep on the stairs to it." As she contemplated the future, she worried about how she would live in Baltimore without Carey. She was unhappy and restless and longed for release. When Carey persisted in making travel plans, Mamie responded, "Your going to Bryn Mawr is unmitigatedly vile, and I *wish* I had discouraged it. I always meant it to be for a very few years, a very short time.

Oh Shimmer, Stag, Pink, did I ever invent all those names for you for you to go swamp yourself in it? I will not *have* you in contact with . . . normal schools."[2]

Mamie showed little interest in seeing the college, and Carey thought it best that she postpone her first look until construction was farther along. After Mamie did visit she tried to squelch Carey's enthusiasm for the college. She wrote to Carey, "Now, I may say, that from the moment I *saw* Bryn Mawr I was very thoroughly out of conceit of it: and have ever since felt that it would not be for my Cecil in any sense an abiding vocation. I was extremely disappointed in the country, and woefully so in the puny hotel-like buildings." Having looked down her nose at the enterprise, Mamie added encouragement riddled with condescension: "I trust my lassie to put a big soul into the little body and make it intellectually supersede the other places: but I doubt if you care to do much more than thoroughly start it."[3]

In Europe alone with Carey, Mamie had attempted to mold her in her own image. As the future dean of Bryn Mawr, Carey Thomas was now cast out on the world. Perhaps sensing Mamie's efforts to rein in the committed self, Carey insisted, despite Mamie's pleadings, on going alone to investigate the women's colleges. While Carey was traveling, Mamie tried desperately to reclaim her. As she renewed questionable associations, Mamie was particularly uneasy. In February, Carey visited Gertrude Mead in New York. Mamie wrote, "I *beg* you not to compromise yourself with her." Knowing Carey's fondness for Gertrude, who had made a play for her in Leipzig, Mamie tried to put it tactfully. It was not, she wrote, that she feared that Carey would indulge in the kind of relation she once had with Libbie Conkey or Carrie Ladd, but that she regarded "*a marked intimacy*" with Gertrude "about the same kind of thing relatively to your present maturity, as those intimacies once were."[4]

After receiving Carey's letter from Vassar she wrote, "It sounds as though you were carried away: as though you were 'going it': in which case you never have a particle of dignity or discrimination. Forgive me, but 'tis true. Pray assume both qualities forthwith and meet every one coolly and impersonally. Force yourself to feel indifferent till 'tis all over: please, dear baby."[5] Mamie did not understand Carey's "going it" because she did not appreciate that Carey was moved by Herbert Spencer as well as Swinburne. Swinburne was the light of her private side, guiding her as she imagined herself as one of "nous autres." Spencer directed her public course, her scholarship, and her work for women. In the Quaker world of Baltimore and Philadelphia, Spencer as well as Swinburne had to remain hidden. Only as she emerged in the twentieth century as a spokeswoman for reform causes did her positivist, Social Darwinian side surface visibly; but her life as an institution builder was founded on it.

While Carey was away, Mamie found being apart from her agony, and she pled for the chance to join her. At this point, Mamie felt she could not "bear to think of Bryn Mawr," and regretted deeply that it had entered Carey's life. "Were it not for the temporary benevolence of the action," she wished she had always advised against Carey's association with it.[6] Carey, however, was not to be won over, so Mamie joined in, throwing herself into plans for Bryn Mawr. She could do this because one side of her was deeply ambitious for Carey. In addition, perhaps not consciously at first, she began to see that Bryn Mawr might be the way out of her own personal trap. In the spring and summer of 1884 Mamie was painfully unhappy in her parents' Baltimore home, with its "sad life-sucking, disappointed monotony." She thought of death. In early May, before she joined Carey in Boston, she wrote to her, "I keep wondering and wondering whether you had not better keep some position for me at Bryn Mawr!"[7]

Mamie Gwinn began to offer counsel. With her eye for detail, she scrutinized stationery, advising Thomas, for example, to add "Ph.D." after her name on her official letter paper. Carey Thomas began to scheme. By July she had the idea that Gwinn might become her secretary. Gwinn reacted to this with excitement. "My Secretaryship runs in my head." With the position dangling before her, Gwinn became bold. She offered advice, not always taken, about the organization of the college and the hiring of professors and about the need for constant publicity to keep the college before the public. She supplied text, not always used, for reports and circulars. For example, in August, she criticized Thomas' draft of the Bryn Mawr circular for omitting what was "the cornerstone of your policy as once expounded to the board," philology, language, and comparative literature, taught through lectures. She urged that Thomas emphasize that German and French literary works would be used. She argued strenuously, and to no avail, against the position in history. She fought hard to convince Thomas that she must insist on a salary of three thousand dollars for her year of organizing for the college, not the one thousand dollars that the trustees had offered; and, once the college opened, Thomas did receive three thousand dollars a year. Whereas Thomas could give or take Gwinn's advice on policy, she found it hard to accept Gwinn's editing of her prose. Gwinn responded, "You are presumably, dear Cecil, in your usual bad humour, when I have taken the trouble to correct your manuscript? Pray remember that your indignation is usually transitory, and keep your affection for Yours affectionately." When Thomas was low, Gwinn encouraged her. The college "deserves in its organization all your heart and all your soul and all your strength. People *are* fired by great ideas."[8]

Mamie Gwinn was caught, and she, too, had her mind revolving around the gymnasium, faculty appointments, schedules, and the sequence of courses. At one point she exclaimed, "How much of my time though I waste in plotting about Bryn Mawr you can't conceive." Bryn Mawr became part of Mamie's relationship to Carey, part of her claim for its special quality. College issues were among "the many things concerning which we have neither of us a friend who thinks and feels with us in the same degree."[9]

Mamie Gwinn offered Carey Thomas help with course preparations. As Thomas worked on lectures in the summer, Gwinn wrote, "I am becoming curious as to the details of Bryn Mawr lectures. You have begotten in me the habits of an organizer—or a reviser at least. My brain clappers like a sewing machine without stuff." Thomas was also writing an article about Dante Gabriel Rossetti, one of their shared enthusiasms, and Gwinn asked to see it, as "it keeps us en rapport." At times she encouraged Thomas to think of her work as Bryn Mawr's professor of English literature as more important than that as dean—"there your province, your honor, your legitimate reputation." She would help Thomas in this. In August 1884 she proposed to Thomas that they work together and each make a brief extract of any book read in preparation for literature courses. "We would not duplicate our researches, and the stones of the mosaic would be ready in half the time."[10] Little did she understand how her offers to help Thomas would come to haunt her.

A position as the dean's secretary was dependent upon the trustees, a slender reed, given the trustees' parsimony. Gwinn suggested that she be hired to work with students on their compositions. She regretted that she had not gotten a degree abroad that might enable her to teach at Bryn Mawr. A solution was found: in September 1885 Mamie Gwinn entered Bryn Mawr as the first graduate fellow in English. Carey Thomas was the professor under whom she worked.[11]

Carey and Mamie spent vacations together. They went to Newport in May 1884, and in late August, Carey joined Mamie and Mrs. Gwinn there. In 1884 Carey's notion of a vacation was very vigorous. She walked six miles a day, drove in a cart, rowed, or swam. Her mother was a little alarmed at reports and wrote, "Do not injure thyself riding on rough horses, or playing tennis too steadily." Mary Thomas could not resist the further counsel that she try and help her friends to true repentance. Carey did not take her mother's advice on either score. Strenuous physical activity fit with Carey's notions of health, and it also was for Carey plain fun.[12] As Carey and Mamie traveled in the White Mountains of New Hampshire, she wrote to her mother, "Mamie is a great satisfaction. We can talk forever about books and theories and Bryn Mawr."[13] Gradually a plan emerged for them to live together. Carey had initially assumed that she was to live in Merion Hall, but in late summer 1884 the college assigned to her an eight-room frame cottage that in its many transformations was to be her lifelong residence. She named it the "Deanery."

It began very simply. In August 1884, Mamie even advised Carey to do without a dining room, as she wrote, "You will not, you know, be really keeping house." Carey had other ideas, and planned from the outset to make the Deanery a true home. Through her mother she arranged to have Lena Manluff, a family servant who had nursed Carey during the long convalescence after the burn, take charge. In anticipation, Carey wrote Mamie that Manluff "would buy and cook and do everything so that I would have no care. Otherwise, beloved squirrel, I could not have you even pay me long visits." Pleased with the cottage, she wrote to Mamie that its porch was "one mass of vines" and looked like a "little bower of Paradise." Trying to encourage Mamie, she wrote in June 1885, "There are trees, sweetheart, and green grapes and many things that will do your heart good next year."[14]

The Deanery was altered in the summer of 1885 to have a fireplace in the first-floor parlor and sitting room and in an upstairs sitting room. Because work was unfinished when the college began, Carey Thomas had to dine initially in one of the cottages shared by the young men of the faculty. Embarrassed, she had Harry visit so that he might accompany her to the table. In the first months of the new college, wallpaper, carpets, and upholstery filled her days along with lectures, students, and deanly duties. By the end of October, she could write to Mary Garrett that "I already like my little cottage, and I think I can care for it when it has been filled with a few years' memories." In the early years, on a salary of three thousand a year Thomas managed the household simply, yet generously. In addition to the rent paid to the college, the Deanery cost $88 a month, or the equivalent of almost $1,400 in 1994. Thomas spent $29 a month for Manluff and a second servant. Fifty dollars a month, an unusually generous sum, went to food, but that covered the entertaining required of a dean.[15]

On September 14, 1885, Carey Thomas moved into the Deanery. Mamie Gwinn, preparing to join her, wrote her from Baltimore on her "first morning among the roses," sending her love enough to keep her "from being ever unhappy again." Mamie hoped that in the new house they would make a new beginning: "Let us try to love each other in the new house. . . . We shall have a real epoch: and shall surely keep the future quite clear and import no past naughtinesses into it." In the early years without a salary, Mamie was able to pay only a small fraction of expenses. She told Carey that to insist on more from her father might threaten the larger sum she hoped he would one day give her.[16] Beginning in this dependent position, Mamie accepted from the outset that, as its name suggested, the Deanery was Carey's house, not hers, though she lived there until 1904, first as a graduate student, then as an associate, and finally as a professor of English.

Carey never staked all on Mamie. A letter to Mary Garrett, written in June 1884 after a trip to Boston, told her about looking up Emma Culbertson, who had aided her through her Ph.D. examinations in Zürich. Carey found her living with Dr. Smith in a flat in an elegant Boston apartment hotel. Carey dined with them and returned with Mamie for lunch. Their reaction to the devoted medical couple was revealing. Carey reported that Mamie had found that "Dr. Culbertson met her approval, but not Dr. Smith, nor indeed did she mine; it is a case of beauty and the beast." Carey continued, "They are neither of them one whit more sensible than when Dr. Culbertson was in Zürich, and I believe Mamie considered that we were not 'flattered by being made the confidants of their foolishness.' " Carey predicted a bad end for Culbertson: "An absorbing passion in a person who has nothing to turn to, if it fail, is so dangerous. I think matter-of-fact people are apt to stake everything on one throw. We have so many chances ~~the~~ nous autres apart from people."[17]

Carey used the occasion to expound on the importance of books rather than persons. But what seems to have been on her mind was the issue of fidelity. These were months in which she and Mamie were living in the houses of their parents and seeing each other every day that Carey was in Baltimore. Although they were an intimate "twosome," Carey was reserving for herself another option. Something of her continuing attraction and admiration for Mary Garrett (and for Mary Garrett's wealth) remained.

In the letter that Carey wrote to Mary about Emma Culbertson, she began very sentimentally. She was using stationery from Leipzig that reminded her of a time "before a great many things, before Pontresina [the site of Mary's ankle injury], before I tried to forget you, before America was more than a name (it did not exist for me during those first years), before I knew how very much I could sympathize with you and think about you when in trouble and anxiety. I have often wondered if you at all knew; it has been so impossible for me to say anything all this winter and spring." It was at this point that she recounted to Mary her meeting with Culbertson and Smith. She went on to suggest that relations with books and art were more important than with persons.[18]

Letters to Mary in this period are particularly hard to decipher. As early as her Cornell years, as she wrote of her delight in Margaret Hicks, she was undoubtedly trying to tease and provoke Anna Shipley back to an earlier intimacy. In Europe she began to write to her mother in a manner calculated to win the admiration of her trustee uncle James Whitall. Letters to Mary Garrett in the 1880s add a further complication. Carey had to write in such a fashion that, were her letters read by Julia Rogers, Carey would not stand accused of seeking a special friendship. They seem, therefore, to be written in code. Carey opens her heart to Mary, but at the moment in which one thinks she is writing about her love for Mary, she substitutes books and pictures, suggesting that she and Mary are linked not by their feeling for each other but by their appreciation of finer things.

An important instance of this comes in an April 1884 letter to Mary. Following a visit with Mary in Lakewood, New Jersey, Carey had viewed a private Baltimore collection of engravings and photographs of old masters. She reflected on the personal strength that the love of art gives. "Yet caring for such things is like being in love with a person in this—one may succeed for days and weeks in forgetting them, when a word, a photograph *undoes all*, and the pulses beat and the heart longs in the same old way. Of the one kind of lovers there are many; of the other, few . . . Mary, I often wonder what we have done that we are among them, and what we can do to prove our worthiness." In another letter Carey pressed the strength of her claim (over against that of Julia) for Mary's love on their mutual love of art. Carey recalled seeing Mary saying goodbye to the statues in Rome: "I remember watching you walk up between the long lines of gods and heroes, the Athena resting on her spear (the only remotely satisfactory Athena I remember) on one side, and this Caryatid on the other, and thinking then as I have thought sometimes since that sharing one or two great loves in common *ought* to be more in a friendship than daily companionship in little things."[19]

Until 1887, Mary never responded to Carey's overtures. She remained in a twosome with Julia Rogers. Mary's mother died just as Carey returned to America. Mary turned to preoccupation with family concerns, especially the care of her mourning and dying father. She took on the administrative burden of the three Garrett houses—the town house on Monument Street in Baltimore, the country estate of Montebello, and the sylvan retreat, Deer Park. Suffering from physical weakness, she was often emotionally unavailable, as her own apologies and Carey's criticism of the unsatisfactory nature of the time they spent together suggest. Mary's infrequent letters are practical, self-involved, and filled with the obligations that prevent her from responding to Carey's needs and demands. Nonetheless, Carey continued to write at length about herself. She explained, "Because you never answer them *subjectively* . . . it is like writing into one's waste paper basket . . . or between the leaves of a journal. . . . My caring for you touches the spring which sets in motion the mechanical process of getting pen, ink, and paper, and the rest is a sequitur."[20]

In addition to Mary's inattention, Carey was finding herself distracted by men. At times she was overcome with professional jealousy and attraction. One evening after spending three hours with Marshall Elliott of Johns Hopkins, she wrote to Mary that their exchange of professional gossip, "the inner scandal of German scholarship," left her "rather faint hearted because I am a woman. I have a chance, of course, but were I a man everything would be open to me. I could have all that sympathy and ~~scholarship~~ fellowship with other scholars, not here in Baltimore, of course, but all over the world. I could write to all these men on terms which sex would not determine." She thought about praise that Francis J. Child of Harvard had given her when she spoke with him in Cambridge: "I am thrown upon men for that kind of companionship; and as yet it seems to me that I had rather have none." Here Carey crossed out: "It brings so much trouble with it."[21]

What was Carey thinking of? She gave some indication on another occasion when she related her encounter at Smith with John Henry Niemeyer, Yale's teacher of art. She had a talk "of a kind that I never expected to have with a man again." They conversed at lunch, "then he stood with his hand on the front door, opening it as the boarders went in and out, and talked, for one and a half hours, as I afterward found, but it seemed to me a moment and to him also." Though he looked ordinary, "some god had touched his lips." Niemeyer talked to Thomas about art, research, Europe and America, life. "Everything was what I cared to hear. . . . There was magic at work, the unwonted charm of hearing one's own theories, and better than one's own theories, from the mouth of a man whose life had been spent on such things, the pleasure of having every thought understood almost before I expressed it!" Clearly Carey was again attracted to a man, something that her plans for her future could not contain. She wrote that the last time she had had such a conversation with a male stranger, it was followed six months later by a proposal, "which did not seem to me as unjustifiable as it in reality was." This time she did not even want to know whether Niemeyer was married, "in order to have no alloy in my remembrance."[22]

But nothing was as powerful as the secret attraction that she intended to confide in her diary February 2, 1885. Carey's journal provided her with a window into her past emotional life, and on that February day she reread it. She had not made an entry in the four years she had been abroad or in her first year back in America. She was particularly interested in her "Stürm and Drang period," perhaps because she was feeling many of her old impulses again. Once more she took up her pen: "I entreat that no one will read this part of my journal, as it is *entirely private*, and I beg that Mamie if she loves me will not read it as it is something I have kept from her. I write it down as an experience and a madness, a temptation and a delusion. Just as the pages about Mr. Gummere seem to me impossible, so this will doubtless in as many years as have passed since my last entry." At this point she reflected on the months in Baltimore since her return from abroad. She had given herself over to Bryn Mawr, saving Taylor's great endowment for women "even if it be not what Mamie and I have planned." Since her journal was "a mortifying record of avocations, not vocations, especially of emotional disturbances, I will proceed to take my bearings and then describe my last trial of that kind."[23]

She returned to her relation with Mamie. They were "still intimate. We have seen each other almost every day since we returned in November of 1883. I still think that our friendship and love will outlast our lives. She is in person and intellect, taste and belief perfectly satisfactory to me. I owe her everything except the isolation of mental life which thing no one can have who loves another person very dearly." And there the passage and the journal end. The remainder of the notebook pages are left blank. It is an odd and tantalizing passage. The reference to Francis Gummere suggests that Carey was about to write about her feelings for a man when she was either interrupted or censored herself. Who was he?[24]

In an April 1884 letter to Mary Garrett, Carey related taking tea with James Rendel Harris, a British scholar at Johns Hopkins. She described him as "the only man for some years whom I find charming, ~~narrow often~~ limited ~~oftener~~ of horizons, yet within his circle he revolves musically. Literary, poetical, first-class Cambridge classicist and mathematician and above all gifted with a better silver string than most men or women." This is the language Carey used in writing about Gummere and in describing Percy in the Friday Evening's group novel, suggesting by "silver string" that Rendel Harris had the poetic gift of song. Harris and she had desks near each other in the Peabody. Rhoads and the board were eager to hire him as a part-time lecturer to teach Bible to Bryn Mawr students. In May 1885, Harris' strong stand against vivisection put him at odds with the Johns Hopkins scientific community, and he decided to return to England. As he prepared to sail, Carey wrote to Mary, "I cannot help regretting him as (to me) the most agreeable man in Baltimore." Although Carey's words did not say it at the time, Rendel Harris was married.[25]

Moreover, it was 1885 not 1878, and Carey Thomas was dean of Bryn Mawr, not a floundering graduate student. She stopped writing in her journal, and the matter was never heard of again. If her "trial" was Rendel Harris, when she visited him and his wife, Helen, in England in the summer of 1886, she wrote in letters home of his narrowness, not his attractiveness.

Mary Thomas may have had Carey's infatuation on her mind when she wrote to Hannah in August 1885 a letter of sympathy on the occasion of the marriage of Hannah's daughter Mary to Frank Costelloe. The letter reveals a great deal about Mary Thomas' feelings about marriage and Carey. The letter, written two weeks before Carey moved to Bryn Mawr, contains several references to Mamie, who had often been in the house. Mary was worried about the difficulties that Carey would face living on her own with the family servant in the Deanery, but added, "Mamie Gwinn will be with her, however, which will be everything to her." Hannah had before her a different prospect. "I know it is terrible for thee—I do think it is more than a mother can stand to see her daughters get married—but we've all got to stand it." Although it was especially hard for Hannah because Costelloe was Catholic and English, Mary offered the consolation that any marriage would be horrible. Mary continued, "There certainly is a sacrifice in marriage for women, or we would not feel so about it." Though she herself had been happy, marriage was "an awful risk for a girl, and while I should not wish my daughters not to marry, yet it will break my heart to see them marry." Carey, in contrasting herself with her cousin Mary Smith, had said to her, "I should think a daughter such as I am would be a solid satisfaction to a mother." Mary agreed but added to Hannah, "I tell her that I have not absolute confidence that her heart might not be touched, but I am sure her principles would come to her aid and prevent her yielding."[26]

What explains the inner Carey during these years, still in love and committed to Mamie, yet doggedly pursuing Mary and fascinated by men? To apply to her the model of romantic heterosexual monogamy that assumes that a single partner fulfils all emotional needs, leads nowhere. For Carey had different needs, and different persons helped to satisfy them.

Once she had conquered her desire to succumb to Francis Gummere, she looked to men like Gummere, Cadbury, and, later, Niemeyer and Harris for wit, intellectual challenge, and confirmation that she was a full player in intellectual life. They provided her with fire—witty repartee and intellectual gossip. Near them she could believe that she might become a creator, that she might play the lyre. But men were dangerous. A relationship with a man could mean a marriage that would destroy her autonomy.

As dean of Bryn Mawr, she possessed a license to have exciting and safe conversations with the intellectually engaging men of the faculty. She regularly entertained them at dinners in the Deanery. Yet she had to be extremely careful. She quickly learned she must not establish a personal friendship with any of the professors. In her early years as dean, she had long talks with the college's classicist, Paul Shorey. As he revealed many years later, Shorey had noticed her at the University of Leipzig: her "shapely head . . . had arrested" his "roving gaze . . . as the only relief in a waste vista of beefy, duel-scarred Teutonic cheeks." They shared literary interests and their professional relation developed into a personal friendship, though one marked by frequent quarrels. When the college year began in 1888, for example, Shorey paid her a Saturday evening visit to talk about Mrs. Humphry Ward's *Robert Elsmere* and stayed "till long past any writing hour." Carey invited him for dinner in November 1889. At the end of the summer of 1890, as they returned from Europe on the same steamer, Carey found his shipboard attentions a burden, and, she wrote Mary, "I had to pretend to be much more seasick than I really was and never moved from my chair. Otherwise my engagement to him would have been all over Philadelphia." Her actions effectively squelched what she regarded as the budding romancer, although Shorey persisted for a short time in pursuing a personal friendship back at Bryn Mawr.[27]

A different and more complicated danger came in the guise of George W. Childs, the sixty-year-old publisher of the *Philadelphia Ledger* and a wealthy Bryn Mawr neighbor. He began to make gifts to the college, and Thomas relied on him for counsel. Childs clearly enjoyed mixing business with the pleasure of her company. Carey wrote to Mary in January 1889 about one such visit: "He ended, as always, with my marriage and again asked me whether I was entirely sure that I should not. His preoccupation with it is entertaining. He goes through the arguments of the supposed suitor and requires me to answer them, which I do in short order as you may imagine." As Thomas sought a major gift from Childs, he clearly misconstrued the nature of her overture. Carey described to Mary a dinner party in the autumn of 1891 that was suddenly ruined. She reached down to pat his dog, and Childs "to my horror" caught her fingers under the dinner table. "I took them away by force." In 1892, Childs kissed her in his office. Carey wrote Mary that when he did, she told him "he must not do it," that since he had told her how young he was she had "considered him almost a contemporary and could not allow it." As she got up to leave his office, he kissed her again. She could not make a scene because they were in "full view of a lady waiting to see him in his ante room." In this case Carey did not exaggerate the risks. Some years later, Childs' wife left Philadelphia after the scandal broke that he had a second family.[28]

Throughout her life Carey Thomas sustained stimulating intellectual conversations with men, but she became more cautious. She could not allow even the chance of rumor. She was becoming a local celebrity in Philadelphia. As a visible unmarried woman, she was at risk. As a result, she chose to go to evening gatherings unaccompanied. As she told Mary about the reception at the Art Club for the poet Edmund Clarence Stedman, she explained, "You see, I must go by myself. I can never appear anywhere with one [of] our professors (I even have to plan so as to avoid entering at the same time) or even with Dr. Rhoads." Any perceived relationship with a man might damage her reputation.[29]

By 1892 Carey insisted to Mary Garrett that she had no interest in men. She wrote to Mary Garrett that "men have no attraction for me." This was, she added, "a mere happy accident, steeped as I have been always in love poetry and French novels." Mary, then abroad, was facing medical judgments that her depression derived from her unmarried state. Carey was angered by doctors' advice that married women profit from regular sexual intercourse. She pointed to the women of her family to illustrate that healthy women became weak, wretched, or ill with marriage. She cited Rendel Harris' wife, Helen, as a case: strong as a young woman, she had become an invalid after her marriage. Helen had told Carey that "it was so with many women she knew in England, that it was a physical change of the gravest character and one no intellectual woman ought to take without realizing it." Carey asked, if celibacy was "unnatural," why were she, other unmarried women, widows, and women separated from their husbands "in such *perfect* health . . . while so few married women are well"? She did not deny women's sexual desire. But saw it as a "temporary" need "for a few years" and no cause to require "the lifelong companionship and continuous physical connection of a man."[30]

Although Carey came to deny the role that men played in her life, she recognized and affirmed her passionate friendships with women. They did not threaten her power. She knew better than to suggest, however, that such friendships simplified life. Carey's relationships with Mamie and Mary were complicated. In both, love and work were intricately bound together. The patterns in each, however, were different.

Mamie was linked with Carey's aesthetic passions. Once, trying to mollify an angry Mamie, Carey promised to swear by the oath of Saint George always to tell the truth: "I will never again, so help me St. George and St. Ruskin and all the rest of the children of light—St. Victor Hugo, St. Swinburne— never even evade with you, sweetheart."[31] The names tumbled out casually. Behind them was a world of shared meaning. They were the two devotees of a personal religion of art. Together they pursued pictures, heard operas, and went to plays. As Mamie entered into daily life at Bryn Mawr, drafting and revising circulars, aiding with writing lectures, and studying literature for her Ph.D., she was an enduring and invaluable constant. She was a coworker in all Carey's projects, generally in the background, but a full partner and a master of detail. Demanding and moody though she was, she was abiding. Sharing Carey's aesthetic aspirations, her work, and the mundane details of their joint life, Mamie was woven into the fabric of Carey's life.

Mary was more distant and a challenge. She was three years older than Carey and very wealthy. Though she never obtained higher education and fought illness all her life, her enormous wealth and her strong will and manner made her attractive. Her exposure to culture and all the accoutrements of wealth made her an additional guide, training Carey in the arts, manners, and style of the American plutocracy. Carey pursued Mary doggedly for decades, despite sustained efforts on Mary's part to discourage her.

Carey realized that through Mary's wealth she and her friends of the Friday Night might be able to extend the reach of their work for women. The first inkling that this was on Carey's mind came during her 1884 spring trip to the women's colleges. Mary was then caring for her ailing father, whose death later in 1884 left her a third of a major fortune built on the Baltimore and Ohio Railroad. Carey wrote of her enthusiasm for doing something for women: "It is the curse of belonging to an unfree race to care for it so foolishly, I suppose. I am so glad, Mary, to think that you will have money someday. There is so much good to do, and what some of us do in another way you can do in that way, and after all it is rarer than the other ways and does not exclude them."[32]

In the first years of her deanship, Carey constantly begged Mary to visit her. These were difficult years in their friendship. Carey felt that Mary did not really understand her Bryn Mawr life or even want to. In late January 1886, as she asked Mary to come, she wrote, "it is not very flattering that you seem to care so little to see my college—that ought to have a little general interest apart from the special." Unlike many of the others, this was an entreaty that Mary responded to. She not only visited Carey at Bryn Mawr, she made a donation to the library of books that her friend needed. Carey was delighted. "Of course, I could not help being embarrassed as I had, in common with all other things, talked to you about it with such un-Greek abandon" but she realized that she should not let her awareness of this spoil her "pleasure in something that it was very nice in you to think of."[33]

Given that Carey was committed to Mamie but vying for Mary, who remained in a twosome with Julia Rogers, relations among four of the five friends were, understandably, intricate. Bessie, suffering probably from tuberculosis, was simply the object of solicitude. After Rome, Carey and Julia maintained a level of civility, but nothing more. Mamie, often jealous of Carey's friendships, became increasingly pained by Mary. With Carey's position as dean came a new threat. Mary was as attracted to power as Carey was to wealth. Mamie began to realize that Mary posed a danger.

During the mourning period after the death of Mary's mother, Carey and Mamie put aside reserve and called on Mary repeatedly at her country estate. Quickly, however, Mamie quarreled with Carey over Mary. As Mamie explained, Mary had begun "with the assumption that we were so intimate we *had* to a certain extent to be invited together to Montebello, and that she could not have you without courtesy to me." But Carey had undermined that. "Little by little, you showed her that we were completely separable, and that no rudeness or coldness toward me diminished in the least your affectionate attentions." As a result, Mary had come to snub Mamie, ending each call with a tête-à-tête with Carey that excluded Mamie. During the last visit Mary had not spoken to Mamie, but had only arranged to come into town to sleep with Carey.[34]

Mamie listed the many aspects of Carey's relation to Mary that she had once opposed: Carey's " 'childishness' and the consequences" by which she meant Carey's smashlike devotion to Mary; Mary's being "in love" with Carey; and Mary's expensive presents to her. They had fought over these issues in the past. Mamie could now accept them, but she would not tolerate Mary's new rudeness. As Mamie clarified in the subsequent letter, Mary's behavior toward her was "a direct cut of a kind which you may use when you are entitled to express contempt and prefer that it should be resented." It was Carey's task to make Mary apologize. It was not that Mamie did not like Mary, "I have always thought her personally attractive. I was very fond of her, in old times."[35]

Mary's forced apology incensed her the more, and Mamie withdrew from the conflict with her anger unappeased. Months later, after they had again quarreled over Mary, Mamie wrote that she was willing to accept Mary's place in Carey's affections. Though there remained "some question of manner and degree," she believed that "as much friendship, as much attention as left to your own judgment and your feelings you would under other circumstances give Mary, belongs to her."[36]

However, there was one condition upon which Mamie insisted: she was to come first. In June 1885, Mamie wrote a letter that revealed much about the construction that Carey and she placed on their relationship. The two had again quarreled about Mary, this time about Carey's hiding the fact that she had visited Mary before leaving for Bryn Mawr. Mamie was angry at what she believed was a lie. It also rankled that Carey seemed to be treating her identically with Mary. Mamie wrote, "Now if you and I, as we have sometimes said, love each other in a different kind of way, and wish to work together and live together—and are only very glad we're not man-woman because that spoils the best part of such affection—I think the way to behave is to other people kindly and sweetly and affectionately: only still more so to each other." This was not unusual. In fact there were models all around: "All married people (and there are some who have dear friends) and even all devoted sisters have their friendships on that understanding."

Mamie was also unhappy because Carey refused to acknowledge their special relationship among their close friends. Carey had been uneasy when it had been assumed that the two were to share a room. "It would seem strange to me, if the acknowledged and binding love between two people were there, that after four years' living together, and more years of talk about living together, that when one room was assigned them at a friend's house, there should be an anxiety to do away with the impression that they may make on a third person." From the tone of her letter, it is clear that Mamie was asking for nothing new. She was only trying to protect in America the life that the two had shaped in their years abroad.[37]

II

IT WAS in her intimate life with Mamie, in her visits and correspondence with Mary, and in her excited conversations with intellectual men that Carey nurtured her aesthetic self. Passion and art were intertwined.

Because Carey resided with Mamie, the primary record of her personal and aesthetic life during these years is her correspondence with Mary Garrett. As at earlier points, Carey's language of intimacy with her close friends was poetry, painting, and music. When she wrote to a contemporary whom she loved, the appropriate letter was not about scholarship or deanly duties or social causes. These she disparaged as the "shop" or "business" or the "war-path." Although she asked others to write of their health, when she did, she apologized for being self-centered. A real letter—the kind she wanted to write and to receive—was about art and feeling. To Mary she wrote many. What they reveal is a Carey for whom books and art are intertwined with passion and yearning. While a studious Carey read for scholarship, and a socially aware Carey for insight into political and economic questions, a passionate Carey read for self-culture and ecstasy.

Because her position at Bryn Mawr required it, outwardly Carey remained a Quaker. Although she attempted to avoid Meeting whenever possible, she was careful in public never to act in ways that violated the tenets or practices of the creed. Inwardly, by the time of her return to Baltimore the search for religious faith was finished. In its place had come the religion of culture. Reading for Carey was the source of spiritual renewal.

In the fall of 1885, she wrote to Mary Garrett that she needed time to read. The two of them, consumed by practical concerns, had "made the mistake of trying what prophets, saints, and martyrs, Christian and pagan, have failed in—to keep good without some outside assistance." This had been easy in Europe. In America it required conscious effort. "I think that I shall have to begin to do a little religious reading every day, whether Antigone or Pindar or Shakespeare, to supply artificially the lack." Without this she feared going the way of Turgenev's heroes, "reclaimed by the world of the flesh and the devil."[38]

The term "nous autres," which in 1880 had stood for passionate souls committed to artistic freedom, was now coming to be redefined as the small band of women who shared the preserve of culture. A letter written to Mary in 1884 captures this transformation. As Carey wrote about reading, she realized that it was vicarious living, but for her it was all the more glorious. Through reading "we rejoice or sorrow with genius," knowing what is worthy in both the present and the past, "sensitive to the splendid passions of our own generation," but capable of being moved "with the passions of past generations." Through art, "we, who cannot live ourselves one noble life, yet . . . live many lives, not like our own but pure fire from which the smoke and ashes have vanished. This *is* splendid."[39]

In the summer of 1884 as she read John Ruskin and declared her allegiance to him, she listed her litany of literary gods: Algernon Charles Swinburne, Dante Gabriel Rossetti, now joined by Walter Pater and Violet Paget writing under the pseudonym Vernon Lee. As she wrote of one of her favorite authors, she declared that he had "the power of bringing tears to my eyes, of touching a heart string on every page."[40] This is the way that she wanted to feel as she read. Yet it is necessary to remember another purpose that was served by writing to Mary about reading and art. Carey was trying to get Mary to love her, and she used art as a lure.

In the summer of 1884, she sent to Mary a poem meant for her eyes alone.

> *These many years within the sanctuary*
> *Which is my heart, alone I break and eat*
> *The bread and wine of dreams. I hear the beat*
> *Of hurrying thoughts that wing from over sea,*
> *From some far land of passion crying to me*
> *Until at morn or eve I go—to meet*
> *Mid dreams and thoughts made manifest her feet*
> *Mid many hearts her heart's deep mystery.*
>
> *For in that hour, afar or near at hand,*
> *When I shall pass beyond her eyes and know*
> *The very dreaming thought of her to grow*
> *One with my thought and splendid, understand*
> *Why I have loved her silence, I shall go*
> *Content, not lonely in the passionate land.*[41]

A year before, Mamie and Carey had seen the exhibition of Rossetti's paintings in London. The poet now recalls the recurring figure in many of his great paintings, imagining Rossetti's heroine as the Ideal "over sea" sending thoughts from "some far land of passion." The self, severed from religious belief, exists within the "sanctuary" of the heart, taking communion with art, breaking and eating "the bread and wine of dreams." God is absent, but the Ideal—Rossetti's compelling woman—calls from the land "over sea." Death—passing "beyond her eyes"—will bring the self union with her. The "I" of the poem will then "know the very dreaming thought of her to grow one with my thought" and joined with the Ideal, will go "content, not lonely in the passionate land."

This poem of yearning does several critical things. It calls to mind the compelling Rossetti figure, identified with Swinburne's poetry. It substitutes art for religion and the female Ideal for the male God. It places the Ideal across the sea, calling its home "the passionate land." It is thus a poem charged by an erotic image of union with the aesthetic Ideal, and it identifies that Ideal with Europe.

It is not certain who wrote the poem. It follows an elaborate preface in the letter to Mary: "Sometimes when I have been reading a book, as during this week, that has made a difference in me, whether it lie in me or in the book or poem I can never tell (I think perhaps it is a habit of thought which blindly works on behind a veil until some sentence on the pages of a book or in the mouth of a person rends it and with a passion of appropriation the thought is mine.) I wonder what you would think of the book or the thought." After having said that she did not know the difference between her own thoughts and those she had read or heard, she dilated, "As one grows older such things become the real life, and reaching thus horizon after horizon, the land becomes in time a new land upon whose possession we must enter. I will enclose you a few lines which have no merit except that of expressing more clearly a little of what I mean." And then, as if to protect herself still further, Carey asked Mary not to show the lines of poetry to anyone and to destroy them after reading them.[42] Why all this effort if the poem was her own? What makes one particularly suspicious about the poem's origin is that Carey never wrote a poem as good as this one.

Is it possible that, just as Mamie had supplied part of the text of the Swinburne paper, she was now, without her knowledge, the author of a poem that Carey sent to Mary? Some of the language of the poem is linked to words used to describe Rossetti's paintings in 1883. Carey had written movingly to Mary about the women in many of his great paintings, calling them "inhabitants of a land of dreams."[43] By her accounts, Carey was transfixed before the paintings, staring at them for hours at a time. But in describing them to Mary did she put them into Mamie's words? Did Carey sometimes purloin Mamie's phrases when she wrote to Mary? Without Mamie's conversation to set against the letters, there can be suspicion but no certainty. Both women had been drawn to Swinburne and Rossetti. Carey was profoundly influenced in these years by Mamie's aestheticism and may have been attracted to her language by natural affinity. But Carey also had a design: to win Mary's heart. It is possible, therefore, that the poem and some of Carey's aesthetic prose were borrowed, without asking, from Mamie Gwinn.

In Carey's effort to elicit Mary's love, she wrote about many aesthetic passions. Her letters give a long record of reactions to paintings, opera, and drama, as well as literature, in which the language of art merged into the language of courtship. As a girl she had often written about one love to another. Although to Mary she never wrote about Mamie, she did write about operatic and dramatic personalities. As she pursued Mary her letters were deliberately provocative, though covered by a veil of the higher morality. On Mary's birthday in 1891, for example, after sending her birthday kisses, Carey wrote that she was "so tattered and torn by the emotion of Tristan and Cleopatra" that she could not get her a proper present. She went on to tell her of seeing Richard Wagner's *Tristan und Isolde*. It was "the most glorious of all Wagner's operas, flawless from first to last, the most triumphant rhapsody of love ever thought, rapturous, soaring, heavenly high, winging through the Empyrean, without a touch of earth, all human emotion sublimated into godlike passion and longing, panting and throbbing through thousands of memories of the splendid things of seas and stars and plains and marble and pictures and poetry

until all together are blended into one in the rapture and fire of the music."
One thinks during the wedding night of Tristan and Isolde, "as she lies in his
arms while this glorious chant rises and falls," that "passion has said its last
word, but when the dying Tristan hears of Isolde's approach and tears open
his wound in the wildest excitement it rises higher and over his dead body in
the death song of Isolde, so high that one fairly breaks down under its weight
of splendor. I never in a public place came so near to losing my self-control."[44]

At another more retrospective moment Carey wrote to Mary about the
"tempestuous effect" on her of a talk they had had about Europe and Wagner
and pictures. It recalled the "nonsense I used to indulge in before I went
abroad, aesthetic nonsense that is better than sense, reading Carlyle and Ruskin
and Wordsworth or anything of the kind, in one's nightgown or waists and
drawers (chemise in the language of romance), half undressed, all undressed,
in bed or out of it, as it happened, just as the fever came, with tears of
admiration until two or three o'clock and then looking at the stars or moon or
darkness with ineffable wertherlike sensations." There had been no tears and
stars after her talk with Mary, but otherwise, her reactions were the same. "I
dedicated a vigil to the thought of Europe and read myself into cloudland and
daydreamed."[45]

III

IN THE fall of 1887 Carey expressed to Mary Garrett a sense of satisfaction that
Bryn Mawr was solidly begun and her teaching was going well. The only thing
keeping her from being "perfectly happy" was that she had too much to do.
Later she realized she should not have so tempted the gods. The day before
Thanksgiving, 1887, Mary Whitall Thomas summoned Carey home to tell
her she was dying of cancer.[46]

Despite the wedge that unbelief and art had wrought between mother and
daughter, Carey had nourished a fantasy that when her mother was old she
would take care of her and make her happy. In this dream the two were again
alone, and Mary was free of the clutter of her husband and seven other
children. Instead, at age fifty-one, Mary was doomed to an agonizing death.
Increasing Carey's pain was her knowledge that Mary had partly brought it on
herself. She had known of the lump in her breast for a year, but had hid it
from her doctor-husband in the belief that she could cure herself by faith.
When she was finally examined by a doctor, he told the family it was too late
for surgery. For Carey, there was no God, no mind cure, no afterlife. Although
skeptical about male doctors, she trusted science and medical research.

Immediately Carey (along with her father and brother Harry) got her
mother to the Philadelphia cancer specialist Dr. David Hayes Agnew. On
Thanksgiving Day he suggested surgery. Mary chose an alternative caustic

approach available in northern New York and, joined by Hannah, the family went immediately to Dr. Kinsley's cancer establishment. The doctor refused to operate and told them "she must die." In despair the family left. On the way home, they stopped in New York City, where Carey insisted that Mary be seen by cancer specialist Dr. Henry Burton Sands. He agreed that Mary had come too late: an operation would only increase her suffering. The family "returned home perfectly hopeless." Dr. Sands gave Mary six to eighteen months to live, but warned the family that they should not wish it to be too long.[47]

The family gathered. They recalled Grace, who was abroad with her husband Tom Worthington. Harry, who had dedicated himself to Mary's care, learned that he had tuberculosis and himself had to take a cure in Saranac Lake, New York. Carey considered resigning from Bryn Mawr, but, if she did, only a "desolate future without some outside active interest" loomed before her, and the possibility that after the years of hard work Bryn Mawr would come down like a "house of cards." She arranged for a woman who had just received her Ph.D. in Germany to lecture in her stead on Fridays, and in the months that followed returned to Baltimore to care for Mary for the long weekend. The family had repapered and furnished the front room for Mary's comfort. Carey filled it with flowers, cushions, books, and reproductions of beloved paintings. There she recited poetry and read to Mary, often throughout the night.[48]

The cancer spread and pinched the nerves of Mary's back and shoulder, and she had to be moved, dressed, and fed. She did not experience the severe pain that Carey feared, and remained cheerful, but each Friday Carey was shocked by the ground lost in the week. Still hoping that medicine might save her mother or at least diminish her pain, Carey investigated every cancer cure. Accepting her sister's wish to be cured by faith alone, Hannah sent word of a mud treatment, especially to be favored because it was "Scriptural . . . for Christ Himself used it; See John 9:6, so it must be in the Divine plan."[49] At one point Hannah wired a prescription from London. Carey hoped desperately that her mother might live until the summer, when she could be with her full time.

Mary weakened, but held on. In June the family moved her by private railway car to Coombe Edge, the retreat that she and Hannah had built in Blue Ridge Summit, Pennsylvania. By then Mary longed for death. There in the shelter of the summer house, Carey was able to tell her how much she loved her. The religion for which Mary had lived and died provided no hope to her eldest daughter. As Carey faced the "tide of oblivion" that was soon to close over Mary, she took a strange satisfaction in the steadfastness of her unbelief. "It has been one little ray of light to feel that a more personal theology has not been the thing I have felt the need of."[50]

Mary's final days were peaceful, and Carey gave herself utterly to her care. She hovered close to her mother's bedside, rubbing her legs when that helped, spooning gruel when she could take it. As Mary neared the end, she could barely speak. She told Carey, "I want to get through, but I did not know it would take so long." James sat near her so that she could see him. She added a codicil to her will that put aside five hundred dollars for a Women's Christian Temperance Union building and reserved Coombe Edge for the use of her unmarried children. On Sunday morning Hannah's telegram arrived, and James roused Mary to hear her sister's words of comfort: "I am thy God even unto death. . . . If thee goes to heaven Jesus will receive thee." Carey sat up with her, watching her sink, "the worst and most heart-breaking thing" she had ever imagined. Early the next morning, July 1, the family gathered. Carey described to Hannah her last moments: "Father held her in his arms and said all sorts of loving words while she looked at him for fully a minute, then as softly as a baby without any struggle for breath she closed them, and when Father laid her back on the pillow she was dead."[51]

Carey wired Mary Garrett: "Six o'clock Monday morning; the rest is silence." Carey and her sisters washed the body, dressed it, and laid it on a sheet surrounded by ice. Carey wrote to Hannah that her mother "looked beautiful, with a majesty of beauty that I had never seen." Her father and brother lifted the body into the coffin: "no one except ourselves touched her."[52] The family traveled with the body to Baltimore for the final services of parting. In the funeral procession Carey placed the carriages of Mamie Gwinn and Mary Garrett immediately behind those of her relatives.

In 1887 and 1888 Mary Garrett, concerned about the health of her brother Robert, had traveled with him and his wife around the world in the hope of restoring his tone. It was on this trip that she received word of Mary Thomas' fatal cancer. Her response was swift, empathetic, and loving. Although on the other side of the globe, she was with Carey completely. Remembering her own losses, the illness and impending death of her friend's mother touched her as nothing else had. Carey took comfort in the outpouring of Mary's warm and generous understanding. Although still bound to Julia Rogers, Mary's response opened the possibility to Carey that the special friendship she had long been seeking might be hers.

IV

EUROPE was for Carey Thomas the location of the Ideal, the place where she could locate her aesthetic self. But Europe was also where the scholarly Doctor Thomas, the third self, needed to repair each summer to research and write. And herein lay a conundrum.

For Carey Thomas scholarship was important. Her Ph.D. summa cum laude from the University of Zürich made her deanship possible. It was the basis of the respect that she commanded in the world. The scholar self was also her public persona. Carey Thomas valued this self and normally regarded its work as intrinsically important. In becoming Bryn Mawr's dean, Thomas realized that she had to forgo living the aesthetic life abroad, at least for a time; but she thought she would be able to develop herself as a scholar. She was, after all, not only dean but Bryn Mawr's professor of literature.

In the months after her appointment she applied herself steadily to preparing her lectures. Still living in Baltimore, she had to protect herself against the intrusion of personal concerns. Carey worried about the distractions to her work caused by her passionate friendships. Once the college opened she found lecturing satisfying, even exhilarating. In the fall of her first year of teaching, as she apologized to Mary Garrett for the abrupt tone of her letter, she wrote, "The college and trustees accounts and faculty are in a snarl: only the students are a very great pleasure. I care more about my hour's lecture than all the rest of the day." Her literature class gave her the chance to teach all Bryn Mawr students, to reach them about the authors who mattered to her most.[53]

As she reread some of her favorite authors, Shakespeare, Shelley, and Keats, their published letters, and biographical treatments, she felt the inspiration to write. During her vacations in Baltimore, she read in the Peabody Library and the library of Johns Hopkins to gather material for lectures. In her early summers abroad her serious task was course preparation, not research. She took especial pride in the graduate students who came to study under her, and she worked very hard to prepare her classes with them.

One of her graduate students—Mamie Gwinn—gave more than she took. Gwinn worked so closely with Thomas in preparing the lectures that they must be seen as their joint creation. Gwinn assisted in planning. In 1886, in reply to a request for help with a lecture on ballads, Gwinn wrote from Baltimore that she had been to the Peabody Library but had not found anything important. "Just tell them the nicest ballads and the probable dates of the chief cycles thereof, and something about the extraordinary differences of the same ballad-stuff in various countries, and something about the modern interest in ballads, Swinburne's early ones, 'King's daughter,' 'well water,' Lord Sands, etc., ditto Rossetti." She then began to establish the sequence of points Thomas should make and finally wrote an outline of the lecture. At times Thomas relied on Gwinn's words completely. As the academic year began in September 1888, two months after Mary Thomas' death, Thomas wrote to Gwinn, "I do not meet my class till Tuesday morning, so anything you send will be in time. I have one college professor of English and three new graduate students in English in my classes—Alas!"[54]

Gwinn's help was part of the fabric of their life in the Deanery. Carey Thomas threw herself into everything, teaching as well as deaning. She was of an era that believed in the necessity of regular habits and ordered, measured days ended by early bedtimes. She continually wrote to others to protect themselves from work and worry. But in her late twenties and early thirties, she was reckless about her own reserves of strength. On a normal day she awoke at six, prepared for teaching for four hours, transacted college business, and spent two-and-a-half hours in study for teaching in the evenings. But, of course, many days were not normal, and she had to work well into the night. During her mother's final illness, she mentioned to Mary that she had stayed up the night before until five in the morning, "getting some work ready for my graduate students." No matter how busy she was, she reread assigned texts. [55]

As a professor of English, Carey Thomas knew the rules, at least the Johns Hopkins rules to which she held her own faculty. She must herself be an active scholar and publish her work. To a German-trained philologist, scholarship in the 1880s had nothing to do with literary passions. It was precise examinations of texts, such as she had done in her dissertation. Thomas learned quickly that her duties as dean did not allow time for this kind of research, that it was the work of the summer. Moreover, philological research required the libraries of England and the Continent. Beginning in 1886, she went abroad with Mamie each summer to study.

Her first goal, however, was to soak up the culture that she had missed. In 1886, in her first eight days in London, she saw five plays and two operas. When she got down to work, it was to prepare lectures for the history of English literature. She read in the British Museum between one in the afternoon and seven in the evening. Her enjoyment was not dimmed by her sense that she had made little progress because of fatigue. She wrote home, "Nothing, nothing since I left Germany has been as nice as my hours of reading in the British Museum." Hannah Smith and family provided diversions, especially the campaign of Frank Costelloe, Mary's husband, for a seat in Parliament. Carey went to Newnham College, where she was invited to lunches and teas with college notables. Best of all were evenings of theater and opera and times alone with Mamie looking at their beloved pictures and then traveling to Devon. [56]

The following summer Carey and Mamie set their sights on Paris, where again Carey planned to work primarily at her lectures. Instead she reveled in the city's museums. It was sheer delight. She wrote to Mary, "To be young (comparatively) and in Paris, to see again as we did the first day, in a fever of excitement . . . some of our old haunts, and to feel that four years . . . have only increased one's power of enjoyment of it all." As she viewed the Salon exhibit, she wrote, "I think my eye for drawing and color has grown, like a bulb in a dark cellar, for I was ravished by everything one misses in England, all the dash and style and verve." She went to see an exhibit of the plein air school and found, "the whole salon . . . in full tilt for vivid blues and greens. . . . I see blue shadows everywhere." Indeed Paris was so filled with pleasures that Carey and Mamie retreated to Switzerland to study.[57]

Summer reading was often light. For example, Carey read Guy de Maupassant's *Les Soeurs Rondoli* with great relish. Maupassant, she wrote Mary, has "developed into an inimitable teller of impossibly indecent stories, short stories of depravity with such an irresistible grin of humour in them that one laughs instead of throwing the book out of the window." Distressed perhaps by the author's portrayal of a woman's passion for another woman, she felt "almost for the first time" that she recoiled "before something literally good and think it is a pity it should have been written." It was to such works that she turned in the summer, not scholarship. In contrast to her earlier notebooks, those from the mid-1880s are pathetic, consisting largely of lists of books, written in her hurried hand. Reference to an article by Friedrich Zarncke, her beloved Leipzig professor, suggests that she was aware of the need to keep up, but only that.[58]

With her mother's illness and death, Carey remained close to home in 1888. Still numb with grief, she devoted the summer of 1889 to recovering, traveling to Paris, Munich, Constantinople, and Athens. Paris evoked in her what was becoming a now familiar reaction. First came the longing to be an artist: "It seemed almost as if, could I live there à la Bohemian again for a year or two, I could do something." Second came her pleasure in the galleries and theater. Sarah Bernhardt sent her into raptures: "Her 'voice of gold' rising and falling, thrilling and murmuring is the greatest nonintellectual pleasure I can imagine. It is a sensation like that of music only more—desperate." In a single fortnight, Carey had made up for seven years' "famine of sensation."[59]

In 1890, she went abroad for the long summer on a trip that began in London and then took her to Scandinavia, Russia, Germany, and Paris. In London she experienced something of a social whirl among the literary set, going to a ball where she conversed with John Morley; a garden party at the Gladstones', where she looked into the "beautiful dark eyes" of her host as he told her stories; a supper given by Sir Edmund Gosse, where she sat between Frank Millet and a close friend of Henry James; and an evening where she and Mamie argued with Sidney Webb over the woman question until the early morning. She initially tried to work in London, as she explained to Mary, but decided to give herself "one more summer of pictures and impressions." Away, she felt well for the first time in the nearly three years since she had learned of her mother's illness, better perhaps than she had felt since becoming dean. As she gloried in the pleasures of art and leisure, she penned a revealing statement: "It seems to me that I have had everything possible, and for an American, a Baltimorean, my love for pictures and beautiful things (things so far away) is like a taste for horse racing, or drink, or women, and equally to be regretted."[60]

The United States in the 1880s and 1890s was developing art museums, symphony orchestras, and opera houses, and sustaining a lively tradition of theater. Despite her approval of this appropriation of European high culture, her native land continued to Carey to feel like a "prison house." She allowed herself relatively few indulgences, and those few were taken discreetly in trips to New York City. Alone with a book or privately with Mamie or Mary, Carey was able to sustain only a shred of her artistic self through the nine months of the Bryn Mawr academic year. To protect her deanship she had to keep that self far away from trustees' ears or eyes. But in Europe Carey could let down her guard and take open pleasure in the arts forbidden to Friends. She could spend whole days with Mamie in picture galleries, hear the entire Wagner *Ring* cycle. In Europe, Carey returned to the life that she and Mamie had lived together in their four years abroad. Each summer she felt restored, whole. If America was the prison house of reform, Europe came to represent the indulgence of art.

In Europe, Carey Thomas found it impossible to sustain the discipline of scholarship. It is not hard to understand why. Bryn Mawr was taxing. To teaching and the deanship she was to add new enterprises in education. By June of each year Dean Thomas was exhausted and needed rest. She also felt starved for the aesthetic pleasures that Europe provided. And there was Mamie, who, despite her graduate work at Bryn Mawr, was literary and aesthetic rather than scholarly. Each summer Doctor Thomas went abroad determined to work. Each summer she found herself deflected from her labors to the pursuit of art. In the meantime the thesis lay there unrevised and unpublished.

During the academic year 1890–91 Thomas made a resolution not to go to Europe so that she might give the summer to scholarship. Her teaching, both to the seventy-six undergraduates in her general English course and to her small group of graduate students, had been going very well, and that had reinvigorated her scholarly ambitions. She wrote to Mary, "This summer I am going to try so hard to publish something." She would sink herself "fathoms deep in books and read and read and read." Because her father was traveling abroad, she had the Baltimore house, but rather quickly retreated from the heat to Coombe Edge. Toward the end of the summer she took Frank and Helen to the Maine coast. Bryn Mawr pressures intruded constantly.[61]

Her days were not entirely taken, however. She had quiet weeks in which to work. The curious thing is that a summer to be devoted to scholarship became a period of study much like the one she had maintained in Baltimore before taking her Ph.D. abroad. In the early summer she read Homer in the morning with Mamie, spent an hour on Greek grammar, studied Italian, read Greek philosophy, and then had the evenings for more pleasurable reading. Later in the summer she read works in anthropology, history, art history, and science, changing her texts each hour to keep from getting tired, and gave her nights to Plato's dialogues. There is nothing ignoble about such reading. With it Thomas reaffirmed her old loves and kept abreast of the newest thought of the day. But in the one summer in which she protected herself from the aesthetic indulgences of Europe in order to undertake scholarly study, she failed even to begin.

A telling remark at the end of her summer suggests how far she was from such work. On the way to Baltimore from Maine, she went to Boston to try to further Bryn Mawr College appointments. She spent part of a day in the Harvard library looking up books on Elizabethan drama. She found few, "but in other directions, especially my Arthurian saga, the library is delightful." That she might have begun her summer in Cambridge she did not suggest.[62]

She concluded that her summer had been wasted, and she immediately began planning for the next summer abroad in Paris, Italy, and Bayreuth. During the year she wondered if she were not giving up too much of herself and of her chance to make a reputation by her constant work and worry. She wrote longingly to Mary, "I wish I could tell you how I long to make a reputation, and how far away any possibility seems with all this business on my hands and all this correspondence." At some point she put aside revising her thesis for publication and began to consider a study of the sixteenth-century dramatist Christopher Marlowe, to serve as an introduction to Shakespeare. Marlowe would have brought her out of narrow philological studies, close to her teaching and her literary passions, near, as she put it, to "the soaring, transcendent beauty and tenderness of Othello speeches."[63] However, to undertake a new project almost a decade after her Ph.D. pushed into the far distance any chance of publishing a scholarly work.

Ultimately one begins to understand that, despite her many statements about the value of scholarship and her own expressions of frustration and regret, Carey Thomas never made the commitment that could have enabled her to publish a literary study. She understood well that if she were a man, it would have been different. She would have had easy contacts, support from the emerging academic network, and no necessity to be dean as well as professor. But, though choices were constrained, by the 1890s, a woman could be principally a scholar. Cornell courted her in 1891 both as a professor of literature and as the dean of Sage College, a relatively minor administrative position; she did not consider it. At Bryn Mawr, she had made it possible for Charlotte Angas Scott to be a mathematician and nothing more. But Carey Thomas wanted to be more, she wanted to change higher education for women, she wanted power. As time passed, scholarship and the engaged life proved to be incompatible.

One index is that, although Bryn Mawr offered sabbaticals to its faculty, Thomas did not seek one until well into the twentieth century. It would have meant giving up her position for a term or a year. To Dean Thomas, this was unthinkable. The trustees might undo her work. President Rhoads might make mistakes in appointments that would bedevil the college for years. The residence hall or the science building might be built without her scrutiny. No, Carey Thomas was committed to the cause, even if it wore her down, used her up.

Thus the cycle continued. Each summer as she rested and renewed herself she made resolutions to put order into her life and to protect her strength. Each year in September she embarked on an exhausting round of work and scheming and new tasks. She always added, never limited. During the nine months of the year there was no surcease. The pressure mounted and with it shortness of temper, conflict, and headaches. June would come, and with a fury of final tasks, Carey would end the year, board a steamer with Mamie, and collapse.

As the Ph.D. moved further back in time, she found herself less able to concentrate on scholarly work. She took more time abroad to explore museums and galleries. With more money to spend, she began to indulge in the luxuries of travel and acquisition. Although even to herself she continued to present travel abroad as necessary for scholarship, it became a time of release and pleasure, a time when she became again the passionate, aesthetic Carey.

What emerged, de facto, was that only two of her identities developed— the committed, zealous, effective dean and the lover of art. Over time the scholar Thomas atrophied. Carey Thomas remained for years a charismatic teacher, but the scholarship she believed must support teaching was missing. Ultimately, Thomas understood this. In 1895, a former student, now immersed herself in administrative work, wrote a poignant letter that was, Thomas felt "all true—every word of it. I saw clearly for myself that in managing the college I was giving up all hopes of scholarship. The combination is impossible, totally impossible."[64]

CHAPTER 12

The Wee Bit of Practical Good

CAREY THOMAS' early adult life poses a particularly difficult challenge. She is best understood not as a single identity, distilling the forces of parental influence, historical era, and inner urges, but as a bundle of conflicting aspirations. She hoped to change the educational outlook for women, to live a life committed to art, to be a scholar. Over the course of her adult life, her scholarly hopes atrophied and her dreams of art came to center on intimate friendship, appreciation, and travel; but she remained a complex, divided being.

Her contending natures were, of course, not totally separate, and they did not exist in discrete chronological time. In any year, month, or even day, one might overlap the other. The image that comes to mind is a braid. Aspects of Carey Thomas are like its three strands. At any one moment in her life, one element is dominant, guiding her actions, emotions, and thoughts, only to give way to another. The image, however, should not conjure up the smooth braids of a proper daughter; but a much scruffier plait, uneven, with lots of knots, one that holds together in sections and becomes unraveled in others.

How does one write about such a life? The strands need to be described separately. Yet the life itself is no individual piece, but a braid of the three. When one returns to the engaged strand, left at the outset of the academic year 1885–86, it becomes clear that key notions rooted in the artistic self affected the direction and boundaries of reform efforts.

Carey Thomas' work in creating Bryn Mawr was located squarely in that side of her committed to the cause of women, shaped initially in the Thomas household but transformed through reading. As she threw herself into turning Joseph Wright Taylor's bequest into a college, Thomas believed that she was gaining for women precious resources for education. The Ph.D. that she had won with such difficulty she now put in service to the cause. She also understood that creating Bryn Mawr was the beginning and must be followed by constant vigilance and growth.

Carey Thomas saw her efforts in a light distinct from those of her mother and aunt, the two most powerful women in her early life. During the years of Carey's young adulthood, Mary Thomas had moved from her parlor to the larger world of reform. Hannah Smith, no longer preaching after Robert's disgrace, sustained her reputation as a religious writer. Although Carey loved both of them dearly, she regarded them as provincial, religious, and old-fashioned, still caught in the woman's net of family obligation.

By contrast, Carey saw herself as secular, cosmopolitan, modern, and free from the burdens of husband and children. She had emerged from her crisis of faith both as one of "nous autres" and as a positivist and Social Darwinian. Her reading of Herbert Spencer had given her a rationale for iconoclasm and a commitment to building a progressively better world through science. Set on her course, she espoused modern causes and kept herself current in the latest literature on socialism, land nationalization, and science. She carried the truth of a world evolving to higher forms through the application of scientific thought.

While mother went out on the streets to preach to the unconverted, daughter worked in a study. One of the primary ways that Carey had come to define herself as different—more up-to-date—than Mary was in her attention to social distinctions. It pained her that her mother opened her parlor so freely, that she associated with "inferiors." Carey found it embarrassing that Mary went out on the streets and into brothels to reform sinners. Although daughter was impelled by some of the same enthusiasm, energy, and sense of the world's wrongs that drew mother into reform, in critical ways she diverged. As she dedicated her adult career to offering to women opportunities through education, Carey Thomas did not mean all women. She meant a woman like herself who was, or could aspire to be, a lady. It never occurred to her to include African-American women, with whom she had close, affectionate, though hierarchical, contact in her Baltimore household. It did not mean Jews, with whom she had little association but strong negative feelings. And it did not mean any women, such as those who were working-class, whom she regarded as vulgar.

On a certain level her mother's world had not made such distinctions. Mary had been cordial to mathematician James Joseph Sylvester, the first Jew on the Johns Hopkins faculty. In 1884, when the American Congress convened in Baltimore, she breached the greatest barrier in a Southern city: she invited African-American women into her home as honored guests at a tea for the delegates. As she wrote to Hannah, "We had a first-rate time at our tea. I invited some of the very nicest ladies in Baltimore to meet the Congress Women, and all enjoyed it ever so much. Mrs. [Frances] Harper and her daughter (colored) were here in the midst, and it really did not make any difference. . . . I am sure it has done the cause of *Woman* good." Carey and her brothers urged that Mary not speak. Mary wrote that she had acceded to her children's wishes, and "Mrs. Harper spoke *admirably* on the Temperance question so they got along without either of us."[1]

Although Mary Thomas opened her reform world to include individuals who were Jewish and African American, she nonetheless sustained boundaries for her children. As a child Minnie Thomas had learned that all were equal in the eyes of God, but that her mother preferred that she make friends only with Friends. The boys and young men acceptable as suitors had been even more narrowly defined; much of her parents' prohibition against socializing with men at Cornell came from fear that Carey would make an unacceptable match. As they chose wives and husbands, her brothers and sisters drew from a restricted social circle; the most favored marriages were among cousins.

Although Carey Thomas had begun to assert some class distinctions at Howland and Cornell, it was in the years abroad that she sharpened her sense of discrimination. Under Mamie's tutelage, Carey had established a clear sense of herself as one of the small band of lovers of beauty. Abroad this had largely been a way that Carey affirmed her own identity vis-à-vis her mother, but after she returned to America, the meaning to her of "nous autres" shifted. It became less "we, the others" than "we, the not-them." America was the land of barbarians. The few lovers of beauty, especially the women whom she loved, had to band together. No longer a Quaker except to the outside, Carey practiced with Mamie and Mary the religion of art. Increasingly it became a religion of exclusion. Only a few had the breeding and the taste to enter its temples. She believed that her task as a reformer was to create opportunities for those few.

Several handsome photographic studio portraits from this period present Carey Thomas as an elegant, refined woman. In one, posture erect, her head held proudly, her heavy-lidded eyes wide open, she stands at a doorway, book in hand. She is dressed in an exquisitely trimmed high-necked dark gown. Her hair catches the light. Another, taken in London by Frederick Hollyer in 1886, has her seated at a small-paned window, reading a book resting on the windowsill. Her long brown hair is braided and secured in a bun at the neck. Her dress is a Liberty print silk, with a high white collar and white lace at the cuffs. Images of her well-proportioned, strong features and her slender form, these photographs suggest how she hoped the world would see her: a woman of dignity and taste.[2]

II

IN JANUARY 1887, asked by Hannah to speak on higher education at the Evening Hour Club, Carey Thomas refused. She explained that, unlike her aunt, she was not a person who felt "called upon to speak." For Bryn Mawr she would do whatever was necessary, but she did not think it was a good idea to speak in public: "I do not believe in general addresses." Her response was of a piece with decisions that Thomas was making in the same years about other causes. When asked to lend her name, or to work for an issue, she found herself reluctant for she did not want to dilute her efforts or hinder the nascent college. Implicitly she had to answer two questions: would outside philanthropy take time from her work? would identification with particular issues threaten in some way her mission at Bryn Mawr? For these reasons, in the early years at Bryn Mawr she refused all invitations to speak before general audiences, making it her rule, as she explained to Hannah, that she never spoke "on any subject in public."[3]

Her urge to work for women did find paths compatible with her position as dean. The first effort sprang from the difficulties of her sisters in getting an education, reminding her of the void in secondary schooling for girls in Baltimore. Carey Thomas joined with Mary Garrett, Mamie Gwinn, Bessie King, and Julia Rogers to found the Bryn Mawr School. The five friends, who had in 1878 met informally as the Friday Evening, constituted themselves the governing committee or board of managers. They sought to use their connections, especially Thomas' contacts in higher education, to gather excellent teachers. From the outset, the school's requirement for graduation was that the student pass the Bryn Mawr College entrance examinations. In February 1885 Carey wrote to Mary that her heart was set "upon the success of our school, the wee bit of practical good we have tried to do, as associated together." As she reread the passages in her journal from years past, "the ethical justice of our enterprise struck me afresh."[4]

The committee met in Baltimore and in the Blue Ridge mountains, at Coombe Edge. In the spring of 1885 Carey Thomas and Mary Garrett traveled to visit girls' preparatory schools in New England. The Bryn Mawr College board of trustees agreed to the use of the name, and in May a public announcement was made. The committee hired Eleanor A. Andrews, a graduate of Newnham College, as secretary or headmistress, and selected a faculty of five. They leased a three-story building at 715 North Eutaw Street, adjacent both to the Friends' Meeting House and to Johns Hopkins University. The school opened on September 21, 1885.

By then Carey Thomas was at Bryn Mawr College; she kept in touch with the school by letter. As she monitored the college's first French and German entrance examinations, she wrote a personal letter to the committee in Baltimore. Bessie, Mary, Julia, and Mamie had gone to the station to see her off to Bryn Mawr. From the train Carey looked at them standing on the platform, looking "so unusually uncommitteeish," and was touched by the sight. For Thomas, the Bryn Mawr School began as a way of doing good with friends. In time, it was to become an important sideline, but it never took center stage.[5]

For Mary Garrett, it became her work and the focus of her energies. In

1884 Garrett's father died. She was no longer burdened by the authority and the care of parents and for the first time in her life was free to make decisions. As one of her father's heirs, she had responsibility for the wise use of one-third of the Baltimore and Ohio railroad fortune. As her initial benefaction she chose to underwrite the Bryn Mawr School and, as the school prospered, to give it a handsome building. Though all policy decisions were made collectively by the committee, Carey Thomas' and Mamie Gwinn's residence in Pennsylvania, Bessie King's constant illness, and Julia Roger's relative lack of interest meant that Mary Garrett assumed primary responsibility, confirmed by the title of president. The board appointed the secretary to act in some respects as headmistress; but kept to itself all disbursements of money and all decisions about personnel, curriculum, and schedule. Because Garrett was meticulous about financial matters, she took over the books; and because she cared that her money be well spent, she supervised the construction and maintenance of the school building.

As the school developed, the members of the board had reason to feel proud of its accomplishments. It succeeded in its central mission. Within a few years, real proof of its success came with the admission of its graduates to Bryn Mawr College. In arguing for exhibit space in the Liberal Arts Building of the 1893 World's Columbian Exposition in Chicago, Thomas pointed out the distinctive features of the school. Unlike any other private school, it prepared all its female students according to an "inflexible college standard." Each pupil began Latin at age ten or eleven and took Greek for the last three years. All students were examined by Bryn Mawr College examiners.[6]

Yet pride in accomplishment did not lead to harmony among the creators. What began as a medium of practical philanthropy among five close friends became a source of tension and discord. Each was strong and willful and used to having her own way. Thomas, moreover, added planning for the school to her heavy burdens of teaching and administration. During the early years her primary tasks, beyond the joint committee work, were interviewing prospective teachers, visiting classes, and arranging the schedule with Gwinn. She often felt overwhelmed with work and unrecognized for what she contributed.

Conflicts became bitter and difficult to resolve, spilling over into the intricate web of personal relationships among the five, which were exceedingly complicated in the late 1880s and early 1890s. At some moments, school business threatened Carey Thomas' rapport with Mary Garrett. Until the committee formed, Carey's relationship with Mary was centered on visits and letters and a mutual love of the arts, but as they began to work together in the Bryn Mawr School, their friendship became frayed.

There were clear differences of power on the committee. Carey had position, clear ideas, a direct and articulate manner, and growing insight into the way that institutions worked. Mary had money, vast amounts of money on a scale that exceeded her luxurious manner of living. Between them, they generally governed the other three, who had some influence and independence. Mamie had claims based on her father's position and on her closeness to Carey. Bessie had illness and a powerful father. Julia had a private income and a connection to Mary.

The Bryn Mawr School is particularly important in Carey Thomas' story, for it reveals her social attitudes in action at the end of the nineteenth century. Unlike the college, where she was constrained by many external forces, the school offered a freer scope for her fears and prejudices. In 1889, for example, she queried an educational adviser about a candidate for secretary, asking not about her educational qualifications but about the length of her hair and her church attendance. In justification for what she knew would be perceived as "a very foolish question," Thomas wrote, "We are so revolutionary in all main points that I do not know whether our headmistress or secretary could afford to differ from other people in non-essential trifles which arouse prejudice."[7] Thomas would most likely have justified the Bryn Mawr School's decision to restrict the number of Jewish students in just these terms. Yet, at another level the school provided a field on which she could play out a deep prejudice. To understand this one must explore the evolution of Thomas' anti-Semitism.

Carey Thomas had grown up in a family with a great interest in Jews buttressed by reverence for the Old Testament and the people to whom it had been addressed. But, although the Thomases held great respect for the historic people, in a local world consisting of Quaker Meeting and kin and the evangelical Christian reform community they had no social contact with members of the sizeable Baltimore Jewish community. However, when Johns Hopkins hired James Joseph Sylvester, an English mathematician who was Jewish, Mary sought to know him and to learn of the state of his soul.[8]

Carey Thomas shared some of her family's curiosity about the Jewish people. When she was in Europe, she visited Prague in 1880, going to the ghetto and viewing the graveyard and synagogue. She wrote, "My inherited taste is strong enough to make Jews awfully interesting to me." She was also learning about the rise of a new German anti-Semitism. She reported to her mother what she had heard in Leipzig: "There is an agitation against the Jews here. A society called 'worry Jews Society' met in Dresden and stated that there are five hundred thousand Jews in Germany who are so nationally separate that they privately consider they owe no allegiance to the Empire. It stated that every newspaper except one was under their control. The conclusion was to disfranchise them. Of course, this is as yet a very small movement."[9]

In Europe, part of the separation that Carey Thomas effected from her religious, tolerant, reform-minded parents was to open herself to new waves of thought that included anti-Semitism. Mary had continued to write to Carey of her own religious beliefs, as a form of self-expression and as an effort, however late, to bring her daughter around. In response to one of Mary's disquisitions on the Old Testament, in October 1882, Carey wrote a defense of the New, curious in the light of her continuing rejection of Christianity. In the course of arguing that the greatness of the New Testament came from its inspiration, Carey digressed into a diatribe against Jews: "The Jews are the same now and were the same then, a most terrible set of people to my thinking, and grand only as a very deep narrow rift between two giant cliffs is grand which from its very narrowness enables one standing at the bottom to see the stars at noon day." Of whom she was thinking when she wrote this is not clear, for, with the exception of Sylvester, she had virtually never met a Jew.[10]

Although nurtured in Europe, Thomas' anti-Semitism found fertile ground in the United States, where such attitudes were rising in elite circles. At the Bryn Mawr School Thomas had the power to take discriminatory actions against Jews. In the opening year, the school received an application from Sadie Szold, a child the secretary described to Garrett as "a quiet, ladylike girl, most interested about her work and promising to make a good student." Garrett, who wanted to admit her, insisted that the school would have to do so or to "refuse point blank," an act that would become known publicly. Garrett forced the issue in such a way that, as Thomas put it the following year, "there seemed nothing else to be done."[11]

It was Thomas' understanding—or misunderstanding—that there were to be no more Jewish students in the school. Supported by Rogers, Garrett insisted that enrollment be open to Jews. On June 12, 1886, perhaps egged on by Gwinn, whom Garrett earlier described as the one "who has throughout been so emphatically against it," Thomas wrote scorchingly to Garrett: "I have just heard from Mamie what you have done about the Jews, and I am very much worried. I think you should have waited one day longer after my emphatic telegram. I should on *no* account take them, and I register my *strongest* protest. The understanding was that Sadie Szold would be the last." In the margins Thomas continued, "*Cannot* your action be withdrawn: we should not risk all that we care for in the success of the school for such a thing and I think at least I should have been allowed to give my reasons. . . . I wish us to escape from them at all hazards. It is so important."[12]

By this letter Carey Thomas so offended Mary Garrett that their friendship was strained for months. In the summer that followed, they were both in London—Carey with Mamie, Mary with Julia—but they did not meet, though Carey saw Mary from afar in a London theater. In September, Carey wrote that she had been very tired in June and therefore had not been kind. In November, she apologized, not for the substance of her letter but for its tone. Although anti-Semitism was intensifying in the United States in this period, the depth of the conflict that Carey Thomas' action caused belies any simple explanation that in her anti-Semitic acts Thomas merely conformed to the notions of her era and social circle.[13]

After agreement was reached in the board that there would be a few Jewish students admitted, Thomas worked to hold down the numbers. In an undated letter to Gwinn, written around 1890, Thomas wrote that she was enclosing Bessie King's letter which "recalled the whole committee discussion and [it] is simply impossible to admit Siliger Jew—after our decision then—we cannot do it. I have just telegraphed Mrs. Colvin not to admit her till further advice. We simply cannot have her." Thomas then suggested that the school secretary, Mary Colvin, "say that she regrets very much that on account of the absence of members of the committee she did not know that the rule of the school had always been not to admit more than a fixed number of Jews and that the limit had been reached." Thomas went on to say that before admitting a particular applicant, the committee should check with their fathers to be certain she was not Jewish.[14]

In 1890 The Jewish Exponent, after an inquiry, charged that the Bryn Mawr School arbitrarily limited the number of Jewish students, a policy that, it editorialized, "smacks of that kind of hateful intolerance" of Europe in the Middle Ages. Colvin had been visited by a reporter, who she assumed was a rabbi wishing to enroll his daughter. Colvin had told him, as she wrote to Thomas, "politely, according to your instructions that we took a certain number of Jewish girls, but that our number was filled." Thomas wrote a letter to the paper denying Colvin's statement, stating that the school was open to all qualified children, "without discrimination on grounds of race or religion," a policy about which "all the members of the board of the Bryn Mawr School feel very strongly." To ground her point, Thomas presented evidence of Jewish students at the top and bottom of ability, a statement that did not, however, address the issue, that there was a quota on the absolute number of Jews.[15]

Colvin's response to the reporter, that she had said it was the school's rule "not to admit more than a certain number of Israelites," repeated Thomas' instructions and accurately represented board policy. Thomas could insist to the contrary because the Bryn Mawr School had one strength that the Jewish community lacked. Francis T. King was called on to write to the Baltimore newspapers to ensure that there would be no reporting of the controversy.[16]

The admission of Jewish students was one of a number of sources of discord among the five friends on the board. When Mary Garrett decided to build a large building for the school, she occasioned new conflicts. Carey, anticipating divisions about the plans, wrote to Mary that they "must try to agree to disagree," if necessary. The Bryn Mawr School seemed to her like a "deformed child" that cost dear time in its formative years; now that it was getting established, the five must "all do our best by our troublesome offspring."[17]

M. Carey Thomas, c. 1884

Carey Thomas presenting herself as an elegant, refined woman

M. Carey Thomas, 1886, by Frederick Hollyer

A woman of quiet dignity and taste in a Liberty print silk

"Bryn Mawr College Group '86"

Dean M. Carey Thomas sits to the right of President James E. Rhoads in the row just below the (standing) faculty. Charlotte Angas Scott stands in academic dress to Thomas' right. The men on the faculty are, left to right: J. James Stürzinger, Edmund B. Wilson, Edward H. Keiser, Paul Shorey, E.W. Hopkins, and Woodrow Wilson. Among family members pictured in the student group, cousin Alys Smith is standing in the front at the far left, sister Grace Thomas stands in the front at the far right, and Margaret Thomas is sitting in the center with a piece of white paper on her lap

Above: M. Carey Thomas, 1896,
by James L. Breese

*A vigorous woman in early middle age;
her erect stance conveys a sense
of confidence and a mature force and
power, and her jeweled dress signals
a clear break with Quaker codes*

Mary Garrett, by Frederick Hollyer

M. Carey Thomas (far left) and Mary Garrett (center) at a meeting of the Naples Table Association, 1907

A buoyant M. Carey Thomas, happy in her joint work with Mary Garrett

M. Carey Thomas and Marion Edwards Park, c. 1922

Capturing a moment of transition, difficult for both women

Helen and Simon Flexner
and their two sons, c. 1910

M. Carey Thomas
surrounded by her brothers
and sisters and their spouses
(n.d.); *left to right*:
Bond Thomas, Simon
Flexner, Josephine C.
Thomas (probably Mrs.
Bond Thomas), Margaret
T. Carey, Grace T.
Worthington, Helen T.
Flexner, M. Carey Thomas,
John Thomas, Josephine C.
Thomas (probably Mrs.
Henry Thomas), Frank
Thomas, and Henry (Harry)
Thomas

M. Carey Thomas in Egypt, 1929

Left: Traveling "en princesse"

Right: On the back of this photograph, Thomas wrote:

> *Desert Camp*
> *In the Pyramid Field,*
> *Feb. 11, 1929,*
> *Seeing the World at 72 —*

M. Carey Thomas, 1933

Garrett spared no expense on the building, designed by New York architect Henry Rutgers Marshall, or on its furnishings, art reproductions, or grounds. Completed in 1890, it stood until the era of urban renewal on Cathedral Street in a fashionable section of Baltimore. Garrett had her lawyer draw up a legal agreement establishing a constitution for the school that required the signatures of the board of managers. In Thomas' judgment, the constitution proposed was unthinkable, for were Garrett to die, the property that she had left the school would be insecure and members of the committee vulnerable for the school's debts. Satisfied that they were appropriately protected, on January 25, 1890, the five signed a simple document of incorporation.

As the year progressed, conflict deepened. A rift came between Julia Rogers and Mary Garrett. Little can be learned about this dispute because afterward Mary and Julia reviewed their correspondence and cleansed it. But glimmers can be seen from Carey's letters to Mary. At last Carey had the opening that she had been seeking for over a decade. In an 1891 New Year's letter she asserted that Julia had been working against Mary ever since Carey had returned from abroad: "There is never a time when I see her that she does not imply, or say, something disloyal to you. Long ago I realized, even at Deer Park, that if I wanted to keep my faith in you I could not talk to Julia." Julia had attempted to poison Mary's relations not only with Carey but also with Bessie, Mamie, and Mary's New York friends Lou Knox and Julia de Forest. Carey hoped that by finally telling this to Mary she might help Mary break through the "ever contracting net of personal difference and friction and nervous strain" that bound her. Carey wanted Julia to resign from the Bryn Mawr School board. If not, the friction would continue. Carey promised always to side with Mary: "as long as I love you, I shall agree, for my agreement is part of my loving and one does not exist without the other." In the meantime she argued that the committee should cease to meet.[18]

Julia Rogers quit the board. She remained active in Baltimore civic affairs and is remembered as a major donor to Goucher College. The marked shift in tone in Carey's subsequent letters to Mary suggests that Julia resigned simultaneously from the Bryn Mawr School board and from her intimate friendship with Mary.

III

INTERSECTING with the Bryn Mawr School was the friends' second major effort at joint philanthropy. Discussion among them began in the fall of 1888, and quiet conversations were held with George W. Childs, the Bryn Mawr College donor. Late in December 1888 Carey Thomas paid a call on President Daniel Coit Gilman of Johns Hopkins and presented him with a startling proposition: a committee of women would raise $100,000 to endow the Johns Hopkins

medical school—a sum comparable in 1990s dollars to over $1.5 million—
if it were open to women on the same terms as to men. Gilman and the Johns
Hopkins board had already dealt with Mary Garrett. In March 1887 they
refused her contribution of $35,000 to be given annually to establish a coeduca-
tional school of science on land near Montebello. Now they faced a bribe
enabling the long-desired medical school on the condition that it admit women
students.[19]

Before his death in 1873 Johns Hopkins had incorporated not only a
university, but also a hospital—and therefore a potential medical school.
Delay postponed the hospital's opening. By 1886 several Hopkins professors
constituted themselves a medical faculty, and in 1888 William Osler came to
the university as professor of the theory and practice of medicine and as
physician-in-chief of the hospital. Less than a month before, Francis T. King,
who was chairman of the Hopkins hospital's board of trustees, had asked
Gilman's help in creating the hospital, and negotiations had begun that were
to lead to Gilman's assuming the position of hospital director in late January.
With the anticipated formal opening of the hospital in May 1889 all would
be in readiness for the Johns Hopkins medical school—with the exception of
the necessary means, an endowment. It was an unpropitious time. Johns
Hopkins' will had required the trustees to retain the endowment in Baltimore
and Ohio Railroad Company stocks. Though in many good years the stock
yielded 10 percent, from 1888 to 1890 the company offered no dividend. To
keep the university afloat, the Hopkins board of trustees authorized a campaign
for an emergency fund; the women's committee agreed to defer their own drive
until it was raised.

Although Thomas initially believed Gilman would aid them, he proved to
be an obstacle, and Thomas and her friends shifted their efforts to the boards
of the university and the hospital. Francis T. King encouraged them strongly,
as did James Thomas and Charles J. M. Gwinn, Mamie's father. Once the
emergency fund was secure, the four principals (Julia Rogers had withdrawn
by this time) moved into action. They established the Women's Medical
School Fund and called on a vast network of friends and associates to start
committees in fifteen cities, including New York, Philadelphia, Boston, Washington, Chicago, and St. Louis. They attracted important women: the wife of
President Benjamin Harrison headed the Washington committee; the writer
Sarah Orne Jewett lent her name. They went after society figures, writers,
famous women, and female physicians. On May 2, 1890, with an article
placed in The Nation, the campaign to raise $100,000 for the Women's
Medical School Fund officially began.

By October the money was raised. Nearly seven hundred gave to the Fund.
Mary Garrett's gift was by far the largest: $47,787.50. The money was offered
to the Johns Hopkins board on October 28, 1890, on the condition that the

medical school admit women students on equal terms with men, a stipulation drafted by Charles J. M. Gwinn. Urged by the faculty, the board accepted the gift, but stated that the medical school could not open until $500,000 was raised. Delighted that his cousin had brought off the seemingly impossible, Francis King wrote to Carey Thomas, "Thee never did a better week's work in thy life." On November 11, 1890, the Women's Medical School Fund held a preliminary victory celebration. Notable members of the local committees were feted by a luncheon at the hospital followed by a reception at Mary Garrett's house.[20]

When *The Nation* printed criticism of the Johns Hopkins trustees for their decision to open the medical school to women, Thomas rose to the defense. Her letter in the January 1891 issue placed responsibility (and credit) for the effort with the Women's Medical School Fund committee and clarified the limited nature of the Johns Hopkins decision. She argued opportunistically that coeducation in the medical school did not require coeducation in all branches of the university, for the scientific course required of all entering medical students could be had in existing colleges open to women.[21]

In February 1891, *The Century Magazine* published a set of open letters, later reprinted as a pamphlet, *The Opening of the Johns Hopkins Medical School to Women*. In the distinguished company of James Cardinal Gibbons, physician Mary Putnam Jacobi, reformer Josephine Shaw Lowell, and physician William Osler, Thomas began her argument where *The Nation* letter ended. The Johns Hopkins medical school would "raise the standard" of women's higher education, as colleges developed courses to meet its entrance requirements. She then went on to broader ground. Medicine was the only learned profession completely open to women, and it was one in which they had a peculiarly important place. A woman physician was necessary in schools and colleges not only to deal with cases inappropriate to a male doctor, but also as a wise counselor who knows that "intellectual activity is the keenest of possible lifelong pleasures and a safeguard against a multitude of evils." Such a woman doctor, with a balanced ideal of women, would not "prescribe sheer idleness" for schoolgirls and college women or "secure physical health for her patients at the expense of intellectual development."

A second reason to support women's entrance into the medical school was that graduate education was fundamentally different from undergraduate. More costly than college training, graduate work could not be easily duplicated. Its students could be trusted with coeducation, and they benefited by the association and competition with the best talent. In a presage of future addresses on women and creativity, Thomas argued that women scholars needed to compete with men and associate with them: "to exclude women from such association is, speaking generally, to exclude them from the delights of intellectual competition and the possibility of fame."[22]

The Century Magazine contribution and the fight for the medical school mark a critical change in Carey Thomas' life. In her early years as dean, she centered her working life on the Bryn Mawr campus, leaving during term only to visit her family in Baltimore or to take an occasional trip to New York. She seldom even went into Philadelphia. She kept a low profile. In her desire to do nothing that might injure Bryn Mawr, she engaged in no public efforts or controversies. But in working for a cause she believed in, Thomas forgot her reticence and her rule never to speak in public. As she tentatively found her voice, she began to develop arguments that were to carry her to a national stage.

Carey Thomas emerged into the public arena, but Mary Garrett fell backward. In her work for the Bryn Mawr School and the Women's Medical School Fund, Mary overstretched her psychological and physical limits. Her intimate friendship with Julia Rogers ended. The distress this caused Mary one cannot know. She had some kind of breakdown and in February 1891 began a long period in which she sought cures in America and Europe. Whenever she was away Thomas had to manage affairs both at the Bryn Mawr School and for the Fund. Garrett agreed to donate more money on the condition that the $500,000 be raised.

On December 24, 1892, the trustees gathered at Mamie Gwinn's Baltimore house as Charles J. M. Gwinn read a letter from Mary Garrett with a new offer. She promised to meet the trustees' requirement herself, by giving over $300,000—almost $5 million in 1994 dollars. She coupled her contribution with added stipulations, however, designed to turn the medical school into a full graduate school. Gilman found the requirements too binding on the faculty, and the medical faculty feared they would limit the number of incoming students. After much discussion and consultation, Mary Garrett wrote a letter clarifying that her intent had been only to insure that the medical school be at the graduate level and that the faculty had full freedom to determine the specific course of study. On February 4, 1893, the medical school faculty voted on requirements for admission. Harry Thomas was sent to Bryn Mawr to explain them to his sister, giving ground to rumors in Baltimore that Carey Thomas was actually making decisions for Mary Garrett. After a period of negotiation, the trustees and Garrett came to full agreement, and the Johns Hopkins University School of Medicine opened in the fall of 1893, offering graduate medical training for women and men. As a final condition Garrett required that the trustees' resolution to accept the Fund appear annually in the university catalogue, and that if the stipulations were ever violated—if the school ceased to be coeducational—the principal of her gift and the interest accrued would fall to Bryn Mawr College.[23]

Drawing on her personal ties and professional position, Carey Thomas was the chief negotiator of the many compromises among the remaining four friends, and between them and Johns Hopkins. These were not cool business arrangements between rational intelligences. Creating the material base for the Johns Hopkins medical school was rather like a performance of Italian opera at its most fevered. Thomas' state of mind is captured in a letter she wrote to Hannah Smith a full year after the conflict had ended. She wrote that Garrett had decided on her large gift to Johns Hopkins "to *force* the trustees to open. Many of them, and President Gilman, above all, preferred never to have a medical school at all rather than to have one to which women were to be admitted." The trustees did not fight openly but "in the dark with treachery and false reasons. Trustees, doctors, professors (Mr. Gwinn and Father leading our forces) became involved in a tangle of hatred, malice, detraction that beggars description." Carey Thomas, Mary Garrett, and Mamie Gwinn were "wire-pulling and lobbying all winter." Garrett became so involved and angry at the trustees that Thomas had to take over the conversations, requiring her to go to Baltimore as much as twice a week. "I often sat up all night preparing campaign broadsides."[24]

Carey Thomas was on trickier ground than she had ever been in her life. She was guiding her beloved Mary Garrett, battered by illness, in her decision to use creatively her money in the service of women—guiding but not controlling. Mary had clear ideas and an imperial manner bred in the household of her father. Mamie, who normally was a dependent ally in their combined causes, had a central role as the daughter of Charles J. M. Gwinn, who, as the executor of Johns Hopkins' will, had drafted the articles of incorporation for the Johns Hopkins hospital and university and now advised the Women's Fund Committee. Bessie, physically weak, and also irrational and demanding, had to be treated with special care as the daughter of Francis T. King, president of the board of trustees of the hospital and powerful trustee of the university (and president of the board of trustees of Bryn Mawr College). Carey, who had been somewhat estranged from her father during her mother's illness and death, drew close to him as her chief ally and mainstay. Through him she gained background and perspective and specific knowledge about positions of the members of the board.

During the negotiations Francis King died, leaving Bessie bereft and without a household of her own, though with a substantial income. Relations among Bessie, Carey, and Mary had become strained as they attempted to work together for the medical school. By the time that the school opened, Bessie had gone the way of Julia and had withdrawn from the joint enterprises. As Carey wrote afterward to Hannah, the medical school struggle cost her Bessie's friendship: "She got angry with Mary Garrett where Mary was clearly right, and I was forced to decide against her. She has not spoken to me since then." Carey had steeled herself many times for a final break with Bessie. When it came, she was numb and never looked back. It is worth noting that Carey allowed the breach to happen only after the death of Francis King.[25]

IV

As CAREY THOMAS labored for a decade for the Bryn Mawr School and the Johns Hopkins medical school, she remained clear that these were extracurricular activities added on to her central commitment: Bryn Mawr College. She understood that creating Bryn Mawr was just the beginning. She had to protect her college and to devise a strategy for growth. Overseeing Bryn Mawr was not like bringing it into being. Members of the faculty turned out to be real men and women, with human needs, feelings, and demands. Students were girls turning into women, challenging, unpredictable, and sometimes disappointing. They were pupils to be polished into scholars, and wards to be cared for in sickness and mischievousness. They were also sisters and future sisters-in-law and, later, nieces. Trustees were members of the family and Orthodox Friends, with ideas of their own, strong wills, and mortal bodies. Donors were intimate companions and neighbors as well as wealthy strangers. Schemes for Bryn Mawr College got entangled in other efforts that were bound up in complex webs of friendship and the private corners of the self reserved for art.

Carey Thomas' days were long and full. She often worked for fourteen hours, seven days a week, with only an occasional half-hour walk. As professor of English, she lectured, saw students, and graded examinations and papers. She prepared for classes late into the night. As dean, she answered correspondence, conferred with faculty, trustees, and President James Rhoads, and saw endless streams of students. The Deanery became the unofficial residence for guests of the college, and Thomas frequently entertained college visitors. She held an "at home" afternoon for students each week and regularly had professors to dinner. She represented the college at Philadelphia gatherings and was invited out often. Emergencies called for her to attend to ill students (and their parents). It was a busy, even frenzied life, and Thomas drove herself beyond her strength. But one side of her would have had it no other way. As she contemplated her thirtieth birthday, she wished for a moment to be ten years younger so that she might still have before her the first view of Rome. Were she about to be twenty, she wrote, "I think I should put my head in the yoke of Bryn Mawr all over again."[26]

To get through such a life, Carey Thomas often tried to lay private considerations aside during her working days at Bryn Mawr, at least until late in the evening when she sat down to write to Mary Garrett. But time and again, the personal intruded. Mamie's presence in the Deanery remains a blank, for the nature of correspondence with Mary did not allow Carey to write about Mamie.

One fascinating letter to Mary about other subjects revealed a tangled web of feeling and college obligation. In her adulthood Carey said harsh things about the Howland School, which had served her well in her youth. She was embarrassed by visiting classmates who struck her as crude and unmannerly, a reminder of her own middle-class household. A constant thorn was Carrie Ladd, who served as Bryn Mawr College's first instructor of physical education. In the third year of the college, Elizabeth Lore, a Howland classmate, became Rhoads' choice as the head of Merion Hall. Carey welcomed her with dinner. To her titillation, Bessie Lore had a story to tell.

Now thirty years old and engaged to be married, Bessie talked about an event that had traumatized her Howland years. In relating it to Mary, Carey set Bessie's story in the context of the smashes that were common at Howland and of her own feeling for Libbie Conkey. In the heated environment of Howland, "Bessie became subject to swoons for the first time in her life, was out of school for three months, came back, only to have Mariana [Bessie Lore's smash] undergo a long illness which forced *her* to leave school. Then Anna Shipley who roomed with me that term was affected in the same way and lay awake night after night in tears, then she, too, from sheer misery . . . became ill, left Howland, and did not get over it for two or three years." At the time it seemed coincidence, but from Bessie she learned that these breakdowns came from intense emotions. Bessie's illness "was simply caused by the fact that she was not strong enough to bear being with Mariana." Her mother removed her from school but she came back to Howland because she was miserable at home. Bessie told Carey that she knew in a room of seventy girls "the moment Mariana's hand touched the door outside." For many years Bessie was like "a burnt child and did not dare to be friends with a man or a woman lest this unhappiness *should* happen again."

After retelling Bessie's story, Carey Thomas went on to relate to Mary the parallel one of a Bryn Mawr junior, "one of the cleverest students in college." Thomas had taught her five hours a week for her first two years and now had her in her advanced Anglo-Saxon class, where her work was admirable. Despite the fact that the student had some unappealing traits, Thomas was clearly drawn to her, for "when she translates, even my uncouth Anglo-Saxon prose, it is as if her lips had been touched with Apollo's lyre." Thomas was delighted when the student selected English as her major. "And now what do you suppose has happened? As ill luck will have it, her, out of all the college, and alone in the college, this stroke of lightning has struck. She is miserable about a perfectly ordinary girl whose whole mind is not worth at least one corner of her own, and my Anglo-Saxon poet is spoiled, I fear, for this year." Thomas wondered what she would do "if any other such cases should occur, but I am glad to be able to say that I see no signs of it."[27]

Told by Carey to one of her own life's loves, these linked stories provide glimpses into both boarding school life in the early 1870s and women's college culture in the late 1880s. They also provide a rare instance in which an adult Carey Thomas wrote of smashes or crushes. Carey relished telling Bessie Lore's story, for at some level she was relating to Mary as she had earlier to Anna Shipley, using a tale to provoke feeling in her correspondent. She was intrigued, and she presented Bessie's story unadorned. About her student, she had more complex feelings. Almost two years before she had written to Mary, "It sometimes fills me with regret to look at our girls here, so eager and interested in things as remote as, for instance, *The Elder Edda*, and to feel that a time will come for each of them when some little personal incident, love, or jealousy, or friendship, will outweigh all these things, that it may now for all I know." Now, to Carey Thomas' distress, this had happened to her Anglo-Saxon scholar. Although she noted that the object of her student's love was commonplace, that she was female was so unexceptionable that it received no particular comment. [28]

Carey Thomas' reaction makes clear the sense of intense personal connection that she felt toward her early Bryn Mawr students. She believed that she was giving each of them a better chance than she had had. She had gotten them a university faculty, trained largely at Johns Hopkins or abroad, kept alert by graduate students. She had insisted that students not be burdened by domestic chores and that their lives be regulated only by their own good judgment. She campaigned for suites, to give each student a study with a fireplace as well as a separate bedroom. She struggled to get them everything that could encourage their independence and scholarship. When the members of the class of 1889 brought back Oxford undergraduate gowns and asked to wear them throughout the week, she agreed. Though she tried to be very careful not to develop personal relationships with students, she identified with them and their dilemmas. Reading with Mamie the Lesbian poems of the Roman poet Catullus led her to think about the college society of young women removed from men: "In watching these girls, as, of course, I cannot help doing, I think that the chastity of women (at least during their student life) will give them an advantage over men and make it more possible for them to attain results that come from a union of work and enthusiasm and that come less often when only work is given. I should like to make a Balzac study of women; they have as yet been analyzed only from their emotional side." The early classes of Bryn Mawr students returned her interest in them. On her first Valentine's Day at Bryn Mawr, she received from her English class a large box of roses and many violets. Harry's future wife Zoe, then a Bryn Mawr student, told her of the class' "idolatry" of her. [29]

Toward her gifted students, she felt a special bond. Immediately after writing about the Anglo-Saxon scholar, Thomas described another student, Emily Greene Balch, whom she found "all round the most civilized girl in college. . . . She is brilliant and earnest and steady and thoughtful, and a lady, and as wily and wise a sophomore as I ever expect to see again." At moments Thomas wished that she were Balch, "beginning over again. I might avoid so many mistakes." Thomas would not, however, seal "the bond of exchange" unless promised four years of foreign study.[30]

This she had helped to provide. In April 1889 Emily Balch won the first fellowship for graduate study abroad. The award meant a great deal to Carey Thomas, for the fellowship was her creation, a statement of the serious intent of a Bryn Mawr education. It became a means to encourage talented students to pursue advanced work, and to ease their way. Thomas wrote to Mary Garrett, "Our European fellowship is given after such *excitement* and discussion last night (and given to my candidate Miss Balch). I could not sleep from excitement and delight. Here she is, and I must congratulate her."[31]

A scheme had become a fellowship, and Emily Balch had won it. What had been an abstraction, had become a person. The story of Emily Balch suggests that, once Bryn Mawr was a reality, behind Carey Thomas' sense of mission was intense identification with Bryn Mawr students. Propelling Thomas was the memory of her own frustrating struggle in her Baltimore years and her release into true scholarship in Europe. With Bryn Mawr she could make a path for those such as she had been—young women of breeding who sought advanced education—but a path that was smooth and even. For Emily Balch the fellowship took her to the Sorbonne in Paris, the first step in a distinguished career as an economist, social reformer, worker for peace, and Nobel laureate.

The realization of Carey Thomas' dream for Bryn Mawr required the rest of her professional life. The college, opening with seven professors, was far too small to be the center of the newest scholarship that Thomas envisioned. She convinced President Rhoads and the trustees that by adding more residence halls, the college could accommodate more students; more students meant more tuition and thus more money to hire the brilliant professors who were the glory of Bryn Mawr. Thomas took Bryn Mawr's growth as her goal.

Her early years as dean were filled with success. In 1887, Radnor, the second residential hall, was built. Joseph Taylor had intended four residential buildings, and Addison Hutton, the original architect, had sketched out a symmetrical grouping around the academic building, Taylor Hall. Landscape architect Calvert Vaux had created a plan for the campus that confirmed the siting of buildings. To design Radnor the trustees hired the young Quaker architect Walter Cope, a nephew of board member Francis Cope and the brother of a member of Bryn Mawr's first class, and his partner John Stewardson. In 1891 Cope and Stewardson planned Denbigh, the third hall. In England Thomas had envied the life of Oxford men and saw Oxford and Cambridge as the ideal settings in which to educate the upper class. Unlike the other two residence halls, Denbigh was placed at the campus's edge. It was a long, low structure in a hybrid style that the college called Jacobean Gothic. With Denbigh, Bryn Mawr began to echo Oxford quadrangles in elegant buildings and courtyards.[32]

In 1893, the college built Dalton Hall, the new science building, to supplement the rooms in Taylor devoted to classes and libraries. Rhoads and Thomas had found it very difficult to convince the trustees of the necessity of Dalton Hall, and when they did, the trustees informed them that they had to raise most of the money for it from outside donors. Only gradually did the trustees come to the realization that Bryn Mawr must seek to attract the wealthy. Only reluctantly did Carey Thomas accede to their wish that she court Philadelphia's intellectual and monied society.

Begging for Dalton Hall signaled a decisive change in Carey Thomas' working life. Previously her fundraising had been not fully conscious, but part of the complex relationships she bore to Mary Garrett and to George W. Childs. As she began to raise money for Dalton Hall, she had to develop a systematic approach. She faced it with dread. In April 1891, she wrote to Mary of a severe headache brought on by "the naked prospect of the absolute necessity of beginning upon our laboratory subscription. I have waited all winter for Dr. Rhoads to do something, hoping there might be a small hole to creep through, but as he will not or cannot, I have forced myself to think of it." She set out her plan to involve trustees and students and to call upon the wealthy. "I do not suppose it is any worse to ask for five thousand dollars than for one thousand and all they can do is to refuse; so think of me as perfectly miserable." Despite her agonies, Thomas was successful, and Dalton Hall launched her career as a fundraiser.[33]

Having drawn the brightest and the best trained scholars, Carey Thomas found she had a challenging and demanding faculty with which to contend. She wrote to Mary Garrett in the spring of 1886, "Your ambitious [Edmund] Wilson refuses to give his second year's course without fifteen hundred dollars of apparatus, which makes me very cross. Shorey is a little provoking, too. In fact your true professor, sensitive and devoted to books and opinions, is a most inflammable article; and I think we have enough scholars in the faculty to make the management of the college an affair of diplomacy."[34]

Bryn Mawr suffered the indignity of raids upon its faculty. Of the initial professorial staff, only Charlotte Angas Scott finished as well as began her career at the college. Talented men were picked off by the new research universities. With each loss, Thomas felt a mixture of betrayal and relief. Woodrow Wilson's departure came while Thomas was numb with grief over her mother's death. Thomas anticipated a welcome change when Paul Shorey left for the University of Chicago. Each resignation, however, meant a frenzy of work, often at the last minute, to find a replacement. Thomas was generally successful, and as each young male professor left, he was followed by another of equal distinction. Sociologist Franklin Henry Giddings and, later, historian Charles McLean Andrews took Woodrow Wilson's place; geneticist Thomas Hunt Morgan, that of Edmund Wilson; organic chemist Elmer Peter Kohler, that of Edward Keiser.

Carey Thomas' many successes as dean were never hers alone. They were the combined achievements of Dean Thomas and President Rhoads, a testament to their effective partnership. Rhoads complemented Thomas very well. Thomas was slow to trust a man. She came to trust James Rhoads implicitly. Seldom deferential, she was willing to defer to his judgment. Throughout the decade of their collaboration she came to rely on his sound sense and his painstaking attention to detail. He gave her personal praise often and handsomely. Although he never withheld criticism when called for, he couched it in gentle respect. Seemingly without ego, he embraced her ideas quietly, content to be in the background unless implementation required his advocacy; then he was a strong defender.

With him, as with no one else, Thomas could differ without that difference becoming personal. Their views occasionally put them at odds. As a friend of Taylor and a trustee, Rhoads felt the weight of the founder's intent and the charter. That Bryn Mawr was a Quaker college seemed to him obvious. Compared to Thomas, he worried more about finances and less about standards. There were distinctions in administrative style. Thomas tended to be abstract and rhetorical, while Rhoads attempted to judge the particularities of a situation, paying close attention to emotional factors. Thomas' strength was exposition and analysis. Rhoads was a good listener. Thomas was willing to stake all and lose gloriously, but Rhoads knew the value of compromise and incremental gains. It was an effective collaboration: Thomas convinced Rhoads on policy, and Rhoads taught Thomas the necessary means.

Thomas won over Rhoads, and Rhoads sought to convince the trustees. How did the trustees respond? The religious leader of English Friends J. B. Braithwaite, writing to Thomas upon leaving Baltimore, may have expressed more than his own judgment when he stated that he was "very thankful that it has pleased our Heavenly Father to place" her mental gifts "at the disposal of the college."[35] The Quaker community may have regarded itself as blessed in having a brilliant daughter with a Ph.D. summa cum laude from the University of Zürich. Yet, from the outset, there was uneasiness among trustees that found expression in the effort to reinforce the college's Quaker identity and to restrain budget excesses.

Taylor had chosen as members of the board trusted male Orthodox Friends. Many of them felt deeply the responsibility he had placed on them to carry out his wishes for a Quaker college for women. As Thomas shaped Bryn Mawr into a cosmopolitan secular institution, they did not fight her on major questions. They gave her free rein to choose Bryn Mawr's faculty for its qualifications, not adherence to the sect. Initially the trustees attempted to have a secret religious test for graduate fellows, but Rhoads insisted that all requirements be either in the catalogue or not imposed, and the matter was dropped. The first group of students to come to Bryn Mawr were attracted through Friends' publications and networks, but within a few years, the proportion of Quakers began to drop. What then did Bryn Mawr's founding and charter mean? In the attempt to come to terms with this question, the trustees waged a number of symbolic campaigns.[36]

James Whitall, long an important presence in Carey Thomas' life, gave a sense of how significant these symbols seemed when he wrote to Thomas in November 1886, that "the four-footed beast"—the symbol of the End of Days—had entered the grounds of Bryn Mawr. He was writing about a practice piano moved into a college-owned house. The piano was anathema to many Orthodox Friends, though not to James and Mary Thomas, who had one in their house. Whitall sketched several alternatives and advised Thomas that the best course was to "*clear it all out*, and make up our minds to dispense with the presence and patronage of the girls to whom it is a necessity." Whitall was a businessman who constantly watched the ledger, but it was better to lose students and income than to tolerate a piano on the Bryn Mawr campus. In the early years the trustees tried to affirm the college's religious purpose. In 1890 trustee Francis Cope criticized the President's Report, and his view was shared by others. The trustees sought an explicit statement in the report of the effort at the college "to uphold the standard of *broad catholic orthodox Christianity* as held by the Orthodox Quakers."[37]

Extravagance was equally troubling. To attract its first stellar faculty, the college offered relatively high salaries and allowed professors to select books for the library. The trustees were deeply conservative in their approach to investment, requiring that Bryn Mawr use only interest on its principal for its academic budget. Four months before the opening of the college, Rhoads understood that the endowment was inadequate for the commitments he and Thomas had made.[38] Thomas' solution to balancing the budget was to bet on growth. If the college could attract and house more students, their tuition payments would support more professors' salaries and more books.

James Whitall disagreed. By February 1886, it was clear to him that if the college was to grow, it required more endowment as well as more students. As he wrote his niece, if the college continued to expand without new contributions, it would "come to financial disaster and ruin." The trustees would have to close it for a time to let the principal recover and then reopen as a smaller institution. Were this to happen "those of us who have favored the present plan of organization and method, against immense opposition, will, of course, be thoroughly humiliated." He urged that, in the face of uncertainty about future endowment, the college scale back.[39]

Carey Thomas did not heed her uncle and, with Rhoads' approval, pushed ahead. The trustees generally found it hard to resist their double campaign. In April 1890, however, when she sought higher faculty salaries, they bucked. In a confidential letter Thomas' father explained to his daughter that she and Rhoads needed to present to the trustees a proper budget. The trustees believed that they were being asked to exceed "the income available, and that the extension of the college was impossible." James Thomas carefully instructed his daughter as to how to construct a budget and in doing so conveyed the tenor of the trustees' deliberations. A budget would mean that "the natural increase of salaries could be made without haggling over each and saying that we were coming to a stone wall, as James Whitall did, or that we must give up some departments, as Edward Bettle did."[40]

Given the conservative direction of the college's board, Thomas' hopes for Bryn Mawr were threatened by high-spirited students. In her early years as dean, Thomas had deep rapport with the undergraduates. She was twenty-eight when the first students entered, and her intense and lively manner minimized the social distance between them. As she taught each of them English literature, she commanded their respect and admiration. This was important because Bryn Mawr did not follow the pattern of many of the women's colleges, which had set up long lists of rules to be obeyed by students. Smith had pioneered with one rule, the ten o'clock rule of lights out, and the expectation that students conduct themselves as ladies. Bryn Mawr found this approach consistent with Quaker philosophy, and Carey Thomas believed that each student should be self-governed. From the outset Rhoads had insisted that it was inappropriate for him, as a man, to have anything to do with student behavior and relinquished all authority to Thomas. She held frequent conferences with students and with them determined the informal regulations that governed their college lives.

However, within a very few years, students' conduct set them on a potential collision course with the trustees. During the illness and death of her mother, Thomas was repeatedly absent from the college and unable to monitor students closely. In the years that followed, undergraduates began to get out of hand. Their misdeeds were minor, such as staying up late in friends' rooms and entering residence halls through windows in the middle of the night. In May 1891 Thomas called all the students together—130 by that time—to appeal to their better natures. She worried that as their numbers increased, she might lose the personal hold that she had on them and "all would be over with our student freedom and self-government." Susan Walker, one of the students, came to Thomas to ask if they might take full responsibility for enforcing such rules as might be necessary. Over the summer, Walker wrote a circular letter to fellow students to propose the idea. In the fall of 1891 discussion began.[41]

In midyear 1891, Thomas talked to the students' association to get them "to bind themselves to take charge of all matters of conduct and behavior." She found them very responsive, "more charming to me than could be imagined." Thomas realized that it was important to work things out when the college was small: "while they love and trust me, I want to outline the paths for the future, because later they may be too many for me to know so well personally."[42]

The result of this conversation and the many private ones that had preceded and were to follow it was the charter, accepted by the trustees in January 1892, of the Bryn Mawr Students' Association for Self Government. Headed by a president and executive board, the Self-Government Association established the rules of community life (What is noise? "Noise is what disturbs other people"), enforced penalties for minor infractions, and made recommendations in serious cases to the dean and college president. It was the first such body in an American college. Late in her life M. Carey Thomas recalled it as one of her most important achievements.

Faculty governance was more difficult to achieve. The strong independent scholars attracted to Bryn Mawr quickly found that the monarchical system of American colleges required the tempering of constitutional rights. In the fall of 1888 they applied to the trustees for formal recognition of their power. The trustees were in no mood to grant it. From their perspective, they made decisions that the president and dean, their employees, were to execute. The two college heads governed the faculty. As James Whitall wrote to Thomas, "We have got on well for three-and-a-half years without any such rules, the Faculty receiving their powers from the *authorities above them, resident at the college*; and this is the right source for them to derive their powers from." Whitall continued, "The trustees will never, by written law, set up the authority of the professors over that of the president."[43] Whitall normally advised his niece to listen to others and compromise, but as he dealt with her relation to the faculty he urged her to stand firm. It was counsel that served her ill in the years ahead. At Bryn Mawr, it took a painful, bitter, public fight for the faculty to win rights that in other institutions were granted quietly, peacefully, and piecemeal.

V

IN 1892, the University of Pennsylvania opened its graduate department to women and asked Carey Thomas to make an address as part of the public ceremony commemorating the occasion. In the audience were professors of the university, important Philadelphia women, professors and students of Bryn

Mawr, and Dr. S. Weir Mitchell, the noted expert on women's nerve disorders. Realizing the importance of the occasion, Thomas researched the subject and struggled to find appropriate words. Her talk, given only five years after her statement to Hannah Whitall Smith that she did not believe in speaking in public, presaged her emergence as an important voice in the higher education of women.

Taking the long sweep, Thomas surveyed the universities of Europe and their policies toward women. In her recounting, the story rang with the heroism of battles won. The high rank of the women in the tripos, a common public examination of all English university students, served as the clearest "proof of the power of women to endure prolonged intellectual strain." The 1890 success of Miss Fawcett of Newnham "who outranked, it is said, by four hundred marks the senior wrangler in the mathematical tripos" rang "through the land."[44]

Turning to the United States, Thomas treated the range of coeducational and single-sex institutions. She argued that in undergraduate education "women themselves have expressed a marked preference for separate colleges." In the West women had no option, but in the East, given a choice between Cornell and Wellesley, they overwhelmingly selected Wellesley. Were all equal, Thomas argued that this would be wise; but unfortunately most colleges for women were not up to the standard of those for men. Here she took her shots at the competition: Smith and Wellesley had teachers who had not taken a college degree; as an annex, Radcliffe drained professors' energies needed for scholarship; and every institution but Bryn Mawr suffered by not having a graduate school. Casting her argument in the widest terms, Thomas used her speech to promote her chief end, the greater glory of Bryn Mawr. It was a strategy to which she returned in her 1900 book *Education of Women.*[45]

Despite her pride in Bryn Mawr's graduate school, the central argument of the address was that graduate education should be coeducational. The University of Pennsylvania, by opening its school to women, was in line with the best thinking of the age. Graduate education was for the few and the mature. Because each scholar offered unique instruction, students should be free to pick the specialist under whom to work, they should be able to travel "like wandering scholars of the middle ages . . . from one great teacher to another." Drawing on Herbert Spencer's scheme of the progressive stages of human evolution, Thomas argued that the trustees of the University of Pennsylvania, by opening the graduate school to women, have acted "in entire accordance with the main course of thought and feeling in the modern world."[46] As her career as a public speaker commenced, Carey Thomas announced at the outset its key themes.

CHAPTER 13

Mammon for Righteousness

O N DECEMBER 3, 1892, M. Carey Thomas reached a crossroads.
President James Rhoads told her he planned to resign. She had been in
harness since she had assumed the deanship in early 1884. With Rhoads'
decision she had to think again about the direction of her life. Did she want
to be president of Bryn Mawr? Could she return to a life of art or scholarship?
She wrote to Mary Garrett, "You have never yet heard my full arguments,"
against becoming president, "nor how sure I am that without it I could win a
reputation that I should care very much for and have a life that would be very
happy and very good."[1]

But 1892 was not 1884. Any decision that she now made not only involved
her own career, it affected the work and life of Mamie Gwinn. Gwinn had received her Ph.D. in 1888 after writing a literary study of *Beowulf.* She had requested and been given a faculty appointment, contingent on Thomas'
remaining at the college. She started as the critic of student essays, but gradually began to teach English literature. Not a professional woman by inclination,
Gwinn was easily exhausted by the pressure of work. Carey admired her literary
gifts and hoped as president she might give Mamie the help she needed to publish the study of *Beowulf.* "As soon as I become president I shall arrange for her
to have only the kind of work where her peculiar genius will tell best and leisure
to write things that will bring reputation to the college and herself." To protect
Gwinn by her power required Thomas to give up her own scholarly career.[2]

Many elements beyond Mamie Gwinn were now shaping Carey Thomas'
decision. Thomas was at a point of sharp conflict with the board over the
building of Pembroke, a double residence hall, critical to her strategy of
growth. When she presented its plan and site, the trustees balked; and well
they might, for Pembroke's scale, architecture, and level of decoration were
something no women's college had ever seen. The two Pembrokes, East and
West, formed a long building line that walled off the campus on the south,
defining the campus from the outside and partially enclosing it from the inside.
At the joining of the two residences, a monumental arched gateway, with four

battlemented towers, framed the carriage entrance to the campus. Even the name was significant. Unlike the Welsh place names that adorned many other Bryn Mawr buildings, Pembroke was named for the House of Pembroke important in Shakespeare's life and work. Thomas wanted to have the Pembroke coat of arms carved on the gateway. In name, plan, and actuality, Pembroke was a courtly building. At various points the trustees, concerned about Quaker tradition and economy, tried to block its construction, and Thomas threatened to resign. The trustees resolved that after Pembroke no more Bryn Mawr buildings were to come from Taylor's endowment.[3]

Beyond the specific controversy raging at Bryn Mawr were critical issues of personal autonomy and self-support. As dean, Carey Thomas commanded a salary of $3,000 ($500 more than a professor's and the equivalent of approximately $50,000 today) and had the use of a large house. Few women of her time were able to live by their wits on such a scale. James Carey Thomas kindly and repeatedly offered to take his daughter back into his household, but Carey enjoyed her salary and the Deanery.

However, even with her salary and regular money from a trust managed by James Whitall, Carey Thomas could not make ends meet. Although the financial record cannot be fully clarified, letters to Garrett tell of significant debts. In February 1892 she owed $200 to Mamie, apart from a larger debt of $1,900 backed by life insurance. She owed $1,000 to another source. The total exceeded $50,000 in 1994 dollars. In February she asked Mary for a loan of $200; in August, for another $1,000. In her late mother's household she had learned that capital could be spent and that debt was a temporary condition relieved by the gifts of others. As Mary Thomas' daughter, debts did not trouble Carey Thomas, and in April she ordered $200 worth of dresses, purchased a soup ladle, and had her lawn sodded. Given her propensity to spend, a presidential salary was an important base for the way of life to which she wished to become accustomed.[4]

Finally, Mary Garrett wanted her friend to be president of Bryn Mawr College. Plagued by ill health and despondency, she admired Carey's strength and purposefulness. To every complaint Carey made about her life, Mary answered that, despite her cares, Carey was fortunate. Traveling in Italy in 1891, Mary wrote that "even with such possibilities before me, how I envy you the doing of the work!" As Carey seesawed about her future, Mary remained clear and firm. Bryn Mawr was important for American women, and Carey had a responsibility to keep it on track. Travel and scholarship were far less urgent than her work at Bryn Mawr.[5]

Mary Garrett was the pivotal force. This was the moment of Garrett's greatest public activity. Thomas urged Garrett to spend not only her income but her principal for their causes. As Thomas succinctly put it, "I happen to have health and . . . very great ability of a certain kind," but Garrett's money was "the very rarest thing in the world for anyone with your and my views."[6] In December 1892 Garrett made the final gift of over $300,000 to the Johns Hopkins medical school and set the new stipulations that required intense negotiation. She and Thomas worked feverishly during January and February 1893 to insure that the school be a graduate school of medicine. In this period both women felt the flush of battle and victory.

In the midst of their work, Mary and Carey found each other. Years later Carey recalled to Mary the decisive moment when "you told me in a passion of tears at the time of the medical school that Julia was not, had not been, and would not always be, your first interest." It was January 2, 1893, Carey's thirty-sixth birthday: it was perhaps the most important day of her life.[7]

Much must be teased out of indirect references in a letter designed to be received on Mary's birthday, March 5, 1893. Carey recalled that on January 2 the two of them had been in Mary's bedroom "on the lounge and on the window seat." Much of the visit had not been very happy, but there had been "the mistletoe part." In response to Mary's wish to celebrate her birthday "not in a tiring way," Carey sent her a thousand kisses, but wondered if "this is the tiresome way you referred to." The same letter accompanied birthday gifts to Mary, and Carey wrote of her "wholly impossible wish" for Mary "never to use anything" that Carey did not give her. She mentioned her frustration at their last visit together when Mary had not been affectionate: "Perhaps it is only Romeo's perpetual 'and wilt thou leave me so unsatisfied?' " And to Mary's worry that Dr. Elizabeth Cushier, the woman physician who was treating her, had overheard them during a Deanery visit, Carey answered, "I said nothing except I called you once 'my darling.' "[8]

A letter such as this is filled with tantalizing half-statements, but the meaning is clear. With love came a feeling of protectiveness: Carey wanted to clothe and provide for Mary. When unsatisfied, Carey identified with Shakespeare's Romeo. Mary was uneasy lest their private relation be perceived by another. On January 2, 1893, after fourteen years of seeking, Carey at last received confirmation of Mary's love. In an emotional moment Mary had declared herself free of Julia. The reference to mistletoe, the thousand birthday kisses, and Carey's uncertainty about what Mary meant when she used the word "tiresome," are codes that tell us that the two women kissed passionately.

Carey had long sought such a kiss but Mary had always denied her. In March 1891, as she wrote Mary birthday wishes, she had asked, "Shall I venture to send you thirty-seven birthday kisses? I fear you would say 'do not do that' many times if they were not gray paper in substance, but made of the fire and ethereal elements of real ones. Still as there is no danger of transubstantiation, consider them sent." A letter of Carey's of December 1892 suggests that Mary had warned her not to be physically demonstrative. Carey wrote that Mary need not fear a loss of self-control in her presence. In all the years, Carey had only lost it once before, in the emotional last visit with Mary before she left for Germany. Mary should not have mistrusted her or spoken about it. "I think in all my life I have never repeated anything I thought you would not like." Clearly Mary was attempting to ward off the embrace that she knew was coming.[9]

To Carey a passionate kiss meant that her love was requited. In October 1891, Carey had sent to Mary a love sonnet, presumably of her own composition. In the poem a viewer of a painting is drawn to its beauty. By analogy, the voice of the poem is drawn to a beloved. A few months earlier, Carey had told Mary that "when you come I will explain what I meant the other night in your bedroom by being swayed too much from my orbit by my love of you. When you are better you, too, must sway a little." In the sonnet that Carey sent are these lines:

> . . . *she sways*
> *My life towards hers, and her remembered gaze*
> *Draws after it my heart to love's far springs.*
>
> * * *
>
> *My lips meet hers within the cup enchanted.*
> *And, lo, at last, mid visioned mysteries*
> *In imminent hour supreme, love's dues are granted.*

At long last, "love's dues" were "granted."[10]

After January 2, Carey's letters contain new words of intimacy. That these outpourings are intertwined with discussions both of the medical school and of the Bryn Mawr presidency is telling. Carey Thomas was living at a fevered pitch, and her passions fed each other. On February 5, 1893, for example, two days after the Johns Hopkins board voted to accept the terms set by Garrett, Carey Thomas made a decision that she would accept the Bryn Mawr presidency if she were made a trustee and given a salary of five thousand dollars. Then she wrote, "I thought about you in Meeting and wanted to ask you a hundred questions of the kind I am never tired of hearing you answer. They have remained unanswered so long that I am like a child with a new and charming toy. I cannot believe my doll will speak with such silver accents when I pull the string. I wonder if you know what I mean." She then quoted lines of longing from two Dante Gabriel Rossetti poems, "The seeking to fill with colour and body those 'hours which might have been yet might not be,' the 'though in years of sight and sound unmet' time . . . which have, I fear, had but one application for me since I first read them how many many years ago." In recalling a conversation she had had with Mary a week before, Carey commented, "Was it only last week we were lying in the bed in my room looking or not looking then at the Apoxyomenos, which it was very sweet in you to put there in memoriam of our goodbye in Rome."[11]

Carey had tried since 1879 to win Mary Garrett's love. Mary's parents and Julia Rogers had been in the way. Death had taken Rachel and John Garrett in 1883 and 1884. Julia Rogers had withdrawn from her intimate friendship with Mary in the period between 1888 and 1891. Beginning January 2, 1893, Mary was hers alone. As Carey put it, she had crossed the mountains to reach her "passionate land."[12]

A marked shift in Mary's behavior accompanied the change. Before 1893 Carey visited with Mary on Sunday afternoons in infrequent trips to Baltimore. Beginning in early 1893, Mary started to travel regularly to Philadelphia. Initially she did not go to Bryn Mawr, but took rooms at the Lafayette Hotel, and Carey went in to stay with her. It had long been Mamie Gwinn's pattern to return to Baltimore for vacations and many weekends to visit her mother. Hesitantly and gradually Mary and Carey began to plan times together during the periods Mamie was away. Carey repeatedly told stories to Mary and to herself in which events and places were a shorthand for stages in their relationship. Since her years abroad, Pontresina (where Mary had fallen on the ice) and Rome (where Carey had fought with Julia) had stood for pain and the breach in their intimacy. Beginning in 1893 Carey linked the fulfillment of her and Mary's love for each other to the medical school and the Lafayette Hotel.

What about Mamie? In 1893 Carey remained committed to her. As Mary and Carey planned times with each other, Carey took great care not to offend Mamie and to clear with her any visit by Mary. Even as she constantly reassured Mary of her love, she reminded her of Mamie's place in her life. In a second birthday letter to Mary, written March 5, 1893, Carey determined "that this next year must be a happy one for us and for Mamie and me." In a most extraordinary letter, March 12, 1893, filled with detailed news of Bryn Mawr and the hurdles in the way of the presidency, Carey wrote of her pleasure in Mary's changed nature. She recalled the Sundays they had spent before their work together on the medical school: "You were so unutterably, so inexplicably different from yourself as I know you now. Oh, how surprised I have been to find you so, so—satisfactory, so unlike your shadow self of all these years." Carey wondered how the shift had come about, whether it were real, and "whether it is possible that the overwhelming thing that has happened may not really and truly have transformed you a little." Carey reassured Mary that even in the earlier period, she had loved even her "silence." Now Carey felt fully blessed: it was spring, she was relatively young, she admired the right things, "and to have such a charming thing have happened as our caring for each other, when my love for Mamie and hers for me is really as much as one lifetime deserves."[13]

Carey and Mamie had lived together as intimate friends since 1879. In Europe, Carey had referred to their relationship as a marriage. Since moving to Bryn Mawr in September 1885, they had shared the Deanery. Mamie paid for her portion of the expenses of the household. Although Carey regarded Mamie's $1,900 and $200 as loans to be repaid, in certain ways their resources were blended. As Carey tried in mid-April to explain to Mary how precarious her financial situation would be if she did not have a Bryn Mawr salary, her complicated statement reveals much about her relationships with Mamie and Mary. She wrote that she could use Mamie's bonds. Though she could borrow from Mary, she was stopped by her love of Mamie and by the fact of their shared household. "From the first Mamie's and my things have been each other's." She and Mary might have been in a similar situation were it not for Mamie. During this period Carey insisted on paying for her own accommodations when the two were together, or at least the amount that it would cost in a reasonably priced hotel. "I feel as if it were a rather foolish distinction without a difference to insist on paying my share of, or rather a share of, expenses when we are together. But it is on account of that other thing being so."[14] The "other thing," of course, was her established twosome with Mamie.

Carey often repeated to Mary that their love had to coexist with Carey's fundamental relationship with Mamie. After all, she lived with Mamie and their work was mutually intertwined. Carey wrote in early April, after a particularly satisfying time with Mary in New York, that she was enclosing a letter from Mamie because "I want you to realize, as I think you do in part, how wonderful it is, after so long, to have anyone so devoted and worthy of devotion as Mamie, and how it seems often like committing all the sins of the decalogue to do the least, not to speak of the greatest, thing she would disapprove of."[15]

The letters that passed between Carey and Mamie when they were apart in these years continued their loving tone. On her birthday in 1891, Carey had written, "A thousand happy returns of the day and twenty-nine kisses on your mouth. . . . How nice it is to love each other through so many years of birthdays since '78, thirteen years, is it not? And I hope it may be many times thirteen more until we are passing a green old age together in Italy." In the letters that follow January 2, 1893, there is no change of tone, no lessening of Carey's affectionate banter or expressions of longing.[16]

What did Mamie know? Although Mary had to know about Mamie and accept Carey's ties to her, Mamie did not have to have parallel knowledge of Mary. Everything about Carey's past behavior suggests that she tried to hide from Mamie the transformation in Mary's feelings and commitments, as she had always hid from Mamie her love of Mary. Mary entered the Deanery under the cover of mutual friendship with both women.

Mamie had long been jealous of Mary and angry at her incivility. Upon their return from Europe she had insisted that she be Carey's recognized special friend. Mamie continued to require her primacy. As she wrote Carey in July 1891, "You are engaged to me for all the future old years of your life, you know." As the fight for the medical school brought the three together, ties between Mary and Mamie were somewhat reknit, but Mary's danger grew more threatening. Carey and Mamie fought in November 1892. Carey had raised questions about the depth of Mamie's love. Mamie answered that Carey's questions were merely a defensive strategy: "That I have loved you dearly we both know. That you know past the slightest doubt that I have not transferred my love to anyone else. You know likewise: that if it does not go out to you it is there, making me miserably uncomfortable for lack of an outlet. You are well aware: that if it anyway ceases to go out to you, it ceases because of conduct of yours the pursuit of which you cold-bloodedly prefer to my love for you." Given Carey's behavior with Mary, whom Mamie called "the enemy," Carey should keep speculations about Mamie's love to herself. "I have ceased, cease, or shall cease (as you like) to love you dearly, only in so far as it is past my power to believe in you and your love for me." The quarrel was spent. On Christmas Eve, Mamie wrote, "I should like to have time to give a long kiss to both sets of long lashes."[17]

Hiding her new understanding with Mary was a tricky business for Carey, for Mamie was clever and knew how to read the signs. In mid-January, Mary gave Carey the gift of a chain, and Mamie objected. Carey attempted to make peace. She wrote Mamie, "By the way, I told her about the chain, that she must give me nothing more at all." Carey closed with these words: "I love you, sweetheart, more than ever and will do all you say."[18]

Carey worked hard to restore relations between Mamie and Mary. Mary sent Mamie flowers and performed other courtesies. Carey encouraged Mamie to accept Mary more graciously. In February, Mamie even cared for Mary in the Deanery when Carey was away, kissing her each night and morning, the two so well mannered, Mamie wrote, that "there is not a ghost of a risk of explanations." Carey had Mamie invite Mary to visit. Though Mamie did so, she explained to Mary that it was unnecessary, as "in all households the various members invite their friends on their own account, and the others have their welcome taken for granted." Mamie wrote, probably at Carey's behest, to reassure Mary that she never opened her letters. In this period Carey tried on occasion to be with both women at the same time.[19]

This pattern has appeared before. Carey Thomas had always delighted in triads. She now had one that fully satisfied her, one in which she was at the center. To her "marriage" with Mamie Gwinn she added a special friendship with Mary Garrett that worked in many ways as an "affair."

How could Carey sustain at the same time two such intense relationships? Years later Mamie gave a clue. She was writing to Hannah Whitall Smith's son, the writer Logan Pearsall Smith, about Carey and the pursuit of culture.

The question that interested her was why, in 1893, Carey did not simply go abroad on Mary Garrett's money rather than seek the Bryn Mawr presidency. Mamie suggested that Carey did not do so, "conceivably because what Mary liked in her had been precisely her careerist, active side, as I had liked her passive side."[20]

Ever since their years abroad Carey had been balancing conflicting identities. With the assumption of the deanship of Bryn Mawr, the woman of action had come into ascendancy, and the person who longed for art had largely been relegated to travel abroad. When Carey and Mamie were in Europe, they were alone, as they had been in Leipzig, and Mamie could encourage in Carey the self that she valued—the "passive side," the Carey who was the lover of art. Yet Mamie lived with Carey the dean. As friend and counselor, graduate student, and faculty member, Mamie came to work with Carey in all aspects of Bryn Mawr life. An early budget for the college is in her diary, and a number of key college documents exist only in her hand. She was coauthor, reviser, and amanuensis. In the Bryn Mawr School she was a full contributing member of the Committee. She entered fully into the work of creating the Johns Hopkins medical school.[21]

Withal, Mamie had doubts. During her years in the Deanery, she never fully accepted the path that Carey had chosen for the two of them. In a telling letter in late December of the fateful year 1893 she wrote to Carey, "our life seems to me so starved!" Yes, there were vacations in Italy to "fall back on." But at Bryn Mawr she lived with questions: "Is it right? Has it been right all along? Is any good done to any one that compensates such hideous waste of the existence of a reasonable being?" Her days at the college seemed an "incredible blank waste." All her life, including her years at Bryn Mawr, she had compromised her wishes to please her parents. "Wouldn't a garret and one's own way have been better?" Carey's position made that impossible. "Of course, I know at the bottom of my heart that there is nothing to be done now, and that a garret today would separate me from my respectable and well-to-do Cecily, as well: but still it gnaws the worm that never dies." What did it mean for Carey to live daily at the Deanery with Mamie's constant displeasure at her life and disapproval of her fundamental choice?[22]

Legend has made Mamie Gwinn into the Emily Dickinson of Bryn Mawr, the ethereal recluse who inhabited the Deanery's upper stories, communicating with students largely by letter. This portrait is exaggerated. Carey's seating charts in letters to Mary have Mamie often at the table for dinner parties. On a number of occasions Carey boasted to Mary of Mamie's popularity with students. And yet the legend carries a kernel of truth. Mamie did remain upstairs on many Bryn Mawr occasions. Until Alfred Hodder came to Bryn Mawr in 1895, she had no college friend, and no friend from the outside ever visited her at the Deanery.

Mary offered Carey from the outset a commanding presence in which personal attractiveness was indissolubly linked with great wealth. In addition, she gave Carey confirmation of the basic direction of her life. In contrast to Mamie's disrespect for Carey's career, Mary constantly proffered words of encouragement. Valuing Carey's work for women at Bryn Mawr, Mary insisted that Carey be strong enough to face the conflicts and pains of power. She refused to let Carey give in to pressure or give up her work. As Mary moved into ascendency in Carey's life, she strengthened her engaged side.

Mary's encouragement was a mixed blessing. It felt good to have a lover admire, rather than denigrate, one's work. Carey could write about the manifold tasks of her day knowing that Mary wanted to know its many details. When she gave lectures outside the college, Mary was an audience who wanted to hear precisely how it went. Although it took Carey years to learn this, for Mary the language of love was not really the language of art; Mary relished the language of power. But the other side of this was that Carey also longed for escape. Mary offered her devotion and understanding, but never a way out. Often Carey chafed at the bit.

Thus Carey needed both Mamie and Mary. To give Mamie up was to relegate a critical part of her self-image and aspiration to the past. To have Mary was to validate the direction her life was taking. That to have them both was utterly selfish was beyond her comprehension.

II

RHOADS delayed a month longer than he had intended and offered his resignation at the March 10 board meeting, effective at the end of the summer or with the appointment of a successor. His resignation had been anticipated for a year. He had given a decade to the college. Since Francis T. King's death he had been both the college's president and president of its board of trustees. He was tired and ill. Rhoads stated to the trustees that he wished M. Carey Thomas to succeed him, but key trustees were in no mood to take that step. The board formed a nomination committee.

Rhoads wrote to Thomas that he hoped that the nomination committee would soon "exhaust all other alternatives" and select her as president. "To this end we must wait and be patient." Rhoads minimized what was happening in the board: certain trustees were using his resignation as an occasion to rethink the nature of the college and to return to a narrow, sectarian conception. Carey Thomas knew the stakes. As she explained to Mary Garrett, she had built a "house of cards that thirteen irresponsible men can in a moment destroy."[23]

In her conversation with James Whitall the following day, Thomas learned that she confronted no competition for the presidency and that the trustees had not "faced for a moment the alternative" of her leaving, "but they are terrified at the thought of putting a *woman* in sole power." Their hope was to have Rhoads remain as nominal president while Thomas did all the work, a possibility Thomas would not accept. Realizing "the feeling of the trustees about a woman," she determined that she must insist on becoming a trustee.[24]

In the frenetically busy days that ensued, as Carey Thomas worried about the trustees, her debts, and her obligations to Mamie, she began to have serious second thoughts about vying for the presidency. On March 12 she wrote to Mary that as she drove to Quaker Meeting she "thought that at least it was the last of Meetings and pretense if I left Bryn Mawr." Two days later Rhoads broke down completely, and his physician prescribed total rest for six or seven weeks. As Thomas took over all his duties, her life assumed a new dimension. She wrote to Mary, "Again, a day full of a rush of business, architects, workmen, contractors, printers, a sort of hell on earth, a foretaste of what you wish me to live for." John Garrett (a Bryn Mawr trustee, unrelated to Mary) told her "that never would they put a woman in sole authority, that they all never dreamed I would refuse to work, do all the work, through a nominal president, etc., etc., that it was my duty to sacrifice myself. . . . Oh, it was shameful." Thomas planned to resign in May. On March 23 she tried one last gambit and contacted the swing members of the board to gain support. She wrote to Mary that once she had gotten in touch with the board, "my conscience will be clear, and women's education must take its chance, which seems to depend, at Bryn Mawr at least, on my being able to persuade six men that I am *not* a woman." She went to bed completely discouraged and spent the night determined to give up and reconstruct her life.[25]

The next morning, without prior warning, Carey received a letter from Mary with a startling proposal. Carey must now radically shift tactics, for all legitimate arguments had failed. The time had come to "work the interest factor," Mary Garrett's great wealth. Carey should appeal to the trustees' baser instincts and tell the trustees that Garrett's promised gift of $2,000 to the English department was to have been only a beginning. Garrett's interest in Bryn Mawr, however, would "cease wholly and entirely" when Thomas' "connection with it was severed." Thomas might add that Garrett had intended, providing Thomas were president, giving her "to expend, *at your sole discretion* for the college $5,000 next year and each succeeding year that you remained president, in the same way, $10,000." What Mary Garrett was proposing was that if Carey Thomas were made president, Garrett would give to the college each year a sum considerably more than 10 percent of its annual budget.

Mary stated her case in this manner because she feared that Carey would not approve. Carey needed to understand that her bribe was "a legitimate use to put that awful power, money, to, and you surely cannot hesitate about it." Mary, required to rest by Dr. Cushier's orders, was trying to do something to help Carey through a difficult period. She worried that her letter was badly written and made her sound "as if I thought having the power of giving some money really makes my opinions of some value." With some fear she wrote that she hoped that Carey would read it in the right spirit. Had she understood Carey better, she would have known she need not have been so modest and self-abnegating.[26]

Mary's proposal overwhelmed Carey with pleasure. As she immediately wrote to dispel Mary's fears, she stated that she understood fully "such a sweet and clever attempt to use Mammon for righteousness. . . . If you can afford to do it, I shall be delighted to accept it and spend it as we decide." Stunned though she was, Carey kept her head. She proposed that Mary present her offer in a letter to President Rhoads, a draft of which she enclosed. All doubts Carey harbored about the direction of her life were dismissed. At this moment she set her course and there was no going back.[27]

Mary Garrett's March 28, 1893, letter to the Bryn Mawr board of trustees, as crafted by Carey Thomas, was a masterpiece. Garrett wrote that after she made gifts to the college, Thomas had told her, "knowing as she did that my interest in the college depended upon her connection with it and her influence in its administration," that the successor to President Rhoads and Thomas' own continuing connection were "apparently uncertain." This change would be "one of the gravest misfortunes that could befall the education of women in this country." The trustees needed to know "that it has always been my intention, whenever Miss M. Carey Thomas should become president of your college, to pay into her hands the sum of ten thousand dollars yearly, so long as I live and she remains president, to be used, at her discretion, for the English department in the first instance, and then for the other departments of the college, but not for buildings." Because of her commitments to the Johns Hopkins medical school, in 1893–94 she could give only $5,000; but beginning in 1894–95, she could begin the annual $10,000 gift. She closed, "I ought to add that I write without consultation with Miss Thomas," although she was sending her a copy of the letter. "I have never had occasion to express to her any part of my intentions in regard to Bryn Mawr College, although she must, of course, have been aware of the certainty of my support of any institution of which she was president."[28]

Rhoads did not react as Thomas had hoped. He saw the proposed gift as likely to hurt her cause. It could increase trustee questions about her autonomy and her pattern of spending beyond the endowment. As he wrote to Thomas, from the perspective of a trustee such a gift could put "great power in the hands of an officer which would be wholly beyond the guidance of the board." Rhoads discussed two issues on the trustees' minds. First, what did Bryn Mawr's founding as a Quaker college mean? "Several of the board sincerely feel an obligation to make the college more Friendly than it is, rather than less so. . . .

They think thou wilt make the college less Friendly and practically discard the intentions of the Founder." And second, who controlled Bryn Mawr? "They think thou art too unwilling to respect the seriously expressed views of the board and that they will have responsibilities on their consciences which they will be powerless to fulfill, in short that the college will pass absolutely into the control of an officer, who, especially with $10,000 a year at her own control, will be independent of the board." Rhoads did not mention the third issue on the minds of members of the exclusively male board, that Carey Thomas was a woman.[29]

James Thomas confronted the gender issue squarely. He was solidly behind his daughter. He encouraged her to have confidence in her judgments and actions, for "I shall be sure, whatever turns out, that thee has acted for the best and desired to do the right thing." He promised his full support in words that must have felt deeply reassuring, coming as they did from a father who was also an influential trustee: "I may be depended on to help thee the best I can and to stand by thee. I need not tell thee how much I love thee."[30]

Although initially he felt inhibited because Carey Thomas was his daughter, he now resolved to act. On the March day that the Garrett gift was announced to the trustees, he wrote an official letter to the board to record his vote for Carey Thomas. He believed that his "personal relationship to the dean" should not stand in the way of his advocacy. He was an original trustee chosen by Joseph Wright Taylor; he had played a large role with his cousin Francis T. King in the initial creation of the college; and he had observed closely Carey Thomas' capable direction of the curriculum, student life, and fundraising. He gave her credit for Bryn Mawr's plan and the group system. The success of Bryn Mawr's organization was "an evidence of her power to grasp the problem of the needs of education of women and to carry them out in a practical and practicable manner." She had chosen excellent faculty and had kept the college running smoothly. Because of her sympathy with individual students, they had given her "their enthusiastic love and admiration." She had the ability to raise money and had won for herself a place in important circles in Philadelphia. President Rhoads had chosen her as his successor.[31]

To James Thomas there was only one bar in the mind of his fellow trustees: his daughter was a woman. In his letter he tried to turn the argument around. "That she is a woman, is a reason why she should be president of a woman's college. . . . It would be a poor commentary in establishing a college for the higher training of women to refuse to the dean, because she is a woman, the recognition of her acknowledged gifts and ability for this position. If the dean had been a man, the trustees could hardly have hesitated."[32]

Empowered by her father's unqualified support and by Garrett's gift, Carey Thomas again made the rounds of the trustees. Trustee Philip Garrett, John Garrett's brother, continued firm in opposition. Thomas gave this account of their conversation: "I said everything there was to say. I kept my temper and was absolutely calm (I am thankful to say) but it was such a comfort at least to have him listen, to make him listen." She wrested from him the curious confession that he would not, in her place, remain at Bryn Mawr. But that was because he was "very imperfect and a man." Thomas, as a woman, could be expected to act out of higher and purer motives. She had a "duty" to sacrifice herself "for the good of the college."[33]

Despite Rhoads' strong support, Mary Garrett's gift, James Thomas' letter, and the votes of her advocates James Whitall, James Thomas, and Rhoads, the board stalled. Trustees John and Philip Garrett, Edward Bettle, Jr., and Francis Cope remained opposed. In the middle were swing trustees, capable of being convinced by either side. David Scull, Jr., loyal as a cousin but conservative by inclination, served as mediator.[34]

Given the strong sentiment against her, yet the need to keep her as dean, the board wrestled with the question for months without making a decision. During this period, James Whitall was her closest adviser, conveying to her the reactions of his fellow trustees. He also advised his brother-in-law James Thomas and insisted that they hold firm. In May, James Thomas was ready to accede to a majority vote against his daughter. Whitall was unwilling to compromise: "If Francis R. Cope has a majority, I expect to vote with the 'saving remnant,' kindly but steadily, and consistently. I could not possibly assume the slightest responsibility for the disaster which he is trying to bring on the college."[35]

Controversy over who should be president led to debate about the direction of the college. The nomination committee asked James Wood, a wealthy New York Quaker, if he would consider the presidency. At their July 1893 meeting, after a committee study on the role of religion, the board adopted a series of resolutions: Quakers should be given preferential treatment in faculty appointments; students must register their religious affiliation; the president had to record attendance at Sabbath worship; and the academic standard of the college, according to Joseph Wright Taylor's wish, was to be that of Haverford. Carey Thomas was outraged at this effort to roll back the secular, cosmopolitan Bryn Mawr that she had created.[36]

III

IN THE meantime Carey had gone with Mary and Mamie to Chicago to see the World's Columbian Exposition and to travel to Colorado. She worked hard to get Mary to be kind to Mamie and Mamie to be forgiving to Mary. "You see," she wrote Mary, "so much of our being together in future depends on your relations with Mamie being pleasant. I cannot leave her for long and if you and she and I could be together, and you and I sometimes alone, you see, it would mean much more companionship." Months earlier, Mary had invited Mamie to join her party to preview the fair. At that point Mamie refused kindly. She was, after all, caught up in Mary's scheme to make Carey president, and she was anticipating her own appointment as associate professor. In thinking about the excursion, Mamie wrote, "I wish we were both rich and free"—we, Carey and Mamie, not Mary.[37]

It was a bittersweet time. The debate over Bryn Mawr's future was excruciating, for it threatened the entire edifice, what Carey had called in the spring "my beautiful, almost perfect, college that Mamie and I have created out of impossible elements like a fairy palace in a desert." The erection of Pembroke Hall only added to the pain, for as it emerged that summer it looked "ravishing, like an old castle keep." Much of the summer Carey Thomas stayed at the Bryn Mawr Hotel, close to home. With Rhoads convalescing, Thomas took over his tasks. At Coombe Edge, where she had gone to please her father, she thought of Mary and wanted time to savor her love: "What I have thought of and dreamed of and tried not to think of has come. I should like to have a year clear to turn my happiness over and over in my hands." Back on duty at Bryn Mawr, as Mamie worked in the adjoining room on her study of *Beowulf*, Carey wrote to Mary, "I wish I could take you in my arms and kiss you." In September Mary and Carey spent three weeks together in the Adirondacks.[38]

Once Carey told Mamie that she was going to the Adirondacks with Mary, Mamie knew all that it was important for her to know. What she had most feared had happened. Carey had violated the promise made in the spring, never to travel with Mary and without her. Now she was doing just that and—most significantly—at Mary's expense. "You have served the very first opportunity of taking pleasure without me. . . . Somehow I trusted and believed you a little, just a little, after all and in spite of all—and now!" For Mamie, the trip had clear meaning, "You have gone so far in travelling without your mate, and with a wrong one." With great prescience she realized that, having taken this step, Carey would be reluctant in the future to spend her own money on travel. Moreover, if Mary found it worthwhile to pay Carey's expenses in the Adirondacks, she could take her anywhere: "It is self evident that if Mary pays your expenses she invites you, and might equally invite you to go to Norway, or to England, or round the world."[39]

Of course, they patched things up and returned to their life together in the Deanery. And yet, Mamie knew that she now lived under different rules. Mary now had a fixed hold. Carey continued to tell Mamie that she was her first interest, that she loved her and longed for her whenever they were apart, but Mamie knew she had been at least partially displaced.

Mary went to Chicago for a final look at the world's fair—and a chance to purchase its wares. Her brother Robert took ill, and Mary stayed on to care for him. Carey, back at Bryn Mawr in late September, suffered from severe headaches. Her letter to Mary conveys something of Carey's expectation about closeness and gives knowledge of their physical intimacy in 1893. She wrote that she could not conceal her anger any more than "if we were sitting side by side with your cheek against mine, as I hope we may be before long." She was angry at Mary for her secrecy about her brother's illness. "In a very deep love there are no shallow places, and I wonder sometimes if there are. I wonder sometimes if you were here and my lips were on yours if I should feel as I felt after reading your long letter."[40]

IV

DEBATE about the presidency continued. When James Wood withdrew, the trustees devised a plan to keep Rhoads as titular head but bring in a male vice president to be in real command. Carey Thomas was angry and threatened to resign as dean. The board could find no suitable man to take the job of vice president. By the November 17 board meeting, all alternatives to naming Thomas president had failed, and the trustees had to make a decision about her. Carey wrote to Mary, "We are tight in the hands of Fate now, and the Lord knows what cards will come uppermost tomorrow. I do not."[41]

By a vote of seven to five, the Bryn Mawr College board of trustees elected M. Carey Thomas president. She was not made a trustee. Carey cabled Mary: "One half all right. Other half will surely be arranged, they think." Later in the day, Rhoads told her of the board's deliberations. After her name was proposed, Francis Cope had made a motion for delay that was voted down ten to two. In a secret ballot, seven trustees voted for Thomas. Of the five in opposition, two were not really opposed. Of the remaining three, Thomas anticipated that both John Garrett and Francis Cope would resign. When Albert Smiley brought up the question of making Thomas a trustee, Cope said that "the minority had gone through so much and had suffered so keenly in defeat, he thought the further details might surely be left to some other meeting." After exhortations to unity, the meeting adjourned.[42]

Thomas learned that before voting on the presidency, the board had dealt with policy issues. Rhoads was vague on this, and reassuring: "he is *sure* nothing in it will interfere with our success, or doing just as we do now."[43] However, two matters were substantive and necessary to persuade the hesitant to vote for Thomas. A resolution that the Garrett annual gift could only be used for temporary expenses mollified those trustees who feared that the Garrett money would only add to Thomas' independence; and Rhoads agreed to stay on for a trial first year.

The board announced the decision to the press. In a faculty meeting Rhoads was overcome and "nearly wept, and altogether it was a most melancholy occasion." Carey Thomas shook hands with the professors, who "congratulated me, and many of them added the college also." Despite this reassurance, it was not the occasion of which she had so long dreamed. The year had taken its toll. She wrote to Mary, "It is too bad to have a victory so like a defeat from the effect of nine months of steady fighting."[44]

In time, Carey Thomas rallied. At the alumnae tea the following week, the genuine enthusiasm of former students moved her. "They said, of course, they had all expected it, but now they felt the future of the college *assured*." Professors told her "they all felt that my presidency meant the assurance of the graduate work [on which] . . . rested Bryn Mawr's claim on them and on the public." And she had Garrett's $10,000 to spend. The first steps that she and Garrett took strengthened Bryn Mawr's commitment to graduate work and scholarship. Garrett established a graduate European fellowship of $500 a year and two graduate scholarships of $200 each. Her money also went to build the library. Nine days after the board's decision, Carey Thomas wrote to Garrett in high excitement: "The best private library (classical) in Germany is for sale," the collection of Professor Sauppe of the University of Göttingen, and could be had for $5,000. Would Garrett be willing to advance the money before Thomas assumed the presidency? Yale was also after the library, and Bryn Mawr had to act immediately. Garrett agreed, and the library of 16,000 books—"probably *the* finest in America," Carey Thomas bragged—came to Bryn Mawr.[45]

As the euphoria wore off, Carey Thomas realized she was in a bind. She had stated at the outset that she would not accept the presidency without the trusteeship. What had seemed merely a delayed vote emerged as a veto by the opposition. As she made the rounds to lobby for the second position, she found that members of the board were conciliatory to her personally, but refused to bend. They urged her to accept the presidency as offered. Aware that Thomas was troubled by a premature public announcement of the decision, Edward Bettle, Jr., wrote, "May thee not, however, consider this is in the Providential ordering and as an indication that the right plan is to accept the high position to which thee has been called, without proviso or conditions." David Scull, Jr., who thought Thomas' presence on the board would rob it of independence, shifted the ground to mutual trust. Since Thomas could attend all meetings of the board, to insist on being a trustee "carries with it the idea of attack and defense, and consequently invites suspicion." Thomas needed to cultivate a spirit of gentleness, that though "manifestly out of place in the battle-field, finds its true exercise, in such high spheres of action as thee is called to move in, and adds to any success, however brilliant, in other aspects a brighter lustre."[46]

Such sermons did not sway Carey Thomas; reality did. Ultimately convinced she could not win, Thomas gave in. These months in the winter and spring of 1894 were particularly difficult. In February 1894, Mamie's father became gravely ill and died. Rhoads took a turn for the worse, and Thomas had to assume all his tasks. The combination of caring for Mamie and the college weighed heavily. In her mourning, Mamie's emotional fragility and dependence on Carey became painfully evident. Carey could not leave Mamie even briefly to visit Mary in New York. In late May as Mamie retreated into illness, Carey called for Mrs. Gwinn to come to the Deanery and thereby added another dependent. Because of her severe headaches, Carey's doctor feared she had malaria. After many doses of quinine, James Thomas tested his daughter and found no trace of the disease. Carey wrote to Hannah Whitall Smith that the year had been "fiendish . . . the worst, except that terrible one of Mother's illness, that I have ever lived through."[47]

Unlike other summers, that of 1894 saw few pleasures. For the second year in a row, Carey remained close to home. Twice she joined Mary in Montauk, Long Island. With her return to work in the fall, M. Carey Thomas became the president of Bryn Mawr College. It was a sober prelude to a twenty-eight-year term. Bryn Mawr held no inauguration.

CHAPTER 14

Shriveled Up
and Parched and Dying

M. CAREY THOMAS became president of Bryn Mawr College on September 1, 1894. A few months earlier she had summed up her feelings in a letter to her aunt Hannah Whitall Smith. If the trustees had decided against her, she would have taken it as "a sign that I could set my wings for an attic in Paris and Bohemia and a reputation." It was painful to renounce her aesthetic and scholarly aspirations, "but the conditions were so favorable, too favorable, and the *Cause*, that troublesome *Woman*, with a capital C and a W, too near my heart, after all these eight years of service, for me to crawl out, so here I am." Of course, in writing to Hannah, it was necessary to hide as well as to reveal, and much was missing in this account: her ambitions, her need for money, her committed relationship to Mary Garrett, her difficulty with writing, her weakened hold on scholarship. But she did express an aspect of her decision in language that her aunt could understand. At Bryn Mawr she was the reformer, "going it," as Mamie Gwinn once said, for women.[1]

I

To RECOUNT her first years as president is to reexperience her feelings of fragmentation, pressure, and frustration. She often complained of headaches during this period, and no wonder. She had too much work to do. She rushed from one activity to another. When Carey Thomas became president, Bryn Mawr lost its only other academic administrator, the dean. The trustees anticipated that Thomas would continue her old duties as she took up the new, and she did. Her initial staff consisted only of young Bryn Mawr graduates who served as typists.

At the beginning of each term she interviewed candidates for admission and their parents. She met regularly with individual Bryn Mawr professors.

Any dispute in the college came to her to resolve. She developed a mounting correspondence, occupying two and later three full-time typists. For five hours each week she was available in her office for consultation, and for three hours she held her weekly "at home," an informal reception at the Deanery for the college community. Faculty meetings took up some evenings. Her social life required frequent dinners away. The Deanery, enlarged to twelve rooms, was the unofficial guest quarters of any speaker or important visitor to Bryn Mawr. For a few years she continued teaching, and this required her to prepare lectures and examinations and hold office hours with students.

To her work as dean—building and supervising a faculty and students— Carey Thomas added the responsibilities that had belonged to President James E. Rhoads. She had to see to it that the physical plant was maintained. It was in her court when pipes leaked and gymnasium equipment broke down. She met with engineers and worked out contracts for such matters as gas fixtures. She managed all Bryn Mawr property, regularly tramping the grounds. If negotiations were required to acquire land or close a street, it was her task. Because she insisted that Bryn Mawr meet her aesthetic standards, she constantly interrupted her other work to choose a paint color, a fabric to upholster a chair, the location for a statue or painting. She was the one who had to deal with a campus robbery, an outbreak of illness, an errant student. She had drafted reports to the trustees before, but now she had sole responsibility for the annual President's Report and worked with the treasurer on the Financial Report. As she came to learn, the trustees held her accountable for all money spent. If outgo exceeded income, as the trustees defined it, she was personally responsible for the deficit.

In the press of daily work, Carey Thomas found it difficult to concentrate on long-term projects. Each year she faced the ritual of the President's Report. She generally started out with good intentions, leaving herself plenty of time to gather the material for the appendices and to draft the text, but each day's dramas forced her to push the report to the side. Finally she had no choice. The trustees' meeting was upon her. In a fury of work, using all her assistants, she organized and corrected the data. She stayed up late at night writing the text. Annually she repeated with only slight variations her initial experience in 1895: she stayed up until 2 A.M., dictated to the last possible minute, read proof and made corrections at the printers, and took the report, with print still wet, to the trustees' meeting. She always worked down to the wire.[2]

In these years she began, somewhat cautiously, to speak in public. Preparation for these talks had the same rhythm as for the reports. She started well in advance, reserving time to read and write. Interruptions deterred her from her intended course. As the date for the speech loomed, she became increasingly anxious. Finally, immediately before the talk, even on the day itself, she admitted no interruptions and forced herself to concentrate. If there was time, she gave the text to Mamie Gwinn for editing, but often there was no time.

Outside interests called. In 1897, she became an alumni (and the first woman) trustee at Cornell, serving until 1901. This required her to travel to Ithaca, New York, for the regular meetings of the board. Thomas was an important presence at Cornell in those years, and she took her responsibilities as trustee seriously.

In addition, Carey Thomas continued her involvement in the Bryn Mawr School. There was real satisfaction in these years because a significant number of the school's graduates were choosing to attend Bryn Mawr College. Mary Garrett kept Thomas and the other members of the board of managers informed about the details of managing the school, its building, and its finances. The board, which now included Bryn Mawr College graduates Margaret Thomas, Carey's sister, and Ida Wood in the place of Julia Rogers and Bessie King, continued to make all decisions of any consequence.

In 1896 the school took one of the most important steps in its history: it hired Edith Hamilton and gave her the title of headmistress. A Bryn Mawr College graduate of great ability, Hamilton had spent a year as a graduate fellow in Latin. She won the coveted European Fellowship and studied in 1895–96 in Leipzig and Munich. She had aspirations as a classicist (and late in her life fulfilled them in her widely read books on the ancient world). As a young woman facing the practical necessity of earning an income, she agreed to manage the school. From the outset, Thomas and Hamilton had a tense and difficult relationship. Both held clear educational ideals and high standards. Thomas and the board of managers, however, were unwilling to give up power, even over minute details. Hamilton had to get permission for every school expense. As Mary Garrett became preoccupied by other matters or suffered from illness, the school was unable to get answers or action about the most routine matters. Finally, despite repeated efforts over many years, the board kept Hamilton from hiring as a teacher a friend and Bryn Mawr College graduate, Clara Landsberg, because she was Jewish.[3] Although she worked within terrible constraints, by persistence and force of will, over the course of a twenty-six-year tenure as headmistress, Edith Hamilton helped build a remarkable school.

The other side of the headmistress' lack of autonomy was the obligation of the board and thus of Thomas to handle school detail. The Bryn Mawr School was often the one thing too much in Carey Thomas' overcrowded day. In a letter to Mary in the spring of 1895, Mamie conveyed something of the chaos that Carey's commingling of school and college work involved. Mamie was writing for Carey, who was ill with influenza. She described the scene: "It has been a sort of pandemonium all the forenoon, what with secretaries and outsiders waiting for answers, enough to make a well person ill." Mamie was out of sorts because, in addition to assistants being unavailable, she had to deal with a bad cook and a bungling waiter. "Whatever papers are handed to Carey are presently stowed away somewhere by that secretary, who vanishes into space, and therefore I can't send you, or myself lay hands on, sundry applications and the like that I think you ought to see." The following autumn, as she apologized to Mary for sending a telegram directly to the head of the school on the heels of one giving contradictory instructions, Mamie reported a sense of the rush of Carey's life: "The first telegram was sent in hot haste, the messenger boy waiting, and Carey in a fume over her opening address to the students."[4]

Carey's daily letter to Mary Garrett is a recital of unremitting work and constant pressure. Although on most occasions, she merely listed her commitments, on a few she recounted her work with a detail that conveys the texture of her days. In late March 1895, for example, she reported, "Today has been spent in first losing my temper with Miss Kirk of Merion totally. She behaved outrageously and I fear I spoke very unkindly. Then [Professor] Kohler and I wrangled pleasantly about his engagement: it is the last. All the other men have signed contracts." She continued, "Then the men on the place had a grand quarrel about a ladder, and I had to call them all to my office, and then I engaged an engineer, a nice one, and then saw the superintendent of our heating plant and quarreled fiercely with him." In the afternoon, she learned that one of the residence hall mistresses she sought had accepted. She interviewed another applicant and saw three of the existing dormitory heads. "Mamie and I located a fence. I dictated three letters, and then John Stewardson and I saw about the location of Dr. Andrews' house from 4:30 till 6:45. It is a knotty problem. I corrected and sent off the Board of Trade notice and will send the other tomorrow."[5]

The narratives to Mary expose days of hectic work and frustration. Carey wrote of her constant irritation and deep fatigue as external demands shaped her life. In her telling there were no challenges or problems to solve, there were only burdens. She often described herself as being spent, used up, exhausted. Yet letters can be misleading. Carey was writing to Mary when she was living with Mamie. Her letters were often designed to tell Mary why she could not write a good letter, why there was no time. In addition, at some level, Carey held Mary responsible for her life. Her complaints are thus indirect efforts to blame Mary for the pains of the day. As she wrote to Mary, she was reminded of her dream of a different life, one devoted to scholarship or art.

Once she was president, Carey Thomas' alternate identities no longer existed as real possibilities; but they continued in her imagination. Although she accepted the fact that she did not have time to be a scholar, her letters to

Mary express her longings for a life of art. In reality, art had been pushed into the summer and some weekends, but Mamie's daily presence was a haunting reminder of the leisure and pleasure that she had given up. Carey Thomas never resolved the basic question of her life. She never clearly and firmly chose the life of action. As a result, she felt that she was kept from what should have been hers. As she faced the rigorous demands of her work, she seemed to herself less an actor than an agent of other persons and forces. She had to be president of Bryn Mawr for Mamie, who needed to remain at Bryn Mawr. She labored for Mary vicariously, serving the cause of women for her.

One element of her discontent in these years may have been her incomplete understanding of work. She desired power. She did not, however, realize or accept the imperative to serve an institution. Tasks of the Bryn Mawr presidency thus constantly intruded on time and space that she felt should have been hers. At some level she felt work violated her.

To be sure, Carey Thomas needed a wife. A late-nineteenth-century household required much labor, and if the tasks were done by others, a great deal of supervision. Mamie, who was dependent upon Carey for a home, was totally uninvolved in the details of housekeeping. It was Carey who hired and fired maids and cooks. When bedbugs or mice infested the Deanery, it was Carey who had to find a way to get rid of them. If new napkins were needed or broken pieces of china had to be replaced, Carey shopped for them in Philadelphia. When coupons were to be clipped from Mamie's bonds, Carey went with her to the bank. The crises of Mamie's life weighed heavily, often at the most stressful periods at Bryn Mawr.

The result was that, in her first years as Bryn Mawr's president, it all felt much too difficult, and Carey Thomas retained profound doubts about her life. Her correspondence with Mary Garrett is scattered with unanswered questions. In January 1895 she wrote, "I am rather shriveled up and parched and dying for a let up and wondering whether days of students and professors and workmen are worth the candle if one's personality goes to pieces."[6]

At a very different level, underlying the frenzied life that Carey Thomas led was a problem she shared with other college presidents of her day. Bryn Mawr in the 1890s was at a point of transition in the American college presidency. The collegiate community ceased to be an enclave isolated from the world, yet lacked the bureaucratic structures that were emerging in American corporate life. In some colleges the beginnings were there. Many nineteenth-century colleges had a treasurer's office to oversee not only receipts and disbursements but also the physical plant and the work force to build and maintain it. But most administrative offices were still to come. In the early twentieth century, colleges created the offices of admissions to enroll students, of dean of students to safeguard the health and discipline of undergraduates, and of registrar to oversee their course credits and transcripts. Infirmaries added

a director to the nursing and medical staffs. In time, many other offices—
financial aid, development, public relations, alumnae affairs—removed the
burden of daily oversight from the president. In addition, beginning in some
places in the late nineteenth century, faculties took over much of the work of
organizing and managing themselves. Departments, committees, and faculty
assemblies gained virtual control over curriculum, appointments, and promotion and tenure.

Bryn Mawr was slow to develop an administration. It had begun as a very
small college, and Thomas wanted to save all resources to hire more professors.
When the faculty consisted of seven, a president and dean must have seemed
ample. But more than size was at issue. Even a small enterprise can establish
methods of work that have order and regularity. President Rhoads did not do
this. However trusted he was, he had been a physician and Indian rights
reformer, not a manager. His Quaker style of governing emphasized vital
conviction and judgment and placed little value on tradition. James Thomas
complained to his daughter that Rhoads did not prepare a full and correct
budget. Yet Rhoads worked so hard that his health suffered.

James Whitall wanted his niece to have an adequate staff to assist her.
Carey Thomas never achieved this as dean, but in 1895 as president she had
the good fortune to get as her secretary Isabel Maddison, a Bryn Mawr graduate
student (and later a Ph.D. in mathematics). Maddison's careful work in preparing letters gradually expanded. Thomas also hired a competent bookkeeper to
serve the college as bursar. Yet although Thomas gained assistants, there was
no delegation of authority or responsibility.

The competent staff she assembled were by and large Bryn Mawr graduates
whose loyalty to her and to the college overrode distaste for the pressured office
atmosphere. Alumnae were an important ally. They were a card she knew
how to play. Even as dean she began to have lunches with alumnae. In the
early years she could count on Bryn Mawr graduates to support her vision of
the college. In time alumnae infiltrated the college at a number of levels.
They served Thomas in her office as secretary, typists, and bursar. Although
Thomas looked for new professors through her connections at Harvard and
other male institutions, bringing to Bryn Mawr primarily men, she developed
a second tier of readers who were Bryn Mawr graduates. Her sister Helen
Thomas and Lucy Donnelly were among the alumnae who taught the essay
course in the English department designed to instruct students in the art of
writing. Bryn Mawr graduates increasingly served as house mistresses.

Assistants, teachers of essay writing, and house mistresses were all subordinates. Carey Thomas was willing to bring alumnae into the college as her
agents, but she was not willing to share power. From the outset she maintained
absolute control over all administrative decisions. In the twentieth century,

this became a major source of tension and conflict at Bryn Mawr; in the nineteenth, it was largely accepted as the way a college worked.

Carey Thomas' inner drives intensified structural imperatives. A perfectionist, she did not delegate because she insisted on control over minute decisions. For example, at times when she was frenetically busy, she read proof because she feared no one else could catch mistakes. Every element of the college had to be held to her standard. If the college was to attract and keep the kind of students that Thomas wanted, then she needed to insure that all elements of their life be above reproach. Thomas took note of every additional student. She was particularly pleased with the increasing entry of "swells" from the upper classes. Her desire for wealthy students from New York and the South intensified her efforts to insure pröper management of the halls, ladylike mistresses, competent housekeepers, and well-prepared food. Professors had to be observed closely to verify that they had the gift for teaching. Although students were to be assigned reading and have regular quizzes, they must not be required to do so much that they would be overwhelmed and then withdraw. Perfectionism, attention to detail: to give up control over any element might lead to sloppiness that would undo her work.

II

ULTIMATELY, at the heart of Carey Thomas' struggles in these years lay a basic conflict over the identity of Bryn Mawr. It was not only the nature of the American college presidency, Bryn Mawr's informal procedures, and her own drive for control that compelled Carey Thomas to work so hard in the 1890s; she also had to fight because she had a clear agenda, and she confronted trustees who opposed her. In understanding both the difficulties of her presidency and its achievements, one must remember that until well into Thomas' tenure as president she faced a board of trustees many of whose members were hostile or indifferent to her goals. In conflict with a board bent on undoing her work, Carey Thomas had to watch everything, keep everything moving ahead. She believed that only she stood between the college and a conservative and arbitrary body of men. As she saw it, her "fairy palace" was fragile. It was, as she often said, a house of cards that thirteen men, the trustees, could destroy in an instant.[7]

Bryn Mawr's board of trustees was divided. There were those such as her father who sympathized with her aims; and there were others, such as Philip and John Garrett, who opposed them. The measure of the opposition was its success in preventing her from becoming a trustee. From 1894 until 1902 Thomas engaged in a continuing struggle to be named trustee. Initially she had few allies. In January 1895 James Rhoads died. After paying him tribute,

Thomas eyed his seat on the board. James Whitall wrote to James Thomas about the February meeting to elect Rhoads' successor as trustee: "I voted for Carey, but I was the only one who did. It is manifest that the board will not consent to electing her as a trustee at present, and it will be wise for her to let that subject rest at present. It is somewhat trying to have strife stirred up every time a trustee is to be elected." The board chose Henry Tatnall, an officer of the Girard Life and Trust Company and a brother-in-law of trustee Edward Bettle, Jr. Unlike the uncompromising stand that Whitall took in an earlier vote for the presidency, he was willing to bend when the issue was making his niece a trustee; and he moved to make the vote for Tatnall unanimous.[8]

At times Carey Thomas fought fiercely to become a trustee; at other times she was resigned, realizing that as president she held many strings. As she wrote to Mary in January 1895, "If I could only keep from getting tired and worrying over trifles, they can do but little, so long as I am here enthroned in your office and mine." She now went to all meetings of the board, as well as many of its committee meetings. The unsympathetic Philip Garrett was chosen president of the board and began to pry into details of her administration, making her work harder and more conflictual. Once, when Philip and John Garrett attempted to keep her from attending board meetings, she held her ground. Because most meetings were in Philadelphia, she spent a good deal of time on the train. When an important issue was before the board, she also visited individual board members in their offices.[9]

The conservative trustees who had opposed her appointment spent the early years of her presidency trying to find a way to reestablish the Quaker college they believed Joseph Wright Taylor intended. This effort had two elements. The first was to restore Bryn Mawr as a sectarian college of the Society of Friends. The second was to keep the college small and preserve its endowment.

At one level, the conflict they waged was personal. For example, Thomas reported to Mary Garrett that at the November 1896 trustees' meeting Philip Garrett read "a *long* paper of which the upshot was I was not a truly religious woman and the influence they wished." This time he was stopped by James Wood, a new trustee (who some had hoped would take the presidency), who told the trustees that Carey Thomas was "one of the remarkable women in America . . . and asked Philip *what* he expected." When Garrett attempted to read an anonymous letter, he was ruled out of order.[10]

Personal insults could be confronted and overcome. The larger aim of the conservative trustees—to return the college to its Quaker roots—was more difficult to combat. The religious committee of the board wrote a statement for the official college program expressing their understanding of the college. Thomas was deeply opposed and rallied her father to object. As the fight resumed in the spring, the conservatives gained the upper hand. At the last moment, she got David Scull, Jr., to add moderating language. The result was a statement in college documents that hedged: "Dr. Taylor was a member of the Religious Society of Orthodox Friends. . . . It was his desire that the college should be pervaded by the principles of Christianity held by Friends, which he believed to be the same in substance as those taught by the early Christians, and an endeavor will be made to promote this end; it was, however, his evident purpose that the college should be nonsectarian, and the trustees accordingly established it on that basis."[11]

Carey Thomas knew better than to regard debate over the religious statement as merely an abstract discussion without practical meaning for the college. In March 1897, she received a visit from trustees David Scull, Jr., and Edward Bettle, Jr., both of whom she regarded as personal supporters. They had insisted that the college censor the reading of students. As she wrote to Mary, the two men "pitched into me about books; they think *nothing* with anything improper should be bought and absolutely wanted me to supervise the books bought privately by the students and read in their rooms." Thomas found this deeply offensive. "Of course, I flatly refused to police the students. I told them they might but I would not." Thomas insisted on no censorship of purchases for the library.

In fact, Carey Thomas' response was more equivocal. She took a strong verbal stand, but she had, in anticipation of the two trustees' visit, already cleansed the library. After Bettle looked over the English books and found one to oppose, John Addington Symonds' *Wine, Women and Song*, it was removed. Thomas felt confident that in the future the trustees would limit themselves to efforts to persuade her.[12] Committed personally to intellectual liberty, she had to operate in a milieu of censorship. Hedged in as she was, she stood rhetorically for full freedom of artistic expression, but practically she was willing to accept some limitations.

There were dangers to Bryn Mawr. Her "fairy palace" was fragile. The other side of a faculty of independent-minded, brilliant professors was the possibility that one of them might make an impolitic public statement. Carey Thomas herself, hardly conventional according to Quaker standards, might make a slip. Then, of course, there were the students. At any moment they might expose the liberality of their education. As dean she had derived her power over students from her personal influence on them as their teacher. As president, though she tried to keep her hand in, she virtually had to give up teaching. In 1893 she stopped teaching graduate students. In 1894 she had a substitute deliver her lectures in the undergraduate course, and after 1896 she gave up regular teaching entirely. Chapel talks became her principal means of reaching students, though when conflicts arose, she held mass student meetings. From 1892 on, the students handled their own discipline through the Self-Government Association. Thomas could not act in violation of its charter, but could attempt to persuade.

By the 1894–95 academic year, it was clear that the hold Carey Thomas had once had over students was weakening. The larger college of 234 undergraduates was attracting more playful, less serious students who no longer sustained the sense, held by those in the first classes, that they were participating in an important experiment. They quickly signaled that a new era had begun. In November, Thomas saw a notice of a play and dance held by students, "all about the Earl of Pembroke and me and my English pronunciation and the girls' beards and wigs and men's costumes." Thomas called a meeting of students to tell them it was necessary to keep reports of their events out of the newspapers and even to avoid talking where reporters might hear.[13]

Throughout the year Carey reported to Mary many incidents in which students violated her standards. They were dining out a good deal, pretending that they were chaperoned by an aunt. A vandal among them painted a mustache on a terra cotta Hermes. Two students cribbed sections of their senior essays. A student set a bad example by eating the whole plate of asparagus meant for her table. Students were leaving their bicycles in the drawing rooms of their halls and the corridors of Taylor.

The climax came in May 1895. As she returned from a trip, she learned that "half the college has been going in *naked* in the pool." "Half the college" turned out to be only twenty students, but they were convincing many others to join them. As she dealt with this breach of decorum, Carey Thomas reacted in a manner that typified her encounters with students. She had learned her mother's lessons well. She herself did not disapprove of nude swimming on any moral grounds, but she knew that if knowledge of it got out, it would hurt the reputation of the college. "Of course, it must be stopped at once, as it would do us more harm than anything I can think of, but there is really no harm in it." She met with the student Athletic Committee to try and convince its members they must not swim without clothes. As Carey Thomas constantly watched over students, she was placed at times in a peculiar position. She had to keep students from engaging in practices that she herself accepted.[14]

In time, Carey Thomas became a censor. Her grounds were never moral, only practical. In May 1897, Georgiana Goddard King, an undergraduate, wrote an article on Rudyard Kipling for the college literary magazine, the *Lantern*. Thomas liked it, but it contained much "objectionable" material, written mostly by Kipling. She spent three hours revising it. As with nude swimming, there was a wide gap between her public actions and private standards. King's piece provoked Thomas' curiosity: "Can the younger generation really think him the greatest of poets and prose writers? Has he indeed thrown Browning and [George] Meredith and Swinburne into twilight?" She made a private decision to study Kipling's poetry.[15]

As in the past, it was not just religion and morals that separated Carey Thomas' conception of Bryn Mawr from that of the trustees, it was their differing ambitions for the college. For Thomas, the Bryn Mawr of the mid-1890s was only a beginning. She had taken Taylor's endowment and created of it a secular and cosmopolitan institution of higher learning. She had attracted a brilliant, well-trained faculty of 26, to which 298 talented students came for instruction at the undergraduate and graduate level. But Carey Thomas dreamed of a college great in size as well as talent.

With the exception of Mary Garrett, Bryn Mawr had not found a major donor. Garrett saw her annual gifts as adding embellishments, such as fellowships, lectures, and books, and had specified that her ten thousand dollars was not to be used for buildings. In addition, other donors contributed funds for specific purposes, especially for scholarships. But in the 1890s no significant endowment came to the college.

How was Bryn Mawr to grow? Carey Thomas believed that once the college attracted more students, their tuition would support a larger faculty. But the trustees had ordained that Pembroke was the last residence hall to be built with Taylor's endowment, and they extended this principle to the purchase of land and buildings. The only growth they allowed was through schemes whereby friends of the college bought land and houses and then leased them to the college. In 1893, George W. Childs and Mary Garrett assumed the interest payments for the Kennedy lot that added nine and a half acres to college property. Thomas and Henry Tatnall assumed the mortgage for Dolgelly, a large cottage purchased in 1898. But in every case, the trustees were careful to insure that the acquisition entailed no capital costs. When they decided not to purchase the Bryn Mawr Hotel, the board minutes declared, the "testamentary endowment" required "rigid protection." Trustee determination to prevent infringements on the endowment was absolute. Not only did this block growth, but given mounting deficits, it also led to continuing conflict with the president.[16]

From the outset, the board of trustees had worried that James Rhoads' and Carey Thomas' ambitions for Bryn Mawr far exceeded the endowment. One of the objections to Thomas becoming president was a fear of fiscal liberality. It was a fear well founded. In pursuing her vision of Bryn Mawr, Thomas constantly spent to the limit—and then some. The issues involved with Carey Thomas' handling of Bryn Mawr's finances go beyond a reasonable pursuit of ambitious goals. Her relation to money is a complex one, derived from her mother's household and deeply entwined in her intimate life. There was convergence between extravagance in her personal accounts and deficits in the college.

In her first year as president Thomas went $8,000 over college resources—over $140,000 in today's dollars—constituting slightly under 10 percent of the college budget. Mary Garrett donated to the college some of the money needed to balance the books. For almost a decade, as Thomas well knew, Garrett had been making up the deficits of the Bryn Mawr School. When Thomas applied to her on behalf of the college, Garrett assumed the burden. Thomas was continually angry about the manner in which the college's financial dealings were carried on. The objects of her wrath could be either Philip Garrett or the Girard Trust, which managed the endowment. On their side, the trustees clearly worried about her fiscal supervision. At the end of Thomas' second year as president, the deficit was ten thousand dollars.[17]

The following fall, Henry Tatnall, the chairman of the board's finance committee and an officer of the Girard Trust, began to give close oversight to Bryn Mawr's books. He undertook a review of expenses, requiring Thomas to come into Philadelphia for frequent meetings. In addition to the detailed financial report that Thomas' office was preparing, Tatnall wanted a full accounting of the costs of buildings. Thomas reported to Mary that because the three college bookkeeping assistants were "working day and night at the financial report, I had to get them out myself," and this required her to work until midnight.[18] Beginning in the fall of 1897, Thomas' office made clear projections of the year's expenses. This task took much of her time. She worked with the college bookkeepers, traveled frequently into Philadelphia to see Tatnall, and regularly reported to the building committee and the executive committee. By 1898, she could tell Mary that her books and Tatnall's agreed and that he was satisfied.

This careful oversight may have started to bring order into Bryn Mawr's accounting, but it did not lead to black ink. In April 1897 Thomas again discovered a $10,000 deficit, which grew in a later estimate to $14,000. Although Thomas had a number of reasons why outgo was greater than income—a smaller yield on the endowment and slightly fewer students—she nonetheless knew she was accountable. She reported to Mary that she had dreamed of bankruptcy and immediately tried to cut some minor expenses. The problem, however, went beyond superficial extravagances. The primary component of Bryn Mawr's budget for 1897–98—$70,000 out of roughly $98,000—was salaries, and these were fixed. Though Thomas did not say so, Bryn Mawr simply had a larger faculty than it could afford for the tuition that it charged. Much against Mary Garrett's intention, a significant portion of her annual gift was redirected toward meeting general expenses.[19]

In 1897 Carey Thomas had no plan to bring Bryn Mawr College's budget into balance and no proposal for growth, just as she had no strategy to protect the college's commitment to intellectual freedom. She could only hang on and fight it out with the trustees issue by issue. As she confronted debt, obstreperous students, and the grind of unending work, her life was filled with frustration. Carey Thomas was overwhelmed by the tasks before her. Her problem was not really the pressure of her days; it was the limits that confined her. She faced trustees who were trying to return the college to the religious goals and modest educational hopes of the founder and to protect its endowment. If Bryn Mawr was a chess game between an inspired president and a conservative board of trustees, in the first years of Carey Thomas' presidency, the trustees held her in check.

CHAPTER 15

To Have the Love of
and to Love Two People

I N THE mid-1890s, held at bay by trustees, Carey Thomas experienced
Bryn Mawr College as frustration. In her personal life, new issues and
conflicts emerged. She had seen herself as one of "nous autres," a special
woman devoted to aesthetic pursuits shared with a few women, but she had
become a drudge in the service of Bryn Mawr. As her relationships took a new
turn, the structures of meaning that she had erected in her early adult years
were challenged. Mary Garrett showered her with gifts, and Carey's feelings
for her grew in intensity. But Mary had her own agenda for Carey, one that
kept her at the grindstone. Mamie began to withdraw and then, alarmingly,
redirected her affections.

I

IN 1894 Bryn Mawr College may have held no formal inauguration for M.
Carey Thomas, but Mary Garrett made certain that the college knew that she
was president. She paid for the renovation of Thomas' suite of new offices in
Taylor Hall and decorated the rooms with some of her finest pieces of art. The
striking of the clock that Garrett had placed there reminded Carey of Mary's
own clocks in Baltimore. Carey was deeply grateful, and wrote her in December 1894, "I cannot tell you how different these long days have been spent in
the office because of its beauty."[1]
    Garrett began to bestow upon Bryn Mawr an abundance of material gifts.
To the $10,000 she gave the college, she added a fund of $1,000 for Thomas'
use that made possible such college entertainments as the 1894 fall reception
for freshmen. Garrett paid for and supervised the decoration of the drawing
rooms of Pembroke. She gave to Bryn Mawr her collection of Braun photographs and many original works of art. She began to furnish the Deanery with
exotic furniture and works of art, including some of Thomas' favorite paintings.

In the summer and fall of 1896, Garrett helped underwrite a major expansion and redecoration of the Deanery. Cope and Stewardson redesigned the house, adding to its existing twelve rooms a two-story wing and a third floor, and giving it a shingled exterior. Comfortable and commodious from the outset, the Deanery evolved into a very large and luxurious house at the heart of the campus. Carey understood Mary's gifts as a loan contingent upon her success at Bryn Mawr. Once, when she was profoundly discouraged, she asked Mary to itemize her gifts of rugs, furniture, and works of art, so that if the trustees drove her out of the president's office, Carey could return them.[2]

When Carey and Mamie set up their household in the Deanery in the 1880s, Carey enjoyed a salary of $3,000, far larger than any she had ever known. In the first few years, it seems to have covered their needs. Mamie contributed a regular sum (by 1896, it was $431.88) for board, as well as money for washing and coal. Mamie also began to lend Carey money, at least $2,000 by 1897. After Carey came to a new understanding with Mary Garrett, Mary became a new and open-handed source of funds.[3]

After she became president, Carey continued to spend well beyond her income. She now had a salary of $5,000, close to $90,000 in 1994 dollars. In addition, she received an annuity from her mother's estate, and Mary Garrett contributed $1,000 to enable entertaining. The college charged her only $750 annually for the use of the Deanery. Even with proportionately low housing costs and an income exceeding $6,000—over six times that of an average working-class household of four—Carey could not pay her bills. Because she kept poor records, she did not know what was in her bank account, nor even where her bankbook was. Mary came to her rescue, and, more costly, she contributed at least $3,000 and as much as $4,500 to removing the college's deficit.

What did Mary's generosity mean to Carey? One cannot really know, but there are patterns and one can guess. For Carey, money and material possessions carried immense emotional import. As the eldest child Carey had always sought to reclaim her place at the center of her parents' life. At age seven, her life-threatening burn brought her mother back. In the years of her youth the possessions that she took for herself were freighted with meaning. The material things that she garnered symbolized for her the love and attention of her mother distracted by nine other children, religion, and reform. As a young girl she was drawn to the wealth that eluded her in her parents' comfortable, but sometimes impecunious, household. Her mother had relied on relief from her own father and brother, and had occasionally passed it on to her eldest daughter. Carey figured out early how to demand what she needed and hold her ground. In her sojourn with Mamie in Europe, Carey learned to live with someone wealthier than herself. In her mid-thirties, when Carey gained the love of Mary Garrett, one of America's richest women began to shower her with possessions. Carey's love for Mary was indissolubly fused with the sense of well-being that Mary's wealth and largesse bestowed.

Unlike Mamie, Mary did not hold back. Mamie had always spoken of her "little love" for Carey. At the outset of their intimacy, Mamie had told her, "I love you dearly, more than anyone else, but I do not love you all I can love." In the years they lived abroad, nothing found in the written record recalls this sentiment. But back in America, Mamie returned to those words. Once, after a quarrel, Mamie wrote, "On t'aime toujours un petit peu." Much later, at a difficult moment, Carey wrote to Mamie from abroad, "I miss you very much and love you the little you love me, as you always say." What this suggests is that, at least in significant phases of their relationship, Mamie held back. Carey was Mamie's abiding love, but not her grand passion.[4]

But for Mary, after 1893, Carey was everything. Carey was her work and her life. As Mary saw it, with her money she had installed Carey in the Bryn Mawr presidency. Mary had her requirements: Carey had to remain in office. But as long as she was there, Mary was hers. At last Carey found her love for another woman fully requited in both physical embraces and in gifts of money. As Carey experienced it, Mary gained for her the presidency of Bryn Mawr and surrounded her with precious possessions. Mary's seemingly unending munificence symbolized to Carey the depth of her love. As Mary's gifts increased, Carey's love for her became more intense. She often told Mary of her complete satisfactoriness. In June 1894, she wrote, "My darling, I cannot tell you how I loved you this last time. You are so sweet and so satisfactory. I love you so much it gets harder to say it, it is so inevitable."[5]

As profound as was her love for Mary, Carey could not and would not give up Mamie. Carey was deeply bound up with Mamie Gwinn. They shared a house, a college, lectures, a life. Love, commitment, mutual dependency, aestheticism, and Mamie Gwinn's unacknowledged authorship of Carey Thomas' lectures tied Carey to her. In February 1894 Mamie's father died suddenly. Carey wrote her a letter exhorting her to have courage, "Think how much is left and above all our love for each other. . . . Write me just what you do and how you are and how your mother is and if you love me as I do you. And be brave, my schätz, my love, my sweetheart. I kiss you and love you and think about you all the time." In other letters she emphasized that she thought of Mamie always, whether or not she was with Mary. In November 1895, when Mamie was in Baltimore and Mary was visiting Carey at the Deanery, Carey reminded Mamie: "I love you, sweetheart mine. You are the light of my eyes and my heart of hearts." Letters continued to invoke their pet names of the past, adding "Cloud" to compliment Mamie's whitening hair. As Christmas of 1897 approached, Carey wrote a Christmas greeting to "My dear, Cloud, Schätz, Squirrel, Rabbitkins."[6]

To Mary, Carey was explicit about her bond to Mamie. She explained to

Mary in February 1894 that, as much as she wanted to see her, "When I am away from Mamie long, I am unhappy. So there it is. Mamie has been so sweet lately and always." And yet, Mamie was not enough. In her next letter to Mary, Carey told her how much she wished for a long talk with her and a "long embrace." She tried to find ways to think about both women. In March she wrote, "I wondered whether it was not too great good fortune to last, to have the love of and to love two people like you and Mamie." Throughout the 1890s, she repeated this to Mary with only minor variations. In May 1897, for example, she wrote Mary, "I love you so dearly that between you and Mamie I do not care to see or speak to anyone else. I am perfectly satisfied with love."[7] But what Carey said to Mary, she did not say to Mamie. Carey's letters to Mamie acknowledge Mary's existence, but they never suggest that Mamie and Carey's relationship is altered or diluted by Mary. Carey was careful not to appear in public with Mary in ways that might demonstrate any shift in allegiance.

Although Mary knew of Carey's commitment to Mamie from the outset, it was hard to live with, and Carey was remarkably insensitive to her feelings. Though she wrote to Mary as many as three letters a day, constantly reassuring her of her love, the very fact of the letter reminded Mary that Carey was with Mamie. Often Mary was lonely and despondent.

In the decade after 1894, Mary's life fell apart. She was suffering from pain in her back and foot during this period and subject to breakdowns. Carey attempted to put her on a schedule that insured afternoon rest and relaxed evenings. She insisted that Mary send her an accounting of her hours. She helped Mary find secretaries for correspondence, personal maids, and masseuses. As Mary consulted a succession of doctors, Carey fretted continually about the medical advice Mary received. Carey advised Mary on her wardrobe and suggested for important events the dresses that Mary should bring. Carey pressured Mary to break with many of her relatives and some of her friends. In 1896 Carey helped Mary choose a New York apartment in the Ava, a building at 9 East Tenth Street managed by Julia de Forest's friends and next to the house of her brother, the designer Lockwood de Forest. When Baltimore rumors surfaced in the spring of 1896 that Mary was suffering from delusions of poverty and living in one room in New York City, Carey insisted that she return to Baltimore, open her 101 Monument Street house, and resume entertaining.[8]

In every way possible, Carey tried to protect Mary and bring her (and her money) closer to her; and yet, in the critical way, she could not and would not. Mamie remained firmly ensconced as Carey's primary partner, and Mamie's needs came first. If the two women were ill, it was Mamie who demanded and received Carey's first attention. It was Mamie who set the schedule that allowed Mary to have Carey's company for some weekends and parts of holidays. And for most of the 1890s it was Mamie who traveled with Carey in the summer.

Carey's obliviousness to Mary's feelings of loneliness and despair was most dramatic in the summer of 1895, following a time of great intensity in their relationship. Carey traveled to Europe with Mamie. The heart of the trip was the Pyrenees. For two weeks Carey spent full days on horseback. She felt wonderful, better than she had in years. In August she wrote Mary, "How am I? Brilliantly well. I feel like myself. Of course, [I] sleep well, have a splendid appetite, and am exactly as brown as an Indian. So is Mamie."[9]

Mary had asked Carey to write a little a day, even if the letter could be posted only twice a week. Carey insisted she could not: she had no private place to keep the partially written letters and she was simply too tired "after so many hours in the open air." Both answers argued Mamie's primacy. With egregious insensitivity, Carey insisted on her 1895 return from Europe that Mary not meet her in New York but at the Bryn Mawr Hotel (Mamie was going directly from New York to Baltimore) where Carey hoped Mary would be "unpacked and ready," having already had her massage. In such moods, at whatever cost to Mary (or Mamie), Carey would have it all.

Mary's most profound crisis came in the summer of 1897. Carey was with Mamie in Spain and under her spell. Mary had remained in the Deanery at Bryn Mawr determined to put order into Carey's finances (and, to some degree, into those of the college). Alone, what Mary described as a tide of unhappiness overwhelmed her. Deeply depressed, she thought about what might have been. Forgetting her own ties to Julia Rogers, Mary wrote that if Carey had loved her enough on her 1883 return from abroad, Mary might have been healthy, studied and gotten her degree at Bryn Mawr, and been able to do more good. Carey, in the midst of her own second thoughts, could not really answer her. As she searched for words, Carey recast their relationship. Mary's love of her was "a great misfortune," she judged, as "almost anyone else whom you had loved would have been free to be with you, and you could have had the happy full life you speak of." Mary had chosen to love someone who was not free. Putting a whole new gloss on their affair, Carey now shifted the burden to Mary. In 1893 when Mary had, "in a passion of tears," told Carey that Julia was not her "first interest," Carey was bound to Mamie. "And you know perfectly well that, if I had not loved Mamie so much, I should have and do now and have for a long time loved you so much as to want to be with you all the time. That you are sure of, are you not?" By 1893 Carey was also bound to Bryn Mawr. Recasting her own history, Carey wrote that had Mary made her move earlier, and had Mamie not been intertwined in Carey's life, Carey might have chosen a life with Mary of leisure, travel, and art: "You see, the college was such a lottery, and the conditions were so unfavourable and the

chances so small of making anything but the narrowest sectarian school that
. . . I went there with the utmost reluctance. You had money, and the
temptation to have gone abroad and reveled in everything worthwhile might
have been too great for us to resist."[10]

At this point any effort to reassure Mary was complicated by Carey's own
feelings. She was yearning for the life of art and scholarship that she had given
up. As she daydreamed in Spanish cathedrals, Carey wrote Mary that she felt
"a longing to gather myself together. Ever since you came back—how many,
six years ago?—I think I have rather let things go in order to be with you every
leisure, and before that it was Mother's death and the Medical School, and
before that Bryn Mawr and all the stress of starting it." Alone with Mamie in
Spain (and Mary and Bryn Mawr in the background), Carey was reconnecting
with a part of herself that she had largely lost in the years following her
European sojourn of 1879–83, the life of Carey the lover of Mamie and of
art. It would be the last time.[11]

In the summers that followed, except for an unhappy trip to Paris with
Mamie in 1900, she traveled abroad with Mary. Carey would no longer lose
herself on horseback or in picture galleries. Her trips with Mary were purposeful explorations of architecture, looking for examples to guide new college
buildings, and visits to health spas. Beginning in 1898, Mamie's worst fears
of 1893 were realized, and Mary took Carey away.

During the 1890s relations between Mamie and Mary remained civil but
icy. After the failure of the initial experiment of being with both women
together, Carey took increasing care to keep the two from encountering each
other. Mamie lived at the Deanery during the week. When she returned to
Baltimore to visit her mother, Mary visited. If Mamie's departure from Bryn
Mawr was delayed, Carey sent a flurry of telegrams to Mary so that she
might hold her arrival. If Mamie canceled her weekend in Baltimore, Carey
discouraged Mary from coming to Bryn Mawr. Carey was not straightforward.
She gave another reason, citing Mary's obligation to the friend she was visiting
or raising a fear that Mary's health might be harmed by a quick visit, objections
that were immediately erased if Mamie changed her mind again and departed.

Why did Mamie remain with Carey? Much as Mamie might be enraged
at Mary's hold over Carey, she was still bound to her in many ways. Moreover,
Mamie was in a difficult position. Although she returned to her mother's
house to visit on many weekends and holidays, she needed a home separate
from that of her mother. In the 1890s she could not imagine herself living
alone. Mamie Gwinn was dependent upon Carey Thomas for providing her
with a job at Bryn Mawr and a home at the Deanery. In the second instance,
Mamie was dependent upon Mary. It was Mary Garrett's backing of Carey
Thomas that ultimately secured Mamie Gwinn's position at the college. After

Garrett's gift of $10,000 a year to gain the presidency for Thomas, Gwinn could not legitimately put limits on her coming to Bryn Mawr, the place of her benefaction.

Although it was not a steady downhill slope, relations between Carey and Mamie began to deteriorate in the mid-1890s. Mamie's intense need for privacy and for time alone with Carey were violated by Carey's life as Bryn Mawr's president. In October 1894, Mamie had written an apology to Mary for the ill temper she displayed in her presence: "I was annoyed, for reasons that do not interest you, with Carey, and that annoyance would certainly not have shown itself in public, were there, in Carey's present state of activity, any 'private' and were I not very tired." Again, the note of Mamie's distaste for Carey's public world—her work and increasingly her life. Moreover, Mamie no longer liked Mary, and now she was surrounded by her presence, her wealth, and Carey's unacknowledged special relation to her. Finally, after the death of her father in 1894, Mamie became responsible for her mother's summers. Carey, relying on the long vacation to restore her for the year, refused to share the burden in any way.[12]

In the mid-1890s Mary made the fateful decision to seek a legal division of her father's estate. This meant conflict with her sisters-in-law and, ultimately, a rupture in their relations. Carey encouraged Mary and counseled her on instructions to her attorneys. When Baltimore and Ohio stock plunged, Carey feared that Mary was about to lose her fortune. Carey repeatedly urged her to sell and use the capital to pay what she still owed to Johns Hopkins. She felt Mary was being held captive by her advisers who, because of their own personal stake in the railroad, had a conflict of interest. She nudged Mary, step by step, to allow her access to her records and securities. Always she couched her suggestions in terms of Mary and her needs. For example, in asking Mary for a key to her safety deposit box, she put it this way: "Suppose you ever should wish me, in the dim future, to cut off your coupons?"[13] Any such single question appears innocent of self-interest; the sum of many questions over many years suggests a careful campaign to gain knowledge and influence over Mary's enormous wealth.

Mary Garrett was a careful businesswoman. However she may have characterized herself, she was, in fact, an investor and the manager of her portion of her father's estate. She spent all her mornings and much of the rest of the day in handling her financial affairs. She tried to bring order into those of Carey. By the mid-1890s she took over Carey's accounts, making out the checks and addressing the envelopes.

Carey's indebtedness to Mary increased in the years after 1895. After paying for extensive reconstruction and decoration of the Deanery, in the summer of 1897, Mary moved into the refurbished Deanery and attempted to organize Carey's household and financial records, paying Carey rent for the privilege.

Carey and Mamie were traveling in Spain, and Carey wrote from Grenada, in an anti-Semitic aside, "As Mamie says, I am a Shylock to take rent from so competent and hard worked a housekeeper." In the past Carey had been able to accept Mary's benefactions with a light heart; this time she knew that she had exceeded some sort of limit. "I cannot tell you how much I mind this, even if it is the last time, my darling. I expect in every way to turn over a new leaf when I return, both personally and collegiately."[14]

In fact she did not. On her return she continued to overspend. The enlarged Deanery operated on a grander scale. In addition, Carey spent lavishly on clothes, household furnishings, and food. In a normal season she spent $250 for three garments; a summer bill at a Parisian dressmaker might run over $400. With a clear understanding of Carey's expenses, Mary determined that she needed at least $5,000 in addition to her existing income and agreed to provide it.[15]

At some point Mary decided to make Carey her heir. There is no written statement of her intention, and it may have been part of the commitment that bound her to Carey from January 2, 1893, onward. The first clear reference came almost as an aside. In the fall of 1899 Carey reported to Mary, who was abroad, a local news account regarding a will. "It augurs ill for our carrying out your will without a contest. If a university can be held to exert undue influence, how much more an intimate friend. Clearly, if we have due warning, you will have to give outright any moveable bonds, etc., and let the struggle come on the real estate only."[16]

In the late 1890s Mary and Carey called the Ava apartment in New York "our flat." As Mary furnished it with her favorite possessions, Carey wrote, "Think of all the charming days we may have there and the music and the pictures and the books and the love." Joining her for a weekend, Carey relished their freedom from others and their ability to shape a life of their choosing. Mary arranged for them to see plays and opera, and Carey took special delight in the many productions of Wagner. In January 1899, Carey wrote to Mary, "I feel much refreshed spiritually, if not morally, by my holiday: such glorious music as we heard and how sweet was our flat."[17]

In these years, as Carey became increasingly dependent upon Mary for money and financial management, her love for her grew. By 1899 she was writing to her of the love that she believed could survive the many blows of their complicated lives, ill health, quarrels, and separations. As she returned to America after a summer abroad, leaving Mary in Europe, Carey wrote, "I have been, oh, so blue this voyage. . . . Often waked at five and longed to have you to talk to. . . . Please think all the time you are abroad how dearly I love you and depend on our love for each other. Nothing can make me forget you or love you less unless you cease to want my love, beloved." Mary had expressed some doubt about Carey's love for her. Carey responded that "it makes me feel as if you could not love me as much as you think you do when you doubt it. . . . Among other blue things I have wondered whether your being less demonstrative means any difference in your sureness."[18]

Carey and Mary had grown physically more intimate. Though specific evidence is fragmentary, Carey's letters to Mary make clear that the two embraced, sat cheek to cheek, and kissed on the lips. In the late 1890s Carey and Mary shared a bed in the Deanery at times and a bedroom in Mary's apartment. After she had returned to the Deanery, Carey wrote to her that she was reading her letters in bed with the Deanery cat "in your place, the place where you said you should like to be." Aroused by her aesthetic passions, Carey lived in a romantic and erotic universe that a letter to Mary, written during a New York visit in the same period, captures: "It seems as strange, as always, to be here without the joy of arriving at your flat and you. Ah, if we could have some champagne and sandwiches and a talk in our pretty bedroom under the Rossetti and the Ariadne!"[19]

II

IN THE mid-1890s, as the sands of her relations with Mary and Mamie shifted under her feet, Carey found a literature that offered her a new understanding of herself and her emotions. It began with a challenge to her aesthetic gods. As one of "nous autres" she had reveled in the paintings and poetry of the Pre-Raphaelites and their followers. In the spring of 1895, Carey read *Degeneration* by Max Nordau, a German work newly translated into English. It filled her with "unspeakable disgust," because of its denigration of Dante Gabriel Rossetti, one of her favorite artists and poets. Nordau's book indicted all of Carey Thomas' aesthetic passions—Swinburne, Wilde, Wagner, as well as the Pre-Raphaelites—and argued that such "degenerate" artists appealed to sexual psychopaths. Nordau noted the contemporary literature of sexual eroticism and perversion, including the work of Richard von Krafft-Ebing. Carey wrote Mary that Nordau's book had its uses, for its references gave "the names of many new books for us to read."[20]

The year 1895 was an important historical moment. In England, Oscar Wilde was on trial for homosexuality. Beginning in her years abroad, Carey had read Wilde, regarding him as a lesser literary descendant of Rossetti and Swinburne. She followed the Wilde trial closely, and her letters expressed sympathy for him. In April she clipped and sent to Mary an article on the creation in England of a moral vigilance committee against homosexuality, or, as the piece put it, "to combat a strange, unspeakable vice." In late May she had noted, "Oscar Wilde and Lord Alfred [Douglas] are clear and it is most clever. I have hopes he will get off."[21]

In the summer of 1895, as Carey traveled abroad with Mamie, there was much gossip about Wilde in the household of Hannah Smith. Hannah had always meant a great deal to Carey, but the meaning changed as both aunt and niece went through metamorphoses. Hannah was now living in England, the matriarch of three interesting adult children who were making their way in Europe's intellectual and aesthetic world. Mary Smith Costelloe had left her husband and children to live and work with Bernard Berenson in Italy; Alys Smith had married Bertrand Russell, the future philosopher and mathematician; and Logan Pearsall Smith had just published his first book. In 1895 Hannah herself was part of the distinctive world of upper-class English reform of Lady Henry Somerset, then linked by love and philanthropic support to the American Frances Willard, president of the Women's Christian Temperance Union.[22]

In late July, Carey reported to Mary the information about Oscar Wilde that she had gleaned from Hannah. "Oscar Wilde was notorious . . . everybody knew he took boys with him wherever he went." All the guests at Lady Henry's "knew he had a boy in the village." When he visited Oxford he was "surrounded by adoring men to such an extent that if it had been possible the authorities would have forbidden his going." Carey added that Hannah told her that the kind of relations between men of which Wilde was charged was "absolutely prevalent throughout England" and that a friend had told her that her brother "was so bothered by men offering themselves to him, that he often used to beg her to come with him to protect him."

Comments about Wilde were surrounded in Carey's letters by news of her visit to Lady Henry Somerset. Before going abroad Carey had written to Mary about Lady Henry and Frances Willard, calling them "our lovers" and suggesting to Mary that she invite the two of them to her Baltimore house. Carey thought that she and Mary would enjoy a visit with them unencumbered by others. As she put it, "We will have them to ourselves. They are great fun." When Carey visited Lady Henry in 1895, Frances Willard was absent, and Lady Henry seemed to want to make a play for her. Carey wrote to Mary, "If Mamie had not been there, I really do believe Lady Henry would have been demonstrative. She took my hand repeatedly, etc. She seems to me quite capable of it—a downright flirtation." Carey enjoyed this and linked Lady Henry to two women with whom she had once contemplated intimate relationships. Lady Henry was "certainly *very* nice and romantic looking. . . . Next to Miss [Agnes] Irwin I like her better than anyone I have seen since Gertrude." In 1895, as in 1875, Carey enjoyed both attracting the attentions of one woman and evoking jealousy in another. Her words, framing the gossip she relayed about Oscar Wilde, suggest that she saw some relation between Lady Henry and Wilde and yet categorized them differently.[23]

Later in the summer, Carey reported to Mary that she was sending her the book *Onanism*, purchased in Paris. This work by M. Tissot, originally published in 1766 and reprinted throughout the nineteenth century, is primarily a moralistic treatment of masturbation, but also deals with homosexuality. In its abbreviated consideration of masturbation among women, it discusses a woman's "clitorical" masturbation with another woman in simulation of sexual intercourse, "the known origin of which is to be traced so far back as the time of the second Sappho." Tissot found this a common practice in his day. He concludes, "Women have been known to love girls with as much fondness as ever did the most passionate of men, and conceive the most poignant jealousy, when they were addressed by the male sex upon the score of love." Carey wrote to Mary that *Onanism* "solves all questions raised by French novels *and all others.* I think I shall mail it to you as I do not care to bring it through the custom house." One recalls that French novels Carey had read included such works as Théophile Gautier's *Mademoiselle de Maupin*, with its depictions of women's erotic arousal of each other. Although few titles of books that she read in the 1890s are available, Carey did continue to read depictions of woman-to-woman love.[24]

Such fragments give tantalizing glimpses into Carey Thomas' mind at this critical juncture in her life. Up to the mid-1890s Carey belonged to an intervening era. In her mother's generation, women loved women in the model of sentimental friendship. By 1880 Carey had come to understand herself, by contrast, as one of the band of rare spirits capable of intense and passionate feeling. She and Mamie were among "nous autres." As she read Swinburne, looked at the paintings of Rossetti, listened to the operas of Wagner, and dreamed of the "passionate land," art and love for another woman were fused. Female emotional bonds were forged and strengthened in shared aesthetic appreciation.

As the youthful Carey experienced passionate feelings toward Mamie and Mary, she interpreted them as full of "rapture and fire," as in the Pre-Raphaelite poems she loved. She assumed, however, that this passion was not sexual in nature because its objects were women. In her mind her intense feelings had no connection to the realm of the sexual, which was reserved for men's lust and women's response to it.[25] Beginning in 1895 she learned of a new interpretation of her feelings and her nature. At least as early as the Wilde trial, Carey was exposed to discussion of homosexuality. Nordau linked sexual perversion to the art and poetry that she admired. Tissot gave examples of woman-to-woman sexual behavior.

Probably at this point Carey Thomas became curious about the emerging literature on homosexuality in women. In her files are note cards with reading lists. Although there is no way to determine when she took the notes, the writing has the density of her hand in the late nineteenth century, not its looseness in the twentieth. Several cards are labeled "Lesbianism," and one is entitled "Books on Sapphism." Most of the works listed are from the 1880s, including the third edition of Krafft-Ebing's *Psychopathia Sexualis*, published in 1888 in German. Though she may not have read the third edition, she did read Krafft-Ebing's book, because in two cases she cites sources from it. One card contains Krafft-Ebing's list of novels depicting lesbianism (he includes *Mademoiselle de Maupin*). Another card, prefaced by "Authorities given in Dr. R. v. Krafft-Ebing, *Psychopathia Sexualis*, p. 272," illuminates Carey's woman-centered perspective in thinking of same-sex love, for it is curiously mislabeled "Lesbianism *In Men*."[26]

The 1888, third edition of *Psychopathia Sexualis* contains discussion of homosexuality in women, although not the lengthy section of the better-known 1906 edition translated into English. This work by a professor of psychiatry at the University of Graz is an effort to ground emotions and sexuality in late-nineteenth-century science. The author states that in women, as in men, same-sex love is a perversion. Its cause is not to be found in the contours of physical organs, but "as with all sick perversions of sexuality, the cause must be looked for in the brain." In attempting to understand what he alternatively calls urning, amor lesbicus, or sexual inversion among women, the author states that although, due to female reticence, little is known, he believes the phenomenon "is not rare." Lack of knowledge did not limit assertions, some of which would have been of interest to Carey Thomas.[27]

As an admirer of Sarah Bernhardt and the paintings of Rossetti, Carey must have been struck by Krafft-Ebing's list of the characteristics of the "woman-loving woman": not only does she wish to dress and act as a man, her interest in the theater is excited by female artists, and in art "only female statues and pictures awaken her aesthetic sense and sensuality." In the third edition Krafft-Ebing narrates only two case studies, but, as in the 1906 edition that contains many more, these are explicit and highly charged. In the case of Mrs. R, a woman of thirty-five, he describes her affair at age twenty-eight with a woman four years younger: "The love was a very sensual one and was satisfied by mutual masturbation." In the case of Mrs. C, "particular indications" argued for a similar method of sexual satisfaction.[28]

In M. Carey Thomas' papers is a tantalizing fragment of a letter from Dr. Emma Culbertson, the doctor studying in Zürich whose "Boston marriage" with Dr. Smith gave Carey an important model. The date has been removed from the first page of the letter but internal references suggest that it was written around 1902. Culbertson was answering Thomas' query: "In regard to the subject of your second note, there does undoubtedly exist a form of reciprocal masturbation between women." Culbertson wrote that "the *unnamed* practice about which you inquire has never been confessed to me," but that she had read about the subject in an article in a medical journal published six or eight years before and had learned of its physical signs. She continued, "It is undoubtedly pernicious for both mind and body; not more so perhaps than unlicensed intercourse between the sexes, but worse than ordinary marital relations where no effort is made to prevent conception." Culbertson knew that masturbation was practiced by school teachers and was "apt to produce nervous prostration." She had found it could be cured "by a plain warning of the results and hygienic rules." She added, "I hope that college life will not tend to develop any such features!" She then sent the regards of her and Dr. Smith to Carey Thomas and Mamie Gwinn and the wish to see them. Late in her life, at a time when she was self-consciously reimagining herself for her autobiography, Thomas put the letter in her files and labeled it "Dr. Culbertson" and "Masturbation." Carey Thomas' reading of *Onanism* and her notes to *Psychopathia Sexualis* clarify, however, that she knew more than her question to Emma Culbertson suggests.[29]

Knowledge that Carey Thomas had information about the physiology of mutual masturbation is significant for understanding her thought, but its meaning for her sexual practice is less clear. Although some elements of her behavior can be known, not all is disclosed. The many hundreds of thousands of pages that Carey Thomas wittingly or unwittingly left for posterity contain no clear, unambiguous statement revealing that her physical expressions of lovemaking with Mary (or with Mamie) included genital contact. Absence of evidence, however, proves nothing at all. Testimony to the most private pleasures of lovemaking does not usually rest in archives.[30]

What is known is that beginning in 1893 Carey and Mary kissed passionately. Over the course of the decade, as Mary gave Carey money directly and indirectly, their physical intimacy grew. Mary took an apartment in New York, and the two frequently shared a bed. Beginning in 1895 Carey read about homosexuality among women. Texts linked the pleasures that she enjoyed in the theater and opera, the emotions toward women that she had long felt, and physical love-making. Tissot and Krafft-Ebing told her that she was not merely one of "nous autres," a passionate being enthralled by the poetry of Swinburne and the paintings of Rossetti. *Onanism* and *Psychopathia Sexualis* told her that passion was sex and that she was lesbian.

Did Carey Thomas' reading change her consciousness? Did it give a new language for her experience? Coming as it did at a point of increasing physical closeness in her relationship with Mary, did it offer a new explanation for her feelings? Questions are easier to raise than to answer. A critical part of Carey Thomas' identity was forged in an earlier era; by the time the new knowledge about homosexuality became available to her, she was approaching forty. She retained a sense of self nurtured in Pre-Raphaelite aestheticism.

Yet there is a tantalizing scrap of evidence that suggests that by the end of the 1890s Carey Thomas began to absorb some elements of the new understanding of sexuality. Carey's many passionate expressions of devotion to Mary, her "Beloved," frame a letter of January 1899. Carey relayed to Mary an "unsuitable" dream that had been induced by taking nitroglycerine: "Last night I was receiving far too many and much too impassioned kisses from Mildred Minturn [a young woman who had been a student at Bryn Mawr] and rather enjoying them in a passive way, and looking down from the beautiful Monaco terrace into the blue depths I saw Harvard student after Harvard student flash through the water with beautiful white bodies like Greek heroes. As I only saw them dive from behind, I do not know whether they had fig leaves or not."[31]

The dream provides a graphic moment when the elements that composed Carey's aesthetic and erotic sensibilities in the late 1890s are fused: the kisses of a woman, Europe, the backs of Greek statues (or the figures on vases) come to life as Harvard students. The troublesome element to Carey, what made the dream "unsuitable," was the intrusion of nude men. Given her love of antiquity and her appreciation of Sappho, the appearance of the young men who appeared "like Greek heroes" may have been linked through the late-nineteenth-century euphemism "Greek love" to male homosexuality. With the 1899 telling of this dream comes additional confirmation of Carey's letters from the winter of 1892–93, writing to Mary of their kisses. Carey wrote with the clear expectation that Mary understood "impassioned kisses" enjoyed from a woman: it formed part of their shared experience. Although Carey may have continued to interpret her love for Mary and Mamie partially through the prism of Pre-Raphaelite aestheticism, this intriguing glimpse into Carey's psyche reveals that at some level she now knew that her feelings included sexual love.

For Carey Thomas, gaining a new understanding of what it meant to love women only affirmed her life and choices. She had long loved Mamie. In Mary she found a love that was fully requited and forged in bonds of aesthetic communion, mutual savoring of power, economic dependency, and physical expression. It was a love that felt as solid and enduring as Mary herself. There is no evidence that Carey absorbed from writers such as Krafft-Ebing any negative portrayal of women-loving women.[32] In the late 1890s Carey Thomas accepted herself and her passions completely. In her letters and journals there is not a single expression of guilt or unease about her love of women. Though she worried constantly about discovery, her anxiety was never about disclosure of the nature of her relationships. She feared that if her letters got into the wrong hands, they might betray her atheism or aestheticism to college trustees. Both before and after she learned about female sexuality and lesbianism, Carey Thomas believed her attachments to Mamie and Mary were right and fitting, that love of a woman for a woman was better than any love for a man.[33]

III

As CAREY had drawn closer to Mary, Mamie Gwinn was left to confront her own life. In 1895, at age thirty-four, her life and interests were to change as dramatically as Carey's. An associate professor of English, Gwinn had made no college friends. On her weekends in Baltimore she had her mother's company and that of her childhood friend Nancy Howard. Though to the outside Gwinn's life seemed independent, she felt intensely isolated.

In February 1895, Carey Thomas interviewed a candidate for the position in English literature who utterly charmed her—Alfred Hodder. By all accounts, he was a stunning man. The author Hutchins Hapgood wrote that, when they were first introduced at Harvard, Hodder appeared to him "like a young god." It was not just that Hodder was exceedingly handsome. As Hapgood put it, "He had the laughing insolence of the conscious intellect. . . . Indeed, there was something Byronic about him." At twenty-nine, Hodder had all the qualities that Thomas desired: he had studied in Berlin; knew Greek, Latin, French, Italian, and Spanish; and was a philosophy graduate student at Harvard. William James and Josiah Royce recommended him highly. Thomas expressed her delight to Mary, "He is a gentleman down to the ground, and more attractive personally, I think, than any other member of the Faculty." After his appointment went through the board of trustees, Thomas learned that Harvard had rejected his dissertation, delaying his degree, but this did not change her view of him.[34]

Hodder arrived on campus in fall 1895 without his wife, Jessie, who came in November. As the term began, he attended Gwinn's first lecture and admired it. President Thomas welcomed the new faculty member at the Deanery with luncheons and dinners. She had him over in mid-October, and noted to Mary, "He talked very well and is very brilliant but never shall we keep Pegasus in harness for long." A week later she included him in a dinner for ten. In early November, in the midst of a rush of work, she allowed the unthinkable: "Hodder to dinner uninvited when I got back." Later in November when Mamie was ill and Carey had to go to Philadelphia for the afternoon, Alfred came to lunch and read a new philosophical article to Mamie.[35]

Although guarded in her letters to Mary about Mamie's involvement with Alfred Hodder, Carey was alarmed. In this central drama in her life, lasting over a decade, many elements were fused. One was that Alfred posed a threat as a person who shared Mamie's (and therefore Carey's) secrets. As Mamie clarified in a late November letter to Carey, Alfred was a thoroughly modern man who spoke flippantly about controversial Bryn Mawr subjects—"self government, and cigarettes, etc."—in keeping with his "general Harvard frivolous manner." If he knew about Carey's disbelief and aestheticism, he might reveal it.

Immediately before Thanksgiving 1895 Carey insisted that Mamie stop seeing Alfred Hodder and threatened to fire him if she refused to comply. The two fought before Mamie boarded the train for Baltimore. From her Baltimore home, the day after Thanksgiving, Mamie wrote that what Carey had feared had happened: "The milk is absolutely spilt. . . . I have since talked to Mr. Hodder about every subject under heaven—life and death and immortality and all the rest of it." In all her years at Bryn Mawr, Mamie had been prudent and discreet. She had seen herself in a position "a little like the wife of the President of the United States. . . . There has been a wall around you and me" that barred her from friendship with other members of the faculty or Bryn Mawr neighbors. Alfred was now "within that wall." He was the only person Mamie had met since Gertrude Mead who was a person like the two of them, sharing their interests and their tastes. "He is exactly one of the people that I for one have been looking for for all these years."

It was too late to suggest that Mamie not become Alfred's friend. "As regards the cordiality of my relations with Mr. Hodder, the milk is spilt. I never dreamed that I hadn't any friendship to bestow, and we are really old and fast friends." Mamie absolutely refused to break relations with him. "I shall never change my manner to him, or give him in any sense the cold shoulder, or lay myself open to the charge of indifference or of a sort of odious flirting with him, without telling him that it is a case of force majeure." She would continue to talk with him at parties. Her talking to him was less conspicuous than what she called her "old conspicuous isolation, and poodle-like edging" after Carey. In others' houses, she would only talk to him half an evening, for there they were in "enemies' land": "But in the Deanery, in my own house . . . the only enemy is you, and such a position taken on your part I should be bitterly ashamed. It would spoil my love for you, it would spoil my pride in you."

Carey Thomas threatened to dismiss Hodder. If Carey did so, Mamie would regard it as "the sharpest sort of lash in the face." Its only ground would be "his friendship" with her. Mamie reflected, "It would indeed be a lesson as to my share in *our* college, as well as in *our* house." If there were a choice between the two of them, Hodder must stay at Bryn Mawr. He was poor and had a family to support. If Alfred Hodder were forced out of Bryn Mawr, Mamie would resign. Mamie called Carey's bluff: "If I am to go, say so: and if not, let us hear of this no more."

Mamie wanted Carey to accept her new friendship and to extend herself to Jessie and invite them to luncheon. Mamie should have a dinner for Jessie and invite Carey's brother Bond and his wife Edith Carpenter, now making a name as an author and dramatist. Though Mamie hoped to be friends with Jessie, she insisted that her friendship with Alfred not be limited to times in which he was with Jessie. It was a question of trust: "I should like to be at least as proud and confident in my relations to you, and as visibly happy in them, as he is in his to Jessie."

Because her relations with Alfred Hodder were "intimate as distinguished from pleasant, . . . if they ceased to be intimate they certainly could not be pleasant." Mamie argued that the real issue was that someone other than Carey was close to her: "The complication has arrived in our life, if it be a complication that I, actually, have a friend; and that that friend knows something about me." Although she understood that their position had prevented her from "finding the pleasure that might be found in intelligent general society and in intelligent chance conversation: I did not understand that it precluded us from ever again in the world finding a friend." Living at some remove, Alfred was a good risk for a friend. And since he now knew everything it would be better to keep him one. Mamie added, "I should think that you would be rejoiced at my having a friend: and that your one instinct would be to say to Mr. Hodder (initially) 'How nice in you that you should have found her out! So few people do ever find her out!' " Mamie hoped that Carey would become his friend, that there would be a "joint friendship all round." Mamie's letter, as all her writing, was clever in what it revealed and in what it left out. Carey knew almost from the outset that more than friendship was at work.[36]

Carey did invite Jessie Hodder to luncheon. As she explained to Mary, "Now I have done my duty." She hoped that Mamie would not keep up the friendship with Jessie and Alfred for long. "However, if it amuses her, and she really sees no one and I suppose it is not to be wondered at, I will try to endure their being here enough to carry it off. Once every few weeks I can stand." Within a week, she had the dinner that Mamie had demanded, inviting the author Agnes Reppelier, Bond, and Edith. This time the Hodders truly offended Carey, by presuming to be her social equals. Carey had been in a frenzy of work and was exhausted. She had left the writing of the President's Report to the last moment and had to stay up very late to compose it; at the final minute, she was reading the printer's proof. As she left Bryn Mawr, she knew that Mamie was in the company of Bond and Edith. She reported to Mary, "Well, the Hodders are born to make trouble." On Saturday they called on Mamie, Edith, and Bond. Edith "took a violent fancy to them," and returned the call the next day, "and what did they do but go down with her to the ferry and over to Camden, and she invited them to visit Bond and herself in Millville." Carey had clearly never intended this, that one of the members of her faculty should insinuate himself into her own extended family.[37]

She wrote philosophically to Mary, "It has got to be stood and so long as Hodder and *his wife* are in question I cannot object." There was some relief that Alfred was now accompanied. Since her arrival four weeks before, he always brought Jessie when he came to call on Mamie, and Jessie had "decided to spend the winter, not to leave him again." Carey got an inkling that Alfred was of questionable morality when Bond told her that he was a good friend of Bernard Berenson and fully approved of Berenson's scandalous liaison with her cousin Mary Smith Costelloe. Although Thomas had to call in Hodder to insist that he require reading of his students, she remained satisfied with his work. Ironically, $500 of his salary came from Mary Garrett's $10,000 annual gift.[38]

In February Carey and Mamie went to dinner at the house of Lindley Miller Keasbey, a Bryn Mawr professor. Among the guests were Dickinson Miller, an associate in philosophy, and Alfred and Jessie Hodder. It was a festive evening, a gathering of young, interesting faculty who talked well and enjoyed the pleasures of the table. Carey reported to Mary, "all kinds of wines, cocktails before dinner and mint cordial afterwards flowed gaily." Carey saw that Miller, the Hodders, and the Keasbeys were good friends. She also observed, but did not report at the time, that Mamie was trying to take Alfred away from Jessie.[39]

Students saw what was happening as well. In *Fernhurst*, Gertrude Stein's fictional portrayal of the Carey-Mamie-Alfred triangle, the author conveyed what students perceived, understood, and misunderstood. Stein's representation of Carey as Dean Helen Thornton is hostile, but Mamie is portrayed sympathetically as Janet Bruce. She is the Mamie Gwinn that students knew and admired. Tall, her wavy hair tinged with gray, the brilliant and elusive, innocent and regardless Miss Bruce is above all detached from human contact. Stein explains that it is "not because she loved best dreams and abstract thought, for her deepest interest was in the varieties of human experience and her constant desire was to partake of all human relations but by some quality of her nature she never succeeded in really touching any human creature she knew." Miss Bruce did not want to avoid life; "her desire was to experience the extreme forms of sensuous life and to make even immoral experience her own. . . . A passionate desire for worldly experience filled her entirely and she was still waiting for the hand that could tear down the walls that enclosed her and let her escape into a world of humans." It is this woman that Alfred Hodder, as the fictional Philip Redfern, meets and admires. Miss Bruce's emerging feeling about him is transparent to all but the dean. Stein chronicles, "It was interesting to see what every one but the Dean did see the slow growth of interest to admiration and to love in this awkward reserved woman, unconscious of her meanings and oblivious of the world's eyes, and who made no attempt to disguise or conceal the strength of her feeling. Many students long remembered her as she then appeared slowly sinking from the clouds to the earth under the influence of the brilliant Redfern, her eyes following him first with interest, then admiration, then love, her body slowing filling with yearning and desire, her shy awkward manner making apparent to all what she never thought to conceal."[40]

Students could see Mamie falling in love, but they did not know what Carey knew. Nor could they have any understanding of what Mamie's new feelings might mean to Carey Thomas. At its simplest, in her pursuit of Alfred Hodder, Mamie was challenging the structure of Carey's life. To lose Mamie was to lose her hold on her past and the aesthetic dreams that it contained. To lose her to a man was to challenge the basis of their friendship. As much as she loved Mary, to be left alone with her was to be left alone with Bryn Mawr: work, conflict, and no escape.

CHAPTER 16

A Great Blank Where
There Used to Be Certainty

BY 1896, Carey Thomas was in crisis. As Mary generously showered gifts
on her and Bryn Mawr, Carey felt a new level of passion. She read texts
that suggested that women and men had similar sexual drives and that the
basis of a woman's love for another woman was sexual. Mamie was throwing
herself at a married man. Then came a series of shocks. In the summer of
1896, Carey had surgery. Mamie demanded recognition for their collaborative
work. Scandal threatened as family members proved unruly. And the deaths
of male mentors left Carey free and exposed. In midlife Carey Thomas was
battered by multiple blows. How she refashioned herself in their wake set her
on her ultimate life's course.

I

ON MAY 11, 1896, Carey required surgery. She had experienced some sharp
pain that turned out to be a rapidly growing though benign tumor. Dr. Howard
A. Kelly, professor of gynecology and obstetrics at the Johns Hopkins University
School of Medicine, performed the surgery in his private clinic in Baltimore.
Later letters clarify that because the operation ended menstruation but not
other periodic indications that Carey was "unwell"—headache and fever blis-
ter—she underwent a partial hysterectomy that removed her uterus but left
her ovaries.

Carey was insistent that no one know why she was indisposed. Not realizing
the need of a college head to keep surgery to remove a female organ secret,
her brother Harry was amused by her elaborate efforts at disguise. As he wrote
to his father, James Thomas, traveling abroad for the summer, "Carey goes
under the name of Miss Martha Carey, Miss Garrett is Miss Grey, and Miss
Gwinn delights in a name which I never can remember. . . . Miss Grey . . .
is constantly having things sent to her here [at Harry and Zoe Thomas' house]

which we have to surreptitiously pass on to the Sanatorium." A week after surgery, he reported to his father that Carey was finding it hard to keep from working. "I believe it will not be many days before she is attending to the affairs of the nation." He told of Mary's attentiveness. Following Carey's instructions she had cut nightgowns off a few inches below the top of the sheet and sewed them with ribbons. She brought to the sanatorium her silver service and her watercolor by Dante Gabriel Rossetti, *Mary in the House of St. John.*[1]

Helen Thomas described to her father the luxury with which Mary surrounded Carey. Carey lay in an Indian bed covered in richly dyed cashmere shawls and drank out of a golden china cup. Helen was a friend and admirer of Mamie; thus her comments about Mary are telling: "Miss Garrett I am trying to get up an affection for, so I will only tell thee of her extreme kindness and devotion to Carey, of her patience in performing the most humble service, and we'll pass by her lack of charm which seems to me so absolute, especially in contrast to Carey's vivacity."[2]

In the long convalescence that followed, Carey was painfully ill with a bladder infection caused by a carelessly applied catheter. She had planned to go abroad with Mamie (and to have Mary also in Europe) but surgery forced the cancellation of these plans, and Carey spent the summer in Montauk, Long Island, nursed by Mary. Her recovery was further hampered by a burn brought on by applying pure carbolic acid rather than a 2 percent solution. Although Carey did not know it, during her recuperation Mamie began a correspondence with Alfred Hodder.

In planning her return to Bryn Mawr, Carey Thomas made careful preparation to cover up the continuing signs of surgery. Her Bryn Mawr doctor had reported that she had left in the spring because of a cold and rheumatism. Owing to the inflammation of the bladder that had followed surgery, she was not to walk the stairs in Taylor Hall. The doctor suggested that she put her foot in a splint and use that as her excuse. She continued to feel wretched. She now weighed 156 pounds, twenty more than she felt right for her 5-foot-4½-inch frame. She was taking many medications that caused uncomfortable side effects: arsenic, for example, brought on double vision. Bladder pain kept her from walking. Later when she resumed exercise, her added pounds felt like "a leaden weight."[3]

Mary's care bound them closer together. Carey's mother had given herself over to nurse her after the burn. The adult Carey now had Mary's comfort. Over and over again in the years that followed, Carey recalled what Mary had done and how it had made Carey love her even more. Three years later, writing to Mary in her Baltimore house, Carey remembered the surgery and its aftermath and their increased intimacy: "Goodnight, beloved. Je t'aime. Don't get blue in the room we have been in so often since the 11th of May '96."[4]

Mamie's presence, however, remained central to Carey. Mary brought to her relationship with Carey her immense wealth. Mamie brought her intense learning. In the years that Carey was frenetically busy first as dean and then as president, she was also teaching undergraduates and graduate students. Mamie was her first English doctoral student. They worked closely together, more closely than Carey was willing to admit.

In the summer of 1896 as Carey Thomas was convalescing, Mamie Gwinn prepared to teach the English literature courses that Thomas had given. Since the opening of Bryn Mawr, Thomas had taught the two-year lecture course surveying Western literature that was required of all students. It was the basis of her hold over the first generation of Bryn Mawr students. Gwinn sought from Thomas public acknowledgment that Carey Thomas' Bryn Mawr lectures in English literature were a collaborative work and had been for eleven years. Gwinn wanted it clear that she was not simply giving lectures written by Thomas, that the lectures had been written by the two of them.

Carey Thomas replied, "I have thought over my lectures in my paroxysmal hours," the distress caused both by surgery and by concern over college finances. "I am not willing to say that we worked over them together, as I have been giving them as mine for eleven years, and it will surely be misunderstood." Gwinn would soon embellish the lectures with her "purple patches" that will make them "much nicer than they ever were, and that will be bad enough." Thomas insisted that Gwinn say nothing: "Remember the fact that you helped me out is a secret that must be kept—entends-tu—faithfully." Thomas explained that she feared that if students knew about Gwinn's help in one course, they would assume her hand in all her courses "and we could never explain." What Thomas wanted Gwinn to say was that she "had undertaken to give the lectures on the same general lines." Gradually Gwinn could then "change them out of all recognition."[5]

This letter makes comprehensible what had been bewildering. The lectures themselves are unlike any of M. Carey Thomas' published writings. All her other writing—her annual reports, lectures to a public audience, and commissioned articles—were composed with great anguish, but her letters record little strain in writing the college lectures. An 1892 typescript of the lectures exists. The lectures roam far and wide and bring in contemporary references. Rossetti informs the presentation of Dante. As the lecturer ranges with authority over a large number of subjects, the words flow. The language bears no resemblance to Thomas' published writing, which, at its best, is straightforward, witty, and hard-hitting.

For example, the discussion of French poetry in the lectures treats the difference between poetry, prose, and poetic prose. It suggests that in poetic prose there was a "kind of vibration caused by the unintermittant succession of pregnant thought and phrase." Praise for La Pléiade, French poets of the sixteenth century, takes this form: it was La Pléiade that demanded "that poetry should have this richness in the thought and rhythm of its separate lines: and their verse vibrates. They created for French literature the splendid Alexandrine, which is as our blank verse and heroic verse in one."[6]

One possible theory that explains the difference between the lectures and Thomas' other writing is that teaching provided a bridge to span her dedication to Bryn Mawr and the world of culture. The lectures to undergraduates were a way that she expressed publicly some of her life passions. Italian and French literature and the poetry of nineteenth-century English Romantics gave her a chance to bring her disparate worlds together. In the classroom at Bryn Mawr, she could be Carey Thomas the lover of art. At one level, this is true.

Only to it must be added that in the classroom, Carey Thomas was, at least at times, the speaker of Mamie Gwinn's words. The boundaries between them were blurred. In the life Carey Thomas shared with Mamie Gwinn, art and love were fused. The stuff of the lectures was the stuff of their relationship. In 1884, it was Mamie Gwinn who suggested that they combine their notes and who offered help with Carey Thomas' writing as a way of keeping them "en rapport." Gwinn became her graduate student. It was natural for her to help Thomas, who was so rushed. When Thomas was giving the lectures, it may not have been clear to her where her prose ended and Gwinn's began.[7]

But it is clear in the historical record. The word "vibrate" is a key: the lectures are in the language of the Swinburne essay, written at least in part by Gwinn, not in the language of Thomas' unassisted *Sir Gawayne and the Green Knight*. Nowhere in Thomas' unaided academic writing does any form of the word "vibrate" occur.

And it was clear to Mamie. Carey's refusal to give public recognition of her work was a shattering moment in their relationship. In 1900, when Mamie drafted a will, she left to Carey all her possessions in the Deanery, with the exception of some jewelry to a close friend and all her "manuscript lectures and notes for lectures" for her college courses. In 1907, during their final rupture, as she wrote to Carey her side of their story, she included this accusation: "You left unacknowledged all my share in the executive labour of making the college as you left unacknowledged all my share in the English lectures of the college not actually delivered by me." In 1897 Thomas had overseen Gwinn's full professorship as it was approved by the trustees; but Gwinn conveyed to Lucy Donnelly a larger, unfulfilled expectation, that in return for her work for Thomas, she was to have been given the position of dean.[8]

To know that Carey Thomas' lectures were written with Mamie Gwinn and contained Gwinn's words and that Thomas refused to acknowledge the collaboration is particularly troubling. It was Thomas' lectures above all that established her reputation at Bryn Mawr as an intellectual presence. Gwinn had her way in one regard. She withdrew from the survey. In 1896–97 Abby Kirk, a reader, delivered the lectures. In ensuing years new members of the department were hired to give the course. Perhaps it is fitting that Mamie Gwinn's courses on Ruskin, Arnold, Pater, and Swinburne came to set the tone for the college. A few years later, when Gertrude Stein characterized a faculty reception at Bryn Mawr as imagined at second hand by students, it seems all Mamie Gwinn: the professors "moved about drinking tea, making epigrams, talking of college matters, and analysing Swinburne, Oscar Wilde and Henry James."[9]

Mamie kept Carey's secret during the years of her presidency, but from 1896 onward, Carey must have feared that Mamie might unmask her.[10] As Carey returned to Bryn Mawr in the fall of 1896, threats of exposure met her at every turn.

II

CAREY THOMAS' family had been her mainstay. Respected, upright, and powerful, James and Mary Thomas, Hannah Smith, James Whitall, and Francis King had buttressed her. Now a danger appeared from within the Thomas family. Thomas Worthington divorced her sister Grace. Not only was divorce itself a scandal among Orthodox Quakers, the particular issues in this divorce threatened to reveal Carey Thomas' views to the world.

Although Grace had attended Bryn Mawr, she was not won over to art or scholarship. Grace married Tom Worthington and had three children. In October 1896 Grace told the Thomas family that Tom had divorced her. Three years earlier the two had "signed a paper stating that they had determined to live together as brother and sister for three years." Tom could no longer accept the terms of a continent marriage and sought a divorce on the grounds that Grace's denial of sexual intercourse constituted legal desertion. Grace wanted the divorce to be amicable and assisted Tom during the trial that took place in Hagerstown, Maryland. She hoped that by granting Tom a divorce he would come to love her and want to return. Although the divorce was granted, during a thirty-day period the decision could be challenged. Carey believed that Grace was being deceived and had one of Mary Garrett's employees get a copy of the divorce decree and investigate Tom. Carey suspected that he was involved with another woman, a nurse named Miss Higby who had taken care of him when he had scarlet fever. Carey was distressed that Grace did not seek an adequate financial settlement from Tom. Under the divorce, she got custody of the children and a monthly alimony payment of two hundred dollars.[11]

As the details of the divorce became known, Carey received some alarming information. At the trial Carey's brother Bond testified that before her marriage to Tom, Grace "was brought into contact with women who held peculiar views in regard to marriage, and that she frequently heard these views expressed." When asked to state these views, Bond answered, "These women believe that ordinarily marriage is a great disadvantage to a woman, that it interferes with her career. Some of them believe that ordinary sexual relations are wrong. Some believe that it [is] degrading, many of them believe that marriage would not hurt a woman if she did not have to have children, and advocate a platonic relation between husband and wife." Edith Carpenter supported Bond's statements. Carey learned all of this from her father, who quoted to her from the typewritten record. James Thomas attempted to reassure Carey that she was not named in the trial and that Grace knew many young women with these views. However, because Grace had attended Bryn Mawr, James Thomas knew that were the trial publicized, the college and its president would be implicated. Most immediately, he feared that Carey Thomas would be criticized by the Bryn Mawr trustees.[12]

Carey sensed danger and knew that she must protect herself and the college even if it required that she disguise her convictions. She wrote Mary that although, following Tom's instructions, her sister had stated these views at the trial, Grace did not hold them, for "she said the other day that one of the greatest griefs of the whole matter was that she could never have another baby." Working with Mary to help silence rumors, Carey labeled the views that Bond had summarized as "preposterous." In addition, she wrote to Judge William Fisher, Garrett's attorney and the person who had actually retrieved the court documents for the family. Carey stated that Tom had dictated to Grace what she, Bond, and Edith were to say in the trial. Then Carey added, "I fancy it is scarcely necessary to say to you that so far from inculcating what Mr. Worthington calls the 'degradating doctrine' I never even heard of it till I saw what you found out in regard to the evidence. It seems to me too evil and wicked for words and I fully agree with General Douglas in thinking that any one who held such a view would be unworthy of any confidence." She asked Judge Fisher to deny "that I hold it or indeed any other view Mr. Worthington says I hold."[13]

The divorce was made final, Grace went to live in England with her children, and Tom married Miss Higby. Carey's efforts to obtain documents and to learn of Tom's affair deeply offended Grace. Statements made at the trial by Bond and Edith did not become public, and Carey and Bryn Mawr were spared. But not for long.

Immediately following the divorce, Carey welcomed Bertrand and Alys Russell for an extended visit. Alys was her first cousin, Hannah's younger daughter, and a graduate of Bryn Mawr College. Bertie, as Carey called him, came to Bryn Mawr to give a series of lectures on the foundations of geometry. Carey also invited Alys to lecture, and suggested "German Women and Socialism" as an appropriate topic. Carey had seen the couple, just married, in England the summer before, a visit she had anticipated with some apprehension because, as she wrote to Mary, she would have to listen to their views: "They are rabid anti-Christians and absolute free lovers as well as extreme socialists." During their November 1896 visit to Bryn Mawr, Carey was still recuperating, and was living in a rented house while the Deanery was being rebuilt. Her days were rushed, and the three-week visit added a heavy burden of entertaining. Before they arrived, she wrote to Mary, "I look forward with the darkest gloom to Bertie and Alys." She hosted them properly, however, planning small dinner parties to amuse them throughout their stay.[14]

Russell's mathematical lectures attracted great interest. The couple were feted at student teas, and at the end of their visit, Alys and Bertrand each gave lectures to students on social and political topics. Bertrand spoke on "Socialism as the Consummation of Individual Liberty," and Alys talked on suffrage and temperance. Frantic with work and exhausted, Carey was utterly unprepared for the firestorm that followed. Letters from two angry mothers announced that scandal was now at her door. Carey Thomas talked with students to find out what Alys and Bertrand had said. Before the Christmas holiday she spoke to the undergraduates in chapel, explaining to them that after their parents received exaggerated reports, the reaction to the Russells' visit had reached "serious dimensions." She asked them to make it clear "that the college in no way approved of or had [foreknowledge] of these discussions." It was appropriate for students to discuss social problems, "but I do not think it suitable that questions on which there is great diversity of opinion should be presented to you from one point of view only by older persons . . . even slightly and temporarily connected with the teaching force of the college." Thomas spoke in generalities with the exception of one particular. Parents had understood that the Russells had stated that "it was right to deceive" a mother "on all occasions." Thomas did not deny that her guests had made such a statement, but she wanted students to know that Alys herself had been "all her life the most devoted and self-sacrificing daughter to her father and mother," a child of whom her father said he had seen her "with her wings and halo on."[15]

James Thomas could not comprehend how his daughter could have allowed Alys to talk, especially in the wake of Grace's divorce trial. "I thought I warned thee as to utterances made at Bryn Mawr on the relations of men and women, on which subject Alys is utterly astray. I do not wonder what she said was misunderstood—what she meant, she did not say. Alys is regardless, always has been, and what she said and did while she was a student at Bryn Mawr is still remembered." He was hosting the couple when Bertrand Russell gave his lectures at Johns Hopkins. He would do his best, he wrote, to prevent Alys "from deploying her views, but I have no authority over clubs of women." On the most fundamental grounds he disapproved of Alys (and therefore, although he did not say it, indirectly of his daughter's mentality): "I shrink from people who have, as I fear, lost any real standard of right and wrong and regard all questions as debatable."[16]

Alys was planning a speech on "Renunciation" in New York. Carey Thomas wrote to her not to invite any Bryn Mawr students. It was a tricky business. Carey felt afterward that she had handled the situation as well as she could. She had managed to disapprove publicly of Bertrand and Alys without saying "anything against them." Alys, she thought, was "offended but sweet about it." The matter was, however, not so easily ended. In the most fundamental way, the Russells' 1896 visit shaped the historical rendering of M. Carey Thomas. Negative impressions that Bertrand Russell received during this visit formed part of the perceptions of a larger circle that included Lucy Donnelly, the companion of Helen Thomas in the 1890s and of Edith Finch in the 1930s. Finch wrote *Carey Thomas of Bryn Mawr*, the authorized biography of Thomas published in 1947, some years before she became Bertrand Russell's fourth wife.[17]

During Bertrand and Alys' visit, Mamie filled a diary with her reactions to Grace and Tom. It provides an intriguing glimpse of Carey as Mamie saw her in 1896, measuring the growing distance between them. Mamie was sympathetic to Grace's tale of love and loss: "One held her hands and wanted to go down on one's knees to her." Grace was trying to get her father, brothers, and sisters to allow her to live her own life as she chose, which meant continuing to see Tom after the divorce and remaining in Philadelphia to attend the Women's Medical College. She tried to enlist Mamie's help in persuading Carey to get their father to accept these decisions. Mamie promised to talk with Carey, but privately she doubted if she could help Grace: "One found her in her office at Taylor Hall, and her passionate invective against Tom—and against Grace—filled all the first interview. . . . Carey was not in a mood to go down on her knees to Grace!"

Mary Garrett had come into Philadelphia to visit Carey ("the third time, one notes with some amusement, that Mary has come to Philadelphia to meet her within the past two weeks"). Mamie saw Mary as a force strengthening Carey's insistence on propriety. "And Mary Garrett that afternoon at the hotel, with brow knit and eyes glaring at the very thought of Grace's bringing her disreputableness, her shadiness, into the neighbourhood of the college (a phrase about desire for nearness to the Medical College being interpreted for a moment as nearness to Bryn Mawr). Mary was in no mood for going down on hers." While Mamie was absorbed by the personal element, Carey and Mary could see only the impact of Grace's decisions on Carey's position at Bryn Mawr.

Carey was harshly judgmental. If Grace remained in Philadelphia and continued to see Tom, Carey would have "to cut Grace dead." Carey criticized

Grace for not seeing that marriage was not merely a private concern. Grace had offended the family by not consulting them on a matter that affected them and by letting herself be put in the wrong. There was a right and a wrong way for the matter to have been settled. Mamie quoted Carey's assessment: "The only decent and manly course was to make the other woman his mistress and live with her publicly, and leave Grace to get a divorce 'on proper grounds'!" Mamie went on to paraphrase Carey's judgment that Grace had "shown herself throughout an idiot too unspeakable to be thought of even with patience by any reasonable person, she has never been supposed to have much sense, but no one knew she was such a fool as that."

A statement about Tom's sexual drive upset Carey. Learning that Dr. William Osler had told James Thomas that Tom suffered from "monomaniatic insanity on sexual questions," Carey responded that Tom was "Mad! mad as men have been from the beginning of time, mad about some other woman." Grace had hopes that if she gave Tom his freedom, he would return and they would be married again. Again Carey had a sharp reaction: "Grace be married to him again, why, if she ever went back to him again, she would have to be a perfect Messalina to content him." By this reference to the infamously wanton Roman empress, Carey meant that she would have to have inordinate sexual energies, but Mamie saw it differently, "it seems to be—well, the existence of our grandmothers—that she means by Messalina's."

Unlike Carey, Mamie delighted in complexity and nuance. Fascination with Alfred Hodder, a married man, underlay her words. She tried to understand the divorce from the man's perspective. Grace may have hurt Tom and he may have found in the nurse someone "whom he loved and who he thought or knew would love him with a love that he calls love." He might have felt himself to be morally free and eager to be legally free to give her "the love the first woman hasn't wanted," and to give to Grace "the friendship that she gives him." In her musings, was Mamie working out a rationale for Alfred to leave Jessie for her?

She and Alfred had been befriended by Edith and Bond Thomas, whose testimony in the trial enraged Carey. Mamie noted Carey's judgment: "With an ass and idiot like Bond hereafter she would surely have no more to do: and it was a comfort also to know exactly what sort of woman Edith was." Bond and Edith adored Grace, and so did James, her father. James had said that Grace's "one fault had been too much goodness." To this came Carey's response: "He tried that sort of cant to me but I stopped it very fast." Mamie was sorely troubled by the facets of Carey that she demonstrated in responding to Grace's trouble: "it irks one to find Carey more violent always, more heavy-handed, than any of the rest: with her one cannot talk." Carey was lost to her now: she had come under Mary's aegis. "One feels the harder influence behind her, or beside her. I could once have softened all this much more."[18]

Emerging from Mamie's portrait is a harsh, unbending Carey, quick to anger, in no mood to forgive. It was a Carey that Mamie had seen a year earlier demanding that she cease to be Alfred Hodder's friend. Did Mamie fear that she might see the hard Carey direct her full rage against her?

III

ANGER linked to self-righteousness can come out of fear. Between 1895 and 1897 Carey suddenly became intensely aware of her vulnerability as the deaths of the men closest to her reminded her of the fragility of life itself.

In the late 1890s death dealt a heavy hand. Earlier in the decade, Francis T. King had died. As president of the board of trustees, he had been an important supporter, but Carey felt no personal sense of loss. In January 1895, James Rhoads died. Despite their close partnership during the early years of the college, Carey again showed little emotion, although she sought to pay him due homage at his memorial service. She praised him for his open mind and his commitment to freedom of conscience. In his work for women, he had the capacity "to feel for them and with them, to be concerned for them and for their fortunes in this world as it is sometimes thought that none but women can be." He supported the opening of all professions to women, their equal pay, and woman's suffrage.[19] Carey Thomas gave Rhoads a loving, although politically pointed, tribute, but her real energies went into confronting the results of his death. Rhoads had been the president of the board of trustees. When the board met to choose his successor, to Thomas' horror, the majority chose Philip Garrett, one of the twin brothers who had most ardently opposed her election to the Bryn Mawr presidency. Rhoads' death also left a vacancy on the board of trustees, and Thomas had lobbied unsuccessfully for the seat.

Carey was aware of the importance of James Whitall's final illness and death in 1896. At every phase in her evolving relationship with the college, Uncle James had been an important mainstay. It was after her discussions with him in England about Taylor's college in 1881 that she fixed her ambition to join its first faculty. When she became dean he advised her, kindly but firmly. He had been a powerful and independent trustee who thought about the college constantly. In his carefully composed and beautifully penned letters, he offered advice on what she should say and how she should say it, inquired after her personal well-being, and gently gave his assistance. He took a principled and uncompromising stand in support of her as president. Loss of him closed an important window into the minds of orthodox trustees.

Of a wholly different order was her father's death on November 8, 1897. In late October, James Carey Thomas had come to Bryn Mawr for a board meeting and stayed for a reception and dinner at the Deanery. During the night he had terrible pain about his heart that he thought was from indigestion, and Carey nursed him with everything they could think of: mustard plasters, emetics, hot water, and paregoric. He returned home to Baltimore feeling better, and two days later he and Carey gave a reception for the women of the Johns Hopkins medical school. Carey left for a trustees' meeting at Cornell. During the days she was away James suffered intermittently from pain that the Johns Hopkins physicians assumed was caused by gallstones. As he rested at home, he seemed to be improving; then, as Frank and Harry were visiting in his room, he made a joke and suddenly died. His gallstones had masked angina pectoris. His sons could not believe he was dead. Frank sat up all night with the body in the hopes that his father was alive. Harry did not allow the undertaker to come for fourteen hours. Carey rushed to Baltimore. There she found her brothers beside themselves and the city in mourning.

As Carey received callers and went through the funeral ceremonies, she began to have some understanding of the impact of her father's life. Each of the major groups with which he had been associated—the Johns Hopkins trustees and faculty, the YMCA, Bryn Mawr College trustees—met in a body to march to the Meeting house. The medical school faculty, Baltimore physicians, and businessmen crowded the vestibules and galleries. She was "amazed by the expression of grief his death has caused." President Gilman of Johns Hopkins repeatedly said that his most important adviser and friend had died and he did not know "where to turn." Most touching to Carey were the formal tributes by the Bryn Mawr faculty and students. James Thomas would be especially missed in morning chapel.[20]

Carey's first report to Mary, after three days, conveyed a sense of her grief: "I slept better, but waked early and cried hard." Eleven days after her father's death, Carey wrote extensively to Hannah of the loss felt by family, friends, and associates. Her letter is measured, more an observer of the scene than one of the mourners. What evoked intense feeling were the moments when she linked her father's death to that of her mother nine years before. Rufus Jones' talk at the Quaker Funeral Meeting "completely upset us all by speaking of Father's reunion with Mother." An era had ended. She wrote to Hannah, "I have been very much knocked up, of course. It seems like the breaking up of everything, and this is quite apart from Father's loss. As I wrote thee last summer, he has been an angel of goodness to us since Mother's death. He has loved us and admired us and helped us in all our plans, and to me he was the greatest stay and support and counselor and colleague in Bryn Mawr and in all my plans."[21]

At the death of her mother, Carey had given herself weeks to mourn. She understood what had been at stake emotionally between them. James Thomas' death was different, for she did not have an emotional context in which to understand what a father meant to her. She returned immediately to work.

She even thought that she would attend the trustee meeting ten days after James' death. She decided not to go, not because of her own feelings, but for appearances' sake: "Anything would be better than their thinking I had failed in respect to Father's memory, and they will look at it as if their own daughter was attending a business meeting within one week of their own funeral." Moreover, there was no important business scheduled for the meeting.[22]

Grace's grief, written from abroad where she had gone after the divorce, brought Carey to some recognition of her loss. Grace felt acutely the degree to which, during the divorce, she had been unkind to her father; yet James Thomas had loved her none the less. In response Carey wrote to Grace, "It is like something gone out of my life, and it gets harder and harder to bear." What Carey was beginning to realize was that "there is a great blank where there used to be certainty of his intense interest and sympathy. It seems to me that a parent's love is unlike any other love—a child knows that it is always there like a haven of refuge to rest on. I find myself twenty times a day thinking of how much Father would delight in or dislike this or that."

James Thomas' death was both personal loss and a loss to Carey's work. "I shall miss him unspeakably in the college. How I shall get on without him I do not know! . . . He was so proud of the college and took such pleasure in it that I feel now as if I did not care for it when he is not here to see." As she summed up, Carey took the full measure of the toll that the recent past had taken. "Francis King, Dr. Rhoads, Uncle James and now Father, all dead within the last few years and all my counsellors and supporters in the Bryn Mawr board."[23]

Yet, as with her letter to Hannah, Carey was philosophizing. Raw feelings were far from the surface. She was not letting herself grieve. She was numb. In this state, she found it difficult to work. As she "fumbled along," she wrote to Mary, "Nothing in the world seems worth doing and nothing interesting. If they elected the devil a trustee I should sit indifferently next to his cloven hoof. The fact is our life is not worth living and that is all there is about it." She hoped that this mood would pass. Ultimately it did, but not for a long time. James Thomas' death continued to haunt her. Two months later, working with an instructor to learn gymnastics, she reported that she was feeling better. "I sleep well and am trying to forget about Father. Why should one mourn?" However, in the spring, an attack of influenza made her wonder: "I suppose I have never got really over Father's death, and that and overwork together make me subject to these colds."[24]

These deaths had many ramifications for Carey. Cousin Francis, Dr. Rhoads, Uncle Jim, and especially Father: the generation of men that had stood behind her was gone. They had been her interpreters to the skeptical and the naysayers, and by the power of their presence they had won for her many battles. But they had for Carey another meaning. They were the men for whom she had to be a good Quaker daughter. They loved her and questioned her, admired her and presumed to guide her, praised her and admonished her. To lose them was to lose both guide and millstone.

IV

As A GIRL and young woman, Carey Thomas had lived vigorously in the out-of-doors. On summer vacations she hiked, rowed, and bathed in the sea. In winter she skated on the ice and rode. In the mid-1890s, perhaps influenced by instructors in physical education and the physicians who spoke at the college on women's health, she began to exercise quite consciously for health. She tried to walk each afternoon, when the ice was good she skated, and she began a routine of gymnastic exercises.

Carey Thomas believed in an aggressive approach to any physical symptom, major or minor, and constantly dosed herself with a wide variety of remedies. For example, in October 1895, she got a headache, a forewarning she feared of an illness to come. For this she took the "muriate of cocaine snuff Aunt Mary gave me [that] completely checked my cold." She frequently took the medicine quinine to ward off the malaria that headaches or lassitude seemed to threaten.[25]

After her 1896 surgery, she resumed regular exercise and tried without lasting success to lose the extra weight that she carried. In the fall of 1897, after she returned from a summer in Spain with Mamie, her father noticed that she was limping. Later that winter, as she skated, her right leg gave way, and she fell on the ice. On May 10, 1898, as she was walking from the railway station to the college, Carey "met with a misfortune" that she described as sciatica in her right leg. She endured a faculty meeting and then had such pain during the night and the following morning that she thought she would be unable to dress or make the public announcement of fellowships. Her doctor suggested a hot soda bath and iodine painting. The pain continued, however.[26]

Carey and Mary went abroad for half of the summer. She was, as she wrote Hannah when she appealed to her for tickets to Covent Garden to hear the Wagner cycle, "absolutely starved for music" after the seclusion of mourning for her father. The day after a performance of Wagner's *Twilight of the Gods*, she awoke with "great pain" and the feeling that her right leg was "much shorter" than the left.[27] When she returned from abroad, she canceled a camping trip with Mamie and instead went with her to try and get help for her leg at a spa in Hot Springs, Virginia. All sorts of possibilities occurred to Carey and her doctors: sciatica, rheumatism, paralysis of the spine, infected tissue remaining from the 1896 surgery. All, except the correct one—changes in the scar tissue of her childhood burn.

Returning to Bryn Mawr, Carey began a series of treatments, based on the differing advice of doctors: daily massage, baking of her leg at 240 degrees at the Bryn Mawr Hospital three times a week, strict diet, injections, and using a cane. She wrote to Hannah Smith: "I am determined to get well, especially as I hear on all sides of obstinate cases of sciatica lasting years." This regime did her little good. In February 1899 a trip with Mary in New York set her back, and she realized that she should not walk until her leg improved. In March, learning that the problem was with her hip not her leg, she began to sleep with a hot water bottle, as suggested by her doctor, and gave herself vaginal douches, a remedy of her own devising. "If heat is so good this may do good, too." She brought her weight down to 142, but felt she should weigh 130. She put herself on an exercise regime of rowing and lifting chest weights and planned to bicycle. She also suffered from heart palpitations that periodically frightened her. She was careful to consult a doctor and asked him specifically if she could exercise. In October 1899, after an examination, the doctor told her that she had "a very nervous heart, so nervous that it missed a beat every now and then but that it was organically absolutely sound and would come right soon." He gave her permission to exercise as much as she chose.[28]

In the summer of 1899, she went with Mary to the famous spa in Aix-les-Bains, France, to consult with specialists and to attempt their cure. After careful examination, her condition was diagnosed as sciatica brought on by the childhood burn. She was given hope for a full cure. As she wrote to Hannah, she revealed that a doctor in Philadelphia and one in London had given her the same diagnosis, a judgment about which she had been silent at the time: "so it must be true, I suppose, but it is hard luck to have my burn come to the front after thirty-five years of good behavior."[29]

Yet still she refused to accept the judgment. In April 1900, she fell on the stairs, and although "the pain was very great in all the burned tendons," she carried on and went into Philadelphia. The following day, she could not walk. When Dr. Gerald Gebhard, her regular physician, gave her an examination, he confirmed the source of the problem: "Gebhard . . . looked at my scar again. He feels quite sure it *is* the cause, says if he had ever seen it he should have been sure." In the many months that he had treated the leg, Dr. Gebhard had dealt with a dressed patient and had not seen the scar tissue fully exposed. Aided by codes of modesty, Carey had continued to deny for twenty-one months the obvious source of her pain and immobility. Carey Thomas brooded little about this turn of fate. All her energies went into hiding knowledge of her infirmity from others. As she faced a college reception, she worried over how she might appear: "if I stand *very* still I think my excessive lameness will not be too much remarked."[30]

For the next thirteen years, from 1900 to 1913, the years of her greatest prestige, Carey Thomas was lame and was forced to use a cane. She learned to move quickly, her billowing academic robe and cane a familiar sight on the Bryn Mawr campus. Her recurring pain was a secret for herself, her doctor, and her few intimates. At one level there is a heroism here, an unwillingness to be daunted or to make others a party to personal suffering. Carey Thomas knew she represented women. She believed that she must represent them in strength. She was also a person of an era in which bodily reticence constituted public virtue. The removal of a uterus was not to be mentioned; nor was a scar covering hip and midsection. But more was at stake.

As a child Carey Thomas had suffered a life-threatening burn. From the time that she forced herself to walk until the wound healed, she hid her pain even from her family. In the years that followed, her scars were covered by clothing, and she appeared completely normal to the outside world. The contraction of scar tissue in 1898 was a terrible personal blow that recalled for her the terror and suffering of her childhood injury. Coming as it did following the death of her father, it must have reminded her of the thin line that separates death from life.

V

PHOTOGRAPHS taken of Carey Thomas at the turn of the century show dramatic change. In May 1896 her image is of a vigorous woman in early middle age. Although lines under the eyes give evidence of life lived, her smooth skin and dark hair are that of youth. Only her erect stance conveys the confidence and sense of latent power of maturity. Images from the early twentieth century convey a different woman, older not by years but seemingly by decades. The body is now stocky and the hair is growing white. In studio portraits the posed face is severe, even when composed, fatigued, and strained. Candid photographs in student scrapbooks give a different set of images of the older woman of the early twentieth century. Their spontaneous Carey Thomas is transformed by her many moods: laughing, talking, scolding, seldom posing.

Examining the many strands of Carey's life makes it clear that she was at a point of crisis in the late 1890s. She had attained at Bryn Mawr the position of which she had dreamed, and yet her life was an unending battle with trustees. There was no real chance that she could recover the parts of herself that yearned for poetry or scholarship. Her love of Mary and Mamie's gradual retreat threatened the basic structure of the daily life that she had lived for two decades and challenged her understanding of herself. The deaths of James Rhoads, James Whitall, and James Carey Thomas removed the supportive older presences that accepted her and interpreted her actions to the board.

Carey Thomas no longer had need to explain herself in traditional terms. The vigorous body that had sustained her was threatened by the return of childhood pain. There was much to fear.

Carey's first reaction was to seek cover. Her parents had taught her how to present to the public world a blameless image. She recalled their lessons. Carey's letter to Judge Fisher, lying about her approval of conventional marriage, is a graphic example of the public face that she assumed. So, too, was the elaborate masking of her gynecological surgery. To the outside she would be unassailable.

Her second response was to clothe herself in the protections of class. She had come from Quaker stock in a household that had combined abundance and scarcity. In the 1870s her physician father had not been able to pay the bills for his burgeoning household. Carey Thomas invented for herself a background of great wealth. In 1899, she wrote to Hannah Smith that neither she nor her daughter Mary should mention her income because the fact that "everyone, even the trustees, thinks I have an independent fortune from Mother and thee is a great help to me among such a set of rich old codgers as they are." In fact, her inheritances from the estates of her mother, father, and Uncle James were small relative to her income and expenses. It was important, however, for her to present herself not as a woman on a high salary—although the trustees certainly knew that—but as a woman of independent means.[31]

She would array herself in an armor of class. She wanted to create for herself the aura that had surrounded Mary Garrett when they first met. Carey Thomas' extensive buying had many sources, but one of them was her inner need to declare herself a lady. It was to enhance her power that she ordered the many silk dresses from the dressmaker. More and more she began to surround herself with the appearance of upper-class status. Mary Garrett's redecoration of the Deanery gave her not only a deep cushion of material comfort, but also the appropriate stage setting of enviable prosperity for the drama of class that she sought to play. She engaged a private teacher for elocution lessons, to change the sounds and rhythms of her speech.[32]

For some years she had been accustomed to a level of disguise. She had been appearing as a Quaker since returning to America in 1883. What happened following the crisis of the late 1890s was that she began to expand this public posture to a whole range of conservative opinion and practices. What began as a thin overlay of convention required by her position at Bryn Mawr expanded to become a thick covering. The passionate, free-thinking Carey was dangerous. A carefully constructed M. Carey Thomas grew around and encased her.

What were the rules of this new order? What were the limits at Bryn Mawr? The loss of the older generation of male counselors left her exposed. It also left her free. Rhoads was no longer there to bend or moderate her plans. James Whitall could no longer provide counsel with a generous spirit and kind firmness. James Thomas no longer implicitly chastened his daughter by his knowledge of her personal weaknesses. As Mamie retreated, Carey was left without critics. Mary fought over Carey's sloppy financial accounting, but supported her in her actions at Bryn Mawr. The major external forces that had constrained her were gone. The calls of the aesthetic life no longer resonated. Carey Thomas could develop into a full-time, consummate administrator. Given that she did not delegate or share power, that she commanded minute detail as well as policy, and that she always felt embattled, the stage was set for Carey Thomas to become Bryn Mawr's autocrat.

At midlife Carey Thomas set herself on a course from which there was no return. She lived fully in the realm of action. She sustained a level of activity that drowned out alternative voices. She became imperial in her dealings with others. She sought to overwhelm, not to argue. Her desires for possessions no longer were contained, and she cushioned herself with ever more abundant things. Her privilege led her to make harsher judgments of others and to broaden her sense of exclusiveness to a more active racism and anti-Semitism.

Of course, much of this evolved as Carey Thomas grew into adulthood and middle age. Character develops gradually. However, an individual contains multiple possibilities, and chance, will, and changing external conditions play their part. Only with the personal crisis of the late 1890s did Carey Thomas set her final course. At the end of the 1890s, as she unfolded in her forties, she became herself with a vengeance.

Although the results are often not pretty, there is another side. Carey Thomas matured into a woman who exercised power directly and openly, a woman unburdened by the constraints of indirection and moralism that informed and shaped many other women leaders of her time. She could thrust herself forward, walk energetically, speak clearly and forcibly. She was confident. Like a male politician, she could demand, cajole, and intimidate. At Bryn Mawr College, she was able to turn a small, excellent college and graduate school, largely of her own devising, into a larger, grander version of itself. As handsome buildings rose, the quality of intellectual life at the college was sustained. Again, opposed by a board unsympathetic to her goals, she was able to bring a vision of the future into full realization.

She was also able to survive painful life blows that might have felled a less resilient woman. The later years of her midlife contained more than their share of loss and physical pain. Personal tragedies led her to stumble and fall, but she got up again to finish her work with a creative flourish. She moved also to the larger stage to become a noted speaker and writer on education, take an active role in the suffrage movement, and help secure needed institutions for women's intellectual advancement. Her own complex life story, with its struggles, disappointments, and successes, gave her a unique vantage point from which she could address the question of women's creativity.

For worse and for better, from the crucible of the late 1890s emerged the powers and passions of M. Carey Thomas of the twentieth century.

CHAPTER 17

To Spread the Fame
of the College

THE YEARS between 1898 and 1906 sealed M. Carey Thomas' reputation as the leading national spokeswoman for women's higher education and as the consummate college president. Out of personal crises of the 1890s, she emerged with a carefully constructed public persona, a vision of Bryn Mawr, and a renewed will.

The era began well. In March 1898 the alumnae decided to commission her portrait, and Carey Thomas chose John Singer Sargent to do it. A year later she arranged to sit for him. The portrait arrived at the Deanery in the autumn of 1899, and the alumnae planned a formal presentation in November. Carey wrote about the painting to Mary Garrett, who remained abroad. After a private viewing, Mamie Gwinn had declared herself "delighted with it and thinks it one of the very nicest Sargents she has ever seen, a new era in his style." Mamie's reaction went beyond that, Carey wrote, giving a sense not only of Sargent's work, but also of Mamie's feeling for Carey in 1899. "She thinks it very stately and full of the detachment of a great work of art, *very* melancholy, not at all 'all there' as she considers I am, a youthful, knightlike, St. George conception of me, more like the im werden Minnie in 1877—all of which she thinks shows his high artistic conception."[1]

Mamie's use of masculine imagery is striking—a "melancholy . . . youthful, knightlike, St. George conception." It recalled to her the Carey of their youth. Mamie brought distinctive memories to the portrait; to a later viewer, outside their relationship, the middle-aged figure of the portrait is hardly knightly. It is, however, regal. Carey Thomas, swathed in an academic robe, fills the canvas. She sits in a chair as if it were a throne, at a point above the viewer. Unlike the well-dressed women in fashionable portraits of the era who were posed in partial profile in beautiful rooms, Thomas looks straight out from a black background that blends imperceptibly into her black robe and blue hood. Only her hair, face, and hands are clear. She is handsome. Her oval face with its widely spaced, heavily lidded eyes under dark brows and her defined chin are congruent with photographs. But by overemphasizing the brow, the artist underplayed Thomas' strong nose and jaw. The hands with their long slender fingers are sheer fiction.[2]

What Sargent got right was the demeanor that Carey Thomas hoped to project to the world. She is serene, confident, neither masculine nor feminine. Sargent, however, failed to capture her most notable quality, her energy. Sargent's portrait is an image of a composed M. Carey Thomas, not the driven administrator that Mamie criticized, the one who was "all there." Sargent himself felt that the painting recalled Bronzino, the sixteenth-century Italian Mannerist, known for his allegories and portraits. The link is an intriguing one. Was Sargent thinking of Bronzino's technical achievements in his highly glazed portraits? Or was he thinking of Bronzino's presentation of his principal subjects, the ruling Medici family, as powerful yet remote? In her memoirs a Bryn Mawr graduate noted that Sargent was known to bring out character cunningly. The clue in the portrait was the manner in which Thomas' hand "grasped the carved arm" of the chair: "it clutched and held an oaken ornament as though it had to dominate the nearest thing within its reach."[3]

The presentation was a triumph. It was a gala occasion at which trustees and alumnae spoke. Louise Brownell, a Bryn Mawr graduate who was the dean of Sage College at Cornell, pleased Carey Thomas with her remarks. Carey reported to Mary that Brownell spoke of the ideals of Bryn Mawr, "which she said were mine, first and last, conception and accomplishment." She turned from Bryn Mawr to education in general to say that M. Carey Thomas was admitted to be "by friends and foes the person who had already done most for women's education." At the end of the speech the portrait was unveiled. Carey Thomas took off her academic cap and "assumed the attitude" of the image: "the applause was, of course, tremendous and unending." The trustees, who had been diffident about the event, seemed "absolutely overwhelmed by the tribute of the students, as did the faculty." Carey Thomas knew that she could no longer be denied. In 1894 she did not have an inauguration, but the presentation of the Sargent portrait in 1899 was her coronation.[4]

The portrait brought M. Carey Thomas widespread fame. It traveled to exhibitions of Sargent's work and of higher education both in the United States and abroad. Its regal image of calm strength contributed to her heightened national prestige, and she was called on increasingly to speak for women and education.[5]

Gradually, Carey Thomas had been building a reputation. After her address at the opening of the graduate school of the University of Pennsylvania to women, she continued to talk to local audiences on issues of education. She gave two important and controversial speeches to the Educational Section of the Civic Club of Philadelphia in 1895, arguing for the broadest training for teachers, the elevation of standards, and the new pedagogy based on psychology. She began to be active in regional bodies of organizations such as the Association of Colleges and Preparatory Schools, sharing the podium with the important college presidents. In November 1896 she praised Charles W. Eliot as speaking "magnificently," and then noted to Mary her growing sense of confidence on the podium: "I suppose I am getting known to Philadelphia audiences. I *think* it went well. Eliot had said so much of what I wished to say that I almost spoke it. I felt almost for the first time that perhaps I could learn to speak in time without notes, not so well as Eliot or Lady Henry [Somerset], but much better than [Daniel Coit] Gilman." Once Francis Gummere had fired her competitive spirit; now she fastened on Charles Eliot, the president of Harvard University and one of the nation's preeminent educational leaders.[6]

By the turn of the century she felt an obligation to accept all important invitations to speak. As she wrote to Mary, "I want to spread the fame of the college and do what I can. Really worthwhile occasions to speak are few, and the few that come I must embrace." She began to speak freely without a written text. She was on her own: Mamie Gwinn no longer gave her substantial help. Two sessions each week with Samuel Arthur King, her elocution teacher, focused on increasing the variety of voice tones and learning strategies to avoid hoarseness. More importantly, it gave her an ally who worked with her and built her confidence as she faced large audiences. As her self-assurance mounted, she began to publish her speeches as articles.[7]

In 1899 M. Carey Thomas attracted national attention when in a Bryn Mawr chapel talk she took on Charles Eliot. Her annual speech at the opening of the college year had been delayed by the inauguration of the president of Wellesley College. The highlight of the Wellesley ceremony was the Harvard president's address. Thomas had long been offended by Eliot's recurring demand that the higher education of women be different from that of men. At Wellesley he again called for a distinctly female college curriculum. As familiar as Thomas was with his position, hearing it at the Wellesley inauguration enraged her. She wrote to Mary Garrett, "Eliot disgraced himself. He said the traditions of past learning and scholarship were of no use to women's education, that women's words were as unlike men's as their bodies, that women's colleges ought to be schools of *manners* and really was hateful." She later wrote to Garrett that his Wellesley speech was "so brutal, it made me hot from head to foot." A few years earlier, Thomas had noted that she admired Eliot's speaking ability and determined to learn to speak extemporaneously, as he had done. Now she had a chance to take him on. The following week, as she welcomed students, she replied.[8]

She began with an articulation of her hope that college life would lead to the creation of the Bryn Mawr type. In the "mutual association" of new and returning students in the residence halls she hoped there would "be fashioned and perfected the type of Bryn Mawr women which will, we hope, become as well known and universally admired a type as the Oxford and Cambridge man." In the halls younger students would be influenced by "the scholarly point of view of the older students," and they would learn good manners. Bryn Mawr was to become a school of "good breeding. . . . Manners do, as President Eliot says, matter immensely and if the Bryn Mawr woman should add to scholarship and character gentle breeding and could join high standards of behavior and usages of culture and gentle observances to high standards of scholarship we should have the type we are seeking to create."

Having established this, she went on to attack Eliot's central premise that the world of knowledge "existing from the time of the Egyptians to the present existed only for men," and that therefore the curriculum and methods of men's colleges were no guide for women. This was, Thomas retorted, nonsense. "He might as well have told the president of Wellesley to invent a new Christian religion for Wellesley or new symphonies and operas, a new Beethoven and Wagner, new statues and pictures, a new Phidias and a new Titian, new tennis, new golf . . . in short, a new intellectual heavens and earth."[9]

Reaction was swift. She wrote to Mary, "I succeeded in hitting the nail on the head today. . . . And the students were touched and delighted." Reporters attended the talk and seized on her criticism of Eliot. Newspapers across the country found the story of the president of a women's college taking on the president of Harvard good copy. As she received the published accounts, she was flattered by her fame. She wrote to Mary that though before the talk she had palpitations from anxiety, she had chosen not to soften her words to placate Eliot. He had never been kind to her, influenced perhaps by Daniel Coit Gilman's coolness to her. Now she was pleased that, after her criticism, Eliot would "never again venture to say such a shocking thing in just that unrelieved awful way again." The publicity she received meant that she would be given many future occasions to speak on women's higher education.[10]

In 1899 Nicholas Murray Butler, the president of Columbia University, asked Thomas to write a book on women's education for the Monographs on Education Series he was editing, to be published by the United States government for the Paris Exposition of 1900. She agreed, and *Education of Women* established Thomas' international reputation as the authority on American women and higher education.

Knowing its potential importance, she found writing the monograph a difficult, almost intractable, task, and she had to get repeated extensions throughout the fall and winter of 1899–1900. In the midst of college business, it was difficult to find time and quiet. Perhaps her inability to write came from her loss of Mamie Gwinn as a helper; she wrote to Mary that Mamie was "no longer any good, it has got too much outside her line." With Isabel Maddison's aid, she gathered material and tabulated it, but felt frustrated at having little reliable data.[11]

The monograph stands as M. Carey Thomas' only book. It is, on its face, a straightforward exposition of women's higher education. It gives tables, maps, and pages of data gathered from different schools. Although presented as an impersonal study, Thomas' commitments and self-promotion come through in the organization of material and in the judgments rendered. The monograph establishes Bryn Mawr's place as the leading women's college. Over ten of its forty pages are given to eleven independent colleges for women, ranked in three groupings. Bryn Mawr appears prominently as one of the four of highest rank. Bryn Mawr is shown to its advantage throughout. In such statements as these, Thomas celebrates Bryn Mawr's student self-government, graduate school, and faculty: "Among the professors the most successful in their teaching at Princeton, Chicago and Columbia are men whose whole experience had been gained in teaching women at Bryn Mawr."[12]

The closing section deals with contemporary questions in higher education, such as women's health and the low marriage rates of college women. It establishes as a fact American women's academic success. The number of women college graduates in the United States—Thomas tallied 14,824—"formed . . . a larger body of educated women than is to be found in any other country in the world. . . . The higher education of women has assumed the proportions of a national movement still in progress." Although it may be possible to guide its development, it "can no longer be opposed with any hope of success. Its results are to be reckoned with as facts." Her last topic is the value of coeducational versus single-sex colleges: Although coeducation is less expensive and is thereby necessary in thinly settled regions, in the east, there is a clear and natural preference for separate women's colleges. Conservative parents value the protection it offers their sheltered daughters. "There is undoubtedly serious objection to intimate association at the most impressionable period of a girl's life with many young men from all parts of the country and of every possible social class." Moreover, only in women's colleges do female students have a chance for a full college life. Given this preference, women's colleges equal in quality to those of men must exist. Thomas ends with a ringing commitment to an identical curriculum for women and men.[13]

The Sargent portrait and the response to Eliot had established M. Carey Thomas' public reputation. *Education of Women* sealed her position as the nation's leading authority on the higher education of women. The book gave Thomas a chance to have her judgments established as fact grounded in data and to present them in a government-sponsored publication under the Columbia University president's editorship to an international audience. Until 1900, Carey Thomas had been working in an isolated setting confronting conservative trustees. After the publication of *Education of Women*, she spoke as the legitimate voice of enlightened public opinion.

M. Carey Thomas also became a celebrity. Newspapers across the country carried articles with provocative titles such as "Woman Merely Man's Drudge: Throw Off the Yoke, Says the President of Bryn Mawr College, and Broaden your Mental Horizon." In "Girls Must Wear Pockets," she was reported as insisting that all Bryn Mawr students copy men by incorporating pockets into their gowns. Thomas was photographed with an international leader and a caption read, "She is one of the foremost educators of the day." She was paired with Jane Addams as one of the two women having most influence over girls. Magazine articles appeared that listed her with other notable contemporaries as the most important women of the era. In one piece on women college heads, she was touted as "an extraordinary woman," "an executive of rare ability," a scholar, and a woman of character. Her many years of preparation could not create "the poise, the judgment, the energy, the courage, the insight and progressiveness, nor her capacity for deep and logical thinking and for inspiring sympathy and faith in her fellows," but could and did enrich these natural powers. Her opening convocation speeches were regarded as newsworthy in Topeka, Kansas, and Rochester, New York.[14]

In the fifteen years that followed, Carey Thomas received many invitations to speak and write on women and higher education. Interest in education and in women was keen during the Progressive period. Thomas gave well-publicized addresses on important ceremonial occasions, such as at the St. Louis World's Fair in 1904. Hers was the strongest and most consistent voice in the United States insisting on women's equal opportunity at all levels in higher education.

Her talks were published in leading American educational journals, such as the *Educational Review*, and constitute a significant body of work. These addresses follow the pattern set by the monograph: normally they combine careful presentation of data with Thomas' judgments and prejudices. As was Carey Thomas herself, they are an intriguing mixture of forward thinking and backward glances. In preparing the monograph, Thomas had, with Maddison's help, mastered the statistics of women's higher education. But as she became a social scientist, she followed the pattern of her day and linked careful research in data with the rhetoric of religion and tradition.

In her speeches Carey Thomas developed the several themes of greatest concern to her: women's education and the world of culture, the need for standards, and the question of which institutional setting—single-sex or coeducational—served women best. As her attack on Eliot's Wellesley address announced, Thomas firmly believed women should take no separate courses, such as psychology or domestic science, to prepare them for their life's tasks, nor should existing subjects be presented from a woman's point of view. Women's education must be identical to that of men, for the life of the mind had no sex. As she put it, "Science and literature and philology are what they are and inalterable." Science and culture belong to women, but they have been robbed of opportunity. "The life of the intellect and spirit has been lived only by men. The world of scholarship and research has been a man's world." Her task was to change that. Women's colleges have a special mission. They uphold the highest standards. They offer a place where the woman student can be the focus. They give employment to women scholars and researchers.

In 1901, as she took on the issue of graduate and professional training, she reasserted her nineteenth-century positivistic belief in scientific truth. As women enter professions, the education they receive must be the same as men's. "Given two bridge-buildings, a man and a woman, given a certain bridge to be built, and given as always the unchangeable laws of mechanics . . . it is simply inconceivable that the preliminary instruction given to the two bridge-builders should differ in quantity, quality, or method of presentation because while the bridge is building one will wear knickerbockers and the other a rainy-day skirt." Driving home her point, she argued for identical medical education for men and women: "There is no reason to believe that typhoid or scarlet fever or phthisis can be successfully treated by a woman physician in one way and by a man physician in another way. There is indeed every reason to believe that unless treated in the best way, the patient may die, the sex of the doctor affecting the result even less than the sex of the patient." The career paths of women and men must be identical. Thus all fields and positions should be open to women. Because the world of knowledge is the same for both sexes, "the objects of competition are one and the same for both men and women—instructorships and professors' chairs, scholarly fame, and power to advance, however little, the outposts of knowledge."[15]

Having established the identity of women's and men's education, what was it to be? Carey Thomas had participated in the great change that had brought German scholarship to America and that had substituted the lecture and the seminar for college recitations. She had opened the curriculum through the group system. But she moderated her Continental enthusiasms with elements from American and British experience. She insisted on a range of requirements for graduation. She valued the residential college and its associated campus life. After regrounding tradition and making it available to women, she now sought to preserve it.

Beginning in 1900 Carey Thomas took on Eliot's belief in the elective system. In college studies as in entrance requirements, Thomas firmly believed that some subjects were more important than others. Eliot had based his arguments on his belief in the individuality of human intelligence. Thomas saw young people as more similar than alike and dismissed their preferences as childish and irrelevant to their proper intellectual development. All students should be required to take classics and mathematics.[16]

In 1904 Thomas argued against the increasing emphasis educators were placing on practical and professional training. Having worked so hard for women's access to higher education, Thomas opposed any change that might dilute the college course. As she spoke at the International Congress of Arts and Science at the St. Louis World's Fair, Thomas opposed the effort to shorten the four-year college course by combining the final year with professional training. Once again she took on Eliot, who allowed Harvard students to take the B.A. in three years. Warning that the college was endangered, she declaimed that the college "has more to fear from the Judas-like kisses of its friends in high places than from the mob." She defended the traditional four-year liberal arts course as "the glory of our past, the source of stability and sanity, the radiant center of all our gallant action and liberal thought." She appealed to the desire for prestige and class, conjuring up the aristocratic image of the Oxford and Cambridge graduate. The British university, "isolated from the outside world among green lawns and mediaeval buildings of wonderful beauty and charm," has given the world "men of thought and action who have guided the destinies of the English-speaking races." Citing statistics, she compared the favorable chances of the college bred against those of less-fortunate others in contests for national political office and inclusion into Who's Who.[17]

Given that women and men should receive an identical liberal arts education, should the colleges that served women be single-sex or coeducational? Here the answer depended on the audience. Her principal commitment was to foster opportunity for women—some women—in higher education. She did not want any school closed to women, and thus strongly supported coeducation. If she spoke before a coeducational institution, she tended to give the arguments for coeducation.

In 1898, after the death of Henry Sage, the donor of Sage College at Cornell, Carey Thomas, as the university's first woman trustee, delivered an address at the memorial service in his honor. She placed Sage and his 1872 gift in the international story of women's advancing opportunities in education. She located the cause of the subordinate place of women students in coeducational universities in their exclusion from future professional life. Arguing that full coeducation requires that women serve as trustees and as members of the faculty, she stated, "Education does not end when the last degree is taken; it is not to have equal facilities for education, for scholarship, to be debarred from just those posts in which alone a scholar may devote to scholarship the working hours of life and not its playtime merely." As long as women in coeducational institutions are still unequal, women's colleges are needed.

"Separate education for men and women cannot ultimately prevail," however, for it wastes money and scholarly power. All students should have access to great teachers, men as well as women. "At the close of the twentieth century it will seem as absurd that only men should be taught by men and only women by women, as it would seem at the close of the nineteenth century that only men should read Thackeray and only women George Eliot."[18]

Carey Thomas was not consistent on the issue of coeducation, however. She was, after all, the president of a women's college. When she addressed the audience that gathered in 1900 to celebrate the twenty-fifth anniversary of Smith College, she emphasized the value of higher education in an all-women's setting. Women need a place where they are honored and where women hold power. In addition, at a women's college there is a different feeling in the air. Students know that they do not come second to the table; in their own colleges "everything exists for women students and is theirs by right and not by favor." In such places, undistracted by men, they have a chance to develop the rich traditions of college life.[19]

Although Bryn Mawr began with a graduate school, it was many decades before Thomas recognized the distinctive value of one connected to a women's college. In her 1892 address at the opening to women of the graduate school of the University of Pennsylvania she argued that the mature and disciplined graduate student, male or female, seeks to study under a particular scholar, and all doors must be open to women.[20] In time, Thomas saw the complicated barriers that women faced and came to support a graduate school for women as a means to foster women's genius.

Such speeches, especially when reprinted as journal articles, strengthened M. Carey Thomas' reputation. They established her as a spokeswoman in support of women's full participation in higher education, the need to blend electives with the traditional college course, and the right of women to receive the culture and science that they shared with men. As Carey Thomas found her voice, she became an important advocate for women. She also solidified her place in the public mind as an expert and established the legitimate claim of Bryn Mawr College for philanthropists' dollars. Her fame as a speaker undergirded her success in raising money for Bryn Mawr.

II

IN JUNE 1898, Carey Thomas rose to answer a toast at the Bryn Mawr College alumnae banquet. In this setting of loyal supporters she set out for the first time her vision of the college of the future. She began by restating Bryn Mawr's animating spirit. Bryn Mawr was a college not in the sense that it was primarily committed to undergraduates; it was a college because it concentrated all its resources in a single school, in contrast to a university, which dissipated energies in teaching everything. When Bryn Mawr's school of philosophy (the liberal arts in today's parlance) was compared to that of many in large universities, Bryn Mawr offered a higher standard. This was what the world required, "there is yearly greater need for at least one college of the widest, freest, most liberal culture." To hold its place as an undergraduate and graduate center for scholarship of the highest order, Bryn Mawr had to continue "expanding and perfecting this one school."

Bryn Mawr had begun auspiciously; now it must grow, adding professorships and books. If it remained small, it was in danger of becoming provincial. But how could Bryn Mawr expand? Taylor's large gift did not invite others: the college had received no significant additional endowments. The only path to growth that Thomas saw was greater enrollments—more paying students to create a larger pool of tuition. But the trustees had resolved that no more of the original endowment be used to build residence halls.

As Carey Thomas envisioned the future of Bryn Mawr, she saw it as a much larger college. To the 325 current students, she would add 550. This would require eight new residence halls, and a library—all to support her "one great college." She described an early plan by Frederick Law Olmsted that projected a series of residence halls "continuing the march around our boundaries in one unbroken line." In addition, Thomas envisioned a great library of 100,000 volumes, with a building in the design of an "English Gothic chapter house with tall Gothic windows." What was needed was money: each residence hall would cost $90,000; the library, $1,400,000.[21]

Carey Thomas' immediate goal was to get the alumnae behind two projects, one modest, the other large. The first called for individual backing for the Low Buildings, an apartment house for female members of the faculty and staff. The second sought collective support for her plan for the library. Thomas had hit on the scheme for the Low Buildings in December 1897. Essentially, it enabled the college to take in 38 more students. Although the trustees were not willing to use the endowment for new residence halls, they had been amenable to partnership schemes that brought additional property to Bryn Mawr. They had agreed to allow Thomas and Henry Tatnall, the treasurer, to take out a mortgage on a large cottage the college called Dolgelly and lease it to Bryn Mawr for rent to cover the mortgage payments. Dolgelly initially served as a residence for female staff. If it could become a student cottage, and all staff were turned out of the residence halls and the house that James Rhoads had used during his presidency, 38 more students could be admitted. But the staff required housing. In an unintended pun, she wrote to Mary Garrett that the Low Buildings was necessary, for "the success of the college depends on our keeping them [women teaching assistants and staff] here satisfied on low salaries."[22]

Thomas' scheme was to float a stock company for the residence, with 23 shares, each worth $1,000. Subscribers were to get 4 percent interest, and the college to put aside annually a small amount from its operation to be used to buy the building. Thomas believed that many of the trustees would purchase stock shares. Cope and Stewardson drew up a plan. In June 1898 the trustees approved of the scheme, and building began in the summer. In her 1898 response to the alumnae toast, Thomas asked individual alumnae to invest in the Low Buildings, announcing to them that she was taking five shares.

It was part of M. Carey Thomas' persona to appear as a wealthy woman whose own philanthropy benefited Bryn Mawr. But this was an illusion she created out of Mary Garrett's wealth. In the case of the Low Buildings, Garrett paid for most of Thomas' stock, but did so in a manner hidden from view. Garrett wrote a check for $4,000 (in return for a mortgage on Thomas' securities) that Thomas then deposited into her bank. Thomas then wrote her own check to Tatnall. She explained to Garrett that handling it this way would keep Tatnall from ever determining the origin of the funds: "He cannot trace it then at all."[23]

The Low Buildings opened in October. It was an important advance for professional women (joined by a few men) for it offered them attractive suites and independent living. More students entered the residence halls. Thomas' easy scheme, however, turned out to be a nightmare of financing and personal supervision. The tenants, especially her sister Helen, proved to be very demanding. Within two months of its opening, it was clear that the Low Buildings was running a serious deficit. Again, Thomas turned to Garrett for a check.[24]

In her 1898 talk to the alumnae, Carey Thomas' second and more important goal was to get them to share her larger dream. From the outset she had linked plans for staff flats with her hopes for a library building that contained faculty offices, seminar rooms, and classrooms. When trustee and cousin David Scull, Jr., agreed in January 1898 to her approaching Cope and Stewardson about drawings for the Low Buildings, he also agreed that they might begin plans for the library, and the building committee that he chaired approved. Students immediately started to try to raise money, but their efforts netted only $100. Thomas turned to the alumnae, still young in 1898, and in October got their agreement to use the alumnae fund for the library. But nothing happened. In May 1899, forced by obligation to attend Meeting, she used her time wisely and, as she wrote to Garrett, "thought hard about how to get our library building." In December 1899, she asked the board of trustees to give her authorization to raise money for the college and requested a trustee committee to help.[25]

For a time no path opened, and she despaired. In November 1900, the alumnae association issued a formal appeal for $939,118, almost half of which was for a library, a dormitory, and a general heating and lighting plant for all buildings. Thomas hated begging, as she called fundraising, but during the next year she forced herself to pay calls on wealthy parents of Bryn Mawr students. After years of excoriating the rich, she now developed a new appreciation. After she visited Henry and Louisine Havemeyer, possessors of a fortune derived from sugar refining, listened to the music they provided, and viewed their collection of Japanese and Impressionist art, she wrote to Mary, "It was rather a revelation to me to find such wealth with such civilized tastes."[26]

At this point M. Carey Thomas' position as the voice for the higher education of women paid off. By the turn of the century John D. Rockefeller had shifted from making money to giving it away. Advised by the Baptist leaders he trusted, Rockefeller had underwritten the rebirth of the University of Chicago. One of his principal advisers was James Monroe Taylor, the Baptist minister who was president of Vassar College. Rockefeller's daughter Bessie was a Vassar student in the 1880s, and he became a trustee. Beginning in 1893, Rockefeller gave generously to Vassar. He also made smaller gifts to Barnard and Mount Holyoke. Thus, in 1901, Rockefeller was familiar with the needs of women's colleges.

In February 1901 Evangeline Walker Andrews, the alumna chairman of the students' building committee and wife of Bryn Mawr historian Charles McLean Andrews, wrote to Rockefeller asking to speak to him of the needs of Bryn Mawr. Impatient to have a students' building, undergraduates had decided to raise money through a May Day fete, inaugurating a treasured Bryn Mawr tradition. Andrews, a young alumna living in a faculty house alongside the campus, organized the event. She also helped develop and publish a decorative Bryn Mawr calendar. On the strength of these accomplishments, Andrews wrote to Rockefeller, describing her modest but effective efforts to raise money for Bryn Mawr. She told him of her hope that he would donate money to the college and stimulate other contributions by making his gift conditional on further donations. Rockefeller's office responded by granting Andrews an appointment with his son, John D. Rockefeller, Jr., and his philanthropic adviser, Frederick T. Gates. An agent for Rockefeller came to the college after commencement to examine its facilities. Carey Thomas spent a day with him in the effort to convince him of the need for a new academic building.[27]

In the fall of 1901 Carey Thomas began to confer with Rockefeller's advisers, and requested an interview with Rockefeller himself. Thomas was more than the president of a small women's college under Quaker auspices in a suburb outside Philadelphia. She was the international authority on women's higher education. She headed the college that the only study of higher education for women—her monograph—reported to have the very highest standards. John D. Rockefeller, Jr., agreed to listen to Thomas' appeal.

On December 4, 1901, Carey Thomas reported to Mary Garrett, Rockefeller did "just what I asked for." He offered to give $230,000—a sum greater than $4 million in 1994—to Bryn Mawr for a residence hall and a power plant for heating and lighting the college, if his contribution were matched by gifts of a roughly equal amount for a library. He set a deadline of Commencement Day 1902. In a handwritten letter Thomas thanked him for endowing the college with "the very things we wanted most and could least easily get given us." At last Carey Thomas had done something to please the trustees. Henry Tatnall was "really delighted and congratulated me over and over." Thomas met with reporters and put out an announcement on the Associated Press wires.[28]

The Rockefeller gift forced Thomas to become a master fundraiser. Bryn Mawr had no development office in 1901, or rather Carey Thomas was it. She had a formidable goal—$250,000 to be raised in six months for a library. Thomas threw herself into the effort. The day after the Rockefeller gift, she tried to explain to Mary Garrett: "It is clear," she wrote, "massage, Christmas, everything must bend to this necessity. Nothing in the world matters but this really."[29] Carey Thomas pursued the wealthy, using every connection she could find. Her policy of appealing to elite students bore fruit, and she got gifts from alumnae, their parents, and the parents of students. In addition, Thomas got Bryn Mawr's neighbors to give, along with wealthy trustees such as Justus Strawbridge. This time, she did not have to call on Mary Garrett.

In the course of the spring, Austin D. Houghton, a man on Rockefeller's staff, studied carefully the heating and power system of the college. His estimate of the cost of an adequate power plant rose markedly, and Thomas appealed to John D. Junior to get his father to raise his contribution. Houghton dictated the letter that Thomas wrote. Thomas confidently predicted to Garrett, "They are going to see us through by hook or by crook in short, and it is by crook." John D. Senior increased his gift to $250,000.[30]

Carey Thomas went right down to the wire. Immediately before commencement 1902, she announced to Mary, "I think we *are* complete, though I haven't time to count before the mail goes." By June 4 she received checks totaling $256,000. Thomas immediately wrote to Rockefeller of the campaign's success and her deep gratitude. The building of the dormitory and power plant began.[31]

Rockefeller's gift gave Carey Thomas the leverage she had been seeking for almost a decade. She had argued to the trustees that only if she were a trustee could she effectively convince potential donors. She was successful only after the fact. In the spring of 1902, John Garrett, one of her enemies on the board, determined to resign: to raise money the alumnae had sponsored a production of Gilbert and Sullivan's *HMS Pinafore,* and his Orthodox Quaker convictions could not countenance such a break with tradition. Thomas promptly mounted her campaign to take his place, insisting that for a president not to serve as a trustee was a defect in college organization. Philip Garrett wrote a letter to each trustee, nominated five others, and noted that he had not mentioned the name "of a person who is seeking her own election," an act that he believed should itself "put her election out of the question." David Scull, Jr., who had become Thomas' champion, responded with a letter of support for her. At the November 21 meeting, Justus Strawbridge nominated her, and she withdrew from the meeting. At the railroad station, Scull met her with the good news: the trustees had voted her in unanimously. She wrote to Mamie, "I am *most* pleased as it shows as nothing else could that the old opposition is dead."[32]

Carey Thomas was convinced it was her growing importance as a speaker in educational circles outside Bryn Mawr that had changed their minds. "I am now," she wrote to Hannah Smith, "the best woman speaker on educational subjects, and I rank high among men." Victory was sweet, and she savored it. To Hannah she exulted, "Francis King, Uncle James, Dr. Rhoads, and Father would wave their haloes, if they only could receive a Marconigram of this election."[33]

With construction of the power plant and residence hall, Carey Thomas' life became a knot of work. In the summer of 1901, she and Mary studied college buildings in Oxford. The summer of 1902 found her unable to travel. She wrote to Hannah that since commencement she had been working harder than she ever had to supervise the workmen sent by Rockefeller. When Walter Cope, the creative partner in Cope and Stewardson, died, Carey Thomas felt she had lost a kindred spirit. Her job was to see that Cope's aesthetic treatment was not lost in the process of construction. "It is a terrible business being modern and up-to-date in buildings that must look Jacobean, and I require the eyes of Argus to save our Medievalism from vanishing away." Rockefeller Hall was the most costly dormitory on campus, with thirty-nine single suites, each with a bedroom and sitting room, and basement service rooms for sewing and hairdressing. Continuing in the Jacobean Gothic mode that Cope and Stewardson had established in Denbigh and Pembroke East and West, Rockefeller Hall stretched the line of Pembroke West to the southwest border of the campus, extending the enclosure of the campus in the manner of Oxford and Cambridge. At the corner, a monumental arch in the tall tower created Owl Gateway, a pedestrian entrance approached by stairs.[34]

No one had anticipated the disruption that construction would cause in existing buildings, and Thomas coped with loss of heat and water. All this was magnified by a serious fire in Denbigh on March 16, 1902, that required its rebuilding. A national coal strike forced Thomas to find coke. The amount of detail that Thomas oversaw was staggering. If the college needed horses, she bargained for them. She chose electric light fixtures, curtains, carpet, and furniture. In February 1903, during a cold rain, she went outside to examine the wall of Rockefeller Hall. She reported to Mary, "The masons were laying it like cut stone and chiseling off all the irregularities. I simply felt as if everything would be ruined if it went on that way." She called out the supervising architect to teach the stone masons to build a stone wall that looked right. [35]

As a way of saving the college money, Rockefeller lent Austin Houghton from his staff to serve as contractor, continuing to pay his salary. As an agent of one of America's foremost capitalists, Houghton had access to materials at lower prices. Thomas worked closely with him, liked him, and appreciated his loyalty. When conflict arose at Bryn Mawr over financial or construction issues, Houghton would take Thomas' part. But, though he may have been loyal, he was also careless about money and possibly corrupt. He did not keep proper accounts. He may have taken for his own personal use some of the money Rockefeller had given to Bryn Mawr to pay construction bills. At one point Houghton told Thomas that he paid a bill using money from "a fund that helped Negro education."[36]

Carey Thomas faced two kinds of indebtedness. The first was capital cost overruns for construction. The second was the mounting deficits in the college's annual budget. Thomas believed that as additional students filled the new residence hall, greater resources would more than balance the deficit; but, in the short run, she had to face large transitional expenses.

Henry Tatnall, the treasurer of the Bryn Mawr board of trustees, had been in conflict with Thomas for years over college finances. A banker, he had taught Thomas the way that he wanted books to be kept, and she had complied. Although he had not been able to keep Bryn Mawr from deficits, for a decade he had made Thomas and Garrett personally responsible for making them up. With her successful fundraising, Thomas had moved the college to a different plateau. [37]

With a larger budget, however, the gap between income and outgo widened. A serious fire in Baltimore leveled some of the property Mary Garrett counted on for income, and she had to cut back on expenses, but, in any case, cost overruns and budget deficits now went beyond her ability to pay. To enable the college to operate, Tatnall agreed to two instruments. For the annual budget deficits, he oversaw the Contingent Fund to receive surpluses in good years and underwrite deficits in bad. For construction overruns on Rockefeller Hall, he allowed the college to borrow from the Library Building Fund Interest Account.

Debts from construction overruns on Rockefeller Hall mounted, and Carey Thomas was frightened. When the power plant exceeded estimates, Rockefeller had refused to give more than $250,000, leaving its additional construction expenses of over $30,000 to be saved elsewhere. John D. Junior suggested that the college plan a more modest dormitory. This, of course, was a compromise Thomas could not consider, and she went ahead with an expensive hall, justifying her action with the hope that Houghton might be able to build the library for less. Using interest from the Library Building Fund for Rockefeller Hall was a questionable action that had to be hidden from donors.

Clearly, then, one major factor in Bryn Mawr's financial quandary—in addition to Houghton's failings and the difficulty of predicting construction costs during this period—was Carey Thomas herself, always pushing, seeking more. In the years of construction, her long history of spending and debt took on new dimensions. In her negotiations with the Rockefellers, Thomas took a gamble, though she may not have been fully conscious of it. She took the money she had in hand, used it, and hoped that when the time of reckoning came, she could return to the source for more. In the past she had overspent and manipulated her private relations both in her personal life and in the college. She had turned to Mary Garrett to meet debts in the thousands. Now, as she confronted debts measured in the hundreds of thousands, an amount that in today's dollars would be many millions, she turned her persuasive gifts on John D. Rockefeller, Jr.

In the spring of 1903, as the plans for the library took shape, Thomas learned that its expense had been vastly underestimated: $250,000 yielded a library far smaller than had been proposed. In a tight spot, Thomas wrote to John D. Rockefeller, Jr., asking for a loan from his father of $100,000, to be repaid by future gifts. Carey Thomas was beginning to be aware of the personal hold that she had on the younger Rockefeller. She had learned that at a recent dinner he had spoken repeatedly to one of Thomas' friends "of his admiration" for her, and, as she put it to Tatnall, she hoped that "the fact that he seems to have taken a fancy to me may be of service to the college."[38]

John D. Rockefeller, Jr., met with Thomas twice in late spring 1903. After the first interview, Thomas reported, "Well, he saw me for one and one-half hours and was most jolly and not a bit displeased. . . . He seemed amused as well as sympathetic." Based on these conversations, Rockefeller drafted a long letter to his father, detailing all the cost overruns of the power plant and the dormitory. John D. Junior grounded his recommendation not only in the moral injunction that by this his father would fulfill his original pledge, but also in his belief in Bryn Mawr and Carey Thomas: "Mr. Gates feels, and I agree with him, that Bryn Mawr is unquestionably the leading woman's college in this country. . . . I know of no abler woman than Miss Thomas or one whose efforts you could more wisely support." The younger Rockefeller conveyed something of the hold that Carey Thomas had over him when he expressed the hope that his father would act quickly so that she might learn of this deed before she left to go abroad. He wrote that Thomas' travel was necessary "since she is almost broken down in health because of the time and thought which she has given to these improvements and the strain which this large indebtedness has brought upon her."[39]

John D. Junior's appeal was successful. He met with Carey Thomas again and told her that his father would increase his gift by $120,000. Furthermore, after seeing the college's final figures, he personally added $5,000 to total $125,000. Yet construction costs continued to mount, going far beyond the estimates of June 1903. By the time Rockefeller Hall was completed in April 1904, the college had borrowed $50,000 and had taken $26,000 from interest belonging to the Library Building Fund. Houghton suffered a breakdown and withdrew from the college from February 1904 until January 1905. When Thomas took over his books, she discovered the full extent of his financial carelessness. Although the library had been cut down and was being built without one of the planned wings, it, too, was going over budget. As annual budget deficits had continued to soar, the board had raised tuition. The Academic Committee of the Alumnae Association protested: "In the community at large, the opinion is not uncommonly expressed that Bryn Mawr is a college for the rich, and while we know that there has been little foundation for this report, we should be deeply distressed to have the idea justified in fact." Abandoning their effort for a students' building, the alumnae initiated a campaign to raise endowment for the academic program.[40]

In May 1905 Carey Thomas again appealed to Rockefeller through his son, this time for $122,000 to be matched by other gifts. Her letter is a masterpiece of manipulation. Why not appeal to Bryn Mawr's donors for funds rather than return to Rockefeller? To this essential question Thomas provided a lengthy and indirect argument designed to ensnare Rockefeller by implicating him. When Houghton broke down and Thomas took over the books, she realized that Houghton had exceeded his revised estimates by almost $50,000. "The knowledge of this dreadful deficit . . . crushed us to the earth." Because the college had used the interest from the Library Building Fund to pay for Rockefeller Hall, Thomas could not raise additional money without explaining to givers "the difficulties we got into in building Rockefeller Hall, about which your great kindness has made it unnecessary for us to speak up to the present time." In this circuitous way, she was suggesting that Rockefeller had not paid for the hall in full. In addition, she was alluding to Houghton's difficulties and maneuvers that may have included his getting money from the Rockefeller funds designed for African-American colleges. Moreover, the alumnae had responded to the operating deficit by making a request to the board of trustees to raise a million-dollar endowment to support academic programs. This had forced Thomas' hand, and she was compelled to help their campaign, making it impossible to simultaneously raise funds for the library. Andrew Carnegie, her one outside hope, had turned her down.

Carey Thomas played on her own weakness. She stated to the younger Rockefeller that she found herself during Houghton's absence so overwhelmed with work "that it was a question whether it would be possible for me to go through the year without breaking down utterly." That Thomas did fear for her health was true, for she wrote of it in her private correspondence. However, in her public life Thomas had always hidden her physical frailties, even when she had to lie to do so. She must have known this personal revelation would be effective with John D. Junior.[41]

It was. He urged his father to give Bryn Mawr $75,000 to cover the costs of the dormitory. This time, the father was vexed. He wrote to his son that the report of costs so far exceeding estimates "leads me to inquire seriously whether they really act in good faith with us. If they do not, it would be a pretty serious charge against the administration." He suggested that in the future, his pledges of money be stated in ways that did not continue the obligation beyond the specific gift. But he gave his son leave to give Bryn Mawr up to $75,000.[42]

On Thomas' letter urging more money is a new kind of notation by John D. Rockefeller, Jr.: in its margins, at the points in which she suggested that he had promised more funds to the college, are the penciled comments "never" and "no." In his letter to Thomas he denied that he ever suggested that his father might be willing to contribute further to the library fund: "I cannot recall that any such thought was ever in my mind, much less in my lips." He asked for strict accounting.[43] Carey Thomas complied with full reports and every ounce of her persuasive powers. Although in this period Thomas had efficient stenographers to type her professional correspondence, all of her letters and reports to the younger Rockefeller are handwritten. She was relying on the force of personality.

Her success was absolute. On Christmas Eve 1905, she received a check for $80,000 to cover the loan and the interest taken from the Library Building Fund. She confided to her diary that she wept, "the relief was so unspeakable." Both Rockefeller Hall and the power plant were free of debt, and the college could complete the library, minus the wing. As she later reported to Caroline McCormick Slade, the younger Rockefeller authorized the large additional sum after she had laid "the whole situation before him and told him that the trustees held me responsible for the deficits of the contractor." Ultimately Rockefeller's total contribution came to over one-half million dollars, a sum greater than $8.5 million in 1994 dollars.[44]

CHAPTER 18

Soaring Eagle

BUOYED by fame, Carey Thomas moved into the new century with an outward confidence. Yet she still had inner doubts. In writing to Hannah Smith during this period, Carey reflected on Hannah's literary son and son-in-law, Logan Pearsall Smith and Bertrand Russell, and her daughters, Mary Berenson, nicknamed Mariechen, now an art historian, and Alys Russell: "Logan and Bertie are doing the things that seem to me most worth doing; and Mariechen the second nicest, pictures; and Alys the third nicest, *women*." Carey Thomas still had her hierarchy: to be a writer or a scholar was a higher calling than that of a reformer dedicated to the cause of women.[1]

On occasion she could still hear the siren calls of Europe and dream of art. When important visitors came to the college, she was bewitched by their presence and basked in the glow of their reflected light. Reality always intruded, however. The Italian actress Eleanora Duse, in Philadelphia to perform, came to Bryn Mawr and was trailed about by adoring students. In her diary, Carey Thomas wrote that Duse was "very, very attractive and clever and lovable," and to Garrett, "I am fathoms deep under her charm"; but the fear of scandal followed as Duse was heard to say of Thomas that she was "unmarried sans rancoeur." William Butler Yeats spoke at the college and enthralled Carey Thomas with his presence and his poetry, but as she faced her tasks, she had to conclude, "He is, however, a great interruption to unpoetical life." Mary and Bernard Berenson were a different story, and when they visited in 1903, she felt the contrast between her life and that of her cousin keenly: "It makes me long for Italy and pictures to have so much talk. . . . An American college seems to me a desolate affair."[2]

These moments were infrequent, and they were quickly drowned out by the press of work. Carey Thomas' life had taken a definite shape. She was supported by Mary Garrett, who was committed to the cause. With the Bryn Mawr School and the Johns Hopkins medical school on solid ground, Mary turned to back Carey in her work at Bryn Mawr. Thomas was now without critics who could reach and influence her. Her father, James Rhoads, and

James Whitall were no longer around to pressure her to modulate her tones or alter her strategy. The Quaker trustees who remained were there to be outwitted. As Mamie Gwinn withdrew, she took with her the force of her implicit criticism. Utterly believing in her work, Mary only wanted Carey to perform it more efficiently, to put order into her accounts, and to give her a little time. Carey Thomas was free to become the single-minded president of Bryn Mawr College.

She worked very hard. Although the administration of Bryn Mawr remained completely in her hands, she began to get the help that she needed. She gave up teaching, except for an occasional stint. Isabel Maddison, who had become her secretary in 1895, performed an increasing number of tasks of a technical nature and gradually assumed many of the duties of today's college registrar as well as some of those of a dean of the faculty. Thomas found capable secretaries. When she was not preoccupied by other matters, she sorted her mail to determine what must be answered immediately and dictated for several hours each day, as many as fifteen letters.

That is not to say that Carey Thomas' life was serene and happy. It never was. She was and always would be rushed, overworked, and angry at the demands that her life required. In late October 1899 she tried to tell Mary why she could not write better letters. Her days were filled with uninterrupted work: "I have been here solidly, and my office work has been incessant." Between 8:00 and 8:45 in the morning, she saw the cook, went to the water closet, sorted the letters of the day before, and answered her secretary's written questions. "From 9:00 to 1:30 I have a succession of interviews and so far have not averaged one hour a day dictating. Usually I have gone back for two or even three hours. . . . I have not shopped at all, paid no calls, written no private letters, done nothing."[3]

During these years she did begin to take time to care for herself. She had her hair washed in Philadelphia and saw dressmakers regularly. She tried to have a regular lunch at one, followed by an afternoon walk (or possibly a drive) for an hour or more. She normally had a massage. But in addition to her regular work, she frequently had to entertain a lecturer, give a Bryn Mawr dinner, attend a trustee meeting, or lobby with individual trustees. She gave chapel talks and public speeches. In 1902–03 she resumed teaching, lecturing an hour a week. With all she had to do, she continued to feel rushed. In one of her many low moments, she described herself to Mary in this way: "I have been living from hand to mouth like a beast of prey, and it seems hopeless to get order out of anything." She simply demanded too much of herself and of others. She could not release her drive for perfection nor her insistence on complete control.[4]

In the letters that she dictated on those busy days, one can see Thomas' skill as an administrator. The professional correspondence has been preserved in neatly kept letterpress books containing copies of the letters that she sent to faculty, trustees, and associates. The first twelve official letterpress books of the college have never been found; but to read number 13, beginning in 1898, is to read the correspondence of an experienced administrator with command of every detail of the college.

At the turn of the century she acted alone, making decisions large and small without committees, administrators, or college advisers. If a professor was to be hired, she searched and negotiated. She fired. She set courses, suggested readings, determined student work load. When the Undergraduate Association requested that the hated German and French senior oral examination be rescinded, she alone kept it in place. She supervised work on college land and buildings. She acted as landlord for college property leased to professors and therefore managed aspects of their housekeeping. She oversaw the living conditions of students and constantly fretted over their food. Minor details did not escape her.

Major decisions were hers to make. Two examples can suffice. In spring 1898, frustrated that she could not bring the students' dining up to her standards, she decided to change the system of residence hall mistresses. She wrote to Garrett, "They *are* stupid old cats and will not admit they are wrong." In their places she determined to install college graduates, who were to have nothing to do with the kitchen, supplemented by a single buyer for all food and by competent cooks. With one stroke she created the system of house wardens, putting at the head of most college residence halls youthful Bryn Mawr graduates. In 1899 she learned that many younger women on the staff, Bryn Mawr graduates in the main, were smoking. She determined that the college could not allow this. It was still unthinkable that undergraduates be allowed to smoke, and, as she wrote to Mary, "I do not see how the students can be expected to give up what graduates of the college in responsible positions do." The decree that no women on the staff smoke either at the college or in their own dwellings made a sharp distinction between male and female and ultimately required the resignation of one of the college's most dedicated essay teachers.[5]

In her fictional presentation of Bryn Mawr in *Fernhurst*, Gertrude Stein reflected on Thomas' need for control as it shaped her dealings with students and discipline. Stein wrote that self-government was a sham because, in fact, the students' regulation of their own conduct was in the hands of the college head "who dominated by a passion for absolute power administers an admirable system of espionage and influence which she interrupts with occasional bald exercise of authority and not infrequent ignominious retreats." Stein accurately caught the paradox of a college president who believed in broad liberty, in allowing women the freedom of men students, and yet was so constituted that "it was impossible for her to be in relation with anything or anyone without controlling to the minutest detail." These judgments were secondhand, for Stein knew Thomas only from the reports of the young Bryn Mawr alumnae at the Johns Hopkins medical school. Although they cannot be corroborated, they merit attention because they are consistent with Thomas' behavior elsewhere in the college.[6]

Carey Thomas' effort to know and direct all could work for good as well as for ill. When sophomore Margaret Emerson Bailey fainted in class from fatigue, Thomas called her to the Deanery. Why, Thomas wanted to know, had she been painting on the floor of a filthy neighborhood barn? Before explaining that to stay in college she had to work and the barn gave her space to make large illustrations of embryo chicks for the biology department, Bailey accused Thomas of following her and peeking in the windows. Thomas retorted that "peeked" was "not a word with any dignity. We shall prefer to say I looked." As they discussed her job and her courses, Thomas seemed to have learned a great deal about Bailey. After a stout tea of sandwiches and cake— Thomas "took two helpings unabashed" and persuaded the young woman to do the same—she proposed that her undergraduate guest tutor during the term and prepare a girl for college during the summer. Bailey's judgment: "Here was a backer who might use devious means, but who'd never let a student down."[7]

In her own mind Carey Thomas could see gold and dross among students. She worked so hard, controlled all, did not delegate, and insisted on perfection because only she had a clear vision of Bryn Mawr. At the turn of the century, confronting trustees who opposed her, and scornful of subordinates' abilities, she alone had to turn dreams into reality.

II

IN THE early twentieth century Carey Thomas faced a faculty becoming restive. While she was achieving fame as a speaker and attracting John D. Rockefeller and other donors, they were at home. In 1905 Bryn Mawr had thirty-three on its faculty, thirty men and three women. Unlike newspaper reporters, philanthropists, or other college presidents, they saw Thomas from the inside. Her college manner was distinctly different from her public persona. As she emerged after the deaths of the men with whom she had worked most closely in her first difficult years as president, what held her in check? She had always been willing to tell a partial truth when it served her. Now she began to lie when it suited her and when she could get away with it. She had a passionate temper and could flare in anger.

Most of Thomas' actions cannot be tracked, for they existed orally, and when they were set down, they were done so many years later, by partisans. In most cases, there are no records of her conferences with students, members of the faculty, or trustees. An exception is her dealings with Professor William Allan Neilson. He was a special case. He tended to write out his concerns, for he was an ambitious and careful man. After teaching at Bryn Mawr, he had a distinguished career as a professor of English literature at Harvard and as an outstanding president of Smith College. His papers allow a glimpse into the mind of a young male professor living in Yarrow, the boarding house for faculty men.

Neilson was particularly important to Carey Thomas and Mamie Gwinn. Alfred Hodder's replacement, he took over the two-year course on the history of English language and literature that Thomas (with Gwinn's silent help) had created. A Scot, trained at the University of Edinburgh and Harvard, Neilson initially appealed to Thomas, and she pronounced him on arrival "charming." In his first months, Neilson was curious about his college president. To his brother he described his first invitation to the Deanery: "We had a very nice dinner, Quaker simplicity appearing only in the absence of wines. She [Thomas] did her best to make up for it by an abundance of rum in the frozen pudding. Conversation was good—the president having a marvellous power of making what she knows go a very long way."[8]

Like many of his colleagues, Neilson was young and a bachelor, but he stood out. His course on English and Scottish popular ballads pitted him against Mamie Gwinn's refined aestheticism. He had an open manner that he later thought Gwinn misunderstood as flirtatiousness. In the spring of his first year of teaching, Thomas called him in to tell him of student criticism of his too-great informality during quizzes. Neilson responded that she should not allow such reports to be circulated. Thomas wrote to reassure him that she had called him in only to see that there was no basis to the students' reports; but she clearly intended the conference to serve as a warning to him to change his behavior, for she went on to state that she felt that he should know "the feeling among some members of the class in regard to the English quizzes (a feeling that is wide spread)." Because of the quality of his work, Thomas wrote, she was the more concerned that he "deal with the English quiz question promptly." Neilson had asked that "if a report is to be listened to at all, its source should be investigated and the instigator made to show grounds."

Thomas pointed out to him the impossibility of this by giving him an example: "Two or three years ago an instructor in the college heard, not through me but through a student, that a certain remark had been made about his work in the presence of another member of our teaching staff. He thereupon insisted on calling the student who had made the remark, the instructor in whose presence it was made, and the student in whose presence it was made, and held a little court of justice, reducing the offender to tears and publishing the remark to the whole college, the result being that his success as a teacher was practically gone from that moment. . . . The whole college sympathized

with her [the student] for the inhuman manner in which she had been treated."
Because the full archival record of Bryn Mawr College, including daily letters
to Mary Garrett, contains no other mention of this incident, it is likely that
Thomas' narrative to Neilson came from her imagination.[9]

Neilson was certainly aware of the young women whom he taught. During
Sunday worship he and his closest faculty friend, Charles Bakewell, lectured
at the Ethical Society, and by February some students followed them there.
Neilson met students informally at the many meetings, lectures, receptions,
and teas of the Bryn Mawr term; their mothers seem to have invited him with
their daughters to luncheon. In the all-female society of students, the male
professors were called the "Temptations." Romances between male professors
and students did occur. Bakewell courted and then married after graduation a
Bryn Mawr student. In their apartment, the Bakewells entertained faculty and
students on Sunday evenings, and Neilson was part of their circle.

Many of the unmarried men lived in Yarrow, the bachelor's apartment
house, where criticism of Thomas was rife. They were in a situation, unusual
at the turn of the century, of working under a female head. Carey Thomas
herself, then in her early forties, found it hard to lead this body of independent,
highly trained professors. As she wrote to Mary Garrett the following year
about a faculty meeting, "it is always somewhat anxious for me to preside over
so many men, 27 in all, 4 of them women." Something of male faculty
disrespect for her is caught in Neilson's report to his brother of the presentation
of the Sargent portrait. He mentioned that he had not really seen the portrait
well and could not judge it. He noted that all the speeches at the presentation
were given by alumnae and trustees: "The faculty declined to take any part
except by being present, and I suspect the old woman was pretty mad. There
is a point in hypocrisy beyond which even a college professor cannot easily
go."[10]

At the end of his second year, Neilson requested the increase in salary that
Thomas had orally promised him when he was hired. It was a time of budget
stringency, and Thomas had to hold all salaries constant, but she did not tell
him this. On March 13, 1900, she reported to Mary Garrett that she saw
Neilson "and asked him to extend his engagement one year at the same salary
for $1,000 till we saw where we were and could tell more about his work.
He said he could not live on $1,000, which is true, and seemed bitterly
disappointed."[11]

Neilson gave his brother a quite different report. At their conference,
Thomas launched an assault on his record at Bryn Mawr "of the most absurd
sort." Her principal accusation was that he had failed in graduate work because
his students had not published and because his courses attracted a large following. As Neilson conferred with his friends at Bryn Mawr and Haverford, "the
universal opinion is that first, she wants me cheap, as she wants everything

cheap," and that second, "she and Gwinn are piqued at my success in work which they have attempted less successfully, and have tried to use their position of authority to get their revenge." In the course of the meeting, Thomas had softened her accusation to state that Neilson's graduate work was now fully satisfactory. Neilson was bewildered and angry: if he was so successful, "one wondered what she had been talking about. Her absolute lack of honesty made me sick."[12]

Neilson immediately wrote to his Harvard mentor to see if there were positions available elsewhere. Thomas informed him that the trustee executive committee met and did not increase his salary because the full board had already passed the budget for the following year. To give himself time to reflect and to learn of his chances elsewhere, Neilson waited a fortnight to write to Thomas that he declined to accept a continuation at Bryn Mawr on his $1,000 salary. When Thomas answered that she would recommend him for a position at another institution and that she would state that he was leaving Bryn Mawr because the trustees would not give him an increase, Neilson would not cooperate. As she put it to Mary Garrett, he "refused to be palmed off on another place if he was not good enough for Bryn Mawr."[13]

He wrote a letter to Thomas, carefully outlining the accusations against him and defending his teaching, and requested that she read it to the trustees. It was a sticky situation for Thomas, because Rufus Jones, a trustee, was Neilson's close friend. Jones was a relatively young, but already eminent, Haverford professor of philosophy and the editor of *The American Friend*. He had taken James Thomas' place on the board. Conveniently, Thomas "lost" Neilson's letter before the trustee meeting. Neilson learned from inside that there had been no criticism on the board of his teaching, that the only objector was the president. He left enraged at Thomas' deception.[14]

On the day that he wrote to the trustees, Neilson composed a poem that he circulated among an informal group of his faculty and student friends in their humorous private publication *The Midnightly Fill-a-Stein*. In a play on a poem by Rudyard Kipling, he began by stating that in all his dealings he had met a range of men,

> *But our Minnie was the toughest of the lot.*

> *   *   *

> *She squatted on my 'ead and blocked my courses;*
> *She cut my feelings up an' tore my fur,*
> *And you never yet could tell her what remorse is.*

> *So 'ere's to you Minnie Carey, in your College in Bryn Mawr*
> *You're a rather shaky Quaker, but at dodging you're a star.*

You give us our new contracts, and if we want 'em signed
We've got to go and jolly you, whenever you're inclined.

She's always oil and honey when we're hired;
But, 'fore we know, she's got us on the run.
She blames it on the Board when we get fired,
And for reasons she can always take the bun.

She's a daisy, she's a ducky, she's a lamb,
She's a modern educator with a twist,
She's the only thing that ever brings a damn
From professor's lips that maidens never kist.[15]

Thomas' view was less poetic, but equally hostile. As she faced Neilson's likely departure for Harvard, her view of him shifted markedly. He was, she wrote to Mary Garrett, "*not* good." The day Neilson wrote his letter to the trustees, she reported, "he has made a fiasco in graduate work." Several days later he had "behaved like a fool—and how thankful I am to be rid of him!" In mid-April, Thomas called Neilson "a liar." At the point that Carey Thomas' judgment of a person became clouded by conflict, she turned from support to enmity.[16]

III

IN THE course of the friction over Neilson, as a way of demonstrating that Harvard University remained eager to place its men at Bryn Mawr, Thomas presented psychologist Hugo Munsterberg's letter in support of a candidate to the trustees. Rufus Jones criticized it as presumptuous. Forced to backpedal, Thomas wrote to Jones that the letter was offensive, especially since Thomas knew Munsterberg only slightly. "It makes me hope that we shall never have a Jew in our Bryn Mawr College faculty."[17]

In 1891, she had hired the German physiologist Jacques Loeb, a Jew, a decidedly advanced step for an American liberal arts college. (Later, as a member of the faculty of the University of Chicago, he won the Nobel Prize.) To her credit, she also insisted on official tolerance among students. In 1898, when a mother bore her daughter's complaint about being placed with a Jewish roommate, Thomas wrote the mother that she would not force the Jewish student to move. If she did so, "the college . . . [would] take part in what has grown to be a religious controversy, and our great desire is to show the strictest impartiality." In fact, she moved both students. As she wrote to Garrett, "it became a race question" involving a quarrel "between the anti- and pro-Jews." She added, "It is a lesson. Never again shall we put a Jew and Christian together." This private thought led to no change in Bryn Mawr College's official toleration of Jewish students. Appropriate to this policy, in 1915 Rabbi Stephen S. Wise was one of several visiting clergy to deliver a sermon.[18]

In the 1900s, Carey Thomas' professional correspondence is riddled with statements asserting the need to prevent Jews from receiving faculty positions. A clearly documented instance in which Thomas sought to bar from the Bryn Mawr College faculty a person she suspected of being Jewish came in September 1906. Upon her return from Europe, she found the college without a necessary economist. To locate one, she immediately contacted her network of senior professors in the field. From Professor Hollander of Johns Hopkins she received a high recommendation for Dr. A. M. Sakolski. Thomas wired Sakolski to find out if he was free to accept a position and if he could come for an interview. She read his monograph and was greatly "impressed with its ability and also with the excellent language in which it . . . [was] written." In the meantime, she wrote to George E. Barnett to find out what she regarded as necessary information—Sakolski's nationality and if he were Jewish. She asked Barnett to telegraph her in the "following order . . . 'Russian' ('Pole', etc.); 'native born' (or 'not native born'); 'Hebrew' (or 'not Hebrew')."[19]

Professor John B. Clark of Columbia wrote recommending T. McWilliams, a man with a safe name. It was with relief that Thomas could respond to Clark, "It is much more satisfactory to have a faculty made up as far as possible of our own good Anglo-Saxon stock." Her decision made, Thomas had to inform Sakolski that he was no longer a candidate. She regretted, she wrote to him, that her initial letter to him was "not clear." She had not meant to invite him for an interview; she had only written to inquire if he was "willing to come . . . in case I telegraphed" with the request. Since her letter to him, she learned that Mr. McWilliams, her first choice, could come to Bryn Mawr for the interview. She did not convey that she had inquired about Sakolski's ethnic origins or that it was in the interim that she had first learned of McWilliams. Thomas was ultimately left without an economist and had to request that Henry Raymond Mussey, the head of the department, take on extra teaching to cover the courses.[20]

IV

THERE was in Carey Thomas' dream of Bryn Mawr a deep fault. Her college was not for all women, but only for some. Since girlhood, she had been elitist. She valued discrimination. When she thought about women she imagined those like herself, privileged and educated Anglo-Saxon Protestants. All others were essentially nonpersons.

Her attitude toward African Americans had roots in her Baltimore child-hood. Although her mother had entertained the writer Frances Harper and her daughter in her parlor, Carey met African Americans only as servants. In her early adulthood her prejudice was so widely shared, so pervasive, that it did not have to be mentioned. As she moved into midlife and came in contact with prominent African Americans, what had been a largely tacit racism took a different cast, and she began to voice her animosities. In March 1902, after dinner with Booker T. Washington, she wrote Mary: "Washington was disappointing, very, although he tells admirable stories, but he is like a Negro in the way his mind works, and he relapses into Negro pronunciations." In 1902 Carey Thomas normally wrote disparagingly of dinner companions. What was interesting in this instance was that she framed her negatives in racial terms.[21]

In 1899, the question of the admission of African-American students came up hypothetically in a statement in *Nineteenth Century*. Thomas wrote to William H. Ward that the discussion in the periodical was untrue, that since the opening of the college, "the question of the admission of a student of African blood has never been brought before either the faculty or the trustees. The difficulty of our entrance examinations and the fact that we do not admit on certificate may perhaps account for this."[22]

Carey Thomas had worked for years to improve the public schools of Philadelphia and to develop good relations between them and Bryn Mawr College. In 1893 the trustees established a set of four scholarships, each of which paid full tuition at Bryn Mawr College for four years for an outstanding graduate of the new Philadelphia High School for Girls. By the turn of the century the number of these scholarships had increased to eight. In the spring of 1901, Jessie Redmon Fauset, an honor student at the High School for Girls, was in a position to win the Bryn Mawr scholarship. Normally she would have been welcomed as an entering student. However, Jessie Fauset's blood was African.

Thomas had not faced the issue of the admission of an African-American student to Bryn Mawr College because nonwhite young women simply knew better than to apply. Jessie Fauset did not have to apply in any official way. It was her strength as a student that positioned her for the opportunity that a white student similarly placed could expect, the Bryn Mawr scholarship. Working quietly to avoid any publicity, Thomas diverted Fauset from Bryn Mawr to Cornell. In an understanding with Mrs. George W. Kendrick, Jr., Thomas agreed to help raise the money for Fauset's tuition to Cornell for four years, personally paying 10 percent, and taking responsibility for subscriptions of 50 percent. In the correspondence relating to Fauset, Thomas made it clear she wished there were alternatives: "I feel, of course, pledged to help raise the money for Miss Fawcett's tuition fees if no other arrangements can be made, but I need not say that I should be very much pleased to be relieved from the necessity, in view of the fact that there are, as no one knows better than you, so many pressing needs for which to raise money." In 1904, she wrote in response to a reminder that the tuition of "the colored girl, Jessie Faussett" was due, that "it seems to me that it is taking her a very long time to get her degree."[23]

In addition to the correct spelling of her name, what Carey Thomas refused to learn was that Jessie Fauset had a brilliant career at Cornell, where she was elected to Phi Beta Kappa. Her subsequent important work as high school teacher, literary editor of *Crisis*, novelist, and midwife to the Harlem Renaissance was to be equally ignored. The Jessie Fauset case has remained hidden in the college's letter books. Although there is no record that Fauset ever knew the full story of Thomas' deception, she knew something, for in her novel of 1926, *There Is Confusion*, Fauset located white evil masked by hypocrisy in a Quaker family in Bryn Mawr, Pennsylvania.[24]

Carey Thomas' racism was such that no specific could ever challenge it. After steering Fauset to Cornell, Thomas continued to dissuade potential African-American applicants and to assert that no student with African blood had ever applied to Bryn Mawr. In 1906 she wrote to a teacher in Washington that though "the question has never come up at Bryn Mawr College as to whether it would be possible to admit a student of the Negro race," she would advise such a student "to seek admission to a college situated in one of the New England states" where she would derive the benefits of close association with other students, which was not possible at Bryn Mawr with its large number of students coming from the South and Middle States.[25]

V

BY THE early twentieth century Carey Thomas was willing to lie and to act surreptitiously to gain her ends. In her mind it was always the good of the college. But who was to judge where considered judgment ended and personal enmity and prejudice began? Thomas believed in no standard higher than herself. With the loss of her father's generation on the board of trustees, she accepted no loyal opposition.

Moreover, the college suffered from Thomas' sense of rush. With so much to do, some of her tasks got laid aside. She found it increasingly difficult to write extended pieces, perhaps because she had once depended upon Gwinn's help, which was no longer there. In a five-year period beginning 1899–1900 she did not write her president's reports.

A subterranean current of criticism was growing within the faculty. But although certain trustees opposed her policies, no opposition could be seen on the surface. In these years, M. Carey Thomas appeared in full control, a national spokeswoman for higher education, a consummate fund-raiser, and the champion of an expanding women's college upholding the highest standards. In 1905–06, however, a serious crisis erupted that threatened to bring Thomas down. Its origins lay in the conflicts of the preceding years. The specific elements came from many different strands.

Evangeline Walker Andrews, once a major supporter, had become a thorn in Thomas' side. Their history was long and complex. An unusually attractive student, Evangeline Walker entered Bryn Mawr College in 1889. Her sister Ethel, also an alumna, was the founder of the Ethel Walker School; her cousin Susan Walker was the first head of student self-government. Thomas chose Evangeline Walker as one of her secretaries upon her graduation, but her service was cut short by marriage to one of the college's most promising professors, the U.S. historian Charles McLean Andrews. As a faculty wife living on the edge of campus, she remained deeply involved with the college. In 1900 she single-handedly produced the college's first May Day; and in the years to come ran it as a fundraiser for a students' building. She chaired the students' building committee and in that capacity made the initial approach to John D. Rockefeller. In 1901–03 she served as junior bursar. Thomas encouraged many of her efforts, but thwarted others. Andrews applied for a position as reader in the essay department, but Thomas rejected her both because to hire a teacher not going on with academic work would lower standards and because Thomas could not see how Andrews could negotiate both teaching and child care. When Andrews sought to use the May Day funds to open a teahouse for students, the profits to be added to the endowment of the students' building, Thomas lobbied against it. Ultimately the teahouse was established, but the conflict created a breach between them. By 1905 Carey Thomas saw Evangeline Andrews as an irritant. As Thomas wrote to Garrett, after describing a minor matter that Andrews had brought to the board of trustees, "I do not know how I can run the college if Mrs. Andrews is always interfering."[26]

In the early twentieth century, Thomas confronted a changed student body. Her work had paid off: Bryn Mawr had become fashionable. But as wealthier, more pleasure-loving students came on campus, so, too, came their relaxed notions of college life. During these years Thomas was losing touch with students. She had once been their slim young dean and teacher of English literature. Now she was a stocky, white-haired, middle-aged presence who spoke to them in chapel or who strode rapidly with her cane across campus, her robe billowing. She knew them only en masse. Forty years later Margaret Emerson Bailey recalled the moment that Thomas, escorting wealthy parents of a prospective student around the campus, used her to assure them that she took a personal interest in each undergraduate. Knowing Margaret not at all at that point, Thomas smiled directly at her and said firmly, "Good morning, Nancy." Bailey reflected, "Old rascal that she was, Miss Thomas trusted to a student to play up to her game and not betray her. . . . Just for an instant, the President had let her share a joke and then sailed off."[27]

Carey Thomas did not have student friends in this period. Although she still registered freshmen, conferred with Self-Government, and administered the senior language oral examinations, she normally did not teach, and she was away a great deal of the time. Only a very few came to her at-homes or senior receptions. A snapshot taken of Thomas talking informally to students from the Deanery porch shows students distracted in the crowd. Though some undergraduates saw her as a power-driven manipulator running a spy system, the most common memory was that she was a distant figure who inspired both awe and its accompanying humor. After hearing recent graduates describe Thomas, Gertrude Stein imagined her as "a dignified figure with a noble head and a preoccupied abrupt manner. She was somewhat lame and walked about leaning on a tortoise-shell stick the imperative movement of which made a way through all obstacles." Bailey remembered her as seeming "a very hand-some, rather jolly-looking witch who found a kind of secret merriment in bamboozling her professors and hoodwinking everyone and managing the college with a strong, imperious will."[28]

No longer able to compel by her personal appeal, Thomas turned to prohibitions and rule-making in an effort to control behavior and raise standards. Students were not to smoke. They were not to receive Haverford students who serenaded them under their windows. They were not to become members of Haverford's Cercle Français but to organize their own. She was joined in this by faculty who voted a series of changes to regulate students. New rules made class attendance mandatory. The college established a "Merit Law" setting the minimum grade level necessary for a student to graduate. The merit law led to painful controversies as students, not all of them wealthy and irresponsible, who had attended for four years and passed courses suddenly found themselves blocked from graduation. By the merit law, Laura Alice Bartlett, whom Thomas later described as a "protégée" of Evangeline Andrews, was denied a degree and barred from ever receiving a Bryn Mawr B.A.[29]

In October 1905 Bartlett petitioned the college. She argued that she had worked during her student years and could only take courses at hours when she was not employed. She had passed all her courses. Denial of the degree would be a particular hardship for her, limiting her ability to earn the income necessary for both her own support and that of her mother. The trustees denied the request, but Bartlett persisted. In April, she petitioned the board to cancel a semester or a year of her college work so that she might return to the college and retake her examinations. Although the faculty insisted that it, not the trustees, had the power to determine standards for degrees, it made a report to the trustees answering the petition point by point, and recommended that it be rejected. The board spurned the faculty report and in private, as Thomas wrote to Garrett, "behaved shockingly. . . . [They] said it was their business to investigate every complaint, that the faculty had no rights in the matter." Thomas felt that the board was usurping her authority and that of the faculty. At the June meeting, James Wood came to Thomas' defense and insisted "that absolute justice had been done, that careful and prolonged discussion covering a year had discovered only justice and fair dealing toward a most unworthy girl." The board voted unanimously to deny Bartlett's petition and passed a resolution that petitions about degrees were to go to the faculty.[30]

Faculty began to make their restiveness known. The budget crises precipitated by construction limited Thomas' ability to raise faculty salaries. In theory Thomas was on their side, for she knew that higher salaries were needed to get and keep professors. The academic year 1905–06 was a crisis year. As she worked over estimates with the college bookkeeper, Thomas realized, as she wrote to Garrett, "We simply have not enough money to run the college with our present organization, and I must make a big cut in salaries. Nothing else can be pared down." Professors were getting outside offers that she was unable to match.[31]

As was the case with Neilson, when Thomas faced an individual professor and her hands were tied, she directed her anger at him. In March 1905 Lindley Miller Keasbey asked for an additional $1,000. She had once had high regard for him. It was in reference to Keasbey that at an earlier moment, when she confronted the possibility of losing him to a university, she had first uttered what became one of her famous statements, "I am tired of being the nursing mother of the famous scholars of this country." Now she was willing to let him go. The directors of the Alumnae Association met and offered to donate $1,000 to keep Keasbey. After Thomas successfully talked them out of making an offer to the trustees in this form, Evangeline Andrews made an offer to the trustees to supplement Keasbey's salary alone. Most likely she was willing to use for this purpose the college tearoom money. Thomas wrote to Garrett that she had presented the board of trustees with Andrews' offer, and "the trustees were properly impressed with the unsuitability but refused to act on such an irregular proposition and accepted Keasbey's resignation with enthusiasm." Lindley Keasbey went to the University of Texas, where he continued his distinguished career.[32]

The Keasbey episode illustrated some of the dangers of alumnae involvement in the college. Yet Thomas also knew how important alumnae could be. They had been her early supporters in the library campaign, and many of them sympathized with her dream of a greater Bryn Mawr. Each year she held a two-day meeting with the Conference Committee of the Alumnae Association that systematically examined areas of the college and suggested changes. The Alumnae Association had long sought representation on the board of trustees, and in December 1905 formally requested a conference with the trustees to consider it, a meeting to which the trustees agreed.[33] Thomas initially opposed alumnae trustees, for she feared further meddling in decisions that she believed were hers alone, but she came to support the effort. She had lost "fathers" on the board; perhaps she could replace them with "daughters." Moreover, because only a few alumnae were Friends, Thomas saw alumnae representation on the board as taking the college even farther from its Quaker moorings, and she regarded as welcome anything that could reduce Quaker influence at Bryn Mawr.

The founder's will limited the board of trustees to thirteen members of the Orthodox branch of the Society of Friends. Working with the college's lawyer, John G. Johnson, Thomas found that a peculiarity of Pennsylvania law gave an opening to alter the college's governing body. Pennsylvania required an educational institution to be governed by a board of directors. In compliance, each year the trustees had elected themselves directors. Johnson agreed with Thomas' proposition that the trustees name additional directors (who would not have to be Quakers) and that the directors become the working board. In December 1905 the trustees agreed. The board of directors could include the two alumnae positions that the association had requested in May. In addition, the augmented board could include an important donor to the college. Carey Thomas expressed it to Mary Garrett in quite personal terms: "Your director-ship finally passed the Board, that is, sixteen directors were approved with the distinct understanding that you were to be elected." The legal agreements were drawn up. By the fall of 1906, all the necessary preliminaries were complete.[34]

Pressure against Carey Thomas was mounting from members of the faculty, a powerful alumna, and an angry student. In 1906, however, the only opposition that could threaten Thomas' position came from the trustees. At this point the board was divided. There were strong Thomas supporters, especially James Wood and her cousin David Scull, Jr. But Thomas had enemies on the board. Francis Cope, Jr., possibly Rufus Jones, and most definitely Henry Tatnall. Two issues from the past haunted her: unbelief and fiscal irresponsibility.

By the early twentieth century Carey Thomas felt personally opposed to her Quaker origins. Her aestheticism made her cringe when she confronted traditional practices. She had continued to attend Meeting, at least irregularly, as something necessary to her position. However, the faith of her parents had no hold over her, not even a sentimental one. In October 1900 after she attended a Friends' wedding, she wrote to Mary, "It was a melancholy assembly to me of bygone days and things that are as obsolete as the mastodon." Though she kept her discomfort with Quakerism secret, her encouragement of college ritual suggested that she was far from traditional practice. In March 1904 Thomas reported to Garrett that at the Founder's lecture held in chapel, trustee Edward Bettle, Jr., and his daughter were enraged by the singing of "Pallas

Athena," the college anthem: "They said it was irreverent and pagan and a hymn to a heathen goddess, sung like a benediction standing. He has been fairly raving to every one." By the early twentieth century both the Orthodox Quaker trustees and Carey Thomas understood what divided them.[35]

The dangerous issue in 1906 was fiscal. The board of trustees in its resolution of acknowledgment to John D. Rockefeller, Jr., thanked him for "continuous kindness and interest."[36] Officially the trustees were grateful, but privately a storm was brewing. Although the deficit was erased, and the library under construction, Henry Tatnall was on the warpath. He and Carey Thomas were locked in a conflict of wills. Minor issues flared into major battles.

The library was a deeply symbolic building that laid bare the contest between the college's Quaker foundations and Carey Thomas' aspirations. An elegant stone building in Jacobean Gothic, the library stood in Thomas' mind for Bryn Mawr's combined dedication to scholarship and class, an architectural demonstration of "the Bryn Mawr type." She obsessed over its design and construction. She wanted it to be a beautiful building at the heart of the campus. Before architect Walter Cope's untimely death, Thomas had provided him with a plan and with drawings for details. Upset that Cope had copied his plans for Pembroke in his work at Princeton and at Washington University in St. Louis, Thomas made him promise that the library would be a unique design. In her summer architectural trips to Oxford, she found appropriate prototypes: Oriel College for the entrance, Wadham College dining hall for the vast, ornate main reading room lit by tall windows decorated with tracery. The building had an enclosed cloister at its center, with a fountain. Thomas delighted in concealed faucets to water the courtyard and electric outlets to be used to light Japanese lanterns for student fetes, "modern inventions," as she put it, in the service of "medieval buildings." After Cope's death, Lockwood de Forest designed the interior, and he planned a teakwood staircase. The result, she wrote to Hannah in the summer of 1905 was "most beautiful and satisfying, and wonderful to say, is admired both by the elect and the Philistines."[37]

Tatnall lost a symbolic campaign to shift the site of the library, but his action led to serious construction delays. He moved on to oppose the elegant treatment of the interior and to limit its costs. As he and others viewed the overruns and deficits with mounting alarm, Lockwood de Forest's teakwood staircase became the symbol, and the board refused to authorize it. When the architectural firm of Cope and Stewardson threatened legal action to recover fees, Tatnall sided with them. As Thomas wrote to Garrett, "Of course, he hates Cope and Stewardson, but he hates me even more just at present."[38]

For her part, Thomas hated Tatnall: "I never saw as cocksure and ignorant a man in my life, nor a more d—— disagreeable half-cut one. His manner to me is awful before the college men and everyone."[39] She could not understand his pettiness. She had won for the college the largesse of John D. Rockefeller, the nation's biggest philanthropist, and had gotten Bryn Mawr's graduates, neighbors, and wealthy patrons to donate a quarter of a million dollars for the library. Arising were the most magnificent college buildings in America. If teakwood was needed to adorn the interiors, then it should, despite trustee prohibitions. Bryn Mawr would fulfill its destiny. The deficits the college faced in the short run would be wiped out as the student body grew. Thomas had felt alarm when the cost of the buildings came in higher than anticipated. But she was able to convince Rockefeller to increase his gift, something the penny-pinching trustees could hardly do. How dare Henry Tatnall hold her to account!

Moreover, if Tatnall had invested the college's endowment correctly, there would be much more money to spend. The conservatism of the Girard Trust, the Philadelphia bank holding Bryn Mawr's endowment, meant that Bryn Mawr was not getting a fair return for its money. And if Tatnall could harass her for overspending, she could show him how to keep books. She delayed sending a resolution of thanks to Rockefeller because she found a 51-cent discrepancy in the accounts.[40]

In 1906, an unexpected legacy of $50,000 enabled construction of the library wing for classrooms and professors' offices, completing the original design. Tatnall threatened to resign. Thomas wrote in her journal, "He is now my open enemy." Tatnall wrote to the board asking for an investigation of the financial position of the college. In addition, he stated that he believed that "many of the criticisms of the management of the college may have more foundation than the trustees have realized," that Thomas was assuming too many duties, and that she was operating independently of the trustees. He called for a committee to inquire. His fellow trustees accepted his recommendation and appointed Howard Comfort, Rufus Jones, and Francis Cope, Jr., to the committee. Trustees were outraged that after they had explicitly refused to authorize teakwood for the library interior, Thomas had gone ahead. Rufus Jones, in talking about Thomas to his daughter many years later, told her, "This was the hottest thing that ever happened, and it came near ending her career."[41]

At the meeting to establish a committee for inquiry Thomas reported that she had found her order for the teakwood and that she would pay the excess seven hundred dollars if, at the completion of the library, the board requested it. Once again she saw herself facing a narrow board. She wrote to Mary Garrett that the trustees, influenced against her by Rufus Jones, Haverford professors living in the neighborhood, and the wife of religion professor George Barton, "are absolutely *without* any broader sense of large issues, and for the reputation of the college and the faculty they care nothing at all. They would just as lightheartedly dismiss president and faculty at one blow and never know the difference if it were to be replaced by Haverford." As she now saw it, the deaths of the 1890s had given the reactionary forces, led by Francis Cope and Henry Tatnall, the upper hand. Carey Thomas drew on language of an earlier period to remind Mary Garrett: "It is a house built on cards as I have always known." She was determined to persist, however. In her diary, she wrote, "Very blue. Have decided to hold on at college [in] spite [of] reactionary movement."[42]

In late May Thomas went to the Lake Mohonk Conference on International Arbitration to lobby among the more liberal trustees. After she spoke to James Wood, she saw that the conflict had been initiated by "tales from Alice Bartlett and professors who have failed at the college." Wood promised her that he would "see fair play and have no anonymous charges made if he can help it." In further conversations she learned of the specific criticism that she did not allow freedom of expression or action at Bryn Mawr College. At Mohonk, Wood consulted with George Barton and Henry Raymond Mussey, and both professors reassured him that "there was the freest possible discussion on every point, that my attitude was strictly judicial and fair on every question, that any such statement was utterly absurd and malicious."[43]

As the 1906 academic year began, the committee investigating Thomas' management of the college remained in session. David Scull, Jr., her gentle cousin, helped Thomas prepare her case. At his request, Thomas drafted a document of particulars against Tatnall, citing his neglect of treasurer's duties. Scull also confronted her on the issue of the teakwood staircase, now in place, and forced her to pay for the extravagance with her—or Garrett's—personal funds.[44]

In October 1906 the board met without Thomas to hear the report of the investigatory committee. They were ready to make peace and appointed a committee of her supporters to confer with Thomas about the report. On her part, Carey Thomas was also willing to conciliate. Her response, dated November 19, carried these words: "I shall strive to promote the highest spiritual and ethical ideas for their own sake. My dealings with the faculty shall be open, candid, straightforward, and, while necessarily exacting, they will be sympathetic. My intercourse with the students shall be affectionate and confidential, and I will use my best efforts to plan and develop in them those principles of honor and duty which will make them useful and good women, and to this end I will seek divine assistance." She asked for trustee suggestions and pledged that she would attempt to follow board direction. Despite the letter's conciliatory gestures, behind the scenes she was working to see that the executive committee second her in the future. In one of her last requests to David Scull, Jr., before his death in 1907, Thomas asked him to change its membership to bring in her supporters.[45]

At a special meeting of the trustees on January 24, 1907, the trustees received Thomas' letter and formed a committee to study the office of dean of the college and consider how the board and college administration might work together more effectively. The struggle had spent itself. In 1906–07, there was no public condemnation of Carey Thomas. Although the crisis was managed within the board of trustees, unquestionably, opponents old and new, such as Neilson and Andrews, learned of the discussions and their outcomes. The practical consequence of the conflict was the creation of three new administrative offices: a comptroller to oversee the financial affairs of the college, a business manager responsible for buildings and grounds, and a dean of the college to supervise advising and to handle questions of student life.[46]

The January meeting was the last substantive meeting of the board of trustees. A month earlier the board had formally accepted new by-laws that gave over its powers to a board of directors. This augmented board had three new additions. Mary Garrett was named director-at-large. The Alumnae Association appointed two representatives. Because the wives of faculty members were explicitly barred from serving as alumnae representatives, Evangeline Andrews could not be chosen. Henry Tatnall resigned. Carey Thomas' victory was complete.

CHAPTER 19

Women . . . Preparing
to Have Their Fling

IN THE early twentieth century, as M. Carey Thomas' public reputation
swelled, her private life hit rock bottom. Mamie Gwinn increasingly withdrew from their relationship. Carey tried to maintain the complicated texture
of her weeks with Mamie and her weekends with Mary Garrett. Both Carey's
own nature and the codes of the day meant that private dramas were shielded
from public view. As a woman of her era, Carey had long before learned to
separate her public persona from her private passions. Because in her case the
gap between public and private was so great, she was exceedingly careful about
her public reputation.

Carey Thomas had learned the lessons of her mother well. Although she
inhabited a sensuous fin de siècle universe of Wagner's music, Rossetti's
paintings, and Swinburne's poetry, she appeared in public—as she had to—
as an upholder of traditional morality. Gradually she had tested the waters to
find that she could safely attend opera and theater in Philadelphia without
bringing trustee censure. As the college began to hold pageants and to host
historical dramas, she moved cautiously to reassure trustees of their innocence
and inherent literary worth. Her dress, always expensive, became more colorful. But in the early twentieth century great gaps remained between her actions
and her public postures. She insisted that no student or woman on the faculty
smoke in private or in public. She never allowed alcohol to be served at Bryn
Mawr and in the twentieth century took a principled stand for prohibition.
However, she urged Mary to drink whisky three times a day as a "tonic," and
when Mary and she met, they enjoyed champagne suppers both in Mary's
New York apartment and in hotels.[1]

Propriety's most important lesson and greatest gift was that only intimates
had the right to know about personal relationships. It was only when the law
intervened that the public gained knowledge. Had Carey been a man, her tie
to Mamie would have required marriage; their estrangement, separation and

divorce. These legal proceedings would have become public and, because Thomas was a college president, would have evoked a scandal. But, as a woman living with another woman, relationships had no legal element and thus remained outside the realm of public scrutiny or comment. As resident observers, Bryn Mawr students were intensely curious and saw a great deal. Stein's fictional telling of the Carey and Mamie tale in *Fernhurst* came in part from the talk of Bryn Mawr graduates that Stein knew at the Johns Hopkins medical school. However, with the exception of this account, not published in full until 1971, Deanery gossip did not make its way into the researchable record. In the years of public triumph it is only in private letters that one finds the confusion and anguish that Carey Thomas experienced in her personal life. Carey's drama is a complicated one with a number of subplots. In it Mamie played a leading role, but Mary provided her own intense moments, as did Helen Thomas.

I

THE NARRATIVE of Mamie Gwinn and Alfred Hodder resumes in 1898. In Gertrude Stein's *Fernhurst*, the dean's eyes are opened after she overhears two students exclaiming, "Isn't it a pretty story, look at her and at him"; the dean exposes her male adversary to his wife; the wife's discovery of a love letter forces him to withdraw from the college and from his love affair with the professor of English; and ultimately the dean and the professor of English repair their relations and return to their life together "in their very same place."[2] In real life it was not so simple. Yes, Hodder did leave Bryn Mawr. He did not, however, leave Mamie Gwinn.

In late March 1898, Alfred Hodder told Carey Thomas that he intended to resign from Bryn Mawr for personal reasons, with no intention of taking another position. Carey wrote to Mary, "He said Mrs. Hodder had gone to Italy, that he expected to join her in June." She added, "If it only were the early part of June." Thomas wanted him to leave immediately at the close of the term, because she had gotten Mamie's agreement that she might travel abroad with Mary in the first half of the summer. Unstated, but clearly in her mind, was the realization that if she were away and Alfred Hodder were around, Mamie had a free field. Carey told Mary that Hodder's resignation was to be kept quiet. "I have not mentioned it to Mamie, though I suppose she knows. I suppose this resignation results from the complications with Mrs. Hodder, etc. I hope it does not—I cannot believe it does—mean living here."[3]

Alfred Hodder did not join Jessie Hodder in Europe but moved to New York. There he roomed with the writer Hutchins Hapgood in the Benedict and drank at the Griffou, a French hotel that was the haunt of writers and artists. Hapgood remembered that he "had no job, but was engaged in writing metaphysical and philosophically romantic novels," staying up all night after carousing with his friends. He had broken "entirely with academic life, for which he acquired an unreasonable contempt," and thought it "far nobler of a man to get drunk, and to meet the denizens of the Haymarket, than to be a dignified professor." Through Josiah Flynt Willard, Hodder entered the circle of Gerald Jerome, the hardworking, hard-drinking district attorney of New York, a man Hapgood characterized as "a perfect sport." Hodder became Jerome's private secretary, living at his headquarters—as well as "his personal companion in poker, song, and drink." Under the pseudonym Francis Walton, Hodder collaborated with Willard on *The Powers That Prey*, a series of stories about the New York underworld. Hodder wrote about his experiences with Jerome in *A Fight for the City*. In 1901 he published his dissertation, *Adversaries of the Sceptic*, a defense of agnosticism.[4]

In the summer of 1898 Carey Thomas took the step that Mamie had anticipated in 1893: she began to travel abroad with Mary Garrett. Although what Mamie had foreseen and feared came to pass, her own interests were shifting. Somewhat to Carey's chagrin, when she broached the possibility that she might go abroad with Mary, Mamie "did not really disapprove." Throughout the summer, Carey was uneasy about Mamie. As she wrote soon after arriving in Paris, "I miss my mouse out of my pocket sorely and feel as if I should never get her back safe and sound." Later she wrote, "I . . . wish I had never come."[5]

Yet the following year, she returned to Europe with Mary. In anticipation of the 1899 trip, she wrote to Mary that along with obligations would come "London in the season and all sorts of adorable things, and the temptation is great." Carey's travel with Mary was largely purposeful. In England they studied the architecture of Oxford, looking for models for the library, and Carey sat for John Singer Sargent; on the Continent they devoted themselves to medical treatments at Aix-les-Bains. Yet it was still delightful. Europe gave her back a little of the self that she had created in her years of study abroad. She wrote to Mamie, "Really, I am constitutionally unfitted to be an American. All my feathers bristle in foreign air." Mary stimulated her even more as she began to plan out "an early Byzantine palace" that she would build on Venice's Grand Canal and fill with church relics.[6]

In these summers, Carey visited with the members of her family who were settled in England: her aunt Hannah Smith, now a widow; her cousins Alys Russell and Logan Pearsall Smith; and her sister Grace. Edith Carpenter, the wife of Bond Thomas, was nearby some of the time, as were Helen Thomas and Lucy Donnelly, who were on an extended leave from their positions as readers in English at Bryn Mawr.

Carey was always respectful to Hannah Smith. Hannah loved her, knew her very well, and was an inspired gossip. Carey had been careful to frame her relationships with Mamie Gwinn and Mary Garrett in ways that she thought Hannah could accept. As she planned her 1898 trip abroad with Mary, she wrote Hannah in this fashion: "Mamie has to stay with her mother, who has lost a sister and Mamie's father's sister and is not very fit. So I can only come for a few weeks, as I want to be back to go to Canada with her as soon as her mother can let her take a vacation. I think, however, I can persuade Mary Garrett to come with me for a glimpse of thee, a week of Paris, and two weeks of rest in Normandy."[7]

In July 1899, when Carey met Hannah, she expressed regret at leaving Mamie behind. Hannah answered, "Oh, but she has a man to console her." This shocked Carey, and the next time she saw Hannah she asked her what she meant, citing the good of the college. Hannah then relayed to her the rumor circulating for months that Mamie was secretly seeing Alfred Hodder, that Mamie met Alfred before and after Jessie's departure "in all sorts of clandestine ways and places, even going in to New York repeatedly to see him and *stay* with him."[8]

In the year following Hodder's resignation from Bryn Mawr, Carey had been relieved he was gone and convinced herself that Hodder was out of Mamie's life. Now she learned from Hannah that she was wrong. She wrote immediately to Mamie, "I am very much distressed by the horrible fact that Aunt Hannah and all of them have heard the most abominable things about your behavior with Hodder." It all sounded like a replay of Grace's story, but this time with Alfred Hodder in the place of Tom Worthington and Mamie in that of the nurse.[9]

Carey was convinced that the rumors had started with Edith, but that all her family in England knew. As she wrote to Mamie, no one "mentioned your name to me. Not Grace or Logan or Alys or Bertie or Mrs. Sidney Webb." The hard Carey that Mamie had observed dealing with Grace in her divorce, concerned about reputation and position at Bryn Mawr, was ascendent in Carey's letters. She wrote to Mamie that Hannah's rumors threatened Mamie's position at Bryn Mawr. Alfred Hodder was beneath Mamie, his wife Jessie was vulgar, and he was a man who took as his confidants Edith Carpenter and Georgiana King. "I knew just what would happen when you let a married man look at you and talk to you as Hodder did."[10]

To this Mamie replied only obliquely. She had offended Edith, Alys, and Bertie, which is why they had not spoken of her. Moreover, Mamie wrote, it was she who was in the position of the spurned first wife. " 'Carey and Mary Garrett' are become as familiar or more familiar than Carey and Mary Gwinn: people do not ask very frequently after first wives. And but for that change Mrs. Smith would never have ventured to unload to you her pack of fantastic lies. Fancy her doing it had I been with you!" Carey immediately replied that Mamie was wrong about Hannah. "She knows I love you better than anything else. I told her so last summer and this too."[11]

A storm of letters to Mamie from her friends in Carey's family followed. They reveal deep hostility to Carey. To them Carey Thomas was a tyrant. Edith wrote Mamie that Carey must have "exaggerated frightfully. . . . You know she is always perfectly unscrupulous when she wishes to make an effect, and her cue was to frighten you as badly as she could." Edith reminded Mamie of Carey's lies at the time of Grace's divorce. Edith surmised that Hannah had learned about Mamie and Alfred through general rumors "that you and Mr. Hodder were in love with each other and were often seen together in trains and in the Broad Street Station." She guessed that when Jessie went to Europe, Hannah thought Mamie was the cause. Edith reassured Mamie that she should feel secure that none of her friends "who have sympathized with you in this affair and hated Carey for her tyranny over you, rendering a pleasant natural friendship on the ordinary basis impossible—that none of us could dream of criticizing any means you have taken not to let the friendship go entirely. . . . Carey simply said it herself, partly to frighten you, and partly to get everything out of you by pretending to know a great deal more than she did know." She hoped that Mamie would not let the trivial gossip—"no matter what terrors it takes on in passing through the crucible of Carey's jealous imagination"— harm her friendship with Alfred Hodder.[12]

Helen took Mamie's side completely. "I wish I could go out with you into open warfare, and at a word from you I will most gladly." Helen had tried to convince Carey that what she was hearing in England was only old gossip from before Hodder left Bryn Mawr, but she warned Mamie that it was possible that "Carey, her suspicions having once been aroused, and we all know how suspicious and jealous she is, may take underhand measures to find out whether you really ever did see Mr. Hodder." Almost a year later Helen wrote that when Hannah questioned her, she lied to her. As Helen asserted her affection for Mamie, she wrote that Mamie's struggle with Carey—"mere struggle as it is for an ordinary liberty"—evoked in her the greatest sympathy.[13]

By this time, however, Carey had buried her fears. On her return to Bryn Mawr in the autumn she observed to Mary that Mamie Gwinn was pleased with her large and intelligent classes and that "she seems to me just as she was before Hodder's apparition." Yet, at some level Carey was frightened. She had repeated dreams of Mamie's death.[14]

In early June 1900, Mamie was ill with the measles. Carey opened the mail in her usual fashion, "mechanically, envelope after envelope, throwing the envelopes away and laying the letters in piles to be read." She read a letter "in a strange handwriting so disgusting in its maudlin endearments that at first I thought it was written by an insane man." Round kisses were drawn over the letter. She hunted through her wastepaper basket to find the envelope. There were two envelopes. The one that had enclosed the letter was addressed to an unknown. In the same handwriting was an envelope addressed to Mamie. Carey realized, "It was a letter from Hodder to Mamie . . . they must be on impossible terms for him to write in such a way."[15]

On June 4, with Mamie now recovered, Carey confronted her. They "had it out" from four in the afternoon until midnight. What Mamie told Carey cannot be known, but Mamie's papers make it clear that she and Alfred had been seeing each other since the summer of 1896 and that when they were absent from each other they wrote long and affectionate diary entries that they sent to each other. In her letters Mamie called Alfred "playmate," and she signed them "princess." She also wrote to him various dramatic scenes from Bryn Mawr in a code in which she was Valentine and Carey, Sabina.

According to Carey's report to Mary, Mamie insisted that their meetings had been proper. "She says she has never met him except on trains, never anywhere in Philadelphia, only six times this year, at the Deanery in the mornings, except that once." Carey brought up marriage, but Mamie said that "she does not want to marry him, only to carry on this affair with absolute regard to conventions." Carey wrote to Mary that she was "dreadfully troubled." She needed time to think out what to do. "I am nearly beside myself."[16]

The next day, Carey wrote that she was resolved to stand by Mamie: "I cannot possibly desert her." She had no hope that Mamie would give Alfred up, "I think it will end in but one way, but I cannot do anything that will hasten such a terrible thing for her and for me." Mamie had convinced her "that the worst I thought and suspected was not true." Mamie's only crime was concealing her correspondence and her meetings with him at the Deanery. Mamie also promised that "in the future she will tell me the exact truth." In a letter to her sister Helen many years later, Carey recalled that she had asked Mamie on June 4 to marry Alfred, but she "refused and said she would not *dream* of marrying him (she had told me he had been divorced by this time), that if I insisted on her leaving, it would ruin her life." Carey had not persisted because she "felt that if there were a shadow of a chance of saving her I must take it and do what I could, that otherwise I should reproach myself forever."[17]

It was at this point that Mamie Gwinn drafted a will. It is an intriguing document, expressive of her ambivalence toward Carey. Mamie specified that the assets from her mother's trust, that became hers upon her mother's death, go to Carey. All letters from Mamie to Carey were to be burned; all from Carey to Mamie were to be returned to Carey unread. Carey was to receive all items in "her house" in Bryn Mawr, including all those jointly owned, and her books, with two exceptions: Mamie left some of her jewelry to her Baltimore friend Nancy Howard; and to Alfred Hodder she left "the manuscripts, lectures, and notes for lectures of my courses on Burke, Carlyle, and Ruskin,

and on Arnold, Pater, and Swinburne, and the books used in those courses."
This was a poignant reminder of Carey Thomas' refusal to honor Gwinn's
request in 1896 that she acknowledge that the English lectures that Thomas
had been giving for eleven years were their joint work. Thomas had once
possessed this material as she gave the lectures; now Gwinn made certain that
at her death her intellectual property remained out of Thomas' grasp.[18]

In the summer of 1900 Carey and Mamie took their planned trip to Paris
for the Exposition, as if nothing had happened. It was a tense, unhappy
summer. Thomas was an official commissioner of education, holding an
appointment from the U.S. government. She had come with copies of the
monograph, and she was asked to make an address. She wrote to Hannah
Smith, however, "I am lying perdu and have not even summoned courage to
give my address to the United States Commissioner as requested." Mary was
also in Paris, but Carey had little time to see her, and they quarreled. There
is no reference to it in the Paris letters, but Carey later wrote that Alfred had
followed them to Paris "and dogged our footsteps, although I refused to speak
to him or see him." Something of Carey's unhappiness came out in a mid-
July letter to Hannah, written after a weekend visit with her. She congratulated
Hannah on her steadiness, then added "but people under forty are subject to
wonderful transformations." Hannah had given her pages of the autobiography
she was writing, and they had obviously discussed the scandalous world in
which Mary Berenson lived. This led Carey to comment on the immorality
of the present generation in contrast to those over forty. Yet, there was a
dilemma. Moral people were dull. How could a person be both interesting
and moral? "It cannot be solved in this generation. We shall see things much
worse, I fancy, before they get better. It looks to me as if women were preparing
to have their fling after their centuries of repression, and who can blame them,
poor things; but it is shortsighted in them." Carey was forty-three; Mamie, just
under forty.[19]

This was the last time that Carey traveled with Mamie. From 1901 until
1904, Carey and Mary traveled to Europe, while Mamie, caring for her
mother, spent the hot months at Cape May. Carey later wrote that "Mamie
and Hodder played their game undisturbed," but in actual fact it was she who
had the freedom to travel abroad with Mary, while Mamie was tied to family
responsibility. Carey refused to help Mamie in any way. Arguing that she
needed the summer respite to recover from the academic year, she even refused
to allow Mamie to bring her mother to the Bryn Mawr Hotel. As she traveled
with Mary to England, France, and Italy, Carey wrote loving letters, reassuring
Mamie that she thought only of her as she revisited their old sites. From Paris,
she wrote, "How I longed last night for my garret with you and without
Gertrude!" From Oxford, "Dear Rabbitest, if I can have you I will live in attics
and eat currant buns and pigeons."[20] But Mamie knew better.

During these years, Carey did not acknowledge what was immediately in front of her. Mamie was in love with Alfred Hodder. She tried to return to their "marriage" as it had been, one that since 1893 had included her intimate relationship with Mary Garrett. But now Mamie, too, was involved in an outside affair. Evidence was everywhere at hand. Mamie wrote Alfred daily letters. During Mamie's summers at Cape May, Alfred was nearby. He visited her at the Deanery. Yet Carey continued to act as if Alfred did not exist. She had a short-lived moment of recognition in late 1901, when *The New Americans*, Hodder's book of stories, was published. Carey found his book lacking in ideas, drama, and containing notions of women "medieval under a pretence of liberality. I should say they were like Tom Worthington's." What she meant was that they pointed to a new, more openly sexual view of women. Mamie, however, insisted that the book "will live forever." Carey wrote to Mary that "I love you, my beloved, and that wretched book makes me love you more. If Mamie really admires the author of such a second-rate book, there is no trust to be placed in her." Carey Thomas conveyed her thoughts about Hodder indirectly in writing to William James. His article "The Ph.D. Octopus," published in the *Harvard Monthly*, had been provoked by Hodder's difficulties. In rising to Hodder's defense, James had stated that a degree in philosophy was no preparation for teaching literature. In rebutting James, Thomas suggested that when a candidate failed to get a degree, its cause was "a roving and inconstant disposition, often joined to irresponsibility toward obligations," a succinct summary of her judgment of Hodder.[21]

Although William James could not admit it in 1903, there was something troubling about Alfred Hodder, an insufficiency that Gertrude Stein tried to analyze in *Fernhurst* through the character of Philip Redfern. How could this brilliant man who in short order published a philosophical tract, a novel, and a book on politics not find the recognition he deserved or even be able to earn a living? In *Fernhurst* different voices pass judgment. Redfern himself suggests that unlike a man who lies with an air of truth, "I tell the truth as if it were a lie." A colleague says of him, "A sad example of a literary man without character." The narrator objects: "He had character . . . but his instincts always thrust him into danger and his chivalry bound him to a losing fight. . . . He only learned to dread the fire, he never learned to keep his fingers from it." To Gertrude and Leo Stein who knew him from Harvard, Hodder was a puzzle. Hutchins Hapgood, a roommate in these New York years and a close friend, believed that Hodder was a romantic living in a realistic era, "gifted, learned, with a proud sentiment which preferred to be misunderstood rather than sacrifice any dignity." Though Hapgood himself faulted Hodder only for not being candid about his personal life, he quoted the harsher assessment of their mutual friend Josiah Flynt Willard: "Alfred wouldn't know the truth if it was stripped naked and put to bed with him."[22]

To Mamie, however, Alfred Hodder was her "playmate" and "prince." She took ill repeatedly, and as always Carey cared for her. Mamie's dependence during this period was conveyed in a letter to Hannah Smith. Mamie, Carey wrote, was "just as usual," tied to her mother, teaching effectively, but not writing her great work. "She neither keeps house, nor takes any care of her clothes, nor packing, nor mending, nor fills her inkstands, nor sharpens her pencils, nor orders her own books. These trifles are the only things I can do to help her, or rather have done for her." Carey's philosophical tone hardly fit her day-to-day mood. It was an exceedingly busy period, and Carey felt often exhausted and overwhelmed. As seen from the outside, it was a time of public triumph, and Thomas traveled a great deal to represent higher education and to raise money for Bryn Mawr.[23]

II

MARY WAS lonely and frequently ill. She found it hard to understand why Carey had so little time for her, why Mamie's needs always took precedence. Each time Mamie took to her bed, Mary had to abandon her trip to the Deanery or forego Carey's company in New York. They fought frequently. Since the robust years of her early twenties, Mary Garrett had never been well. She suffered from a variety of ailments that both she and Carey believed were largely psychosomatic in origin. She often tried a home version of a health cure, a period of extended rest and massage under medical care. Throughout the 1890s Carey tried to regulate Mary's hours in the belief that if she found her natural limits, she could keep herself from exhaustion and depression. If her illnesses had a psychological source, Carey's systematic isolation of Mary from family—brothers, sisters-in-law, and aunts—at a time when she was separated from Carey's daily companionship by Mamie could have hardly been therapeutic.

In April 1899, Mary had a breast tumor that required surgery. Mary and Carey both were frightened, and feared that Mary might die. Eleven years before, Carey's mother had died after she had hidden her cancer from doctors, including her doctor-husband. To Carey's great relief, Mary acted quickly. Carey wrote to her: "I feel like a man reprieved who had been sentenced to capital punishment. We all must take our chances. You may die, I may die, Mamie may die but now I feel that your chance is as good as the rest." With the surgery safely accomplished, Carey wrote that she could "rejoice . . . that we are going to be able to love each other and see and do charming things so much longer than we feared. . . . To go through so much emotion in a week makes it seem an eternity." Although the tumor was benign, Mary did not heal quickly. In late May, Carey wrote that she was encouraged "by the pain stopping even for thirty-six hours, and certainly the breast *does* look better. I am sure healing has begun." Although the record is not fully clear, a letter in late June suggests that Mary had to have a breast removed.[24]

The nature of their intimacy was not to be revealed even to a female physician, such as Dr. Elizabeth Cushier, who herself was in a Boston marriage with Dr. Elizabeth Blackwell. In November 1900 Mary experienced breast soreness that turned out to be a medically insignificant cyst. Carey wanted her to show it to Dr. Cushier or to another woman doctor Mary Sherwood: "you can cut a little hole in a towel and show it through this without any exposure." Evidently Carey had first suggested that she might describe Mary's breast to the doctors, and then had second thoughts. It would be unwise to do so, because, as she wrote to Mary, "If I were to do what I suggested, it might seem as if you minded me less than a physician."[25]

Carey's secrecy in revealing her knowledge of Mary's body to a physician was in contrast with her full acceptance of her own feelings of love for Mary and Mamie, delight in female beauty, and interest in other women's passion for each other. Her correspondence contains many testaments to her admiration of Sarah Bernhardt. In January 1901 Carey wept during a performance in which Bernhardt played Camille: "Sarah was divine as Camille and adorably beautiful and not one particle of overacting. . . . Her neck is ravishing, and her dresses far more splendid and her jewels, too, than I remembered." After seeing Bernhardt in a performance of Hamlet in which she took the male lead, Carey wrote to Mary: "Sarah was absolutely divine. She *was* Hamlet." Carey then relayed that Bernhardt had become enamored of a wealthy young American woman and was begging her to come to Paris. "Of course, she will follow Sarah's beckoning and so would I. I would follow that Hamlet over the cliff or where not."[26]

For Carey and Mary, these were ragged times. Carey constantly pleaded innocent and placed the fault on Mary. In February 1901 she wrote "the fault is largely yours because you are really suspicious and unbearably distrustful. I never never lie to you. You are my friend and my sweetheart, and I could not lie." At issue between them was not only Mamie but the whole host of their common concerns: Mary's investments, policies of the Bryn Mawr School, and the money that Mary gave to the college and Carey. Mary had suffered great losses in her Baltimore and Ohio stock and was convinced that she could not live on her income, given that she still underwrote the Bryn Mawr School and paid to Bryn Mawr College $10,000 each year. For long periods she economized by shutting her Baltimore house. She moved out of the New York flat and traveled in Europe. It was difficult for her to find traveling companions and, somewhat to Carey's distaste, spent time with the writer Sarah Orne Jewett and Mrs. James Fields. Carey urged her to return to Baltimore and reviewed with Mary her income and expenses to convince her that it was feasible. Carey revealed that in 1901 Mary was giving her $3,000 a year, paying $750 for the Deanery, and spending $2,000 for their summer trips together. Income from real estate gave Mary $20,000; and in addition she held investments and other potentially income-producing properties. Carey insisted that Mary had enough money for a useful life in Baltimore and a summer of pleasure.[27] Mary was not so certain.

In an informal, unwritten way, Mary had put aside $100,000 for Carey's perpetual use and gave Carey the annual interest it yielded. Carey sought to insure that this annuity would be secure if Mary died. In February 1902, she wrote to warn Mary, "All use of giving me that $100,000 is done away with unless you keep the coupons in envelopes in your box marked as my property. Unless this is done, I cannot take possession of them if you died, nor should I have anything to fight your will with, if necessary."[28]

Despite Mary Garrett's generosity, Carey continued to overspend and was often in debt to Mary. In addition, in times of difficulty she appealed to Mary Garrett for money to tide over the college. For example in September 1902, the college needed $5,000 immediately for operating expenses. The treasurer pleaded that he was too busy to take out the loan and asked Thomas to carry it for four days. Thomas immediately appealed to Garrett. After the first years, Garrett had insisted that her annual gift never be used to make up deficits. In 1904 the college was in debt and needed to borrow. Thomas pled with her to release the $10,000: "As you have it lying there, why not waive principle once and save me this. Answer yes or no, please."[29]

Mary Garrett was giving so much, and yet she was invisible. Her accomplishments were ignored, and her relationship with Carey unacknowledged. In February 1902, she was angry when she was not invited to march in the inaugural procession for Ira Remsen at Johns Hopkins. Thomas tried to explain that Baltimore was a conservative city and that she herself had been invited only because she was a college president. In November 1902, Garrett attended a talk by Thomas in New York and ended up sitting on the platform with honored guests. Carey felt that Mary had been presumptuous and lashed out, "I thought you were completely out of place walking in with Professor Harrison. . . . I *tried* to insist on you going on the floor but you did not back me up at all. At Haverford, also, you would not say positively you wished to have a seat in the audience." Carey warned that she would never again ask for an invitation for Mary unless she promised not to sit on the stage. Carey was also offended by what she called, "the gross impropriety" of Mary's dress: "For a woman of nearly fifty to wear a *hat* and a gown three inches from the ground of the roughest travelling description is a great discourtesy when everyone else is in gala attire. I should as soon have thought of going in my nightgown."[30]

Mary felt that she had some rights to Carey, particularly the right to be with her on holidays. In December 1901, she demanded that the two stay alone together at the Deanery, putting Carey in what she regarded as an impossible position. "It is exceedingly difficult for me to turn Mamie out of the house. I can go away and leave her here if I choose. I cannot turn her out. I should think you would see this. This is her home and for four months in the summer she has to be with her mother, and I cannot begrudge her the time she stays here, nor have I the right to prevent her staying."[31]

At moments, Carey dreamed of the life together that they might have abroad, only to pull back, "I know we could have life that would be a dream abroad, only I never could desert Mamie. How I should adore to read and see things the rest of my life no words can tell." Yet, with all their conflicts and disappointments, there were times of private pleasures, as in March 1901, when Carey traveled to Baltimore to be with Mary: "I want you to let us sleep in your bedroom which would be like old times. . . . Let us have a bottle of champagne for dinner and a mince pie and broiled lobster."[32]

For Carey family issues also intruded. In May 1901 Edith Carpenter committed suicide. When Carey first learned the details—that Edith shot herself when her husband Bond Thomas was in the house—she was incensed. After Harry Thomas, now a prominent nerve specialist, explained that Edith had long feared killing herself and had fought against it, that it "was probably an irresistible obsession coming from her overworked state," Carey only felt its grisly misery.[33]

On January 18, 1903, Helen Thomas came to lunch and "broke the fact after luncheon to Mamie and me that she is engaged to Dr. Flexner." Simon Flexner, the brilliant Johns Hopkins research doctor, who had known Helen for seven years, had proposed.[34]

Carey had always feared marriage to a man—first for herself and then for those closest to her. Her relationship with Helen, her youngest sister, was unique. Redheaded, partially deaf, and never in sturdy health, Helen had gone to Bryn Mawr, graduating in the class of 1893. She had formed a deep attachment to Lucy Donnelly, a classmate, and together the two had studied abroad. Carey had been instrumental in aiding Helen in a life to replicate her own. She encouraged her with words and money. Such a relationship to a younger sister can evoke complicated feelings: pleasure, satisfaction, but also jealousy. Carey expressed these in an 1894 letter to Hannah Smith: "As thee knows I have launched Helen's little craft Leipzigwards and Lucyward. She sails for fairyland in two weeks. It will be, I hope, the happiest time of her life, and I envy her."[35]

Helen and Lucy returned to Bryn Mawr to teach English composition and served as readers in the English department from 1896 to 1903. The two dreamed of a life of scholarship and writing. Helen was never strong, and in 1901 her health broke down. The two announced their plan to leave the college to write in the country. They went abroad instead. Helen tried to write, but collapsed and was forced to remain quiet for months.

Although from the outside, it may have looked as though Helen were Carey's dependent, in fact Helen reserved her independent judgment. Increasingly deaf, she was also more quietly literary than Carey. She was Mamie's friend more than Carey's. Bertrand Russell, who since his 1896 visit to Bryn Mawr had judged Carey with a critical eye, was Helen's companion abroad and her correspondent. She experienced her sister's college policies as a reader and lecturer, one of the second tier of faculty, who read student essays, lived in the Low Buildings, and earned salaries of $1,000 or less. In the fall of 1902, she and Lucy Donnelly confronted President Thomas: Helen Thomas accused her of being a slave driver, and Lucy Donnelly wept.[36]

Helen's engagement to Simon Flexner was her own doing. Years earlier she had checked him as he had declared his love. In 1902, she wrote to him to renew the relationship, and their engagement followed immediately. Her happiness was alloyed, however, by her need to tell Lucy and Carey. The two took it very hard. For Lucy, Helen's marriage tore their life asunder, and she was plunged into despair. Carey explained Helen's choice of Simon over Lucy to Mary: "The truth is she has read a great many French books, and the physical side has great attractions. . . . And after he spoke, her imagination has dwelt on it."

For Carey, the issue was both the choice of a man and the fact that Simon Flexner was a Jew. As she broke the news to Mary, she reported, "He is a Jew and utterly insignificant looking and of no social qualifications." She had never understood her brother Harry's fondness for him, nor the adulation he received. Flexner had been offered and accepted the position as director of the new Rockefeller Institute for Medical Research in New York. "It is a blow, I confess, but I shall have to make the best of it for Helen's sake, and at least he is very eminent and has the prize position in the country in pathology," one claiming a salary of $10,000 a year. In the next months, Carey returned repeatedly to the theme, the contrast between Flexner's high reputation and his Jewishness. After a dinner for him later in the month, she commented to Mary, "He is intelligent and talks well and is presentable in manner but *you* would know him as a Jew." Two weeks later, she wrote to Mary, "He is Jewish to a degree and as ugly as sin. To think I shall have such a brother-in-law and lots of little Jew nephews and nieces!"[37]

What was the source of Carey Thomas' particular antipathy to Jews? During her adulthood, anti-Semitism was fashionable in polite society. It was a hatred that could be spoken in homes and clubs of the upper class, to speak it helped solidify one's identification with elite status. With each letter, as she voiced her venom, Thomas had a correspondent who she assumed shared her antagonism. [38] Thomas in the twentieth century was ever attuned to such potentialities. However, Thomas never passively received ideas, even those justified by scientific authority. It was fashionable to believe women had smaller brains than men: she dedicated her life to proving that tenet wrong.

As Carey Thomas emerged from her personal crisis in the 1890s, she was fully on her own. She no longer had to temper her ambitions or moderate her manner for father or uncle. Her dreams of a great college had a chance; but she constantly had to outmaneuver a board of trustees who mistrusted her. She hardened herself to the outside. Inside, however, conflicts roiled. Her passion and her greed entwined her with two women who loathed each other, who each had to be satisfied but kept apart. Her life was a frenzy of activity—college work, travel, purchases. She was in debt personally and collegiately. She was always grabbing, grasping for more; and she had no sense of where the college's needs ended and hers began. As she moved into her forties, the scars of her childhood burn immobilized her and caused her pain; she fought ever harder against the new limits her body imposed. As scandal and personal illness surrounded her, she hid behind a smokescreen of propriety and acquisition. There were inner torments that had to come out. Jews became for her a convenient, an intellectually and socially respectable way to objectify her anger.

Carey kept her feelings about Helen's marriage and Simon's Jewishness private, and when Helen married, on September 17, 1903, Carey assumed the role of parent. The printed announcements read, "M. Carey Thomas announces the marriage of her sister," and Helen and Simon were married in an Episcopal ceremony in the Deanery garden. [39] Over the years, Carey came to respect and admire Simon Flexner. As she traveled to New York, she visited their apartment and noted that Simon provided well for Helen. Carey came to enjoy William and James, the two nephews the union produced. In his professional capacity Simon Flexner became an important adviser to Carey Thomas about the foundation world and about personal medical care. Yet however much Carey eventually changed her view of Simon, this had no effect on her anti-Semitism.

As these personal dramas swirled about her, drawing her in, Carey Thomas carried on her duties at Bryn Mawr, spoke publicly, and raised money. She found herself overwhelmed by the combination of public and private responsibilities that she shouldered, and she burst out in anger. She tried to explain to Mary that she was worn down by the demands of week and weekend: "I should not have lost my temper if I had not been horribly tired. You see, unless I have quiet at the end of a busy week, hours of quiet, I go to pieces, and that, beloved, is the reason you so often see me cross, because I am with you only at the weekend, and those weeks I never have any quiet at all." At times she pleaded for male prerogatives. She faced the rough world and needed the comforts a man had. Once, after she had lost her temper, she explained, "The fact is my daily life uses up all my energy and temper, and when I undertake to be agreeable outside of it I can't succeed, it seems. Many men are unbearably cross at home, and I see how they feel." She had to be creative and needed license. On November 15, 1902, after delivering a difficult and well-received speech, she wrote to Mary about her short temper the day before, "You cannot have both pleasantness and excellence. It is like a genius who must be allowed his little infatuations and love affairs."[40]

III

IN THE winter of 1903–04, Mamie's health deteriorated. She had long been exhausted and filled with aches and pains, but she reached a new level of weakness. Carey later wrote that Mamie "spent days and weeks lying down too weak to get up" and asserted that Mamie brought on her illness in an attempt to get her mother to give her an annuity of $3,000. At the time, however, Carey feared for her life. Terrified that Mamie's stiffness, making her unable to move, might be the secondary symptom of cancer, Carey wrote an urgent letter to Dr. William Halsted. On April 4, 1904, Carey wrote to Mary that she believed Mamie was going to die. Mamie's attacks reminded her of those of her mother in her last illness. Mamie Gwinn arranged for a leave of absence for ill health for the coming year. Carey confessed, however, "I cannot trust Mamie to tell me the truth about it, and I think it is very probable that she is only waiting to have her mother's money to marry Hodder. . . . I should much rather have her die."[41]

A week later, Carey's worst fears were realized. She wrote to Mary, "Mamie *is* going to marry Hodder this summer, and Mrs. Gwinn has given her $3,000 a year to do it with, which makes her independent." The next weeks were agony. Mamie fell, and Carey once again had to nurse her. She begged Mary not to ask to see her: "You must let me be for a little while now and not try to see me. I cannot go into Philadelphia at all if you are there. It will upset me." It was not just that Mamie was going to marry Alfred. It was that for the first—and last—time, Carey realized that her actions had played some part in Mamie's drama, that Mamie had been responding in part to Carey's involvement with Mary. "I feel that I am getting what I deserve in Mamie's marriage. I have left her alone summer after summer to go abroad with you. I have not helped her with her mother but have deserted her. I deserve it all. . . . Much as she is to blame I am infinitely more so toward her." This moment of truth soon passed. Ten days later, Carey's defenses had returned. She invited Mary to come to Bryn Mawr's May Day and to stay with her at the Deanery. "Mamie will not be downstairs so it will make no difference whatever to her, besides which I do not care if it does."[42]

For Carey, April and May, 1904, were a nightmare. She had lived with Mamie for twenty-five years. Their lives, possessions, and work were intimately intertwined. That for these same twenty-five years she had also pursued Mary and that for the last eleven years Mary had shared Carey's life were as naught. Carey was losing a central pivot in her life, the person in reference to whom she had defined much of herself. For years Carey had not had an active artistic or scholarly life, but only one in relation to Mamie. When Mamie walked out of the door, Carey's link to the aesthetic passions of her young womanhood was severed.

In the spring of 1904, as the day approached, Carey found it increasingly difficult to cope. Bryn Mawr had an exhibit at the 1904 World's Fair in St. Louis. Carey Thomas took a trip in May to check on the arrangements and preview the fair. She wrote to Mamie on board the train, "I'm afraid you thought me careless today about saying goodbye, but I have to be careful about things, and I could not let myself think that it was the last time I should ever leave the Deanery and come back to find you there." In St. Louis she felt out of sorts. Mamie wrote of her wedding plans. Carey replied, "It makes little difference to me what the arrangements are so that they are not at Bryn Mawr, or Philadelphia." As Mamie prepared to move out, Carey asked her to make a complete list of her furniture and books. Before breaking up the household Mamie sought to have a photographer take pictures of the Deanery interiors. Carey gave her a suggestion, but wrote that she wished no copies. "I do not care for any photos. There are some things I want to try to forget, if only there were any hope of it."[43]

In the last weeks of their life together, she and Mamie quarreled continually. Thomas could not write a public address, and by May 30, she was frantic. She wrote to Mary, "You will find me in a prickly, not-to-be-spoken-to stage over my speech." As Mamie's marriage approached, she was in despair, "I believe she is walking into such disaster that it wrings my heart. I dare not let myself think of it."[44]

Carey planned to be in Europe with Mary when the actual wedding took place. In June, as she prepared to go abroad, she sent Mamie money for her to buy her own wedding gift. The moment of parting was more than she could bear. "I completely lost my self-control in the train and last night. You have been my first interest and care for twenty-seven years, and to feel that I shall not be able to care for you in the future is like losing one's eyes or legs." There was nothing that she could do. Carey was now prepared to put her face to the wind: "appalling accidents do happen in life, and it has to go on." She asked Mamie to write her "till the fatal day. Then cable me." Mamie was not to write on her honeymoon. "I do not feel as if I could bear to write or hear this summer unless you are in trouble, which God forbid. Write me when you get back."[45]

On June 22, 1904, Mamie married in New York. Traveling in Europe with Mary, Carey noted in her diary simply, "Mamie married to Hodder."[46]

CHAPTER 20

Le roi est mort: vive le roi

WHEN CAREY THOMAS returned from abroad in the fall of 1904, Mary Garrett immediately moved into the Deanery, this time to stay. Carey was in a humor quite different from that of the spring, ready to take command of a new life without Mamie Gwinn. Evidence of Mamie, however, surrounded her in Mamie's possessions, material objects that both Mamie and Carey regarded as important symbols of the spirit. With an urgency, Carey set about to remove all traces of Mamie Gwinn's occupancy of the Deanery.

Nothing was to stand in Carey's way, not even Mamie's unsettled state. Mamie and Alfred Hodder had taken a wedding trip to Europe. As the new Mrs. Hodder organized her life in a New York apartment on her return, she was not ready to receive her things. Without consultation, Carey hired packers, sent Mamie's furniture and objects to a storage warehouse, and forwarded the bill to Mamie. Carey described the ordeal to her aunt Hannah Smith: "dividing Mamie's and my things (the accumulations of twenty-five years) has been an enormous task before which my spirit has quailed." One of Mary's bookkeepers looked up the records of their purchases in old account books. "Many things we bought together, and these it would have required a Solomon to divide satisfactorily."[1]

Carey began to worry about the letters she had written to Mamie. She could not find the locked tin box that contained them in the dormer closet. Two days after Mamie's return, Carey wrote to Mamie, "I know it was there when I left. Did you take it?" Something needed to be done about their letters. "Such dreadful things happen to letters when the writer's dust should be at peace." Carey found the box, and the two began to review their correspondence. They were following the well-understood practice of friends who, at the close of intimacy, returned letters to the sender. In the year that followed, many of Mamie's letters left the Deanery, and many of Carey's were returned.[2]

Mamie was angry at the damage done to her possessions by the packers and movers, and noticed items missing. Gradually the two women disentangled their things and worked to deal with each other on a civilized basis. From

Rome, Mamie had sent Carey a small volume of Shelley, and she continued to sent her gifts for important occasions. Carey wrote letters and even sent plans of the library for Mamie to see. They did not visit, as Carey could not "endure with calmness" seeing Mamie "under such changed conditions."[3]

Asked by Hannah if Mamie was happy, Carey responded that she would be the last to know for Mamie gave her little information. As to the critical question—"how she likes it"—Carey answered, "Certainly, I should not be the first person to whom Mamie would express her true sentiments." And then, more revealingly, Carey gave her early-twentieth-century views on heterosexual marriage: "if people are really in love, I usually give them two, three, or four years to reach bottom rock."[4]

This interlude of strained civility between Carey and Mamie was not to last. Carey had assumed that Alfred and Jessie Hodder divorced after Jessie went abroad to live. In 1907 Carey learned that not only had the two never divorced, they had never been married. Despondent at the death of Alfred's and her elder child, Olive, Jessie Hodder returned from Europe with their son, J. Alan Hodder. William James and his wife introduced Jessie to the Boston philanthropic community. She became a house mother at the Industrial School for Girls in Lancaster, Massachusetts, and began a long and honorable career as a prison reformer. Encouraged by her Boston mentors, she hired a lawyer and sued Alfred Hodder for bigamy, claiming her rights as a common-law wife. Carey learned all this when William James and a lawyer visited her and presented her with Jessie's evidence. They were seeking to get Thomas to testify in Jessie's behalf that Alfred Hodder had officially introduced her to the Bryn Mawr community as his wife.[5]

Mamie and Alfred fought back. They hired lawyers and prepared a defense. The central tenet of their case was that Jessie was never accepted as Alfred's wife. Alfred attempted to portray Jessie as a college-town hussy who had set her sights on landing a Harvard man. Bryn Mawr College was a stumbling block, for Alfred had brought Jessie to Bryn Mawr as his wife, the mother of Olive, and it was during Alfred's years at Bryn Mawr that Jessie had given birth to their son, Alan. From many sources Mamie gathered letters in a vain effort to prove that Jessie Hodder had never been a recognized wife.

Carey refused to testify for Jessie but, in the course of conversation with Jessie's lawyers, she learned details of Mamie's relationship with Alfred and some of the contents of Mamie's daily journal. According to Jessie, Mamie had agreed to marry Alfred if he got rid of Jessie. Worst of all, as she wrote to Mamie, she learned that Mamie had connived "with Mr. Hodder to hide the knowledge . . . that he was living here at a college for women with his mistress." Mamie had known that he and Jessie were not married, and had said nothing, although she knew "the students were constantly going to her house and he was bringing her to college receptions and introducing her as his wife." Mamie should have insisted that Alfred leave the college, and, if he refused, should have told Carey "so the intolerable scandal might have been done away with." Carey was particularly hurt by Mamie's remark that if "I had deserved to know, I might have known." Mamie had put Carey in the "impossible position of a trusting dupe."[6]

As part of Alfred's defense, Mamie was preparing to claim that the president of Bryn Mawr College had been aware he was not married. Unknown to Carey, Mamie had kept some of Carey's letters, including one that was potentially damaging. Once she had unthinkingly written to Mamie that Alfred and Jessie Hodder were both "so preoccupied with sexual questions" that she "should not be surprised if they themselves were unmarried." Mamie intended to introduce into court this and other personal letters from Carey.[7]

Carey Thomas had faced scandal before, but Mamie's planned defense would bring it inside the Deanery and raise questions about her judgment as president. If she had known that Alfred and Jessie were unmarried and "had permitted him and his mistress to be asked to all college entertainments and had allowed the students to go to his house . . . and had not reported the situation to the trustees and recommended that his resignation be asked for immediately," the trustees would have properly insisted that she resign. In both her own opinion and that of others, she would been found "unworthy of any position of trust or confidence in the future."[8]

Frightened for Bryn Mawr as well as for her career, on August 13, 1907, Carey broke off all relations with Mamie. In a letter of great dignity, written when she was abroad, Carey stated that she had erred in writing to Mamie about her relations before marriage with Alfred and begged her pardon. She restated her indictment of Alfred: "To beget illegitimate children and leave them to suffer all the obloquy and misery that are the lot of such bastards in twentieth-century America among people whom we know is the most dishonourable crime I can conceive of. To introduce as one's wife, among conventional people, and above all in a college for women, a mistress who was later to be cast off like an old shoe—is only second to the first crime." Alfred could have resigned from Bryn Mawr for personal reasons at any time. "Nothing can ever alter these two facts of the gravest social and moral misconduct. No testimony in the witness box can change them." Carey was giving this judgment because Mamie had written lengthy explanations to her. Carey demanded that if a suit were brought to court, her name not be introduced. In her last two letters Mamie had quoted her. If Mamie did so in court, Carey warned, "I must appear and speak for myself."

Mamie and she differed "so radically that any further words about it are absolutely useless between us." Mamie could count on her if she ever needed her. Carey would never say anything against Mamie, even to her family. She would not write again. "I have loved you so much that I cannot bear us to

continue writing letters such as yours to me and mine to you." Carey closed
with Hamlet's last words, the line she had written to Mary when her mother
died: "The rest is silence."[9] Mamie was dead to her now.

By this point, however, any real danger of a court trial and scandal had
passed. On March 3, 1907, Alfred Hodder died. He had suffered from intesti-
nal pain for three years, had lived a riotous life, and may have been an
alcoholic, but his death took Mamie by surprise. It also ended Jessie's suit
against him. Mamie, however, did not give up her efforts to prove the legitimacy of her marriage and to restore Alfred's good name. With his death,
Mamie's love turned into adoration. Mary Berenson, who admired Mamie's
mental gifts, was fascinated and appalled by her efforts to claim sainthood for
Alfred. On a visit in 1909 Mamie said, "He was a reincarnation of Christ,"
and spoke of him as "St. Alfred . . . a real Knight of the Round Table."[10]

For the rest of Mamie's long life, she lived to pay tribute to Alfred Hodder.
After a short period in Baltimore, she moved to an elegant house in Princeton.
She took up Hodder's causes, transcribed and edited their correspondence for
publication, and spoke with him in séances across the grave. She returned to
her literary studies, but, despite the urging of former Bryn Mawr colleagues,
never published any of her writings. With her will she endowed the Hodder
Fellowship at Princeton University, which, by its generous support each year
to an artist or scholar in the humanities, perpetuated her understanding of the
relation of leisure and creativity.

Carey never saw Mamie or wrote to her again. Although she had promised
Mamie never to speak against her, Carey systematically insisted that all members of her family break with her. When Alfred died, Helen traveled with
Mamie to his funeral in Baltimore. In a forty-page letter Carey explained to
Helen why she saw this as an act of personal betrayal. By putting herself in
the position of "chief mourner," Helen had "stabbed" her "in the back." Carey
Thomas had long learned to make a distinction between her personal views
and college policy, and she depicted her breach with Mamie to Helen in this
light. Marriage was not the issue. Mamie "might have loved the devil himself,
and I should only have been sorry for her and helped her to marry him, if that
was what she wished." What forced the break was the court battle and the
knowledge she gained of Mamie's treachery.

Yet this was hardly all. Carey likened Mamie's marriage to Tom Worthington's divorce and remarriage: "It seemed to me that thee had acted to me as I
should have acted to Grace if Tom Worthington's second wife had died and
I had gone with him from Baltimore to Lancaster to support him during her
funeral." Such an analogy makes it clear that what was at issue for Carey
Thomas was Mamie's desertion. Just as Tom had left his wife to marry another
woman, so Mamie had left Carey. To think this way meant that Carey denied
her own emotional entanglements, her own commitments to Mary. It also

meant that she presented herself as being as unselfish and self-abnegating as Grace. She wrote to Helen, "The saddest thing about it all is that after twenty-five years of what I believe was unselfish devotion and love on my part, in which I tried to meet Mamie's every wish and shield her in every way, it became clear to me years before she left Bryn Mawr that she had no real love or affection for me—and never had had. . . . I had wasted and thrown away twenty-five years of love and affection on her."[11]

Mamie hardly perceived things this way. Perhaps under Alfred's tutelage, she had come to see herself at Bryn Mawr as trapped by Carey, forced into total dependency, an unwilling witness to Mary's growing power, or as she ultimately put it "a prisoner in the dwelling of an ogress."[12] Mamie, in fact, knew that, despite Carey's seeming friendship with her after her marriage, Carey now regarded her as a nonperson. In 1905, when Mamie did not receive an invitation to graduation at the Bryn Mawr School, she wrote Carey bitterly that she had expected no less, remembering what had happened to Julia Rogers.

Mamie was, in fact, in the position of the discarded wife. Her contributions to Carey Thomas' work as lecturer, and as schemer and planner in their common enterprises at Bryn Mawr College, the Bryn Mawr School, and the Johns Hopkins University School of Medicine had never been recognized and were now destined to be erased. Her threat to Carey to involve her in the bigamy trial may have been not so much careless or selfish as vengeful.

Late in her life Mamie put on paper reminiscences and judgments, provoked by Logan Pearsall Smith's published recollections in 1937. Penned three decades after her break with Carey, drafts of statements, obsessively reworked but never sent, reveal Mamie's bitter feeling. She recalled Carey's words as they parted: "I shall have everything that money can give, but I have loved you better than anything in the world. And my heart is broken." Perhaps Carey said this, perhaps not. Memory at such a distance is not trustworthy. Mamie's final judgment of Carey, however, carries a different weight, because it rests on the twenty-five years they lived together. Although Mamie captures only one facet of a complex person, her verdict carries an element of truth: "She was created—so it seems to me in retrospect—as incapable of an altruistic feeling or thought as my cat . . . and in so far was innocent as he or any beast of prey. She was incapable of ever concerning or imagining another person's personality or inner life 'as in itself it really is.' "[13]

II

"Le roi est mort: vive le roi," Carey wrote to Hannah, supposedly about the professor that Bryn Mawr hired to take Mamie Gwinn's place. But she followed immediately with this statement: "It consoles me when I think of leaving the college myself for Mary's and my Venetian palace." What she was really writing about was Mary Garrett's assumption to the Deanery.[14]

With Mamie's departure, Mary closed her Baltimore house, except for rare occasions. She set about remaking the Deanery in a grand fashion, one befitting a railroad heiress. Once before she had expanded and redecorated, but this time she rebuilt the Deanery on a larger scale and filled it with her possessions. At a cost of $100,000—over $1.6 million in 1994 dollars—she extended the guest-room wing, adding a bathroom; built a housekeeper's apartment, servant rooms, and rooms for storing linen and china; and greatly expanded the rooms for receiving and entertaining. Photographs show it to be a vast house on the scale of the great shingled "cottages" that once lined the New England seacoast. Lockwood de Forest, the brother of Mary's friend Julia, designed the alterations. A member of Tiffany's firm, he was an aesthete who delighted in intricate patterns and textures. Mary and Carey imagined the Deanery as an English country house, suitable for entertaining on a grand scale. The interior was filled with bright colors and works of art garnered in travel abroad. The primary entertaining room was modeled after the Dorothy Vernon Gallery in the British country house Haddon Hall. Leaded windows and a copper-beamed ceiling surrounded a vast space filled with Tiffany glass, Persian rugs, and Indian chests. To staff such a house required a cook, two waitresses, two chambermaids, a laundress, and a cleaning lady for the servants' rooms. Carey also had a personal lady's maid. The trustees agreed to grant to Thomas and Garrett the right to live in the Deanery as long as either desired.[15]

Mary had John C. Olmsted design the Deanery garden. The plan that Carey described as "an English garden behind a tall stone wall" was to her "wholly irresistible." It was a green garden with only a few flowers in the borders, decorated with statuary and tilework by de Forest. With the Deanery and its garden Carey aspired to an American version of Bernard and Mary Berenson's I Tatti. She hoped to lure distinguished foreign visitors, enlivening the dull social scene of Philadelphia and the college.[16]

These were active years for both Carey Thomas and Mary Garrett. The two women, now without Gwinn, continued their collaboration in the Bryn Mawr School. Garrett, for her part, pushed Thomas into the suffrage movement, and, in her more quiet manner, joined her. Thomas shared her college work fully with Garrett, including her professional mail. In 1906 Garrett became the first non-Quaker director of Bryn Mawr College, and served on its two most important committees, buildings and grounds, and finance.[17]

During Mary's first two years in the Deanery, Carey was not always certain that the two were making the right choices. These were years of raising money and supervising the construction of buildings. Conflicts with the board of trustees were reaching a climax. Carey Thomas no longer eschewed the political arena outside Bryn Mawr's gates. By working so hard was she making a mistake? Hannah had long thought so. In late May 1906, as she rode on a train to the peace conference in Mohonk, she mused in a letter to Mary: "I wonder if we are wise in not taking these next ten years to travel and see the world. In another ten years it will be too late." With extraordinary insensitivity, she wrote a week later that she wanted Mary to see a doctor to be certain that her heart was sound: "If I were sure about it, I should be inclined to sail away with you in the not too far-off future, but if there is a shadow more than the ordinary possibility of your leaving me alone (of course either of us may die or be killed in an accident), I should have to have the college to console me."[18]

Carey had had these questions since 1884, but now Mary asked them, too. Although, as Mamie was later to state, Mary loved Carey's active side, she was tempted to take Carey away from Bryn Mawr and enjoy a life of leisure with her. And yet, for neither woman were the questions real. Carey was enmeshed in the college; and Mary still needed her to be. Mary Garrett wanted to use her great wealth for good. She longed for a meaning for her life. To some degree Garrett put her money into Carey Thomas as she had put it into the Johns Hopkins medical school: to achieve something for women. To give it up, for the two women to withdraw to live abroad, involved failure for Garrett as well as for Thomas. Garrett's primary wish was to make life as luxurious for Thomas as she could, paying for their annual summer in Europe on a grand scale; but she understood her gifts as philanthropy, not indulgence—its end, Bryn Mawr College.

The years together held for both women the intimacy for which each had longed. They were seldom apart from each other after 1904, so there are relatively few letters. But the ones that exist contain expressions of love and comfort in each other. Carey wrote to Mary in 1908, "I shall miss you awfully, beloved, tonight. No one to sit opposite me in the easy chair and go to sleep, and no one to curl up with tonight."[19]

The two had bad times as well as good. They were both headstrong women who found it difficult to compromise. Breaks that Mary had made in the past—with friends such as Julia Rogers and Bessie King and with members of her family—were not merely Carey's doing; they arose also from Mary's imperial manner. In the 1880s and early 1890s, Carey had often commented on Mary's bossiness, and she continued to do so after 1904. Once when Mary was recovering from illness, Carey wrote that she knew she was better: "You scolded me quite like your own managing self yesterday, and I have been happy ever since." Carey's family never liked Mary, associating her with crass plutocrats. Mary Berenson's description to Hannah during a 1908 Bryn Mawr visit gives a revealing glimpse of Mary Garrett and of the Deanery household. She wrote that she "fusses more, Mother, than I imagined a person *could* fuss. Not over herself, but over this house. And the results are disastrous. She and all the servants and secretaries are on the verge of nervous prostration."[20]

Mary had often been subject to Carey's angry outbursts. Before 1904 Carey had attempted to explain them away as springing from their complicated weekend life. After she moved into the Deanery, Mary found a different explanation. In 1909 she wrote that Carey's rage was like a "demoniac possession" that in earlier eras required exorcism. When angry, Carey said "cross (and, oh, so often, far worse than cross) things." Carey promptly forgot the episodes, but Mary nursed her wounds. "Such horrible scoldings and tirades I am subjected to. I feel sure that if you could once realize what you looked and are like for the time, in one of your fits of temper, you would try never to let yourself give way to another." And yet their quarrels did not tell Mary about the essentials: she loved Carey and was committed to her vision.[21]

In the years surrounding 1910, buoyed by Mary Garrett's money and support, the trustees submerged in a board of directors and seemingly compliant, Carey Thomas was happier in her work than at any other time. She wrote to Hannah, "Mary, my Mary, has been very well this winter. If it were not for the begging we should be very well content. We like our harness and our traces and have no desire to run away and upset our academic load." In observing her cousin in the Deanery Mary Berenson felt awe and sadness. Carey was "a 'life-enhancing' person." She could put together a lunch for forty Whitall cousins the day after giving a dinner for college trustees, but her life took too much work, canceling out essential pleasures. Each day Carey got up at six-thirty in the morning and went "hard all day" until six-thirty P.M. As a result, by nine P.M. she and Mary Garrett were "fit for nothing." Mary depicted them after dinner, as "dropping with sleep, and their eyes got narrow and half closed like cats!"[22]

For her part Carey wrote of her well-being as never before. To Hannah she regularly stated how happy and satisfied she was, that she loved life, that she was never bored. She once laid it to good fortune, "a mere matter of health and lack of nerves." She did have to work at her health, however. She could no longer exercise as she had before 1898, but almost every day she took a massage and tried to spend time in the open air. Along with Mary, she struggled unsuccessfully to keep her weight down, losing pounds in the strict regime of health spas each summer, only to regain them (and then some) during the academic year. As she wrote to Hannah, at age fifty she "began steadily to gain." She found it a problem, with her inability to exercise, "to remain stationary in weight and eat enough to do as much work as one wishes to." She knew that her increasing girth was unhealthy, and doctors in Philadelphia gave her strict instructions to cut down on fats; but she liked to eat rich food. It was typical on a busy day for her to accompany a sandwich with a glass of cream, and she could eat a half pound of chocolates at one sitting. Part of the hospitality at the Deanery was its generous table. Good food, as their age defined it, was an ingredient in the common life that Carey and Mary enjoyed, and it showed on both of them.[23]

From Mary Garrett's perspective, the partnership was successful. Bryn Mawr assumed its form on the land, an endowment campaign raised capital, secularization was complete, and the quality of the college's intellectual life was sustained. M. Carey Thomas remained the leading national spokeswoman for women and higher education. The eagle soared.

III

THE 1906 expansion of the college's board of trustees into a board of directors and the creation of new administrative positions consolidated Carey Thomas' authority. The college moved into a new phase. The enlarged governing board now consisted of twelve male Orthodox Friends, Thomas herself, Mary Garrett, and two Bryn Mawr alumnae. A dean, a business manager, and a comptroller lessened the burden of day-to-day administration. Marion Reilly, as dean, took responsibility for what is today called academic advising, as well as student affairs. Isabel Maddison, who had arranged courses and worked with the faculty, continued to combine the duties of a registrar with some of those of a dean of the faculty. The comptroller took over financial management, what had been Thomas' most time-consuming activity. Carey Thomas wrote to Hannah Smith that after a year of adjustment, she would "have time to *live*" and hoped that she might begin to take the three sabbaticals to which she was entitled.[24]

Carey Thomas, however, did not begin to "live," but only to work ever harder. Relieved of certain tasks, she held onto others tenaciously. She continued to administer the oral examinations in French and German to all Bryn Mawr students. She retained sole power to set the college's curriculum. She gave minute attention to the content of specific courses. She hired and fired all members of the faculty and set the particular terms of each professor's contract. In 1885 presidential authority was the norm in American colleges; by the early twentieth century, Carey Thomas' control at Bryn Mawr was becoming an anomaly.

The building program of 1902–06 was followed by the endowment campaign of 1910 to raise $500,000. Thomas had hoped that she could expand the intellectual life of the college by building new residence halls to increase the number of students. Expansion, however, had not worked because the college lost money on each collegian. In 1909, with a student body of 424, the college had a deficit of approximately $16,500 on a budget of $210,000, and a total deficit of $74,000. Prominent alumnae had not agreed with Thomas' strategy to build from a material base, and beginning in 1904, the alumnae association initiated a campaign to increase the academic endowment for the college, setting $1 million as their goal. Progress was modest but steady, and by 1907 the alumnae had raised almost $100,000. After the new buildings were in place, Thomas joined the alumnae effort.[25]

Her first thought was John D. Rockefeller, Jr., and in a letter to him of March 6, 1907, she broached the subject. She set out her dream of Bryn Mawr as a "great school of productive scholarship and research," citing statistics of the graduate school. In a departure from what had been her own position, she argued vigorously for the value of a women's graduate institution. Not only did it inspire female students, it could serve as a center for gathering statistics about women and education. But an important change had occurred: between the initiation of Rockefeller's benefactions to Bryn Mawr and 1907, he had channeled his philanthropy into a new foundation, the General Education Board. Carey Thomas did not want to lose her direct line to the younger Rockefeller. She asked John D. Junior if it was appropriate to request of the Board a gift to match each alumna dollar by two. Advised by Frederick T. Gates, the GEB's head, Rockefeller replied that Thomas needed now to address her inquiries directly to the Board, but he warned her that though he supported separate undergraduate colleges for women and men, he did not think it "wise or necessary" for postgraduate education to be single-sex.[26] On January 26, 1909, Thomas got word that the General Education Board would give Bryn Mawr $250,000, if it were matched by $280,000 in gifts by Commencement 1910. The Board's promise decided her work for the next eighteen months. She and Garrett immediately invited 175 alumnae to lunch at the Deanery to begin the campaign.

Raising endowment money proved very difficult. The GEB increased the sum that the college had to raise, and Carey Thomas went to New York to talk with Frederick Gates, but got nowhere. The days of personal appeals to Rockefeller were over, and Gates was now limited by a board that included Charles W. Eliot. As much as she had enjoyed getting money from Rockefeller, she hated campaigns. As she put it, fundraising was "a horrid business, only second in indignity to stealing but preferable because it does not put you behind prison bars." She wrote to Ray Costelloe, Mary Berenson's daughter, "Life is simply not worth living with begging to be done. It is a nightmare and sits on my pillow and poisons my thoughts. I can neither read or write in the hateful intervals. I can only try to forget my horrid occupation in novels or in the theatre or opera." The board of directors gave her leave to absent herself from her office and concentrate all her energies on raising money. In the course of the campaign Thomas came to believe that colleges made a mistake in not charging the full cost of undergraduate education. The principle was all wrong, she felt. "College education should not be given away. It should be paid for like everything else in the world." By paying less than what it costs to educate them, students require the college to make up the difference "by begging and underpaying our professors. Privately endowed colleges ought not to subsist on the charities of the rich."[27]

As Carey Thomas sought big gifts, she inquired in New York about wealthy potential donors, and she asked Frank Thomas, her brother now living in New York, to look up the financial status of Bryn Mawr fathers. She wrote to Hannah in late January 1910, "Since Christmas I have been sitting like a spider weaving my nets in my beautiful Deanery den, getting up lists of people whom I can ask to give $10,000, $5,000, $1,000, $500 and so on. Every few days I emerge and rush on to New York and back to ask for advice in making up my lists or I drop into a Wall Street office to ask a fatted victim for a subscription." The alumnae gave successful fundraisers that put Bryn Mawr in the public mind. In Boston they staged *Medea,* and in other cities arranged concerts, readings, operas, and parties. Thomas knew, however, that the alumnae could get very little and that the large sums were her task. Late in the campaign, Thomas appealed to the owners of Philadelphia newspapers for editorial support. She sent out written appeals to four thousand potential contributors, which she followed by letters, telegrams, and personal calls. Evangeline Walker Andrews wrote to the board of directors to attach a condition to the alumnae gift that all funds had to be used solely to increase professors' salaries. Because she had stepped on what the directors regarded as their turf, she got nothing of what she sought and a wrist-slapping to boot.[28]

As always, Carey Thomas worked up to the wire. She wrote to Hannah: "we have completed our fund in agony and drops of blood. Up to 4:00 P.M. on the day before Commencement we were $6,000 short, and I telegraphed in all directions for help and telephoned everyone I could reach with the final result that checks and promises by telegram and telephone and messenger came pouring in." By 9:00 A.M. on the morning of Commencement, the $416,000 needed to qualify for the GEB grant was raised, plus an extra $36,000, "towards our second half-million," as Thomas confidently put it. The occasion was made even more noteworthy by the presence of President William Howard Taft, the father of undergraduate Helen Taft, as commencement speaker.[29]

On October 21 and 22, 1910, Bryn Mawr celebrated its twenty-fifth anniversary. It was a glorious occasion, marked by intellectual debate and congratulatory speeches. As presidents of women's colleges honored Bryn Mawr, they linked the college and M. Carey Thomas. Mary Emma Woolley, the president of Mount Holyoke College, set the tone when she stated that "the progress of Bryn Mawr College, its place in the educational world, is, to an unusual degree, the work of the woman whose name has been identified with it from the beginning." On the following day, filled with contrition that praise of the college had become praise of herself, she wrote letters of apology to James

Rhoads' daughter Anna and to the trustees. "I was greatly distressed to have things thrown out of perspective by over emphasis on my own services." She sent paragraphs from her undelivered speech that paid tribute to James Rhoads and to trustees, past and present.[30]

As a reward for her exertions, the directors voted to give Carey Thomas a four-month leave of absence. She and Mary went to Egypt in the winter of 1910–11. It was the first leave Carey Thomas had taken in more than twenty-five years of running Bryn Mawr. In what was probably her last letter before Hannah's death in 1911, Carey wrote, "Everybody approved, and I have got myself to the point of going and letting the college do without me."[31]

Philanthropic gifts gave Carey Thomas the ability to support two projects that took Bryn Mawr in important new directions. In her work with the Philadelphia school board, Thomas had argued for scientific preparation for teaching. As early as May 1901, Thomas laid out a plan to Mary Garrett for a practice school for teacher training. In 1910, at the end of the endowment campaign, Samuel Thorne offered to the college $150,000 to underwrite the Phebe Anna Thorne Model School, in conjunction with the college's department of education. The school opened opposite Pembroke Arch, in Japanese-inspired buildings and two renovated structures that once housed students. Under the direction of Mathilde Castro, the model school offered an innovative curriculum combining the arts with the traditional subjects required for Bryn Mawr entrance and kept pupils out-of-doors for much of the school day. It was, despite its endowment, a venture on a shaky financial base. The college advanced funds for construction on the expectation that it be repaid from the Thorne funds, but the endowment did not prove large enough to fund the operating costs of the school, and it continued to run a deficit until it was closed in 1931.[32]

The second project took Bryn Mawr further afield from its initial design. Carola Woerishoffer, a wealthy young graduate of the class of 1907, died in 1911, leaving the college $750,000. Bryn Mawr needed the money, for deficits had continued even after the successful 1910 campaign. Although much of the bequest went into general funds, Carey Thomas could not forego the opportunity for a new venture. In 1915, influenced by the new social consciousness of students, the settlement house, and the larger spirit of Progressivism, she proposed a graduate school of social work named in Woerishoffer's honor. Thomas approached Susan Kingsbury, a professor of economics at Simmons known as both an innovator and a difficult personality, to found the Carola Woerishoffer Graduate Department of Social Economy. It was an important departure both for the profession of social work and for Bryn Mawr. It was the first graduate school in the field to offer a Ph.D. Under Thomas' direction, Bryn Mawr had committed itself to the liberal arts in their purest forms, and now suddenly had in its midst a school of social work prepared to engage with the world. Social work education at Bryn Mawr College proved to be a volatile but creative mix.[33]

IV

DURING these years Carey Thomas' anti-Semitism grew more virulent, supported by a rising hostility to Jews among the American Protestant upper class. In letter after letter, personal and professional, she singled out and labeled Jews. At Bryn Mawr College, Jewish students ran the gamut of excellence and failure, but whether it was their candidacy for the European fellowship or an accusation of plagiarism, Thomas invariably focused on their Jewishness. Jewish parents presented Thomas with problems to solve and potential donations to give. Jews sought admission to the Bryn Mawr School. They were recommended for professorships at Bryn Mawr College and as teachers at the Bryn Mawr School. As Thomas traveled, she encountered Jews in hotels and resorts. They were the medical specialists she was advised to consult. Whatever the context, she fastened on their Jewishness as their salient characteristic; and normally, this led her to an angry derogation.[34]

Carey Thomas also continued anti-Semitic actions. At the Bryn Mawr School Edith Hamilton sought repeatedly to have Clara Landsberg join the faculty. Thomas insisted each time that Hamilton be informed that Jews were to be excluded from teaching positions. At Bryn Mawr College, Thomas spared herself potential embarrassment in faculty negotiations after 1906 by making certain beforehand that she was not dealing with a Jewish candidate. That she could make such inquiries and state her preferences to graduate school mentors and college presidents suggested that they shared or accepted her prejudices. With her own faculty she may have been on shakier ground. For example, in 1916 in a long letter to Bryn Mawr professor David Tennent she stated her unwillingness to consider either of two scientists because they were Jewish. She asked Tennent to frame the rejections in terms only of their inexperience, adding "if you say this, it seems to me that the question of race need not be raised." Thomas was not certain that Tennent was willing to speak as she directed. If not, then he should choose one of the two to come to Bryn Mawr for an interview, after which Thomas would select a candidate for the position who was not Jewish.[35]

Although Carey Thomas' anti-Semitism had specific roots that date from her young womanhood, it melded in these years into the stream of a broader racism stimulated by travel. In the early twentieth century, as she and Mary took their regular trips abroad, she began to comment disparagingly on other passengers in terms of their nationality and color. As she began to reflect on world politics, her position became clearer. In November 1903, she reacted to efforts to enforce the Monroe Doctrine in Panama. She wrote to Mary

Garrett, "I am infinitely disgusted by the Panama Incident. It is not only horribly dishonest but it means we shall have all mongrel South America in our possession. I have always so understood our Jingo politics to aim at that, but I hoped it would not come in my lifetime."[36]

The real change came in 1911, as she traveled in Egypt. It was her first trip with Mary beyond Europe. When she had gone with Mamie to Gibraltar and Tangier in 1897, her response to those from northern Africa had been that they were exotics, not important in themselves, but as providers of local color or background. In Egypt in 1911 Thomas took the measure not only of ancient sites but also of colonial rule. As an avid reader, she kept up-to-date on contemporary works on imperialism and racial theory. Scientists and popular writers had proposed a genetic theory of civilization that put the human races in a hierarchy with Northern Europeans at the top and native Africans at the bottom. As Thomas looked at Egypt through this lens, everything she saw strengthened her conviction that the British had brought civilization to a backward people. In setting forth her observations to her family, she began to reveal the depth of her revulsion against African Americans. "It would be as absurd for England to give back Egypt to the Egyptians . . . as it would be for us to turn over the government of the United States to our Negroes." The Egyptians themselves were quite content. As she tried to understand the contrast between the people around her and the ancient Egyptians who had built glorious monuments, she resolved it by the theory of racial mixing. Contemporary Egyptians "are one of the untrustworthy, untruthful mongrel races, totally ignorant, superstitious and without any intellectual curiosity. Like our Negroes they seem unable to sustain intellectual work."[37]

Travel is thought to broaden one, and Carey Thomas certainly believed that it did. As she went to faraway places—Japan, China, Palestine, and Syria—she wrote letters to be circulated among the members of her family, confident that she was bringing to others the insights of her travels. These letters demonstrate that Thomas delighted in energetic travel, gloried in natural scenery and works of art, but found herself revulsed by people who looked and acted in a manner different from her own. She used racial categories and the racial arguments of contemporary eugenicists to explain and solidify that revulsion. In her case, travel narrowed her.

Perhaps the most interesting example was her response to the Japanese. Beginning in the 1890s, Thomas cooperated with a committee and Umeka Tsuda, a Japanese woman who had studied at Bryn Mawr, to bring female students from Japan for two years of preparatory school and four years at Bryn Mawr or other Pennsylvania institutions. Her papers document this activity, but evidence little personal interest in the project or curiosity about the recipients. When she traveled with her nephew Harold Worthington to Japan in the summer of 1915, she was met at Yokohama by three Japanese women who had graduated from Bryn Mawr, and she spoke at Tsuda's school. She admired the beautiful land and its monuments. She was treated with especial courtesy in hotels. She liked the seriousness and silence that she observed from the train. When she wrote to her family her reflections, however, she had nothing but scorn for the Japanese as a people. She and Harold decided that the Japanese were "orientals and savages and that in spite of their wonderfully intelligent government they can never compete with *us*. They are radically unintelligent, I feel sure." In the case of the Japanese, all evidence evaporated in the face of her racial hostility.[38]

V

IN THE twentieth century Carey Thomas' relationship to students shifted. She spent more of her time away to speak or raise money. When she was on campus she was involved in performing routine administrative tasks or developing programs. A dean now served to advise all students in planning their courses. Thomas was also older and saw Bryn Mawr undergraduates less as sisters than as nieces. She had lost the connective thread of teaching.

Bryn Mawr College had begun with a liberal approach to students. As a young dean, Carey Thomas had insisted that students were adults, responsible for their behavior both in class and out. When they first began to get out of hand, she worked with them to create the Self-Government Association, a student judicial system that executed college policy. In the early years of her presidency, Thomas focused on students' comfort. As she tried to attract wealthier students to the college, she worried about overwork and the quality of the table. Numbers grew, and the college attracted more high-spirited young women. In the twentieth century Thomas' focus shifted, and she attempted to regulate students to maintain standards. Self-Government continued to be the court that tried students for the breaking of college rules, but administration and faculty increasingly intervened to set new requirements and monitor them. The college adopted rules that required student attendance at lectures. Through the merit law, the college set a minimum on the number of low grades a student could have and graduate. In time, students below the minimum were forced to withdraw from the college. The old informality was replaced by record-keeping.

Formerly each student had known Carey Thomas as professor and adviser. In the twentieth century, how did students know their president? For them, she was the court of appeal for Self-Government and the censor of college publications. She was the one who rushed across campus with a cane. She was the sometimes amusing, sometimes challenging giver of daily chapel talks. A distant yet familiar figure, Thomas in the twentieth century inspired both awe and humor.

She had a potential link with students in the daughters of Richard Cadbury and other friends from her youth. Letters to their parents, however, suggest that she did not reach out to them. Beginning in 1906, however, Carey Thomas had a special tie to the student body. Grace's daughter Mary Worthington, who had lived most of her life in England, came to Bryn Mawr with her tuition and board paid by Mary Garrett. Mary Worthington was a delightful niece, and Thomas and Garrett—her "Aunt Carey" and "Aunt Mary"—loved her dearly and saw her often. Mary Worthington spoke to Carey Thomas freely about student life. When her younger brother Harold came to attend Yale, Carey hosted them both frequently. Mary Worthington's years at Bryn Mawr were productive and happy. She was chosen May Queen by her classmates. After Bryn Mawr, she began training to be a doctor at Johns Hopkins medical school. But tragically, her body gave way, and she died of heart disease in 1912. Carey's many long, loving letters to her during her illness convey what she had come to mean to her. Carey wrote to her in 1911, "Do you know, long ago I made up my mind that I would never care too much about a younger person, but you and Harold have made me break my good—or bad—resolutions. You are really so very nice that if I had had a daughter I should have liked her to be just like you. Only the fairies around your cradle, when they gave you all the other good gifts ought to have added a little better heart."[39]

In addition, Mary Berenson's daughters Ray and Karin Costelloe came to Bryn Mawr. Through their eyes Carey Thomas began to understand some of the forces that were impelling undergraduates. Karin was delightfully happy, but Ray, very much her cousin Carey's kindred spirit, was critical and outspoken. From the younger members of her family, Thomas learned that twentieth-century college students were a changed breed. They were in college for the life, what Woodrow Wilson, now president of Princeton, was calling "the sideshows" swallowing up "the circus" of the curriculum. Their round of activities in the dormitories and in college organizations gave them little time to study or to read. Thomas discussed these matters at great length at her annual conference with the Academic Committee of the Alumnae Association in 1909. To these informed alumnae, she was sharply critical of twentieth-century Bryn Mawr students, far more so than in her public pronouncements. She told them that her view "from the inside," allowed her by the younger members of her family, had made her understand that the "whole academic point of view is different now. It is very much less intellectual." Ray had told her that once students finished their work for the day, they got together in their rooms, and "the evenings are spent in telling funny stories and in shrieks and shouts of laughter, and that this is repeated evening after evening." She sought alumnae support in the college's efforts to limit student dramatics. Dean Marion Reilly disagreed with her criticism of students and insisted on the educational value of informal drama. Thomas retorted that students' assessments were hardly to be trusted. Her nephews had attempted to convince her of the educational value of hazing. "They think it is a magnificent institution, and that compelling the freshmen to walk to Villanova carrying pails of water on their heads is a magnificent education."[40]

In time Carey Thomas was to understand that the primary difference between her college generation and the students of the 1910s was in their insistence on practical fields leading to social service. In a generous mood, she wrote about her college nieces and nephews to Hannah, "It is a joy to see virtuous youth about one even if it is virtuous in its own way and if it cares about reading and art so little and about people and causes so much."[41] Through the Phebe Anna Thorne Model School and the Carola Woerishoffer Graduate Department of Social Economy, Carey Thomas attempted to bring to Bryn Mawr the fields, the training, and the practical experience that met undergraduates' needs and desires. She also sought to win them to her sense of what was important in her chapel talks.

VI

CHAPEL was the one activity that, after she gave up teaching, allowed Carey Thomas to span the two worlds of college and art. No longer subjected to the discipline of scholarship, she could speak directly to undergraduates of her enthusiasms. On becoming president she had inaugurated short chapel talks with no religious message. In her early years as president she had prepared the talks carefully and anticipated them with anxiety, but over time she realized that she could talk to students extemporaneously. She wrote to Mary in October 1900, "Oh, I am so pleased I can speak easily. Even if it is not better, which I think perhaps, it is no longer such a nightmare to look forward to addressing the students."[42]

Gradually Carey Thomas learned that in chapel she could say almost anything. An alumna from the early twentieth century recalled that she spoke "freely and openly," with a spontaneity that riveted student attention. Thomas amused her chapel audience by her many slips of the tongue and malapropisms. An especial favorite was her assertion that "in X years 17 percent of you will be married, and 25 percent of you will be mothers." A former student insightfully suggested that such slips happened because Thomas "gave immediate expression to thought as it took shape in her mind without waiting to adapt its utterance as tact or social form might have directed." Thomas always insisted that she stated, "Our failures only marry," just as she had written it; but students' remembrance of "Only our failures marry" may have been the misreading that expressed her actual views.[43]

It is the nature of chapel talks to speak to the occasion, to use an event or a controversy on campus to invoke a larger issue. Thus there is seemingly a great deal of variety in Carey Thomas' talks. But underneath this surface are a few major themes that recur over the course of the almost three decades in which she spoke to students—the nature of higher education for women, the Bryn Mawr standard, ideal womanhood, women's rights, and the love of literature and art. It is her chapel talks that demonstrate most clearly Thomas' personal prejudices and her hopes for Bryn Mawr students.

In her best-known chapel talk, her 1899 retort to Charles W. Eliot of Harvard, she asserted women's right to education and culture. Both in college and to the world outside her most important theme was that the education of a woman should be exactly like that of a man. At Bryn Mawr she used the words of her addresses beyond college gates: the life of the mind had no sex; men and women must study the same subjects, have the same ideas, and contribute to the advancement of the same body of knowledge.

In the 1899 talk, she also discussed manners. She began with the change in college residence hall policy by which each dormitory got a roughly similar mix of the four undergraduate classes and graduate students. She stated that this facilitated a mutual association that would perfect the Bryn Mawr type. Along with the diffusion of a scholarly perspective would come good manners. Living together, "angles should rub off, awkwardness should disappear." As she told students that Bryn Mawr would become a school of "good breeding," she indicated its lessons: "we all have an opportunity to correct provincialism, uncouth pronunciations, to get rid of expressions that no person of culture could possibly use." The typescript of the talk shifts to lists, rather than sentences, but they are revealing: "table manners . . . toothpicks, knives in fish, salad, pie."[44]

In the early years when Carey Thomas had spoken about the Bryn Mawr standard, she had in mind the high intellectual goals of German scholarship. Her plan for Bryn Mawr was designed to sustain this standard through its combination of high entrance requirements, a faculty composed of foreign-trained scholars, the group system, and the graduate school. As Thomas moved into the twentieth century, however, the Bryn Mawr standard increasingly defined a social type, the scholarly student who was a lady. Alice G. Howland, an alumna who later became head of the Shipley School, recalled that in 1902, as Thomas was being paid tribute by a speaker from the podium, she rose, and "suddenly the interest of the audience was electrified. Could it be— but yes. Nevertheless she was! Pulling up the skirt of her dress! Bunching it under her right arm with a massive gesture, she plunged into the folds of her underskirt until she found a pocket from which she came up with a small folded handkerchief." What Howland's affectionate recollection reveals is that, despite all her efforts, Carey Thomas was no lady. The household of her origins had been comfortable but informal; it cared more for goodness than for polite manners. Carey Thomas worked hard to overcome the relaxed manners of her Baltimore upbringing. Under Mamie's and Mary's tutelage, she attempted to assume the formal standards of the American upper class. She spent beyond her means to dress elegantly and to present a grand table. She took elocution lessons. Her shocking breach of decorum in 1902 suggests how unnatural the ways of the lady were to Carey Thomas, how much labor and learning they required. [45]

All of this effort she projected onto Bryn Mawr. The college was to be a place for proper social training as well as intellectual development. Carey Thomas used her chapel talks to train students in the way she felt they should be trained. Some of what she asked of them was for the college. They were not to "embrace each other in the streets" and were to wear hats on Sunday because they belonged "to the fraternity of college-bred women" and had a responsibility to "uphold its banners." But most of what she demanded was a projection of what she wanted for herself. They were to take baths each day, never to put peas on a knife. Thomas spoke to them about these issues because she truly believed in the redemptive power of manners. They brought one into the magic circle of the elite. [46]

Carey Thomas' third theme in her chapel talks was the ideal woman and the part that college played in bringing her into realization. Bryn Mawr was to strengthen what she regarded as the Anglo-Saxon ideal of frank and open womanhood. Thomas frequently talked to students about relationships, especially those with men. A college education should make false relations inconceivable. She counseled students to choose a good father for their children, one to ensure for them "a proper heredity." Though she knew that "rakes were attractive," she advised students that they should "never marry a man to reform him." She also employed the knowledge or half-knowledge of the day to speak to students about health, hygiene, and sex. She warned students about behaviors that caused venereal disease. On one occasion she told them of a New York party where kissing games were played: "One man caught seven girls and kissed them. These seven girls have syphilis. Every effort is being made to suppress it. One of the girls committed suicide." As Thomas became more involved in the drive for suffrage she brought more women's issues into chapel. She introduced insights from Charlotte Perkins Gilman and defined an emerging feminism. [47]

Sprinkled amid the talks was perhaps Carey Thomas' most enduring theme, her literary and artistic passions. As she talked about women's independence, she spoke of Johann Wolfgang von Goethe; loyalty provoked a reference to William Shakespeare. Once she recalled her own book-besotted youth, a college life filled with "voracious and limitless reading of poetry and unending discussions of abstract questions." Frequently she turned to the literature and art of the day, bringing to students her assessments of new cultural movements.

In 1913, for example, she commended to students the exhibition of avant-garde painting in New York known to history as the Armory Show, and a story in the same mode by Gertrude Stein. In such moments she conveyed her intense aestheticism and her openness to the new. As she spoke of the Armory Show, she recalled an earlier moment, her first look at the "purple pictures of Impressionists" as a young woman in Paris. She was captivated, "and now I see you all purple." In returning to the present, she continued, "There is everything in a point of view. It is possible that you may grow to see me in cubes." All that Thomas once so carefully hid from her trustees, she now brought into the open in her chapel talks.[48]

There were risks even in the twentieth century. Carey Thomas had once carefully separated the Carey who worshipped art from the President Thomas who stood for the higher education of women. Now she was blending the two. Carey Thomas' literary heroes were not those of the Quaker members of the board or faculty, and they could still hold her to account. Many years later, an alumna recalled such a moment. "We were sitting in Chapel. The poet Swinburne had died—she always gave these little talks before daily Chapel—and she gave her recollections of hearing his poetry. . . . She was absolutely carried away. Evidently Dr. [George] Barton, the poor, learned Quaker who always was there at the same time for the religious part of the service that we had, evidently he told her it wasn't the proper thing to show such enthusiasm for Swinburne before young ladies." Thomas learned she was not so free to speak in chapel as she had supposed. And the following day she recanted, making "an absolutely deadpan speech about Swinburne's less commendable qualities."[49] George Barton did not forget such breaches in decorum.

These chapel talks sustained and amused undergraduates in the early twentieth century. Elizabeth Shepley Sergeant remembered the impression that Carey Thomas made on her and other classmates at chapel, standing before them, "her fine, sculptural head, with wiry-wavy hair . . . snowy, drawn back in a knot at her neck, her strong handsome regular features, her straight-cut, energetic body which Bryn Mawr graduates will always think of in a black loose-sleeved gown banded with bright blue." As Thomas looked down on them from behind the low reading desk, "how passionate, yet how aloof and impersonal, almost cold, was the concentration" with which she regarded them. Sergeant knew that Thomas did not see them as individuals, that she did not know any of their names. She saw them as women of the future, able to achieve. Students responded to her messages "in a spirit that varied from delight and admiration to sharp opposition or tolerant amusement; but never with placid acceptance, never with sentimental adoration. . . . Those ten minute speeches, if the truth be told, were a charge of dynamite."[50]

They also open a window into Carey Thomas' consciousness at the peak of her presidency. In the midst of her busy life as the administrator of a successful college, she paused to talk to students about some of her deepest commitments. In words profound and trivial, she tried to get them to appreciate standards and manners, to open them to new political, literary, and artistic currents, to frame for them a sense of the importance of higher education for women, and to provide a model of ideal womanhood to which they could aspire. In so doing, she spoke as much about her own concerns as about those of her youthful audience.

Woman, *with a Capital* W

I N THE early twentieth century, M. Carey Thomas became a committed suffragist. Mary Garrett was in ascendency, and she had been a supporter of women's rights her entire adult life. It goes against expectations to think of a wealthy heiress, raised to fashion, goading a Quaker daughter and college executive into sympathy for women's suffrage, but over the course of decades that is what did happen. Mary Garrett wanted Carey Thomas to head Bryn Mawr for the cause of women, and when Thomas got discouraged, Garrett continually reminded her of why she must get back to work. Yet Garrett realized that Bryn Mawr College, the Bryn Mawr School, and the Johns Hopkins medical school were not enough. Women had to gain their full political rights. By the early twentieth century, Mary Garrett publicly joined the suffrage cause, and took Carey Thomas with her.

Carey Thomas had always seen her work at Bryn Mawr and her advocacy of higher education for women as contributing to the cause. She was, after all, Hannah Whitall Smith's niece. However, she had held back from identifying herself with the political movement for women's rights. Led by pre–Civil War leaders and at its low point in popular esteem, the late nineteenth-century movement held little appeal. As Garrett attempted to persuade her, Thomas resisted. In 1892 she wrote to Garrett, "I am sure what you say about woman's suffrage is true; it is the keystone of the whole, and for the past year or two I have felt that my attitude is a cowardly one. . . . But the means seem to me hard to find." Their discussion continued throughout the 1890s without resolution. In 1898, Thomas wrote to Garrett, about her work in preparation for a speech at Cornell: "I have been stirred to the depths by my women's rights reading. I feel as if I never could give up the struggle and go to Italy, or my attic, while these poor slaves were in chains." Thomas knew that when she wrote to Garrett about her commitment to women, as opposed to that of art or scholarship, Garrett would understand; but she also wanted Garrett to accept her work in education as fulfilling all her commitments to women's rights.[1]

In 1899 Charlotte Perkins Gilman, then known as Charlotte Stetson, spoke at Bryn Mawr. In preparation Carey Thomas had read her *Women and Economics* with appreciation. She wrote to Garrett, "Every word she says seems to me fatally true, and I have not yet found one word too trenchant." In 1899 Thomas feared controversial politics on campus and asked Gilman not to speak about women's economic independence. But, given Thomas' indebtedness to Garrett, more was at issue. After hearing Gilman speak, Carey Thomas reported, "She thinks all economic dependence under *all* circumstances degrading, and we pressed her hard about geniuses and artists. That love can continue to exist under such circumstances she denies. . . . I love you very dearly, more so each time I see you, my sweetheart. Mrs. Stetson [Gilman] doesn't know everything."[2]

Carey Thomas told herself and others that she held back from open support for women's suffrage because, as a college head, she feared an association that might bring criticism on Bryn Mawr. In 1902 she stated that she could not write for a woman suffrage leaflet because she feared it might alienate conservative Bryn Mawr parents. It was her elitism, however, that restrained her. As Carey Thomas struggled to become a lady and a spokeswoman for higher education, the American women's righters seemed wanting in manners and taste. While in England, she enjoyed the hospitality of Lady Henry Somerset, the aristocratic British temperance leader who supported women's rights; but she felt the American temperance and suffrage movements lacked class. As she wrote to Hannah Smith in 1903, reformers in America were a disappointment: "In the case of the woman's suffrage movement, I am especially sorry. I am heart and soul a suffragist, but the leaders here, both speakers and writers, are so uneducated that I cannot afford for the sake of the college to identify myself with them. If I could give the time to try to reorganize them with younger or rather with better material I should feel differently."[3]

In 1902 Dr. Howard A. Kelly, the gynecologist who had performed Carey Thomas' surgery in 1896, presented to Bryn Mawr a medallion of Susan B. Anthony, sculpted by Leila Usher. Anthony, then in her eighties, came to Bryn Mawr for the occasion in her honor. The immediate impact on Thom~ was minimal.[4]

II

FOR DECADES Carey Thomas acted on the belief that sh~ women's broader interests through efforts to open up ~ Her work for the Bryn Mawr School and the Joh~ was an important beginning, and she contir~ into the twentieth century. Thomas was a p~ campaign to fund a scientific research position station in Naples, Italy. The physiologist Ida Hyde, a former assistant in the biology laboratory at Bryn Mawr College and the holder of a Ph.D. from the University of Heidelberg, responded to the plan for endowment of the Naples institution by proposing to endow a research position (or table) reserved for women. She contacted Thomas as early as 1896 with a scheme, and Thomas worked on a subscription circular. They created the Naples Table Association, composed of representatives of women's colleges and other women's educational groups, each of which agreed to subscribe $50 a year to the required annual $500 for a position. Bryn Mawr College subscribed, and Thomas became the president of the association and later one of its board members.

Carey Thomas understood that women suffered from a lack of opportunity not only for study but for professional competition, and that men refused to recognize their accomplishments. Under her leadership, the Naples Table Association established a research prize of $1,000 for the best piece of research by a woman on a scientific subject.[5] This was the first of many such awards for women's excellence that Thomas attempted to institute. Influenced by Thomas, the Naples Table was also the first association that brought together the heads of women's colleges in a cooperative endeavor. Thomas was later to be a founding member of the committee to establish a hostel for women students at the American School of Classical Study in Athens and was to work with the International Federation of University Women to install club houses for college women in Paris and Washington, D.C.

The 1900 monograph had convinced Thomas of the need for statistics on women, higher education, and health. She began to develop data under the aegis of the Association of Collegiate Alumnae, later to be called the American Association of University Women. After an initial period of reticence, Carey Thomas took an active part in the ACA and began to lobby and argue, warring with Laura Drake Gill, former Dean of Barnard College. She gave major convention addresses. She presented motions, including the controversial proposition that in each institution women should compose the same proportion of the faculty as of the student body. As chairman of the ACA Publications Committee, she undertook a comprehensive study of three thousand college women. With Alice Upton Pearmain, Thomas sought to collect more accurate data, pairing college women with college men and those closest to them in social position. For a decade she gave spare moments to work on the data and engaged Isabel Maddison as statistician. Thomas was never able to complete the study, and in 1917 Maddison published it privately.[6]

III

t was before audiences at the Association of Collegiate Alumnae that Carey
as developed her most important contribution to feminism. In two

speeches in 1903 and 1907, Thomas tackled the most difficult question the opposition posed to an advocate of women's higher education: why are there no women geniuses? To her answer she brought the data she had collected and special insights from her experience in higher education. Thomas understood male power in institutions of higher education, even in those devoted to women. At Bryn Mawr she had worked under the thumbs of a board of trustees composed of thirteen men. She knew that their interests and her own were often opposed.

More than a decade earlier, as she had schemed with Garrett for the Johns Hopkins medical school, she had voiced her dream to turn Bryn Mawr into "a great university of women scholars, where publications and investigations . . . done by women should prove original thinking power."[7] In the early twentieth century she posed against that dream the realities she had encountered, the dilemmas of talented women. From the outset the women on the faculty of Bryn Mawr had the same salary as the men at their rank and lived the same independent lives; but what had they produced? What of Bryn Mawr graduates whose promising careers proved disappointing to her? She herself had been in an unusually favored position to become a scholar, and yet she was unable to revise her Ph.D. manuscript. She had given Mamie Gwinn the work and the leisure to complete her book, but it was never written. She had supported her sister Helen's ambitions, sending her to Leipzig, employing her at Bryn Mawr, allowing her an extended leave; and yet Helen did not publish. Both Mamie and Helen were choosing marriage and an end to scholarly work.

Carey Thomas had long puzzled over the problem of how women might combine work and marriage. As early as 1887 she had written Hannah Smith, at the birth of her first grandchild, that the next question after suffrage was that of marriage and children: "how to have them without periling this education we have got and the life that is worth so much more to an educated, than to an uneducated woman." She realized even then that not all women could be like herself, nor should they be: "All of us cannot, I fear, forswear marriage, and indeed for *woman* to triumph, women must be born." She jocularly gave her aunt the commission: "Solve this before thee furls thy wings!"[8]

Out of these elements Carey Thomas constructed an understanding of women, their problems and possibilities, unique to her era. In her speeches and articles in the first decade of the twentieth century are extraordinary insights. In 1903 and 1907 Carey Thomas anticipated many of the concerns that only gained broader attention beginning in the late 1960s. In 1903 she began by stating that women have proven that they can study successfully side by side with men at all levels. They have demonstrated the error of detractors who argued that study would harm female health. As she put it, the delusion that certain subjects were specially suited to women's nature "has finally melted away before the avidity and rapture with which girls devote themselves to

Greek and Latin and mathematics." But one last hurdle remains: some would deny women "the crowning gift of all, the power of original thought and research."[9]

This is women's secret fear. Is it possible that women—who live "in closest companionship" to men and who receive their fathers' as well as their mothers' characteristics—fail to inherit "the highest qualities of all"? Are they condemned to "only acquire like parrots the results of men's scholarship, and work over again like calculating machines, without adding anything original of their own, the mathematical, electrical, and mechanical problems by which famous men have solved the secrets of nature"? Thomas answers no. For her it is a matter of faith. Like eternal damnation, it simply can not be. Women must have the same creative potential as men. Whatever they fail to achieve is due to social circumstances, not to inherent limitations on female intellect.[10]

Carey Thomas avers she has no full proof of her assertion of women's equality of genius. There is, however, some evidence providing a reasonable basis for her belief. Twenty-five years earlier, similar arguments were made about women's inability to successfully compete with men in university examinations and to teach boys and girls in German and English high schools. "We may conclude that if women did not before prove their capacity for hard intellectual work or their ability to teach subjects of high school grade, it was for some reason circumstances did not permit them to show the power they had always possessed. I believe that it is exactly the same in the case of original research."[11]

Carey Thomas develops her case for the circumstances inhibiting women's creativity. Of the millions born, only a very few possess "original power of the highest kind." Very few of these "are enabled by circumstances to develop and use this power so as to become famous as scholars, scientists, or inventors." Assuming that women are equally endowed with men, they have not had the chance to develop their power. Throughout the world, only fifty thousand women have graduated from college. It would be fortunate if "one genius in research" were produced for every fifty thousand male graduates. But women's disabilities go beyond access to higher education, beyond even access to graduate school. Although they have written doctoral dissertations, they have not produced an outpouring of first-rate work. Thomas speaks from the most profound of personal experience. She argues that real scholarship is produced in social circumstances still denied to women. It comes "under the spur of competition for professorships, and of a struggle for a livelihood." Because there are so few women attempting scholarship, and the force of social convention is so strong, "women are cut off almost wholly from the companionship with other scholars which is the most important factor of all in original production." By contrast, in the theater, where artistic association among men and women is not limited, women have achieved fame and salary equal to men.[12]

Beyond the social conditions of work are the pressures of personal life. A professional woman is not allowed the luxury of a man. While men have their summers and holidays for creative work, a professional woman is tethered by the family claim. She must do the work of two women—"the old-fashioned woman and the new rolled into one." She must give her time away from classroom or office to her family as its unpaid nurse and companion. "I defy a Kepler, a Newton, an Edison, a Sir William Thomson, or a Pasteur, to make great discoveries under such circumstances."[13]

The final and most important limitation that women face is their inability to both marry and sustain careers. "Women scholars who feel within themselves the wonderful gifts of originality and power and who desire above all other things to give these gifts free play, must as [a] rule deny themselves the companionship of married life." Carey Thomas personally understood this dilemma on many different levels, emotional and practical, but when she came to write of it, she reduced the issue to economics. To marry all but the wealthiest of men means that women scholars "must occupy themselves with household cares of the most unintelligent and mechanical kind, which would kill in any man, and does kill in most women, the desire and the power for original work." Thomas reassures her audience that this problem need not be permanent. Women graduates in the field of household economy are at work attempting to solve it. For a woman to remain single, for her to trust her genius, demands a confidence that few have. Thinking of herself as a young woman or of Mamie or Helen in midlife, she states that women, like men, come to a time in life when their greatest desire is to marry. A decision of a woman to remain unmarried is "so seldom made because, without prolonged trial throughout a long life, no one can be sure just how much he or she can add to human knowledge."[14]

At the close, Carey Thomas answers a question she had asked at the outset. Has there ever been a woman genius? If so—if there has been "even one woman" who "possessed creative power of the highest kind"—then the case is proved. It is circumstances that prevent women's attainment, not absence of natural gifts. Thomas clinches her argument with her woman genius: Sappho, "the greatest lyric poet of the world," whose poems had never been equaled. Closer to the present, Thomas notes the achievements of British women novelists and poets and French and American women artists. Just as a hundred years ago they would have been denied the power to accomplish their work, in the early twentieth century women are kept from the circumstances that allow scholarly creativity. Thomas ends on a note of hope that present changes allow the belief that "we shall have many women scholars and inventors of eminence before the century closes."[15]

The issues raised in 1903 resurfaced in 1907, when Carey Thomas addressed the ACA at its twenty-fifth anniversary convention. As she returns to the theme of the social conditions of genius, Thomas argues for the first time the value of a women's graduate school. She bases her new commitment to the promotion of graduate schools in women's colleges on the need to cultivate women's gifts. "The highest service which colleges can render to their time is to discover and foster imaginative and constructive genius." Women students need particular help. "As I watch their gallant struggles I sometimes think that the very stars in their courses are conspiring against them." Women scholars can help women students "tide over the first discouragements of a life of intellectual renunciation." Women educators must work to create conditions in their colleges to foster creativity. They must found research chairs, allowing time for independent investigation. They must establish traveling fellowships for those showing potential. They must pressure coeducational universities to allow women to compete for academic chairs, what Thomas calls the "last and greatest battle to be won." Genius is rare and precious. "If the graduate schools of women's colleges could develop one single woman of Galton's 'X' type—say a Madame Curie, or a Madame Kovalewsky born under a happier star—they would have done more for human advancement than if they had turned out thousands of ordinary college graduates."[16]

As she again takes up the argument that women have creative ability of the highest type, Carey Thomas sweeps away the arguments of male educators, lost "in a maze of platitudes about women's receptive and unoriginative minds." She asks, "What do we ourselves, what do we women, think?" Her answer is unambiguous: "I, for one, am sure that women possess this ability." In 1907 Thomas brings new evidence. Contemporary work on heredity shows "conclusively that boys and girls inherit equally from both mothers and fathers in mathematical proportion." She surveys the studies of Alfred Odin in France, Havelock Ellis in Britain, and J. McKeen Gattell in the United States that demonstrate the degree to which male genius is shaped by opportunity and social conditions. Gattell's work shows that great regional variations exist in the proportion of eminent scientific men: in Massachusetts, for every million in the population, there are 108.8 important scientists; in Pennsylvania, there are 22.7; in Georgia, 2.8; in Mississippi, 1.3. "Only women know how true it is that in the development of the highest scientific and scholarly qualities women have today far less favorable conditions than even men in Mississippi."[17]

In turning to the studies of Britain and France, Carey Thomas reports that one out of twenty persons of genius are women, but that women form a greater proportion of actors and distinguished prose writers. In these two fields talented women have had greater chance to develop. Thomas avers that it is likely that equally talented women have a natural aptitude for scientific research but that they are "crushed by their unfavorable environment." The task of college women of the present generation is to see that "girls of the next generation are given favorable conditions for this higher kind of scholarly development. To advance the bounds of human knowledge, however little, is to exercise our highest human faculty. . . . I am convinced that we can do no more useful work than this—to make it possible for the few women of creative and constructive genius born in any generation to join the few men of genius of their generation in the service of their common race."[18]

Carey Thomas spoke many more times in her life, yet never again with such a profound understanding of her subject. In these two addresses she joined personal experience to data and analysis to shape a convincing argument about women's intellect. In doing so, she imbued with meaning her long career as a reformer committed to creating new social conditions for women's creativity. One only wishes that she could have extended her thinking to include women outside the circle of privileged white Protestants.

IV

IN 1905 Mary Garrett and Carey Thomas welcomed Susan B. Anthony a second time to Bryn Mawr, this time accompanied by Anna Howard Shaw, the president of the National American Woman Suffrage Association. Anthony told Thomas and Garrett of her fear of holding the next national suffrage convention in the conservative Southern city of Baltimore. Garrett and Thomas responded in their distinctive manners. Garrett agreed to open her Baltimore house, welcome Anthony and other distinguished women as personal guests, and give a series of lavish entertainments. Thomas committed herself to organizing a college evening for the convention program.

Carey Thomas was now ready to link herself with suffrage. What had happened in the preceding years to change her mind? The most important element was that she now shared the Deanery with Mary Garrett. But, in addition, there were changes in the wind. The suffrage movement was shifting to emphasize social issues needing women's conscience and care. Friends and members of her family, such as her sister Helen, were becoming socially conscious. And the suffrage movement was becoming respectable in polite circles.

Carey Thomas was drawn to some elements of Progressivism. Although, unlike reformers such as Jane Addams, she had no animating vision of a just social order, she shared a belief in the value of trained intelligence applied to government. In her private correspondence she used the language of muckraking reporters to rail over corporate power. She rhetorically supported the little man in his struggles against the corporate giants.[19] In the abstract she supported the eight-hour day. She wanted to see bosses replaced by educated representatives. Despite her own personal habits, she advocated prohibition.

There were, however, limits to Carey Thomas' liberalism. When Bryn

Mawr's interests were at stake, her commitments faded. In the conflict between big labor and big business, Progressives often stood for neither but for the middle class. Thomas was a manager and took the side of business. She barred union members from employment at Bryn Mawr College. Thomas once explained her reasoning in this way: "At the college I positively refuse to employ any union men, otherwise it would not be run. Our painters and carpenters and plumbers and engineers are devoted to the college, and do anything we ask of them to help out in emergencies, or when work is dull; but, if they were union men, they would not be allowed to do this." In stating what she believed to be a positive principle of open shop, Thomas failed to take into account the possibility that she might take advantage of nonunion workers unable as individuals to defend themselves.[20]

There is evidence that take advantage she did. This was revealed in 1913 when Pennsylvania enacted a labor law regulating women's work. At its passage Carey Thomas feared that its provision of a fifty-four-hour work week might apply to the college's staff of ninety-nine African-American maids. If the college cut the working day to nine hours and the working week to six days, it would have to hire additional workers. Although she was to speak movingly about men's exploitation of women and write privately with enthusiasm for the 1910 New York shirtwaist workers' strike, that she was exploiting women workers never occurred to her. Because domestic workers were exempt from the law, the college continued to require their services from seven A.M. to ten P.M., seven days a week, paying them an annual salary of approximately $333 (roughly $5,000 in 1994 dollars). Only years later, when the head of the nearby Shipley School, Alice Howland, pointed out the inconsistency between words and practice and its danger to Thomas' position as a suffrage leader, did Thomas grant the college's domestic workers a day off once a week.[21]

Carey Thomas' public support of suffrage was buttressed by class consciousness. She increasingly chafed over the disparity between her power as a college head and the limitations she faced as a woman. There were critical local elections whose outcome affected Bryn Mawr College's property. As a woman, she could not vote, whereas the college workmen could. She felt keenly the irony of her position when she sent letters to all male employees of the college, from faculty to grounds men, rallying them to vote. She once told an anecdote about her mother. Mary Thomas was being driven around Baltimore in her carriage in a fruitless effort to convince local politicians of the need for police matrons. She stopped at a polling booth "to let her ignorant Negro coachman, who could neither read nor write, vote for these very men whom she had implored in vain." Whether or not the story was true, it accurately captured Carey Thomas' feelings about her own work and civic powerlessness.[22]

This anecdote is a reminder of the limits of Carey Thomas' vision of women. She worried over the elite woman in the carriage, not the wife of her coachman nor the domestic worker at Bryn Mawr College. In her restricted vision of "woman," Thomas was, of course, not alone. The mainstream of the women's suffrage movement adopted rhetoric similar to Thomas' and also allowed its Southern branches to remain segregated. Immigrant and African-American women fought for recognition that was largely denied them in NAWSA.[23]

The College Evening of February 9, 1906, was a triumph. Carey Thomas assembled a panel of leading women academics, professors, and college presidents to give major addresses: Mary Woolley, president of Mount Holyoke College; Lucy Salmon, professor at Vassar College; Mary Augusta Jordan, professor at Smith; Mary W. Calkins, professor at Wellesley, and Maud Wood Park, graduate of Radcliffe. President Ira Remsen of Johns Hopkins University lent his distinguished presence as presiding officer. Carey Thomas closed the program with a masterful speech demonstrating the inevitability and the desirability of women's suffrage. "Just as surely as the seasons of the year succeed one another, or the law of gravitation works, just as surely will this great body of educated women wish to use their trained intelligence in making the towns, cities and states of their native country better places for themselves and their children to live in. . . . The logic of events does not lie. . . . [Women] are being irresistibly driven to desire equal suffrage for the sake of the wrongs they try to right."

She closed with a statement of tribute to Susan B. Anthony, who attended the session in spite of illness and pain. Its final words to Anthony offered Thomas' distinctive rhetoric, uniting the older language of Christian reform with the newer strand of modernism: "In those far-off days when our mothers' mothers sat contented in darkness, you, our champion, sprang forth to battle for us, equipped and shining, inspired by a prophetic vision of the future like that of the apostles and martyrs, and the heat of your battle has lasted more than fifty years. . . . Of such as you were the lines of the poet Yeats written:

> *They shall be remembered forever,*
> *They shall be alive forever,*
> *They shall be speaking forever,*
> *The people shall hear them forever."*

At the evening reception at 101 Monument Street that followed, Mary Garrett and Carey Thomas received. As they stood on the right of Anthony and Julia Ward Howe, who were placed on a divan at a large bay window, they joined themselves fully and publicly to the cause.[24]

During the Baltimore convention Susan B. Anthony took ill, and Mary Garrett arranged for medical care, calling in the woman physician Dr. Mary Sherwood and Henry Thomas, Carey's brother. Carey Thomas and Garrett asked Anthony what they might do for her, and Anthony told them of her desire for a fund to underwrite suffrage work. Garrett and Thomas agreed to find other suffrage supporters to contribute a total of $12,000 for each of five years. Garrett invited the business committee of NAWSA to dinner and pledged that she and Thomas would attempt to raise the money. Reversing their usual roles, Garrett assumed chairmanship of the committee, and Thomas became treasurer. They brought philanthropically minded women into the committee. In February 1907 the campaign began, and by May the money was raised. The list of contributors drew on known liberal, wealthy women, but it also found support in the Philadelphia world that Bryn Mawr inhabited. Garrett herself gave $2,500. The $60,000 fund proved critical because it kept NAWSA alive during its "doldrum" years. As Carey reflected to Hannah in 1909, "Does it not seem wonderful that Mary and I were able by raising that $60,000 . . . just when we did, to tide over the few years before people of means came forward to help? It has been a great joy to us."[25]

Despite this achievement, Carey Thomas still lacked an ongoing way to engage herself in suffrage work. She let her college evening address be printed by NAWSA as a pamphlet in their Political Equality Series, but this did not lead to other writing for suffrage. In February 1908 she had the idea that she might get President Theodore Roosevelt to speak out for women's suffrage if she offered him the forum of a Bryn Mawr commencement address, and she traveled to Washington in the hope that through contacts she might get an interview with him. She wrote to Hannah Smith that she hoped that at Bryn Mawr he might consider *"woman,* with a capital W. . . . If he came out strongly for woman's suffrage, he might go down in history as the second Lincoln of the disfranchised." It was a maverick gesture that did not even net her a commencement speaker.[26]

Later in 1908 she found the aegis that she needed. It had been there since the 1906 convention, in fact since 1900. In that year Maud Wood Park, who had attended Radcliffe College, had formed in Boston the first chapter of the College Equal Suffrage League. In 1904 she began to organize chapters in New York State and elsewhere. At the 1906 NAWSA College Evening, Park presented the objects of the league: "to bring the question of equal suffrage to college women, to help them realize their debt to the women who have worked so hard for them," and to make them feel the debt that they bear for the privilege of higher education. For the 1908 NAWSA convention in Buffalo, Thomas, Mary E. Woolley of Mount Holyoke, and others issued a call to the college chapters to form the National College Equal Suffrage League under the NAWSA umbrella. Carey Thomas assumed the presidency; Mary Garrett became the chairman of the finance committee, and subsequently treasurer. Maud Wood Park became vice president. Privately Carey Thomas took full credit for the organization. She wrote to Hannah Smith with news of Ray

Costelloe, her granddaughter, "We took Ray with us to Buffalo, where Mary and I went to organize the National College Equal Suffrage League."[27]

The league was just the forum that Carey Thomas needed. It gave her a way to express her long-held belief in women's rights and suffrage at the same time that she asserted herself as an educated, elite woman. The English militants gave her a model that linked social prestige and suffrage. As she wrote to Hannah in 1908, "We have been thrilled by reading of the great Votes for Women processions. England is gradually arousing our American women. There is a vast change in woman suffrage sentiment. It has become respectable." A year later, she continued, "Thee would be amazed to see how eager American women are becoming about suffrage. In New York, and Boston and Chicago, it is becoming the fashion. I flatter myself that I have made it respectable among college women."[28]

In the years between 1908 and 1917, when it disbanded, the National College Equal Suffrage League sought to bring debate about suffrage onto college campuses and to rally educated women to support suffrage. It had college chapters composed of students, faculty, and governing boards, and it had state societies of former college and professional students. The league offered to local chapters a traveling suffrage library. In the great suffrage parades, college women marched holding aloft the banners of their schools.[29]

Leadership in the league gave Carey Thomas and Mary Garrett power within NAWSA. They attended conventions, when health allowed, and hosted smaller meetings. Working relationships with Jane Addams and Sophonisba Breckinridge opened Thomas to broader social issues and introduced her to the settlement house. The complicated story of the politics of the women's suffrage movement in its final years is still to be written. Scattered evidence suggests that Carey Thomas remained a supporter of Anna Howard Shaw and her faction against all comers; that Thomas sought to minimize the impact of the more radical Congressional Union on NAWSA; and that she saw herself as a bridge to Southern white women. Active at the point of the change within the suffrage movement that substituted broad-based organization for the personal ties and rhetorical skill of an earlier generation, Carey Thomas was something of a maverick, and she has not been given serious attention by recent suffrage historians. Eleanor Flexner has characterized her as "a vital and compelling personality who aroused antagonism by her impatience and self-assurance." Carrie Chapman Catt, the leader who emerged to take suffrage to victory, called her "Her Holy Smokes."[30]

V

AT THE 1908 NAWSA Convention in Buffalo Carey Thomas gave a major address, which the National College Equal Suffrage League reprinted for wide distribution. As an actor in the suffrage drama, Carey Thomas was one of many players in a very large field. Her special gift was her oratory. In "A New Fashioned Argument for Woman Suffrage" she brought a fresh voice for women's emancipation. In suffrage, as in so much else, she was a bridge between generations. Her talk is fascinating both in the way that it reveals Carey Thomas' mind and as a harbinger of elements of late-twentieth-century feminism.

Carey Thomas constructed an understanding of women, their problems and possibilities, unique in her era. Unlike many of her contemporaries, Thomas did not accept the central conception of separate male and female spheres. She saw one universe of thought, expression, and action. In her work for women, she sought to open doors for them that led to the center stage of intellect and power. Yet she was aware that women as a group had interests different from those of men. As a single woman whose emotional life centered on other women, Thomas did not participate in the central construction of womanhood as wife and mother. She did not share in the mythology of the family. She saw men as sexual exploiters of women, able to use the power of the law to gain their ends.

Suffrage was for her a means for women to get the power to change their condition. Although she was not above relying on Progressive rhetoric to add to her arguments, at base she was not interested in women reforming society but in women attaining their rights. Her examples are of women acting in their own self-interest. As women gain the vote, they change laws defining the age of consent for females. They write legislation to allow them to teach after they marry; they vote for university regents committed to hiring women professors on the same basis as men.

The new argument for women's suffrage is that women are working. Carey Thomas cites statistics to buttress the claim that a social revolution has occurred as women have joined the work force. As workers, women need to protect their interests with their votes. Women must demand no labor without representation: "a disfranchised class cannot protect its labour." Although much of the female labor force was in the working class, the example Thomas gives is of middle-class women teachers. "Is it conceivable that the state of the future in which women as well as men will vote will deprive women of bread because they wish to marry?"[31]

Women, as a class, have interests as a class to protect. In this argument Carey Thomas anticipates modern feminism by understanding difference in terms of sexual power. Thomas argues that on some questions, "mostly those which affect women themselves, all women and a minority of good men think differently from the majority of men." Although Thomas lists a range of social welfare issues, including sanitation and health, the main thrust of her rhetoric—and her concern—involves morality and sexuality. She does not use the word *patriarchy*, but she clearly understands the concept: "It is an outrage against decency and morality that every vital question in the lives of women and children should be controlled by this masculine majority, indifferent or worse, to women's interests. Women are one-half of the human race. Why should they be born, educated, married, divorced, buried under laws made exclusively by men?" These laws regulate women's labor, determine the guardianship of their children, and control "women's power of will."

"Why," Carey Thomas asks, "should women be arrested and confined in police stations, accused, defended, tried by jury, sentenced by a judge, imprisoned, and executed solely by men?" The legal example that she chooses is pertinent, the law establishing a girl's age of consent to sexual intercourse, a clear example of men serving their sexual interests at the expense of women. In one state, the age of consent is ten; in another, twelve. These laws make it impossible for mothers to regain their daughters seduced by "human brutes" or held by brothels. In the four woman suffrage states, voting women who could not tolerate these laws raised the age of consent to eighteen.

Although Carey Thomas' primary argument takes her in a direction that became critical for feminists after the suffrage era, it is expressed in the terms of the day—the debate over "race suicide" launched by those opposed to women's advance. The phrase "race suicide" was coined by eugenicists to denote the apparent inability of Americans of Anglo-Saxon stock to reproduce, unlike the immigrants from central and eastern Europe. Demographic studies appeared that examined the marriage and reproduction rates of college women and blamed the college woman for her failure to marry and have children. Developing ideas first treated in a 1901 article in *McClure's*, Thomas returns to the charge that women's higher education, especially in women's colleges, has led to a decline in population by the white Anglo-Saxon middle class. In 1901 she insisted that the issue was not higher education but the failure of middle-class men to marry. Using the ACA statistics to mount a rebuttal to the demographers, she asserted that if one alters the focus of data collection to include noncollege sisters and college brothers of college women, it becomes clear that class rather than education is the principal deterrent to marriage. Middle-class men and women, college-educated or not, are not marrying in the same proportion as those in the lower classes.[32]

In her 1908 speech she begins with what she calls the second revolution (the first being women's higher education), "taking place before our eyes," the economic independence of women. She presents statistics demonstrating the increasing importance of women's paid labor. Women at both ends of the economic spectrum—the poorer and the leisured classes—marry because both contribute to the income of the family. Working women continue to work after marriage; women of independent means bring their fortunes. But middle-class women, "the dowerless," are prevented by social custom from working after marriage. As a result, only one half of them marry.

Carey Thomas turns the argument away from women's higher education. The problem is caused by middle class men, not by female college graduates choosing not to marry. The "men of the classes which formerly supported their wives and daughters in comfort are now unable to do so and are becoming increasingly unwilling to marry and assume responsibilities which they cannot meet." The women who have been passed by must then work to support themselves. For the sake of argument, Thomas accepts the language of the opposition. She states that the thousands of unmarried women teachers in the United States, England, and Germany compose "a celibate class like the monks and nuns of the Middle Ages, and like them an ever present menace to the welfare of the state." One might question the choice of such language to describe the single state, for its use narrows women's options. In Carey Thomas' case, it is particularly troubling because it denies what she herself values. Never rigorous with words, Thomas probably did not make a carefully calculated statement, but allowed herself to get carried away in a rhetorical flight.

She continues in the same vein: "If it is ill, as we all admit, why do we not encourage the women of these middle classes to work and marry like the women of the poorer classes who are practically all married?" Here she comes to her clincher. Women teachers, a large component of educated middle class working women, cannot marry because if they do so in the United States, England, or Germany, they lose their jobs. To those who argue that it is bad for children if women work, Carey Thomas answers that whether or not such a debatable proposition is true is not the point. "The question is simply and solely this, is it not better for these myriads of unborn children to have married working mothers than to have no mothers at all?" The solution is a change in the laws by female voters enabling women to teach and to marry.

Carey Thomas understands how profound a change women's full emancipation will bring. From her own experience she knows how great is the resistance, even of good men, to change. As she reviews the principal objections of those opposed to suffrage, she rebuts them using the conventional arguments of her day. None of these, she argues, really blocks suffrage. The true objection lies deeper: "Giving women the ballot is the visible sign and symbol of a stupendous social revolution, and before it we are afraid." Then she turns back to describe what she, as a young woman imagining her future, had feared. It was a world in which "women lived a twilight life, a half-life apart, and looked out and saw men as shadows walking. It was a man's world. The laws were men's laws, the government a man's government, the country a man's country." Through struggle, women have gained the right to go to

college and to work. Suggesting that much has been won, but much remains
to be overcome, Thomas closed, "We cannot go back. The man's world must
become a man's and a woman's world."[33]

In 1908 Carey Thomas was fifty-one. She belonged to the era of the
suffragists. With many in her generation she shared elitism, an embrace of
racial and social exclusions, moral energy, and attachment to solving social
ills by prohibition and good government. Where Carey Thomas differed was
in her ability to ask new questions and raise new issues. She considered the
complicated interactions between social conditions and creativity, the myriad
ways in which women's interests differed from those of men, the question of
sexual power, the use of the vote by women to protect their interests as a class,
and the knotty problems posed by the negotiations of marriage and career. In
her 1908 suffrage address, as in her 1903 and 1907 speeches to the ACA,
Carey Thomas pointed part way to women's future.

VI

IT SHOULD come as no surprise that by 1913 Carey Thomas identified herself
with the new word being used to encompass the ideas of a younger generation
of women: feminism. To Thomas the term gave a name to all that she had
been striving for since early girlhood. It meant not the narrow pursuit of legal
rights but women's broader effort to open opportunity and to inject a distinctive
point of view.

In 1913 she announced her allegiance to feminism in a chapel talk to Bryn
Mawr students. Since 1907 she had been openly discussing women's rights as
she spoke to students. In many of her chapel talks Carey Thomas spoke in
broad terms that began with the animal kingdom and moved through the stages
of human development. She placed reform within the framework developed
by Charlotte Perkins Gilman and grounded in progressive Social Darwinism.
Sharing Gilman's philosophical underpinnings, Thomas also saw traditional
women's culture as dragging down the human race. She urged her students
to bring the highest culture into their own homes and to move beyond the
confines of domesticity to embrace the broader issues of the day.[34]

As she addressed students in 1913, she defined feminism as a worldwide
movement of women and men that sees "the emergence into the life of
the state, . . . into literature, into scholarship, medicine, philosophy, art,
wherever the human spirit manifests itself, of the woman's point of view." She
gave a list of pure feminists and partial ones. It is an unusual list, linked more
to her aesthetic passions than to politics. For Carey Thomas the true feminists
were Walt Whitman, George Meredith, Henrik Ibsen, Richard Wagner,
George Bernard Shaw, Havelock Ellis, William Salter, and Charlotte Perkins
Gilman. Into the camp of partial feminists or those lacking in its full spirit she

placed Theodore Roosevelt and, tellingly, most of the women educators and suffrage leaders of the day. As her iteration made clear, for Carey Thomas feminism was more than women getting the vote and attaining equal opportunity and pay; it was "the coming into our social, artistic, literary, civic life of the woman's point of view for the first time honestly expressed."[35]

This new identity was to stick. For the rest of her life, in public and private, whatever the conflicts or pressures, Carey Thomas understood that she was a feminist.

CHAPTER 22

A Knockdown Blow

THE YEARS 1904 to 1911 were the high tide. Supported by Mary Garrett, M. Carey Thomas dominated Bryn Mawr College, represented women and higher education, lent the educated women's voice to the suffrage movement, and added a note to the national chorus of rising racism and nativism. Ensconced with Mary in the Deanery, rebuilt as a grand villa, surrounded by precious objects, served by eight in help, she attained the life she had sought since girlhood. She had power, prestige, wealth, and love. There were a few disturbing reminders of the past. Mamie's campaign to prove her marriage legitimate reevoked the agony of their separation. Recurring leg pain from the scar tissue of the childhood burn forced Carey to acknowledge her vulnerability. But, on the whole, life seemed in these years to have moved to a new plateau. For the first time since the period of study abroad with Mamie, Carey Thomas was satisfied. It would not last long.

I

As EARLY as 1912, Mary's health began to fail. Carey had long been convinced that Mary's physical difficulties were psychosomatic. Mary and she spent many summer weeks at European spas. This time, however, there could be no resort to health cures: the Johns Hopkins doctors diagnosed Mary's illness as leukemia. Carey was frightened. When Mary went to the hospital, Carey wrote to her, on returning alone to her room: "What I should do if you ever left me I do not know. I cannot imagine it." Committed to heroic medicine, Carey wanted to press onward. Mary was in a different frame of mind. Carey wrote her in April 1912, "We must not give up hope. . . . Please do not . . . say things that look like giving up the fight for I simply cannot bear it. I have the greatest difficulty in keeping myself from crying all the time when I am not with you. I have to tell everyone you are much better because I cannot find the composure to say anything else." Carey wrote to William Halsted, who was Mary's and her doctor and an important friend, "It seems to me that

I cannot face it. I suppose we all of us meet a knockdown blow some time or other—and this is mine."[1]

During the spring of 1913 the two women spent alternate bouts in the hospital. Carey had a tumor removed and underwent repeated skin grafts for her scarred right leg. Halsted's surgery was successful, and for the first time since the late 1890s Carey stood and walked straight. She also required treatment for inflammatory cystitis. Doctors were subjecting Mary to a wide range of procedures. In Mary's behalf, Carey enlisted Simon Flexner and the resources of the Rockefeller Institute in New York to search for a cure. Carey again begged Mary to keep up hope. In late April 1913 Carey wrote, "Unless, as we hope and believe, you are going to get strong enough to enjoy things again, the old fashioned way of leaving people in peace was better. These inoculations and vaccinations and X rays are terrible to go through with, and yet one must do everything possible or one, at least I, should be unable to bear it if anything happened to you."[2]

In the spring of 1914 Mary suffered terrible pain, and the doctors recommended the removal of her spleen. Carey wrote to a friend that Mary did not want to consent to surgery, "and did so only for my sake." Immediately after the June commencement Mary underwent an operation and began a slow process of recovery. Initial hope began to fade in the summer of 1914, however, as she became ill in a different way. The surgical wound did not heal. Halsted returned from abroad to attend her, and for the remainder of her illness alternated with Simon Flexner and Harry Thomas in coming to Bryn Mawr to visit her on Sunday. Carey was then suffering from a bone out of joint in her pelvis and was unable to walk even the short distance from the Deanery to Taylor Hall. She wrote to her brother Harry that Dr. Halsted was insisting that she should ask another doctor to "put my pelvic bone in joint so that I could lie in bed beside Mary. He does not know how poor I am. But I wish thee would ask him what I had better do." Although she needed medical attention before the academic year began, she could not leave Mary for the twelve days it required. Halsted diagnosed Mary as suffering from an infection that could have caused anemia, and he inoculated her in the hope of a cure. Carey wrote soberly, "Mary and I have no such hope." Carey's realism was well founded. By March 1915, Mary's condition was desperate.[3]

Mary's last days were terrible. Carey cared for her until the end. On April 3, 1915, in her final hours, Carey recited to her Elizabeth Barrett Browning's "Little Ellie." Mary went to sleep before Carey had finished and "never waked again." In her diary Carey wrote simply, "Mary died."[4]

Carey arranged Mary's funeral and her burial in Greenmount Cemetery in Baltimore and went into deep mourning. She wrote to Rufus Jones, "As thee knows, it is a complete breaking up of my home life. I feel as if it could not be faced." With the close of the academic year, she traveled to Hawaii and Japan with her nephew Harold Worthington, who was just finishing a year's course at MIT. In late June she wrote to Harry, "I think I am really climbing up a little, although I still cannot let myself think of Mary without collapsing, and I dream incidents of her illness over and over again."[5]

Her usual ways of coping returned. She kept herself busy, tired herself out, and did not let herself feel. From Japan she wrote in late July that energetic travel was having its therapeutic effects and she was gradually getting back her "grip." Then she stepped back, "I do not know how I shall pull through Mary's death. It is unlike anything else that I have ever been through and leaves me terribly desolate in spite of my dear family. Losing one's daily companion is different from any other loss." She returned to work in the fall and had to face the many projects that she had let go during Mary's illness. She wrote to Halsted that for three years she had been "so overwhelmed by emotion" that it had been impossible to accomplish anything other than routine tasks. "Now that there is no more hope or fear, I find that my power of work is coming back again." She began to sleep outside under the stars and to go for an automobile drive each day. On April 3, 1916, she reported to Harry that she had spent the anniversary of Mary's death alone in Mary's room. In her autobiographical fragments, written near the end of her life, lies this bleak note: "After Mary's death, Poetry—forgotten."[6]

II

IN CAREY THOMAS' life, there is a pattern. With personal loss comes challenge to her public power. In 1887, after the death of her mother, Bryn Mawr students got out of hand. With the help of undergraduate leaders, Thomas created Self-Government. In 1904 during a tumultuous period of fund-raising and construction, Mamie Gwinn left the Deanery. Reeling from the loss, Carey Thomas confronted a trustee-treasurer bearing down relentlessly. She overstepped and was called to account. After facing investigation and potential censure, she returned with her forces strengthened and her opponent defeated.

Now, as she dealt with the most heart-wrenching loss of all, Mary Garrett's death from cancer, challenge came from the faculty. In 1916, the world learned how M. Carey Thomas governed Bryn Mawr College. Distinguished scholars and a prominent alumna offered testimony in the Philadelphia *Public Ledger* about her administration. She had set herself up as the single authority in the college. She played to students, manipulating them, and then used her interpretation of their judgments as the basis of her actions. She was the one intermediary between the directors and the faculty, and she misrepresented each in order to control the other. She retained absolute power over professors and their courses. In her exercise of authority, she was uninformed, arbitrary, and dictatorial. She lied.

Were these reports true? The historical verdict is, yes. Although the collective judgment is one-dimensional and thus distorted, what it asserts is correct. In the years between 1898 and 1916, Carey Thomas acted in this manner, at least on some occasions. She had emerged from the crisis of the late 1890s more vulnerable and more determined. As she guarded herself ever more carefully on the outside, her protective armor, which included lies, grew thicker. She no longer had critics able to reach her. Unlike James Whitall or Mamie Gwinn, those who opposed her after 1898 could be dismissed as the enemy. Mary Garrett's wealth did more than cushion her, it fed her drive to power.

She did not become an ogre. Carey Thomas was a woman of many sides: generous and acquisitive, warm and hard, straightforward and manipulative. As a college executive for many decades, she balanced a conservative Quaker board, a secular and increasingly professional faculty, assertive and intrusive alumnae, and all the variety of human nature that students present. But she was behind the times. In 1885 when Bryn Mawr began, governance was a simple equation. The trustees hired the president, and the president governed the faculty. This notion of college authority was broadly shared by presidents and trustees in colleges across the country. But by 1915, much had happened outside Bryn Mawr's gates. Issues of academic freedom had galvanized the American professorate to organize and to establish standards in their colleges to protect them from willful presidents and trustees. In many other colleges, faculty had gained a measure of power over curriculum and appointments. The American Association of University Professors was debating, and was to approve in January 1916, a set of proposals governing faculty reappointments. Thomas resisted all such encroachments, reserving to herself every decision, large and small.

Moreover, Carey Thomas was a perfectionist who had difficulty delegating responsibility. She wanted every element of Bryn Mawr to meet ever higher standards. She intruded into specific courses to suggest topics and select readings. As time went on, Bryn Mawr professors felt an increasing sense of violation from her encroachments and a growing disrespect for her professional judgment. Her own scholarship dated from the early 1880s: professors in the 1910s found her dictates arbitrary and uninformed. In the academic year 1915–16, as Carey Thomas struggled to regain her equilibrium after Mary's death, the Bryn Mawr faculty revolted. This time, the conflict could not be contained within the secret proceedings of a board of trustees.

In 1915 Thomas brought in a young scholar from Harvard, Howard J. Savage, to assess the essay section of the English department. Bryn Mawr required that all freshmen and sophomores take a two-year composition course. Regina Crandall, who had come to Bryn Mawr in 1902, had supervised the work for several years, but never to Thomas' satisfaction. Savage wrote a long report, harshly critical of existing methods, and Thomas gave him the task of reorganizing the program, beginning in the fall term of 1915. Thomas made him head, demoting Crandall from director to the teaching staff.[7]

Protest began. Crandall delivered an ultimatum. The essay department readers, Crandall loyalists all, threatened to resign. Alumnae in Baltimore attempted a protest meeting. Evangeline Walker Andrews sent off a letter to the members of the board of directors and others. Thomas was determined to tough it out. Savage came to her with his resignation, but Thomas refused it, telling him that she "never yielded under any circumstances to storms." She may not have yielded, but she certainly bent. Thomas worked to appease Crandall, writing her in a conciliatory fashion to remind her that she was only removing her from her executive position, not firing her. In January and February Thomas went further. She commended Crandall for her teaching, promised her elective English courses, and created a new position for her as a regular member of the faculty at the level of associate with a two-thousand-dollar salary. Under these terms Crandall agreed to cooperate with Savage and remained.[8]

The Crandall affair touched a sensitive nerve. That President Thomas could bring in a younger scholar from the outside over a friend and colleague crystallized resentment that had long festered in the faculty. There were long-standing specific grievances. Bryn Mawr regarded a term contract for a specified number of years as binding both on the college and on the professor. Beginning in 1911 the college refused its faculty permission to teach summer school in other institutions, an important means of adding income and professional experience. The college had always required attendance at commencement. Although the faculty had committees that proposed rulings to trustees on curricular matters, Thomas determined departments and positions—hiring, promoting, and firing at will. She decided on specific courses to be taught and their content. Professors talked to Thomas, and Thomas talked to the board. Faculty members had no way of knowing what Thomas said as she represented them, individually or collectively, or if she said anything at all. Moreover, Bryn Mawr was not only employer but, in many cases, landlord; and professors felt Thomas' arbitrary power as they sought affordable rents and repairs.

A movement to address these issues began in the fall of 1915. On November 1, thirteen professors wrote to President Thomas to demand that the college modify the memorandum of agreement that served as their contracts, listing particular elements, such as the ban on summer teaching, that they felt needed change. Thomas entered into negotiations with the full professors and drafted a set of changes, but the faculty found them unacceptable.[9]

In the middle of these negotiations, Thomas fired Richard T. Holbrook, a specialist in old French and Italian who had been a member of the faculty since 1906. At the time of his hiring, Thomas had heard negative reports from

Columbia that he was quarrelsome, but decided that it did not matter, as he was to work independently at Bryn Mawr.[10] In the intervening years, Holbrook had sought promotions without success, and Thomas had limited his teaching to Italian. Holbrook hoped to hang on and outlive Thomas' reign. Unlike the many talented professors who had left angrily but silently in the past, when Thomas fired him, he protested and contacted his wide professional circle outside the college. Word got to the editor of the *Public Ledger*, H. B. Brougham, and on March 15 and 16 he sent a letter of inquiry into "the state of affairs" at Bryn Mawr to alumnae and members of the faculty. In his net Brougham caught Evangeline Walker Andrews.

Andrews had left the environs of Bryn Mawr in 1907, when her husband Charles McLean Andrews took a position first at Johns Hopkins and then at Yale, but the college remained her calling. She founded the *Bryn Mawr Alumnae Bulletin* and was its editor from 1907 until 1913. She played an active role in the 1910 endowment campaign. At critical moments she attempted to shape college policy, often at odds with Thomas' plans. Ambitious, but checked by life in New Haven as a professor's wife, she seemed to see herself as a shadow president of Bryn Mawr. The Crandall affair propelled her again into action. Carey Thomas now regarded her as her enemy. Thomas wrote to Lucy Donnelly, on leave in Japan, that Andrews was "a stormy petrel appearing whenever there is any difficulty." Savage further angered Andrews when he decided not to rehire two of the essay readers. At a meeting of the New York Bryn Mawr Club called to draft a memorial to Mary Garrett, Andrews rose to make a personal attack on Thomas.[11]

Brougham's letter was a fishing expedition to gather information on M. Carey Thomas' administration of Bryn Mawr. It framed the issue in terms of academic freedom. It addressed specifically the firing of professors and focused on the case of Richard Holbrook. Citing an anonymous friend of Holbrook and other informants, Brougham asserted that Holbrook had an outstanding record and was fired only because he angered Thomas in seeking promotion to full professor and in rebelling against the rule forbidding summer school teaching. He had not been judged by his peers but only by students questioned by Thomas, students "who are habitually overawed into making any statements which she wishes to elicit in matters of opinion." The thrust of Brougham's accusations was that "Bryn Mawr, for a long period of years, has been regarded by its president as a proprietary institution, to be managed as she, the proprietor, and controller of its board of trustees, sees fit." As the only link between the board and the faculty, "she reports back to either body whatever she chooses and feels free to withhold information which may be pertinent to subjects of complaint or appeal." Finally, her "habit of dealing arbitrarily with the careers of members of her faculty has produced a state of intimidation in the college in which no one ventures to speak in protest, and . . . members feel that their opportunities for a wholesome, untrammeled, sound and progressive academic career is menaced." Brougham then listed seven cases, in addition to that of Holbrook, in which members of the faculty had been dismissed without cause.

The letter contained an additional accusation: after the two examining teachers had failed a socially prominent student in the oral examinations in German and French, Thomas asked her a few questions and then summarily passed her. This was an example of Thomas' more general interference in the college's academic life. Brougham stated that critics charged Thomas with " 'riding two horses,' one the Johns Hopkins ideal of work of high quality, and the other that of favoritism such as might be manifested in a fashionable private school."[12]

On March 29, Carey Thomas prepared a lengthy retort to the Brougham accusations. She responded to the Holbrook case by citing college policy, the practice of other institutions, and reference to his sharply declining enrollments. The only reasons his appointment was not renewed were "his insistence on being made a full professor and the increasing lack of response to his teaching." To the charges of improperly dismissing faculty members, she answered case by case. Brougham had been careless enough to make this easy. The sanctity of the language oral examinations was the most serious charge, and Thomas presented letters to document their propriety. The orals that tested seniors' reading knowledge of French and German were a central ritual of the college, always administered by Thomas, a member of the French or German department, and another member of the faculty. Thomas had guarded them as a critical symbol of the college's high standards, and now she successfully attested that all protocols had been followed. To the larger question of authoritarian rule, Thomas replied philosophically that she believed that "inherent difficulties exist in the present system of college and university management" in the United States, but that Bryn Mawr was already taking steps to alter it. The American Association of University Professors had issued a report on changes in college governance, and at the point of the controversy, committees of the Bryn Mawr board of directors and the Alumnae Association were studying it. Bryn Mawr's faculty had already approved certain of the AAUP's suggestions.[13]

To Andrews, Brougham's letter appeared as the chance to press the Alumnae Association and the board of directors for change. She began her own investigation, speaking to directors and alumnae. The *Public Ledger* campaign was a lever she could use, and she threatened to respond in print if she failed to get the Academic Committee of the Alumnae Association to act. Andrews and Brougham had a brisk correspondence. Brougham was convinced that tyranny reigned at Bryn Mawr, yet he found himself frustrated that he could get little information. Specific cases were dissolving for lack of evidence. He had confidential information he could not publish. It appeared to him that

Andrews was conducting a separate inquiry that was keeping his from success. He was being betrayed, he felt, by "narrow, selfish, individual interests and stupid pride in the institution." He begged Andrews to come forward with details.[14]

When Andrews spoke with directors, they requested that the faculty make complaints directly to them. The full professors had continued to meet and were now ready. On March 29 they approved and signed a letter to Thomas requesting that the 1916 AAUP proposal be adopted by the college, especially the provision that five senior professors elected by the faculty be consulted on matters of reappointment and that a representative of the faculty serve on the board of directors as a voting member. The full professors were attempting to establish a new constitution for Bryn Mawr, to turn an absolute academic monarch into a constitutional one.[15]

The directors held a special meeting on March 30 to receive the senior professors' letter, and appointed a committee of inquiry. In 1916 Carey Thomas had no real enemies on the board. The committee they chose was a balanced one, embodying different interests: Charles J. Rhoads represented the link to the past; Elizabeth B. Kirkbride, the alumnae; and Rufus Jones, progressive Friends. The committee met on a number of occasions and heard the disparate voices of faculty, administration, and alumnae. On April 10, it conferred with all the full professors to discuss the letter and, as it turned out, to hear their candid opinions. The abbreviated transcript of the meeting is a revelatory document.[16]

What it offers is the judgment of Bryn Mawr's senior faculty, uncensored and unrestrained. Over and over again, the full professors stated that Thomas was untrustworthy, arbitrary, interfering, and deceitful. When a director asked if there was a reason to complain of Thomas' treatment of individuals, Arthur Wheeler responded, "One obtains consideration only when her will is not thwarted."

Thomas, as the sole intermediary between the directors and the faculty, had deceived both. On matters of important college policy, Thomas had failed to report faculty advisory votes to the directors. For example, the faculty had unanimously rejected her proposal to take attendance in lecture, but she had not told the directors of this before their vote. On matters that affected an individual professor's career, she reported to the faculty that the directors fully deliberated the case, when they never discussed it but took action based only on her recommendation. Rufus Jones, perhaps remembering Thomas' treatment of Neilson, responded to one example of a professor's petition to the board by stating, "The letter was not read." Charlotte Angas Scott stated, "I would not accept the president's word unless corroborated." George Barton asserted, "She tells untruths calculatingly." Wheeler added, "You can't count on her word."

Thomas' lies extended beyond her intermediary role between directors and faculty. William Roy Smith accused her of lying as a means of dividing the faculty against itself, "by falsely quoting one member to another." Charlotte Scott asserted that she "misunderstands or misrepresents students and directors." She also felt that Thomas attempted to exert undue influence by lobbying committee members before they met. The professors refuted Thomas' statement that no faculty member had been dismissed without the recommendation of a department head, by giving several instances in which heads had objected, only to be ignored by Thomas.

An element deeply disturbing to the professors was Thomas' interference in their teaching. Without consultation, she changed their courses—subject, content, and schedule. James Leuba stated that he would have been willing to make the changes Thomas required, but she did not consult him or even directly notify him. By his understanding Thomas acted as she had from no legitimate reason, but "simply because she is autocratic." What disturbed Theodore de Laguna was both the fact of her meddling and that it was not grounded in scholarship or reasoned argument. It was his judgment that Thomas, in determining the sequence of courses in philosophy, "invents her criticisms as she goes along. It is a case of ignorant interference."

Charlotte Scott, the only person remaining from the 1885 roster, spoke with sorrow about what she saw as Thomas' "change in ideals" since the college's founding. In recent years Thomas had shifted from building a faculty to building a campus. As she considered her teaching staff, her judgment had become "warped" by a "desire for popularity, numbers, in a course." George Barton interjected a different note as he condemned Thomas' influence on students. "Her tone has degenerated. Chapel is made a place for propaganda, suffrage, feministic questions, etc., in a manner which encourages lax moral standards. She has the zeal of an evangelist in expounding feministic books by women who lived in immoral relations with men." A professor of religion and an Orthodox Quaker with many ties to Haverford College, Barton did not see how a board of the Society of Friends could allow "a person of such a character" to remain in office. Most of the full professors seemed to be urging more than a change in the rules. Only Barton stated it directly, but the implied judgment was that Thomas must go. As Leuba summed up, "It is doubtful if any men would remain here with such complete absence of confidence. We are unanimous in our distrust of the president."

Only Susan Kingsbury, the head of the Carola Woerishoffer Graduate Department of Social Economy, demurred. New on the faculty, she stated that she remained neutral. In double negatives, she explained that she had "no connections" with Thomas that bore out others' testimony, and thus she could not "sit quietly and not remark that she has experience which points to it not being impossible to carry out a new charter." A younger scholar, brought in by Thomas in one of her innovative ventures in the 1910s, a woman attuned to the stirrings of social change on campus, Kingsbury did not share the grievances of her more battle-weary colleagues.[17]

Toward the end of her life, as Carey Thomas advised the headmistress of the Bryn Mawr School about the difficulties of bringing about change, she reflected on the resistance confronted by a school head once the teaching staff becomes entrenched. At the outset of Bryn Mawr, "when we were all young together, everybody approved of change." But after the faculty had been teaching for a long time, they became "the most conservative people in the world" who "always dread anything new. In every move that we have taken at Bryn Mawr College we have had to fight the opposition of the older teachers of the college." Clearly she was remembering 1916.[18]

Not only was Susan Kingsbury neither entrenched nor scarred by old battles, she did not share the predominantly masculine perspective of Bryn Mawr's professors, which may have fed hostility to Thomas. Much light is cast on this by a letter from a former member of the faculty. Louis Cons, an associate in French from 1911 to 1914, wrote from the war front near Verdun a record of his own experience at Bryn Mawr, intended to strengthen Holbrook's case. It is a complicated letter, for mixed into the report of Thomas' meddling with courses, shared in common with the full professors, was his frank reaction to her as a woman.

Cons had found much to admire in Thomas, "one of the most vigorous personalities of our time." She had "an energy, a power of action which I should characterize as virile if . . . not so rare in men." But there was also much to scorn. Thomas was not "satisfied to preside and direct: she wishes to dominate." It was not enough that Bryn Mawr be her work, "she wishes it to be her own property, her fief." Her command extended not only to the faculty but to courses. "Science itself, the Truth must bend to the demands, to the special categories that are posed upon them by . . . Miss Thomas." She willfully determined subjects for courses, topics for examinations, and texts for translation with "that imperious fierceness of which she holds the secret," a quality that would be admirable were it linked to competence. Conversations with her were joined by an invisible presence, her invocation of "the students." Toward the men on the faculty, she was "more or less unconsciously aggressive. Too broad-minded or too prudent to pick quarrels" with them on general ideas, she would attempt to dominate them on details. In this capacity Cons could imagine her "reigning over a college exclusively feminine and feminist, a sort of laical abbey of later days."[19]

Cons' letter and the transcript of the April 10, 1916, meeting must be read in the light of familiar patterns from the past. Carey Thomas' willfulness and lying in both her personal and public life have been apparent before. How one judges these actions is the problem. When Thomas was the underdog, fighting against the odds, it is possible to perceive and judge her actions with at least partial sympathy. Early on she learned to attain her ends through manipulation, partial truths, playing one person against another. She used all her resources, good and evil, to get to Bryn Mawr and to create of a small sectarian college an institution dedicated to cosmopolitan scholarship. She was known to lie on occasion. Her attention to detail has been noted. Again, it was how she built an institution, stone by stone, or, as she put it, card by card. But once Thomas attained control, it is appropriate to judge her actions by a stricter measure. In the years after 1906 she was at the height of her powers; she was in command and had attained her ends. The house of cards was not about to topple. Yet Carey Thomas could not stop. She had gotten into a habit of dominating and interfering. She knew no other way.

But that is only half the story. The other half reveals some of her dilemma. Bryn Mawr was different. It was not only an institution of high academic standards and handsome buildings; under Carey Thomas it was directed toward feminist goals. Thomas used her influence in chapel to encourage scholarship, teach standards and manners, and convince women to lead autonomous lives. To at least some of the men on the faculty, Thomas' effort to get students to break with gender codes rankled. Moreover, the fact that they experienced their willful, arbitrary president as a woman made her leadership all the more galling.

On April 12, the *Public Ledger* printed its condemnation of M. Carey Thomas on the front page, under the headline "Bryn Mawr Alumnae Inaugurate Plans for Reform." The article accused Thomas of arbitrarily demoting Crandall and firing Holbrook. It briefly outlined Evangeline Andrews' efforts to restore Crandall and get the alumnae to bring about change. With Andrews' permission, it printed an edited version of her letter of April 1 responding to Brougham's inquiry. In her letter Andrews stated that the evidence Brougham had gathered was "accurate and damaging." Any investigation would only do harm if it were not accompanied by a full-scale reform in the college's organization. She asked for four weeks in which to attempt modification from within before joining an exposé from without. By allowing the letter to be printed, she announced indirectly that her internal effort had failed.

Andrews' indictment of Thomas was thoroughgoing. The heart of Bryn Mawr's problems was that it was "overadministered," bound by red tape and a plethora of rules governing details of student and faculty life. Members of the faculty were not able to change this because they were dependent on Thomas for their positions and their reputations: "They are not free to express themselves as regards their own work and their own departments, and cannot, without risk of losing their positions, express their disapproval when members of their own body are unfairly treated." Professors had no way to communicate directly with the trustees and had no redress in the case of misunderstandings.

Students, too, suffered from Thomas' imposition of rules and her meddling. Andrews placed blame on the trustees, who kept in office a president who misrepresented them and the faculty. Andrews' plan supported the full professors' effort to shift power from the president to the faculty, especially in faculty appointments. In addition, she called for the college to break all ties to the Society of Friends, opening the board to greater alumnae participation.[20]

In an earlier, unedited version of her letter, Andrews expressed a fear of halfway measures that did not give power to the faculty. Anything short of full-scale change would "mean that President Thomas would be more firmly entrenched than ever and would have power to harm the college even more than she has already done." In the published letter, Andrews' language was more respectful, but equally damning. She wrote that although the alumnae appreciated "the fine work that President Thomas has done for Bryn Mawr, especially in the early days of the college," for many years they had "hoped against hope that her affection for Bryn Mawr and her real and deep interest in the education of women would bring her to a realization of the fact that her later administration was seriously injuring the institution that both she and we love."[21]

Thomas was given an opportunity to respond in a letter published with the article. She first hit the low road. The complaints aired in the *Public Ledger*, she wrote, were all too familiar. It is the "old story" of the president "over whose devoted head breaks all the storms of abuse and of successive generations of discontented alumnae who wish the college in which they studied happily 20 or 30 years ago to remain forever unchanged; of discontented students who are forever insisting on change; of discontented professors whose teaching is not appreciated and whose salaries do not equal their own opinion of their merits." All that happens or does not happen in a college is judged the president's fault. "In all other professions except the teaching profession a man's failures are his own. It is only the college professor who is so happily situated as to be able to attribute his failure to the president of his college." Her spleen vented, Thomas moved to higher ground. The real issue was a system that was wrong at its roots. Professors needed to share in the responsibility and the burden of college administration. Toward this end, Bryn Mawr had begun the process of reform in its governance several months prior to the public controversy. Thomas could not resist a vindictive stab: let professors take their turn and fire colleagues who "cannot teach and lazy scholars who have gone to seed."[22]

The second day of exposure was more inflammatory than the first. Under the front-page headline "Committee Sits on Case against Bryn Mawr Head," the *Public Ledger* reported on the April 10 meeting between the trustee committee of inquiry and the full professors. The paper portrayed it as a meeting of a committee "working vigorously and thoroughly with the mass of charges that has accumulated covering several years of alleged maladministration of the college." The newspaper then printed letters it received from professors who had left Bryn Mawr, without stating that these letters were solicited by Brougham.

Compared to these statements from former faculty members, Andrews' letter emerges as balanced and tactful. William Allan Neilson, in 1916 a professor at Harvard, recalled his termination and accused Thomas of lying. "I know many former Bryn Mawr instructors, now in important positions in the large universities, who hesitate to recommend good students to accept appointments at Bryn Mawr on account of the capricious and arbitrary nature of the treatment they are liable to receive." He concluded with this biting statement: "Those loyal alumnae seeking to free their college from elements which are seriously hampering its development deserve the support of all who are or have been in a position to know the root of the evil." Other former members of the Bryn Mawr faculty, J. H. Huddilston, Alvin Johnson, and Frederick H. Getman, were no less hard-hitting and gave further examples of her despotic power, what one of them called her "academic Prussianism"— inciting words in 1916.[23]

One cannot know directly the impact of this public controversy on the critical body of decision-makers, Bryn Mawr's directors, for they kept their deliberations private. Some guesses, however, are possible. On the one hand, the newspaper accounts clearly required of them some action. On the other, the headlines probably protected Thomas' position as president. No board could bend to the demands of a newspaper for impeachment.

In his 1934 autobiography, Rufus Jones wrote that Carey Thomas was "a person of creative educational leadership and she was endowed with rare qualities which may, I think fairly be called qualities of genius." She was, he added, difficult to work with and a formidable opponent. "She produced a kind of august spell; she was adept in the art of carrying her point and of getting what she was after; she had strong emotional forces behind her strong will, and she had the subtle advantage of being a woman, so that an encounter could never be quite that of 'man to man'!" Several years later, after Thomas' death, Jones was asked in an interview to reflect on her. His remarks, taken down in abbreviated form by the interviewer, give an affectionate gloss on what others called lies: "MCT never grew up. Childish mind at times always. Had family trait of being able to imagine things so strongly that she believed them true . . . her gift of simplification—responsible for much." In 1916, however, Jones and the other directors on the committee of inquiry were discreet. Keeping their own counsel, they met with faculty, alumnae, Deans Reilly and Maddison, and Thomas herself. On May 19 they presented their recommendations to the full board. A statement they voted to enter into the minutes reflected the gravity of the situation as they perceived it. Their many conferences impressed the committee of inquiry with "the feeling of distrust and antagonism which is manifested toward the existing administration of the college. Whether justified or not, this feeling is profound and widespread throughout the faculty and exists to some extent among the alumnae, the patrons of the college, and in the collegiate world." The committee believed that this condition worked against the college's interests and required that the board of directors take action.[24]

After hearing the report, the directors fundamentally altered the way the college was governed. As they set out the specific terms of change, they increased faculty power and forced the president to operate in full view. The board and the president were no longer to meet alone: three professors were given the right to attend and speak at board meetings, though not to vote. The directors authorized the faculty to establish its own committee to consider reappointments and terminations of appointments, and created tenure in deed, if not in name. The board established a set of faculty committees that gave professors more power to shape curriculum, library, and laboratories. It gave professors direct access to the directors, allowing the faculty to report in writing to the board all its important actions—a board on which three professors now sat as nonvoting members. In many matters critical to their work, the faculty had forced Thomas to share power. But they did not get all they sought. They did not get power over new appointments. They did not get voting positions on the board of directors. And they did not get a new president.

Carey Thomas was present as the directors made all these changes. She was the one who presented the faculty letter to the board. She voted for the changes in governance. When a motion was made that the committee of inquiry remain in place as a "committee on the state of the college," she voted for it. In effect, this was a vote to make permanent a watchdog committee to oversee her actions. In 1916 she tacked to the wind. She gave where it was necessary, but she did not give all that was desired. She emerged limited in her powers, tarnished in the public mind, but still in place.[25]

A letter that Carey Thomas wrote to her sister Helen Flexner after the newspaper attacks reveals her state of mind. She saw herself as the victim of a conspiracy, cooked up by Holbrook and a Philadelphia editor who was his intimate friend. "The *Ledger* has, we believe, been made the instrument of private revenge. One of Holbrook's friends on the faculty told me that if I would nominate him for full professor of French the *Ledger* attack would be called off; otherwise it would be directed against my administration." Evangeline Andrews had been "stirring up trouble all winter." That the crisis of 1916 was provoked by personal vendettas for which she was not responsible, Carey Thomas believed for the rest of her life. Her fullest expression came in 1933, when she wrote asking to have an amusing reference to the 1916 conflict excised from the minutes of the executive committee of the board. Remembering what was the most serious blow in her professional life, she recalled herself as totally in the right, her detractors as totally in the wrong. "It was," she concluded, "a terrible experience and I cannot help being still sensitive about even joking references to it."[26]

These were private thoughts or words written seventeen years later. Her public face at the end of the crisis demonstrated her resilience and sense of humor. Carey Thomas used her speech at the 1916 June commencement to close the episode. She stressed the college's many accomplishments, including moving toward a democratic form of governance. As she turned to the events of the spring, she took a light touch: Bryn Mawr had set its house in order and found that like all housecleaning it was "unpleasant for those who live in the house. Indeed some of the linen that we ourselves did not know was dirty has been washed on the housetops and for us a wilderness of skeletons that we did not know were housed in our many college closets have been persuaded to stalk about horribly clanking their chains." But now the sheets were clean, and the closets filled with light and air. If her own excoriation in the press was a "public sacrifice" that stirred Bryn Mawr graduates to care for the college's welfare as "her spiritual children should," then "all that has happened has happened well." Such domestic and forgiving language was odd coming from Carey Thomas, but it provided healing balm at the end of a brutal conflict.[27]

CHAPTER 23

Really Almost Satisfied
for the Moment

WHEN COLLEGE resumed in fall 1916, M. Carey Thomas greeted students with her customary opening address. This time she chose to speak on both education and politics. After exhorting the freshmen to engage in disciplined study, she asserted that the difference between the educated and the uneducated was the difference between the elite and the mass, the cultured and the uncultured, the historically saved and the damned. She asked each student to begin "that solitary voyage that must be made . . . across the dim waters that now divide you from the shining country of the chosen people of light and leading." Her words were consistent with her elitism and her belief in the ennobling power of education.[1]

In the middle of the talk, Thomas shifted ground. Only certain cultures had proven themselves capable of educating their young. Those, it turned out, were from the temperate zone of Western Europe, North America, and parts of Russia and South America. Then she changed the terms: the issue was race, not climate. "The pure Negroes of Africa, the Indians, the Eskimo, the South Sea Islanders, the Turks" among others had "never yet in the history of the world manifested any continuous mental activity nor even any continuous power of organized government."[2]

America was in danger. "Our first immigration was made up of the dominant races of the world"; but American power and intellect were being threatened by "the backward people of Europe," Czechs, Slavs, and southern Italians. By the laws of heredity, "we are jeopardizing the intellectual heritage of the American people by this headlong intermixture of races." The new immigrants brought diseases threatening America with epidemics. Although war harmed a nation, killing off the best and bravest men, "how much more insidiously dangerous is the lowering of the physical and mental inheritance of a whole nation by intermixture of unprogressive millions of backward peoples." After a war, an advanced nation can restock. But if Americans "tarnish our inheritance of racial power at the source," it can never be replenished. The solution was clear: "we must close our doors."[3]

For years Thomas had asked students to tell her the country of origin of their families and the number of generations they had been in America. From this she learned that "almost all of our student body are early time Americans . . . They are overwhelmingly English, Scotch, Irish, Welsh, . . . of other admixtures, French, German, Dutch largely predominate." They thus "belong by heredity to the dominant races . . . have the best intellectual heritage the world affords," and live in a temperate zone. Having clearly established that Bryn Mawr students were the highest racial type, Thomas urged them to study hard, attend classes, and respect student self-government.[4]

The speech, an odd mixture of politics and education, is important for an understanding of Carey Thomas. To her repertoire of educational topics she was adding in these years her developing concept of race. What was once a working assumption about other groups became publicly articulated ideology. In the early twentieth century, racism and reform were linked in the eugenics movement that promised progressive improvement through breeding of the fit. Eugenics gained a significant following among white Protestant Americans. Eugenic concerns fed the debate over "race suicide." They also fueled the demand to restrict immigration. Thomas' background in Herbert Spencer and Charles Darwin predisposed her to endorse eugenic theory. However, in her effort to refute the charge that women's colleges contributed to "race suicide," Thomas had shown considerable independence from early-twentieth-century thought, rejecting many of the scientific arguments of her day. In the case of eugenics, she claimed its rationale for racial purity and the cultivation of the higher races at the expense of the lower because it buttressed her own deep-seated prejudices. She accepted the doctrines of Nordic racial superiority, and its accompanying denigration of Eastern and Southern Europeans, Jews, and African Americans. Notions of the proper breeding of American stock— promising cleanliness and careful choice, in contrast. to passion and messiness—meshed with her views on appropriate relations between the sexes. Her elitism fit growing opposition to immigration and its accompanying demands to restrict newcomers, especially those not from Britain or Western Europe.[5]

It is significant that Carey Thomas went public with her racial views in 1916. Despite the face she put on the 1916 crisis at its close, she had endured a public humiliation in which members of her own faculty had turned against her. Her powers as president were curtailed, her reputation stained. She stood alone, without Mary Garrett to defend her. At one level racism objectified her anger and dignified her position as one of the elect. As she took up the reins of Bryn Mawr again, she could face the world as an Anglo-Saxon. To see Carey Thomas' racial statements as a solution to personal pain is neither to justify nor to excuse, but only to understand.

II

In 1916 Carey Thomas was fifty-nine. She had lost Mary. She had no close friend. It was as if a piece of herself went with Mary. There remained no one from the past, no one who had known her as one of "nous autres." In the years that followed she framed a world for herself of family and friends. She turned to her brother Harry and her sister Helen for familiarity and comfort. She dipped into the faculty world of Lucy Donnelly and Georgiana Goddard King for friends and companions. But it was a different world. She was now the older, wealthy one. It was she who provided travel and gifts.

The texture of her life story is different in the years after Mary's death. As she is without intimates, many of her private thoughts were not recorded. Letters to Harry, Helen, and Helen Taft expressed something of her thinking, but she was always more guarded with them, less revealing, than she had been with Mary, Mamie, or her mother. With only a partial internal record, one must examine Carey Thomas increasingly by her actions and the reactions of others.

Mary's death made Carey Thomas a rich woman. By Mary's will, Carey was her principal heir and received outright her considerable estate. Newspaper accounts across the country (carefully preserved by Carey) celebrated that the wealthiest single woman in America had given her fortune to a woman and a college president. At the time, estimates placed Garrett's estate as high as $15 million. Although this was exaggerated, nonetheless, Carey Thomas had considerable resources at her command. In 1915 assessors, who undervalued the estate to shield Thomas from taxes, appraised Garrett's investments, three houses, and furnishings at slighter greater than $1 million, a sum which would, in 1994, be close to $15 million. Although by her death in 1915 Mary Garrett's estate was eroded by investment losses, a Baltimore fire, and generous benefactions, as her primary heir, Carey Thomas had at her disposal one third of what remained of the Baltimore and Ohio Railroad fortune.[6]

In fact, the will states it differently. To the Bryn Mawr School Garrett gave outright its building and freed it from indebtedness. She gave Thomas only life use of the 101 Monument Street house, which was to revert to Johns Hopkins University. She established a trust for her Aunt Rebecca Harrison and specified that her mentally incompetent brother, Henry S. Garrett, was to receive home care. She then left her estate to Carey in these words: "The said M. Carey Thomas and myself have been closely associated in our work for the higher education and I am confident that an appropriate and wise use will be made by her of my gift to her." Garrett saw herself as the steward of wealth, not its owner. She gave it to Carey in the belief that she would make wise use of it. It was given "without any trust, reservation or restrictions whatsoever . . . my said sympathy with and confidence in her judgment and wisdom being one of the motives only for said disposal of my property and in no sense a condition thereof." The provisions that Garrett made, however, should Thomas predecease her, suggest what she had in mind. The objects that she had accumulated or inherited, such as her wardrobe and silver, were to go to persons, but her great wealth was to go to the Johns Hopkins University School of Medicine, Bryn Mawr College, the Bryn Mawr School, and the National American Woman Suffrage Association.[7]

The Garrett family contested the will. Both Carey and Mary had always feared this, and as early as the late 1890s had thought about ways to protect Mary's estate in the courts. The inevitable battle that followed Mary's death coincided with Carey Thomas' struggles at Bryn Mawr. In an illuminating letter to Mary Berenson in the summer of 1916, Carey told her of her troubles in the preceding "long difficult year." The letter seemed to promise an accounting of the Bryn Mawr crisis. What Carey actually wrote to Mary Berenson—what was on her mind—was a description of the fight over Mary Garrett's will.[8]

At Mary's father's death, he left his sole daughter one third of his estate, his three houses, and their contents. In 1915–16 lawyers for the Garrett family argued that Mary did not have power of will over the property but only life use, that her brothers and their heirs retained ownership of two thirds of the land and buildings. As the crisis at Bryn Mawr was unfolding in 1916, Thomas' lawyers were arguing before the courts that Mary had full title to the houses and the absolute right of will. In December the arguments were heard, and on January 7, 1916, as the Crandall affair was heating up and as the Bryn Mawr faculty were negotiating changes in their memoranda of agreement with the college, Thomas learned that the court had decided against her. The case then went to the Maryland Court of Appeal, and on April 7, right before the *Public Ledger* printed its attack, a telegram came from her lawyer, D. K. Este Fisher: "Garrett case decree reversed. We have won out completely." Carey wrote to Mary Berenson that John G. Johnson, Bryn Mawr's lawyer, went to Annapolis, "and won it for me, as he always does win, wonderful man!" On July 1, 1916, Carey Thomas officially became Mary Garrett's heir and executor.[9]

When Carey had written to Johnson to enlist his aid, she had assumed the mantle of steward. She needed Johnson because a decision against Mary's will would "mean ultimately a loss of over half a million to the Johns Hopkins University medical school and Bryn Mawr College, as well as, during my lifetime, the loss of the income on this amount which I should hope to use to help women's education and other things in which both Miss Garrett and I have been so deeply interested."[10] But once Mary's wealth was in her hands, Carey saw it as hers absolutely. Although she took up and sustained Mary's causes, Carey had no compunctions about living life on a grand scale.

Carey Thomas' wealth was now considerable. In addition to her salary of $5,000, which she put at the service of Bryn Mawr College, she received over $3,000 in rents, almost $9,000 from trusts, slightly under $42,000 in stock dividends, and under $1,000 in bonds. In the years that followed, the sale of Garrett real estate, Deer Park and 101 Monument Street, and its conversion into income-bearing investments augmented annual income. With $60,000 a year (twenty times the salary of the highest-paid Bryn Mawr professor), Carey Thomas did not hold back. She fashioned a life in the grand manner. In 1921, as she tried to entice Alys Russell and Logan Pearsall Smith to come to the Deanery for a long stay, she promised each of them a suite of rooms and described her help: "I have to have eight servants for my entertaining (two waitresses, two house maids, cook, laundress, seamstress and ironer, lady's maid) and [a] housekeeper and they have very little to do. There is also Charles [the chauffeur] and two cars, one open and one closed, Franklin and a Ford— all at your disposal."[11]

In the summer of 1915 she had bought her first automobile and learned to drive. After Mary's estate was settled, she bought herself an additional car, and retained the services of a chauffeur. His task was more to service the car than to drive it. Carey Thomas loved being at the wheel. She was, however, a reckless driver and thoughtless about others' comfort and safety. Edith Finch gave this firsthand account: "Straight and masterful she sat at the wheel, the chauffeur, relegated to the rear, gripping the edge of the seat, apprehensive and unhappy as out of the Deanery driveway, across the campus and through Pembroke arch the car surged, jerking at each change of gear, cutting corners, scattering students from the roadway like frightened rabbits."[12]

Carey's greatest extravagance was travel. It was also her primary interest. During the final years of her presidency, the balance between the academic year of work and the summer of pleasure was reversed. Travel became the central task; Bryn Mawr College was the interlude between trips.

In the summer of 1917, with the world at war, she traveled a second time to Asia, taking with her Harry and Zoe. In 1918, she went west with Lucy Donnelly. Met by her chauffeur in Denver, they toured the Rocky Mountains. In 1919, the trustees granted her a full year's leave of absence to travel around the world. Although Carey Thomas had taken most summers away from Bryn Mawr, and in 1910 had taken a four-month trip to Egypt with Mary Garrett, in the thirty-five years of work at Bryn Mawr this was her first full sabbatical. She began her journey in the summer, continuing to conduct Bryn Mawr College business until September, when Helen Taft became acting president. It was an energetic and well-planned trip. Each stage was taken with a different companion. Helen Taft began the journey; Alys Russell went with her to Spain and North Africa; Logan Pearsall Smith, to Palestine and Syria; Georgiana Goddard King, to Turkey and Greece; Lucy Donnelly, to Italy and France;

and Harry and Zoe joined her for the second summer. Carey paid the expenses of her companions.

It is with the 1919–20 trip that Carey Thomas began to travel on an immense scale. Trained by Mary Garrett, who had been cultivated in the style of nineteenth-century robber barons, Carey had been working up to it for many years. More and more items became necessary for comfort: a coffee maker, reading lamps, candles, fans. As she and Alys moved across the desert in a caravan, six camels carried her luggage, which now included rubber tubs for bathing, wraps, rugs, cushions, and seven suitcases. The two women required not only a guide and a cook, and their four tents and provisions, but ten drivers for their camels and mules. To accommodate her moves through Europe in the spring, she had her chauffeur bring over her Franklin car and hired a lady's maid. Traveling in the grand manner generated in Carey Thomas no sense of conflict with less worldly values. She occasionally thought of herself as a socialist.[13]

She traveled luxuriously, but with driving energy, testing the limits of the possible. With her unquenchable thirst for experience, she toured the battlefields of the late war in France and ventured to a holy city under police guard. The view of the Bay of Naples was such, she wrote her family, "I could hardly take time to sleep from the sheer beauty of the moon and the sea." As she traveled in Italy, Carey returned to old haunts associated with Mary Garrett. She wrote to Helen and Lucy that Italy was like "a dream of beauty," but "it brought everything back most awfully. Every night I lay awake and lived over again all that we had done and said in that place." Only by turning to a novel and reading until one or two in the morning did she regain control of her emotions. On her travels, Carey was determined to make every minute count. Her companions were expected to read during their meals as she did. To Helen Taft she wrote at the end that the long trip had left her "really almost satisfied for the moment."[14]

In a three-part series on "The Mediterranean Basin" in *The Bryn Mawr Alumnae Bulletin*, Carey Thomas gave her "Impressions of a Sentimental Traveller." To an alumnae audience in 1921 she wrote about her aesthetic passions as freely as she had spoken to students in chapel or in lectures, for she knew they understood. The pieces mixed racial theory and enthusiasm for British imperialism with responses to Greece, Rome, and North Africa, but their central purpose was not politics. Thomas wanted to put down on paper her intense reactions to the great monuments of ancient civilizations. Admitting that "aesthetic passion, like any other kind of falling in love, does not admit of argument," she wrote about her loves for the art and scenery of Greece and Rome.[15]

Approaching her middle sixties, battered by loss and a life of conflict, Carey Thomas found solace in the old faith of art, the temple where she had worshiped since her early womanhood. About Greece she wrote, "It makes us proud to belong to the human race to be able to feel that just once in the history of the world a highly gifted people, living in a wholly lovely country washed on all sides by the most beautiful seas we know, speaking the most perfect of languages wonderfully expressive of the loftiest thought, attained to absolute perfection in poetry, prose, temples, and statues." Though she went far afield and searched for new experiences, travel was a return to old rituals in an effort to rekindle earlier emotions. She wrote, "The test of really great art seems to me to be the unquenchable longing it inspires, the desire if possible to spend an eternity in going back and back for one more look."[16]

III

TRAVEL not only reinvigorated Carey Thomas aesthetically, it strengthened twin beliefs in the value of imperialism and the "truths" of eugenics. Rome's successor was now England and the United States. In their hands were placed "the destinies of the civilized world." With this view of the world went an intensifying racism supported by eugenic theory. Thus, in discussing the beautiful ancient schools of the Arabs, she digressed to remark that "The Arabs themselves we found degraded, filthy and idle. For centuries they have been adulterating their proud Arab blood by Negro intermixture from the Sahara, thousands of black slave girls having been bought for harem concubines." To Thomas, Morocco served as "an object lesson of what will happen to us if we ever permit intermarriage with our American Negroes. We shall forthwith lose our place among the progressive races of the world. I came home with a stronger belief than ever in racial integrity and in putting a stop to immigration now before it is altogether too late."[17]

Carey Thomas' increasing opposition to immigration and her prejudice against African Americans went hand in hand. Her household staff was largely white, though she did on occasion have a Black butler. The college residence halls were attended by African-American women working the long hours of domestic servants. Thomas had insured that no one with "African blood" attended Bryn Mawr. There were no Black members of the college faculty or staff.

Carey Thomas almost never encountered an African American in a capacity other than that of servant. If an occasion to do so presented itself, she avoided the contact. In 1920 Thomas was asked to arrange for the distinguished African-American educator Mary McLeod Bethune to speak at Bryn Mawr. Bethune, she explained to Hilda Worthington Smith, then serving as dean, was a "second Booker Washington." Thomas arranged that Bethune speak in Smith's Thursday morning chapel: "it was the easiest way out . . . as we could not, of course, give up an evening for her." Thomas made certain that Bethune left by a morning train to avoid the problem of lunch in the halls, "which might cause difficulty." She herself did not attend the chapel and asked Dean Smith to make apologies on her behalf. Although she may have had a conflict in her schedule that prevented her from meeting Bethune, Carey Thomas' avoidance of her was consistent with her refusal to see evidence that contradicted her prejudice.[18]

I V

WITH THE Garrett wealth came Garrett responsibilities. Carey Thomas became the executor of Mary Garrett's many philanthropies. During her lifetime, Garrett had given roughly $300,000 each to the Bryn Mawr School and the Johns Hopkins medical school, and contributed $450,000 to Bryn Mawr College. Garrett's relationship to these educational institutions had varied, and through her will Thomas inherited that variety.

At the Johns Hopkins medical school, Garrett sat in no official capacity, but saw herself as the unofficial sponsor of women students. Carey Thomas had shared this responsibility with her, hosting the women in receptions, listening to charges of unfair treatment, thinking and rethinking about their life outside the classroom. With Garrett's death, these activities crystallized in the creation of the Mary Garrett Memorial Room and the formation of a committee to supervise it.

At the Bryn Mawr School, the original committee had contracted with the successive departures of Julia Rogers, Bessie King, and Mamie Gwinn. Gradually others were added, and in the twentieth century Margaret Thomas Carey, Marion Reilly, and Florence Sabin joined a reconstituted board of managers. During the long years of Edith Hamilton's tenure as headmistress, beginning in 1896, many of the activities that the board had once supervised came under Hamilton's jurisdiction. But, to an unusual degree, the board, and especially Garrett and Thomas, continued to hold power. After 1915, as the last of the original committee and as the executor of Garrett's estate, Thomas exercised that power at critical moments.

Carey Thomas' relations with Edith Hamilton had been strained for years, and they came to a crisis point after 1917. One of four talented sisters, Edith Hamilton had graduated from Bryn Mawr and had won the European fellowship.[19] In her latter years as headmistress she suffered from ill health and from a sense of deep injury. Carey Thomas' travels with Edith's intimate friend Lucy Donnelly created new personal tensions. In January 1922, Edith Hamilton asked the board for either an immediate leave of absence for rest or her continuance until the end of the year coupled with her resignation. The board accepted her resignation and offered to pay her generously through 1927. Public controversy erupted and parents charged that Thomas was acting arbitrarily and autocratically. Hamilton refused to leave Baltimore as promised and expressed a feeling of betrayal. Ultimately Edith Hamilton moved to New York City and, supported by a circle of women writers who shared her interest in antiquity, began to write a library of books that included *The Greek Way* and *Mythology*. Carey Thomas never acknowledged or commented on Edith Hamilton's unexpected renown. With Hamilton's departure, the school maintained its strong faculty and cadre of loyal supporters and, though plagued by continuing deficits, survived.

Before her death Garrett had made an annual gift of $10,000 to Bryn Mawr College. In addition, she had donated approximately $70,000 for academic purposes and over $158,000 for buildings, including the Deanery. By returning to the college her $5,000 presidential salary, Carey Thomas partially restored Mary Garrett's yearly $10,000, lost to the college with her death. Thomas intended the Presidential Salary Fund to be used, as had the Garrett money, for special gifts, not for routine expenses or deficit relief, and she often favored physical improvements. The Deanery became Carey Thomas' sole responsibility. Garrett's other contribution had been her decisions after 1906 as a director. Her particular concern had been the beauty of the campus. After her death, Carey Thomas considered the design of Bryn Mawr as their joint creation and worked to protect it.[20]

V

DID MARY GARRETT'S death make it necessary for Carey Thomas to remain at Bryn Mawr? If Garrett had been well in 1916, might Thomas have resigned rather than have submitted to the public humiliation of the newspaper war against her? Might she have triumphantly retired to the castle in Venice? One cannot know for certain because more than a job was at stake—the meaning of a life and career. Mary Garrett was as proud as she and might have wanted Carey Thomas to clear her name. It seems likely that Garrett would have helped Thomas win the battle and then have urged her to retire after the victory. Alone, Carey Thomas took a different course. Although presenting a formidable face to the outside, to the board she bent and accommodated. She accepted a Bryn Mawr in which faculty shared power and held her accountable. In 1916 she went to work under the new order and never misbehaved again.

When the crisis was weathered, Carey Thomas must have asked herself, at least implicitly, what are my goals? There is no record of the question, but only of the answer, the tasks that Thomas set for herself in the final years of her presidency. The years that followed 1916 saw her take the trip of which she had long dreamed; assume a public posture with World War I; establish a pension plan; ponder the question of a successor; and retire in a blaze of glory after pushing the college into a new and promising venture, the Summer School for Women Workers in Industry. It was an exit worthy of her.

World War I affected Carey Thomas and the college in important ways. As early as 1902, she had spoken on the relation of educated women to peace at the Lake Mohonk Conference on International Arbitration. However, in 1914 when war came in Europe, she greeted it with excitement, her Quaker background erased. As she wrote to Harry, "We are more and more excited by the War. It is much the most thrilling thing in the world that I can remember. . . . One cares so tremendously to have Germany whipped that it is almost too exciting to open the papers." Even during the period of official U.S. neutrality, Thomas did not rehire professors who showed open sympathy for Germany. Once the U.S. entered, she enthusiastically joined in the war effort. She required that new members of the faculty support the allied cause. As she wrote a series of personal questions to a potential appointment in Spanish, she explained, "We do not wish to appoint to the faculty anyone who is neutral. We wish clearly defined loyalty."[21]

The war gave Carey Thomas a chance for state and national service. She served as chairman of the Pennsylvania Women's Committee of the National Council of Defense. In 1917, she wrote to Zoe Thomas that she was not able to celebrate Christmas with the family because she was going to an all-day conference in Washington. She was working, she wrote, to get the government to free men for military service by hiring college women and paying them the men's salaries. She also reported that she had spent the day at a national defense conference. Thomas joined the propaganda campaign. Believing that Germany might win if Americans lost their faith, she helped organize the college women of Pittsburgh for patriotic speaking. Her highly inflammatory speeches, as filled with anti-German propaganda as those of her contemporaries, declaimed, for example, that "thousands of pro-Germans are spreading abroad falsehoods in our schools and colleges through pro-German teachers and pro-German textbooks."[22]

At the war's close, Carey Thomas saw herself not only as an authority on higher education and women's rights, but as someone deserving of a national political platform on issues of war and peace. She was firmly committed to the League of Nations, and the Republican opposition to it turned her against her party. Although she had borne a grudge against Woodrow Wilson since his peremptory departure from Bryn Mawr in 1887, she admired his leadership in war and peace. In the 1920 election she spoke for the Democratic presidential candidate. In a letter to the *Baltimore Sun*, she argued that women should oppose Warren G. Harding because the League of Nations was the fundamental issue before the United States and the Republicans had made unendurable attacks on Wilson, the Treaty of Versailles, and the League. She also stated that the Democrats, more responsive "to the great movement for social justice and equal financial opportunity" now sweeping the country, promised to pay more attention than the Republicans "to the interests of women as such" and were more likely to give women a chance to work out their "special women's problems in responsible government positions." Carey Thomas relished the opportunity to influence public opinion in this manner and saw her future after retirement as giving her the leisure to write political speeches and articles.[23]

The years of World War I and its aftermath were tough on educational institutions. The inflation that had begun earlier in the century intensified, and the entry of the country into the war made economic planning exceedingly difficult. It was an era before colleges understood that wages must rise according to a cost-of-living index, and faculty salaries took a beating. As the college moved into its fourth decade, its teaching staff was beginning to age. Although Bryn Mawr had been known for its turnover of youthful scholars, it retained Charlotte Angas Scott, who had opened the college with Thomas in 1885. By the 1910s it had a significant number of professors in midlife and needed to plan for retirements. The Carnegie Foundation for the Advancement of Teaching, created in 1905, offered a pension plan for college professors. It was, however, limited to nonsectarian institutions, and Bryn Mawr did not qualify because of the founder's will that required that trustees be Orthodox Friends. Carey Thomas tried hard to convince the foundation that the change in 1906 that had opened the college's board of directors to those outside the Quaker faith met the foundation's requirements, but Bryn Mawr was rejected.

In 1918 the Carnegie Foundation broadened its approach to create in the Teachers Insurance and Annuity Association a retirement and insurance system for college professors. It was a comprehensive scheme that required contributions both from individual professors and from their institutions. On the death of Margaret Olivia Sage the college received a large bequest. The faculty convinced the directors that $200,000 of the Sage funds be set aside for the college's contribution to TIAA. To persuade the Carnegie Foundation that Bryn Mawr was free of sectarianism, Thomas wrote letters, visited the foundation with directors in tow, and marshaled legal arguments. This time she was successful.[24]

The pension plan set the mandatory age for retirement at sixty-five. For Carey Thomas this had personal meaning, for it suggested that she must set an example and retire in 1922. Despite periods in the hospital for successive surgeries on her foot, the scar tissue of her burned leg, and a dislocated shoulder after a fall, she was, in her sixties, a vigorous woman. As she confronted the end of her presidency, she left little word of her feelings beyond eager anticipation. She did, however, imagine a successor and she set out to cultivate and groom her. Helen Taft had been a Bryn Mawr student while her father was President. Entering the college in 1908, she graduated in 1915, after taking several years off to live in the White House. In 1917 Thomas asked her to serve as dean of the college, making it clear that she would be acting president when Thomas took a year of travel in 1919–20. Taft accepted and served as acting president during a difficult year of fundraising. During the year Thomas wrote her encouraging letters and offered the material aid of her car, chauffeur, masseuse, and elocutionist.

Helen Taft saw herself as no one's acolyte. She had her own ideas and her own plans, and they included a man. In the spring of 1920 she announced to Thomas her intention to marry Frederick Manning. Carey Thomas first took it as a crushing blow, but in contrast to her reaction to her sister Helen's marriage in 1903, in 1920 she immediately recovered. She urged Helen Taft to see her marriage as serving the cause of women: she could "make what may prove to be an important contribution to the most important problem still to be solved in the woman question," combining career and marriage. "I am delighted that your generation does not have to turn away and that you can have both a friend and a husband and congenial work—and, if you wish, children, as many, or as few as you want, and when you want them." Both Helen and Fred could complete their Ph.D. degrees, get jobs on the faculty at Bryn Mawr, and Helen might still become president of the college. She begged permission to give the young couple $4,000 to make it possible for them both to finish their graduate training quickly. Carey Thomas insisted that her gift was not personal but for the advancement of education; Helen Taft nonetheless refused it. Fred Manning took a position at Swarthmore, and Helen Taft Manning joined the history faculty at Bryn Mawr. Although she declined all entreaties to be considered for the presidency, she remained an active vital presence at Bryn Mawr, serving the college in many capacities in her long career.[25]

In encouraging Helen Taft Manning, Carey Thomas wrote a good deal about herself. She wanted to travel with Helen and become her friend. She saw her in much the same way that she saw Ray Costelloe, as a spiritual daughter. In long, affectionate letters Carey presented herself to her designated successor in the way she wished to be remembered. In so doing she distorted her past and present. In contrast to the atheism that she avowed to intimate friends and her often-expressed regret at sacrificing her dreams of art and scholarship to Bryn Mawr, she pretended to Helen that she was religious and had been single-mindedly content as a college president. For example, in 1919 she wrote to Helen, "My religion means more to me than anything else but I despair of having it generally understood." In another letter, she stated, "From the first moment I became dean I knew beyond possibility of doubt that I had found what I cared most to do, and dog's life as it has been often, I have never changed my mind."[26]

After Helen denied any interest in fame or power, Carey wrote her that the real value of the presidency of Bryn Mawr was that it was "a very great club to wield in the good fight . . . to help women get free materially and intellectually." As she approached the end of her presidency, she attempted to swing it one more time. According to her later reports, in Morocco she had a vision. As she was celebrating the enfranchisement of British women and thinking about American suffrage, "Suddenly, as in a vision, I saw that out of the hideous world war might come, as a glorious aftermath, international industrial justice and international peace." Her part in its realization was the creation of a school for women workers on the Bryn Mawr campus during the summer months to utilize "the deep sex sympathy that women now feel for each other before it has had time to grow less."

Reality was more prosaic but more interesting than this account. The plan for the summer school grew from the base of Thomas' earlier work in establishing the Carola Woerishoffer Graduate Department of Social Economy. The school's director, Susan Kingsbury, had founded a community center in the town of Bryn Mawr to provide field experience for graduate students in social work. Hilda Worthington Smith, a 1910 graduate of Bryn Mawr with an M.A. in ethics and psychology from Bryn Mawr and a degree in social work from the New York School of Philanthropy, headed the center before she became college dean in 1919. Among its projects, the center offered evening classes for workers. When Smith was dean she welcomed Albert Mansbridge, who spoke on campus. Inspired by Christian Socialism, he led the successful Workers' Educational Association in England, which offered workers nonvocational classes in the social sciences, an education, as he put it, for "life, not livelihood." Spurred by Mansbridge, Bryn Mawr began a program for college employees in which over a hundred college workers, white and black, skilled and unskilled, enrolled in classes taught by Bryn Mawr faculty and assisted by students. At the time of her vision Carey Thomas was traveling in the desert with Alys Russell, one of the British intellectual circle that supported Mansbridge's association. During the year abroad, Thomas had taken time in England to visit schools in which university professors taught workers from factories, farms, and mines.[27]

When Carey Thomas returned to Bryn Mawr in the fall, she consulted with Kingsbury and Smith. They devised a plan for the school that they took to labor activists Mary Anderson, chief of the Women's Bureau, and Rose Schneidermann, head of the New York Women's Trade Union League. As early as 1916 the national league had resolved that women's colleges should open "their doors to women workers for a study program." The constituencies of Bryn Mawr all agreed—board, alumnae, faculty, and students. The critical early decision that the school be "a cooperative venture between college women and industrial workers themselves" proved essential to its success. The Joint Administrative Committee was formed of college representatives, alumnae, and industrial workers. Hilda Worthington Smith became director. Although Thomas had provided the initial impetus, it was Smith's creativity and good sense that shaped the enterprise. Teachers came from outside, a lively and open faculty that included Amy Hewes, an economist from Mount Holyoke College, and Paul Douglas, the future senator from Illinois. Students from Bryn Mawr and other women's colleges served as tutors. Alumnae helped raise money to underwrite expenses. In 1921 the Bryn Mawr Summer School for Women Workers opened with eighty-two students, from forty-nine trades and twenty-five countries of origin, the beginning of a remarkably successful endeavor.[28]

VI

MARY'S death effectively ended the first phase of Carey Thomas' work for women's rights. Thomas attended the 1915 convention that honored Anna Howard Shaw's retirement and helped raise an annuity for her, but without Garrett to encourage her, Thomas regarded her suffrage work as over. Her withdrawal coincided with changes in the movement. Garrett had been an important donor to the National American Woman Suffrage Association. New women with great wealth, such as Mrs. August Belmont, took over the financial support and management of NAWSA. The College Equal Suffrage League disbanded in 1916. Anna Howard Shaw's leadership gave way to that of the independent, politically savvy westerner Carrie Chapman Catt. After a decade of engagement, the suffrage movement virtually disappeared from Carey Thomas' consciousness. Her heart was in the cause so little that when the Nineteenth Amendment passed and was ratified in the states, she made no mention of it in her personal correspondence.[29]

Since 1913 she had identified herself as a feminist committed to broader issues of liberation beyond suffrage. In 1918, as she traveled in the west, she noted differences in dress and deportment that seemed aspects of a new freedom. In Rocky Mountain Park she found women in "absolutely unadulterated trousers," that they wore day and evening. She wrote home in her circular letter, "I cannot tell you how handsome and serviceable the women look, much smarter and more distinguished than the rest of us trailing about in skirts. Women will never be truly emancipated until their dress fits their two-legged bodies." Unlike women in the eastern part of the country, she saw few women smoking. She concluded that "it may take a combination of the smoking smart women of the East and the trousered smart women of the West to make the *new woman* that has almost arrived." Although Carey Thomas never took up pants, she was to approach cigarettes with enthusiasm. Unlike her heavy-handed use of the phrases "women's rights" or "Woman with a capital W," her references to herself as a feminist normally came casually, in light moments. For example, as she traveled with Alys in the North African desert, she wrote home that "as good feminists we were pleased to hear that female camels can work as hard as ever while they are carrying their young, until within the last two weeks."[30]

In 1913 she had spoken of the injection into the broader culture of "the woman's point of view." She returned to this in a speech in 1921 to welcome Madame Marie Curie at the University Woman's Meeting in Carnegie Hall. This was an occasion Carey Thomas relished, a large gathering of university women paying tribute to a famous researcher. In this setting she brought together many strands: her commitment to women's higher education, her hope for female genius, and her feminism. She began by celebrating the importance of the occasion. For university women to meet to honor Madame Curie recalled the ancient women's rites of goddess worship. "But however . . . devoted to the service of their godhead may have been the priestesses of old and their worshipping throngs of women, our meeting today is the symbol of a greater mystery . . . the coming to its own of a new group-consciousness on the part of women . . . a wholly new sex solidarity." At the end of the international struggle for education and the vote, women were seeking freedom "to act as we think best . . . the right to dispose of our own lives and bodies . . . to live worthily and unashamed." She set out what she regarded as women's political agenda: compulsory international arbitration, prohibition, abolition of prostitution, educational reform, and equal pay for equal work. Although Thomas had earlier seen that women as a group had interests different from men, especially protection from sexual exploitation, in 1921 Thomas began to develop the notion of a broader women's culture. "By our age long struggle we women are bound together by bands of steel. . . . Through centuries of different environment and different occupations and different ideals of life there have grown up certain profound differences in character and point of view between us and men. These differences cannot be ignored. For the sake of us all, men and women alike, they *must not* be ignored. Our different woman's outlook must be written large into the laws and life of all civilized nations."[31]

VII

As HER retirement neared, Carey Thomas returned to the issue of succession. Throughout her career she had maintained the position she first articulated to James Rhoads, that the head of a women's college should be a woman. In the twentieth century she argued that "as we are trying to develop ambition and self-confidence in our women students . . . it is a great encouragement to all students of a women's college to feel that the head of the college is a woman."

In the May 1921 issue of *The Bryn Mawr Alumnae Bulletin*, Thomas presented the summation of all her arguments in an effort to rally the alumnae to the cause, adding the new note of women's culture. She asserted that the "differences between men and women which have grown up through centuries of different environment and different ideals of life" give women a common point of view and an "intense loyalty and pride in each other's success and achievement." To the arguments from 1885 that a woman president could understand women students better than a man, that a man cannot truly care for women's education, and that women need positions in their own institutions, Thomas added a trump card, the "enthusiastic moral and financial support" of the alumnae, who believe that "Bryn Mawr must have a woman president."[32]

Carey Thomas was on the nominating committee along with Marion Reilly and alumna Frances Hand. This did not calm her fear that the board might choose a man in her stead. A number of men emerged as likely candidates, including Rufus Jones, Haverford professor and president of the board of directors. Some members of the Bryn Mawr community anticipated that the next president might serve only a short time, agreeing with a professor who suggested that "no one could survive more than five or six years with President Thomas living in the Deanery ready to jump out at intervals like a jack-in-the-box and give everyone a 'crisis of nerves.' " Given the situation, some counseled that a man might best be able to handle the pressures Thomas would inevitably bring to bear.[33]

Carey Thomas' campaign for a woman successor proved effective, and the board was inundated with letters from alumnae and resolutions from alumnae chapters. She later wrote that this drive forced the male members of the nominating committee "to agree that women candidates would have to be tried out first." She believed that because of her article in *The Bryn Mawr Alumnae Bulletin*, the president of the board perceived her as the "arch instigator of this feminist demonstration to which he had to bow."[34]

Ultimately the two possibilities favored by Thomas and the board were Ada Comstock, the head of Radcliffe College, and Marion Edwards Park. Comstock withdrew, and at the January meeting of the board of directors, the nominating committee of directors assisted by three faculty members recommended Park, a Bryn Mawr graduate, M.A., and Ph.D., serving under Comstock as Radcliffe's dean. Park was elected unanimously. Carey Thomas and Rufus Jones called on her in Cambridge to persuade her to accept. When she agreed the following month, Thomas felt relief. The college was safe in the hands of Park, a woman "who knows its past and is triple product of its culture and discipline." Although Alys Russell noted that Carey disliked the "dull, undistinguished but sound" Park, Carey wrote to her brother Harry that she was "the best choice we could have made, and, on the whole, I am satisfied that the college will be very safe in her hands and will go forward. She is as nice as she can be, entirely trustworthy, and intelligent and clear sighted."[35]

Commencement 1922 was the time of formal celebration. Once again, as at the presentation of the Sargent portrait, or the twenty-fifth anniversary, loyal supporters rallied at the dinner held in her honor to praise Carey Thomas' vision and leadership. She invited her close family and friends to stay at the Deanery and to attend the festivities that included a garden party, Russian singers, and Hindu dancers. As in other gatherings, speakers—in this case, sixteen—reviewed the litany of her accomplishments. Thomas had been particularly pleased with the commencement address of William H. Welch, the Johns Hopkins pathologist, for he carefully delineated her achievements within an informed understanding of curricular and educational issues. Although his speech was predictable, representing the often-struck chord of solid praise for Thomas, those that came after dinner were different. What emerged from the celebratory oratory was a reevaluation of M. Carey Thomas.

She was praised not for her accomplishments, but for her presence, her energy, her will. She stimulated others by her example; and she also nurtured the will to resist. In 1899 Louise Brownell had glowingly framed the presentation of Thomas' portrait with admiration of Thomas' work and reputation. Now, as Louise Brownell Saunders, she stated, "It was, above all, contact with her, contagion of the incomparable energy of her spirit, that lighted our spark also to flame. We wanted to work hard, passionately, professionally, because we saw her working harder, more passionately, more professionally than we. . . . Why, the very strength with which we have sometimes opposed her came from her." Helen Taft Manning put it this way, "I think that the greatest tribute to Miss Thomas is that the spirit of no Bryn Mawr student or no member of the Bryn Mawr faculty has ever been killed by her own heroic force." Ada Comstock stated that in contrast to most women in public, who seem to lack vividness, Carey Thomas "brings into every assembly into which she comes a presence as real, as self-directed, as forceful, as any that can oppose her; and therefore she has given innumerable women the faith they most needed—faith in their own possible effectiveness." Comstock declared Thomas "the most colorful, the most vigorous, the most dynamic figure in American education today."[36]

Carey Thomas was an unusual president because she actually cared for the life of the mind. Paul Shorey must have evoked tender memories when he recalled that Bryn Mawr's founding dean had "her favorite poets, whom she actually read and quoted, her chosen French and English critics whose formulas were law and whose definitions of literature, religion, art, life, love, death, and destiny she collected and transcribed in her note-books. Swinburne, Arnold, Pater were something in her young life that we cannot conceive them ever to have been for Presidents Eliot, Hadley, and Harper." It was this "intense and eager mood, this hard and gem-like flame," that Carey Thomas conveyed to students and sympathetic faculty.[37]

Carey Thomas had long believed that women needed the spur of awards and fame to rise to their best work. To her delight the alumnae endowed the M. Carey Thomas Prize Fund to award an American woman $5,000 for outstanding achievement. Thomas herself was the first recipient. In witty and eloquent words Carey Thomas thanked the speakers for their tribute to her, telling her audience that she had experienced "the sensations of a departed spirit accidentally present at the ceremonious laying away of its own ashes." She suggested that she was of a generation of women about to be misunderstood. Women now had the chance for both a life work and a husband and children, "as men have always had both." But as a pioneer for whom this was not possible, "my life has been so happy that I often wonder whether many other people have been as happy as I have been." She had not been a mother, but in her professional life she had nurtured many daughters. "One of the chief causes of my happiness," she continued, "has been the many children of the spirit that have gone out from Bryn Mawr in whom I feel that I have a little share and shall have a share as long as I live." Carey Thomas had never had a need to justify her life and career in such terms but she realized in 1922 that she was seeing the beginning of a new era. As she turned to the future of the college, she embraced the changes that were to come. "It is a very great joy to me to feel the college is strong in the love of her graduates and former students" who will help the new president "build the new Bryn Mawr greater and fairer than our dreams." Those such as she who served the college "in the dawning of her fame" can anticipate "a kind of vicarious immortality as the work of our hands prospers and lives through the years to come."[38]

CHAPTER 24

The Flame of a
Burned-out Candle

W HEN M. CAREY THOMAS retired in 1922 at age sixty-five, she had
already embarked on her new life. She was wealthy beyond her grandest
hopes. World War I had suggested to her a larger field for her endeavors. She
had kept her dignity and left the college in good hands. The commencement
of the Summer School gave her a grand finale. What she most wanted for
herself upon her retirement was pleasure. She had balanced the work of every
year by summers of travel abroad, the harness of Bryn Mawr with the release
of art and indulgence. She now looked on her entire life since 1884 as the
academic year; retirement she imagined as the summer sojourn.

Following the retirement celebration, Carey Thomas received an honorary
LL.D. from Johns Hopkins. Forty-four years after she had withdrawn from
the university, Thomas accepted Johns Hopkins' honor with pleasure. After
greeting the Summer School, she took a steamer to Europe for fifteen months
of travel. Technically she remained president until September. On the final
day of August, she wrote her last letter on presidential stationery to her brother
Harry: "I cannot possibly tell you how happy I am to be free and to have made
a good end. I feel like one of the many little naked souls . . . on the great
western portals of Romanesque cathedrals who smirk and cross their self-
righteous little hands on their tiny breasts in joy because an angel instead of
a demon has got them. I cannot be thankful enough to have been translated
instead of damned."[1]

And yet it was not so simple. Beginning in 1922, Carey Thomas' primary
concerns were her own health, family relations, and friendship; the exercise
of her great wealth and the acquisition and care of possessions; a public
career of influence and work for women; extravagant travel; the writing of her
autobiography; and the disposition of her estate. Freed from constraints that
convention and her work had imposed, she smoked cigarettes openly and
enthusiastically and, in 1927, formally left the Society of Friends.[2] Able to get

away from the Deanery in any season, she was constantly in motion as she traveled, visited, bought, spoke, and politicked. But without Bryn Mawr, the work that had fixed her purpose since 1884, her life was without anchor.

Although Carey remained vigorous until her mid-seventies, in the 1920s illness and injury made her feel vulnerable. Before embarking on the first round of travel in 1922, she dislocated a shoulder, and had to delay departure. In October 1924, on a motoring trip in Greece, she had a terrifying accident. Kicked by a mule, she fell down a rocky bank, cutting open her head, spraining her shoulder, and injuring her burned leg so badly that she required surgery in 1925 and again in 1927. A second dislocated shoulder prompted more surgery. For pain Carey took marijuana, what she called her "wonderful silver pills." Arranging for her hospital care, she was meticulous and demanding, insisting on special rooms and mattresses. She wrote to her physician nephew Henry Thomas, Jr., "You and I are perfectionists and like to make things just as good as we can." The young Dr. Thomas in a letter to Simon Flexner put a different gloss on her behavior: "As you know, Aunt Carey believes from principle that all pain can be avoided; she objects to it even when she imagines that it may be about to hurt. She is not an easy patient."[3]

For a number of years, Carey attempted to reground her personal life in her family. She especially cared about her brother Harry Thomas and mourned his death in 1925. She reached out to her sister Helen Flexner. Toward all of her brothers and sisters and their children she felt a sense of connection and obligation. She jokingly referred to herself as the family "Patriarch." In her travels she paid for the accommodations of family members who traveled with her. When she was away she carefully arranged to have all members of her family get Christmas gifts and cables. When she returned to Bryn Mawr, she gathered her relatives together for an extended house party over New Year's and her birthday, filled with gift giving.

Carey sought as favored traveling companions two alumna members of the Bryn Mawr faculty from Helen's generation, Lucy Donnelly and Georgiana Goddard King. They were, as she explained to Harry, "very satisfactory companions, as I brought them all up. . . . They spoil me by letting me do just as I like and by being nicer to me than I deserve." Despite a stormy relationship with Georgiana, Carey enjoyed accompanying her on art historical studies. It was a return to the years with Mamie Gwinn, though this time with a disciplined, productive aesthete. Georgiana was in an intimate twosome with Edith Lowber, a younger woman and an accomplished amateur photographer. Beginning in the mid-1920s, Carey sought to have Edith to herself. By the end of the decade, Carey had largely succeeded, perhaps because of the attractions of her extravagant wealth, and Edith accompanied her on travels and lived with her on the French Riviera. Triangles, as always, gave Carey particular satisfaction. She expressed both her androgynous sensibility and the link between her erotic feelings and maternal ones when she stated that she would like her younger women friends as daughters, "if I could have had them fully grown out of my side like Athené from the side of Zeus, or, for the matter of that, Eve from Adam's rib."[4]

Certain of these younger women led her to reflect on combining work and family life. She wrote to Helen Taft Manning, who was beginning to have children, about women who combined careers and marriage, "I heartily approve. It is absolutely necessary for them to marry as much as and as often as they wish and have just as many children as they wish, even three." Although she could verbally accept marriage in the younger generation, she wanted promising women to sustain careers. When Millicent Carey became engaged to Rustin McIntosh, her aunt hated her losing her name and worried that she would miss her chance for success. Carey lived to see Millicent McIntosh give birth to twin sons but not to her tenure as president of Barnard College. When Harry's son married Caroline Bedell, Carey delighted in the addition of a woman physician to the family but feared that her new niece's research would be impaired by motherhood. Enthusiastic about birth control, Carey sent books advocating and explaining methods to the marrying career women of her acquaintance. As she wrote to Helen Flexner, "Yes, women must indeed address themselves to the task of uniting jobs and babies. I used to feel almost hopeless before birth control came in but now the rest is comparatively easy."[5]

The fine arts remained her chief resource. Under Georgiana's tutelage, architecture, painting, and sculpture became more important to her. She sustained her love of music, opera, and theater. Her taste for reading continued, and she never lost her ability to confront new works. In the 1920s she read D. H. Lawrence, Gertrude Stein, and Virginia Woolf. She wrote to Helen Flexner of her delight in Woolf's *Orlando*. It was to her "pure gold. . . . She gives me the same kind of intellectual joy that Henry James did—strange thrilling subtleties of thought and emotion . . . and being a woman, she thinks as I do very often."[6]

II

AT SEVENTY, Carey Thomas was a woman with "brown eyes still sparkling, her whole person breathing a rich, strong, restless vitality." So wrote Elizabeth Shepley Sergeant, a writer and Bryn Mawr alumna, after she interviewed Thomas for a biographical sketch. Sergeant saw Thomas as a woman who belonged on a lecture platform, with her fine head and handsome face and "rather squarish body" suited for the black academic robe. (In these years she carried 171 pounds on her 5-foot-4½-inch frame.) In her retirement Carey Thomas "still conveys a sense of buoyant, almost Rooseveltian energy and power. . . . When she laughs, a gay, ruthless vitality bubbles up clear from its own source."[7]

After reading Sergeant's draft, Frances Hand, a Bryn Mawr alumna and director, contemplated a sequel treating her later years: "I can imagine that the next part will be far more difficult. You think she is wandering between two worlds. I rather think that her only real conception of life is 'doing' and active, riotous living and that if she stops that she is without resource. Of course, she won't stop it. We have grown up and old perhaps—she has not grown up." In her private notes Sergeant wrote that she sensed in Thomas a "lack of *spiritual* values."[8]

An unpublished memoir of Carey Thomas, written by her private secretary in the 1920s, tells the story of a woman who is lost. Thomas hired Esther Lanman to assist in writing her autobiography, anticipating that it would be the primary task of retirement. In the three years in which Lanman worked for her, Thomas never began it. Lanman's first duty was to help Thomas establish procedures for the Deanery. In 1923, Thomas had fifteen employees, nine of whom lived in the Deanery. Living outside, along with Lanman, were two bookkeepers, a gardener, a chauffeur, and a laundress. Lanman typed and retyped schedules of the maids' duties and the master plan, as each day Thomas reworked the tasks. In the supervision of the Deanery Thomas was a perfectionist with a rigid sense of protocol. In spying a yellow tulip among the red in her garden, Thomas called her housekeeper to send immediately for the chauffeur to pull it up. She could be formal and cold. When, after a shopping expedition, the housekeeper, a graduate of the Bryn Mawr School, tried to make small talk, Thomas silenced her with, "My dear, I am not in the least interested in anything you may have to say to me."[9]

Lanman's account is confirmed by Katie Doyle, who came with Alys Russell as a maid and worked in the Deanery in 1921–22. Interviewed in 1975, she gave this overall assessment: "She was firm, and she could be tough, but you know, with it all there was a softness and a sadness about her." The details, however, are damning. Doyle recalled that Thomas "was very changeable—very," which made her a difficult employer. She would alter instructions about how she wanted her table set and "claim she'd never said whatever it was she'd said before." In those years Thomas had one longstanding servant, Etta Taylor, a white woman of her own age. Doyle remembered that Taylor got no time off because Thomas "couldn't do without her." Except when making arrangements on her travels, Thomas did not normally mention servants in her own correspondence. She did make one telling statement to Harry, as she planned her 1922 trip abroad, "Etta is going on with me to pack and unpack at the Murray Hill and will go to the steamer and unpack me there before it sails. I thought thee meant a real person not a maid when thee asked who was going with me."[10]

Doyle recalled that Thomas had a quick temper, but her outbursts were short. She was demanding, and "everybody had to be at her beck and call." The rules of the household were strict, and the duties onerous. Thomas slept on a sleeping porch, and her bed had to be rolled out at night, covered with cashmere covers and warmed with many hot water bottles. (In the middle of the night she went indoors to a big bed inside.) She was extravagant and yet she was "tight fisted if it didn't *show*." Though she had a vast wardrobe of dresses for every occasion, the cashmere covers of her bed got ragged. Doyle did not like the way that she gave gifts in a public manner, made a "ceremony out of giving things out." On Christmas, standing by a huge Christmas tree lit by at least five hundred lights, she lined up the servants and gave out money. Worst of all, she dressed the servants down "in front of people," an unusual practice for an employer. She browbeat her housekeepers so much that they stayed only a short time. Her reputation as a difficult employer required her to pay the highest wages on the Main Line in order to get help.[11]

Family recollections reveal a different, more generous side. Many years later, Carey Thomas' nephew Harold Worthington remembered the family New Year's party at the Deanery. At one's place at the table for each of the meals was a gift acquired on her travels, "a paper opener from Toledo [Spain], or engraved scissors from India, some sort of nicknack, usually charming, suited for the person, and from some distant place." On these occasions, as on others, she held a discussion after dinner on a timely subject. When she hosted her Quaker family, she did not serve alcohol. Two of her brothers brought a bottle that they kept upstairs, and retired to it regularly. When Harold became a young man, he was invited to join them in a drink. He recalled that they told him "it was a necessity when visiting Carey." After he had his turn at the bottle, they said, "When thee kisses thy aunt, breathe in."[12]

III

CAREY THOMAS kept her hand in Bryn Mawr College. When she was made a trustee in 1902, it was with her promise to resign from the board at her retirement. By 1922 this was forgotten, and Thomas remained a life trustee and director. Although her extensive travels distracted her, when she was in the Deanery, she observed everything on campus and made suggestions with the mastery of detail that she had exhibited when in office. Some of her guidance could be explained by her position as director and donor. But certain matters showed an interference that must have been distressing to the new administration. When Helen Manning was dean, Thomas sent her specific instructions that ranged from the way to approach the General Education Board, to the need for the college to hire a roofer to check all the roofs. On one occasion she passed over the line and was called back. Convinced that she could get the best candidate for a position in art, she had Lanman book her rooms in Boston for a weekend of Harvard interviews. "Next morning word of her trip and its purpose must have reached President Park," for Thomas asked Lanman to cancel all the arrangements. Thomas felt particular responsibility for several programs, donating money and negotiating with foundations on behalf of the Carola Woerishoffer Graduate Department of Social Economy and Social Research, the Phebe Anna Thorne Model School, and the Summer School. She gave $16,000 to Goodhart Hall, paid for student prizes and a monograph series, financed a greenhouse, had firewood sent from Montebello for the library, and continued to be a mainstay of the Low Buildings and the College Inn.[13]

The Bryn Mawr School continued to claim her attention, even when she was abroad. Since Mary Garrett's death, the school had run repeated deficits. When the managers appealed to Carey Thomas for a major gift to ease the transition of the school to a new suburban location, she refused. Helen Flexner urged her to stand by the school for her own sake and for that of Mary Garrett: in a time of "back wash" the school was necessary to women's education and must be conserved for women "when the tide turns again." The board of managers sent a representative across the Atlantic to bring a personal message from Caroline McCormick Slade, an important contributor to Bryn Mawr College, who promised to go on the school's board and to lead an endowment campaign. Carey Thomas could not refuse Slade. Believing that the Baltimore school would serve as a "permanent memorial" to Mary Garrett, Thomas ultimately agreed to give $100,000.[14]

Carey Thomas continued to be a force in groups that fostered women and higher education: the American Association of University Women, the International Federation of University Women (whose meetings in Europe she attended), and the Seven College Conference. She traveled frequently to Washington and New York for committee meetings. American women's college leaders broadened the opportunities for educated American women by creating bases abroad for them. Carey Thomas was appointed chairman of the International Federation of University Women's Committee for Club Houses, which opened a club house in Paris for women students in 1922, assisted in operating a club house in Washington, and supported a hostel for women students in Athens.

It was the Athens hostel that captured Carey Thomas' imagination during her early retirement. Aware of the need of women students for safe and comfortable room and board in Athens, in 1916 the heads of eight eastern women's colleges had begun a campaign, interrupted by the war, to build a residence for women students at the American School of Classical Study. In 1924, feeling that "the time could not be more auspicious," Thomas took it upon herself to revive the project and made herself an "unappointed agent" to reorganize the Women's Hostel Committee. She went to Athens to meet with architects and officials of the school, settle on the exact site of the building, and revise plans. It was a return to the way of life of her presidency. In anticipation, she wrote to Harry, it is "the hardest and most diplomatic kind of work and seeking lots of people and making myself agreeable which I hate." Launching the women's hostel at Athens proved to be exceedingly difficult. Thomas and the committee had to work with the architect, negotiate an agreement with the managing committee of the American School in the U.S., initiate a fundraising campaign, and appeal to the Laura Spelman Rockefeller Memorial Foundation for money. In the process she had to best the director of the American School and a Princeton classicist in their efforts to turn the women's project into a coeducational residence hall. Throughout the successful effort Thomas managed to stay informed and in control. Letters and minutes demonstrate that she had not lost her touch. In the mid-1920s—when she summoned it—Carey Thomas could have the command over detail and the negotiating skills of 1905.[15]

Carey Thomas hoped in her retirement to return to the prominent position she held during the war, to be listened to as "somebody whose ideas would encompass world affairs." In this spirit she entered the competition for the American Peace Award created by Edward W. Bok. Her scheme called for a Declaration of Interdependence by the United States. By it, the nation was to pledge itself to resolve disputes peacefully, respecting an international judicial system, and to outlaw war. Thomas' proposal was one of twenty finalists and was printed in the collection *Ways to Peace*. Continuing to speak for peace and the League of Nations, she urged women at the Democratic Women's Luncheon Club of Philadelphia to organize politically to unseat senators who opposed the League. In 1928, she supported Herbert Hoover as the candidate most likely to work for peace, support prohibition, and be free of corrupt party politics. On many issues Thomas worked directly, but on others she attempted to influence powerful friends, writing lengthy letters with solutions to what she regarded as key problems.[16]

In 1925 she made an important public name for herself with her strong support for the equal rights amendment proposed by the National Woman's Party. In an argument published with differing statements by social researcher and reformer Mary G. Van Kleeck and by Mary Anderson in the *Journal of the American Association of University Women*, Carey Thomas offered a conception of women as not only equal to men but identical, with similar rights and responsibilities. Healthy "non-child-bearing women" ought to be liable for the draft; fathers should be responsible with mothers for illegitimate children; wage-earning and wealthy women should contribute to their family's support. As she faced the vexing issue raised by the amendment—that it threatened to nullify protective legislation for women workers—she pointed out that nine-tenths of American women suffer disabilities as a result. Existing laws worked "great hardship to professional and non-industrial women workers, in many cases depriving them of well-paid jobs, and in all cases strengthening the injurious assumption that adult working women are not to be classed with adult working men, but with children." Part of Thomas' opposition to protective legislation was its negative psychological impact on women, increasing their feeling of dependency. "If men are to legislate for grown-up women and control their hours of work and their opportunities of work, it seems to me that women will never be free from the leading strings in which they now are."[17]

Thomas argued that the equal rights amendment, helping especially "the large and influential group of 1,517,888 proprietors and professional women," would aid all women morally and materially, raising their wages and status. Her eye was on the middle class and professional woman; but, unlike other equal rights supporters, she worried about the possible costs of ending protective legislation for factory women. It was, as she put it, "out of the question to wipe out protection and throw these millions of helpless women to the wolves of industrial exploitation." She proposed a conference of the leading women's organizations to reconsider redrafting the amendment to exempt welfare laws until protective legislation included men.[18] Eager to gain an audience for her ideas, she ordered a thousand reprints of the three arguments, framed by an introduction and recommendations.

Carey Thomas remained a strong supporter of equal rights principles until her death. In the last year of her life, she wrote to a leader in the Woman's Party that "in the future, women as well as men must work for their living and for the joint support of their children. Women can no longer be supported by men." Women need full rights with men to be "paid by the job and not by the sex of the worker."[19]

IV

THESE many commitments notwithstanding, Carey Thomas' primary activity in her early retirement years was travel. Following her retirement in 1922, she had embarked on one of her longest journeys, a second trip around the world. In 1928–29 she returned to Egypt and the Far East. Her reputation as a legendary traveler, an American empress moving with an entourage in a caravan, was well established. When C. R. Ashbee had met her on March 20, 1920, traveling "*en princesse* with Logan Pearsall Smith . . . she had couriers and carriages, boxes and special bedding, cases of soda water, hampers of sweetmeats, and all the apparatus necessary to the comfort of the president of Bryn Mawr on a visit to Prince Faisal." Her many trunks filled with books and equipment were often noted by her traveling companions. In Paris in

1923 Alys wrote to her sister Mary Berenson that she had stayed with Carey an extra two days "to help her sort and repack her 20 pieces of luggage . . . one trunk of kitchen utensils and tea, one of drugs, one of electric fans (never opened as India is well supplied), five of books she has never read, one of unanswered letters and three of unopened newspapers which follow her in hordes everywhere." As she traveled, Carey Thomas insisted that at each site she have the best room and table, the most capable guide, the perfect view at the right hour. Her cousin Logan wrote in his published memoirs that Carey, "inheriting a very large fortune at the age of sixty, . . . rolled, as they say in money, spending it for the most part in fabulously expensive journeys. . . . She loved money, as few people I have known loved it." Ever her mother's daughter, as early as 1920 she had dipped into principal for income. By 1927 Carey had spent half of what Mary had left her.[20]

These travels confirmed for Carey Thomas her beliefs about the world's peoples and the superiority of Northern and Western Europeans. Her letters to her family continued to comment disparagingly about others. Reading of eugenicist texts in the 1920s led her to feel her convictions more strongly and strengthened her sense of the legitimacy of race as a public issue. In 1922, she sent to her family Theodore Lothrop Stoddard's two books, *The Revolt of Civilization* and *The Rising Tide of Color against White World Supremacy*, believing that they clarified the issues of immigration, Asian exclusion, and the American Negro. She asked especially that her nieces and nephews read them "if they are to hand on to their children our white civilization." She added, "Nothing else in the world seems to me quite so important as this." Stoddard's deeply conservative arguments helped buttress the movement to restrict immigration into the United States that led to the National Origins Act of 1924.[21]

V

AFTER 1927, the autobiography competed with travel for Carey Thomas' attention, and for the first time since 1922 she had work to organize her days. She routinely refused requests that she attend conferences or lend her name to causes. In the summer of 1927 she and Ray Costelloe Strachey sorted family letters. She wrote to her sister Helen that all she saw was "Religion to wallow in. . . . Even I, as a baby, take down sermons for Grandma Whitall and make a little hypocrite of myself. There is nothing real—only a mush of sentiment and religion. What an environment we emerged from! . . . Not one general idea, not one non-religious book."[22]

In the winter of 1927–28, she leased a house on the French Riviera. Accompanied by Edith Lowber and assisted by a French cook, a waitress, and a lady's maid, she read biographies and autobiographies, studied Freudian theory, examined her own papers, and made notes. She described the process as attempting to tap a "sub-conscious self" that "obediently digs up for me worthwhile and worthless memories every morning between sleeping and waking. I have only to select and write them down to be revised later." These notes, largely lists under headings such as "Reading" and "Youth," are valuable (though not always reliable) sources for her biography.[23]

The list entitled "Jews" sheds light on Carey Thomas' anti-Semitism. She began, "My Mother idealized the whole Jewish race on account of the Old Testament, and as a child I accepted everything she told me so I too idealized them." Further down the page she wrote, "Reasons for dislike of them. Like Quakers stick together." The particular traits that Thomas singled out are of interest. They include the special demands that Jews made at Bryn Mawr to have kosher meat and to worship on Jewish holidays; the supposed proclivity Jewish professors had for recommending other Jews for positions; unknown attributes of those who particularly offended her; and "Jews do not play cricket." One statement is of special note: "Things seem honorable to them that do not seem honorable to others."[24]

What is significant about this list is that, with the exception of the failure to play cricket, much of what offended Carey Thomas suggests Quakers and herself. She always made special demands, had special requirements. She supervised a placement network that fostered only those in her image. She had her own scheme of values, at odds with trustees and convention, her own private system of honor. Thomas' jottings suggest a possible additional explanation for the strength of her anti-Semitism. Mary Thomas had established an identity between Quakers and Jews. Rejecting both her mother's religious faith and links to the community of Friends, Carey Thomas may have drawn on Mary's identification of Quakers with Jews to objectify elements of her own self. Carey Thomas hated Jews perhaps in part because she saw them as having qualities as a people that she had as an individual; only in her mind they demonstrated those qualities openly and aggressively.

Another list of great interest is that entitled "Lovers": "Tomlinson, Warren, Halsted, Roland, G——, Cadbury, Boyesen,—— Pension Berlin, P——, Andrew D. White, Justus Strawbridge." The first four were the men who came to call during the two years Carey spent in Baltimore after Cornell. Francis Gummere, represented by the letter G, was a critical actor in Carey's young womanhood, supported by Richard Cadbury. H. H. Boyesen was her professor of literature at Cornell. The two unnamed entries that follow are probably men she found appealing. Andrew D. White, the Cornell president who wrote letters for her in Leipzig, did marry a college contemporary, but there is no indication that he pursued Carey. Justus Strawbridge was a generous donor and supporter on the board of trustees.[25]

More interesting than the specific names is the list itself. The names are all of men. Carey Thomas always enjoyed the conversation of men and may have continued to be attracted to them, but the intimate companions of her adulthood were women. She loved and was loved by Mamie Gwinn and Mary Garrett. Shaped by her reading of Swinburne and Gautier, she understood herself as a passionate woman who loved women. As she worked on her autobiography she had the company and affection of Edith Lowber. Her reading of the medical literature on sexuality and homosexuality in the mid-1890s had given her a new awareness of the sexual component in her relationships with women, but she had not absorbed its negative messages. She continued unself-consciously to see her intimate relations with Mamie and Mary as right and fitting. As late as the first decade of the twentieth century, she wrote of her relationship with Mamie in language analogous to marriage. But by the 1920s she faced a different world. The culture had shifted. The love between women that had once been broadly accepted was now being portrayed in fiction and on the stage as lesbian and deviant.

Carey Thomas worried about the labeling of lesbianism, fearing that it could make it more difficult for women to form with each other the warm attachments that they needed.[26] She may have worried also about how history would treat her. In her list of "Lovers," as elsewhere in the notes for her autobiography, it is possible that she was consciously attempting to rewrite her past to tell the world that she was heterosexual and "normal."

As Carey Thomas read and annotated for her autobiography, her feminist consciousness remained strong. It sometimes popped out in a humorous aside; at other times it appeared in a more straightforward statement. After she learned from Freud about the power of the id, she used the feminine pronoun *she* in reference to it. "I hope," she wrote to her family, "that my It is She for it would be shocking for so good a feminist as I to be ruled by a He." To Helen Flexner she wrote of her discomfort with *he* as a generic pronoun. "We must invent and adopt a neutral pronoun for men and women. . . . The psychological effect of speaking of women as *he* is very humiliating and gives women an inferiority complex. . . . I am writing to Ray and Alice Paul and other feminists."[27]

Working on her autobiography proved to be an irksome task, made more difficult by her study of the genre. After reading *The Education of Henry Adams*, she wrote, "I regard writing my autobiography with terror." Refusing the help of the gifted writer Elizabeth Shepley Sergeant, Thomas wrote that she wanted the book to be hers alone: "I want it to represent my life and opinions as I have lived and thought, and this it could not do if I wrote it with anyone else." She spent 1930–31 at the Deanery to have access to her records. She wished that she had not waited to do her memoirs. Ultimately she saw her autobiography as the impediment to life, much as in her early years she had seen her work at Bryn Mawr. In 1932 she reported that at last, "My memoirs are really getting written. They will take at least a year more, but I feel sure now that they will be written."[28]

What happened to the autobiography after Thomas' death has remained a mystery. Two significant fragments survive: a section on genealogy and childhood rests in the Bryn Mawr College Archives and four folders containing a draft of childhood years are in Helen Flexner's papers at the American Philosophical Society. In 1928, Carey wrote to Helen that her autobiography would be shocking, for she insisted on telling the truth. Helen was herself writing fiction that remains unpublished. In composing her memoir A *Quaker Childhood*, published in 1940, Helen Flexner took notes on the papers in her possession, including those of her eldest sister. Additional notes suggest that for a time she may have herself considered writing Carey Thomas' biography. The best guess is that Helen separated the draft of the autobiography from her sister's papers, returned the genealogy, kept the inoffensive sections on her childhood, and destroyed the rest.

VI

THE DEPRESSION of the 1930s hit Carey Thomas hard. She had been spending principal ever since she had received Mary Garrett's assets. The less than half that remained, largely Baltimore real estate and stocks and bonds, took a tumble beginning with the crash of 1929. In 1930 her income was roughly $26,600, while her expenses ran over $69,000, requiring her to turn a large amount of principal into cash.[29]

In the early 1930s, Carey Thomas attempted to convert fixed assets into liquid ones. In the mid-1920s she had sold Mary's house at 101 Monument Street to the Art Museum of Baltimore and transferred the principal to Johns Hopkins in return for a lifetime annuity. The mansion house at Montebello burned, allowing her to collect insurance, and she had been able to sell some of the property. African Americans had moved into the surrounding area, and this led her to angry denunciations because she believed their presence lowered the value of her land. She had earlier attempted to prevent an African-American college from building on adjacent land. In 1932, five years after she had resigned from the Society of Friends, she asked her financial manager to write confidentially to the president of the Julius Rosenwald Fund to tell him that the owner of the land adjacent to the Negro college of Baltimore "was a Quaker and came of abolitionist stock" and thus might be willing to sell seventy-two acres facing college land. The hypocrisy in this statement is particularly shameless because it came soon after Bryn Mawr College's 1931 decision to admit African Americans. Carey Thomas, that "Quaker . . . of abolitionist stock," had marshaled arguments for exclusion and had visited each of the directors to urge them to oppose racial integration.[30]

Carey Thomas called in Garrett's loans to Bryn Mawr and asked the college to redeem the bonds she held in the Low Buildings, Dolgelly, and the College Inn. The Deanery was a problem, for in 1930 alone it cost her over $21,000 to maintain, not including her own table, entertaining, and servants. Moreover, to live in the Deanery exposed her to the many occasions of the college year, returning alumnae, and college friends. To economize and escape from interruptions she closed the Deanery and rented a villa, Il Nido, in Alpes-Maritimes on the French Riviera. After securing it, she wrote to Helen, "There, if anywhere, I can write my autobiography." She described Il Nido as the "villa of my dreams" and delighted in its great windows and balconies overlooking the sea. She removed her rugs, plates, linens, and silver from the Deanery to furnish it.[31]

On a visit to the United States in 1933 she transferred the Deanery to the college to serve as an alumnae center. It took her months to complete the legal arrangements and to sort her possessions. In addition to books, furnishings, and household effects, there were seventeen trucks of papers that were removed to Coombe Edge, the family summer cottage in the Blue Ridge Mountains. She wanted to look them over for the autobiography. Carey wrote to Helen, "Already, as I write thee, vans full of papers have been burned," perhaps including the missing volumes of presidential letter books. Moving out of the Deanery had been a hard task, but despite the difficulties, she felt it had been worth the trouble. She concluded, "Now with no impedimenta to hamper me I can finish my course in carefree happiness." In October the college held a reception for Thomas to which 850 alumnae came. As Carey Thomas received, she was pleased to be thanked by each alumna.[32]

In autumn 1933 Carey Thomas returned to the French Riviera with Edith Lowber for a second stay at Il Nido. Carey found it necessary to explain why she spent so much time with Edith. Members of the family and other friends had ties keeping them from accompanying her. For example, Lucy Donnelly was "now living with, and traveling with, her new intimate friend Edith Finch." In addition, Edith Lowber, independent and artistic, increased her happiness. "She is devoted to me and takes the best possible care of me. This is a new experience for me as I have always taken care of my friends, Mamie Gwinn and Mary. I confess that I enjoy being taken care of, now that I am older." She had arranged with her family that if she became ill, only Edith outside of the family was to be allowed to see her: "I wish everyone else to remember me as I have been, not as I am ill and wretched and unlike myself."[33]

In March 1934, Edith took sick and suddenly died. Carey arranged for cremation of the body and transport of the ashes for burial in the United States. She wrote to Helen, "I am desolate." Using Mary Berenson's terms, Carey described Edith: "She was life enhancing, more so than any one I have ever known, and she gave me the most wonderful love and devotion. And after all, we had nine years of it." Carey quickly took herself to mourn at the Hotel Danieli in Venice and made plans to spend the summer in England.[34]

VII

It was in England that Carey Thomas completed the last draft of her will, executed in London August 29, 1934. In its printed version, it is a ninety-five-page document. Although Thomas was kept from leaving for posterity her autobiography, her Last Will and Testament can serve as a carefully considered statement of her commitments and hopes in the last years of her life. Because it was premised on a fortune that she no longer possessed, it mixes reality and fantasy.[35]

As Carey Thomas arranged for the dispersal of her material possessions, she conveyed her belief in the magical qualities of things. They were extensions of relationships, they provided solace, they enabled work and pleasure. In designating items, even those long in storage, she recalled when and where they had been purchased or given, how long and for what purposes she had used them, the services and benefits they had provided. Perhaps the most moving gift was that of her mattress "made of old-fashioned down taken from Montebello sheep, now unobtainable," that she bequeathed to her sisters and sister-in-law "in order of age, or by any one of them who may have a long illness." She had derived comfort from it, and she wanted to pass that comfort on.

She had carefully considered the likes and aspirations of each person and attempted to fit the object to them. To Logan went the traveling candlesticks that had lighted their books during evening meals in the Middle East. To Helen Manning, the large leather suitcase "designed by myself for over week-end journeys with pockets on all four sides for small articles and a double top which carries, unrumpled, two dresses, or one dress and several blouses." She attempted to foster the writing careers of several nephews by gifts of writing tables, bookcases, and books. She gave to Simon *The Arabian Nights*, translated by Burton. She directed him to return the volumes to the Deanery Library at his death. She gave many such instructions to recipients, believing that she had a right to give not only in the first instance but in the second and third. Buried in the enumeration were the substantial gifts. She gave the Garrett family silver, "now marked by my initials in great part," to three nieces. Her two automobiles went to Henry Thomas, Jr. She gave outright to Bryn Mawr College the many furnishings and works of art that Mary Garrett had loaned.

Her papers and those of Mary Garrett had long been a concern. She directed that they be burned by her executors, with the exception of those pertinent to the history of the college or to her own life story. She requested that if she had not completed her autobiography by the time of her death, her executors were to "appoint a biographer," approve the book's content, and see that its profits became part of the estate.[36]

The will is divided into three parts. The first arranges for the distribution of her real possessions and papers. The second establishes a fund of $200,000— far beyond her actual resources—to provide annuities for those, such as her sister Grace Worthington and sister-in-law Zoe Thomas, dependent upon her for their living. She made small gifts to persons to whom she felt she owed a debt, the most striking of which was $500 to Zoe to recompense her for the losses she sustained on stock bought at Thomas' suggestion. She left $3000 to Greenmount Cemetery as an endowment to maintain Mary Garrett's tomb and $5000 to Johns Hopkins University for the Mary Elizabeth Garrett Memorial Room Fund.

By 1934 little of Mary's fortune remained. The only significant holdings that Carey Thomas had left were 77 acres of Montebello land; Deer Park, 1,077 largely wooded acres in Garrett County, Maryland; two paintings; and three rugs—all seriously devalued. Logan, perhaps disappointed that he had gotten only candlesticks, summed up in his memoirs what may have been a family judgment: after spending all of Mary's money, Carey took several months in making "an elaborate will . . . leaving large bequests to all her friends and relatives" and then died "heavily in debt." This is true and not true. At her death, Thomas had few liquid assets. Her real estate had potential value estimated at $63,000. Her jewelry, mortgages, and college bonds and loans (both rated at par), estimated at $91,400, were unlikely to bring any such price in 1935. Thomas owed approximately $49,500, the largest element of which was unpaid real estate taxes. With inheritance taxes deducted, the estimated net worth of her estate was $104,900. Its actual value proved to be $80,770—slightly under $745,000 in today's dollars.[37]

Mary Garrett's estate—at its underassessed value, the equivalent of almost $15 million in 1994—had been given to her unconditionally, but nonetheless with the expectation that it was to be conserved for the institutions that the two of them supported. By 1934 Carey Thomas knew it was gone. To be sure, during the preceding decade she had made a major gift to the Bryn Mawr School and had turned over most of the furnishings of the Deanery to the college. But she was aware that she was expected to do more. As she wrote to her sister Helen, "It makes me so very sad to think that owing to my losses in the last three years I can do so few of the things I had hoped to do." Embarrassed, Carey Thomas took every precaution to prevent an announcement of the amount of her estate after her death.[38] The third section of the will, which makes elaborate provisions for gifts to institutions, serves as a record of what she would have done if she could.

Carey Thomas set up a fund that she called the Mary Elizabeth Garrett Endowment Fund for Bryn Mawr College. Under it were the Deanery Endowment Fund to maintain the house and grounds, the Professor Lucy Martin Donnelly Memorial Fund to support Donnelly in her retirement, the President M. Carey Thomas English Prose and Poetry Prize Fund to continue the annual student prize. Finally, there was the Mary Elizabeth Garrett and M. Carey Thomas Bryn Mawr Women's Order of Merit.

The Order of Merit was to be a prize of $10,000 given every five years to honor a woman for accomplished scholarship. It was to be like the "Nobel prizes," and the recipient was to be decorated with a medal. Carey Thomas had thought long about this project and in her will described the design of the medal, modeled after the French palms, and set out the composition of the permanent prize committee. In justifying the award, her words recall her speeches on women and creativity in the early twentieth century. The Order of Merit would "encourage the highest achievements of women by offering them the opportunities, recognitions and financial rewards justly regarded" of their male peers. "The development of one great woman scholar or creative thinker will do more to advance higher learning and research and increase the prestige and authority of women scholars . . . than the sending abroad of many hundreds of well-equipped routine women scholars whose work cannot be expected to rise higher than its source."

Carey Thomas used her will to direct the rites following her death. She instructed her family to hold a "strictly private" funeral attended only by family and intimate friends. "I request that there shall be no words spoken, no prayers offered, and no ceremony of any kind," except for readings that Thomas herself had chosen. She desired her body to be cremated without public ceremony and her ashes buried under the pavement of the library cloisters. She asked that the college hold a memorial meeting attended by directors, faculty, students, workmen, and representatives of the Summer School.

Many provisions of Carey Thomas' will, including the Order of Merit, were fantasy, because the money to back them was gone; yet M. Carey Thomas' larger legacy is enduring. In spending Mary Garrett's fortune over the course of two decades, she did not undo her larger life's work. She bestowed on posterity a wealth of institutions that have enriched many individual lives and served elements of the broader society. Although initially distorted by racial and religious discrimination, her bequest has been redeemed by the more open minds of those who followed her. M. Carey Thomas also left the words of her speeches and articles, some of them vicious, some of them eloquent. Most of all, she bequeathed Bryn Mawr College, the embodiment of her ideas about education and women, a college whose high standards have endured as it has been transformed to serve women of all races and creeds.

VIII

AFTER her will was executed at the office of the American Consulate General, Carey Thomas returned to the United States in the fall of 1934. She renewed ties with family and returned to the autobiography. She moved to Washington, D.C., thinking that she might enjoy its amenities and nearness to Baltimore. With Isabel Maddison's help, she surveyed the correspondence found in a locked cellar closet in the Deanery. In October she and Maddison burned several trunks of letters; in November, seventeen cases and trunks. It is likely that the 1934 bonfire in Maddison's dump in Wayne, Pennsylvania, consumed Carey's letters that Mamie had returned in 1907.[39]

Carey also found many locked tin boxes, including one with Mamie's jewelry. Although Mamie was living in Princeton, and Carey had just asked Zoe to send her a newly found manuscript in her hand, Carey did not return the jewelry to Mamie. After she placed it in a safe deposit box, she fabricated a complicated lie to her insurance agent. She told him that she had found "a number of what seemed to me to be very valuable jewels" in a tin box in the papers at the Deanery that "were left to me by Miss Garrett." She pretended that she had believed them to be stolen by the appraisers and concocted an elaborate story of their concealment by a servant. Carey wrote to her sister Helen that she hoped to sell Mamie's jewelry. Mamie, of course, never knew; but if she had, she would have believed it consistent with the Carey Thomas whom she had left thirty years before.[40]

After Carey found Washington not to her liking, she took an apartment in the Belgravia in Philadelphia, determined to make one last attempt on her autobiography. She traveled to New York and attended meetings of the Summer School board. The college and the Summer School were rethinking their connection. The difficulties of raising money and the radical politics of some Summer School participants had led to calls for ending Bryn Mawr's sponsorship. Thomas at one point believed that the two should go their separate ways so as not to harm the college's fund-raising efforts. At a later point, however, she worked to keep the Summer School at Bryn Mawr. She took pride in the school and in the impact it was having on workers' education in the Roosevelt administration. She continued to fight a battle at Bryn Mawr to preserve the design of the campus. She garnered strength for a radio speech. She thought about an article in the *New York Times* to make a positive case "for sending women at the present time to a separate college for women—more initiative, more independence, more training in executive work." And she schemed for ways to get more money for the Bryn Mawr faculty who were too old to receive the pension benefit of the Carnegie plan. Carey Thomas had been deeply gratified when, after the completion of a new wing, the alumnae chose to name the library after her. "It is," she had written Helen Flexner, "a symbol to me of the academic Bryn Mawr."[41]

In the summer she removed to Coombe Edge, where she suffered a heart attack. Grace came to run the household, and Carey was attended by nurses. Drs. Henry and Caroline Bedell Thomas took over her medical care. She gradually recovered and summoned a last bit of energy to speak on November 2, 1935, at the fiftieth-anniversary celebration of Bryn Mawr College. Refusing to let her words be merely ceremonial, she reviewed the history of the college, recalling the crisis of 1916 that led to the faculty sharing power and responsibility with the president. Now, almost twenty years later, she pronounced her long-withheld judgment: "I have never thought since that time that the creative work of the faculty has reached the degree of excellence which it had earlier achieved."[42]

The exertion led to shortness of breath and overwhelming fatigue. The Summer School rallied her to action for the last time. She argued that the school should return to Bryn Mawr, and when it did, she was content and resigned from the board. She saw plays and ballets. One of her last comments to Helen, only a few days before her final illness, came after reading a contemporary's depiction of Florence: "I think I, too, could have written—if there had been time."[43]

M. Carey Thomas died December 2, 1935. Some years before, she had written to her family about death. She wanted them to know that she did not believe in immortality and had no wish for a life after death. The notion that one lived on as a disembodied spirit with "halos and wings" had no hold over her. She herself was an embodied woman, a mixture of forces for good and ill. That is how she saw others. As she reflected on those she had loved who were now gone—her parents, Mary and James Thomas, her aunt Hannah Whitall Smith, and Mary Garrett—she wrote, "I loved their faults as well as their virtues, their looks and their bodies. As disembodied spirits I have no interest in them and should hate to think that their vivid human personalities had become stupid angels or little puffs of soul without the bodies I love." In facing her own death, she thought of herself as going out "like the flame of a burned out candle." She concluded, "I have been very happy and have enjoyed life to the full, and I should like to live it all over again but as this is impossible I am well content—just to go out."[44]

NOTES

Abbreviations

APS: American Philosophical Society Library

HMT: Henry M. Thomas, Sr.

HMT, Jr: Henry M. Thomas, Jr.

HTF: Helen Thomas Flexner

HWS: Hannah Whitall Smith

JCT: James Carey Thomas

JDR, Jr.: John D. Rockefeller, Jr.

JW: James Whitall

LD: Lucy Donnelly

MCT: M. Carey Thomas

MEG: Mary (Elizabeth) Garrett

MMG: Mamie Gwinn (Mary Mackle
     Gwinn)

MWT: Mary Whitall Thomas

PUL: Princeton University Libraries

RC: Richard Cadbury

Preface

1. Gertrude Stein, *Fernhurst*, in *Fernhurst, Q.E.D., and Other Early Writings*, ed. Donald Gallup (New York: Liveright, 1971); Marjorie Housepian Dobkin, ed., *The Making of a Feminist: Early Journals and Letters of M. Carey Thomas* (Kent, Ohio: Kent State University Press, 1979); Carroll Smith-Rosenberg, "The New Woman as Androgyne: Social Disorder and the Gender Crisis, 1870–1936," in Carroll Smith-Rosenberg, *Disorderly Conduct: Visions of Gender in Victorian America* (New York: Alfred A. Knopf, 1985), pp. 245–96; Edith Finch, *Carey Thomas of Bryn Mawr* (New York: Harper & Brothers, 1947); James Thomas Flexner, *An American Saga: The Story of Helen Thomas and Simon Flexner* (Boston: Little, Brown & Co., 1984), passim; Laurence R. Veysey, "Martha Carey Thomas," in *Notable American Women, 1607–1950: A Biographical Dictionary*, ed. Edward T. James, vol. 3 (Cambridge, Mass.: Harvard University Press, Belknap Press, 1971), pp. 446–50.

2. Lillian Faderman, *Odd Girls and Twilight Lovers: A History of Lesbian Life in*

Twentieth-Century America (New York: Columbia University Press, 1991), although primarily about more recent history, has summarized the scholarship on the late nineteenth and early twentieth centuries and offered fresh perspectives (pp. 1–61). As I reflect on Faderman's presentation of M. Carey Thomas (pp. 28–31), I am aware that I approach the subject with a heightened interest in the specifics of relationships, the precise nature of her thought, nuances of changes over time, and evidence of behavior. Although the Summer 1993 issue of *Signs*, vol. 18, came just as I was closing my work, I was struck by the way that Lisa Duggan's understanding of identity and experience in "The Trials of Alice Mitchell: Sensationalism, Sexology, and the Lesbian Subject in Turn-of-the-Century America" gives definition to my approach (pp. 791–814).

3. For example, in 1922, provoked by the request of a Chilean woman to the League of Women Voters, *The New York Times* asked many experts to name the twelve greatest living American women. Almost all consulted picked Thomas, and she and her photograph made the composite list and the front page of the feature section ("Twelve Greatest Women," *The New York Times*, June 25, 1922).

4. Cynthia Farr Brown has brilliantly analyzed Bryn Mawr's and Thomas' exclusion from the pantheon of white male middle-class colleges and universities and their heads in "Letting in New Light: M. Carey Thomas, Feminism, and Higher Education for Women," M.A. dissertation, Bryn Mawr College, 1984, Bryn Mawr College Archives. Brown has rightly taken on such sources as John S. Brubacher and Willis Rudy, *Higher Education in Transition: A History of American Colleges and Universities, 1636–1976* (New York: Harper & Row, 1976) for ignoring and belittling the contributions of women's colleges and female educators. Reading the influential Brubacher and Rudy text after researching Bryn Mawr is a painful lesson in the erasing of an important woman and women's college from the historical record. Rosalind Rosenberg has accepted this tradition the denial of the importance of women's college in *Beyond Separate Spheres: Intellectual Roots of Modern Feminism* (New Haven: Yale University Press, 1982), pp. 1–27, 52.

5. Stein, *Fernhurst*, pp. 5, 18, 17, 12.

6. She and her brother Leo had known Alfred Hodder at Harvard. Leo Stein read his doctoral thesis, *The Adversaries of a Skeptic*. Gertrude was a medical student at Johns Hopkins, where Henry Thomas was a nerve specialist. When Gertrude joined Leo in England she spent a summer near Fernhurst, the country house of Hannah Whitall Smith. Stein took her title from the house's name. Gathered were members of Hannah's talented family, including her gossipy daughter and son-in-law Mary and Bernard Berenson. In the summer of 1904 on their wedding trip the Hodders visited Gertrude and Leo Stein at rue de Fleurus in Paris and spent time with Hutchins Hapgood, a mutual friend, in Italy. Soon afterwards, in the fall of 1904 or the winter of 1905, Gertrude Stein wrote the tale.

7. Helen Whitall [Thomas] Flexner, *A Quaker Childhood* (New Haven: Yale University Press, 1940).

8. Lucy and Helen's intimate friendship began at Bryn Mawr College during their student years and continued as they traveled abroad for study and taught in the English department of the college. After Helen married Simon Flexner in 1903, the two sustained their friendship. In the last decade of her life Lucy lived with Edith Finch. After Lucy's death, Edith met Bertrand Russell, a close friend of Helen. Russell's first wife was Alys Smith, Carey's and Helen's first cousin. Edith Finch became Bertrand Russell's fourth wife.

9. Edith Finch to Bernard Berenson, Feb. 25, 1948, Berenson Archives, I Tatti, Florence, Italy.

10. Dobkin, ed., *The Making of a Feminist*.

11. Lucy Fisher West, ed., *The Papers of M. Carey Thomas in the Bryn Mawr College*

Archives (printed reel guide and index and microfilm, 217 reels, Woodbridge, Conn.: Research Publications International, 1982).

12. Carolyn Heilbrun, *Writing a Woman's Life* (New York: W. W. Norton, 1988). Although encountered only after my work was largely complete, I have drawn renewed courage from the new collection *The Challenge of Feminist Biography: Writing the Lives of Modern American Women*, ed. Sara Alpern, Joyce Antler, Elisabeth Israels Perry, and Ingrid Winther Scobie (Urbana: University of Illinois Press, 1992).

13. Estelle B. Freedman, "Separatism as Strategy: Female Institution Building and American Feminism, 1870–1930," *Feminist Studies*, 5 (Fall 1979): 512–29.

Chapter 1

1. MCT, Autobiography, folder 4, Simon Flexner Papers, American Philosophical Society Library, Philadelphia, Pa.; MWT diary, Jan. 1857, vol. 2, Lucy Fisher West, ed., *The Papers of M. Carey Thomas in the Bryn Mawr College Archives* (217 reels, Woodbridge, Conn.: Research Publications International, 1982), reel 1, frame 54. I researched the M. Carey Thomas Papers both at the Bryn Mawr College Archives, Bryn Mawr, Pa., and through the microfilm edition. Following the preference of the archives, I cite the reel and frame of the microfilm edition, whenever possible. Unless otherwise noted, the citing of reel and frame indicates the Thomas papers at the Bryn Mawr College Archives. In citing letters, the frame number gives the initial frame of the letter. For ease in reading I have gathered citations in sequence and placed the note at the end of the paragraph. Throughout I have corrected Thomas' grammar and spelling and have spelled out the words that she abbreviated. I have documented all quotations and those details of Thomas' life that I judged required substantiation.

When I use the full name M. Carey Thomas, it is normally to refer to the biographical subject and adult woman who became the college president. She was never addressed by her first name, Martha. Minnie was the name she had as a child, and close friends and family continued to use it long afterward. She assumed the name Carey in 1875 when she went to Cornell, and signed her official correspondence M. Carey Thomas. When I refer to her as a child I call her Minnie Thomas or Minnie. When I refer to her as an adult in her personal capacity, I call her either Carey Thomas or Carey. In referring to her in her professional capacity, I call her Carey Thomas or Thomas.

2. MCT to HWS, Nov. 15, 1903, reel 29, frame 643.

3. Urban renewal and public housing have taken the place of much of the nineteenth-century neighborhood: neither the Thomas house nor the Meeting House stands.

4. MCT to HTF, Aug. 14, 1927, Simon Flexner Papers, APS.

5. MWT diary, Aug. 1859, vol. 2, reel 1, frame 69.

6. MWT diary, Dec. 1859, reel 1, frame 70; MWT diary, Jan. 1860, reel 1, frame 71.

7. MWT diary, Jan. 1857, reel 1, frame 54; MWT diary, July 1857, reel 1, frame 55.

8. MWT diary, July 1859, reel 1, frame 69.

9. MWT diary, Aug. 1860, reel 1, frames 72–73; John M. Whitall to MCT, Oct. 28, 1861, inserted in MWT diary, reel 1, frame 83.

10. Anne Tatum to MCT, Mar. 26, 1858, reel 1, frame 62.

11. MWT diary, Jan. 1860, reel 1, frame 71.

12. Thomas D. Hamm, *The Transformation of American Quakerism: Orthodox Friends, 1800–1907* (Bloomington: Indiana University Press, 1988), pp. 36–73. Hamm lists Mary Whitall Thomas, James Thomas, Francis T. King, Hannah Whitall Smith, and Robert Pearsall Smith among renewal leaders, pp. 43–45.

13. MWT diary, Aug. 1860, reel 1, frame 73; MWT diary, Nov. 1861, reel 1, frame 78; MWT diary, June 10, 1862, reel 1, frame 88.

14. MWT diary, Aug. 1860, reel 1, frame 73.

15. MWT diary, June 24, 1857, reel 1, frame 54; MWT diary, Feb. 22, 1858, reel 1, frame 59; MWT diary, Mar. 1859, reel 1, frames 67–68.

16. MCT, Autobiographical Notes, reel 74, frame 411.

17. MWT diary, Dec. 1858, reel 1, frames 66–67; MWT diary, July 1859, reel 1, frame 69.

18. HWS to sisters, Aug. 2, 1863, reel 1, frame 120; HWS to MCT, Sept. 18, 1861, reel 1, frame 76.

19. HWS to MCT, Sept. 18, 1861, reel 1, frame 76; HWS to MCT, undated [after letter Sept. 18, 1861], reel 1, frame 79.

20. HWS to MWT, undated [July–Aug. 1863], reel 1, frame 124.

21. MWT to MCT, undated [Aug. 1863], reel 61, frame 5.

22. MWT diary, Nov. 1862, reel 1, frame 99.

23. MWT diary, Oct. 1863, reel 1, frame 135.

24. MWT diary, Jan. 1864, reel 1, frame 141; Anne Tatum to MCT, Mar. 26, 1858, reel 1, frame 62.

25. Mary Thomas' account of Minnie's burn is from MWT diary, Jan.–Oct., 1864, reel 1, frames 141–144.

26. MCT's account is from MCT, Autobiography, folder 1, Simon Flexner Papers, APS. Thomas' statement that she did not immediately call for help because her mother was lying down, and because she was afraid that Mary would disapprove of her being in the kitchen, differs from her mother's account.

27. MWT diary, Jan.–Oct., 1864, reel 1, frames 141–44.

28. MCT, Autobiography, folder 1, Simon Flexner Papers, APS; MWT diary, Jan.–Oct., 1864, reel 1, frames 141–44.

29. MWT diary, Jan.–Oct., 1864, reel 1, frames 141–44.

30. MWT diary, Jan.–Oct., 1864, reel 1, frames 141–44; MCT, Autobiography, folder 1, Simon Flexner Papers, APS.

31. MWT diary, Jan.–Oct., 1864, reel 1, frames 141–44; MWT to Mary Whitall, Mar. 1864, Flexner family papers, APS; JCT to MCT, June 11, 1864, reel 60, frame 274.

32. MWT diary, Jan.–Oct., 1864, reel 1, frames 141–44; MCT, Autobiography, folder 1, Simon Flexner Papers, APS.

33. MWT diary, Jan.–Oct., 1864, reel 1, frames 141–44.

34. MWT diary, Jan.–Oct., 1864, reel 1, frames 141–44; MWT to Sarah Nicholson, Apr. 13, 1865, to Mary Whitall, June 28, 1865, to Sarah Nicholson?, Feb. 1, 1866, to Mary Whitall, Dec. 18, 1866, Flexner family papers, APS.

35. MCT, Autobiographical Notes, reel 74, frame 857.

Chapter 2

1. MCT diary, Jan. 8, 1865, vol. 5, reel 1, frame 301; MCT diary, Jan. 4, 1865, vol. 5, reel 1, frame 299. Probably Nathaniel Hawthorne's retelling of classical mythology, *A Wonder Book for Girls and Boys* of 1851.

2. In her autobiography, Thomas recalled that the wound did not heal until she returned from Cornell, but in her correspondence with her parents she reported it healing in the fall of 1872.

3. MCT, Autobiography, folder 1, Simon Flexner Papers, American Philosophical Society Library, Philadelphia, Pa.

4. MCT, Autobiography, folders 1 and 2, Simon Flexner Papers, APS.

5. MCT, Autobiography, folder 1, Simon Flexner Papers, APS.

6. MCT diary, June 20, 1870, vol. 8, reel 1, frame 380.

7. MCT diary, Jan. 1, 1871, vol. 10, reel 1, frame 441. Carolyn G. Heilbrun has written, "Jo was a miracle. She may have been the single female model continuously available after 1868 to girls dreaming beyond the confines of a constricted family destiny to the possibility of autonomy and experience initiated by one's self" ("Louisa May Alcott: The Influence of *Little Women*," in *Women, the Arts, and the 1920s in Paris and New York*, ed. Kenneth W. Wheeler and Virginia Lee Lussier [New Brunswick: Transaction Books, 1982], pp. 21–26, quote, p. 21). I have also enjoyed Catharine R. Stimpson, "Reading for Love: Canons, Paracanons, and Whistling Jo March," *New Literary History*, 21 (Autumn 1990): 957–76.

8. HTF, *A Quaker Childhood* (New Haven: Yale University Press, 1940), p. 64.

9. MCT, Autobiography, folder 4, Simon Flexner Papers, APS; MCT diary, June 21, 1870, vol. 8, reel 1, frame 382–83. The poem was by Jean Ingelow, "The High Tide on the Coast of Lincolnshire."

10. MCT diary, Nov. 12, 1870, vol. 8, reel 1, frame 384; MCT, Autobiography, folder 4, Simon Flexner Papers, APS.

11. MCT diary, June 20, 1870, vol. 8, reel 1, frame 381; MCT diary, Nov. 19, 1870, vol. 8, reel 1, frame 388 (some underlining in original removed). Thomas was probably referring to the four books of Flavius Josephus, a first-century Jewish historian. Barbara Sicherman first alerted me to the importance of reading in shaping the consciousness of late-nineteenth-century educated women. Her paper on women's reading at the June 1987 Berkshire Conference in Women's History at Wellesley College has been published: Barbara Sicherman, "Sense and Sensibility: A Case Study of Women's Reading in Late-Victorian America," in *Reading in America: Literature and Social History*, ed. Cathy N. Davidson (Baltimore: Johns Hopkins University Press, 1989), pp. 201–25. My thinking and research have been stimulated by her thoughtful papers at Organization of American Historians and American Studies Association sessions. The latter paper has been published: Barbara Sicherman, "Reading and Ambition: M. Carey Thomas and Female Heroism," *American Quarterly*, 45 (1993): 73–103.

12. MCT, Autobiographical Notes, reel 74, frame 7; MCT diary, Jan. 3, 1871, vol. 10, reel 1, frame 443.

13. MCT diary, Nov. 26, 1870, vol. 8, reel 1, frames 392–94.

14. MCT diary, Jan. 6, 1871, vol. 10, reel 1, frame 444.

15. MCT diary, Jan. 6, 1871, vol. 10, reel 1, frame 444.

16. MCT diary, Nov. 25, 1870, vol. 8, reel 1, frame 392.

17. MCT diary, [Jan. 1], 1871, vol. 10, reel 1, frame 441.

18. MCT diary, Jan. 2, 1871, vol. 10, reel 1, frame 443.

19. MCT diary, Nov. 20, 1870, vol. 8, reel 1, frame 389.

20. MCT diary, Jan. 8, 1871, vol. 10, reel 1, frame 445. The frame number for all poems is for the poem's beginning.

21. MCT diary, Feb. 26, 1871, vol. 10, reel 1, frames 451–52. François Arago (1786–1853) was a French physicist; Jean Paul was the pen name of Jean-Paul Friedrich Richter (1763–1825), a German writer.

22. Sicherman, "Reading and Ambition," 73–103. Sicherman has focused on the reading of Thomas' early years; my own attention has concentrated on that of her late adolescence and early womanhood, cf. Helen Lefkowitz Horowitz, " 'Nous Autres': Reading, Passion, and the Creation of M. Carey Thomas," *Journal of American History*, 79 (1992): 68–95.

23. MCT diary, Mar. 12, 1871, vol. 10, reel 1, frame 453.

24. MCT diary, May 5, 1871, vol. 10, reel 1, frame 456.

25. MCT diary, May 7, 1871, vol. 10, reel 1, frame 456.

26. MCT diary, May 28, 1871, vol. 10, reel 1, frame 461.

27. MCT diary, May 14, 1871, vol. 10, reel 1, frame 457; MCT diary, June 14, 1871, vol. 10, reel 1, frame 461.

28. MCT diary, June 14, 1871, vol. 10, reel 1, frame 462.

29. Rebecca Marble to MCT, June 16, 1871, vol. 10, reel 1, frame 463; MCT diary, June 16, 1871, vol. 10, reel 1, frame 462.

30. MCT diary, July 10, 1871, vol. 10, reel 1, frame 467; MCT diary, July 13, 1871, vol. 10, reel 1, frame 468.

31. "Oration spoken before the Scholars of Marble Hall," 1871, folder "Intellectual Development," reel 74.

32. MCT diary, Oct. 1, 1871, vol. 10, reel 1, frame 469.

33. MCT diary, Oct. 1, 1871, vol. 10, reel 1, frame 470.

34. MCT diary, Oct. 1, 1871, vol. 10, reel 1, frames 470, 469.

35. MCT diary, Oct. 27, 1871, vol. 10, reel 1, frame 471; MCT to Frank Smith, Nov. 5, 1871, reel 29, frame 395; MCT diary, Oct. 27, 1871, vol. 10, reel 1, frame 472; MCT diary, Nov. 10, 1871, vol. 10, reel 1, frames 472–73.

36. MCT diary, Jan. 1, 1872, vol. 11, reel 1, frame 490.

37. MCT diary, Jan. 1, 1872, vol. 11, reel 1, frames 491–92.

38. MCT diary, Jan. 1, 1872, vol. 11, reel 1, frame 492; MCT diary, Jan. 3, 1872, vol. 11, reel 1, frame 494.

39. MCT to Frank Smith, Mar. 27, 1872, reel 29, frame 415; MCT diary, Apr. 27, 1872, vol. 11, reel 1, frame 506.

40. MCT to Frank Smith, Nov. 5, 1871, reel 29, frame 395.

41. MCT diary, Apr. 27, 1872, vol. 11, reel 1, frames 506–07; MCT to Anna Shipley [ca. early summer 1872], reel 29, frame 46.

42. MCT diary, Feb. 4, 1872, vol. 11, reel 1, frame 497.

43. MCT, Autobiography, folder 3, Simon Flexner Papers, APS.

44. MCT diary, Feb. 4, 1872, vol. 11, reel 1, frame 497. Dinah Maria Craik, *Hannah* (New York: Harper and Brothers, 1872).

45. MCT diary, Feb. 4, 1872, vol. 11, reel 1, frames 497–98.

46. MCT diary, Feb. 8, 1872, vol. 11, reel 1, frame 499; MCT diary, "Rex and Rush," in "My Poetical Effusions," vol. 7, 1869–1882, reel 1, frames 355–56.

47. MCT diary, Mar. 14, 1872, vol. 11, reel 1, frames 500–01.

48. MCT diary, Mar. 14, 1872, vol. 11, reel 1, frames 501–2.

49. MCT diary, Mar. 30, 1872, vol. 11, reel 1, frame 504.

50. MCT diary, Apr. 1, 1872, vol. 11, reel 1, frames 505–6. Women's attributes were underlined in the original.

51. MCT to Frank Smith, May 4, 1872, reel 29, frame 430.

52. MCT to Frank Smith, Feb. 5, 1872, reel 29, frame 407; MCT to Frank Smith, May 4, 1872, reel 29, frame 430.

53. MCT to Frank Smith, undated [after he was accepted to Princeton], reel 29, frame 459.

54. MCT, Autobiography, folder 4, Simon Flexner Papers, APS; MCT diary, Aug. 8, 1872, [actually written Sept. 9, 1872], vol. 11, reel 1, frames 507–8.

55. MCT diary, Aug. 8, 1872, vol. 11, reel 1, frames 507–8.

56. MWT diary, [1872], reel 1, frame 156.

57. MCT diary, Aug. 8, 1872, vol. 11, reel 1, frames 507–8.

58. MCT diary, Aug. 12, 1872, vol. 11, reel 1, frame 509.

Chapter 3

1. MCT to HWS, Aug. 8, 1874 [misdated 1875], reel 29, frame 498; MCT to HWS, undated, 1872 [before going to Howland], reel 29, frame 488.

2. MCT to HWS, undated, 1872 [before going to Howland], reel 29, frame 488; Dorothy Lloyd Gilbert, *Guilford: A Quaker College* (Greensboro, N.C.: Guilford College, 1937), pp. 79–85, 147–49, 239–40; MWT diary, 1872, vol. 2, reel 1, frame 157.

3. MCT diary, Oct. 26, 1872, vol. 11, reel 1, frame 510. At this point Minnie ceased regular entries in her journal and wrote in it only at the end of the academic year. Her correspondence with her mother and her friends, however, give a view both of her life at Howland and of home preoccupations.

4. JCT to MCT, Nov. 12, 1872, reel 60, frame 279.

5. MWT to MCT, Nov. 19, 1873, reel 61, frame 144.

6. MWT to MCT, Nov. 20, 1872, reel 61, frame 49.

7. MWT to MCT, May 1873, reel 61, frame 105; MWT to MCT, Feb. 28, 1873, reel 61, frame 102. Mary spoke of pipe dreams as a castle in Spain.

8. MCT to Anna Shipley [Christmas break, 1873], reel 29, frame 72.

9. MWT to MCT, Sept. 17, 1873, reel 61, frame 138.

10. MCT to HWS, undated [Dec. 1872], reel 29, frame 493.

11. MWT to MCT, May 1873, reel 61, frame 120; MWT to MCT, Oct. 5, 1872, reel 61, frame 23; MWT to MCT, undated [1872], reel 61, frame 83; MWT to MCT, undated [1872], reel 61, frame 70.

12. MCT to HWS, undated [1872], reel 29, frame 488.

13. MWT to MCT, June 12, 1873, reel 61, frame 129; MWT diary [1872], vol. 2, reel 1, frame 156; MWT to MCT, May 7, 1873, reel 61, frame 111. Hannah Whitall Smith, *The Record of a Happy Life; Being Memorials of FWS, a Student of Princeton College, by His Mother, HWS* (London: Morgan & Scott, [1873]).

14. MWT to MCT, May 7, 1873, reel 61, frame 111.

15. MWT to MCT, Jan. 2, 1873, reel 61, frame 91.

16. MWT to MCT, undated [Valentine's Day 1873], reel 61, frame 164.

17. MWT to MCT, Nov. 19, 1873, reel 61, frame 144; MWT to MCT, Nov. 4, 1873, reel 61, frame 151; JCT to MCT, Nov. 6, 1873, reel 60, frame 302.

18. MCT to Anna Shipley, July 13, 1873, reel 29, frame 52.

19. MWT to MCT, Feb. 11, 1874, reel 61, frame 187; MWT to MCT, Feb. 18, 1874, reel 61, frame 192; MCT diary, Aug. 2, 1874, vol. 11, reel 1, frame 512.

20. MWT to MCT, undated [1872], reel 61, frame 78; MWT to MCT, May 20, 1874, reel 61, frame 234.

21. MCT to Anna Shipley, Aug. 3, 1873, reel 29, frame 59.

22. MWT to MCT, undated [day before Thanksgiving, 1873], reel 61, frame 310; MWT to MCT, Nov. 20, 1872, reel 61, frame 49.

23. MCT to MWT, fragment, 1874, Flexner family papers, American Philosophical Society Library, Philadelphia, Pa.; MWT to MCT, undated [day before Thanksgiving, 1873], reel 61, frame 310.

24. MWT to MCT, Feb. 18, 1874, reel 61, frame 192.

25. MWT to MCT, undated [1872], reel 61, frame 83; MWT to MCT, Feb. 18, 1874, reel 61, frame 192.

26. MWT to MCT, Nov. 20, 1872, reel 61, frame 49; MCT to MEG, Nov. 11–12, 1887, reel 15, frame 787.

27. "Given to Libbie Conkey at the end of the Winter Term—Howland—1873," MCT poetry, vol. 7, reel 1, frames 358–59; MCT diary, spring 1873, vol. 11, reel 1,

frames 510–11; "Lines sent to Libbie Conkey at the close of the Spring Term—Howland—1873," MCT poetry, vol. 7, reel 1, frames 361–63.

28. MWT to MCT, Mar. 6, 1873, reel 61, frame 167; MWT to MCT, May 1873, reel 61, frame 105. Lillian Faderman, *Odd Girls and Twilight Lovers: A History of Lesbian Life in Twentieth-Century America* (New York: Columbia University Press, 1991), pp. 1–61, discusses nineteenth-century encouragements of romantic friendship.

29. MCT to Anna Shipley, [fall 1873], reel 29, frame 69; MCT to Anna Shipley, Mar. 5, 1875, reel 29, frame 138.

30. MWT to MCT, May 1873, reel 61, frame 120; MWT to MCT, Mar. 1874, reel 61, frame 202; MWT to MCT, undated [1872], reel 61, frame 81.

31. MWT to MCT, June 4, 1873, reel 61, frame 125; MWT to MCT, undated [Apr. 1874], reel 61, frame 253; MWT to MCT, June 12, 1873, reel 61, frame 129.

32. Thomas D. Hamm, *The Transformation of American Quakerism: Orthodox Friends, 1800–1907* (Bloomington: Indiana University Press, 1988), pp. 74–97, esp. 97; "Mrs. James Carey Thomas," in *Maryland Women*, ed. Margie H. Luckett (Baltimore: Margie H. Luckett, 1937), pp. 390–91; M. Carey Thomas wrote retrospectively of her knowledge of her mother's career in MCT to MWT, May 30, 1880, reel 31, frame 379.

33. MWT to MCT, Oct. 1, [1873], reel 61, frame 269.

34. MWT to MCT, June 10, 1874, reel 61, frame 247.

35. MWT to MCT, May 27, 1874, reel 61, frame 240; MWT to MCT, May 20, 1874, reel 61, frame 234.

36. MCT diary, Aug. 2, 1874, vol. 11, reel 1, frames 512–13.

37. MCT to HWS, Aug. 8, 1874 [misdated 1875], reel 29, frame 498; MCT to Anna Shipley, Sept. 18, 1874, reel 29, frame 114.

38. MCT to Anna Shipley, Jan. 24, 1875, reel 29, frame 131.

39. MCT to Anna Shipley, Apr. 20, 1875, reel 29, frame 142; MCT to Anna Shipley, May 19, 1875, reel 29, frame 88.

40. MCT to Anna Shipley, Sept. 18, 1874, reel 29, frame 114.

41. MCT to HWS, Aug. 8, 1874 [misdated 1875], reel 29, frame 498.

42. MCT diary, Thanksgiving 1874, vol. 11, reel 1, frame 516.

43. MCT to Elizabeth Shepley Sergeant, June 17, 1927, reel 28, frame 1088; Percy Bysshe Shelley, *Queen Mab*, in *The Complete Works of Percy Bysshe Shelley*, ed. Roger Ingpen and Walter E. Peck, 10 vols. (New York: Gordian Press, 1926–30), vol. 1, pp. 55–165, esp. p. 146; MCT to RC, Apr. 8, 1880, reel 13, frame 235.

44. MCT diary, Thanksgiving 1874, vol. 11, reel 1, frame 516.

45. MCT diary, Aug. 3, 1874, vol. 11, reel 1, frame 515; Friedrich H. K. La Motte-Fouqué, *Sintram and His Companions* (London: C. & J. Ollier, 1820).

46. MCT diary, Mar. 15, 1875, vol. 11, reel 1, frames 519–20.

47. MCT diary, July 16, 1875, vol. 11, reel 1, frames 520–21.

48. MCT to Anna Shipley, [1875], reel 29, frame 171.

49. MCT to Anna Shipley, July 14, 1875, reel 29, frame 149; MCT to Anna Shipley, Aug. 11, 1875, reel 29, frame 155.

50. MCT to Anna Shipley, Aug. 11, 1875, reel 29, frame 155; MCT diary, Aug. 15, 1875, vol. 11, reel 1, frame 523.

51. MCT to Anna Shipley, Aug. 11, 1875, reel 29, frame 155.

Chapter 4

1. MCT to Anna Shipley, Aug. 11, 1875, reel 29, frame 155; MWT to MCT, [1876], reel 61, frame 569.

2. MCT to JCT and MWT, Sept. 13, 1875, reel 30, frame 782.

3. MCT to MWT and JCT, Sept. 14, 1875, reel 30, frame 785.

4. MCT to Anna Shipley, Nov. 21, 1875, reel 29, frame 165.

5. *Record of the Class of 1877* (Ithaca, 1923), summarized statement, n.p.; MWT to MCT, Sept. [1875], reel 61, frame 335; MCT to MWT and JCT, Sept. 19, 1875, reel 30, frame 791.

6. MWT to MCT, [1875–76], reel 61, frame 579.

7. MCT to JCT and MWT, Sept. 26, [1875], reel 31, frame 29; MCT to Anna Shipley, Jan. 30, 1876, reel 29, frame 186; MCT to MWT and JCT, [Oct. 1875], reel 31, frame 42.

8. MCT to JCT and MWT, Jan. 23, 1876, reel 31, frame 48.

9. MCT Cornell notebook, vol. 18, reel 2, frame 460.

10. MCT Cornell notebook, vol. 15, reel 2, frame 113.

11. MCT to MWT, Feb. 13, 1876, reel 31, frame 59; MCT to JCT and MWT, Jan. 23, 1876, reel 31, frame 48; MCT to MWT, Sept. 29, 1876, reel 31, frame 84; MCT to Anna Shipley, Feb. 20, 1876, reel 29, frame 191.

12. MCT Cornell notebook, vol. 15, reel 2, frame 182; MCT Cornell notebook, vol. 15, reel 2, frame 205.

13. MCT Cornell thesis, 1877, MCT Papers, Bryn Mawr College Archives.

14. MCT, Notes for commencement address at Bryn Mawr College, June 6, 1907, abridged, quoted in Barbara M. Cross, ed. *The Educated Woman in America: Selected Writings of Catharine Beecher, Margaret Fuller, and M. Carey Thomas*, Classics in Education, No. 25 (New York: Teachers College of Columbia University Press, 1965), pp. 155–56. This volume first drew my attention to Thomas.

15. MCT to Elizabeth Shepley Sergeant, June 17, 1927, reel 38, frame 1088; MCT to MWT and JCT, Nov. 7, 1875, reel 30, frame 806.

16. MCT to Anna Shipley, Jan. 30, 1876, reel 29, frame 186.

17. MWT to MCT, Feb. 8, 1876, reel 61, frame 425.

18. MCT to MWT and JCT, Nov. 14, 1875, reel 30, frame 813.

19. MCT to Anna Shipley, Nov. 21, 1875, reel 29, frame 165.

20. MCT diary, June 12, 1877, vol. 11, reel 1, frames 523–26. It was, Carey wrote, the record of her "fifth friendship," suggesting that she put it on a par with her friendships with Bessie, Anna, Libbie, and Carrie.

21. MCT to Anna Shipley, Feb. 20, 1876, reel 29, frame 191.

22. MWT to MCT, Oct. [23,] 1875, reel 61, frame 356.

23. MWT to MCT, [1875], reel 61, frame 391; MWT to MCT, May 24, 1876, reel 61, frame 499.

24. Carey relayed the conversation to Anna, MCT to Anna Shipley, Aug. 11, 1875, reel 29, frame 155.

25. MWT to MCT, Jan. 23, 1876, reel 61, frame 408.

26. MWT to MCT, Jan. 23, 1876, reel 61, frame 408; MCT to Anna Shipley, Jan. 30, 1876, reel 29, frame 186.

27. MCT, Autobiography, folder 3, Simon Flexner Papers, American Philosophical Society Library, Philadelphia, Pa.

28. MWT to MCT, Aug. 19, 1876, reel 61, frame 315; MWT to MCT, Sept. 22, 1876, reel 61, frame 519. Carroll Smith-Rosenberg has captured Mary Thomas' world tellingly in her landmark article "The Female World of Love and Ritual: Relations between Women in Nineteenth-Century America," *Signs*, 1 (Autumn 1975): 1–29. Mary called her private upstairs parlor the "land of Beulah," or Heaven, giving a sense of its importance to her.

29. MWT to MCT, Jan. 23, 1876, reel 61, frame 408.

30. MCT to JCT and MWT, Sept. 26, [1875], reel 31, frame 29; MCT to MWT, n.d. [fall 1875], reel 31, frame 138; MCT to MWT and JCT, n.d. [fall 1875], reel 31, frame 143.

31. MCT to Anna Shipley, Nov. 21, 1875, reel 29, frame 165; MCT to Anna Shipley, Oct. 1, 1876, reel 29, frame 204.

32. MCT to MWT, [Apr. 1877], reel 31, frame 114; MCT to MEG, May 2, 1892, reel 16, frame 925; MCT, Autobiographical Notes, "Friendship," reel 75, frame 538. I have found no way to determine whether or not Carey Thomas and H. H. Boyesen were at the hotel, but a letter from Anna Shipley (reel 58, frame 316) tells of hearing that Carey had taken the wrong train and as a result had a "horrifying and romantic adventure" that involved *"that* man—whom I hate."

33. MCT to Anna Shipley, Jan. 30, 1876, reel 29, frame 186; MCT to Anna Shipley, Feb. 20, 1876, reel 29, frame 191; MCT to Anna Shipley, Jan. 30, 1876, reel 29, frame 186.

34. MCT to HWS, Nov. 14, 1875, reel 29, frame 503.

35. MCT to Anna Shipley, Jan. 30, 1876, reel 29, frame 186.

36. MCT to Anna Shipley, Feb. 20, 1876, reel 29, frame 191. In discussing Beecher, Thomas mentioned nothing about his adultery trial, despite a reference to it in her later reminiscences about sexual knowledge. Adler, a liberal Jewish scholar, left Cornell and became the founder of the Ethical Culture Society.

37. MCT to Anna Shipley, Jan. 30, 1876, reel 29, frame 186.

38. MWT to MCT, Feb. 14, 1877, reel 61, frame 603. For the influence of Clarke, see Sue Zschoche, "Dr. Clarke Revisited: Science, True Womanhood, and Female Collegiate Education," *History of Education Quarterly*, 29 (Winter 1989): 545–69.

39. MCT diary, June 12, 1877, vol. 11, reel 1, frames 523–26.

40. MCT to MWT, [after last exam], reel 31, frame 119.

41. MCT diary, June 12, 1877, vol. 11, reel 1, frames 523–26.

42. Carol Stoneburner discusses the concept of "Public Friend" in the preface to *The Influence of Quaker Women on American History: Biographical Studies*, ed. Carol and John Stoneburner (Lewiston, N.Y.: The Edwin Mellen Press, 1986), xv.

43. MWT [and JCT] to MCT, Nov. 3, 1875, reel 61, frame 364.

44. MWT to MCT, Feb. 22, 1876, reel 61, frame 446; MWT to MCT, Apr. 3, 1876, reel 61, frame 470.

45. MWT to MCT, Oct. 17, 1876, reel 61, frame 350; MWT to MCT, Oct. 11, 1876, reel 61, frame 534.

46. MWT to MCT, [Nov. 22, 1876], reel 61, frame 370.

47. MWT to MCT, [1876–77; prob. Apr. 1877], reel 61, frame 657.

48. MWT to MCT, [1876–77; prob. Nov. 1876], reel 61, frame 647; MWT to MCT, [1876–77, envelope says Mar. 1], reel 61, frame 657.

49. MWT to MCT, [1876–77, envelope says Mar. 1], reel 61, frame 657.

Chapter 5

1. MCT diary, Sept. 23, 1877, vol. 11, reel 1, frame 527; Hugh Hawkins, *Pioneer: A History of the Johns Hopkins University, 1874–1889* (Ithaca: Cornell University Press, 1960), p. 261.

2. MCT to Anna Shipley, Oct. 31, 1877, reel 29, frame 222; MCT diary, Oct. 4, 1877, vol. 11, reel 1, frame 528.

3. MCT diary, Nov. 1877, vol. 11, reel 1, frames 528–29.

4. MCT diary, Dec. 16, 1877, vol. 11, reel 1, frames 529–30.

5. MCT diary, Mar. 18, 1878, vol. 22, reel 2, frame 876; MCT diary, Mar. 1878, vol. 12, reel 1, frames 557–58; on Godwin, see John R. Clark, *The Philosophical Anarchism of William Godwin* (Princeton: Princeton University Press, 1977), esp. p. 93.

6. MCT, chapter 2, in MMG, MCT, Julia Rogers, and Bessie King, literary draft, vol. 23, reel 2, frames 921–33.

7. MCT, chapter 8, in MMG, MCT, Julia Rogers, and Bessie King, literary draft, vol. 24, reel 2, frames 970–77.

8. MCT diary, Feb. 2, 1878, vol. 22, reel 2, frame 871.

9. MCT diary, Feb. 13, 1878, vol. 22, reel 2, frame 872.

10. MCT diary, Nov. 1877, vol. 11, reel 1, frame 529.

11. MCT diary, Sept. 23, 1877, vol. 11, reel 1, frames 527–28.

12. The long account is MCT diary, Mar. 24, [1878], vol. 22, reel 2, frames 877–82.

13. MCT to Anna Shipley, Aug. 20, 1877, reel 29, frame 215.

14. MCT diary, Mar. 24, [1878], vol. 22, reel 2, frames 877–82.

15. Algernon Charles Swinburne, "Hymn to Proserpine," *Laus Veneris and Other Poems and Ballads* (New York: Charleton, 1867), pp. 75–81; quote from p. 78; Swinburne, "The Garden of Proserpine," pp. 189–92; quote from p. 192.

16. All citations in notes to Swinburne's poetry are from the volume cited in note 15; bill of sale, Cushings & Bailey, Simon Flexner Papers, American Philosophical Society Library, Philadelphia, Pa.

17. Swinburne, "Anactoria," *Laus Veneris*, pp. 64–74; quote from p. 68.

18. Swinburne, "Hermaphroditus," *Laus Veneris*, p. 90.

19. Swinburne, "Sapphics," *Laus Veneris*, pp. 228–29.

20. Mrs. E. B. Duffey, *What Women Should Know: A Woman's Book about Women* (Philadelphia: J. M. Stoddart & Co., 1873). Although James Thomas' medical library could not be reconstituted, an examination was made of medical books published before 1878 that could have been among those in his library.

21. MCT diary, Apr. 6, 1878, vol. 22, reel 2, frames 883–84.

22. Steven Seidman, "The Power of Desire and the Danger of Pleasure: Victorian Sexuality Reconsidered," *Journal of Social History*, 24 (1990): 47–67.

23. MCT diary, Feb. 22, 1878, vol. 22, reel 2, frames 873–75.

24. MCT diary, Apr. 6, 1878, vol. 22, reel 2, frames 883–84, 871.

25. MCT diary, Apr. 21, 1878, vol. 22, reel 2, frame 886.

26. MCT diary, Apr. 21, 1878, vol. 22, reel 2, frame 886.

27. MCT diary, Apr. 23, 1878, vol. 22, reel 2, frame 887.

28. MCT diary, Feb. 13, 1878, vol. 22, reel 2, frame 872; MCT diary, Mar. 2, 1878, vol. 22, reel 2, frame 875.

29. Notes of talk with Mary Gwinn Hodder, Jan. 14, 1939, probably with Alan Mason Chesney, copy in The Archive of the Johns Hopkins University School of Medicine, Record Group 1, Series b, Records of the Women's Medical Fund Committee, 1890–93, Alan Mason Chesney Medical Archives, Johns Hopkins University School of Medicine.

30. MCT diary, Feb. 22, 1878, vol. 22, reel 2, frame 873; MCT diary, Mar. 2, 1878, vol. 22, reel 2, frame 875; MCT diary, Mar. 23, 1878, vol. 22, reel 2, frame 876; MCT to MEG, undated [received Mar. 24, 1878], reel 15, frame 3; MCT, poem, dated Mar. 23, 1878, vol. 7, reel 1, frame 370.

31. MCT to MEG, June 14, 1878, reel 15, frame 15; MCT to MEG, Aug. 27, 1878, reel 15, frame 26.

32. MCT, May 8, 1878, vol. 7, "My Poètical Effusions," reel 1, frame 370; MCT diary, Apr. 21, 1878, vol. 22, reel 2, frame 884.

33. MMG to MCT, n. d. [1878], Alfred and Mary Gwinn Hodder Collection, Princeton University (published with permission of the Manuscripts Division, Department of Rare Books and Special Collections, Princeton University Libraries). Box and folder are unknown. I researched the Hodder papers when the collection was unprocessed. After it was processed in 1992, I returned and made every effort to find all citations in their new locations but not all material in the collection is in order. In this case the original document could not be found. John M. Whitall died in 1877.

34. MCT diary, Aug. 25, 1878, vol. 22, reel 2, frame 894.

35. MCT diary, Feb. 2, 1878, vol. 22, reel 2, frame 871; MCT diary, Feb. 22, 1878, vol. 22, reel 2, frame 873; MCT diary, Mar. 18, 1878, vol. 22, reel 2, frame 875; MCT to MEG, Aug. 27, 1878, continued Sept. 22, 1878, reel 15, frame 26; MCT diary, Aug. 25, 1878, vol. 22, reel 2, frame 894.

36. Mary Gwinn Hodder to Logan Pearsall Smith, early 1938, copy in The Archive of the Johns Hopkins University School of Medicine, Record Group 1, Series b, Records of the Women's Medical Fund Committee, 1890–93, Alan Mason Chesney Medical Archives, Johns Hopkins University School of Medicine.

37. MCT diary, May 2, 1878, vol. 22, reel 2, frame 887.

38. The poem is "Easter Day," Naples, 1849. The correct second line is "We are most wretched that had most believed."

39. MCT diary, June 1, 1878, vol. 22, reel 2, frame 891.

40. MCT to Anna Shipley, Jan. 30, 1876, reel 29, frame 186; MCT diary, July 6, 1878, vol. 22, reel 2, frame 892.

41. MCT to MEG, July 7, 1878, reel 15, frame 20.

42. MCT diary, July 6, 1878, vol. 22, reel 2, frame 893.

43. MCT diary, Aug. 25, 1878, vol. 22, reel 2, frame 895.

44. MCT diary, Sept. 1, 1878, vol. 22, reel 2, frames 898–99.

45. MCT to Board of Trustees of the Johns Hopkins University, Oct. 7, 1878, reel 148, frame 2.

46. MCT to Anna Shipley, Oct. 13, 1878, reel 29, frame 228.

47. MCT diary, Sept. 14, 1878, vol. 22, reel 2, frame 900.

48. MCT to Anna Shipley, Oct. 13, 1878, reel 29, frame 228; MCT, Autobiographical Notes, "Friendship," reel 75, frame 538; M.C.T., "School for Study at Home," *The Quaker Alumnus*, 1 (April 1879): 64; M.C.T., "Education in the Society of Friends. A Plea for Its Continuance," *The Quaker Alumnus*, 1 (Jan. 1879): 36–37.

49. James Thomas Flexner, *An American Saga: The Story of Helen Thomas and Simon Flexner* (Boston: Little, Brown and Company, 1984), pp. 162–65.

50. MCT diary, Jan. 11, 1879, vol. 22, reel 2, frame 904.

51. MCT diary, Jan. 13, 1879, vol. 22, reel 2, frame 904.

52. HWS to MWT, Jan. 17, 1879, Flexner family papers, APS.

53. MCT diary, Mar. 24, 1879, vol. 22, reel 2, frame 905.

54. MCT diary, Aug. 27, 1878, vol. 22, reel 2, frame 897.

55. MCT diary, Mar. 24, 1879, vol. 22, reel 2, frame 906.

56. MCT diary, Mar. 24, 1879, vol. 22, reel 2, frame 906.

57. MCT diary, Mar. 30, 1879, vol. 22, reel 2, frame 907; Statement of F. B. Gummere in regard to connection between Dr. Joseph W. Taylor and himself in professional matters, Sept. 21, 1880, reel 166, frame 802.

58. John S. Brubacher and Willis Rudy, *Higher Education in Transition: A History of American Colleges and Universities, 1636–1976* (New York: Harper & Row, 1976), p. 175.

59. MCT to Dear Girls [MEG and Julia Rogers], June 7, 1879, reel 15, frame 43.

Mr. Jones was probably Richard Jones. I have established the relative value of the dollar using the historical price index in John J. McCusker, "How Much Is That in Real Money? A Historical Price Index for Use as a Deflator of Money Values in the Economy of the United States," *American Antiquarian Society*, 101 (Oct. 1991): 297–373, esp. table A-2, pp. 328–32.

60. MCT to MEG, June 12, 1879, reel 15, frame 50.

61. MCT diary, Sept. 14, 1878, vol. 22, reel 2, frames 899–900; MCT diary, Oct. 12, 1878, vol. 22, reel 2, frame 901.

62. MCT diary, Oct. 12, 1878, vol. 22, reel 2, frame 901; MCT to Anna Shipley, Oct. 13, 1878, reel 29, frame 228; MCT, Oct. 6, 1878, vol. 7, "My Poetical Effusions," reel 1, frame 371.

63. MCT diary, Oct. 30, 1878, vol. 22, reel 2, frame 902.

64. MCT diary, Jan. 11, 1879, vol. 22, reel 2, frame 903.

65. MCT diary, Feb. 24, 1879, vol. 22, reel 2, frame 905; Mary Gwinn Hodder to Logan Pearsall Smith, early 1938, copy in The Archive of the Johns Hopkins University School of Medicine, Record Group 1, Series b, Records of the Women's Medical Fund Committee, 1890–93, Alan Mason Chesney Medical Archives, Johns Hopkins University School of Medicine; MCT diary, July 7, 1879, vol. 22, reel 2, frame 908.

66. MCT to MMG, July 13, 1879, Simon Flexner Papers, APS.

67. MCT to MEG, Aug. 10, 1879, reel 15, frame 71.

68. MCT to MEG, Aug. 18, 1879, reel 15, frame 76.

69. MCT to MEG, Aug. 10, 1879, reel 15, frame 71.

70. MCT to MEG, Aug. 10, 1879, reel 15, frame 71; MCT to MEG, Aug. 18, 1879, reel 15, frame 76.

71. Sarah Whitall Nicholson to HWS, Aug. 22, 1879, Flexner family papers, APS.

Chapter 6

1. MWT to Sarah Whitall Nicholson, Aug. 25, 1879, Flexner family papers, American Philosophical Society Library, Philadelphia, Pa.; MCT to MWT, [August 22, 1879], reel 31, frame 199.

2. MCT to MWT, Sept. 7, 1879, reel 31, frame 209.

3. MCT to MWT, Sept. 7, 1879, reel 31, frame 209.

4. MCT to MWT, Sept. 27, 1879, reel 31, frame 228.

5. MCT to MWT, Oct. 2, 1879, reel 31, frame 237.

6. MCT to MWT, Nov. 15, 1879, reel 31, frame 252.

7. MCT to MEG, Nov. 5, 1879, reel 15, frame 101.

8. James C. Albisetti, *Schooling German Girls and Women: Secondary and Higher Education in the Nineteenth Century* (Princeton: Princeton University Press, 1988), pp. 122–29; MCT to MEG, Nov. 5, 1879, reel 15, frame 101.

9. MCT to MWT, Nov. 15, 1879, reel 31, frame 252.

10. MCT to MEG, [postdated after Dec. 1, 1879], reel 15, frame 108.

11. MCT to MWT, June 20, 1880, reel 31, frame 388; MCT to MWT, Dec. 11, 1880, reel 31, frame 577.

12. MCT to MWT, Nov. 21, 1880, reel 31, frame 565.

13. MCT to Anna Shipley, Jan. 25, 1880, reel 29, frame 252; MCT to MWT, Nov. 20, 1879, reel 31, frame 257.

14. MCT to Elizabeth Shepley Sergeant, June 17, 1927, reel 28, frame 1088.

15. MCT to Anna Shipley, Jan. 25, 1880, reel 29, frame 252; MCT to MWT, Nov. 29, 1879, reel 31, frame 263; MCT to MWT, Nov. 15, 1879, reel 31, frame 252.

16. The journal had a new name by then. MCT, "A Letter from Leipzig," *The Alumnus*, 2 (June 1880): 35–36; "The Study of Comparative Literature," *The Alumnus*, 2 (June 1880): 39–40, quote from 39.

17. MCT to MEG, [postdated after Dec. 1, 1879], reel 15, frame 108; MCT to MWT, Feb. 7, 1880, reel 31, frame 292.

18. Holger Pedersen, *The Discovery of Language: Linguistic Science in the Nineteenth Century*, trans. John Webster Spargo (Bloomington: Indiana University Press, 1962), pp. 89–91, 264–65, 293–94.

19. MCT to Anna Shipley, Jan. 25, 1880, reel 29, frame 252.

20. MCT to MWT, May 12, 1880, reel 31, frame 369.

21. MCT to MWT, n.d. [1880], reel 31, frame 606.

22. MCT to MWT, Dec. 11, 1879, reel 31, frame 270; MCT to MWT, Nov. 15, 1879, reel 31, frame 252.

23. MCT to MWT, Feb. 1, 1880, reel 31, frame 288.

24. MWT to MCT, Jan. 30, 1880, reel 61, frame 709.

25. MCT to MWT, Feb. 7, 1880, reel 31, frame 292.

26. MCT to MEG, Feb. 29, 1880, reel 15, frame 123.

27. MCT to MWT, n.d. [1880], reel 31, frame 606.

28. MCT to MEG, Feb. 19, 1880, reel 15, frame 123. In the letter, this intriguing statement appears: "Mr. Gummere says he gets piles of letters asking everything about the 'wild beast,' " i.e., M. Carey Thomas. It is not clear whether this is Carey's term for herself, that of the letter writers, or a more general sentiment in their Quaker world about her.

29. MCT to Anna Shipley, Jan. 25, 1880, reel 29, frame 252.

30. MCT to MEG, Apr. 14, 1880, reel 15, frame 131; MCT to MEG, Nov. 30, 1880, reel 15, frame 229. Frank visited Carey twice, and Mamie had heard the two conversing through the walls, reminiscing about their times together at Anna Shipley's. Mamie wrote to Julia Rogers about Carey and Frank's friendship in February 1880: "On one point you may be at rest, that is about Mr. Gummere—*M. is not in the least in love with him.* She likes him very much as she continues to do all her old loves you know— but it's after the fashion of Miss Hicks—Of course himself he is more interesting—frank, impulsive, head over heels, loving a strong expression—hampered by his devotion to his mother, half for her sake and more for his own clinging to everyday home-life; never in his life having heard of a woman's having M's opinions and opening his eyes wider every minute as she evangelizes him, greeting everything new which M formulates with excitement and enthusiasm" (MMG to Julia Rogers, Feb. 20 [1880], reel 71, frame 95).

31. MCT to MWT, June 20, 1880, reel 31, frame 388.

32. Francis Gummere to MCT, July 23, 1880, reel 152, frame 2; Francis Gummere to David Scull, Jr., June 15, 1880, reel 166, frame 796.

33. MCT to MWT, Nov. 13, 1880, reel 31, frame 559.

34. MCT to Mr. Wood, May 3, 1912, letter book 49, reel 124; MCT to MEG, Oct. 15, 1898, reel 21, frame 643.

35. RC to MCT, June 19, 1879, reel 37, frame 55.

36. MCT to RC, Nov. 2, 1879, reel 13, frame 225.

37. MCT to RC, [1880–81], penciled on envelope Feb. 10, 1881, reel 13, frame 257; MCT to MEG, Nov. 11, 1880, reel 15, frame 222.

38. MCT to MWT, Feb. 13, 1881, reel 31, frame 638.

39. MCT to RC, Apr. 4, 1880, reel 13, frame 233.

40. MCT to MWT, Nov. 20, 1879, reel 31, frame 257.

41. MCT to MWT, Feb. 22, 1880, reel 31, frame 305.

42. MCT to MWT, Feb. 26, 1880, reel 31, frame 308.

43. MCT to RC, Apr. 4, 1880, reel 13, frame 233.

44. MCT to RC, Apr. 4, 1880, reel 13, frame 233.

45. MCT to MWT, Mar. 26, 1880, reel 31, frame 338.

46. MCT to RC, Oct. 14, 1880, reel 13, frame 242.

47. MCT to RC, Nov. 23, 1880, reel 13, frame 247.

48. MCT to MWT, Feb. 6, 1881, reel 31, frame 633; MCT to MWT, Dec. 4, 1881, reel 31, frame 783; MCT to MEG, May 10, 1882, reel 15, frame 288.

Chapter 7

1. MCT to MWT, July 12, 1880, reel 31, frame 412.

2. [MCT], untitled, *The Nation*, 30 (Feb. 26, 1880): 156; MCT to MWT, Apr. 18, 1880, reel 31, frame 355; MWT to MCT, June 8, 1880, reel 61, frame 758.

3. MCT to MWT, July 12, 1880, reel 31, frame 412.

4. Théophile Gautier, *Mademoiselle de Maupin*, trans. Joanna Richardson (Harmondsworth, Eng.: Penguin, 1981), p. 39.

5. MCT to MEG, Nov. 11, 1880, reel 15, frame 222.

6. MCT to Margaret Hicks, Aug. 30, 1880, reel 32, frame 737.

7. MCT to MWT, Aug. 24, 1880, reel 31, frame 476; Margaret Hicks to MCT, Sept. 15, 1880, reel 62, frame 58.

8. MCT to MWT, Nov. 13, 1880, reel 31, frame 559.

9. MCT to RC, [1880–81] penciled on env. Feb. 10, 1881, reel 13, frame 257.

10. MCT to MWT, Nov. 13, 1880, reel 31, frame 559; MCT to MWT, Feb. 19, 1881, reel 31, frame 643.

11. MCT to MWT, Feb. 19, 1881, reel 31, frame 643; MCT to RC, Feb. 21 penciled on env., reel 13, frame 265.

12. MCT to MWT, Mar. 13, 1880, reel 31, frame 325; MCT to MWT, Dec. 19, 1880, reel 31, frame 582.

13. MCT to MWT, Nov. 21, 1880, reel 31, frame 565; MCT to MWT, Dec. 11, 1880, reel 31, frame 577.

14. MCT to MWT, Nov. 27, 1881, reel 31, frame 780; MCT to MWT, Jan. 16, 1881, reel 31, frame 611; MCT to MWT, Feb. 13, 1881, reel 31, frame 638.

15. Richard Cadbury in begging her for a photograph wrote, "I know you have pretty eyes, I remember that" (RC to MCT, Aug. 4, 1880, reel 37, frame 90).

16. MCT to MWT, Sept. 22, 1880, reel 31, frame 503.

17. MCT diary, Aug. 25, 1878, vol. 22, reel 2, frame 894; MCT diary, Mar. 18, 1878, vol. 22, reel 2, frame 875.

18. MCT to MEG, Nov. 2, 1880, continued Nov. 4, 1880, reel 15, frame 217.

19. MCT to MWT, July 25, 1880, reel 31, frame 428.

20. MCT to MEG, Oct. 18, 1880, reel 15, frame 211; Feb. 15, 1881, reel 15, frame 249; MCT to MEG, Nov. 26, 1881, reel 15, frame 276.

21. MCT to MWT, Feb. 17, 1880, reel 31, frame 303.

22. MCT to MWT, Feb. 22, 1880, reel 31, frame 305.

23. MCT to MEG, July 2, 1880, reel 15, frame 149; MCT to MWT, May 30, 1880, reel 31, frame 379.

24. MCT to MWT, June 22, 1880, reel 31, frame 393.

25. MCT to MWT, June 22, 1880, reel 31, frame 393.

26. MCT to MWT, June 22, 1880, reel 31, frame 393.

27. MCT to MWT, June 20, 1880, reel 31, frame 388.

28. MMG to MCT, [Apr. 23, 1884], reel 53, frame 115.

29. MCT to MWT, Aug. 23, 1880, reel 31, frame 468.

30. MCT to MWT, Oct. 30, 1880, reel 31, frame 544.

31. MCT to MWT, Apr. 20, 1880, reel 31, frame 358; MCT to RC, June 26, [1880?], reel 13, frame 237.

32. MCT to MEG, Dec. 31, 1880, reel 15, frame 241.

33. MCT to MEG, Jan. 11, 1881, reel 15, frame 246.

34. Helen Whitall [Thomas] Flexner, *A Quaker Childhood* (New Haven: Yale University Press, 1940), p. 64.

35. HTF, *Quaker Childhood*, pp. 58, 60; MCT to MEG, Aug. 4, 1881, reel 15, frame 270.

36. HTF, *Quaker Childhood*, pp. 66–67.

37. MCT to MEG, Aug. 4, 1881, reel 15, frame 270; MCT to MWT, Oct. 8, 1881, reel 31, frame 754; MCT to MWT, Sept. 24, 1881, reel 31, frame 739; MCT to MWT, Oct. 23, 1881, reel 31, frame 763.

Chapter 8

1. MCT to MWT, Sept. 8, 1881, reel 31, frame 726.

2. MCT to MWT, Oct. 30, 1881, reel 31, frame 768.

3. MCT to MEG, Nov. 26, 1881, reel 15, frame 276; MCT to MWT, Dec. 27, 1881, reel 31, frame 798; MCT to MWT, Jan. 5, 1882, reel 32, frame 6.

4. MCT to MWT, Mar. 25, 1882, reel 32, frame 60. I have retained Thomas' spelling; contemporary usage is *Sir Gawayne and the Grene Knight*.

5. Martha Carey Thomas, *Sir Gawayne and the Green Knight*, inaugural dissertation before the Philosophical Faculty of the University of Zürich (Zürich: Orell, Füssli & Co., 1883).

6. MCT to MEG, Mar. 18, 1883, reel 15, frame 314. Thomas always uses the form Crestien for Chrétien de Troyes.

7. MCT, *Sir Gawayne*, pp. 23–24, 72–73, 103.

8. MCT to MWT, Apr. 23, 1882, reel 32, frame 87.

9. MCT to MWT, June 25, 1882, reel 32, frame 101.

10. MCT to MWT, July 23, 1882, reel 32, frame 120.

11. MCT to MWT, Sept. 7, 1882, reel 32, frame 156.

12. MCT to MWT, [Aug. 5–21, 1882], reel 32, frame 135; MCT to MWT, Sept. 26, 1882, reel 32, frame 172.

13. MCT to MWT, Nov. 1, 1882, reel 32, frame 196.

14. MCT to MWT, Nov. 25, 1882, reel 32, frame 204.

15. MCT to Allen C. Thomas, July 8, 1882, reel 30, frame 5; MCT to MWT, Sept. 7, 1882, reel 32, frame 156; MCT to MEG, July 24, 1882, reel 15, frame 295.

16. Martha Carey Thomas, "Swinburne's Place in the History of English Poetry," English Seminar, University of Zürich, State Archive of the Canton of Zürich, p. 12.

17. MCT, "Swinburne's Place," 7, 8–9, 8, 11, 23.

18. MMG to MCT, Oct. 15, 1882, reel 53, frame 53; MMG to MCT, Oct.–Nov., 1882, reel 53, frame 103.

19. MMG to MCT, Oct.–Nov., 1882, reel 53, frame 103.

20. MMG to MCT, postmark Nov. 16, 1882, reel 53, frame 92.

21. MMG to MCT, Oct.–Nov., 1882, reel 53, frame 103; MCT, "Swinburne's Place," pp. 20, 16, 15, 17.

22. Heinrich Breitinger, "Report on the Homework of Miss Thomas," English Seminar, University of Zürich, State Archive of the Canton of Zürich.

23. MCT to MWT, Nov. 25, 1882, reel 32, frame 204.

24. MCT to MWT, Nov. 25, 1882, reel 32, frame 204; MCT to MEG, Nov. 26, 1882, reel 15, frame 305.

25. MCT to MWT, Nov. 25, 1882, reel 32, frame 204. Final sentence crossed off in original.

26. MCT to MWT, Nov. 25, 1882, reel 32, frame 204. That there were twenty professors comes from Thomas' drawing of the scene.

27. Heinrich Breitinger, "Evaluation of the Dissertation of Miss Thomas," English Seminar, University of Zürich, State Archive of the Canton of Zürich.

28. MCT to MWT, Nov. 30, 1882, reel 32, frame 212.

29. MCT to MWT, Dec. 20, 1882, reel 32, frame 222.

30. MCT to MWT, Jan. 13, 1883, reel 32, frame 243; MCT to MEG, Mar. 18, 1883, reel 15, frame 314.

31. MCT to MEG, Mar. 18, 1883, reel 15, frame 314.

32. MCT to Anna Shipley, Dec. 12, 1882, reel 29, frame 261; MCT to MEG, June 13, 1883, reel 15, frame 322. Gérard de Nerval was the pseudonym of Gérard Labrunie, a poet, journalist, travel writer, dramatist, and writer of fiction. Arsène Houssaye was a novelist and the director of the Théâtre-Français. With Gautier and Camille Rogier they founded Paris's artistic bohemia in the mid-1830s.

33. MCT to MEG, May 10, 1882, reel 15, frame 288.

34. MCT to MWT, [undated, but ca. July 10, 1883], reel 32, frame 368.

35. MCT to MEG, Nov. 11, 1880, reel 15, frame 222.

36. MCT to MWT, [1881] fragment, reel 31, frame 806.

37. Statement of Francis B. Gummere in regard to connection between Dr. Joseph W. Taylor and himself in professional matters, Sept. 21, 1880, reel 166, frame 802; Francis Gummere to David Scull, Jr., June 15, 1880, reel 166, frame 796; Oct. 22, 1880, Minutes of the Board of Trustees of Bryn Mawr College, vol. 1, p. 32; Apr. 23, 1881, Minutes of the Board of Trustees of Bryn Mawr College, vol. 1, p. 32.

38. MCT to MWT, [1881] fragment, reel 31, frame 806; MCT to MWT, [Mar. 1882], reel 32, frame 65.

39. MCT to MWT, Mar. 19, 1882, reel 32, frame 55; MCT to MWT, Feb. 19, 1881, reel 31, frame 643; MCT to MWT, Mar. 19, 1882, reel 32, frame 55. Thomas cannot be excused on the grounds that, as a woman, she had no alternative prospects. Although her professional opportunities were limited by her gender, academic women contemporaries were obtaining positions at Wellesley, Vassar, and other women's colleges and at coeducational universities in the West.

40. MCT to MWT, July 23, 1882, reel 32, frame 120.

41. MCT to Allen C. Thomas, July 8, 1882, reel 30, frame 5.

42. MCT to MEG, May 10, 1882, reel 15, frame 288.

43. MCT to Allen C. Thomas, July 8, 1882, reel 30, frame 5; Mary Gwinn Hodder to Logan Pearsall Smith, early 1938, copy in The Archive of the Johns Hopkins University School of Medicine, Record Group 1, Series b, Records of the Women's Medical Fund Committee, 1890–93, Alan Mason Chesney Medical Archives, Johns Hopkins University School of Medicine.

44. MCT to MWT, Sept. 13, 1882, reel 32, frame 160.

45. MCT to MWT, Nov. 30, 1882, reel 32, frame 212.

46. MCT to MWT, Jan. 13, 1883, reel 32, frame 243.

47. MCT to MWT, Jan. 30, 1883, reel 32, frame 255.

48. MCT to MWT, May 11, 1883, reel 32, frame 311.

49. MCT to MWT, June 12, 1883, reel 32, frame 323.

50. MCT to MWT, Oct. 24, 1883, reel 32, frame 387.

51. JW to JCT, Oct. 8, 1883, Simon Flexner Papers, American Philosophical Society Library, Philadelphia, Pa.

52. MCT to MWT, [Oct. 1883], reel 32, frame 397; MCT to MWT, Oct. 24, 1883, reel 32, frame 387.

Chapter 9

1. MCT diary, "Books Read, 1873–1887," Dec. 1878, vol. 12, reel 1, frame 561.

2. Théophile Gautier, *Mademoiselle de Maupin,* trans. R. Powys Mathers and E. Powys Mathers (London: The Folio Society, 1948), p. 222.

3. Gautier, *Maupin,* pp. 264, 265.

4. Gautier, *Maupin,* p. 277; MCT to MWT, Dec. 27, 1881, reel 31, frame 798; MCT, Autobiographical Notes, reel 87, frame 1218.

5. MCT to MWT, Feb. 27, 1881, reel 31, frame 650.

6. MCT to MWT, Jan. 23, 1883, reel 32, frame 249; MCT to MEG, Mar. 18, 1883, reel 15, frame 314.

7. MCT to MWT, Feb. 12, 1882, reel 32, frame 36.

8. MCT to MWT, Jan. 5, 1882, reel 32, frame 6.

9. MCT to MWT, Mar. 19, 1882, reel 32, frame 55.

10. MCT diary, Oct. 12, 1878, vol. 22, reel 2, frame 901.

11. MMG to MCT, Mar. 1882, reel 53, frame 41. Carey told Mary that Cecil was the German word for "sweet"; it was probably the way that the two Americans heard "süsse." In "Schimmerle" Mamie may have been playing with the English word "Shimmer," one of her many nicknames for Carey, suggested perhaps by Carey's shining hair. (MCT to MEG, Apr. 7, 1893, reel 17, frame 472). Karen Lystra has challenged notions of Victorian propriety, arguing for the intensity of passion expressed in love letters and behind closed doors. See Karen Lystra, *Searching the Heart: Women, Men and Romantic Love in Nineteenth-Century America* (New York: Oxford University Press, 1989). She is one of a number of historians who have pointed to the difference between the repressive prescriptive literature of the era and actual practice.

12. MCT to MEG, Oct. 18, 1896, reel 20, frame 79; MMG to MCT, Mar. 1882, reel 53, frame 41.

13. MCT to MMG, July 13, 1879, Simon Flexner Papers, American Philosophical Society Library, Philadelphia, Pa.; MCT diary, Jan. 11, 1879, vol. 22, reel 2, frame 903.

14. Carroll Smith-Rosenberg, "The Female World of Love and Ritual: Relations between Women in Nineteenth-Century America," *Signs,* 1 (Autumn 1975), 1–29. I have argued elsewhere that the passionate mentality of M. Carey Thomas and her intimate friends challenges the two-stage chronology of same-sex love: sentimental friendship and medically defined homosexuality. See Helen Lefkowitz Horowitz, "Nous Autres: Reading, Passion, and the Creation of M. Carey Thomas," *Journal of American History,* 79 (June 1992): 68–95. Much important work has focused on the new definition of homosexuality in the late nineteenth century. Although writers differ significantly in their interpretations, especially on what weight to give to the sexologists' influence, they accept an essentially two-stage chronology. See Jeffrey Weeks, "Havelock Ellis and the Politics of Sex Reform," in *Socialism and the New Life: The Personal and Sexual Politics of Edward Carpenter and Havelock Ellis,* ed. Sheila Rowbotham and Jeffrey Weeks (London: Pluto Press Limited, 1977), pp. 139–92; George Chauncey, "From Sexual Inversion to Homosexuality: The Changing Medical Conceptualizations of Female 'Deviance,' " in *Passion and Power: Sexuality in History,* ed. Kathy Peiss and Christina Simmons (Philadelphia: Temple Uni-

versity Press, 1989), pp. 87–117; Jane Caplan, "Sexuality and Homosexuality," in *Women in Society: Interdisciplinary Essays*, ed. Cambridge Women's Studies Group (London: Virago, 1981), pp. 149–67; Carroll Smith-Rosenberg, "The New Woman as Androgyne: Social Disorder and the Gender Crisis, 1870–1936," in Carroll Smith-Rosenberg, *Disorderly Conduct: Visions of Gender in Victorian America* (New York: Alfred A. Knopf, 1985), pp. 245–96; Lillian Faderman, *Odd Girls and Twilight Lovers: A History of Lesbian Life in Twentieth-Century America* (New York: Columbia University Press, 1991), pp. 1–61.

15. MCT to MWT, Sept. 26, 1882, reel 32, frame 172.

16. MCT to MWT, Nov. 14, 1882, reel 32, frame 201.

17. MCT to MWT, Feb. 19, 1881, reel 31, frame 643. Others have suggested a possible relation between the scars from the burn and Carey's passionate commitment to women, that, for example, they might have made her reluctant to undress before a man. It is conceivable, however, that, as a married woman, she might never have undressed before a husband, just as she and Mamie bathed with their backs to each other in Leipzig (see chapter 7). I have consciously chosen not to introduce any relation between the scars and Carey's choice of her life's loves. Nothing in her papers suggests it. It is unnecessary: without scars, I am convinced that Carey would have come to the same resolution of her life.

18. Having said this, Carey quickly restated her position that her own offended taste would "none the less make me anxious to meet him. He is our greatest living genius and I believe he honestly thinks outraging so called decency the right thing to do and he does it in a whole-souled way which wins him my admiration, distasteful as it is. Where he is not either prosaic (another theory of his) or as above, he is glorious. Tell me if they like him as a man. Do approve of Aunt H's having him" (MCT to MWT, Jan. 23, 1883, reel 32, frame 249).

19. MCT to MWT, Jan. 5, 1882, reel 32, frame 6; MCT to MWT, Oct. 3, 1882, reel 32, frame 177. Gertrude Mead later married the artist Edward Abbey.

20. MCT to MWT, Apr. 26, 1883, reel 32, frame 301.

21. MCT to MWT, Jan. 12, 1882, reel 32, frame 14; MCT to MWT, Apr. 30, 1882, reel 32, frame 90.

22. MCT to MWT, [July 1882], reel 32, frame 131.

23. MCT to MWT, Aug. 1883, fragment, reel 32, frame 371.

24. MCT to MWT, [July 1882], reel 32, frame 126; MCT to MWT, Feb. 23, 1883, reel 32, frame 272.

25. MCT to MWT, June 22, 1883, reel 32, frame 330.

26. MCT to MEG, Sept. 25, 1883, reel 15, frame 367; MCT, Autobiographical Fragments, Flexner family papers, APS.

27. MCT to MEG, Aug. 31, 1879, continued Sept. 2, 1879, reel 15, frame 82.

28. MCT to MEG, May 12, 1880, reel 15, frame 143. West Chester is in Chester County, Pa.

29. MCT to MWT, Aug. 12, 1880, reel 31, frame 464; MCT to MWT, Aug. 23, 1880, reel 31, frame 468.

30. MCT to MEG, July 15, 1880, reel 15, frame 154; MCT to MEG, Dec. 31, 1880, reel 15, frame 241.

31. MCT to MEG, May 7, 1881, reel 15, frame 257; MCT to MWT, Apr. 12, 1881, reel 31, frame 678; MCT to MWT, July 17, 1882, reel 32, frame 113.

32. MCT to MEG, Aug. 7, 1881, reel 15, frame 264.

33. MCT to MEG, Oct. 15, 1881, reel 15, frame 300.

34. MCT to MEG, Dec. 31, 1881, reel 15, frame 282.

35. MCT to MWT, Mar. 18, 1881, reel 31, frame 664.

36. MCT to MWT, undated [Oct. 1883], reel 32, frame 397; MCT to MWT, Oct. 24, 1883, reel 32, frame 387; MCT to MWT, undated [Oct. 1883], reel 32, frame 397. *Mary in the House of St. John* (1858) now hangs in the Delaware Art Museum.

37. MCT to MWT, undated [Oct. 1883], reel 32, frame 397.

38. MCT to MWT, Nov. 1, 1883, reel 32, frame 410.

Chapter 10

1. MWT to HWS, Nov. 25, 1883, Flexner family papers, American Philosophical Society Library, Philadelphia, Pa.

2. MCT to HWS, [1883], reel 29, frame 510.

3. HWS to "My dear friend," Jan. 9, 1884, reel 179, frame 335.

4. HWS to "My dear friend," Jan. 9, 1884, reel 179, frame 335.

5. HWS to MCT, Jan. 15, 1884, reel 58, frame 1176.

6. MWT to HWS, Jan. 23, 1884, Flexner family papers, APS; Francis T. King to Daniel Coit Gilman, Jan. 21, 1884, Milton S. Eisenhower Library, Special Collections, Johns Hopkins University; Minutes of the Board of Trustees of Bryn Mawr College, Mar. 14, 1884. Deflation began in the 1880s and continued until approximately 1910.

7. MWT to HWS, Mar. 15, 1884, Flexner family papers, APS.

8. HWS to MCT, Mar. 16, 1884, reel 152, frame 6; MCT to HWS, [1884], reel 29, frame 518.

9. MCT to MEG, Mar. 20, 1884, reel 15, frame 413.

10. MCT budget in MMG notebook [before Apr. 1884 trip], Alfred and Mary Gwinn Hodder Collection, box 36, folder 2, Princeton University (published with permission of the Manuscripts Division, Department of Rare Books and Special Collections, Princeton). The historian and political economist position did not have a tutor assigned, however.

11. Bryn Mawr, Organization of Bryn Mawr, 1884, Note Book I, reel 166, beginning on frame 554, quote from frame 556.

12. Bryn Mawr, Organization of Bryn Mawr, 1884, Note Book I, reel 166, frames 560, 563–64.

13. Bryn Mawr, Organization of Bryn Mawr, 1884, Note Book I, reel 166, frames 564–69.

14. MCT to MEG, Mar. 30, 1884, reel 15, frame 422.

15. Bryn Mawr, Organization of Bryn Mawr, 1884, Note Book I, reel 166, frame 587.

16. MCT to MEG, Apr. 26, 1884, reel 15, frame 432.

17. Bryn Mawr, Organization of Bryn Mawr, 1884, Note Book I, reel 166, frames 594 and ca. 609; MCT to MWT, May 1, 1884, reel 32, frame 420.

18. Bryn Mawr, Organization of Bryn Mawr, 1884, Note Book I, reel 166, frame 594.

19. MCT to MEG, Apr. 26, 1884, reel 15, frame 432.

20. Bryn Mawr, Organization of Bryn Mawr, 1884, Note Book I, reel 166, frame 622; MCT to MEG, May 3, 1884, reel 15, frame 437. Freeman was a close contemporary of Thomas. An 1876 graduate of the University of Michigan and a doctoral student there in history, Freeman received an honorary Ph.D. from Michigan in 1882 after serving as the head of the history department at Wellesley College. In 1881 she was appointed acting president, and in 1882, at age 27, president of Wellesley, the first to act without the supervision of the college's founder, Henry Fowle Durant.

21. MCT to MEG, May 3, 1884, reel 15, frame 437.

22. MCT to MWT, Apr. 27, 1884, reel 32, frame 416; MCT to MEG, Apr. 26, 1884, reel 15, frame 432; MCT to MEG, May 3, 1884, reel 15, frame 437; MCT to MWT, May 1, 1884, reel 32, frame 420.

23. MCT to MWT, [May 4, 1884], reel 32, frame 426; MCT to MEG, May 3, 1884, reel 15, frame 437; MCT to MWT, May 1, 1884, reel 32, frame 423.

24. MCT to MEG, May 28, 1884, reel 15, frame 442. Marion Talbot was later to be dean of women at the University of Chicago.

25. MCT, Report to the President and Trustees, Bryn Mawr College, June 7, 1884, quotes, pp. 3, 11.

26. MCT, Report, 1884, pp. 21, 23, 27, 29, 30.

27. MCT, Report, 1884, pp. 31, 32, 34.

28. MCT, Report, 1884, p. 36.

29. MCT, Report, 1884, pp. 39, 40.

30. MCT, Report, 1884, p. 41.

31. MCT, Report, 1884, p. 44.

32. MCT to MEG, May 28, 1884, reel 15, frame 442.

33. MCT to MEG, July 2, 1884, reel 15, frame 454.

34. H. B. Adams to MCT, June 28, 1884, reel 152, frame 17.

35. MCT to MEG, July 21, 1884, reel 15, frame 460.

36. MCT to MEG, Sept. 21, 1884, reel 15, frame 489; MCT to MEG, Oct. 9, 1884, reel 15, frame 497. Bryn Mawr's oral examination in French and German came to monitor this requirement.

37. Although at the time she gloried in the correction to her astigmatism, no photograph of Thomas in glasses survives. Glasses must have been for her something worn only in private.

38. The name Bryn Mawr, Welsh for great hill, is a reminder of the original settlers of the region. Francis King, June 1879, quoted in Helen Lefkowitz Horowitz, *Alma Mater: Design and Experience in the Women's Colleges from Their Nineteenth-Century Beginnings to the 1930s* (New York: Alfred A. Knopf, 1984), p. 106. Chapter 8 contains a full discussion of the early planning of the Bryn Mawr College campus.

39. M. Carey Thomas, Address to the Alumnae and Former Students of Bryn Mawr College, National Broadcasting Company, Apr. 16, 1935, typescript, p. 4, Bryn Mawr College Archives. Her line is a variation of Strachey's famous statement about Florence Nightingale: "It was not a swan that they had hatched; it was an eagle" (Lytton Strachey, *Eminent Victorians: Cardinal Manning, Florence Nightingale, Dr. Arnold, General Gordon* [New York & London: G. P. Putnam's Sons, 1908], p. 141). I am grateful to Carolyn Heilbrun for the reference.

Chapter 11

1. MMG to MCT, Jan. 16, 1884, Alfred and Mary Gwinn Hodder Collection, box 52, folder 2, Princeton University (published with permission of the Manuscripts Division, Department of Rare Books and Special Collections, Princeton University Libraries).

2. MMG to MCT, Apr. 2, 1884, Apr. 5, 1884, Apr. 6, 1884, Alfred and Mary Gwinn Hodder Collection, box 52, folder 2, PUL.

3. MCT to MMG [1884], Alfred and Mary Gwinn Hodder Collection, box 51, folder 1, PUL; MMG to MCT [Apr. 23, 1884], reel 53, frame 115.

4. MMG to MCT, Feb. 3, 1884, Alfred and Mary Gwinn Hodder Collection, box 52, folder 2, PUL.

5. MMG to MCT [Apr. 23, 1884], reel 53, frame 115.

6. MMG to MCT [Apr. 24, 1884], reel 53, frame 123.

7. MMG to MCT [July 31, 1884], reel 53, frame 177; MMG to MCT, [May 2, 1884], reel 53, frame 152.

8. MMG to MCT, July 1, 1884, Alfred and Mary Gwinn Hodder Collection, box 52, folder 2, PUL; MMG to MCT [Aug. 2, 1884], reel 53, frame 181; MMG to MCT, [Aug. 5, 1884], reel 53, frame 185; MMG to MCT, Aug. 22, 1884, Alfred and Mary Gwinn Hodder Collection, box 52, folder 2, PUL.

9. MMG to MCT [Aug. 5, 1884], reel 53, frame 185; MMG to MCT, [Aug. 8, 1884], reel 53, frame 189.

10. MMG to MCT, June 14, 1884, Alfred and Mary Gwinn Hodder Collection, box 52, folder 2, PUL; MMG to MCT, July 2, 1884, Alfred and Mary Gwinn Hodder Collection, should be in box 52, PUL; MMG to MCT, July 22, 1884, Alfred and Mary Gwinn Hodder Collection, box 52, folder 2, PUL; MMG to MCT, [Aug. 8, 1884], reel 53, frame 189.

11. MMG to MCT, Aug. 5, 1884, Alfred and Mary Gwinn Hodder Collection, box 52, folder 2, PUL.

12. MWT to MCT, Aug. 12, 1884, Flexner family papers, American Philosophical Society Library, Philadelphia, Pa.

13. MCT to MWT, Aug. 24, 1884, reel 32, frame 431.

14. MMG to MCT, [Aug. 9, 1884], reel 53, frame 197; MCT to MMG, [summer 1885], Alfred and Mary Gwinn Hodder Collection, should be in box 51, PUL; MCT to MMG [June 1885], Alfred and Mary Gwinn Hodder Collection, box 71, folder 5, PUL.

15. MCT to MEG, Oct. 31, 1885, reel 15, frame 582; MCT to HWS, Jan. 18, 1887, reel 29, frame 530.

16. MMG to MCT, Sept. 14, 1885, Alfred and Mary Gwinn Hodder Collection, box 52, folder 3, PUL; MMG to MCT, [1885], Alfred and Mary Gwinn Hodder Collection, box 52, folder 3, PUL.

17. MCT to MEG, June 9, 1884, reel 15, frame 446.

18. MCT to MEG, June 9, 1884, reel 15, frame 446.

19. MCT to MEG, Apr. 10, 1884, reel 15, frame 427; MCT to MEG, Mar. 5, 1887, reel 15, frame 730.

20. MCT to MEG, Dec. 6, 1884, reel 15, frame 506.

21. MCT to MEG, July 2, 1884, reel 15, frame 454.

22. Carey may have been fantasizing about the proposal, for her papers contain no mention of it.

23. MCT to MEG, [1885], reel 15, frame 606; MCT diary, Feb. 2, 1885, vol. 22, reel 2, frame 908.

24. MCT diary, Feb. 2, 1885, vol. 22, reel 2, frame 908.

25. MCT to MEG, Apr. 10, 1884, reel 15, frame 427; MCT to MEG, Apr. 19, 1885, reel 15, frame 536. Only in Thomas' autobiographical notes, compiled late in her life, is there reference to this infatuation: she turned to "the man I was in love with," among others, to learn about Woodrow Wilson (MCT, Autobiographical Notes, reel 75, frame 984). Two stray pages surviving from a lost chapter 5 of the Autobiography contain the following: "He replied that he knew I would say that but that he had tried to please me but could not make himself in love again. He said he wanted only to be with me, that our talks inspired him as nothing else did, that only when we were together was he perfectly happy. I was, of course, pleased by this and I remember that as the result of long discussions of the duty of faithfulness I reserved my judgment about his [page break] love affair and we both dismissed it from our minds and gave ourselves up to pure enjoyment of being together" (MCT, Autobiographical Notes, reel 74, frame 675 [the number sequence suggests that two pages are missing after the page break]).

26. MWT to HWS, Aug. 31, 1885, Flexner family papers, APS.

27. Paul Shorey, speech at Thomas' retirement dinner, *Bryn Mawr College, June 8,*

1922, p. 34; MCT to MEG, Oct. 7, 1888, reel 15, frame 922; MCT to MEG, Sept. 25, 1890, reel 16, frame 182.

28. MCT to MEG, Jan. 5, 1889 (misdated 1888), reel 15, frame 821; MCT to MEG, Nov. 1, 1891, reel 16, frame 694; MCT to MEG, Mar. 24, 1892, reel 16, frame 881; MCT to MEG, Jan. 10, 1898, reel 21, frame 31. It was not until December 1893 that Thomas got a pledge from Childs that he would not kiss her, after threatening never to visit his office again if he did so (MCT to MEG, Dec. 7, 1893, reel 17, frame 1069).

29. MCT to MEG, Feb. 14, 1892, reel 16, frame 832.

30. MCT to MEG, Mar. 24, 1892, reel 16, frame 881 (This statement came immediately following her office visit with Childs and his repeated kisses); MCT to MEG, Apr. 7, 1892, reel 16, frame 903. After a visit from Drs. Culbertson and Smith, Carey sent Mary medical literature to back up her points.

31. MCT to MMG [June 1885], Alfred and Mary Gwinn Hodder Collection, box 71, folder 5, PUL.

32. MCT to MEG, Apr. 26, 1884, reel 15, frame 432. At John W. Garrett's death, his fortune was rumored to be $15 million. The artistic talent of a Cornell acquaintance, Gabrielle DeVaux Clements, had prompted the women of Sage College to attempt to raise $1000 so she might go to Europe with her mother to study. Carey herself contributed $75 for Clements' first year abroad and promised $100 for the second. The following year, after giving Mary one of Clements' etchings, Carey persuaded her to help fund Clements' European studies. Thomas' contributions to Clements are documented in her letters to Mary Garrett on reel 15: May 28, 1884 (frame 442); Dec. 23, 1884 (frame 514); July 14, 1885 (frame 542); Aug. 12, 1885 (frame 559). Thomas' and Garrett's larger contribution to Clements' distinguished career came through the Bryn Mawr School, which employed her beginning in 1895.

33. MCT to MEG, Jan. 26, 1886, continued Jan. 27, 1886, reel 15, frame 618; MCT to MEG, Feb. 7, 1886, reel 15, frame 626.

34. MMG to MCT, Apr. 3, 1884, Alfred and Mary Gwinn Hodder Collection, box 52, folder 2, PUL.

35. MMG to MCT, Apr. 4, 1884, Alfred and Mary Gwinn Hodder Collection, box 52, folder 2, PUL; MMG to MCT, Apr. 5, 1884, Alfred and Mary Gwinn Hodder Collection, box 52, folder 2, PUL.

36. MMG to MCT, Oct. 10, 1884, Alfred and Mary Gwinn Hodder Collection, box 52, folder 2, PUL.

37. MMG to MCT, June 24, 1885 [misdated in processing, 1888], Alfred and Mary Gwinn Hodder Collection, box 52, folder 6, PUL.

38. MCT to MEG, Oct. 31, 1885, reel 15, frame 582.

39. MCT to MEG, Dec. 21, 1884, reel 15, frame 511.

40. MCT to MEG, July 31, 1884, reel 15, frame 468.

41. Untitled poem, July 27, 1884, Baltimore and Blue Ridge Summit, reel 76, frame 788.

42. MCT to MEG, July 31, 1885, reel 15, frame 468. Rather than destroying the poem, Mary made a clear copy, correcting Carey's grammatical mistakes, and dated it July 27, 1884, Baltimore and Blue Ridge Summit.

43. MCT to MEG, Mar. 18, 1883, reel 15, frame 314. In 1893, Carey connected the sky in Mary's watercolor *Mary in the House of St. John*, by Rossetti, with "the sky of my passionate land" (MCT to MEG, n.d., postmark Apr. 22, 1893, reel 17, frame 557).

44. MCT to MEG, Mar. 3, 1891, reel 16, frame 381.

45. MCT to MEG, Mar. 27, 1886, reel 15, frame 650.

46. MCT to MEG, Nov. 11, 1887, reel 15, frame 787.

47. MCT to MEG, Dec. 3, 1887, reel 15, frame 795.

48. MCT to MEG, Dec. 3, 1887, reel 15, frame 795.

49. HWS to MCT, 1888, Flexner family papers, APS.

50. MCT to MEG, June 1, 1888, reel 15, frame 841.

51. MCT to MMG [June 30, 1888], Alfred and Mary Gwinn Hodder Collection, box 51, folder 23, PUL; MCT to HWS, July 10, 1888, Flexner family papers, APS.

52. "The rest is silence" are Hamlet's last words; MCT to MEG, July 2, 1888, reel 15, frame 854; MCT to HWS, July 10, 1888, Flexner family papers, APS.

53. MCT to MEG, Nov. 22, 1885, reel 15, frame 592.

54. MMG to MCT, Oct. 6, 1886, Alfred and Mary Gwinn Hodder Collection, box 52, folder 4, PUL; MCT to MMG, Sept. 3, 1888, Alfred and Mary Gwinn Hodder Collection, box 51, PUL.

55. MCT to MEG, Dec. 3, 1887, reel 15, frame 795.

56. MCT to MWT, July 31, 1886, reel 32, frame 491.

57. MCT to MEG, June 24, 1887, reel 15, frame 759; MCT to MEG, July 22, 1887, reel 15, frame 762.

58. MCT to MEG, July 22, 1887, reel 15, frame 762; MCT notebooks, vol. 52, reel 4, frame 278, for example.

59. MCT to MEG, June 29, 1889, reel 15, frame 1087.

60. MCT to MEG, Aug. 4, 1890, reel 16, frame 129; MCT to MEG, Aug. 31, 1890, reel 16, frame 153.

61. MCT to MEG, Mar. 8, 1891, reel 16, frame 396; MCT to MEG, Mar. 22, 1891, reel 16, frame 421.

62. MCT to MEG, Sept. 8, 1891, reel 16, frame 646.

63. MCT to MEG, Mar. 24, 1892, reel 16, frame 881.

64. MCT to MEG, Aug. 15, 1895, reel 19, frame 316.

Chapter 12

1. MWT to HWS, Nov. 13, 1884, Flexner family papers, American Philosophical Society Library, Philadelphia, Pa.

2. MCT to Frederick Hollyer, Feb. 3, 1926, reel 27, frame 330.

3. MCT to HWS, Jan. 18, 1887, reel 29, frame 530.

4. MCT to MEG, [1885], reel 15, frame 606.

5. MCT to "Dear Girls," Sept. 16, 1885, reel 27, frame 316.

6. MCT to Selem Peabody, Sept. 2, 1992, Bryn Mawr School Archives. The examination was Mamie's original idea, expressed in an undated letter to Carey (MMG to MCT, 4:30 A.M. [1884–85], Alfred and Mary Gwinn Hodder Collection, box 52, folder 3, Princeton University (published with permission of the Manuscripts Division, Department of Rare Books and Special Collections, Princeton University Libraries).

7. MCT to Anna Brackett, Jan. 23, 1889, Bryn Mawr School Archives.

8. MWT to MCT, [Nov. 22, 1876], reel 61, frame 370.

9. MCT to MWT, Dec. 25, 1880, reel 31, frame 592; MCT to MWT, Nov. 29, 1879, reel 31, frame 263.

10. MCT to MWT, Oct. 10, 1882, reel 32, frame 182.

11. E. Digby Baltzell, *The Protestant Establishment: Aristocracy and Caste in America* (New York: Random House, 1964), pp. 109–42; MEG to Julia Rogers, Sept. 28, 1885, reel 70, frame 863; MCT to MEG, Sept. 30, 1885, reel 15, frame 569. Sadie Szold was the sister of Henrietta Szold, the founder of Hadassah.

12. MEG to Julia Rogers, Sept. 28, 1885, reel 70, frame 863; MCT to MEG, June 12, 1886, reel 15, frame 675.

13. In her nineteenth-century letters there is no mention of African Americans as applicants to either the Bryn Mawr School or to the college, nor is there any suggestion of anti-Black feeling. This is not because racism and discrimination against Blacks were nonexistent, rather that both were so well accepted that they were not issues. It simply never occurred to Thomas that an African-American student might enter either institution, and none did during her administration. To Thomas they were nonpersons. In the nineteenth century the only racial issue visible in her letters is whether or not one of her white servants is willing to eat in the kitchen with one of her Black ones.

14. MCT to MMG, n.d. [ca. 1890], Alfred and Mary Gwinn Hodder Collection, box 51, PUL.

15. "Religious Tests in Non-Sectarian Schools," *The Jewish Exponent*, Nov. 14, 1890, p. 4; Mary Colvin to MCT, Nov. 19, 1890, Bryn Mawr School Archives; clipping of letter, dated Nov. 25, 1890, published in *The Jewish Exponent*, Bryn Mawr School Archives.

16. Mary Colvin to MCT, Nov. 19, 1890, Bryn Mawr School Archives.

17. MCT to MEG, Aug. 22, 1888, reel 15, frame 897.

18. MCT to MEG, Jan. 1, 1891, reel 16, frame 283.

19. The Johns Hopkins community was somewhat wary of Mary Garrett as the daughter of the late John Work Garrett, the head of the Baltimore and Ohio Railroad, whose stock was the risky principal component of the university's endowment. John Garrett had withdrawn from the university shortly before he died to protest against both the university's unwillingness to offer a practical curriculum geared to Baltimore and its refusal to move from the center of the city to Johns Hopkins' country estate in Clifton neighboring his own property.

20. Francis T. King to MCT, Oct. 29, 1890, reel 152, frame 903.

21. M. Carey Thomas, letter, Jan. 26, 1891, *The Nation*, 52 (Jan. 1891): 114.

22. M. Carey Thomas, letter, in *The Opening of the Johns Hopkins Medical School to Women*, reprinted from "Open Letters" in *The Century Magazine* for Feb. 1891, n.p.

23. Nancy McCall, "The Savvy Strategies of the First Campaign for Hopkins Medicine," in *Hopkins Medical News*, 8 (Fall 1984):2–5; Alan M. Chesney, *The Johns Hopkins Hospital and the Johns Hopkins University School of Medicine: A Chronicle* (Baltimore: The Johns Hopkins Press, 1943), vol. 1, pp. 205–21.

24. MCT to HWS, Mar. 11, 1894, reel 29, frame 557.

25. MCT to HWS, Mar. 11, 1894, typescript copy of letter, reel 29, frame 557.

26. MCT to MEG, Dec. 5, 1886, reel 15, frame 706.

27. MCT to MEG, Nov. 11, 1887, reel 15, frame 787.

28. MCT to MEG, Jan. 16, 1886, reel 15, frame 613. *The Elder Edda* is an ancient Scandinavian verse epic.

29. "The Cap and Gown," *The Monthly Philistine*, Feb. 21, 1902, p. 5; MCT to MEG, Jan. 16, 1886, reel 15, frame 613; MCT to MEG, Feb. 12, 1886, reel 15, frame 629. By mistake the college ordered not the short undergraduate gown but the lengthened gown of the scholar, and this remained the Bryn Mawr dress.

30. MCT to MEG, Nov. 11, 1887, reel 15, frame 787.

31. MCT to MEG, Apr. 2, 1889, reel 15, frame 1041.

32. In the history of campus design Denbigh signaled an important breakthrough. It heralded the entry of women's colleges into the mainstream of collegiate building. See Helen Lefkowitz Horowitz, *Alma Mater: Design and Experience in the Women's Colleges from Their Nineteenth-Century Beginnings to the 1930s* (New York: Alfred A. Knopf, 1984), chapter 9, for a full discussion of the evolution of the Bryn Mawr College campus.

33. MCT to MEG, Apr. 12, 1891, reel 16, frame 444.

34. MCT to MEG, Mar. 4, 1886, reel 15, frame 639. Thomas was referring to Edmund B. Wilson.

35. J. B. Braithwaite to MCT, Dec. 7, 1884, reel 152, frame 50.

36. By 1897, the incoming class had only two Quakers, in contrast to thirty Episcopalians and twenty-four Presbyterians (Monthly Reports of the President to the Trustees, Oct. 26, 1897, Bryn Mawr College Archives).

37. JW to MCT, Nov. 19, 1886, reel 152, frame 358; Feb. 22, 1890, reel 152, frame 783.

38. James Rhoads to MCT, June 2, 1885, reel 152, frame 198.

39. JW to MCT, Feb. 14, 1886, reel 152, frame 273. As dean, Thomas found Whitall a powerful and independent trustee who thought about the college constantly. In his carefully composed and beautifully penned letters, he offered advice on what she should say and how she should say it, inquired after her personal well-being, and gently gave his assistance. He was a kind window into the mind of Bryn Mawr's Orthodox trustees.

40. JCT to MCT, Apr. 14, 1890, reel 152, frame 814.

41. Such were the concerns of Thomas in December 1891 (MCT to MEG, Dec. 12, 1891, reel 16, frame 733). MCT to MEG, May 30, 1891, reel 16, frame 516.

42. MCT to MEG, Dec. 12, 1891, reel 16, frame 733.

43. James Whitall to MCT, Jan. 3, 1889, reel 152, frame 637.

44. M. Carey Thomas, Address, in University of Pennsylvania, *Addresses Delivered at the Opening of the Graduate Department for Women, May 4, 1892* (Philadelphia: Allen, Lane & Scott), p. 12.

45. MCT, *Addresses Delivered*, p. 16. M. Carey Thomas, *Education of Women*, Monographs on Education in the United States, ed. Nicholas Murray Butler (Washington: U.S. Department of Education, 1900).

46. MCT, *Addresses Delivered*, pp. 19, 20.

Chapter 13

1. MCT to MEG, Dec. 3, 1892, reel 17, frame 126.

2. The thesis itself demonstrates Gwinn's conflict between the traditional scholarship of her training and her literary inclinations. Although it refers to scholarly works, it is avowedly "a purely literary enjoyment and appreciation of Beowulf." Although it exists as an unfinished piece of work, it contains remarkable passages that sustain Thomas' belief in Gwinn's potential (Mary Mackle Gwinn, "Beowulf," Ph.D. dissertation, Bryn Mawr College Archives, quote from p. 8). Thomas wrote that to become president would mean "putting aside the other" (MCT to MEG, Dec. 3, 1892, reel 17, frame 126).

3. MCT to HWS, Mar. 11, 1894, reel 29, frame 557. For a discussion of Bryn Mawr architecture, see Helen Lefkowitz Horowitz, *Alma Mater, Design and Experience in the Women's Colleges from Their Nineteenth-Century Beginnings to the 1930s* (New York: Alfred A. Knopf, 1984), chapter 9.

4. MCT to MEG, Apr. 15, 1893, reel 17, frame 524; MCT to MEG, Feb. 26, 1893, reel 17, frame 309; MCT to MEG, Apr. 29, 1893, reel 17, frame 603. M. Carey Thomas' finances are further complicated by the accounts of the Bryn Mawr School. She wrote to Mary that she owed "thousands" to the Bryn Mawr School account (a later letter gives her total debt to the school as $7437.47), but it is likely that she meant that the school account owed this money to Mary Garrett.

5. MEG to MCT, Oct. 11, 1891, reel 42, frame 1023.

6. MCT to MEG, Jan. 17, 1892, reel 16, frame 790.

7. MCT to MEG, July 14, 1897, reel 20, frame 735.

8. MCT to MEG, Mar. 4, 1893, reel 17, frame 339.

9. MCT to MEG, Mar. 3, 1891, reel 16, frame 381; MCT to MEG, Dec. 3, 1892, reel 17, frame 126.

10. MCT to MEG, Apr. 5, 1891, reel 16, frame 436; untitled sonnet, dated Oct. 4, 1891, MCT to MEG, Oct. 11, 1891, reel 16, frame 656.

11. MCT to MEG, Feb. 5, 1893, reel 17, frame 256.

12. The context was a criticism of Julia, that her vulgarity was "one of the mountains I had to cross to reach my passionate land" (MCT to MEG, Apr. 28, 1893, reel 17, frame 593).

13. MCT to MEG, Mar. 5, 1893, reel 17, frame 347; MCT to MEG, Mar. 12, 1893, reel 17, frame 386.

14. MCT to MEG, Apr. 15, 1893, reel 17, frame 524.

15. MCT to MEG, Apr. 3, 1893, reel 17, frame 456.

16. MCT to MMG, Feb. 1, 1891, Alfred and Mary Gwinn Hodder Collection, box 51, Princeton University (published with permission of the Manuscripts Division, Department of Rare Books and Special Collections, Princeton University Libraries).

17. MMG to MCT, July 17, 1891, Alfred and Mary Gwinn Hodder Collection, box 52, folder 11, PUL; MMG to MCT, Nov. 24, 1892, Alfred and Mary Gwinn Hodder Collection, box 52, folder 12, PUL; MMG to MCT, Dec. 24, 1892, Alfred and Mary Gwinn Hodder Collection, box 52, folder 12, PUL.

18. MCT to MMG, Jan. 19, 1893, Alfred and Mary Gwinn Hodder Collection, box 51, PUL.

19. MMG to MCT, Feb. 15, 1893, Alfred and Mary Gwinn Hodder Collection, box 52, folder 13, PUL; MMG to MEG, June 3, 1893, reel 71, frame 363.

20. Mary Gwinn Hodder to Logan Pearsall Smith, early 1938, copy in The Archive of the Johns Hopkins University School of Medicine, Record Group 1, Series b, Records of the Women's Medical Fund Committee, 1890–93, Alan Mason Chesney Medical Archives, Johns Hopkins University School of Medicine.

21. Her role in Bryn Mawr, as in other joint enterprises, was written out of institutional history by Thomas after 1904.

22. MMG to MCT, Dec. 30, 1893, Alfred and Mary Gwinn Hodder Collection, box 52, folder 13, PUL.

23. James E. Rhoads to MCT, Mar. 11, 1893, reel 152, frame 1009; MCT to MEG, Mar. 9, 1893, reel 17, frame 366.

24. MCT to MEG, Mar. 10, 1893, reel 17, frame 372.

25. MCT to MEG, Mar. 12, 1893, reel 17, frame 386; MCT to MEG, Mar. 16, 1893, reel 17, frame 404; MCT to MEG, Mar. 22, 1893, reel 17, frame 408; MCT to MEG, Mar. 23, 1893, reel 17, frame 413.

26. MEG to MCT, Mar. 23, 1893, reel 43, frame 386.

27. MCT to MEG, Mar. 24, 1893, reel 17, frame 421.

28. MEG to Board of Trustees, Mar. 28, 1893, Mary E. Garrett file, MCT Papers, Bryn Mawr College Archives.

29. James E. Rhoads to MCT, Apr. 13, 1893, reel 152, frame 1013.

30. JCT to MCT, Mar. 21, 1893, reel 60, frame 408.

31. JCT to MCT, Mar. 15, 1893, reel 60, frame 406; JCT to Board of Trustees, typescript, Bryn Mawr College Archives, reel 181, frame 169.

32. JCT to Board of Trustees, typescript, Bryn Mawr College Archives, reel 181, frame 169.

33. MCT to MEG, Mar. 25, 1893, reel 17, frame 428.

34. I have profited from the insightful article by Cynthia Farr Brown, " 'Putting a *Woman* in Sole Power': The Presidential Succession at Bryn Mawr College, 1892–1894," *History of Higher Education Annual*, 8 (1988): 79–97. Scull's late wife was James Carey Thomas' first cousin.

35. James Whitall to JCT, May 9, 1893, Flexner family papers, American Philosophical Society Library, Philadelphia, Pa.

36. MCT to MEG, July 31, 1893, reel 17, frame 698.

37. MCT to MEG, Aug. 12, 1893, reel 17, frame 741; MMG to MCT, Mar. 31, 1893, Alfred and Mary Gwinn Hodder Collection, box 52, folder 13, PUL.

38. MCT to MEG, Apr. 28, 1893, reel 17, frame 587; MCT to MEG, July 31, 1893, reel 17, frame 698; MCT to MEG, Aug. 6, 1893, reel 17, frame 717; MCT to MEG, Aug. 9, 1893, reel 17, frame 723.

39. MMG to MCT, Sept. 10, 1893, Alfred and Mary Gwinn Hodder Collection, box 52, folder 13, PUL; MMG to MCT, Sept. 14, 1893, Alfred and Mary Gwinn Hodder Collection, box 52, folder 13, PUL; MMG to MCT, Sept. 20, 1893, Alfred and Mary Gwinn Hodder Collection, box 52, folder 13, PUL.

40. MCT to MEG, n.d., rec. Oct. 23, 1893, reel 17, frame 900.

41. MCT to MEG, Nov. 16, 1893, reel 17, frame 989.

42. MCT to MEG, Nov. 17, 1893, reel 17, frame 994; MCT to MEG, Nov. 17, 1893, reel 17, frame 1001; MCT to MEG, Nov. 18, 1893, reel 17, frame 1004. Garrett and Cope did not resign at that time.

43. MCT to MEG, Nov. 17, 1893, reel 17, frame 1001.

44. MCT to MEG, Nov. 20, 1893, reel 17, frame 1013.

45. MCT to MEG, Nov. 26, 1893, reel 17, frame 1027; MCT to HWS, Mar. 11, 1894, reel 29, frame 557.

46. David Scull, Jr., to MCT, Jan. 20, 1894, reel 152, frame 1053.

47. MCT to HWS, Mar. 11, 1894, reel 29, frame 557.

Chapter 14

1. MCT to HWS, Mar. 11, 1894, reel 29, frame 557.

2. MCT to MEG, Dec. 12, 1895, reel 19, frame 659.

3. MEG to MCT, Dec. 6, 1897; "Requisitions or questions sent to Miss Garrett to which no answer has been given," undated; MEG to Edith Hamilton, Apr. 24, 1899, Bryn Mawr School Archives.

4. MMG to MEG, Apr. 23, 1895, Bryn Mawr School Archives; MMG to MEG, Oct. 18, 1895, Bryn Mawr School Archives.

5. MCT to MEG, Mar. 29, 1895, reel 18, frame 1151.

6. MCT to MEG, Jan. 22, 1895, reel 18, frame 996.

7. MCT to MEG, Apr. 28, 1893, reel 17, frame 587.

8. JW to JCT, Feb. 8, 1895, Flexner family papers, American Philosophical Society Library, Philadelphia, Pa.

9. MCT to MEG, Jan. 16, 1895, reel 18, frame 967; MCT to MEG, Feb. 13, 1895, reel 18, frame 1059; MCT to MEG, May 24, 1894, reel 19, frame 175.

10. MCT to MEG, Nov. 9, 1896, reel 20, frame 154.

11. MCT to MEG, Dec. 11, 1896, reel 20, frame 292; MCT to MEG, Mar. 12, 1897, reel 20, frame 402; *Program of Bryn Mawr College, 1897* (Philadelphia: Sherman & Co., 1897), p. 1.

12. MCT to MEG, Mar. 24, 1897, reel 20, frame 448.

13. MCT to MEG, Nov. 19, 1894, reel 18, frame 828.

14. MCT to MEG, May 10, 1895, reel 19, frame 118; MCT to MEG, May 11, 1895, reel 19, frame 120; MCT to MEG, May 13, 1895, reel 19, frame 136.

15. MCT to MEG, May 13, 1897, reel 20, frame 598; MCT to MEG, May 14, 1897, reel 20, frame 608.

16. Special Meeting, Jan. 12, 1898, Minutes of the Trustees of Bryn Mawr College, vol. III, May 8, 1896–Dec. 19, 1902.

17. MCT to MEG, July 5, 1895, reel 19, frame 224; MCT to MEG, Aug. 23, 1896, reel 19, frame 1122.

18. MCT to MEG, Oct. 8, 1896, reel 20, frame 48.

19. MCT to MEG, Apr. 27, 1897, reel 20, frame 524; MCT to MEG, n.d. [spring 1897], reel 20, frame 579; MCT to Henry Tatnall, Aug. 16, 1898, letter book 14.

Chapter 15

1. MCT to MEG, Dec. 13, 1894, reel 18, frame 896.

2. MCT to MEG, Jan. 23, 1895, reel 18, frame 1000.

3. MMG to MCT, June 8, 1897, Alfred and Mary Gwinn Hodder Collection, box 54, folder 4, Princeton University (published with permission of the Manuscripts Division, Department of Rare Books and Special Collections, Princeton University Libraries).

4. MCT diary, Jan. 11, 1879, vol. 22, reel 2, frame 903; MMG to MCT, Oct. 10, 1884, Alfred and Mary Gwinn Hodder Collection, box 52, folder 2, PUL; MCT to MMG, July 22, 1899, Alfred and Mary Gwinn Hodder Collection, box 51, PUL. A rough translation of "On t'aime toujours un petit peu" is "I love you always a little bit." Julia Rogers had once written about Mamie: "Mamie has too large a capacity of passion . . . not to bestow it upon some man, unless she bestows it upon a woman, and although that is *like*, with all our inherited tendencies, it is but a pale likeness of the passion for a man and if passion must come at all it had best be as golden and throbbing as it may" (JR to MCT, Jan. 6, 1880, reel 56, frame 29).

5. MCT to MEG, June 15, 1894, reel 18, frame 540.

6. MCT to MMG, Feb. 14, 1894, Alfred and Mary Gwinn Hodder Collection, box 51, PUL; for example, MCT to MMG, Mar. 4, 1894, Alfred and Mary Gwinn Hodder Collection, box 51, folder 9, PUL; MCT to MMG, Nov. 2, 1895, Alfred and Mary Gwinn Hodder Collection, box 51, PUL; MCT to MMG, Dec. 23, 1897, Alfred and Mary Gwinn Hodder Collection, box 51, PUL. *Schätz* most likely comes from *schätzle* or *schätzchen*, meaning "precious" or "sweetie."

7. MCT to MEG, Feb. 3, 1894, reel 18, frame 123; MCT to MEG, Feb. 4, 1894, reel 18, frame 128; MCT to MEG, Mar. 17, 1894, reel 18, frame 247; MCT to MEG, May 14, 1897, reel 20, frame 608.

8. MCT to MEG, Mar. 23, 1896, reel 19, frame 858.

9. MCT to MEG, Aug. 17, 1895, reel 19, frame 331.

10. MEG to MCT, June 29, 1897, reel 46, frame 761; MCT to MEG, July 14, 1897, reel 20, frame 735.

11. MCT to MEG, Aug. 24, 1897, reel 20, frame 850.

12. MMG to MEG, Oct. 3, 1894, reel 71, frame 443.

13. MCT to MEG, May 30, 1897, reel 20, frame 668; MCT to MEG, Jan. 19, 1896, reel 19, frame 740.

14. MCT to MEG, July 11, 1897, reel 20, frame 727; MCT to MEG, July 17, 1897, reel 20, frame 747.

15. MEG to MCT, July 18, 1897, reel 46, frame 794. This would bring Thomas' annual income to roughly $200,000 in 1994 dollars.

16. MCT to MEG, Nov. 21, 1899, reel 22, frame 695.

17. MCT to MEG, Mar. 14, 1897, reel 20, frame 408; MCT to MEG, Jan. 5, 1899, reel 21, frame 854.

18. MCT to MEG, Sept. 19, 1899, reel 22, frame 490.

19. MCT to MEG, Nov. 23, 1899, reel 22, frame 702; MCT to MEG, Dec. 21, 1899, reel 22, frame 816.

20. MCT to MEG, Apr. 23, 1895, reel 19, frame 59. Max Nordau, *Degeneration* (London: Heinemann, 1895).

21. MCT to MEG, clipping between letters of Apr. 28, and 29, 1895, reel 19, frame 91; MCT to MEG, May 24, 1895, reel 19, frame 175.

22. Isabel Somerset, known as Lady Henry Somerset (1851–1921), was president of the British Women's Temperance Union.

23. MCT to MEG, Feb. 13, 1895, reel 18, frame 1059; MCT to MEG, July 12, 1895, reel 19, frame 243. As Carey gained more knowledge of Oscar Wilde, her reaction to him was consistent with this distinction. In July 1898, as she learned that Wilde's stay in a Paris hotel was marked by the night visits of "gilded English youth" and "the rabble off the streets," she wrote to Mamie, "He must be a most degraded creature. I fear we must give up his defense" (MCT to MMG, July 5, 1898, Alfred and Mary Gwinn Hodder Collection, box 51, PUL). A week after this, she saw Wilde for the first time and reported that he looked "inconceivably vile," with the "worst and the most cruel face that I have ever seen" (MCT to MMG, July 15, 1898, Alfred and Mary Gwinn Hodder Collection, box 51, PUL).

24. M. Tissot, *Onanism*, trans. A. Hume (London, 1766), pp. 45–47; MCT to MEG, Aug. 27, 1895, reel 19, frame 360. For example, she wrote to Mary in 1897, when she was traveling in Spain with Mamie, that she threw from the train "a very disgraceful French book about a man and two mistresses who were also each other's mistresses, a truly three cornered affair—It had not a merit" (MCT to MEG, July 11, 1897, reel 20, frame 727). Her aesthetic judgment might scorn a book that informed her in other ways.

25. It should be clear that I am discussing the construction of Carey Thomas' mental universe, how she understood her feelings, not describing her behavior or how her feelings and behavior might be interpreted in a later era.

26. MCT, Autobiographical Notes, reel 76, frame 101; MCT, Autobiographical Notes, reel 76, frame 105. By "Lesbianism In Men" Thomas meant same-sex love. It is interesting that Carey Thomas makes no reference to the writings on sexuality of Havelock Ellis. As one who traveled in Fabian Socialist circles, Carey Thomas would have known about his work. She did note him in her lists of books to read as an editor of literary texts. In later years Thomas would cite him in a talk on feminism. In 1895 his "Sexual Inversion in Women" appeared in the *Alienist and Neurologist*, a journal of psychiatry and neurology published in St. Louis, Missouri.

27. Dr. R. v. Krafft-Ebing, *Psychopathia Sexualis* (Stuttgart: Verlag Von Ferdiand Enke, 1888), pp. 65, 72. The edition that is normally used is the twelfth edition, 1906, translated into English by F. J. Rebman (Brooklyn: Physicians and Surgeons Book Company, 1932). The two editions differ in length: the third edition is 177 pages; the twelfth, 614. Krafft-Ebing seems not to have altered his basic ideas about female homosexuality in the later edition. The increase is largely due to extensive additions of case studies in the later edition. I am grateful to Gretel Schuller for translation of the 1888 text. Where the texts are the same, I have relied on the translation provided by Redman.

28. Krafft-Ebing, *Psychopathia*, pp. 68, 116, 118.

29. Emma B. Culbertson to MCT, n.d., reel 38, frame 360.

30. One usually does not deny the sexual history of a childless heterosexual couple with no written record of sexual intercourse.

31. MCT to MEG, Jan. 8, 1899, reel 21, frame 877.

32. Lillian Faderman has clarified the range of reactions possible from reading the work of the sexologists in *Odd Girls, and Twilight Lovers: A History of Lesbian Life in Twentieth-Century America* (New York: Columbia University Press, 1991), pp. 37–61.

33. At the close of her life, aware of growing public stigmatization of same-sex love, she made some effort to rewrite her personal history. See chapter 24.

34. Hutchins Hapgood, *A Victorian in the Modern World* (New York: Harcourt, Brace & Co., 1939), p. 164; MCT to MEG, Feb. 14, 1895, reel 18, frame 1046; MCT to MEG, May 19, 1895, reel 19, frame 155.

35. MCT to MEG, Oct. 16, 1895, reel 19, frame 452; MCT to MEG, Nov. 9, 1895, reel 19, frame 543.

36. MMG to MCT, [the day after Thanksgiving, Nov. 1895], Alfred and Mary Gwinn Hodder Collection, box 53, PUL.

37. MCT to MEG, Dec. 5, 1895, reel 19, frame 636; MCT to MEG, Dec. 17, 1895, reel 19, frame 668.

38. MCT to MEG, Dec. 17, 1895, reel 19, frame 668; MCT to MEG, Jan. 21, 1896, reel 19, frame 756; MCT to MEG, Feb. 11, 1896, reel 19, frame 800.

39. MCT to MEG, Feb. 19, 1896, reel 19, frame 813.

40. Gertrude Stein, *Fernhurst*, in *Fernhusrt, Q.E.D., and Other Early Writings*, ed. Donald Gallup (New York: Liveright, 1971), pp. 19–20, 32–33.

Chapter 16

1. HMT, to JCT, May 19, 1896, Flexner family papers, American Philosophical Society Library, Philadelphia, Pa.

2. HTF to JCT, June 16, 1896, Flexner family papers, APS.

3. MCT to MEG, Dec. 10, 1896, reel 20, frame 288; MCT to MEG, July 17, 1897, reel 20, frame 747.

4. MCT to MEG, Mar. 8, 1899, reel 21, frame 1004.

5. MCT to MMG, [1896], Alfred and Mary Gwinn Hodder Collection, box 51, Princeton University (published with permission of the Manuscripts Division, Department of Rare Books and Special Collections, Princeton University Libraries).

6. M. Carey Thomas, Class Lectures, Bryn Mawr College Archives.

7. In September 1888, after the death of her mother, Carey wrote this rushed note: "I do not meet my class till Tuesday morning. So anything you send will be in time" (MCT to MMG, Sept. 3, 1888, Alfred and Mary Gwinn Hodder Collection, box 51, PUL).

8. MMG, draft of will, June 11, 1900, Alfred and Mary Gwinn Hodder Collection, box 74, PUL; MMG to MCT, July 1907, Alfred and Mary Gwinn Hodder Collection, box 55, folder 5, PUL; Elizabeth Shipley Sergeant, "Notes taken by ESS from an autobiographical talk with MCT in NYC 1927," reel 76, frame 959. Gwinn never seems to have considered employment elsewhere. In 1894, the father of a student came in his capacity as Barnard trustee to inquire if Gwinn would head Barnard College (MCT diary, Mar. 28, 1894, vol. 80, reel 5, frame 281).

9. Gertrude Stein, *Fernhurst*, in *Fernhurst, Q.E.D., and Other Early Writings*, ed. Donald Gallup (New York: Liveright, 1971), p. 12. I am fascinated by the possible links here to women poets, such as H.D., who studied at Bryn Mawr during these years. See Cassandra Laity, "H.D. and A. C. Swinburne: Decadence and Sapphic Modernism,"

Lesbian Texts and Contexts: Radical Revisions, ed. Karla Jay and Joanne Glasgow (New York: New York University Press, 1990), pp. 217–40.

10. In 1927 Lucy Donnelly did tell Elizabeth Shipley Sergeant, "Mamie wrote lectures or at any rate, got up all the backgrounds" (Elizabeth Shipley Sergeant, "Notes taken by ESS from an autobiographical talk with MCT in NYC 1927," reel 76, frame 959).

11. MCT to MEG, Oct. 18, 1896, reel 20, frame 79; MCT to MEG, Oct. 3, 1896, reel 19, frame 401.

12. JCT to MCT, Oct. 13, 1896, reel 60, frame 464.

13. MCT to MEG, Oct. 11, 1896, reel 20, frame 58; MCT to Judge Fisher [MEG copy], Oct. 14, 1896, reel 20, frame 74.

14. MCT to HWS, July 24, 1896, reel 29, frame 575; MCT to MEG, Aug. 20, 1895, reel 19, frame 340; MCT to MEG, Oct. 23, 1896, reel 20, frame 104.

15. MCT, chapel talk, Dec. 8, 1896, Bryn Mawr College Archives.

16. JCT to MCT, Nov. 27, 1896, reel 60, frame 488.

17. MCT to MEG, Dec. 8, 1896, reel 20, frame 274; Edith Finch, *Carey Thomas of Bryn Mawr* (New York: Harper & Brothers, 1947).

18. MMG journal, Oct. 1896, Alfred and Mary Gwinn Hodder Collection, box 37, PUL.

19. MCT to MEG, Jan. 3, 1895, reel 18, frame 936; MCT, speech, printed in *Addresses Delivered at a Memorial Meeting held in honor of James E. Rhoads, LL.D.*, copy in Bryn Mawr College Archives.

20. MCT to HWS, Nov. 16, 1897, and Nov. 19, 1897, Flexner family papers, APS.

21. MCT to MEG, Nov. 13, 1897, reel 20, frame 1054; MCT to HWS, Nov. 19, 1897, Flexner family papers, APS.

22. MCT to MEG, Nov. 19, 1897, reel 20, frame 1070.

23. MCT to Grace Thomas Worthington, Dec. 10, 1897, Flexner family papers, APS.

24. MCT to MEG, Nov. 18, 1897, reel 20, frame 1064; MCT to MEG, Jan. 25, 1898, reel 21, frame 87; MCT to MEG, Mar. 20, 1898, reel 21, frame 223.

25. MCT to MEG, Oct. 20, 1895, reel 19, frame 467.

26. MCT to MEG, May 10, 1898, reel 21, frame 373.

27. MCT to HWS, Mar. 4, 1898, reel 29, frame 587; MCT, note re "Health and Medical Treatment," reel 76, frames 153–54.

28. MCT to HWS, Nov. 24, 1898, reel 29, frame 592; MCT to MEG, Feb. 27, 1899, reel 21, frame 982; MCT to MEG, Mar. 10, 1899, reel 21, frame 1015; MCT to MEG, Mar. 23, 1899, reel 21, frame 1046; MCT to MEG, Oct. 13, 1899, reel 22, frame 568.

29. MCT to HWS, Aug. 10, 1899, reel 29, frame 598.

30. MCT to MEG, Apr. 13, 1899, reel 22, frame 85; MCT to MEG, Apr. 14, 1899, reel 22, frame 97.

31. MCT to HWS, Aug. 28, 1899, reel 29, frame 602. James Whitall's bequest, divided equally among the eight Thomas children, took effect only after James Carey Thomas' death. James Carey Thomas left at his death a house, which went to Harry, and a warehouse and life insurance of $20,000, the proceeds from which were divided nine ways, with Helen receiving the double portion (MCT to HWS, Nov. 26, 1897, Flexner family papers, APS).

32. As early as 1892 Thomas had begun to experience some of the power that expensive dress conferred. Dressed in a new jet and brown dress and hat to "beguile" the trustees, she found as she traveled to the meeting in Philadelphia "both going and coming every door in Broad Street Station was opened for me although in my ordinary costume I always open them for myself" (MCT to MEG, Dec. 3, 1892, reel 17, frame 126).

Chapter 17

1. MCT to MEG, Oct. 31, 1899, reel 22, frame 623. A rough translation of "im werden Minnie" is "Minnie in the process of becoming."

2. Sargent chose to have her pose full face, a pose she had generally avoided. I am grateful to Richard Millington and the students of American Studies 201 for their insights.

3. MCT to MMG, July 26, 1899, Alfred and Mary Gwinn Hodder Collection, box 51, folder 14, Princeton University (published with permission of the Manuscripts Division, Department of Rare Books and Special Collections, Princeton University Libraries); questions on Sargent's reference to Bronzino are provoked by Charles McCorquodale, *Bronzino* (New York: Harper & Row, Publishers, 1981), esp. p. 93; Margaret Emerson Bailey, *Goodbye, Proud World* (New York: Charles Scribner's Sons, 1945), p. 263. The real name of Bronzino (1503–72) was Agnolo di Cosimo.

4. MCT to MEG, Nov. 20, 1899, reel 22, frame 691.

5. Thomas reported in December 1899 that the portrait was to be exhibited at the Philadelphia Academy, and then go to the Paris Exposition (MCT to MEG, Dec. 7, 1899, reel 22, frame 756). It then went to Copley Hall in Boston, in 1901; the Corcoran in Washington, D.C., in 1907; the Roman Art Exposition in Rome, in 1911 (information courtesy of Elaine Kilmurray, Sargent catalogue raisonné project, Northampton, England).

6. M. Carey Thomas, "The Duties of the State and City to Higher Education," Feb. 2, 1895; "The New Pedagogy," Mar. 15, 1895; MCT to MEG, Nov. 27, 1896, reel 20, frame 216.

7. MCT to MEG, Oct. 18, 1900, reel 23, frame 102.

8. MCT to MEG, Oct. 3, 1899, reel 22, frame 540; MCT to MEG, Nov. 3, 1899, reel 22, frame 640; MCT to MEG, Nov. 27, 1896, reel 20, frame 216.

9. Address to Students at the Opening of the Academic Year 1899–1900, Oct. 10, 1899, typescript, Bryn Mawr College Archives. This talk, published as "The 'Bryn Mawr Woman,'" in Barbara Cross, ed., *The Educated Woman in America*, Classics in Education No. 25 (New York: Teachers' College Press of Columbia University, 1965), pp. 139–44, first introduced me to M. Carey Thomas.

10. MCT to MEG, Oct. 10, 1899, reel 22, frame 557; MCT to MEG, Nov. 3, 1899, reel 22, frame 640.

11. MCT to MEG, Dec. 29, 1899, reel 22, frame 838.

12. M. Carey Thomas, *Education of Women*, Monographs on Education in the United States, ed. Nicholas Murray Butler (Washington: U.S. Department of Education, 1900), quote from p. 25, continuation of note 1.

13. MCT, *Education*, pp. 34–35. Thomas' figure is that of those holding the B.A. degree from important colleges.

14. The college kept scrapbooks of press clippings, which are now in volumes, boxes 1–3, reel 87. Quote from Lavinia Hart, "Women as College Presidents," *The Cosmopolitan*, 33, no. 1 (May 1902): 72–29.

15. M. Carey Thomas, "Should the Higher Education of Women Differ from That of Men?" *Educational Review*, 21 (1901): 1–10.

16. M. Carey Thomas, "College Entrance Requirements," Address, Association of Collegiate Alumnae, Nov. 10, 1900, *Publications of the Association of Collegiate Alumnae*, Series III, no. 4, Feb. 1901, quote from p. 12.

17. M. Carey Thomas, "The College," paper read before the International Congress of Arts and Science, Dept. 23, Sect. 3, at the Louisiana Purchase Exposition at St. Louis, Sept. 19–24, 1904, reprinted in *Educational Review*, 10 (Jan. 1905): 1, 15, 19, 15–16.

There is a certain unintended irony here, in that the English university course is three years.

18. M. Carey Thomas, "Mr. Sage and Co-education," *Memorial Exercises in Honor of Henry Williams Sage* (Ithaca: Cornell University, 1898); quote from pp. 59, 60. In these years as she struggled to find her voice, she was fearful of audience reaction. She wrote to Hannah that she had been concerned that she was "too revolutionary" and had been surprised when "they applauded me instead of hissing me as I feared" (MCT to HWS, Mar. 4, 1898, reel 29, frame 587).

19. M. Carey Thomas, Address, *Celebration of the Quarter Centenary of Smith College, Oct. 2–3, 1900* (Cambridge: Riverside Press, 1900), pp. 183–92, quote from p. 189.

20. M. Carey Thomas, address, in *Addresses Delivered at the Opening of the Graduate Department for Women, University of Pennsylvania* (Philadelphia: Allen, Lane and Scott's Printing House, 1892). However, in the medical school debate the year before, she began to develop a distinctive rationale. Women scholars must not work in isolation, but must associate with men and compete with them (Letter, in "The Opening of the Johns Hopkins Medical School to Women," reprinted from "Open Letters" in *The Century Magazine*, Feb. 1891, n.p.).

21. MCT, "The College," June 2, 1898, reel 182, frames 483–92.

22. MCT to MEG, Jan. 25, 1898, reel 21, frame 87.

23. MCT to MEG, Dec. 4, 1898, reel 21, frame 795.

24. Helen Lefkowitz Horowitz, *Alma Mater, Design and Experience in the Women's Colleges from Their Nineteenth-Century Beginnings to the 1930s* (New York: Alfred A. Knopf, 1984), pp. 185–86; MCT to MEG, Nov. 8, 1898, reel 21, frame 699; MCT to MEG, Jan. 5, 1899, reel 21, frame 854.

25. MCT to MEG, May 21, 1899, reel 22, frame 278.

26. Bryn Mawr College, "An Appeal," 1900, Thomas office files, reel 169; MCT to MEG, Nov. 24, 1901, reel 23, frame 903.

27. Evangeline Andrews' role is documented in Rockefeller Family Papers, Record Group 2, Educational Interests, box 54, Bryn Mawr College folder, Rockefeller Archive Center, North Tarrytown, N.Y. All the Rockefeller correspondence that follows is from this file in the Rockefeller Family Papers. See especially Evangeline Walker Andrews to John D. Rockefeller, [Sr.,] Feb. 18, 1901, and Oct. 18, 1901. Thomas' version is found in the Board of Trustee Minutes, Dec. 16, 1904 (beginning p. 145), Bryn Mawr Archives.

28. MCT to MEG, Dec. 4, 1901, reel 23, frame 929; MCT to JDR, Jr., Dec. 6, 1901, Rockefeller Family Papers; MCT to MEG, Dec. 4, 1901, reel 23, frame 929.

29. MCT to MEG, Dec. 5, 1901, reel 23, frame 966.

30. MCT to MEG, May 7, 1902, reel 24, frame 69.

31. MCT to MEG, June 1, 1902, reel 24, frame 132.

32. MCT to MEG, Nov. 16, 1902, reel 24, frame 293; MCT to MMG, Nov. 22, 1902, Alfred and Mary Gwinn Hodder Collection, box 51, folder 17, PUL. As the chairman, Philip Garrett did not vote.

33. MCT to HWS, Jan. 8, 1903, reel 29, frame 629.

34. MCT to HWS, July 18, 1902, reel 29, frame 628; Horowitz, *Alma Mater*, pp. 126–27.

35. MCT to MEG, Feb. 12, 1903, reel 24, frame 509.

36. MCT to Caroline McCormick Slade, Apr. 22, 1935, reel 29, frame 351; MCT to JDR, Jr., Jan. 12, 1904, Rockefeller Family Papers; Thomas wrote to Garrett on October 8, 1903, that "poor Mr. Houghton has begged 9,000 of the 18,000 excess [in Rockefeller Hall construction expenses] from a special fund for educating negroes" (MCT to MEG,

Oct. 8, 1903, reel 24, frame 933). If true, this would be especially ironic given that Bryn Mawr College did not accept African-American students until 1931.

37. Treasurer and vice president of the Girard Trust, in 1900 Tatnall became president of the Franklin Bank.

38. MCT to JDR, Jr., May 30, 1902, Rockefeller Family Papers; MCT to Henry Tatnall, Mar. 4, 1903, letter book 27, p. 284, reel 103.

39. MCT to MEG, May 27, 1903, reel 24, frame 810; MCT to MEG, May 29, 1903, reel 24, frame 826; JDR, Jr., to John D. Rockefeller, Sr., June 9, 1903, Rockefeller Family Papers.

40. June 8 and 15, 1903, and Feb. 19, 1904, Minutes of the Board of Trustees of Bryn Mawr College, vol. IV, Jan. 16, 1903–May 21, 1912, pp. 31–32 and 76. JDR, Jr., wrote to his father, "Miss Thomas was deeply touched by this gift, she could hardly believe the good news, and when I showed her your letter, her eyes filled with tears, and she could not speak for a moment" (JDR, Jr., to John D. Rockefeller, Sr., June 17, 1903, Rockefeller Family Papers).

41. MCT to JDR, Jr., May 27, 1905, Rockefeller Family Papers. Thomas may have learned from this incident that she was better off revealing some of her physical or mental limits, as after this she did write to trustees a number of times about almost breaking down. In addition she may have used the financial concerns to cover her more private distress over Mamie's departure.

42. John D. Rockefeller, Sr., to JDR, Jr., July 10, 1905, Rockefeller Family Papers.

43. JDR, Jr., to MCT, July 5, 1905, Rockefeller Family Papers.

44. MCT diary, Dec. 24, 1905, vol. 101, reel 6, frame 334; MCT to Caroline McCormick Slade, Apr. 22, 1935, reel 29, frame 351.

Chapter 18

1. MCT to HWS, Aug. 10, 1899, reel 29, frame 598.

2. MCT diary, 1902, vol. 95, Dec. 4, 1902, reel 5, frame 763; MCT to MEG, Dec. 4, 1902, reel 24, frame 332; MCT to MEG, Mar. 23, 1903, reel 24, frame 623; MCT to MEG, Dec. 8, 1903, reel 24, frame 1141; MCT to MEG, Jan. 29, 1904, reel 24, frame 1247. A rough translation is "without rancor."

3. MCT to MEG, Oct. 31, 1899, reel 22, frame 623.

4. MCT to MEG, Dec. 3, 1900, reel 23, frame 216.

5. MCT to MEG, Apr. 16, 1898, reel 21, frame 298; MCT to MEG, Mar. 2, 1899, reel 21, frame 990; Helen Hoyt was forced to leave the college because she could not give up smoking. Her parting riposte to Thomas gives a fascinating glimpse into the mentality of a young academic in 1906. As Thomas reported to Garrett, "Helen Hoyt delicately intimated that smoking was a compensation for abstinence in more serious dissipations, and she insinuated that for me who had neither smoking nor these, fame and glory made up" (MCT to MEG, May 22, 1906, reel 25, frame 532).

6. Gertrude Stein, *Fernhurst*, in *Fernhurst, Q.E.D., and Other Early Writings*, ed. Donald Gallup (New York: Liveright, 1971), pp. 5–6, 17.

7. Margaret Bailey, *Good-bye Proud World* (New York: Charles Scribner's Sons, 1945), pp. 265–71, 283–84.

8. MCT to MEG, Oct. 1, 1898, reel 21, frame 610; William Allan Neilson to Robert Neilson, Oct. 30, 1898, Neilson papers, box 5, folder 115, College Archives, Smith College, Northampton, Mass.

9. MCT to William Allan Neilson, Mar. 16, 1899, letter book 16, p. 394, reel 92.

10. MCT to MEG, Oct. 30, 1900, reel 23, frame 129; William Allan Neilson to Robert Neilson, Nov. 19, 1899, Neilson papers, box 5, folder 116, College Archives, Smith College.

11. MCT to MEG, Mar. 13, 1900, reel 22, frame 985.

12. William Allan Neilson to Robert Neilson, Mar. 3, 1900, Neilson papers, box 5, folder 117, College Archives, Smith College.

13. MCT to William Allan Neilson, Mar. 27, 1900, Neilson papers, box 18, folder 300, College Archives, Smith College; William Allan Neilson to MCT, Apr. 1, 1900, Neilson papers, box 18, folder 300; MCT to MEG, Apr. 6, 1900, reel 22, frame 1047.

14. William Allan Neilson to MCT, Apr. 3, 1900, Neilson papers, box 18, folder 300, College Archives, Smith College; Margaret Farrand Thorp, *Neilson of Smith* (New York: Oxford University Press, 1956), pp. 77–82.

15. Quoted in Thorp, *Neilson of Smith*, p. 82.

16. MCT to MEG, Mar. 28, 1900, reel 22, frame 1021; MCT to MEG, Apr. 3, 1900, reel 22, frame 1043; MCT to MEG, Apr. 13, 1900, reel 22, frame 1064.

17. MCT to Rufus Jones, Apr. 23, 1900, letter book 19, p. 369, reel 95.

18. MCT to Mrs. Seth, copy in M. Carey Thomas letter book 15, Oct. 11, 1898, p. 208, reel 91; MCT to MEG, Oct. 10, 1898, reel 21, frame 638; MCT to Mr. Sandy L. Hurst, May 3, 1915, letter book 58, p. 117, reel 133.

19. MCT to George E. Barnett, Sept. 27, 1906, letter book 35, p. 95, reel 111.

20. MCT to Prof. John B. Clark, Sept. 27, 1906, letter book 35, p. 102, reel 111; MCT to Dr. A. M. Sakolski, Sept. 29, 1906, letter book 35, p. 109, reel 111; Oct. 19, 1906, Minutes of the Board of Trustees of Bryn Mawr College, vol. IV, Jan. 16, 1903–May 21, 1912, p. 273.

21. MCT to MEG, Mar. 12, 1902, reel 23, frame 1175.

22. The article makes no specific mention of Bryn Mawr College (Elizabeth L. Banes, "The American Negro and His Place," *The Nineteenth Century*, 46 [Sept. 1899]: 459–74). MCT to William H. Ward, Oct. 7, 1899, letter book 17, p. 424, reel 93. At the turn of the century, there was no "risk" that an African American might apply for a faculty position in a white college.

23. MCT to Mrs. George W. Kendrick, Jr., June 12, 1901, letter book 22, p. 480, reel 98; MCT to Mrs. George W. Kendrick, Jr., Sept. 23, 1901, letter book 23, p. 48, reel 99; MCT to Dear Friend, Feb. 17, 1904, letter book 29, p. 128, reel 105.

24. Jessie Redmon Fauset, *There Is Confusion* (Boni & Liveright, Inc., 1924), reprinted by Northeastern University Press, 1989; see the informative forward by Thadious M. Davis.

25. MCT to Georgiana R. Simpson, teacher of German, M. St. High School, Washington, D.C., May 2, 1906, letter book 34, p. 320, reel 110. A similar letter was sent to an unknown addressee, Mar. 30, 1910, letter book 45, p. 397, reel 120. The college did not accept its first African-American student until 1931, and even at that late date Thomas, no longer president, argued in opposition.

26. MCT to Evangeline Walker Andrews, Feb. 19, 1900, letter book 19, p. 93, reel 95; MCT to MEG, Dec. 9, 1905, reel 25, frame 456.

27. Bailey, *Good-bye*, p. 264.

28. Only ten seniors came to her senior at-home in 1899 (MCT to MEG, Apr. 19, 1899, reel 22, frame 110); Stein, *Fernhurst*, pp. 5–6, 10; Bailey, *Good-bye*, p. 263.

29. MCT to HMT, Feb. 21, 1916, reel 30, frame 290.

30. Oct. 24, 1905, Minutes of the Trustees of Bryn Mawr College, vol. IV, Jan. 16, 1903–May 21, 1912, p. 183; Apr. 20, 1906, Minutes of the Board of Trustees of Bryn Mawr College, vol. IV, Jan. 16, 1903–May 21, 1912, p. 250; MCT to MEG, May 18, 1906, reel 25, frame 521; MCT to MEG, June 8, 1906, reel 25, frame 590.

31. MCT to MEG, Apr. 14, 1905, reel 25, frame 376.

32. MCT to MEG, Apr. 10, 1900, reel 22, frame 1060; MCT to MEG, Mar. 31, 1905, reel 25, frame 345.

33. Feb. 17, 1905, Minutes of the Board of Trustees of Bryn Mawr College, vol. IV, Jan. 16, 1903–May 21, 1912, p. 151.

34. MCT to MEG, Dec. 9, 1905, reel 25, frame 456. Thomas gave Johnson the credit for thinking of the creation of a board of directors, but she actually proposed it to him (MCT to John G. Johnson, Feb. 17, 1905, letter book 31, p. 295, reel 107).

35. MCT to MEG, Oct. 18, 1900, reel 23, frame 102; MCT to MEG, Mar. 18, 1904, reel 25, frame 50.

36. Jan 11, 1906, Minutes of the Board of Trustees of Bryn Mawr College, vol. IV, Jan. 16, 1903–May 21, 1912, p. 227.

37. MCT to MEG, Dec. 4, 1901, reel 23, frame 929; MCT to HWS, Aug. 15, 1905, reel 29, frame 654. In a letter to Abby Kelly, head of the Bryn Mawr School, Thomas wrote, "Before I planned the library cloister I think that Miss Garrett and I must have measured forty cloisters in Spain, Italy, and England to get what seemed to us the right proportion" (MCT to Abby Kelly, Apr. 30, 1930, reel 27, frame 464).

38. MCT to MEG, June 15, 1906, reel 25, frame 615.

39. MCT to MEG, June 15, 1906, reel 25, frame 615.

40. MCT to Edward Bettle, Jr., Jan. 15, 1906, letter book 33, p. 397, reel 109.

41. MCT diary, 1906, Apr. 20, 1906, vol. 104, reel 6, frame 437; MCT to MEG, May 18, 1906, reel 25, frame 521; letter from H. Tatnall, May 18, 1906, Minutes of the Board of Trustees of Bryn Mawr College, vol. IV, Jan. 16, 1903–May 21, 1912, p. 265; Rufus Jones quoted in Elizabeth Gray Vining, *Friend of Life: The Biography of Rufus M. Jones* (Philadelphia: J. B. Lippincott Co., 1958), p. 188.

42. Letter from H. Tatnall, May 18, 1906, Minutes of the Board of Trustees of Bryn Mawr College, vol. IV, Jan. 16, 1903–May 21, 1912, p. 265; MCT to MEG, May 19, 1906, reel 25, frame 526; MCT, diary, 1906, vol. 104, May 18, 1906, reel 6, frame 452. Thomas identified Jones as Neilson's friend.

43. MCT to MEG, May 30, 1906, reel 25, frame 566; MCT to MEG, June 8, 1906, reel 25, frame 590.

44. "Some Instances of Neglect of College Interests Which Have Occurred Since October 1, 1901," Thomas office files, reel 170; interview with Rufus M. Jones, interviewer unknown, June 14, 1935, reel 172.

45. MCT to David Scull, Jr., Dec. 8, 1906, copybook I, p. 1, reel 147.

46. Jan. 24, 1907, Minutes of the Board of Trustees of Bryn Mawr College, vol. IV, Jan. 16, 1903–May 21, 1912, p. 289.

Chapter 19

1. In December 1899, Carey wrote to Mary that she was going to go to a play in Philadelphia. "I am going to try going occasionally to the opera and theatre and see what happens. My impression is the board is much more liberal on such subjects now" (MCT to MEG, Dec. 18, 1899, reel 22, frame 798).

2. Gertrude Stein, *Fernhurst*, in *Fernhurst, Q.E.D., and Other Early Writings*, ed. Donald Gallup (New York: Liveright, 1971), quotes pp. 37, 49.

3. MCT to MEG, Mar. 31, 1898, reel 21, frame 241.

4. Hutchins Hapgood, *A Victorian in the Modern World* (New York: Harcourt, Brace & Co., 1939), p. 165; Josiah Flynt Willard and Francis Walton, *The Powers That Prey* (New York: McClure, Phillips & Co., 1900); Alfred Hodder, *A Fight for the City* (New

York: The Macmillan Co., 1903); Alfred Hodder, *The Adversaries of the Sceptic or the Specious Present: A New Inquiry into Human Knowledge* (New York: The Macmillan Co., 1901).

5. MCT to MEG, Jan. 30, 1898, reel 21, frame 104; MCT to MEG, June 21, 1898, Alfred and Mary Gwinn Hodder Collection, box 51, folder 13, Princeton University; MCT to MMG, June 28, 1898, Alfred and Mary Gwinn Hodder Collection, box 51, folder 13, Princeton University (published with permission of the Manuscripts Division, Department of Rare Books and Special Collections, Princeton University Libraries).

6. MCT to MEG, Mar. 24, 1899, reel 21, frame 1049; MCT to MMG, July 11, 1899, Alfred and Mary Gwinn Hodder Collection, box 51, folder 14, PUL; MCT to MMG, Sept. 3, 1899, Alfred and Mary Gwinn Hodder Collection, box 51, folder 14, PUL.

7. MCT to HWS, Mar. 4, 1898, reel 29, frame 587.

8. MCT to MMG, July 18, 1899, Alfred and Mary Gwinn Hodder Collection, box 51, PUL.

9. MCT to MEG, Oct. 21, 1898, reel 21, frame 680; MCT to MMG, July 18, 1899, Alfred and Mary Gwinn Hodder Collection, box 51, PUL.

10. MCT to MMG, July 18, 1899, Alfred and Mary Gwinn Hodder Collection, box 51, PUL.

11. MMG to MCT, Aug. 1, 1899, Alfred and Mary Gwinn Hodder Collection, box 54, folder 6, PUL; MCT to MMG, Aug. 13, 1899, Alfred and Mary Gwinn Hodder Collection, box 51, PUL.

12. Edith Carpenter Thomas to MMG, Aug. 24, 1899, Alfred and Mary Gwinn Hodder Collection, box 66a, folder 3, PUL.

13. Helen Thomas to MMG, Sept. 23, 1899, Alfred and Mary Gwinn Hodder Collection, box 66a, folder 3, PUL; Helen Thomas to MMG, May 14, 1900, Alfred and Mary Gwinn Hodder Collection, box 66a, folder 4, PUL. Helen told Mamie what she really thought of Hannah: "She is so impossible to calculate upon and so unreasoning and so violent that I have a terror of her, really a panic terror." Deceiving her gave Helen "*Satanic pleasure.*"

14. MCT to MEG, Oct. 10, 1899, reel 22, frame 557.

15. MCT to HTF, Jan. 6, 1909, reel 14, frame 56.

16. MCT to MEG, June 4, 1900, reel 22, frame 1150.

17. MCT to MEG, June 5, 1900, reel 22, frame 1154; MCT to HTF, Jan. 6, 1909, reel 14, frame 56.

18. MMG, draft of will, June 11, 1900, Alfred and Mary Gwinn Hodder Collection, box 74, PUL.

19. MCT to HWS, July 11, 1900, reel 29, frame 607; MCT to HTF, Jan. 6, 1909, reel 14, frame 56; MCT to HWS, July 18, 1900, reel 29, frame 609. "Perdu" can be translated as lost; to "lie perdu" is to hide.

20. MCT to MMG, June 26, 1903, Alfred and Mary Gwinn Hodder Collection, box 51, PUL; MCT to MMG, Aug. 2, 1901, Alfred and Mary Gwinn Hodder Collection, box 51, PUL.

21. Alfred Hodder, *The New Americans* (New York: The Macmillan Co., 1901); MCT to MEG, Nov. 16, 1901, reel 23, frame 871; MCT to William James, Apr. 6, 1903, reel 27, frame 419.

22. Stein, *Fernhurst*, pp. 47–48; Hapgood, *A Victorian*, p. 222.

23. MCT to HWS, Jan. 8, 1903, reel 29, frame 629.

24. MCT to MEG, Apr. 11, 1899, reel 22, frame 68; MCT to MEG, May 29, 1899, reel 22, frame 321. Carey wrote to Mary that no one need detect a change in her appearance. "You can have made a high underwaist going to your neck to be filled in and no one could

possibly guess. I feel so thankful to have you safe nothing makes any difference, even an arm or a leg I could stand, but this is really no disfigurement at all, my darling" (MCT to MEG, June 28, 1899, reel 22, frame 456). Mary wore a prosthesis, for Carey wrote that she feared that "the cast iron" Mary was wearing was uncomfortable and was causing her distress.

25. MCT to MEG, Nov. 5, 1900, reel 23, frame 143.

26. MCT to MEG, Jan. 8, 1901, reel 23, frame 289; MCT to MEG, Jan. 13, 1901, reel 23, frame 308.

27. MCT to MEG, Feb. 23, 1901, reel 23, frame 440; MCT to MEG, Feb. 26, 1901, reel 23, frame 451.

28. MCT to MEG, Feb. 8, 1902, reel 23, frame 1103.

29. MCT to MEG, Sept. 25, 1902, reel 24, frame 168; MCT to MEG, Apr. 28, 1904, reel 25, frame 181.

30. MCT to MEG, Feb. 9, 1902, reel 23, frame 1108; MCT to MEG, Nov. 17, 1902, reel 24, frame 296.

31. MCT to MEG, Dec. 9, 1901, reel 23, frame 947.

32. MCT to MEG, Feb. 26, 1901, reel 23, frame 451; MCT to MEG, Mar. 2, 1901, reel 23, frame 479.

33. MCT to MEG, May 16, 1901, reel 23, frame 631.

34. James Thomas Flexner has written a moving joint biography of his parents and their relationship, *An American Saga: The Story of Helen Thomas and Simon Flexner* (Boston: Little, Brown & Co., 1984).

35. MCT to HWS, Mar. 11, 1894, reel 29, frame 557.

36. MCT to MEG, Sept. 24, 1902, reel 24, frame 164.

37. MCT to MEG, Jan. 18, 1903, reel 24, frame 395; MCT to MEG, Jan. 29, 1903, reel 24, frame 451; MCT to MEG, Feb. 12, 1903, reel 24, frame 509.

38. In some cases her correspondents were men, such as Rufus Jones, respected in other contexts for moral leadership.

39. Wedding announcement, reel 14, frame 55; James Flexner, *An American Saga*, p. 425.

40. MCT to MEG, Jan. 21, 1901, reel 23, frame 337; MCT to MEG, Jan. 20, 1902, reel 23, frame 1034; MCT to MEG, Nov. 15, 1902, reel 24, frame 291.

41. MCT to William S. Halsted, Mar. 28, 1904, reel 27, frame 195; MCT to MEG, Apr. 4, 1904, reel 25, frame 112.

42. MCT to MEG, Apr. 12, 1904, reel 25, frame 139; MCT to MEG, Apr. 17, 1904, reel 25, frame 159; MCT to MEG, Apr. 28, 1904, reel 25, frame 181. At the end of her life Mamie wrote that when Carey learned of her plan to marry, she proposed "that she should give up Mary Garrett and I should give up Mr. Hodder" (Mamie Gwinn Hodder, Reminiscences of M. Carey Thomas, Alfred and Mary Gwinn Hodder Collection, box 46, folder 1, PUL). Nothing in the 1904 record confirms this; and because it would have threatened Mary Garrett's gifts to Carey and to the college, it is difficult to believe that even if Carey said it, she meant it.

43. MCT to MMG, May 17, 1903, Alfred and Mary Gwinn Hodder Collection, box 51, PUL; MCT to MMG, May 22, 1904, Alfred and Mary Gwinn Hodder Collection, box 51, PUL.

44. MCT to MEG, May 30, 1904, reel 25, frame 237; MCT to MEG, May 31, 1904, reel 25, frame 242.

45. MCT to MMG, June 4, 1904, Alfred and Mary Gwinn Hodder Collection, box 51, PUL.

46. MCT diary, 1904, June 24, 1904, vol. 96, reel 5, frame 782. Carey was off by

two days. Actually, for reasons that are not known, she was carrying two diaries. In the other, she gave a few details, and a different date. On June 25, 1904, she wrote "Mamie married New York at Mrs. Rich Irwin by Father Huntington."

Chapter 20

1. MCT to HWS, Dec. 31, 1904, reel 29, frame 649. In Paris Alfred visited the rue de Fleurus, the ménage of Leo and Gertrude Stein; in Italy, Hutchins Hapgood (Leon Katz, "Introduction," Gertrude Stein, *Fernhurst, Q.E.D., and Other Early Writings*, ed. Donald Gallup [New York: Liveright, 1971], p. xxix).

2. MCT to MMG, Sept. 13, 1904, Alfred and Mary Gwinn Hodder Collection, box 51, Princeton University (published with permission of the Manuscripts Division, Department of Rare Books and Special Collections, Princeton University Libraries).

3. MMG to MCT, Oct. 16, 1904, reel 53, frame 262; MCT to MMG, Apr. 21, 1905, Alfred and Mary Gwinn Hodder Collection, box 51, PUL.

4. MCT to HWS, Dec. 31, 1904, reel 29, frame 649.

5. Tamara K. Hareven, "Jessie Donaldson Hodder," *Notable American Women, 1607–1950, A Biographical Dictionary*, ed. Edward T. James, 3 vols. (Cambridge, Mass.: The Belknap Press of Harvard University Press, 1971), vol. 2, pp. 197–99.

6. MCT to MMG, June 16, 1907, Alfred and Mary Gwinn Hodder Collection, box 51, PUL.

7. MCT to HTF, Jan. 6, 1909, reel 14, frame 56.

8. MCT to HTF, Jan. 6, 1909, reel 14, frame 56.

9. MCT to MMG, Aug. 13, 1907, Alfred and Mary Gwinn Hodder Collection, box 51, PUL.

10. Mary Berenson to Hannah Whitall Smith, Dec. 29, 1908; Mary Berenson diary, Jan. 1, 1909, Berenson Archives, I Tatti. After discussing their riotous, alcohol-filled nights, Hutchins Hapgood suggested that Hodder, like Willard, died of "too much bachelor life" (Hutchins Hapgood, *A Victorian in the Modern World* [New York: Harcourt, Brace and Company, 1939], p. 152).

11. MCT to HTF, Jan. 6, 1909, reel 14, frame 56.

12. Mamie Gwinn Hodder, Reminiscences of M. Carey Thomas, Alfred and Mary Gwinn Hodder Collection, box 46, folder 1, PUL.

13. Logan Pearsall Smith, "The Friendly City: Boyhood and Youth," *The Atlantic Monthly*, 160 (1937): 565–72; Mamie Gwinn Hodder, Reminiscences of M. Carey Thomas, Alfred and Mary Gwinn Hodder Collection, box 46, folder 1, PUL.

14. MCT to HWS, Aug. 15, 1905, typescript copy, reel 29, frame 654.

15. "Running Expenses of the Deanery," reel 168, frame 660.

16. Memorandum, reel 168, frame 683; MCT to HWS, Aug. 15, 1905, typescript copy, reel 29, frame 654.

17. MCT to MEG, May 6, 1906, reel 25, frame 499. Thomas remained involved in the most minute details of the Bryn Mawr School. For example, in 1912 she proofread with nitpicking attention the school's *Circular* ("Notes on School," 1912, Bryn Mawr School Archives).

18. MCT to MEG, May 30, 1906, reel 25, frame 559; MCT to MEG, June 8, 1906, reel 25, frame 590.

19. MCT to MEG, Mar. 17, 1908, reel 25, frame 773.

20. MCT to MEG, Apr. 14, 1912, reel 25, frame 1182; Mary Berenson to HWS, Dec. 16, 1908, Berenson Archives, I Tatti.

21. MEG to MCT, Sept. 3, 1909, reel 51, frame 496. On one journey abroad the

conflict became so severe that they briefly went separate ways (MCT to MEG, Dec. 24, 1910, reel 25, frame 993).

22. MCT to HWS, Jan. 27, 1910, reel 29, frame 736; Mary Berenson to HWS, Dec. 16, 1908, Dec. 11, 1908, Dec. 11, 1908 "private," Berenson Archives, I Tatti.

23. MCT to HWS, Aug. 11, 1909, reel 29, frame 717; MCT to HWS, Aug. 15, 1905, typescript copy, reel 29, frame 654.

24. MCT to HWS, July 3, 1907, continued July 14, 1907, reel 29, frame 664. Reilly's title had galled Maddison, and she threatened to resign. Thomas promised to continue to press the directors to give Maddison the title of dean of faculty, and begged her, "Do not desert me if you can help it" (MCT to Isabel Maddison, May, 27, 1907, copybook I, p. 36, reel 147).

25. Bryn Mawr College, "Brief Financial Statement," 1909.

26. MCT to JDR, Jr., Mar. 6, 1907, and JDR, Jr. to MCT, Mar. 15, 1907, Rockefeller Family Papers, Record Group 2, Educational Interests, box 54, Bryn Mawr College folder, Rockefeller Archive Center, North Tarrytown, N.Y.

27. MCT to MEG, Dec. 7, 1909, reel 25, frame 916; MCT to HWS, Jan. 27, 1910, reel 29, frame 736; MCT to Ray Costelloe Strachey, Mar. 8, 1910, typescript copy, reel 29, frame 870. Thomas wrote to Hannah Smith, "I felt as if I must do this before I died" (MCT to HWS, Mar. 15, 1909, reel 29, frame 704).

28. MCT to MEG, Dec. 10, 1909, reel 25, frame 923; MCT to HWS, Jan. 27, 1910, reel 29, frame 736; Minutes of the Board of Directors of the Trustees of Bryn Mawr College, May 5, 1910, adjourned meeting, vol. I, Dec. 7, 1906–Apr. 21, 1911, pp. 307–16.

29. MCT to HWS, June 3, 1910, reel 29, frame 745.

30. *Bryn Mawr College Twenty-Fifth Anniversary*, Oct. 21 and 22, 1910, p. 20; MCT to Anna Rhoads, Oct. 23, 1910, Bryn Mawr College letter book 46, following p. 385, reel 121.

31. MCT to HWS, Dec. 9, 1910, reel 29, frame 752.

32. Cornelia Meigs, *What Makes a College? A History of Bryn Mawr* (New York: The Macmillan Co. 1956), pp. 84–88. The Thorne School reopened in 1952 as a laboratory school for young children (Phebe Anna Thorne Collection, inventory. Summary note, Bryn Mawr Archives).

33. Rita Heller, "Blue Collars and Bluestockings: The Bryn Mawr Summer School for Women Workers, 1921–1938," in *Sisterhood and Solidarity: Workers' Education for Women, 1914–1984*, ed. Joyce L. Kornbluh and Mary Frederickson (Philadelphia: Temple University Press, 1984), p. 113.

34. A most curious—because it is largely positive—example of Thomas' attention to Jewishness came in her recommendation of a Bryn Mawr alumna for a Wellesley College position: "She is a Jewess. She was very able here and was one of a little group of excellent students, closely associated together in a friendly group, very nice socially, who specialized in English and economics and law." She had done "brilliantly" in Columbia graduate work. She would be good for a temporary position, but for a permanent one, "it would depend upon your attitude toward Hebrews in your faculty. If anyone could overcome such prejudices as may exist she should do so because she is really so able" (MCT to Ellen Fitz Pendleton, May 6, 1911, letter book 47).

35. MCT to MEG, Sept. 26, 1900, reel 23, frame 37; MCT to MEG, Sept. 29, 1901, reel 23, frame 762; MCT to David H. Tennent, July 18, 1916, letter book 61, p. 59, reel 136. An example of her consultation with others is the inquiry, in 1909, to Ira Remsen of Johns Hopkins of whether the man he recommended was a Jew and her stated preference not to appoint Jews in faculty positions (MCT to Ira Remsen, May 19, 1909, letter book 43, reel 118, p. 335).

36. MCT to MEG, Nov. 8. 1903, reel 24, frame 1030.

37. Mark H. Haller, *Eugenics: Hereditarian Attitudes in American Thought* (New Brunswick, N.J.: Rutgers University Press, 1963); MCT circular letter, January 14, 15, 1911, reel 33, frame 125. In the summer of 1897 Carey wrote to Mary from Cadiz, "I had never seen Moors before or any thing stranger than Turks and a few Armenians and, of course, Negroes from the interior, wild men, snake charmers, Negroes with huge hats and scanty dirty white togas and all the infinite variety of colour of face and raiment" (MCT to MEG, July 1, 1897, reel 20, frame 705).

38. MCT, circular letter, July 23, 1915, reel 33, frame 174.

39. MCT to Mary Worthington, Dec. 22, 1911, reel 32, frame 1057. Mary Worthington did face what must have been a painful rule, that while she was at college she could not have her father visit her. Carey wrote to Mary Garrett in 1907, "Some one telephoned me she saw Tom Worthington on his way to college from the station. I shall tell Mary while I am putting her through college she *cannot* have him here—If she does she must leave" (MCT to MEG, May 1, 1907, reel 25, frame 744).

40. Woodrow Wilson, "What Is a College For?" *Scribner's Magazine*, 46 (1909): 570–77; Conference of the Academic Committee of the Bryn Mawr College Alumnae Association and the President and Dean of the College, Jan. 29, 1909, Minutes of the Academic Committee, vol. 1, 1894–1911, Bryn Mawr College Archives.

41. MCT to HWS, July 5, 1908, reel 29, frame 691.

42. MCT to MEG, Oct. 10, 1900, reel 23, frame 78.

43. Ellen Deborah Ellis, "Memorabilia: M. Carey Thomas," pp. 1, 11, typescript copy in Bryn Mawr College Archives. In Tacoma, Washington, I was told the story of a Bryn Mawr senior who came to Thomas' party for graduating seniors dressed in a new pink frock. As she responded in turn to the general question of her future, put to all guests, that she was to be married, Thomas replied, "Oh, you poor little pink thing!"

44. Address to Students at the Opening of the Academic Year 1899–1900, Oct. 10, 1899, typescript, Bryn Mawr College Archives.

45. Alice G. Howland, "Memories of M. Carey Thomas," typescript, Bryn Mawr College Archives.

46. Quotes from "Address after Easter," Apr. 7, 1904, Bryn Mawr College Archives.

47. Chapel Addresses, Thanksgiving 1905, and Jan. 10, 1913, Bryn Mawr College Archives. In 1910 she requested that the pamphlet from the Pennsylvania Society for the Prevention of Social Diseases be sent anonymously to all seniors (MCT to Robert N. Willson, Jr., Jan. 10, 1910, letter book 45, p. 20, reel 120). For a full discussion of Thomas' feminism, see chapter 21.

48. "The purpose of the College," Notes for Commencement address at Bryn Mawr College, June 6, 1907 (Bryn Mawr College Archives), abridged, in Barbara Cross, ed., *The Educated Woman in America*, Classics in Education No. 25 (New York: Teachers College Press of Columbia University, 1965); M. Carey Thomas, Chapel Address, Feb. 27, 1913, typescript, Bryn Mawr College Archives.

49. Agnes Goldman Sanborn interview by Florence Newman Trefethen, Nov. 18, 1987, typescript, p. 140, Bryn Mawr College Oral History project (Bryn Mawr College Archives).

50. Elizabeth Shepley Sergeant, "Portrait of a Feminist," reel 76, frames 916–18.

Chapter 21

1. MCT to MEG, Aug. 1, 1892, reel 16, frame 1039; MCT to MEG, Feb. 16, 1898, reel 21, frame 152.

2. MCT to MEG, May 1, 1899, reel 22, frame 168; MCT to MEG, May 2, 1899, reel 22, frame 172.

3. MCT to Ida Porter-Boyer, Sept. 25, 1902, letter book 25; MCT to HWS, Jan. 8, 1903, typescript copy, reel 29, frame 629.

4. Ida Husted Harper, *The Life and Work of Susan B. Anthony*, 3 vols. (Indianapolis: The Hollenbeck Press, 1908), 3: 1253–54.

5. *Association for Maintaining the American Women's Table at the Zoological Station at Naples and for Promoting Scientific Research by Women, 1898–1903*. The prize's first recipient was Florence R. Sabin of the Johns Hopkins medical school.

6. Ada Comstock, speech at Thomas' retirement dinner, *Bryn Mawr College, June 8, 1922*, pp. 32–33; Isabel Maddison, *A Preliminary Statistical Study of Certain Women College Graduates* (Bryn Mawr: privately printed, 1917).

7. MCT to MEG, Jan. 17, 1892, reel 16, frame 790.

8. MCT to HWS, July 1, 1887, reel 29, frame 533.

9. M. Carey Thomas, "The Future of Women in Independent Study and Research," *Publications of the Association of Collegiate Alumnae*, Series III, no. 6 (Feb. 1903): 13.

10. MCT, "Future of Women," pp. 13–14. Two contemporary arguments were not in Thomas' lexicon. She did not argue that women failed to get recognition for the work that they accomplished, nor did she argue that women's culture was equally valid. She believed that the existing standard for achievement was both fair and appropriate.

11. MCT, "Future of Women," pp. 14–15.

12. MCT, "Future of Women," pp. 15, 16.

13. MCT, "Future of Women," p. 16.

14. MCT, "Future of Women," pp. 17–18.

15. MCT, "Future of Women," pp. 18–19.

16. M. Carey Thomas, "Present Tendencies in Women's College and University Education," *Educational Review*, 35 (Jan. 1908): 83, 83–84. "Intellectual renunciation" is a slip: Thomas meant rather the renunciation of normal family life in order to pursue a life of intellect. Sonya Kovalevsky (1850–1891) was a Russian mathematician.

17. MCT, "Present Tendencies," 84, 84–85.

18. MCT, "Present Tendencies," p. 85.

19. MCT to HWS, Feb. 12, 1908, reel 29, frame 682.

20. MCT to Thomas E. Keating, Oct. 28, 1902, letter book 25; MCT to HWS, Jan. 8, 1903, typescript copy, reel 29, frame 629.

21. MCT to Mr. [John G.] Johnson, Nov. 17, 1913, letter book 53; Alice G. Howland, "Memories of M. Carey Thomas," pp. 2–3, Bryn Mawr College Archives.

22. M. Carey Thomas, "Dr. Thomas on Woman's Ballot," Political Equality Series, National American Woman Suffrage Association, vol. 2, no. 2 (1909), n.p.

23. Aileen S. Kraditor, *The Ideas of the Woman Suffrage Movement, 1890–1920* (New York: Columbia University Press, 1965), pp. 123–218.

24. Harper, *Susan B. Anthony*, 3: 1393–95, 1398.

25. Harper, *Susan B. Anthony*, 3: 1399–1401; MCT to HWS, Aug. 11, 1909, reel 29, frame 717. Well-known donors included Mrs. Russell Sage of New York, Mrs. Quincy Shaw of Boston, and Mrs. Henry Wilmarth of Chicago. Mr. and Mrs. Isaac Clothier, Dr. Anna Sharpless, and Miss Ella Mench were among the Philadelphia contributors.

26. MCT, "Woman's Ballot"; MCT to HWS, Feb. 12, 1908, reel 29, frame 682.

27. Eleanor Flexner, *Century of Struggle: The Woman's Rights Movement in the United States* (New York: Atheneum, 1971), pp. 234–35; MCT to HWS, Nov. 14, 1908, reel 29, frame 698.

28. MCT to HWS, July 5, 1908, reel 29, frame 691; MCT to HWS, Mar. 15, 1909, reel 29, frame 704.

29. "Suggestions for Work for College Chapters," reel 174, frame 334; Barbara Miller Solomon, *In the Company of Educated Women: A History of Women and Higher Education in America* (New Haven: Yale University Press, 1985), pp. 111–12; *The History of Woman Suffrage*, ed. Ida Husted Harper (New York: National American Woman Suffrage Association, 1922), 5: 660–64.

30. MCT to Anna Howard Shaw, June 13, 1914, reel 29, frame 4; Flexner, *Century of Struggle*, p. 362, footnote 14. As Simon Flexner's niece, Eleanor Flexner knew Thomas personally; she cites a 1911 letter from Carrie Chapman Catt for the nickname. Unlike the more than twenty references to Thomas in volume 5 of Harper's history, Thomas' name does not appear in the index of Kraditor, *Ideas of the Woman Suffrage Movement*, or in more recent histories of the movement.

31. M. Carey Thomas, "A New Fashioned Argument for Woman Suffrage," Address, College Evening of the NAWSA, Oct. 17, 1908, reprinted 1911, pp. 7, 4.

32. M. Carey Thomas, "The College Women of the Present and Future," *McClure's* (1901). In making her argument, Thomas accepts certain elements of eugenics but rejects others. She agrees with the division of the world into racial categories and the superiority of the Anglo-Saxon. What she seeks to demonstrate is that female education does not pose a threat to the race. Her effort clarifies that Thomas did not passively receive scientific wisdom, but sought ways to refute it when it challenged her commitments to women. That she never questioned her era's racial thinking but allowed it to buttress further her anti-Semitism, hostility to African Americans, and nativism cannot, therefore, be simply attributed to her time and place.

33. MCT, "New Fashioned Argument," p. 21.

34. MCT, Chapel Address, Christmas 1907, Bryn Mawr College Archives.

35. MCT, Chapel Address, 1913, Bryn Mawr College Archives. Salter was a philosopher and Ethical Culture lecturer.

Chapter 22

1. MCT to MEG, Apr. 4, 1912, reel 25, frame 1110; MCT to MEG, Apr. 18, 1912, reel 25, frame 1193; MCT to William S. Halsted, May 12, 1912, reel 27, frame 212.

2. MCT to MEG, Apr. 27, 1913, reel 26, frame 297.

3. MCT to Anna Howard Shaw, June 13, 1914, reel 29, frame 4; MCT to William Welch, Sept. 25, 1922, reel 32, frame 765; MCT to HMT, Aug. 11, 1914, reel 30, frame 244; MCT to HMT, Aug. 15, 1914, reel 30, frame 252. During Mary's illness, Carey became particularly fond of Dr. Halsted. She wrote him in 1913, "Perhaps you will let me venture to tell you that your friendship is one of the nicest things that has happened to Miss Garrett and me since we made the friends of our girlhood" (MCT to William Halsted, Dec. 25, 1913, reel 27, frame 220).

4. MCT to Rufus Jones, Apr. 4, 1915, box 14, folder "letters to, N–Z, 1915," Rufus Jones Collection, Quaker Collection, Haverford College; MCT diary entry, Apr. 3, 1915, five-year diary, 1915+, vol. 132, reel 7, frame 1394.

5. MCT to Rufus Jones, Apr. 4, 1915, box 14, folder "letters to, N–Z, 1915," Rufus Jones Collection, Quaker Collection, Haverford College; MCT to HMT, June 25, 1915, reel 30, frame 266.

6. MCT to HMT, July 23, 1915, reel 30, frame 269; MCT to William S. Halsted,

Nov. 26, 1915, reel 27, frame 225; MCT to HMT, Apr. 3, 1916, reel 30, frame 296; MCT, Autobiographical Notes, reel 87, frame 1165.

7. Thomas had never thought highly of Crandall's executive capacity. In 1907 she had written, "Speaking frankly—as I know you would wish me to speak—neither Miss Donnelly nor I think that you have precisely the qualities needed to take charge of the freshman composition work" (MCT to Regina Crandall, Apr. 26, 1907, letter book 36, p. 432, reel 112).

8. MCT to Lucy Donnelly, Jan. 29, 1916, letter book 59, p. 359, reel 134. Crandall later received an endowed professorship in composition that freed her from teaching required courses to teach only advanced and graduate ones. As the terms of the gift were being worked out, Thomas insisted that the donors could not bind the college to select a particular recipient of the chair, but she also made it clear that Crandall would receive it.

9. Professors to MCT, Nov. 1, 1915, "File on Faculty Uprising, probably from Henry Nevill Sanders" (found after MCT Papers were microfilmed), Bryn Mawr College Archives.

10. MCT to Gonzalez Lodge, Feb. 19, 1906, letter book 33, p. 491, reel 109.

11. MCT to Lucy Donnelly, Jan. 29, 1916, letter book 59, p. 359, reel 134.

12. H. B. Brougham to Mrs. Charles McLean Andrews, Mar. 16, 1916, Charles McLean Andrews Papers, Manuscripts and Archives, Yale University, New Haven, Conn. The letter was sent to members of the faculty, many alumnae, and the alumnae directors, among others (copy, "File on Faculty Uprising," Bryn Mawr College Archives).

13. "Brief reply prepared by M. Carey Thomas . . . to the letter sent out by Mr. H. B. Brougham," Mar. 29, 1916, "File on Faculty Uprising," Bryn Mawr College Archives.

14. H. B. Brougham to Mrs. Charles McLean Andrews, Apr. 6, 1916, Charles McLean Andrews Papers, Manuscripts and Archives, Yale University.

15. Professors to MCT, Mar. 29, 1916, "File on Faculty Uprising," Bryn Mawr College Archives.

16. Notes of a meeting of professors and a committee of directors, Apr. 10, 1916, "File on Faculty Uprising," Bryn Mawr College Archives.

17. Lucy Donnelly was on a year-long sabbatical in Asia, to her immense relief, as she wrote Helen Flexner, for she was caught between her strong tie to a woman whom she admired and her sense that Thomas was in the wrong. She and Flexner had hoped that Thomas would improve after Mary Garrett's death. Donnelly now feared that "she is likely to be more unrestrained without Miss Garrett to hold her back—to act as a brake—in certain ways as she strengthened her in others." Had she independent money, Donnelly would resign, "for I do not believe there is any saving Miss Thomas" (Lucy Donnelly to Helen Thomas Flexner, Apr. 21, 1916, Simon Flexner Papers, American Philosophical Society Library, Philadelphia, Pa.). A month later, after she learned the full extent of the newspaper war, Donnelly took a more balanced view. Although she blamed Thomas for the public scandal and worried that it would make her more frantic to "popularize courses instead of running the college wisely and quietly," what was done could not be helped, and she would remember Thomas' "great virtues and abilities." Donnelly concluded, "I love and admire her so much, it is a personal pain to me when she puts herself in the wrong" (Lucy Donnelly to HTF, May 13, 1916, Simon Flexner Papers, APS).

18. MCT to Abby Kelly, May 3, 1930, reel 27, frame 470.

19. Louis Cons, Apr. 22, 1916, translation, "File on Faculty Uprising," Bryn Mawr College Archives.

20. "Bryn Mawr Alumnae Inaugurate Plans for Reform," *Public Ledger*, Apr. 12, 1916.

21. Evangeline Walker Andrews to the editor of the *Public Ledger*, Mar. 22, 1916,

typescript, Charles McLean Andrews Papers, Manuscripts and Archives, Yale University; "Bryn Mawr Alumnae Inaugurate Plans for Reform, *Public Ledger*, Apr. 12, 1916.

22. "Bryn Mawr Alumnae Inaugurate Plans for Reform," *Public Ledger*, Apr. 12, 1916.

23. "Committee Sits on Case against Bryn Mawr Head," *Public Ledger*, Apr. 13, 1916.

24. Rufus M. Jones, *The Trail of Life in the Middle Years* (New York: The Macmillan Co., 1934), p. 206, 207; interview with Rufus M. Jones, interviewer unknown, June 14, 1935, reel 172; May 19, 1916, stated, Minutes of the Board of Directors of the Trustees of Bryn Mawr College, vol. II, 1912–1940. Jones' biography recounts the many times that Thomas called at his home. In anticipating her arrival, Jones would be apprehensive. His mood on her departure would depend on the success or failure of their talk (Elizabeth Gray Vining, *Friend of Life: The Biography of Rufus M. Jones* [Philadelphia: J. B. Lippincott Co., 1958], p. 190).

25. May 19, 1916, stated, Minutes of the Board of Directors of the Trustees of Bryn Mawr College, vol. II, 1912–1940. Professors with indefinite terms could be removed only after a joint conference between the faculty committee on appointments and a committee of five directors, presided over by the president, made a written report of its findings to the full board. Professors had a right to a fair hearing and "charges against them stated in writing."

26. MCT to HTF, Apr. 18, 1916, Simon Flexner Papers, APS; MCT to Marion Edwards Park, Feb. 11, 1933, reel 28, frame 658. Thomas did get some chance for revenge. In 1917 she attempted to write out of the record Evangeline Andrews' contribution to the college in approaching John D. Rockefeller (MCT to Elizabeth B. Kirkbride, Feb. 9, 1917, reel 27, frame 575).

27. Quoted in a newspaper report on 1916 commencement, entitled "President Jokes over College Row," clipping, "Press Attacks on MCT" folder, Autobiography, reel 75, box 1.

Chapter 23

1. M. Carey Thomas, "Address by President Thomas at the Opening of the College, Oct. 4, 1916," *Alumnae Quarterly*, vol. 10, no. 3 (Nov. 1916): 101.

2. MCT, "Opening of the College," p. 102.

3. MCT, "Opening of the College," p. 103.

4. MCT, "Opening of the College," p. 104.

5. Kenneth M. Luchmerer, *Genetics and American Society: A Historical Appraisal* (Baltimore: The Johns Hopkins University Press, 1972), pp. 7–33.

6. Mary E. Garrett will, inventories, list of investments, Register of Wills for Baltimore City, photocopy, Bryn Mawr College Archives. Thomas later stated that the assessors appraised the contents of the Deanery at roughly 27 percent of their value, $30,000 rather than $110,000 (MCT to HTF, Sept. 5, 1928, Simon Flexner Papers, American Philosophical Society Library, Philadelphia, Pa.).

7. MEG will, Feb. 27, 1908, Bryn Mawr College Archives, reel 171, frame 196.

8. MCT to Mary Berenson, July 20, 1916, Berenson Archive, I Tatti.

9. D. K. Este Fisher to MCT, Apr. 6, 1917, reel 39, frame 699; MCT to James Carey III, Oct. 25, 1929, reel 13, frame 466; MCT to Mary Berenson, July 20, 1916, Berenson Archive, I Tatti.

10. MCT to John G. Johnson, Apr. 20, 1915, reel 27, frame 423.

11. MCT tax returns, 1918; work sheet for tax returns, 1919, Bryn Mawr College Archives; MCT to Alys Russell, Apr. 21, 1921, Berenson Archive, I Tatti. The income

figures suggest that the income-producing assets of the Garrett estate (i.e., not the three houses) were worth roughly $1 million. A yearly income of $60,000 in 1918 is comparable to one of $600,000 in 1994.

12. Edith Finch, *Carey Thomas of Bryn Mawr* (New York: Harper & Brothers, 1947), p. 268.

13. MCT circular letter, Nov. 9, 1919, reel 33, frame 353; MCT circular letter, June 20, 1920, reel 33, frame 410. I have not tended to take Thomas' socialist pronouncements very seriously. They were generally made after reading a book and led to no further thought or any political action.

14. MCT circular letter, Sept. 29–Oct. 9, 1919, reel 33, frame 328; MCT to HTF and LD Aug. 5, 1919, Simon Flexner Papers, APS; MCT to Helen Taft Manning, Aug. 18, 1920, reel 28, frame 64. Helen had married Frederick Manning by that point.

15. M. Carey Thomas, "The Mediterranean Basin: Impressions of a Sentimental Traveller," *The Bryn Mawr Alumnae Bulletin*, Jan., Feb., Apr., 1921, quote from Part III (Apr. 1921): 7.

16. MCT, "Mediterranean Basin," Part II (Feb. 1921): 6; Part III (Apr. 1921): 9; Part III (Apr. 1921): 7.

17. MCT, "Mediterranean Basin," Part II (Feb. 1921): 7; Part III (Apr. 1921); 10–11.

18. MCT to Dean Hilda W. Smith, Nov. 2, 1920, letter book 66, p. 494, reel 141.

19. She won the fellowship over Georgiana Goddard King, much to Thomas' displeasure, for she felt that King was "the ablest student we have ever had" (MCT to MEG, Mar. 17, 1897, reel 20, frame 423).

20. In 1917, for example, she suggested that the Presidential Salary Fund be used for a new service road (MCT to Arthur H. Thomas, July 15, 1917, reel 30, frame 13).

21. MCT to HMT, Aug. 11, 1914, reel 30, frame 244; MCT to Rufus Jones, May 19, 1915, box 14, folder "letters to, N–Z, 1915," Rufus Jones Collection, Quaker Collection, Haverford College; MCT to Dr. Carolina Marcial Dorado, July 20, 1918, letter book 63, p. 394, reel 138.

22. MCT to Josephine Carey Thomas, Dec. 18, 1917, reel 30, frame 994; MCT to William S. Halsted, Nov. 25, 1917, reel 27, frame 240; MCT, "How Shall We Educate Our Children in Patriotism," scraps of speech, MCT Speeches and Articles, Politics file, Bryn Mawr College Archives.

23. MCT, "President M. Carey Thomas of Bryn Mawr College Tells Why Women Should Vote for Cox" and "President M. Carey Thomas of Bryn Mawr College Tells Why Women Should Vote against Harding," Speeches and Articles, Politics file, Bryn Mawr College Archives; MCT to editors of *Baltimore Sun*, Oct. 29, 1920, reel 13, frame 97.

24. Cornelia Meigs, *What Makes a College? A History of Bryn Mawr* (New York: The Macmillan Co., 1956), pp. 112–14; Ellen Condliffe Lagemann, *Private Power for the Public Good: A History of the Carnegie Foundation for the Advancement of Teaching* (Middletown, Conn.: Wesleyan University Press, 1983), pp. 148–53, 168–73.

25. MCT to Helen Taft Manning, Apr. 17, 1920, reel 28, frame 44.

26. MCT to Helen Taft Manning, Sept. 1, 1919, reel 28, frame 22; MCT to Helen Taft Manning, July 18, 1920, reel 28, frame 64.

27. MCT to Helen Taft Manning, Apr. 17, 1920, reel 28, frame 44; MCT, "Address at Opening of the Second Summer School for Women Workers in Industry at Bryn Mawr College, June 14, 1922," Bryn Mawr College Archives, reel 179, address begins frame 732; Rita Heller, "Blue Collars and Bluestockings: The Bryn Mawr Summer School for Women Workers, 1921–1938," in *Sisterhood and Solidarity: Workers' Education for Women, 1914–1984*, ed. Joyce L. Kornbluh and Mary Frederickson (Philadelphia: Temple University Press, 1984), p. 111; Hilda Worthington Smith, *Opening Vistas in Workers' Education*

(Washington, D.C., 1978), pp. 106–7. Thomas' vision in Morocco is reminiscent of Jane Addams' attribution of the origin of Hull House to her disgust at a bullfight in Spain.

28. Heller, "Blue Collars," pp. 109–29; Smith, *Opening Vistas*, pp. 113–17, quote from p. 115.

29. MCT to William S. Halsted, Dec. 19, 1915, reel 27, frame 232. During the war years Thomas' public statements tended to mute her commitment to women. Working to evoke the patriotic response of mixed audiences of men and women affected statements on education. A 1918 article on "Coeducation," for example, was in this vein, insisting that educating women and men together was the national trend that would become universal in all "civilized nations" (M. Carey Thomas, "A Statistical Study of Coeducation in the United States," *Encyclopedia Americana*, new edition, reprint [written June 1, 1918]).

30. MCT circular letter, Sept. 1, 1918, reel 33, frame 270; MCT circular letter, Nov. 9, 1919, reel 33, frame 353.

31. MCT, Chapel Address, 1913, Bryn Mawr College Archives; M. Carey Thomas, "The Woman's Programme," May 18, 1921, *Bryn Mawr Alumnae Bulletin* (June 1921): 7–17.

32. MCT to Bishop William Lawrence, Dec. 17, 1912, letter book 50; M. Carey Thomas, "The Next President of Bryn Mawr College," *The Bryn Mawr Alumnae Bulletin* (May 1921), reprint.

33. Quote from Elizabeth Gray Vining, *Friend of Life: The Biography of Rufus M. Jones* (Philadelphia: J. B. Lippincott Co., 1958), p. 191.

34. MCT to Marion Edwards Park, Nov. 13, 1922, Park Family Papers, Manuscripts and Archives, Yale University.

35. MCT to Arthur H. Thomas, Feb. 27, 1922, reel 30, frame 41; Alys Russell to M[ary Berenson], Jan. 19, 1922, verso of MCT to Alys Russell, Jan. 16, 1922, H. W. Smith Papers, The Lilly Library, Indiana University, Bloomington, Ind.; MCT to HMT, Feb. 26, 1922, reel 30, frame 395.

36. Louise Brownell Saunders, speech at Thomas' retirement dinner, *Bryn Mawr College, June 8, 1922*, pp. 3–4, reel 181; Helen Taft Manning, speech at Thomas' retirement dinner, p. 17; Ada Comstock, speech at Thomas' retirement dinner, p. 33.

37. Paul Shorey, speech at Thomas' retirement dinner, pp. 35–36. Arthur Twining Hadley was a president of Yale; William Rainey Harper, of the University of Chicago.

38. M. Carey Thomas, speech at Thomas' retirement dinner, pp. 41–43.

Chapter 24

1. MCT to HMT, Aug. 31, 1922, reel 30, frame 441. About the Johns Hopkins degree Thomas wrote to William Halsted, "I should rather have it than any other degree in the world" (MCT to William Halsted, June 11, 1922, reel 27, frame 253).

2. There is no statement to clarify why, after all the years of irreligion, Thomas chose this moment to resign. She had remained because of her position at Bryn Mawr, but that had not claimed her for five years. Perhaps it was her brother Harry's death, breaking the last primary tie to her father. She wrote little about religion in these years, except to restate throughout the notes for her autobiography that her liberation came with freedom from it.

3. MCT to Grace Thomas Worthington, July 3, 1930, reel 32, frame 967; MCT to HMT, Jr., Apr. 26, 1930, reel 30, frame 180; HMT, Jr., to Simon Flexner, Dec. 30, 1930, M. Carey Thomas Papers, Box 002-5, Alan Mason Chesney Medical Archives, Johns Hopkins University School of Medicine.

4. MCT to HMT, Sr., Mar. 31, 1922, reel 30, frame 402; MCT to Harold Worthington, June 29, 1923, reel 32, frame 929.

5. MCT to Helen Taft Manning, Aug. 6, 1929, reel 28, frame 176; MCT to HTF, May 16, 1932, reel 14, frame 224; MCT to HTF, Aug. 18, 1935, reel 14, frame 509.

6. MCT to HTF, Nov. 13, 1928, Simon Flexner Papers, American Philosophical Society Library, Philadelphia, Pa. Thomas wrote that Ray Strachey had first called *Orlando* "gold"; Thomas added that Edith said it was a "plate of rubies and diamonds and pearls."

7. The United States of America passport, MCT Papers, reel 81, box 1, file "Important documents"; Elizabeth Shepley Sergeant, "Notes for a Portrait of M. Carey Thomas," reel 76, beginning frame 961. The materials that Sergeant left include a short, polished portrait of Thomas' younger years, "Portrait of a Feminist," intended for a magazine such as *Harper's*; the rough draft of an article on Thomas' professional career; notes from the oral interview, partially annotated by Lucy Donnelly; and some observations Sergeant made as she thought about Thomas.

8. Frances Hand (Mrs. Learned) to Elizabeth Shepley Sergeant, July 12, reel 76, box 2, Bryn Mawr College Archives; Sergeant, "Notes for a Portrait of M. Carey Thomas," reel 76, frame 961.

9. Lanman's recollections are found in Esther Lanman Cushman, "M. Carey Thomas and Her Radcliffe A.B.," typescript, Feb. 17, 1968, Thomas Biographical File, Bryn Mawr College Archives.

10. Katie Doyle Gaffney interview by Marjorie Housepian Dobkin, Feb. 4, 1975, Dobkin materials, Bryn Mawr College Archives; MCT to HMT, July 7, 1922, reel 30, frame 432.

11. Gaffney interview, Dobkin materials, Bryn Mawr College Archives. The housekeepers were middle-class women who supervised the servants.

12. Harold Worthington interview with Millicent McIntosh and Marjorie Housepian Dobkin, Dobkin materials, Bryn Mawr College Archives.

13. In 1902 Thomas wrote to Rufus Jones that she would have put in the minutes the expectation that the president resign both from the office and the presidency at the same time. Although not legally binding, it would be "morally binding and in my case I should, of course, act on it even were there no minute because I really think it is the right precedent to establish for the College" (MCT to Rufus Jones, Oct. 16, 1902, Folder "letters to, 1902," Rufus Jones Collection, Quaker Collection, Haverford College). The aborted trip to fill the art position is documented in Thomas' papers by a letter to the Harvard Appointment Bureau, Mar. 20, 1925, requesting appointments, followed by a cable of Mar. 21, 1925, canceling the letter (MCT to Harvard Appointment Bureau, Mar. 20, 1925, reel 27, frame 300; cable, Mar. 21, 1925, reel 27, frame 302). Thomas' Bryn Mawr College role is best documented in her correspondence with Marion Edwards Park, reel 28, frames 364–774.

14. In 1927, out of respect to Garrett's memory, Thomas sought to close the Bryn Mawr School rather than see it "become less good little by little," and finally close "when it had become a ghost of itself" (MCT to Miss Kelly and other members of Board of Managers, Dec. 11, 1927, Records, Bryn Mawr School). She explained that the school's cumulative deficits would use up in twenty-five years the endowment of $300,000 that she intended to give the school on her death. She required that the reorganization of the school maintain its traditional high standards and insisted that all managers be women, preferably Bryn Mawr School graduates (MCT to BMS Board of Directors, Jan. 2, 1928, reel 13, frame 208). HTF to MCT, Jan. 5, 1928, Records, Bryn Mawr School; MCT circular letter, Mar. 5, 1928, reel 33, frame 623. Thomas resigned from the board of managers.

15. MCT to James B. Wheeler, July 18, 1913, letter book 52; MCT to Mary Woolley, Apr. 8, 1924, reel 32, frame 905; MCT to HMT, Sept. 14, 1924, reel 30, frame 736; MCT to John V. Van Pelt, Jan. 3, 1927, reel 32, frame 700; MCT to Abraham Flexner, May 12, 1928, reel 14, frame 47.

16. Interview with Esther Lanman Cushman by Marjorie Housepian Dobkin, Jan. 31, 1975, notes in Bryn Mawr College Archives; M. Carey Thomas, "To Outlaw War: A Declaration of Interdependence by the United States," *Ways to Peace*, ed. Esther Everette Lape (New York: Charles Scribner's Sons, 1924), pp. 151–70; "How to Get into the League of Nations," Feb. 25, 1924, Democratic Women's Luncheon Club of Philadelphia, MCT Speeches and Articles, Politics file, Bryn Mawr College Archives; "Hoover's Election," MCT Speeches and Articles, Politics file, Bryn Mawr College Archives. For example, she attempted to persuade William Welch that it was his next task to convince John D. Rockefeller, Jr., to give $7 million to endow medical salaries at the Johns Hopkins medical school (MCT to William Welch, Feb. 28, 1928, reel 32, frame 768). When Mary Woolley was appointed as a delegate to the Disarmament Conference in 1932, Thomas wrote her at great length of her plan to end war through implementation of an embargo against any warring nation (MCT to Mary Woolley, Jan. 4, 1932, reel 32, frame 911).

17. MCT to Mary Anderson, Feb. 5, 1924, reel 13, frame 63.

18. M. Carey Thomas, "Argument for a Woman's Equal Rights Amendment to the Constitution of the United States," *Journal of the American Association of University Women*, 18 (Mar. 1925): 22–28.

19. MCT to Mina Kerr, Mar. 9, 1925, reel 27, frame 472; MCT to Mrs. Harvey Wiley, Feb. 9, 1935, reel 32, frame 879.

20. C. R. Ashbee, M.A., *A Palestine Notebook, 1918–1922* (Garden City, N.Y.: Doubleday, Page & Co., 1923), p. 99; Barbara Strachey, *Remarkable Relations: The Story of the Pearsall Smith Women* (New York: Universe Books, 1982), pp. 292–93, quote from p. 293; Logan Pearsall Smith, *Unforgotten Years* (London: Constable & Co., 1938), p. 264; MCT to HTF, Feb. 11, 1920, July 31, 1927, Simon Flexner Papers, APS. In the 1927 letter to Helen, Carey stated that she had spent Mary's estate in "giving to things" both she and Mary cared for. Thomas did make significant gifts, but the more important reasons that the estate was exhausted were her spending of principal for living expenses and investment declines during the Depression.

21. MCT circular letter, Nov. 20–24, 1922, reel 33, frame 442; Mark H. Haller, *Eugenics: Hereditarian Attitudes in American Thought* (New Brunswick, N.J.: Rutgers University Press, 1963), pp. 152–55.

22. MCT to HTF, Aug. 14, 1907, Simon Flexner Papers, APS.

23. MCT to Elizabeth Shepley Sergeant, Apr. 21, 1928, reel 28, frame 1110.

24. MCT, Autobiographical Notes, "Jews," reel 74, frame 929.

25. MCT, Autobiographical Notes, "Friendship," reel 75, frame 538. The Halsted is not William Halsted, the physician. Nothing survives in the record about a man in a Berlin pension until Jack Peters, an archaeologist, came to Bryn Mawr in 1904 as an official guest of the college, and Carey told Mary that she had been attracted to him during her European sojourn (MCT to MEG, Apr. 14, 1904, reel 25, frame 149). "P——" may have been the man who provoked her final diary entry in 1885 (see chapter 11).

26. Marjorie Housepian Dobkin, ed., *The Making of a Feminist: Early Journals and Letters of M. Carey Thomas* (Kent, Ohio: Kent State University Press, 1979), p. 87.

27. MCT circular letter, Mar. 5, 1928, reel 33, frame 623; MCT to HTF, Mar. 29, 1929, Simon Flexner Papers, APS.

28. MCT to Helen Taft Manning, Aug. 6, 1929, reel 28, frame 176; MCT to Elizabeth Shepley Sergeant, Dec. 11, 1927, reel 28, frame 1096; MCT to HTF, May 16, 1932, reel 14, frame 224; MCT to Helen Taft Manning, Sept. 27, 1932, reel 28, frame 207; MCT to Marion Edwards Park, Feb. 8, 1932, reel 28, frame 618.

29. Statement of Cash Receipts and Disbursements, 1930, vol. 194, reel 10, frames

1257–58. In 1994 dollars Thomas' annual income would be about $234,000, and her annual expenses, roughly $620,000.

30. MCT to Grace Thomas Worthington, May 2, 1930, reel 32, frame 962; MCT to John D. Stinger, Feb. 23, 1932, reel 29, frame 805; typescript with MCT corrections in folder "Legal Cases," reel 173, near frame 123. "I am seeing the Directors one by one on the Negro question. I have not yet found one that approves" (MCT to HTF, Nov. 23, 1931, Simon Flexner Papers, APS). None of the Thomases or Whitalls were abolitionists.

31. MCT to Marion Edwards Park, Apr. 13, 1932, reel 28, frame 625; MCT to Josephine Thomas and Margaret Carey, n.d. [ca. June 1932], reel 30, frame 1039; Statement of Cash Receipts and Disbursements, 1930, vol. 194, reel 10, frame 1250; MCT to John D. Stinger, Nov. 16, 1931, reel 29, frame 804; MCT to Josephine Thomas and Margaret Carey, n.d. [ca. June 1932], reel 30, frame 1039; MCT to HTF, July 11, 1931, reel 14, frame 140; MCT to HTF, May 22, 1931, reel 14, frame 115. Deanery servants cost Thomas another $7,000. (Translated into 1994 dollars, the Deanery cost roughly $189,000 annually to maintain, and servants an additional $63,000.) Thomas spent three to four hours each day putting down "everything I can remember" and planned to send her work to London to be typed (MCT to HTF, Nov. 9. 1931, reel 14, frame 187).

32. MCT to Helen Taft Manning, Oct. 7, 1933, reel 28, frame 218; MCT to HTF, June 26, 1933, reel 14, frame 297; MCT to Grace Thomas Worthington, Oct. 26, 1933, reel 32, frame 970. Thomas later wrote to Helen Manning that she did not know where the papers of the early college were. They had been in a black trunk in the attic of Taylor, but may have been lost when the ceiling of the auditorium was taken down (MCT to Helen Taft Manning, Feb. 21, 1935, reel 28, frame 232).

33. MCT to HMT, Jr., Jan. 19, 1932, M. Carey Thomas Papers, Box 002-1, Alan Mason Chesney Medical Archives, Johns Hopkins University School of Medicine; MCT to HMT, Jr., Jan. 18, 1932, reel 30, frame 193.

34. MCT to HTF, Mar. 22, 1934, reel 14, frame 372; Apr. 1, 1934, reel 14, frame 380.

35. "Last Will and Testament of M. Carey Thomas, Executed in London at the Office of the American Consulate General, August 29th, 1934," copy of printed will, Bryn Mawr College Archives.

36. Lucy Donnelly's intimate friend Edith Finch was selected as the biographer. Her *Carey Thomas of Bryn Mawr* (New York: Harper & Brothers, 1947) was written under conditions of censorship.

37. Smith, *Unforgotten Years*, p. 264. After Thomas' death the college administered a single fund that combined parts 2 and 3. After paying annuities to Grace Worthington and Etta Taylor, the college used the entire fund to maintain the Deanery. None of the other subfunds were established ("Memorandum of Informal Meeting Held February 14, 1936, at Provident Trust Company at 11 A.M.," Marion Park Papers, "Thomas, M. Carey, President Emeritus. Bequest" file, Bryn Mawr College Archives; "Income from Miss Thomas' Estate Now Coming to Deanery," *Bryn Mawr Alumnae Bulletin* [March 1942]: p. 8).

38. MCT to HTF, fragment, p. 2, no date [but after MCT wrote her last will], reel 14, frame 562.

39. MCT to HTF, Oct. 16, 1934, reel 14, frame 430; MCT to HTF, Nov. 15, 1934, reel 14, frame 449.

40. MCT to HTF, Nov. 15, 1934, reel 14, frame 449; MCT to James Barton Longacre, Nov. 26, 1934, reel 27, frame 730; MCT to HTF, Nov. 15, 1934, reel 14, frame 449.

41. MCT to Carolyn McCormick Slade, Apr. 23, 1935, reel 29, frame 353; MCT to

HTF, May 22, 1931, reel 14, frame 115; MCT to Marion Edwards Park, Oct. 18, 1935, reel 28, frame 734.

42. Ellen Deborah Ellis, "Memorabilia: M. Carey Thomas," p. 7, typescript copy in Bryn Mawr College Archives. The published written version of Thomas' address recounts familiar Bryn Mawr College firsts and contains a sustained plea for women's colleges to hire women faculty and for women donors to insist that the schools to which they give money be open to women. Comparing it to other Thomas writings from the period suggests that it was composed with assistance (M. Carey Thomas, Address, *Bryn Mawr College Fiftieth Anniversary*, Nov. 1 and 2, 1935).

43. MCT to HTF, Thanksgiving 1935, reel 14, frame 557.

44. MCT, circular letter, Mar. 5, 1928, reel 33, frame 623. The official cause of her death was arteriosclerosis; she was cremated and her ashes were removed to Bryn Mawr College and placed in the Thomas Library cloister (Commonwealth of Pennsylvania Department of Health, burial or removal permit, Bryn Mawr College Archives).

INDEX

A NOTE ABOUT THE AUTHOR

HELEN LEFKOWITZ HOROWITZ received her B.A. from Wellesley College in 1963, and her Ph.D. from Harvard in 1969. She has taught at MIT, Union College, the University of Michigan, Scripps College, and the University of Southern California, where she chaired the Program for the Study of Women and Men in Society. She currently teaches American history and American studies at Smith College. She is the recipient of grants from the National Endowment for the Humanities and The Spencer Foundation. She is the author of *Culture and the City: Cultural Philanthropy in Chicago from the 1880s to 1917*; *Alma Mater: Design and Experience in the Women's Colleges from Their Nineteenth-Century Beginnings to the 1930s*; and *Campus Life: Undergraduate Cultures from the End of the Eighteenth Century to the Present*.

A NOTE ON THE TYPE

THIS BOOK was set in a digitized version of Electra, a type face designed by W(illiam) A(ddison) Dwiggins (1880–1956) for the Mergenthaler Linotype Company and first made available in 1935. Electra cannot be classified as either "modern" or "old style." It is not based on any historical model, and hence does not echo any particular period or style of type design. It avoids the extreme contrast between thick and thin elements that marks most modern faces, and it is without eccentricities that catch the eye and interfere with reading. In general, Electra is a simple, readable type face that attempts to give a feeling of fluidity, power, and speed.

W. A. Dwiggins was born in Martinsville, Ohio, and studied art in Chicago. In the late 1920s he moved to Hingham, Massachusetts, where he built a solid reputation as a designer of advertisements and as a calligrapher. He began an association with the Mergenthaler Linotype Company in 1929 and over the next 27 years designed a number of book types, of which Metro, Electra, and Caledonia have been used widely. In 1930 Dwiggins became interested in marionettes, and through the years he made many important contributions to the art of puppetry and the design of marionettes.

Composed by Crane Typesetting Service, Inc.,
West Barnstable, Massachusetts
Printed and bound by Arcata Graphics/Martinsburg,
Martinsburg, West Virginia
Designed by Virginia Tan

DATE DUE